"Philbrick is both a meticulous histori[an] teller. The book has unforgettable n[otes] contains much astute historical analysi[s] sees Arnold not as the man who almost lost the war so much as the catalyst that helped to win it."
—*The Christian Science Monitor*

★

"A suspenseful, richly detailed, and deeply researched book about the revolutionary struggle that bound George Washington and Benedict Arnold together and the almost disastrous dysfunction of America's revolutionary government that helped drive them apart."
—*The New York Review of Books*

★

"A vivid and in some ways cautionary tale of the Revolutionary War. The near-tragic nature of the drama hinges not on any military secrets Arnold gave to the British but on an open secret: the weakness of the patriot cause.... Arnold's betrayal still makes for great drama, proving once again that the supposed villains of a story are usually the most interesting."
—*The New York Times Book Review*

but on an open secret: the weakness of the patriot cause. . . . Arnold's betrayal still makes for great drama, proving once again that the supposed villains of a story are usually the most interesting."

—*The New York Times Book Review*

"No contemporary author is better suited to reintroduce readers to this high drama than Nathaniel Philbrick. Author of the award-winning books *Mayflower* and *In the Heart of the Sea*, Philbrick has a knack for cinematic depictions and dramatic pacing, and he uses these to great effect in his new book."

—*National Review*

"An engrossing narrative of the war's most difficult years . . . Philbrick argues that the quarrelsome, divided Americans needed Arnold's perfidy as much as they did Washington's greatness to unify their new nation. He pushes aside the patriotic myth to unveil the war's messy reality—and it's still a rousing adventure."

—*BookPage*

"A lively account of our Revolution's most reviled figure." —*Kirkus Reviews*

"Philbrick weaves exciting accounts of Arnold's impulsive battlefield exploits with the activities of self-interested military and civil associates into the demythified story of the circumstances of a tragic betrayal. This page-turner will be valued by both casual readers and historians."   —*Library Journal*

"A compulsively readable and fascinating narrative . . . Philbrick makes vivid and memorable the details of numerous military engagements and reliably punctures any preconceptions that the rebels' victory was inevitable. . . . Eye-openers abound. . . . Philbrick's deep scholarship, nuanced analysis, and novelistic storytelling add up to another triumph."

—*Publishers Weekly* (starred review)

"In the final analysis, *Valiant Ambition* adds to Philbrick's laurels as one of this country's premier historians. His account of the middle years of the American Revolution is a tour de force, popular history at its best."

—*ARMY Magazine*

PENGUIN BOOKS

VALIANT AMBITION

Nathaniel Philbrick is the *New York Times* bestselling author of *In The Heart of the Sea*, winner of the National Book Award; *Mayflower*, finalist for the Pulitzer Prize; *Sea of Glory*; *The Last Stand*; *Bunker Hill*; and *Why Read Moby Dick?* He lives on Nantucket. www.nathanielphilbrick.com

Also by Nathaniel Philbrick

The Passionate Sailor

Away Off Shore:
Nantucket Island and Its People, 1602–1890

Abram's Eyes:
The Native American Legacy of Nantucket Island

Second Wind:
A Sunfish Sailor's Odyssey

In the Heart of the Sea:
The Tragedy of the Whaleship Essex

Sea of Glory:
America's Voyage of Discovery; The U.S. Exploring Expedition, 1838–1842

Mayflower:
A Story of Courage, Community, and War

The Last Stand:
Custer, Sitting Bull, and the Battle of Little Bighorn

Why Read Moby-Dick?

Bunker Hill:
A City, a Siege, a Revolution

VALIANT AMBITION

George Washington,
Benedict Arnold,

* AND *

the Fate of the
American Revolution

NATHANIEL PHILBRICK

PENGUIN BOOKS

PENGUIN BOOKS
An imprint of Penguin Random House LLC
375 Hudson Street
New York, New York 10014
penguin.com

First published in the United States of America by Viking Penguin,
an imprint of Penguin Random House LLC, 2016
Published in Penguin Books 2017

Map illustrations by Jeffrey L. Ward

Credits for other illustrations appear on pages 404–406.

ISBN 9780143110194 (paperback)

THE LIBRARY OF CONGRESS HAS CATALOGED THE HARDCOVER EDITION AS FOLLOWS:
Names: Philbrick, Nathaniel, author.
Title: Valiant ambition : George Washington, Benedict Arnold, and
the fate of the American Revolution / Nathaniel Philbrick.
Description: New York, New York : Viking, [2016]
| Includes bibliographical references and index.
Identifiers: LCCN 2016303785 | ISBN 9780525426783 (hardcover)
Subjects: LCSH: Washington, George, 1732–1799. | Arnold, Benedict,
1741–1801. | United States. Continental Army—Biography. |
United States. Continental Army. | American Revolution (1775–1783) |
Generals—United States—Biography. | Traitors—United States—
Biography. | Generals. | United States—History—Revolution,
1775–1783—Biography. | United States.
Classification: LCC E206 .P48 2016b | DDC 973.3/82092 B—dc23

Printed in the United States of America
1   3   5   7   9   10   8   6   4   2

Set in Adobe Garamond Pro and Americanus
Designed by Amy Hill

To Melissa

As he was valiant,
I honor him.
But, as he was ambitious,
I slew him.

~William Shakespeare,
Julius Caesar

CONTENTS

❧ **PART II**

Secret Motives and Designs   169

PREFACE
The Fault Line

We all know the story: how a defiant and undisciplined collection of citizen soldiers banded together to defeat the mightiest army on earth. But as those who lived through the nearly decadelong saga of the American Revolution were well aware, that was not how it actually happened.

The real Revolution was so troubling and strange that once the struggle was over, a generation did its best to remove all traces of the truth. No one wanted to remember how after boldly declaring their independence they had so quickly lost their way; how patriotic zeal had lapsed into cynicism and self-interest; and how, just when all seemed lost, a traitor had saved them from themselves.

Charles Thomson was uniquely qualified to write a history of his times. As secretary of the Continental Congress from 1774 to 1789, he had functioned as what one historian has described as the "prime minister" of the Congress. While delegates came and went over the course of the War of Independence, Secretary Thomson was always there to bear witness to the behind-the-scenes workings of the nation's legislative body during its earliest and most critical period. According to his friend John Jay, "no person in the world is so perfectly acquainted with the rise, conduct, and conclusion of the American Revolution as yourself."

Soon after his retirement in July 1789, Thomson set to work on a memoir of his tenure as secretary to the Congress, eventually completing a manuscript of more than a thousand pages. But as time went on and the story of the Revolution became enshrined in myth, Thomson realized that his account, titled "Notes of the Intrigues and Severe Altercations or Quarrels in the Congress," would "contradict all the histories of the great events of the Revolution." Around 1816 he finally decided that it was not for him "to tear away the veil that hides our weaknesses," and he destroyed the manuscript. "Let the world admire the supposed wisdom and valor of our great men," he wrote. "Perhaps they may adopt the qualities that have been ascribed to them, and thus good may be done. I shall not undeceive future generations."

The American Revolution had two fronts: the war against Great Britain and a civil war so widespread and destructive that an entire continent was seeded with the dark inevitability of even more devastating cataclysms to come. Many of us have heard of the partisan struggles in the South during the final bloody years of the Revolution. But the middle of the country was also torn apart by internal conflict, much of it fought along the periphery of British-occupied New York. Here, in this war-ravaged "Neutral Ground," where neither side held sway, neighbor preyed on neighbor in a swirling cat-and-dog fight that transformed large swaths of the Hudson River Valley, Long Island, and New Jersey into lawless wastelands.

At the epicenter of this self-destructive furor was the patriot capital of Philadelphia. Before and after it was briefly occupied by the British, the city was the scene of religious and political persecution, profiteering, and massive legislative dysfunction. Rather than the paragon of leadership and eloquence that we associate with the passage of the Declaration of Independence in July 1776, the Continental Congress had become, as the testimony of Charles Thomson suggests, the political incarnation of the confusion and hostility that had overtaken the nation as a whole.

By the summer of 1780, America had reached its lowest ebb. The expectations created by a dramatic victory at Saratoga in 1777 had subsided into disillusionment as the much-vaunted alliance with France had so far done nothing to win the war. Exhausted and dispirited by a struggle that was in its fifth year, the American people appeared to have turned their backs on the cause they had once so ardently embraced. Instead of a unified republic governed by a Continental Congress, the United States had devolved into thirteen scrabbling and largely independent polities. If, by some miracle, General Washington should find a way to win the war against the British, the real question was whether there would be a country left to claim victory.

What follows is the story of how one of Washington's greatest generals came to decide that the cause to which he had given almost everything no longer deserved his loyalty. Although it later became convenient to portray Benedict Arnold as a conniving Satan from the start, the truth is more complex and, ultimately, more disturbing. Without the discovery of Arnold's treason in the fall of 1780, the American people might never have been forced to realize that the real threat to their liberties came not from without but from within.

The Battle of Saratoga is the pivot point of this story, the place where on October 7, 1777, Benedict Arnold suffered the debilitating injury that ultimately set him on the path to treason. It is also where his nemesis Horatio Gates acquired the renown that allowed him, with the help of key members of the Continental Congress, to challenge Washington's position as commander in chief.

Washington is rightly regarded today as one of the greatest military commanders and statesmen in American history. But like every exceptional leader, he made his share of mistakes. Indeed, to insist that Washington could do no wrong is to deny him his greatest attribute: his extraordinary ability to learn and improve amid some of the most challenging circumstances a commander in chief has ever faced.

Though a soldier, Washington recognized at the beginning of the war that if America was to survive the Revolution with her ideals intact she must be governed by her civil, rather than military, leaders. This meant that he had no choice but to submit to the indignity of being continually second-guessed by a legislative body that had a deep distrust of the army and especially its leader. By 1777 Washington had emerged as the preeminent figure, civilian or military, in America, and for many members of Congress, particularly if they were from New England, the Virginia planter had assumed an aura that was dangerously monarchical. Inevitably the legislators began to employ the same strategies against Washington that they had used to overthrow the British king. The danger was that the revolutionaries' almost knee-jerk urge to undermine whoever was in charge would ultimately lead to anarchy. That Washington resisted the temptation to resign in disgust or, at the other extreme, proclaim himself, like Napoleon, emperor, is a testament to his judgment and almost unbelievable patience.

While Washington had the strength of character to see the long view, Benedict Arnold lived in the messy and highly emotional moment. As he once admitted, "I am a passionate man," and without this passion, he would never have accomplished what he did on the battlefield—accomplishments that garnered from Washington the highest praise. But as Washington also came to realize, Arnold's volatility could be dangerous. The son of a bankrupt alcoholic who had been ruined by his pretensions, Arnold lacked the ability to rise above petty and unjustified criticism. He also had a habit of living beyond his means. Later in the war, after being overlooked for promotion and almost losing his leg to an enemy musket ball at Saratoga, he convinced himself that profiting from his position in the military was justified. When combined with his growing disillusionment with Congress, which in addition to denying him promotion, proved reluctant to reimburse him for his considerable expenses at the beginning of the war, Arnold's need for money helped fuel his gradual creep toward treason.

If Arnold was Washington's dark angel, the young Marquis de Lafayette almost always seemed to be in the light. Only nineteen years old when he and Washington first met, this idealistic, confident, and immensely wealthy French nobleman had a charm and charisma that appealed to just about everyone. Even when the reality hardly justified his optimism, Lafayette maintained a buoyant enthusiasm that stood in marked contrast to Arnold's ever-growing bitterness.

This story is also about the British side of the Revolution. Unlike their American counterparts, for whom the war was what Washington called "this glorious cause," the British generals quickly came to see the struggle as a dreary quagmire out of which few, if any, of them were likely to emerge with their reputations intact. Rather than the aristocratic buffoons and bloody hirelings of later American legend, Generals Howe, Clinton, Carleton, Cornwallis, and Burgoyne were bright, ambitious, and conflicted men forced to fight a people whom they considered to be their countrymen.

Ultimately, however, the story is less about battles won and lost than it is about a people who lived through one of the most tumultuous and creative periods in American history. While Washington, Arnold, Howe, and Lafayette will play major roles in what follows, this book is also the story of the long-suffering soldier from Connecticut who almost single-handedly set the record straight as to what really happened in the ranks of the Continental army; of the mechanical genius who, if not for an uncooperative tide, might have ended the war before it had properly begun; of the Philadelphia lawyer who betrayed Washington's trust before pushing Benedict Arnold to the brink of treason; and of the young wife and mother whose loyalist leanings changed the course of a nation.

Finally, this is the story of a country knit together—and potentially pulled apart—by water. At a time when overland travel was laborious and slow, rivers and lakes held a strategic advantage that is difficult for us to appreciate today in a nation crisscrossed by multilane highways. Extending south from Canada was a corridor of water that both the British and the Americans regarded as the strategic key to the conflict. If the British could establish control of both Lake Champlain to the north and the Hudson River to the south, it would be possible to isolate New England from the rest of the colonies and win the war. As a consequence, New York City and the Hudson River, augmented by Lake Champlain's river-like thrust toward Canada, will serve as the jagged fault line of this book, a book about loyalty and betrayal and the fault line that is in all of us.

PART I

The Wilderness
★ OF ★
Untried Things

We Americans . . . are the pioneers of the
world; the advance-guard, sent on through
the wilderness of untried things, to break a
new path in the New World that is ours.

~Herman Melville,
White-Jacket, 1850

CHAPTER ONE

Demons of Fear and Disorder

By the spring of 1776, George Washington had established his army's headquarters at New York, then a wedge-shaped labyrinth of streets and lanes at the southern tip of Manhattan Island. Bracketed by two tidal rivers, New York was the second-largest urban center in America. It was also rapidly filling up with American soldiers as the city braced for an invasion by sea. Five miles to the south of the American encampment in New York, lookouts atop Staten Island's Todt Hill searched the horizon for enemy ships.

Three months before, Washington had formed his elite Life Guard, consisting of more than a hundred handpicked men between five feet eight and five feet ten inches in height. They were all, in accordance with Washington's orders, "handsomely and well made . . . , clean and spruce." As their title suggested, the Life Guards had been entrusted with ensuring the safety of His Excellency, the commander in chief of the Continental army.

During the second week in June, with a British invasionary force expected any day, New York was rocked by the rumor that one of Washington's Life Guards, Sergeant Thomas Hickey, had conspired to betray the leader he had vowed to protect. Upon the arrival of the British fleet, Hickey and a few well-placed confidants planned to turn against the Americans. Hickey had been accused of the blackest of crimes, but the case had a startling legal nuance: how could a people who still called themselves British subjects condemn a soldier for remaining loyal to the king?

Certainly the New York courts, "being as yet held by authority derived

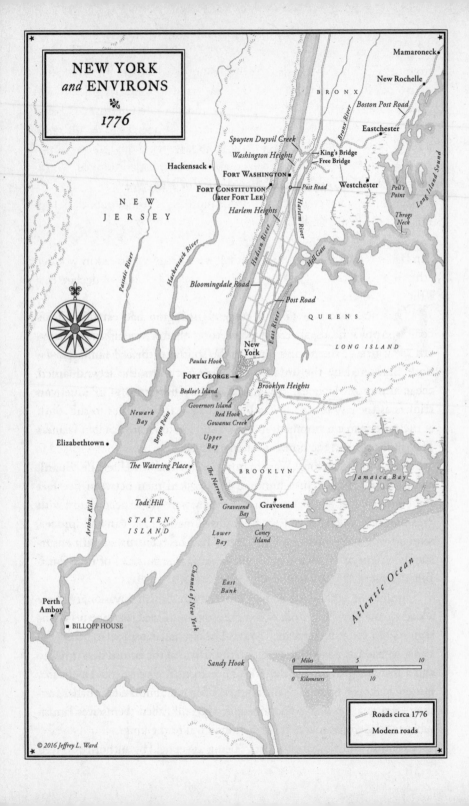

NEW YORK *and* ENVIRONS

1776

Mamaroneck

New Rochelle

B R O N X

Boston Post Road

Bronx River

Eastchester

Spuyten Duyvil Creek

Washington Heights

King's Bridge
Free Bridge

Hackensack

FORT WASHINGTON

Post Road

Westchester

Pell's Point

FORT CONSTITUTION
(later FORT LEE)

Harlem Heights

Harlem River

Throgs Neck

N E W
J E R S E Y

Passaic River

Hackensack River

Hudson River

Long Island Sound

Hell Gate

Bloomingdale Road

Post Road

Q U E E N S

LONG ISLAND

East River

New
York

Paulus Hook

FORT GEORGE

Brooklyn Heights

Bedloe's Island

Governors Island
Red Hook
Gowanus Creek

Newark
Bay

Bergen Point

Upper
Bay

B R O O K L Y N

Jamaica Bay

Elizabethtown

The Watering Place

The Narrows

Gravesend
Bay

Gravesend

Todt Hill

STATEN
ISLAND

Arthur Kill

Lower
Bay

Coney
Island

Atlantic Ocean

Channel of New York

East
Bank

Perth
Amboy

■ BILLOPP HOUSE

Sandy Hook

| 0 | Miles | | 5 | | 10 |
| 0 | Kilometers | | | 10 | |

Roads circa 1776

Modern roads

© 2016 Jeffrey L. Ward

from the Crown of Great Britain," could not try the man. The only alternative was for Washington to try Hickey before a military tribunal.

On June 26 a court-martial board found the Life Guardsman guilty of mutiny and sedition. Two days later, Hickey was hanged on the common of New York before a crowd of almost twenty thousand spectators. A week before the signing of the document that made it official, Washington had issued his own Declaration of Independence.

On the very next day, at nine in the morning, the lookouts atop Todt Hill saw the first British sail.

"In about ten minutes," Private Daniel McCurtin recounted in wonder, "the whole bay was [as] full of shipping as ever it could be. I declare that I thought all London was afloat."

Over the course of the next few hours the dozens upon dozens of sails coalesced at Sandy Hook, the strip of barrier beach at the tip of northeastern New Jersey where ships traditionally anchored before entering New York Harbor. Once the ships had come to rest and the sails were furled, the many masts looked, to McCurtin's eye, like "a wood of pine trees trimmed."

Only three months had passed since the British general William Howe and his army of almost nine thousand soldiers had been forced to abandon Boston when in a single night Washington managed to build a cannon-equipped fort atop Dorchester Heights. After retreating to Halifax, Nova Scotia, to recoup and rebuild, Howe was now back, with an even bigger army and with New York squarely in his sights. It seemed almost unimaginable that King George and his ministry could have responded so quickly and with such force to the setback in New England. But, as it turned out, King George was just getting started.

A few days later the wind shifted into the south, and the hundred or so ships gathered at Sandy Hook started up the channel toward the Narrows, the mile-wide choke point between Staten Island and Long Island through which all ships sailing into New York Harbor must pass. At that moment, Henry Knox, the twenty-five-year-old commander of the Continental army's artillery regiment, and his wife, Lucy, were standing together at the second-floor window of their temporary quarters at Number One Broadway.

Henry had already decided that his wife and their young daughter must leave New York, but Lucy had stubbornly insisted on remaining by his side. Now, with a fleet of enemy warships and transports racing up the channel, both of them knew that she had indeed "stayed too long." "We saw the ships coming through the Narrows," he wrote to his brother William, "with a fair wind and rapid tide, which would have brought them up to the city in about half an hour. You can scarcely conceive the distress and anxiety that she then had. The city in an uproar, the alarm guns firing, the troops repairing to their posts, and everything in the [height] of bustle. I not at liberty to attend her, as my country calls loudest. My God, may I never experience the like feelings again!"

Fortunately, the wind began to die and shift to the north. At first it looked as if the fleet was about to veer off for Long Island, but eventually the ships turned to the west and started to anchor along the shore of Staten Island. Once Knox realized that the immediate danger had passed, he returned to his quarters on Broadway and "scolded like a fury at her for not having gone before." By early July, Lucy and their daughter were safe in Connecticut, and Knox was still lamenting "the extremely disagreeable . . . circumstances of our parting."

In mid-July, the already considerable enemy force gathered at Staten Island more than doubled in size with the arrival of 150 more ships under Admiral Richard Howe, the new commander of the British navy in North America and William Howe's older brother. On August 1 another 45 ships sailed up the Narrows bearing two thousand troops under the command of General Henry Clinton. And then, on August 12, just when it seemed that the Narrows could not fit any more vessels, yet another vast fleet materialized "as if," an American officer remarked, "[they] had dropped from the clouds."

This final convoy, it turned out, contained eight thousand soldiers from Hesse-Cassel in west-central Germany. Britain's determination to put an end to the American rebellion was so great that the ministry had decided to augment its army of native-born troops with these superbly trained and equipped professional soldiers, whose ruler depended on the income derived from hiring out the young men of his impoverished state to finance his government.

By the middle of August, the British flotilla totaled more than four hundred vessels bearing forty-five thousand soldiers and sailors, making it the largest collection of ships and men ever assembled by the British Empire. (Not until World War I would Great Britain amass a larger fleet.) Housed within this giant network of wooden hulls and creaking masts was a floating city of soldiers more populous than Philadelphia, the biggest urban center in North America.

Joseph Reed had recently rejoined George Washington's staff as His Excellency's adjutant general. Reed had been there at the beginning when Washington had faced the daunting task of dislodging the British army from Boston. But nothing had prepared him for what he called "the prodigious fleet they have collected." "I cannot help being astonished," he wrote to his wife in Philadelphia, "that a people should come three thousand miles at so much risk, trouble, and expense to rob, plunder, and destroy . . . because [another people] will not lay their lives and fortunes at their feet."

The Americans were not the only ones surprised by the size of the fleet gathered at the Narrows. Even the British army's commander, the normally imperturbable William Howe, voiced his "utter amazement at the decisive and masterly strokes" exhibited by the new secretary of state, Lord George Germain, in assembling this mammoth fleet. Germain was driven by that most powerful of motives in the eighteenth century: personal honor. Back in 1760 he had been convicted of cowardice at the Battle of Minden in what is now North Rhine–Westphalia, Germany, and for the last decade and a half he had languished in disgrace. But now he had his chance; by pulling off the logistical miracle that ended the rebellion, he hoped, in the words of his friend the historian Edward Gibbon, to "reconquer Germany in America."

Germain had sent this force across the Atlantic with the expectation that Howe would deliver "one decisive blow [and] finish this rebellion in one campaign." But Howe and his newly arrived older brother appear to have had other ideas. Both Howe brothers were political moderates with a long-standing affection for the American colonies. In 1759 the General Court of Massachusetts had paid for a memorial in Westminster Abbey for their older brother George, who'd been killed during the French and Indian War. It was a tribute the Howe family never forgot, and as early as 1774 Admiral Howe had engaged in informal talks with Benjamin Franklin in a fruitless effort to set things right with the colonies. More recently he had insisted that in addition to being named commander of the British navy in America, he also be given, along with his brother William, the power to negotiate peace.

But there was a problem. On his arrival at Staten Island in July, Admiral Howe learned of the signing of the Declaration of Independence—a document that technically rendered all future negotiation impossible because the Howes had only been given the authority to quell a rebellion, and not to recognize the Americans as an autonomous people. This was not enough to deter Admiral Howe, who made several unsuccessful attempts to engage Washington in talks even as he sent communications to Benjamin Franklin and other officials in Philadelphia. But as Franklin subsequently informed the admiral, the "fine and noble china vase" of the British Empire had already been shattered.

Soon after the evacuation of the British from Boston in March, the Continental Congress had commissioned the artist Charles Willson Peale to paint a portrait of His Excellency General George Washington. The timing was unpropitious, but in early July, just as the waters to the south of New York began to fill up with enemy warships, Washington reluctantly agreed to sit for the portrait.

In the finished rendition, he is dressed in a dark-blue, buff-faced coat with a light-blue sash cutting diagonally across his chest. A still vital forty-four, he seems a man with better things to do, and he looks at the painter with a withering impatience, his left hand stuffed inside his vest. His mouth has a puckish expressiveness that will be lost in the years ahead when after a lifetime of cracking walnuts with his teeth he will be forced to wear ill-fitting dentures. He has the pale forehead of someone who regularly wears a hat, his sun-scorched cheeks demonstrating why he often takes an umbrella with him when riding his horse beneath a summer sun.

This is not the steady and pragmatic leader that most of us associate with the Father of Our Country. This is an ambitious, even ferocious warrior caught in a moment of forced tranquillity. This is a man who wants to fight.

Throughout the nine-month Siege of Boston, Washington had wanted desperately to attack the occupying British army and end the war with one brilliant and bloody stroke—a proposal that had repeatedly been rejected by his council of war as too dangerous. Taking up where he had left off in Boston, Washington presented a plan to his generals in New York to launch a bold, preemptive strike against the British at Staten Island. But once again the plan was dismissed as too risky.

As his adjutant general Joseph Reed recognized, Washington's determination to confront the British army was partly a "point of honor" for his commander—a determination that had only increased with the signing of the Declaration of Independence. If America was to be worthy of her status as a new nation, her army must be willing to meet the enemy head-on. But there was another, more personal side to Washington's attitude toward the British army. His formative years as a military officer had been spent in the western frontier during the French and Indian War. Because of that experience, Washington had developed the unmistakable look of a soldier, possessing "so much martial dignity," the doctor Benjamin Rush claimed, "that you would distinguish him to be a general . . . from among ten thousand people." But those years in the wilds of Pennsylvania had also been a time of bitter professional disappointment. Even though he had served with great bravery on Britain's behalf, he had ultimately been refused an officer's commission in the king's army. Like Secretary of State Germain, Washington hoped to obliterate the painful memories of past injustices with a victory at New York.

But to engage this powerful and well-disciplined British force in combat involved enormous risks. By placing most of his own army on the island of Manhattan, Washington had made himself inordinately vulnerable to the enemy, who simply had to sail their fleet up the Hudson and East Rivers and attack his army from the north. With only two small bridges at the Harlem River providing a potential evacuation route, his army would be trapped and most likely crushed. Despite these obvious hazards, Washington remained convinced that occupying Manhattan was worth the gamble. On July 10 he assured John Hancock, president of the Continental Congress, that if the British did take New York, they would have to "wade through much blood and slaughter [and] at best be in possession of a melancholy and mournful victory." The Battle of New York would be, in other words, another Bunker Hill, and, in fact, a well-fortified rise of land that overlooked a large pond on the northern edge of the city had been renamed Bunker Hill in hopes of emulating that battle's result.

Critical to the defense of New York were the heights of Brooklyn at the western tip of Long Island, across a narrow river channel from lower

Manhattan, where an emplacement of cannons commanded any ships that might approach the city from the south. If Brooklyn should fall, so, inevitably, would New York, which made it particularly disheartening when on August 15 Washington learned that the general in charge of the fortifications around this strategic high ground, Nathanael Greene, had been incapacitated by "a raging fever." Washington was ultimately forced to replace Greene with General John Sullivan, just back from Canada and without his predecessor's intimate understanding of the terrain.

The great question for Washington was where Howe would ultimately attack. Because his brother's navy commanded the sea, the British general could move his men in almost any direction in a matter of hours. Already two frigates, the *Phoenix* and the *Rose,* had sailed boldly past the American fortifications at the mouth of the Hudson and spent several weeks terrorizing the river towns to the north. Now the ships were back with the bulk of the fleet, and what was going to happen next was anyone's guess.

By the morning of August 23, the chaplain Philip Fithian had moved with his regiment from New York to Brooklyn, where a string of forts extended from Wallabout Bay down to Gowanus Creek to the south. A violent thunderstorm had erupted over Manhattan the night before, and after a night of little sleep, Fithian was awakened by the sound of cannons. "Crack! Crack!" he recorded in his journal. "An alarm from Red Hook, Crack! Crack! Crack! The alarm repeated from Cobble Hill." He soon learned that "the enemy have been landing for some time down at the Narrows." The long-awaited British invasion had begun.

Amphibious landings were notoriously difficult, but the Howes made it look effortless. Ninety sailing vessels crowded into the Narrows as wave after wave of troops were delivered to the sandy shore of Long Island's Gravesend Bay in a new type of landing craft with a bow section that dropped open like the drawbridge of a castle. From the perspective of Admiral Howe's secretary Ambrose Serle, it all made for a magnificent spectacle: "ships and vessels with their sails spread open to dry, the sun shining clear upon them, the green hills and meadows after rain. . . . Add to all this, the vast importance of the business . . . and the mind feels itself wonderfully engaged." By noon, fifteen thousand men and forty pieces of artillery had landed at Gravesend.

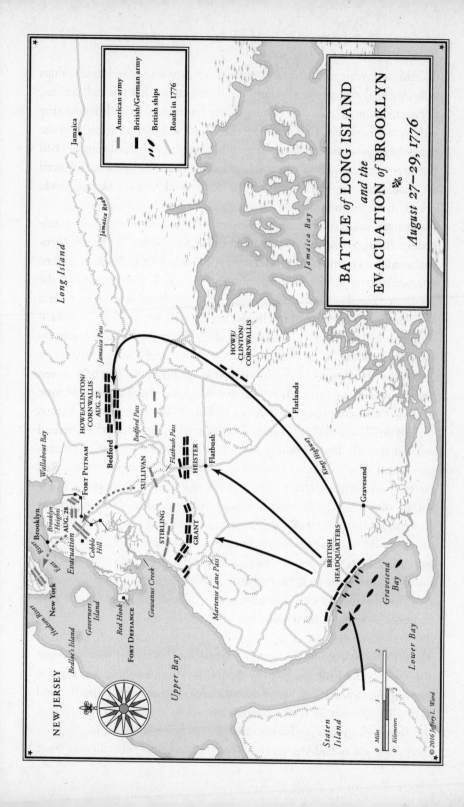

BATTLE of LONG ISLAND *and the* **EVACUATION of BROOKLYN**

August 27–29, 1776

American army
British/German army
British ships
Roads in 1776

Jamaica

Long Island

Jamaica Road

Jamaica Pass

Jamaica Bay

HOWE/CLINTON/
CORNWALLIS

Wallabout Bay

HOWE/CLINTON/
CORNWALLIS
AUG. 27

Bedford Pass

Bedford

FORT PUTNAM

Flatbush Pass

SULLIVAN

Brooklyn
Heights
AUG. 28

Brooklyn

Evacuation

HEISTER

Flatbush

Flatlands

East River

Cobble
Hill

Gowanus Creek

STIRLING

GRANT

King Highway

Gravesend

New York

Governors
Island

Red Hook

FORT DEFIANCE

Martense Lane Pass

BRITISH
HEADQUARTERS

Gravesend
Bay

Hudson River

NEW JERSEY

Bedloe's Island

Upper Bay

Lower Bay

Staten Island

0 Miles   1   2

0 Kilometers   2

© 2016 Jeffrey L. Ward

Brothers with a close and congenial relationship, the Howes interacted without the tensions and miscommunications that typically existed between the army and navy. But if they had the special closeness that only siblings possess, that very intimacy made it difficult for their subordinates to know exactly what they were thinking, especially since both brothers were exceedingly taciturn. (Horace Walpole described William as "reckoned sensible, though so silent that nobody knew whether he was or not" while his brother was "undaunted as a rock and as silent.") While the Howes' stolid reserve might seem impenetrable to many of their subordinates, one officer was determined to let his opinions be heard. With the arrival of General Henry Clinton on August 5, fresh from an embarrassing defeat in Charleston, South Carolina, a new and extremely volatile ingredient was added to the already strange dynamic at work within the command structure of the British army.

No one liked Henry Clinton, especially Clinton himself, who was, by his own account, "a shy bitch." His sense of insecurity brought to a fever pitch after the debacle in the South, he did what Clinton did best: act so obnoxiously that even when he proposed the most logical move, those he was attempting to convince felt compelled to do the opposite. That is what had happened prior to the disaster at Bunker Hill, when he had insisted that the British should avoid a deadly frontal assault by cutting off the rebels from behind, and that is what would happen once again. First Clinton urged Howe to attack Washington from the north of Manhattan Island, a suggestion that appears to have made it inevitable that Howe would land his force at Long Island. Certainly there were considerations that favored this relatively cautious approach. Long Island, like Staten Island, was home to a significant number of loyalists. It also had the farms and grasslands Howe's army needed to sustain itself. But once established in Gravesend, Howe needed to decide upon his next move, and once again Clinton would play a crucial role.

Washington's previous wartime experience had been limited to the western wilderness during the French and Indian War and, most recently, the Siege of Boston. He had never commanded a large army in battle, and during the days prior to the British assault, he displayed the petulance and lack of focus of a leader who had strayed beyond his depth.

Rather than making certain that he and his subordinates were thoroughly acquainted with the terrain between them and the enemy on Long Island, he decided that thirteen of his senior officers must remain in New York to attend the court-martial of an officer accused of selling secrets to the British. Besides providing a needless distraction, the court-martial in New York on August 25 and 26 meant that several of the regiments in Brooklyn were without their commanders when they needed them the most. Colonel William Smallwood of Maryland remembered that when he "urged the necessity of attending our troops, [His Excellency] refused to discharge us, alleging there was a necessity for the trials coming on." Even though a British attack was imminent, Washington chose to indulge his wrath against a traitorous officer rather than confront a far more pressing and complex challenge for which he had no good solution.

In the meantime, the American force in Brooklyn was in chaos, partly because Washington had reorganized the army from regiments into larger brigades. The change was a good one, but the timing could not have been worse. An already tentative command structure was now almost entirely unhinged, and General John Sullivan reported that "American troops were wandering about western Long Island, sometimes miles beyond their position." Adding even further to the confusion, Washington suddenly decided to replace Sullivan with Israel Putnam of Connecticut. A rotund, boisterous, and rough-edged Yankee, Putnam had never been known for a meticulous attention to detail, and on August 25 Washington pointedly reminded him that "the distinction between a well-regulated army, and a mob, is the good order and discipline of the first, and the licentious and disorderly behavior of the latter." Even though he had largely created the problem in Brooklyn, Washington vented his frustrations by lecturing an officer who had not yet had the opportunity to set things right.

On the afternoon of August 26 Washington joined Putnam in Brooklyn to assess the disposition of the American army. By that time, Putnam had established his headquarters at the appropriately named Fort Putnam that anchored the American line of defense near Wallabout Bay. Six thousand men were stationed behind this line of fortifications perched atop the high ground in Brooklyn; another three thousand were stationed outside the lines along a wooded ridge that extended for four miles between the American and British armies. This natural barrier was pierced by three narrow and (from an American perspective) easily defended passes—the Martense Lane Pass near New York Harbor, the Flatbush Pass a few miles to the east, and a few miles beyond that, the Bedford Pass. Even if the British were able to force their way through the passes, they could not avoid enduring considerable losses before the American defenders retreated to the safety of the forts behind them. This did not change the fact, however, that if fighting should occur at these three passes, most of Washington's army would remain bystanders behind the lines, leaving just a third of the army to confront a British force that outnumbered it by more than six to one.

After a final inspection of the lines, Washington returned to New York. That night, at about two in the morning, the British assault began when General James Grant, commanding approximately five thousand men, marched up the road leading through the Martense Lane Pass on the American right. Amid the firing of alarm guns, Putnam ordered General William Alexander to advance with a force of sixteen hundred men.

Alexander was one of the more intriguing figures in the Continental army. In addition to marrying well, he had inherited a large fortune from his Scottish father. Affecting the title of Lord Stirling, he had lived in high style at his estate in Basking Ridge, New Jersey, until the money had run out and he was forced to move to New York. Eager for a new beginning even though he continued to insist on being addressed as Lord Stirling, Alexander had embraced the patriot cause and was now a general in the Continental army. And so it was that a fifty-year-old bankrupt alcoholic with aristocratic pretensions was about to lead the first significant American force to oppose the British army in the open field.

It all unfolded in what one officer described as the "true English taste." Stirling and Grant marched to within two hundred yards of each other's position, and the two armies proceeded to blast away with their artillery, a cannonball every now and then "taking off a head." More than a year before, Grant had famously bragged in Parliament that he could subdue all of the American colonies with just five thousand men, and Stirling now used this boast to encourage his soldiers. For the next four hours, the Americans stood up to the British force "amazingly well," convinced that they were "holding back the invaders." Meanwhile, Sullivan, looking out from a redoubt on the left toward the Flatbush Pass, faced a similar number of Hessian soldiers under General Leopold Philip de Heister. Dressed in blue, the Hessians made a great show of cannon and musketry but, like Grant's division of British soldiers to the west, seemed unable to make any progress against the Americans.

Not until nine in the morning on August 27, with the firing of a British signal gun, did the truth begin to dawn. While Stirling and Sullivan had been preoccupied with the enemy ahead of them, ten thousand British light infantrymen and grenadiers under General Howe had marched to a fourth pass, the Jamaica Pass, which was so far to the east that the Americans had left it undefended. For Washington and his generals, who had several weeks to learn every nook and cranny of western Long Island, it was an inexcusable lapse. For the British general Henry Clinton, who had come up with the idea of a flanking movement through the Jamaica Pass, it marked one of the few times, if not the only one, that another general had chosen to follow his advice.

It was over in about an hour. As Howe's forces swooped in from the northeast and attacked Sullivan and Stirling from behind, Grant and Heister advanced from the south. Those Americans who weren't captured or killed fled in panic toward the fortifications to the north from which the Reverend Fithian looked on in horror and despair. "O doleful! Doleful! Doleful!" he recorded in his diary. "Blood! Carnage! Fire! . . . Such a dreadful din my ears never before heard! And the distressed wounded, came crying into the lines." Fithian watched in terrified disbelief as Stirling and his small band of 400 Marylanders, dressed in scarlet and buff coats, actually *advanced* on the British general Charles Earl Cornwallis's 2,000 soldiers. Stirling and his Marylanders hoped to hold the British back for as long as possible as their comrades floundered through the tidal pond that lay between them and the American lines. Over the course of the fighting, 256 Marylanders were killed and 100 captured (including their leader, Lord Stirling, who one witness claimed fought "like a wolf"), making for a casualty rate of close to 90 percent. By this time, Washington had crossed over from New York and was, like Fithian, watching from the American lines in Brooklyn. "Good God," he is reputed to have said, "what brave fellows I must this day lose!"

Soon the sheer momentum of the onslaught had thrown the grenadiers of the British advance up against the American fortifications. Howe was confident that "had they been permitted to go on . . . they would have carried the redoubt." But to the frustration of Clinton, Howe called them back, claiming that he did not want to "risk the loss that might have been sustained in the assault."

Several British officers later insisted that their commander had made the right decision. One notable American, however, had a different view. Standing on the battlements of the fort that bore his name, Israel Putnam watched as the British grenadiers reluctantly gave up the attack. "General Howe," he said, "is either our friend or no general."

For the next two days it rained, a "pitiless pelting" that further depressed the morale of the already dispirited American soldiers. On the morning of August 29, Washington learned that the British had spent the night building a sizable breastwork less than five hundred yards from the walls of Fort Putnam—the first step in the methodical process of taking a fortress by siege.

That appears to have decided it for Washington. If the British were not going to make another Bunker Hill–like assault, he no longer had a chance to inflict significant casualties on the enemy by remaining in Brooklyn. He must get his army off Long Island before Admiral Howe's fleet (presently held in check by a nasty nor'easter) moved up the East River and prevented him from escaping to New York by water. No longer stymied by a multifaceted strategic problem, he could now apply his naturally aggressive instincts to a single and urgent objective: the evacuation of his army. But first he needed a fleet of boats to transport his men across the river.

Absolute secrecy was essential, so Washington came up with a ruse: claiming that his exhausted soldiers on Brooklyn Heights needed to be replaced with troops stationed across the Hudson in New Jersey, he issued an order to collect every available boat along Manhattan's sixty-five-mile perimeter. If word of the ever-growing fleet of boats leaked to the British, Washington hoped the enemy would assume the vessels were to replenish rather than to evacuate the American army in Brooklyn.

The call for watercraft had already gone out by the time Washington convened a council of war in a mansion overlooking the mouth of the East River. All the officers present soon agreed to the necessity of an immediate evacuation, with General Thomas Mifflin of Philadelphia volunteering to command the last group of soldiers to abandon the works at

Brooklyn Heights. By the afternoon, boats of all types—rowboats, flatboats, whaleboats, pettiaugers (two-sailed workboats equipped with leeboards instead of a keel), and sloops—were being gathered at the ferry landing, near what is today the easterly base of the Brooklyn Bridge. Manning this heterogeneous fleet were sailors from Marblehead and Salem led by John Glover and Israel Hutchinson, respectively, and by 7:00 p.m. the evacuation of the more than nine thousand American soldiers had begun.

From the first, the driving, wind-whipped rain was miserable, but by 9:00 p.m., it was blowing so hard that the sailboats could no longer negotiate the passage. Then the first of two miracles occurred.

At 11:00 p.m. the nor'easter began to moderate and shift to the southwest. With a change in the tide, the once turbulent river suddenly became as smooth as a slick of oil, enabling the sailing craft, some of them so loaded with men that only their hulls' gunwales were visible over the water, to glide back and forth between Brooklyn and New York. Throughout this tense ordeal, Washington seemed to be everywhere: on his horse quietly urging the men to hurry or, in one instance, taking up a boulder in his huge hands and threatening to sink a dangerously overloaded boat if some of its occupants didn't immediately get out.

But as dawn approached, a sizable number of men still remained to be transported across the river. Benjamin Tallmadge, waiting impatiently in the trenches, described what happened next. "A very dense fog began to rise, and it seemed to settle in a peculiar manner over both encampments . . . ; so very dense was the atmosphere that I could scarcely discern a man at six yards' distance." Concealed by a smothering fog, the boat trips continued, with several of the ferrymen ultimately completing as many as eleven trips back and forth across the East River. By midmorning, almost all of Washington's force had returned to the relative safety of New York—with one notable exception.

Around one in the morning, the Reverend Fithian and a fellow chaplain had been advised by the woman who owned the house they were staying in that they "consult immediately for our safety as the army is leaving the island!" Fithian and his friend dismissed the warning as "an idle tale" and went back to sleep. The next morning they made their way through the fog to the ferry landing only to discover that their landlady had been right, and they were about to be marooned in Brooklyn.

Fortunately, a few vessels still remained, and along with Washington and his staff, they "happily came over, among the last boats."

One American officer called it "the best effected retreat I ever read or heard of." Washington's beaten and bedraggled army had been delivered from Long Island by what was, in effect, a lifesaving operation performed by a handful of fishermen from the north of Boston. As it turned out, this was not to be the last time that John Glover and his boys from Marblehead would come to Washington's rescue.

Not until more than a day after the retreat, on Saturday, August 31, was Washington able to inform the Continental Congress of how things stood in New York. After being awake for more than two days straight, he had been, he admitted, "entirely unfit" to take up a pen. "Since Monday scarce any of us have been out of the lines till our passage across the East River," he wrote. "I had hardly been off my horse and never closed my eyes."

In the aftermath of the Battle of Long Island, Washington's army began to fall apart. The militiamen who composed the majority of his force started to desert in droves, and in his subsequent letters to Congress, Washington raged at the inadequacies of his army. "No dependence," he insisted, "[can] be put in a militia or other troops than those enlisted and embodied for a longer period than our regulations heretofore have prescribed." Those militiamen who hadn't already deserted were so "dismayed, intractable, and impatient to return" that they had become useless as soldiers. What was needed to oppose the British was the steady expertise that only a well-trained professional army could provide. "Our liberties must of necessity be greatly hazarded, if not entirely lost, if their defense is left to any but a permanent standing army."

He might fume about the quality of his soldiers, but if anyone had failed to meet the test at the Battle of Long Island, it was their commander in chief. Lieutenant Colonel Daniel Brodhead, who'd witnessed the catastrophe on the American left, was still outraged by the ineptitude displayed by His Excellency and his subordinates. "Upon the whole," he wrote, "less generalship never was shown in any army since the art of war was understood." Colonel John Haslet was more diplomatic: "I fear General Washington has too heavy a task, assisted mostly by beardless boys."

By his own account, Washington did not have, at present, an army equal to the task of taking on a force of disciplined British and German soldiers. He also knew that given the enemy's large fleet of ships, defending a city at the tip of a river-surrounded island was a virtual impossibility. He should have continued what he had so brilliantly begun with his retreat from Long Island and gotten his army off Manhattan as quickly as possible. Washington, however, was unwilling to abandon his original determination to fight for New York.

Part of the problem was that Washington was not his own master. The delegates of the Continental Congress had made it clear that they did not want New York abandoned. The majority of Washington's generals, whom he consulted regularly in councils of war, were also reluctant to leave the city. In addition, there was the matter of public opinion. After the defeat on Long Island, giving up New York without a fight would be difficult to explain. And then there was Washington's inherently aggressive nature. In the early days of September, he appears to have talked—at least to his adjutant general Joseph Reed—about making a stand on the southern tip of Manhattan Island.

Reed did not agree with Washington's decision to remain in this vulnerable position—"cooped up . . . on this tongue of land where we ought never to have been." But if a final climactic battle might serve a greater good, Reed was perfectly willing to go down fighting with his commander. "If a sacrifice of us can save the cause of America," he wrote to his wife on September 6, "there will be time to collect another army before spring, and the country be preserved."

When it comes to Washington's interior life, we are without an essential source: his letters to his wife, Martha, which were destroyed, almost without exception, after his death. But as his letters to his cousin Lund Washington in Virginia reveal, he missed his former life terribly, and that summer and fall, as his army fell apart around him, he sought relief from the pressures of the moment by contemplating the renovation of his beloved home on the Potomac. In one paragraph to his cousin he lamented having ever agreed to assume command of the Continental army: "In confidence I tell you that I never was in such an unhappy, divided state since I was born." In another, he detailed how he wanted the addition at

Mount Vernon to enhance the mansion's neoclassical symmetry and grandeur: "The chimney in the new room should be exactly in the middle of it—the doors and everything else to be exactly answerable and uniform—in short I would have the whole executed in a masterly manner." If he could not control the course of events in New York, he at least had the satisfaction of knowing that his wishes were being followed in Virginia.

In the end, however, Washington was still commander in chief of the Continental army, a post from which he could not resign even if he wanted to. "[I am] told . . . that if I leave the service all will be lost," he wrote to Lund. His only alternative, then, was to fight.

As Washington prepared for the battle to end all battles, the Howes decided to have one more try at negotiation. Two American generals had been captured during the Battle of Long Island—Lord Stirling and John Sullivan—and Admiral Howe was able to convince Sullivan to deliver a verbal message to the Continental Congress: if the Americans agreed to discuss the possibility of peace, the British would suspend current military operations.

John Adams, for one, was not pleased by Sullivan's appearance in Philadelphia on September 2, just three days after the American evacuation from Brooklyn. As the general spoke before the assembled delegates, Adams leaned over to Benjamin Rush and whispered that he wished "the first ball that had been fired on the day of the defeat of our army had gone through [Sullivan's] head." He was, to Adams's view, a mere "decoy duck" for the British. Even though Admiral Howe clearly did not have the authority to negotiate with a newly independent America, Sullivan had provided him with the opportunity of "playing off a number of Machiavellian maneuvers in order to throw upon [the Continental Congress] the odium of continuing the war." So as to avoid the accusation that they had rebuffed the admiral's attempts to settle this dispute, Congress reluctantly decided, after several days of heated discussion, to send a delegation of three representatives to meet with Admiral Howe.

On the night of September 7, Admiral Richard Howe was preparing for bed aboard his flagship HMS *Eagle,* anchored beside tiny Bedloe's Island between the tip of Manhattan and the shore of New Jersey. By that time, the Continental Congress had selected John Adams, Benjamin Franklin, and the young South Carolinian Edward Rutledge to serve on the committee that was to meet with the admiral. Howe would not receive word of the committee's impending arrival until three days later, but on September 7 he was still hopeful that he could settle this dispute peacefully.

It was truly bizarre. Despite having at his command the largest army anyone had ever seen in America, General Howe (aided and abetted, if not led, by his brother) seemed reluctant to use it. George Washington, on the other hand, seemed determined to put his much weaker and disorganized army squarely in harm's way, first on Long Island and now on Manhattan. And then, on the night of September 7, events turned in an even more curious direction.

Unbeknownst to the admiral, whose head was full of improbable dreams of peace, a strange clam-shaped device made of tar-smeared wood and powered by a hand-cranked propeller was making its uncertain way through the dark waters of New York Harbor toward his ship. If all went according to a plan hatched by the son of a Connecticut farmer and approved by Washington, Admiral Howe and his flagship, anchored beside the future site of the Statue of Liberty, were about to be blown to smithereens.

They called it the *Turtle*, an appropriate name for a craft designed to swim both above and below the surface of the water. A submersible vessel was by no means a new concept; already in England more than a dozen patents had been granted to inventors attempting to find a way to explore the depths of the sea. What made this submersible unique was the keg of gunpowder attached to its back, making the *Turtle* the world's first military submarine.

It was the brainchild of David Bushnell, a Yale graduate who during the Siege of Boston began to tinker with the idea of creating a craft equipped with an explosive device that he called a "torpedo" in reference to the torpedo fish, a type of ray capable of stunning its prey with an electric shock. The operator of the *Turtle* gazed out through a glass hatch at the top while holding the tiller to an aft-mounted rudder in one hand and spinning a front-mounted propeller with the other. When it came time to submerge, he filled the bottom of the submarine with water for a dive that could only last as long as a half hour before the oxygen ran out. Once he had succeeded in attaching the torpedo to the bottom of an enemy ship with a hand-crank drill that extended from the top of the submarine, the operator pumped out the water sloshing around his feet and legs and returned to the surface of the sea.

Although a mechanical genius, Bushnell was not, apparently, much of a physical specimen, and he lacked the strength and stamina required to propel his invention through the water. At first his brother was enlisted to man the *Turtle,* but when he fell ill, Bushnell was forced to replace him with Sergeant Ezra Lee. On the night of September 7, Lee was attempting to position Bushnell's submarine under the flagship of Admiral Howe. He'd already consumed several hours fighting against the tide, and with dawn approaching he was desperate to place the torpedo at the stern of the ship, beneath the admiral's cabin.

The *Eagle* was a sixty-four-gun third-rate ship of the line, meaning that she had two gun decks and a crew of over six hundred men. She was relatively small to be the flagship of an admiral of Howe's stature, but given the difficulties of navigating the shallow, current-swept waters of the mid-Atlantic coast, she was the perfect vessel—fast, maneuverable, and just two years old. Howe's cabin was splendidly appointed: lacquered-white walls trimmed in gold and decorated with mirrors and copper engravings. The *Turtle,* on the other hand, was a barely seaworthy contraption without a single amenity (unless you counted barely breathable air) whose sole purpose was to destroy the enemy. By sanctioning a mission to send both the *Eagle* and Admiral Howe to the bottom, Washington was taking a risk that far exceeded anything he was currently contemplating in New York.

Up until that point, the Howe brothers appear to have been motivated by a genuine belief that crushing the rebellion with a brutal show of force would only alienate the affections of the colonists even further. Instead of destroying Washington's army in New York, Howe had opted for the more conservative approach of occupying enemy territory on Long Island. Having so thoroughly humiliated the American army and its commander on August 27, the time was right, from the Howes' perspective, for negotiation. But as the presence of this tadpole of a submarine made clear, the American high command was not yet ready to yield. However, was killing Admiral Howe—which would undoubtedly force his brother to dispense with diplomacy in favor of all-out war—really in America's best interests?

Dawn was approaching by the time Ezra Lee positioned the *Turtle* beneath the *Eagle*'s stern. Now he must fasten the torpedo to the wooden planking of the hull by turning a large screw, which he rotated within the dripping confines of the submersible. But as chance would have it, he had placed himself directly under the thick metal plate that connected the *Eagle*'s rudder to the hull. By the time Lee realized he must reposition the *Turtle*, it was too late. He had to abandon the operation and start back for New York before daylight revealed him to the enemy.

Lee, by this point, was exhausted, and try as he might to propel the *Turtle* across the surface of the harbor to Manhattan, the current kept sweeping him east toward British-occupied Governors Island. When a boatload of British sailors set off in pursuit, Lee once again submerged and this time released the torpedo, which had a clocklike timing device. The torpedo exploded, "throwing up large bodies of water to an immense height," but did no apparent damage, and Lee was eventually rescued by several American whaleboats waiting for him along the city's waterfront.

Lee and Bushnell had failed in their quest to destroy Admiral Howe and his flagship. And yet the voyage of the *Turtle* testifies to the immense wellsprings of ingenuity and audacity unleashed by the American Revolution. A young nation had attempted to negate the superiority of the most powerful navy in the world with a technological breakthrough that was almost a century ahead of its time.

By the morning of September 11, after a two-and-a-half-day journey from Philadelphia, Benjamin Franklin, John Adams, and Edward Rutledge found themselves in the presence of Admiral Howe in the Billopp House at the southwestern tip of Staten Island, just across from Perth Amboy, New Jersey. Howe was, according to Adams, "profuse in his expressions of gratitude to the state of Massachusetts" for erecting the marble monument to his brother in Westminster Abbey. Howe claimed, Adams recounted, that he "esteemed that honor to his family *above all things in this world*. That such was his gratitude and affection to this country, on that account, that he felt for America as for a brother, and, if America should fall, he should feel and lament it, like a loss of a brother." Franklin slyly replied, "My Lord, we shall do our utmost endeavors to save your lordship that mortification."

The conversation quickly went from bad to worse as the Americans came to realize that nothing had changed since the admiral's earlier communications with Washington and Franklin; he still did not have the authority to conduct meaningful negotiations. As Howe's secretary tersely recorded in his journal, "They met, they talked, they parted." Admiral Howe might have been a most capable naval officer, but he was a wretched negotiator. Rather than Washington and his army, it was the Howe brothers' misguided obsession with reaching a peace accord that saved America in the summer of 1776.

On September 5 General Nathanael Greene, who'd been transported from Long Island to New York for medical attention back in August, announced his return from the sickbed that had nearly claimed his life with a letter addressed to George Washington. It was madness, Greene asserted, to remain in the city. "Part of the army already has met with a defeat," he reminded Washington, "the country is struck with a panic, any capital loss at this time may ruin the cause. 'Tis our business to study to avoid any considerable misfortune and to take post where the enemy will be obliged to fight us and not we them." Instead of battling it out in New York, he insisted that "a general and speedy retreat is absolutely necessary and that the honor and interest of America requires it." He also recommended burning the entire city to the ground so as to "deprive the enemy of an opportunity of barracking their whole army together."

Initially Washington appears to have resisted his subordinate's advice, in part because he saw New York as "the key to the northern country." It wasn't the city itself but what it provided access to that made New York so important. At that moment, British forces under General Guy Carleton were in the Canadian town of St. Johns in present-day Quebec assembling their own version of Howe's invasion force for an assault on Fort Ticonderoga near the southern tip of Lake Champlain. If Howe should take the city of New York (which the Continental Congress insisted should *not* be burned in any retreat or evacuation), the British would have unimpeded access to the Hudson River, which was navigable all the way to Albany. By the end of the year, Howe would undoubtedly have linked up with Carleton coming down from Lake Champlain, and America would effectively be cut in half. With the British in command of both the Hudson and the sea, the flow of provisions and soldiers on which the American war effort depended would cease. The longer Washington could hold on to New York, the better.

By September 8, three days after Greene wrote the letter urging the abandonment of the city, Washington had begun to come around to his brigadier general's way of thinking. As he explained in a letter to Congress, even if the British occupied New York, the "strong posts" the Americans had established at Fort Washington at the northwestern corner of Manhattan Island and directly across the Hudson in New Jersey (eventually called Fort Lee) might be enough to block the British, especially since a barrier of sunken ships and other impediments to navigation now spanned the river between these two fortifications. Washington certainly did not feel good about it, but even he had to admit that from a strategic point of view, the time had come to abandon New York. On September 12 he called a council of war where it was agreed to relocate the army to the rocky and highly defensible heights of Harlem fourteen miles to the north of the city.

And so, as on the other side of the East River General Howe moved his army from Brooklyn into Queens County to the north, Washington began the evacuation of New York.

Joseph Plumb Martin was just fifteen years old. His father was an improvident, know-it-all minister with a habit of alienating the members of his congregation, and early on in his life the decision had been made that Joseph should be raised by his mother's parents in Milford, Connecticut. Precocious, restless, and ultimately rootless, Martin had convinced his reluctant grandparents to allow him to join a locally raised company of state troops attached to the Continental army. As dawn approached on the morning of September 15, he was with his regiment at the edge of the East River, dug into a bank of dirt overlooking Kips Bay (today's East Thirty-Fourth Street), almost directly across from Long Island's Newtown Creek at the border of Brooklyn and Queens.

"At daybreak," Martin later wrote, "the first thing that 'saluted our eyes' was . . . four ships at anchor with springs upon their cables, and within musket shot of us." It had been what Martin described as "quite a dark night," and somehow the British had maneuvered four frigates to within just a few hundred yards of the Manhattan shore—an amazing

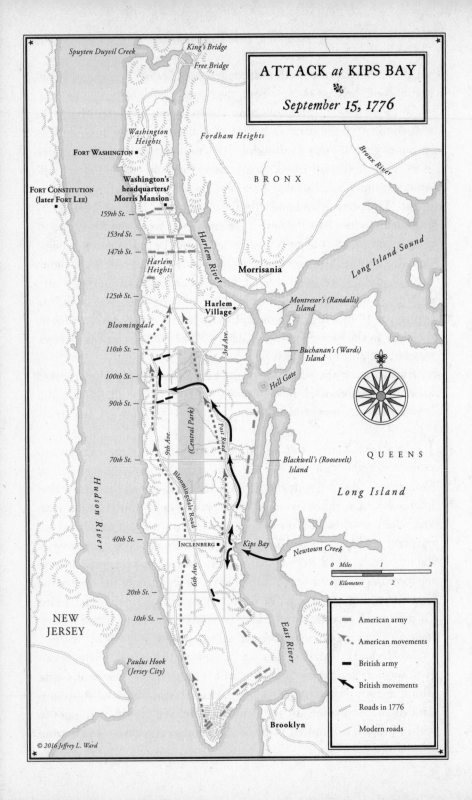

ATTACK *at* KIPS BAY

September 15, 1776

Spuyten Duyvil Creek

King's Bridge

Free Bridge

Washington Heights

FORT WASHINGTON

Fordham Heights

BRONX

Bronx River

FORT CONSTITUTION
(later FORT LEE)

Washington's headquarters/
Morris Mansion

159th St.

153rd St.

147th St.

Harlem Heights

Morrisania

Long Island Sound

Harlem River

125th St.

Harlem Village

Montresor's (Randalls) Island

Bloomingdale

110th St.

3rd Ave.

Buchanan's (Wards) Island

100th St.

90th St.

Hell Gate

Post Road

(Central Park)

9th Ave.

70th St.

Blackwell's (Roosevelt) Island

QUEENS

Bloomingdale Road

Long Island

Hudson River

40th St.

INCLENBERG

Kips Bay

Newtown Creek

0 Miles 1 2

0 Kilometers 2

6th Ave.

20th St.

10th St.

East River

NEW JERSEY

Paulus Hook
(Jersey City)

American army

American movements

British army

British movements

Roads in 1776

Modern roads

Brooklyn

© 2016 Jeffrey L. Ward

feat given the strength and variability of the current in this portion of the East River. Using lines to keep them sideways to the shore, the four frigates presented an awesome show of potential firepower, with close to eighty large cannons now trained in the direction of the Connecticut troops. One of the frigates was so close to Martin's position that he could make out the name *Phoenix* "as distinctly as though I had been directly under her stern."

As the sun rose over the opposite bank of the East River, Martin could see dozens upon dozens of boats coming out of the mouth of Newtown Creek. They were filled with British soldiers dressed in red uniforms, and once the fleet had spread out over the river behind the warships, the bobbing boats imparted a crimson haze across the water's surface that resembled, Martin wrote, "a large clover field in full bloom."

After a few hours of staring quietly at the unfolding scene ahead of them, the American soldiers heard the distant boom of cannons behind them as several British ships that had recently sailed up the Hudson River began to fire on the small community of Bloomingdale on the west shore of Manhattan. This, it turned out, was a feint to distract the Americans from what was about to happen on the east side of the island at Kips Bay.

As the British forces waited for the diversion in Bloomingdale to have its effect, Martin grew impatient. Directly behind him was an abandoned warehouse with its door swung open. Martin stepped inside the old cavernous space and sat down on a stool. "The floor was strewed with papers which had in some former period been used in the concerns of the house," he wrote, "but were then lying in 'woeful confusion.'" Martin, a bright and very curious lad, began to examine some of the papers when suddenly, just outside the doorway into the warehouse, the British barrage at Kips Bay began.

"I thought my head would go with the sound," he remembered. "I made a frog's leap for the ditch and . . . began to consider which part of my carcass was to go first." It was, by all accounts, an absolutely overwhelming show of force. According to Howe's secretary Ambrose Serle, "So terrible and so incessant a roar of guns few even in the army and navy had ever heard before." The Reverend Benjamin Trumbull was a chaplain in the American lines near Martin, and he, like all of them, was awestruck by what he described as "a most furious cannonade." All around the

Connecticut troops, the "sand and sods of earth" were thrown into the air and "made such a dust and smoke that there was no possibility of firing on the enemy to any advantage."

For the next two hours, Trumbull, Martin, and the others lay with their hands over their ears as their earthen fortifications were, according to Martin, "almost leveled upon us." Eventually their officers, "seeing we could make no resistance and . . . that we must soon be entirely exposed to the rake of their guns, gave the order to leave the lines." Even though they were grievously exposed to British grapeshot, which rained upon them, one soldier remembered, "as though a person . . . had thrown his hand full of stones," they had no choice but to run for it. Once beyond the reach of the British artillery, Martin fell in with two fellow soldiers from Connecticut, and the three of them headed west.

They were in a hurry, but apparently not that much of a hurry. On the road leading into the interior of Manhattan, they came upon a small house in which they found two women and several small children, "all crying most bitterly." When asked whether they had "any spirits in the house," one of the women produced a bottle of rum and placed it on the table. "We each of us drank a glass," Martin wrote, "and bidding them good-bye betook ourselves to the highway."

William Howe had hoped to launch the assault on New York two days earlier, on September 13, which was the anniversary of the Battle of Quebec. On that date in 1759, a much younger Howe had courageously climbed the near-vertical cliffs fronting the Plains of Abraham to help deliver a miraculous victory to his commander, General James Wolfe. Wolfe had been fated to die on September 13, 1759, a glorious hero. Howe chose to memorialize that inspiring victory by assigning the passwords "Wolfe" and "Quebec" for the day of the attack on Kips Bay.

The circumstances of the two battles could not have been more different. Wolfe had been at the end of his tether. With the Canadian winter approaching and his army succumbing to disease, he had risked everything in a desperate bid to achieve the improbable triumph that secured Canada for the British Empire. Now, in 1776, Howe, the commander of a seemingly invincible force, was determined to risk nothing. One of his officers recorded that "he declares it his intention not to lose the finger of a single man wantonly."

Accordingly, he had chosen to pound what passed for a breastwork at Kips Bay into oblivion before landing any of his men. Then began a slow and cautious accumulation of soldiers and artillery as General Clinton in the advance seized the nearest high ground, "the height of Inclenberg" (today's Murray Hill), and waited for his commander and the rest of the army to catch up. And so, as the American forces around Kips Bay fled in panic, Howe's army moved with ponderous deliberation toward Inclenberg.

Only the day before, with the evacuation of New York already begun, Washington had moved into his new residence at the Morris Mansion in upper Manhattan overlooking the Harlem River. At approximately 10:00 a.m. on September 15, he first heard the distant sound of the cannons at Kips Bay, approximately eight and a half miles to the south. He was soon riding with "the utmost dispatch" in the direction of the British landing, accompanied by his young staff. As he rode south through the rocky, heavily wooded terrain that skirted the eastern edge of what later became Central Park, Washington must have known that General Howe had once again caught him by surprise.

Washington had divided his army into three groups. In anticipation of Howe's launching his attack at New York or, at the opposite end of the island, the Harlem River, Washington had positioned his two strongest concentrations of soldiers to the south and north. Since it seemed unlikely that Howe would attack Manhattan at its center, Washington had stationed the already disheartened remnants of the Connecticut troops at Kips Bay. To expect these inexperienced soldiers to stand up to the full, unmitigated might of Howe's navy-assisted army was folly, especially after the embarrassing rout in Brooklyn. And besides, Washington had already decided to leave New York City and the majority of Manhattan Island to the enemy. If the British had attacked just one day later, there would have been no Americans left to oppose the landing. So what was the point of opposing them now?

None of this seems to have made any difference to Washington, who arrived at Inclenberg just as the first few companies of Clinton's advance came into sight and began marching toward a cornfield that lay between them and a confused gathering of American soldiers. Washington rode into the midst of the troops and attempted to make some order out of the chaos. "Take the walls!" he shouted. "Take the cornfield!" It fell to the Connecticut general Samuel Parsons to implement these orders, but the men proved uncontrollable even though only a relatively small number of the enemy's light infantrymen were visible to the east.

Also arriving on the scene, but from the direction opposite to Washington, was Private Joseph Plumb Martin, no doubt feeling the effects of his recent glass of rum. "The demons of fear and disorder seemed to take full possession of all and everything on that day," he wrote. The militiamen threw down their weapons and packs and started running to the north. By that time, Washington had worked himself into an almost crazed furor, swatting at the passing soldiers with his sword and snapping his unloaded pistols in a futile attempt to make it all stop. According to one account he repeatedly threw his hat to the ground and cried out, "Are these the men with which I am to defend America?"

Washington was a man for whom discipline and control meant everything, particularly since his own passions were, according to a friend, "almost too mighty for a man." As a teenager he had laboriously copied out 110 "Rules of Civility" and had established what Thomas Jefferson called "a firm and habitual ascendency" over his emotions. Back in July, he had so impressed Howe's adjutant James Paterson with his quietly charismatic air of authority that the British officer had been, according to Henry Knox, "awestruck as if he was before something supernatural."

But now, in a cornfield near the heights of Inclenberg, the mask was off and the floodgates had swung wide as Washington's anger threatened to become dangerously self-destructive. Even though enemy soldiers were just eighty yards away and closing fast, he was, according to Nathanael Greene, "so vexed at the infamous conduct of his troops, that he sought death rather than life." According to another account, "the general, regardless of his own safety, was in so much hazard, that one of his attendants seized the reins and gave his horse a different direction." Washington had lost control of not only his army but himself.

By the end of the day, several thousand American soldiers had evacuated New York and taken up positions among the rocky hills of Harlem Heights, with only the tiny span of the King's Bridge providing a way off Manhattan Island. In the weeks and months ahead there would be brief moments of uplift for Washington's army. On the day following Kips

Bay, several hundred troops from Connecticut, Virginia, and Pennsylvania showed some overdue courage in a skirmish euphemistically called the Battle of Harlem Heights. On October 28 the Americans fought with surprising stubbornness at the more legitimate Battle of White Plains. Mostly, however, the autumn of 1776 amounted to a terrible and embarrassing collapse of the American army in New York and New Jersey. Over the course of four disastrous days in November, both Fort Washington and Fort Lee fell to the British. By the end of the month, Washington's ever-dwindling army was fleeing across the breadth of New Jersey to the Delaware River.

So it was that on the afternoon of September 15, almost within sight of the scene of Washington's disgrace at Inclenberg, General Howe took the time to refresh himself and his staff at the home of Robert Murray, renowned as one of the most elegant and beautiful houses on Manhattan Island. Some later claimed that this pause was what allowed General Putnam and his portion of the Continental army in New York to escape the clutches of the British army. But Howe had reason to savor the hospitality provided by Mrs. Murray and her two daughters, Susannah and Beulah. The first link in the chain that would seal off New England and snuff out the rebellion was in place, and 360 miles to the north another large waterborne British army was on its way to making that fate an accomplished fact.

CHAPTER TWO

The Mosquito Fleet

On the morning of September 15, 1776, the day the British took New York, Brigadier General Benedict Arnold stood on the quarterdeck of a fifty-five-foot schooner anchored in the northern reaches of Lake Champlain, about eight miles below the Canadian border. Surrounding the narrow lake was a wilderness of trees and dense undergrowth, with the distant peaks of the Adirondack and Green Mountains visible to the west and east. During the day the sky was frequently darkened by vast flocks of passenger pigeons. At night Arnold and his men could hear the howls of wolves feasting on deer. But as they had learned from bitter experience, the real danger came from the many native warriors patrolling the margins of the lake. For all intents and purposes, the Americans were prisoners on the dozen or so vessels of their little fleet, with just a single schooner to supply them with provisions and news from Fort Ticonderoga, almost a hundred miles to the south.

Since no roads existed, Lake Champlain provided the only practical route by which the British could invade America from the north. For the time being, Arnold's collection of cannon-equipped schooners and oversize rowboats, which the Americans referred to as the "Mosquito Fleet," had command of the lake. But as Arnold was well aware, about forty miles to the north, in the tiny frontier town of St. Johns on the Richelieu River (the tributary through which Lake Champlain flowed into the St. Lawrence River), the British were working furiously to construct a fleet that could win back control of the lake.

In the meantime, at the opposite end of Lake Champlain, at the

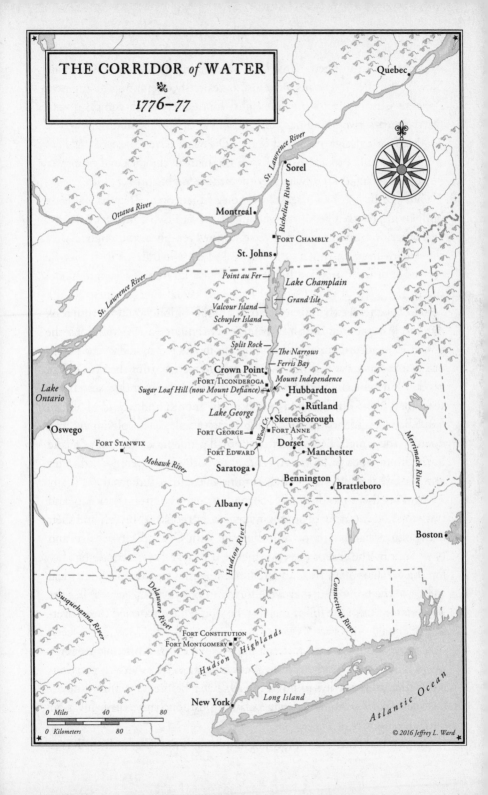

THE CORRIDOR *of* WATER

❧

1776–77

Quebec

St. Lawrence River

Sorel

Ottawa River

Montreal

Richelieu River

Fort Chambly

St. Johns

Point au Fer

Lake Champlain

St. Lawrence River

Valcour Island

Grand Isle

Schuyler Island

Split Rock

The Narrows

Ferris Bay

Crown Point

Fort Ticonderoga

Mount Independence

Lake Ontario

Sugar Loaf Hill (now Mount Defiance)

Hubbardton

Lake George

Rutland

Skenesborough

Oswego

Fort George

Fort Anne

Dorset

Fort Stanwix

Fort Edward

Manchester

Mohawk River

Saratoga

Bennington

Brattleboro

Merrimack River

Albany

Boston

Hudson River

Susquehanna River

Delaware River

Connecticut River

Fort Constitution

Fort Montgomery

Hudson Highlands

New York

Long Island

Atlantic Ocean

0 Miles   40   80

0 Kilometers   80

© 2016 Jeffrey L. Ward

swampy, insect-infested hamlet of Skenesborough (today's Whitehall, New York), the Americans were just as zealously attempting to augment Arnold's existing fleet with four eighty-foot galleys, each equipped with thirty-six oars, two triangular sails, and a bevy of cannons and swivel guns. Modeled on a design perfected on the Delaware River, these row galleys would hopefully provide Arnold with the maneuverability and firepower he needed to stand up to whatever the British might throw at him.

But the British had a secret weapon of their own. They had already built an impressive fleet of two schooners, twenty-two gunboats, and several other even more powerful vessels. However, given the pugnacity of the American navy, which just two weeks before had dared to sail to the very edge of the Canadian border and fire off an impressive cannonade, the British general Guy Carleton had determined that he must build a vessel of such overwhelming size that all opposition would be futile. At that moment, a dozen British carpenters were building a 280-ton, eighteen-gun ship in record time. "Trees growing in the forest in the morning," one commentator admiringly wrote, "would form part of the ship before night." Known as the *Inflexible,* this relatively mammoth vessel was scheduled to be finished by the end of the month and would establish, one officer confidently insisted, "dominion of Lake Champlain beyond a doubt." They might be two relatively small armies at either end of a lake in the hinterlands of North America, but both forces were locked in an arms race that could very well determine the course of the war.

And yet there was one factor beyond anyone's control: the weather. If Carleton and his army of approximately eight thousand British and German soldiers had any hope of linking up with General Howe's army in New York by the end of the year, they had to take Fort Ticonderoga before Lake Champlain froze in late November. If Arnold could delay the enemy to the point that they were forced to postpone the attack on Fort Ticonderoga until the following year, he would have achieved the equivalent of a major victory.

Arnold was not aware of it, but his bold handling of his tiny fleet two weeks before had already won the Americans an extra month by convincing Carleton he needed to build the *Inflexible* before he ventured down the lake. But was it enough of a delay to postpone the British invasion until the summer of 1777?

August had been unbearably hot and humid, but now with the leaves of the trees beginning to take on the colors of fall, what Arnold called "the blowing season" was about to arrive. Northerly gales were sure to cause the temperatures to plummet as they kicked up waves steep enough to intimidate even the most seasoned saltwater sailor, let alone Arnold's ill-equipped assortment of greenhorns. How he was to oppose the British under such conditions was a question that not even Arnold knew how to answer.

He was short, solidly built (one acquaintance remembered that "there wasn't any wasted timber in him"), and blessed with almost superhuman energy and endurance. He was handsome and charismatic, with black hair, gray eyes, and an aquiline nose, and carried himself with the lissome elegance of a natural athlete. A neighbor from Connecticut remembered that Benedict Arnold was "the most accomplished and graceful skater" he had ever seen.

He was descended from the Rhode Island equivalent of royalty. The first Benedict Arnold had been one of the colony's founders, and several subsequent generations had helped to establish the Arnolds as solid and respected citizens. Unfortunately, Arnold's father, who had resettled in Norwich, Connecticut, proved to be a drunkard, and only after his son had moved to New Haven was the boy able to begin to free himself from the ignominy of his childhood. By his midthirties he had enjoyed enough success to begin building one of the finest homes in town. That didn't prevent him from remaining hypersensitive to any slight, and like many honor-obsessed gentlemen in the eighteenth century he had challenged more than one man to a duel.

Prior to the Revolution he had been an apothecary and seagoing merchant captain who regularly traveled as far south as the Caribbean and as far north as the Canadian ports of Montreal and Quebec on the St. Lawrence River. From the first, he distinguished himself as one of New Haven's more vocal and combative patriots. On hearing of the Boston Massacre, he thundered, "Good God, are the Americans all asleep and tamely giving up their glorious liberties?" When in April 1775 he learned of the skirmishes at Lexington and Concord, he quickly seized a portion of New Haven's gunpowder supply and marched north with a company of volunteers. Once in Cambridge, Massachusetts, he convinced Dr. Joseph Warren and the Massachusetts Committee of Safety to authorize an expedition to capture Fort Ticonderoga and its eighty or more cannons.

As it turned out, others had the same idea, and Arnold was forced to form an uneasy alliance with Ethan Allen and his Green Mountain Boys before the two leaders strode side by side into Ticonderoga. While Allen and his men turned their attention to consuming the contents of the British liquor supply, Arnold sailed and rowed to St. Johns at the opposite end of the lake, where he and a small group of men captured several British military vessels and instantly gave America command of the lake.

Abrupt and impatient with anything he deemed superfluous to the matter at hand, Arnold had a fatal tendency to criticize and even ridicule those with whom he disagreed. When a few weeks later a Continental officer from Pittsfield, Massachusetts, named James Easton, dared to question the legitimacy of his authority as the self-proclaimed commodore of the American navy on Lake Champlain, Arnold proceeded to "kick him very heartily." It was an insult Easton never forgot, and in the months and years ahead, Easton became one of a virtual Greek chorus of Arnold detractors that would plague him for the rest of his military career.

About this time, Arnold's personal life took a tragic turn when he learned of the death of his wife. Upon returning to New Haven, he visited her grave with his three young sons at his side. Arnold's letters to his wife prior to the Revolution had been filled with pleas for her to write more often, and his grief upon her death seems to have been almost overpowering. And yet, for someone of Arnold's restless temperament, it was inconceivable to remain in New Haven with his sorrow. "An idle life under my present circumstances," he explained, "would be but a lingering death." After a visit of just three weeks, Arnold left his children under the care of his sister Hannah and was on his way back to Cambridge, where he hoped to bury his anguish in what he called "the public calamity."

In early August 1775 Arnold met the American army's new commander, General George Washington. Washington was without the gunpowder and cannons he needed to dislodge the British army from Boston and was mired in what was to become a nine-month siege. But to the north, in Canada, he saw the opportunity for action. The outbreak of the Revolution had caught the British ministry off guard, and they had not yet been able to reinforce the small army based in Montreal and Quebec. If the Americans could take those two cities before the arrival of reinforcements from England, they might succeed in removing the British threat from the north. General Philip Schuyler in Albany was already formulating plans to use the corridor formed by Lake Champlain and the Richelieu River to attack Montreal. The real challenge was to find a way to surprise the tiny British garrison at Quebec. By following the Kennebec River into what is today northern Maine, it might be possible to lead an army through the forest to Quebec—a heavily fortified castle of a town that loomed imposingly over the fast-flowing St. Lawrence. Arnold, needless to say, was all for it.

He eventually lost five hundred of his twelve hundred men to starvation, exposure, and desertion, but after several weeks of slogging through the boggy, ice-crisped backwoods of Maine, Arnold and the ragged remnants of his command staggered out of the wilderness and proceeded to climb the same riverside cliffs the young William Howe had scaled back in 1759. Even though the British forces in Quebec refused his impertinent demand that they surrender, the sheer audacity of the undertaking won Arnold the title of the "American Hannibal."

Arnold needed a larger army if he was to have any hope of successfully attacking Quebec, and he was soon joined by forces led by General Richard Montgomery, who had just taken Montreal. Not until December 31, 1775, in a blinding snowstorm, did they finally mount a daring two-pronged assault. The operation ultimately proved unsuccessful—largely because Montgomery was killed and Arnold seriously wounded in the left leg at the onset of the attack.

With the arrival of a large British military force on May 6, 1776, what was left of the disease-ravaged American army in Canada had no choice but to evacuate. By that time, Arnold had recovered from the injury to his leg and been reassigned to Montreal, where he took a leading role in supervising the American retreat south to Lake Champlain. In typically dramatic fashion, Arnold was the last one to hop aboard the last boat to leave St. Johns and "thus indulged," his aide remembered, "the vanity of being the last man who embarked from the shores of the enemy."

Once back at Fort Ticonderoga, Arnold, now a brigadier general, was picked by Major General Horatio Gates "to give life and spirit to our dock yard" in an attempt to retain the naval superiority he had helped establish on Lake Champlain more than a year earlier. Up until that point, the American boatbuilding effort had focused on the construction of fifty-five-foot gondolas—very wide and very heavy rowboats rigged with a single mast and a square mainsail. Although perfectly adequate platforms for three cannons, an assortment of swivel guns, and a crew of approximately forty-five men, the gondolas were dangerously low to the water and notoriously "dull" sailers, making them an easy prey for a traditional naval vessel in a sea fight.

Arnold quickly became an advocate for the construction of the larger and much faster row galleys, and by the end of July he was supervising more than two hundred carpenters in building four of these new and relatively nimble craft, whose raised quarterdecks and plumb bows combined with their triangular lateen-rigged sails to give them an almost piratical appearance. Gates was so impressed by Arnold's knowledge of maritime affairs and his ability to get things done that he made him commander of the American fleet. But by the beginning of August, even before he left Fort Ticonderoga, the new commodore of Lake Champlain was already experiencing some unexpectedly stormy weather.

Arnold had a talent for rubbing people the wrong way. And yet, if a soldier had served with him during one of his more heroic adventures, that soldier was likely to regard him as the most inspiring officer he had ever known. By the time Arnold returned to Fort Ticonderoga after the evacuation of Canada, he had accumulated a truly remarkable number of subordinates and colleagues who either worshipped or despised him. One former aide during the evacuation of Canada described him as "intrepid, generous, friendly, upright, honest." A Connecticut physician at Fort Ticonderoga, on the other hand, hated Arnold so thoroughly that he recorded in his journal, "I heartily wish some person would try an experiment upon him—to make the sun shine through his head with an ounce ball; and then see whether the rays come in a direct or oblique direction." No one seemed to lack an opinion when it came to Benedict Arnold.

During the retreat from Canada, Arnold had ordered Moses Hazen, a former British officer and resident of St. Johns who had joined the American cause, to guard some provisions as the Continental army worked its disorganized way south. Due to what Arnold considered Hazen's neglect, the provisions had been lost, and Arnold had ill-advisedly pressed charges. In late July, just as he was preparing to depart with his newly assembled fleet on their mission up Lake Champlain, he was forced to testify in Hazen's court-martial at Fort Ticonderoga. And just as had happened with Washington in New York, the court-martial did nothing but distract him from the matter at hand.

While Arnold had been consumed with building the gondolas and galleys, Hazen had been cultivating the friendship of the young officers who were to serve on his court-martial board. Perhaps not unexpectedly, the officers disallowed the testimony of the only soldier Arnold had named as a witness. Arnold exploded, prompting "a spirited reprimand" from the court's president. Arnold's outrage only increased when Hazen was acquitted, and the court-martial board demanded that he apologize. When he indignantly refused, the court ordered his arrest. Since Arnold clearly had more pressing concerns, Gates felt he had no choice but to dissolve the court, explaining to John Hancock of the Continental Congress that "the warmth of General Arnold's temper might possibly lead him a little farther than is marked by the precise line of decorum." This, however, would not be the end of the controversy as Hazen, Easton, and a considerable list of disgruntled Arnold subordinates took their case to the Continental Congress in Philadelphia.

Over the course of the next month Arnold and his fleet worked their way up the more than 125-mile length of Lake Champlain, a watery pathway through the woods that shrunk down to less than a mile near a fissured cliff of stone known as Split Rock and expanded to as many as fourteen miles near the present site of Burlington, Vermont. In some places, algae-slicked rocks lurked just below the water's surface; in others the lake plunged down more than four hundred feet into the blackness. Only a handful of families lived along the lake, and just past Ferris Bay, named for the household of Peter Ferris on the eastern shore, Arnold paused to entertain his officers, one of whom appreciatively referred to the gathering in his journal as a "genteel feast."

By the end of August they had reached the northern portion of the lake, where the peninsula-like Grand Isle divides the waterway in half as its western fork flows into the headwaters of the Richelieu River. By early September they had ventured so far north that they could hear the British building fortifications behind the trees. At night, native warriors in their birch-bark canoes drifted silently past the American fleet, and to guard from attack Arnold kept two schooners and several bateaux constantly on patrol. When some of his men were killed by Indian ambushes onshore, Arnold thought it prudent to retire more than twenty miles to the south.

Arnold did his best to monitor the British shipbuilding operation in St. Johns, of which he heard sporadic reports through a largely unreliable assortment of scouts and spies. The British to the north had him worried, but by September 15, when he wrote to Horatio Gates from the cabin of his flagship, the *Royal Savage,* there was more on his mind. In August his sister Hannah had reported that his sons, particularly his youngest, Hale, missed him terribly. "Tell my papa he must come home," the boy told her. "I want to kiss him." Hannah also reported that his house in New Haven leaked "more than ever," and that shingles had become impossible to purchase. Even worse, Hannah had been forced to sell his brigantine for a pittance to the Continental army in New York, where it was to serve as a navigational hazard against the British. The irony was almost laughable: while he had been building a new fleet in Lake Champlain, the vessel on which he had once depended for his livelihood had been sunk to the bottom of the Hudson River. "If you ever live to return," Hannah wrote on September 1, "you will find yourself a broken merchant."

But what troubled Arnold the most was a letter he'd received from a delegate in the Continental Congress. The latest gossip being spread in Philadelphia, the delegate reported, was that Arnold had commandeered goods for his own personal gain during the retreat from Canada. "Your best friends," the informant ominously warned, "are not your countrymen."

Arnold poured out his frustrations to Gates, who over the last several months had become both his commanding officer and his confidant. Gates, forty-eight, was a former British officer who had embraced the republican ideals of the patriot cause and now owned a house in Virginia. Although he had begun the war as Washington's adjutant general during the Siege of Boston, he had been quick to establish his own independent identity. Unlike Washington, who had found the local troops who made up the undisciplined core of his army frustratingly uncooperative, Gates had announced that he "never desired to see better soldiers than the New England men made." A virtual love affair had subsequently flourished between Gates and the New England delegates of the Continental Congress, who had hoped to make Gates the new commander of the northern army. As it turned out, that position was already filled by the aristocratic Philip Schuyler, whose family owned vast holdings in upstate New York and who shared Washington's disdain for the militiamen of New England.

A tense standoff had ensued both in Congress and between the two generals that was eventually resolved by stationing Schuyler (who retained the title of commander of the northern army) in Albany, New York, where he oversaw the flow of soldiers and provisions to the north, while Gates remained in the field with the army at Fort Ticonderoga. For the time being, Arnold appears to have been on good terms with both generals. However, it was Gates who had awarded him command of the Mosquito Fleet, and it was to Gates that he complained of how his critics were attacking him in Congress while he was on a boat in the northern reaches of Lake Champlain.

"I cannot but think it extremely cruel," he wrote, "when I have sacrificed my ease, health, and great part of my private property in the cause of my country to be calumniated as a robber and thief at a time too when I have it not in my power to be heard in my own defense." Gates assured Arnold that he was doing everything possible to contradict "the foul stream of that poisonous fountain, detraction." And besides, Gates tactfully suggested, Arnold had other, more important matters demanding his attention at the present moment—namely how to prevent "the enemy's invasion of our country."

Arnold, Gates had made clear, was not to mount an all-out attack; rather, it was "a defensive war we are carrying on," meaning that Arnold must take "no wanton risk" or exercise an "unnecessary display of power." If, however, the British should encroach from the north, Arnold was to "defend in that case . . . with such cool determined valor as will give them reason to repent their temerity." Gates, in the tradition of many a commanding officer before and since, was covering himself as best he could—advising Arnold to take no needless chances even as he urged him to do everything he could to oppose a British advance.

For the last month Arnold had attempted to identify where on the lake he could best accomplish all this—an especially difficult thing to do since he did not have, he complained to Gates, a proper chart. Finally, on September 5, Gates sent him "the draught of the lake as you desire," and within the next week Arnold had begun to focus on "the island of Valcour," just south of modern Plattsburgh, New York, on the western shore of the lake. As it so happened, a young Scotsman named William Hay had built a house overlooking the little bay between the shore and the island. Hay was a devoted patriot and would be, along with his wife and baby daughter, a potentially helpful neighbor during a stay at Valcour.

Arnold knew the enemy would not begin to move south until they had a strong northerly breeze at their backs. If he positioned his fleet at Valcour, between the island and the shore (a distance of less than half a mile), the rocky, tree-topped island would conceal his vessels from the British as they sailed past on their way south. Only after the British were a significant distance below the island would Arnold reveal himself to the enemy, thus forcing them to sail back against the wind if they wanted to attack his fleet. By gaining what was known as the "weather gage," the Americans would have the nautical equivalent of the fortified high ground the New Englanders had enjoyed at the Battle of Bunker Hill. There was no way to predict exactly what the British would do, of course, but Arnold decided that Valcour Island had the best chance of giving his fleet the upper hand in a potential battle with the British.

By September 21 he had sent two boats "to sound round the island of Valcour." He wrote Gates that their crews reported that "it is an exceeding fine, secure harbor." In the next northerly breeze, he decided, he would sail to Valcour.

By that time Arnold was regularly drilling the men in "the exercise of their guns." Unfortunately, they needed all the practice they could get. Most of them had never been at sea and "in general," he wrote, "are not equal to half their number of good men." He also complained that he had received little of the warm clothing he had requested—an absolute necessity if they were not to freeze to death in the weeks ahead. But it was the galleys that he was most anxious about, and he was "greatly at a loss [as to] what could have retarded the galleys so long." "Believe me, dear sir," Gates assured him, "no man alive could be more anxious for the welfare of you and your fleet than . . . myself."

Finally, on October 6, by which time Arnold had relocated to Valcour Island, where snow was visible on the peaks of the Adirondacks, General David Waterbury from Connecticut arrived with the last two galleys, bringing the fleet to a total of fifteen fighting vessels. Waterbury was to act as Arnold's second-in-command, and along with the galleys, he also brought news about Washington's army in New York. Up until that

point, Arnold had heard only the vaguest rumors about some kind of action on Long Island. From what Waterbury reported, it sounded as if the
American army had surrendered New York without a fight. "It appears to
me our troops or *officers* are panic struck," Arnold wrote Gates, "or why
does a hundred thousand men fly before one quarter of their numbers? Is
it possible my countrymen can be callous to their wrongs or hesitate one
moment between slavery or death?"

By October 10 Arnold was convinced that Howe's recent success to
the south almost guaranteed that General Carleton in St. Johns was
about to mount his own attack. "If [the British] hear . . . that Lord Howe
is in possession of New York," he wrote, "they will doubtless attempt a
juncture with him. . . . Their fleet, I make no doubt . . . , will be formidable, if not equal to ours."

On October 12 Gates assured Arnold that he was "pleased to find you
and your armada ride in Valcour Bay in defiance of the power of our foes
in Canada." But by then the Battle of Valcour Island had already been
fought.

After five straight days of southerly breezes, the wind finally changed to
the north, and around dawn on October 11 the British fleet departed
from Point au Fer, about forty miles north of Valcour Island. The flotilla
made for an impressive sight, with all eyes drawn to the *Inflexible,* the
freshwater equivalent of a frigate built in less than a month amid the
wilds of Canada—"a phenomenon . . . never so much as dreamed of," one
British soldier remarked, "in the very heart of the continent . . . and so
great a distance from the sea."

The fleet was under the command of General Guy Carleton, who had
recently been knighted for his brave defense of Quebec the previous winter. However, this being primarily a naval operation, there were some
who grumbled that it would have been better if Sir Guy had left the command to others. "Many blamed his hazarding himself on an element so
much out of his line," Lieutenant William Digby wrote, claiming that
Carleton would provide "very little service on board excepting proving
his courage," of which there was already little doubt.

Carleton's flagship was the schooner *Maria* (named for the general's
wife), on which he shared the quarterdeck with Thomas Pringle, a naval
captain and now commodore of the British fleet. In addition to the *Maria*

and *Inflexible,* there were the schooner *Carleton;* the scow-like sailing barge *Thunderer,* equipped with twenty large cannons; the gondola *Loyal Convert* (originally an American vessel before her capture during the evacuation of Canada); and twenty-two gunboats. Accompanying the fleet in a large number of longboats and bateaux were approximately one thousand British and German soldiers, who were to act as boarding parties if the fighting should become hand-to-hand—a possibility that deeply concerned Arnold, since the gondolas that made up the majority of his fleet were so low in the water as to make boarding relatively easy.

The British fleet was making good time on this cold, clear day with what the German artillery officer Captain George Pausch described as a "splendid and auspicious wind" pushing them to the south. By 9:30 a.m. they had begun to enter the widest portion of the lake, with Grand Isle to the east and Valcour Island, which from their vantage point looked more like a point of land attached to the mainland, to the west. The surgeon Robert Knox was with Carleton and Pringle aboard the *Maria* that morning, and as he looked behind them toward the New York shore, he thought he saw something. "As I was walking the quarterdeck with the general," he wrote, "I descried a vessel close in shore, which suddenly disappeared and almost made me think I was deceived, but my glasses being good I persisted in it and induced the commodore to send a tender . . . with orders to fire a gun and hoist a signal if he saw any ships."

They were now almost two miles to the south of Valcour. With the northerly breeze kicking up the gray-blue lake into whitecaps, the fleet of thirty-six warships backed their sails and waited. As soon as the tender reached what Dr. Knox thought was the mouth of a river but was actually the bay between Valcour Island and the shore, the vessel fired a cannon. Captain Pringle hoisted a prearranged sequence of signal flags, and soon the British fleet was headed back toward the enemy.

Arnold had known from the start that with the wind out of the north, the chances were high that the British would start sailing down the lake. Around dawn he had sent out the schooner *Revenge* to keep an eye to the north, and between 7:00 and 8:00 a.m., her crew returned with word that a large fleet had just passed Cumberland Bay and was headed in their direction. Arnold's second-in-command, General David Waterbury, was a veteran of the French and Indian War, and he worried that by tucking the American fleet inside Valcour Bay, Arnold had given them no way to escape the enemy. All the British would have to do was come at them from both the northern and southern entrances of the bay and they would be surrounded.

That morning, Waterbury rowed from his galley, the *Washington*, over to Arnold's flagship, the *Royal Savage*, which as her name might suggest had originally been a British vessel. Waterbury urged Arnold "not to lie where we should be surrounded" and to fight the British in the open lake "as they were so much superior to us in number and strength." Arnold remained steadfast. It might seem counterintuitive to confine themselves to this little tree-lined cove, where the prospect of adding another thirty or more hostile warships inevitably evoked a terrifying sense of claustrophobia, but as subsequent events proved, what Waterbury proposed would have been a disaster. The British vessels were faster and more powerful than their own, especially if their side-mounted batteries were brought to bear in a sea fight in the open lake. No, Waterbury remembered Arnold saying, "He would fight them in the bay of Valcour."

Around 9:30 Arnold sent out his third-in-command, Colonel Edward Wigglesworth, a mariner from Newburyport, Massachusetts, in a small yawl to observe the enemy. This was the vessel that Dr. Knox had glimpsed from the quarterdeck of the *Maria* before Wigglesworth returned to the American fleet with word that, as Arnold had hoped, the British had overshot the island and were well to the south. By that time Arnold had moved over to the galley *Congress*, from which he planned to lead the fighting from the center of the American line of battle. But first he must make sure the enemy knew where they were. Soon the three galleys and the *Royal Savage* had left their moorings and were sailing out into the lake so as to attract the attention of the British and lure them into the bay.

For the first time Arnold and his officers had a good view of their opponents. Some American prisoners later told the British that on seeing the *Inflexible* looming high above the rest of the vessels on the lake, one man cried out, "Lord God have mercy upon us—there's a three-masted ship!" Another reported that when Arnold saw that so many of the enemy sported the white lapels of a British naval uniform, he exclaimed, "By God, they are all navy people!" Given that five hundred of Arnold's force of approximately seven hundred men were landlubbers, one can hardly blame him.

Once he could see that the British were sailing back toward Valcour, Arnold ordered all the American vessels to return to the bay. The galleys were soon back inside, but the *Royal Savage,* through what Arnold described as "some bad management," fell victim to the *Inflexible.* Despite being as much as a half mile away, the British frigate possessed cannons of sufficient power and accuracy to blow away the schooner's foremast and bring down much of her rigging. With the British fast approaching, the *Royal Savage*'s captain decided he must run the schooner up on the rocky tip of Valcour, where most of her fifty-man crew were able to jump over the side and wade to shore.

Carleton and Pringle were convinced that the swiftness of the British advance was what prevented the enemy from fleeing down the lake. What they either failed to realize or preferred not to admit was that by sailing blindly past the Americans tucked inside Valcour Bay they had not only missed an opportunity to attack the enemy from the north but also rendered the most powerful weapon in their arsenal virtually useless. Being a square-rigged ship, the *Inflexible* was unable to sail against the wind with any effectiveness, and it was now almost impossible for her to reach the enemy. By taking the *Inflexible* out of the fight, Arnold had, in effect, rendered the four weeks spent building the three-masted ship a waste of the enemy's time.

As it was, even the British schooners, with the fore-and-aft sails required to sail higher into the wind, were having trouble reaching the Americans due to the flukiness of the wind coming out of Valcour Bay. Only those British vessels equipped with an ample number of oars were able to follow the enemy into the bay. Not until later did their crews realize that they had ventured into a carefully prepared trap.

First on the scene was Lieutenant Edward Longcroft of the *Loyal Convert.* Longcroft led a boarding party onto the abandoned wreck of the *Royal Savage* and quickly turned the vessel's cannons against the enemy. Before Longcroft and his men could inflict any significant damage, they found themselves surrounded by the three American galleys. As the majority of the British fleet watched in helpless frustration—being too far to leeward to be of any assistance—the Americans made short work of Longcroft and his men, hammering them with a lethal barrage of cannonballs and grapeshot that killed eleven of the original boarding party.

Longcroft ordered his men to abandon the *Royal Savage* and return to the *Loyal Convert,* which drifted off to leeward and was never again a factor in the battle.

That left the twenty-two gunboats to carry on the battle without any support from the rest of the British fleet. Arnold had succeeded in evening the odds in his favor, and for the next two hours his line of fourteen gondolas, galleys, and schooners—arranged in a crescent that stretched across the bay from Valcour to the mainland—slugged it out with the gunboats.

A standard British gunboat was thirty-seven feet long, with a mast stepped in the center of the vessel and a cannon mounted on the bow. Approximately half the twenty-two-man crew were sailors who managed the boat; the other half were artillerymen who fired the cannon. The German artillery officer George Pausch had spent the last few weeks training both himself and his men in the "British way" of firing a cannon—made no easier by the fact that this particular cannon was planted on the bow of a wave-tossed boat. Once the gunboats had formed themselves in a line just 350 yards to the south of the Americans, the battle began. "Our attack . . . became very fierce and after getting to close quarters, very animated," Pausch wrote.

With General Waterbury in the galley *Washington* near the mainland shore on the far right and with Colonel Wigglesworth in the galley *Trumbull* beside the island on the left, Arnold in the *Congress* held the American center. The galleys had been given the most conspicuous positions in the American line, but the gondolas made up the majority of the fleet. Double-ended, wide, and with only a yard or so of freeboard, the gondola looked more like a shallow, oval-shaped bowl than a proper boat. Arnold had attempted to compensate for their lack of freeboard by stacking fascines (bundles of sticks used in constructing earthen fortifications) along the boats' sides and bows, making the gondolas the true floating incarnation of a land-bound redoubt.

Captain Pausch recounted how the enemy's galleys and gondolas used their oars to move in and out of the thick gray cloud of powder smoke that hovered between the two opposing lines. "Every once in a while they would vanish," Pausch wrote, "in order to get a breath and again suddenly reappear." The Americans were apparently backing behind the cloud to reload and then advancing out of the cloud to fire, which, of course, made it all the harder for the British gunboats to fire at them with any accuracy. In addition to helping to coordinate these movements, Arnold, dressed in his blue-and-buff officer's uniform, with his cocked hat planted on his head, aimed the cannons on the *Congress* with what he later described as "good execution."

While Arnold clearly relished being an active participant in the battle, his British counterpart, Captain Pringle, proved to be a far less aggressive leader. Despite having, according to one account, the most weatherly schooner in the British fleet, Pringle showed "no inclination to fight," and the *Maria* "lay to with topsails," well below Valcour Island.

All the while, Lieutenant James Dacres in the schooner *Carleton* had been "endeavoring to the utmost of his power to attack." Finally, around 1:00 p.m., Dacres caught a fortuitous shift of wind that carried his schooner past the line of gunboats and up to within just a few hundred yards of the American line, where he anchored and, using a spring line, drew his vessel sideways to the enemy so as to unleash a volley from his battery of half-a-dozen six-pounders.

It was a brave but perhaps foolhardy maneuver on Dacres's part. Since the *Carleton* was well beyond the line of gunboats and in full view of the Americans, the schooner inevitably became, like the *Royal Savage* before her, the sole target of the entire enemy fleet. One witness recalled how over the course of the next hour, American cannonballs "bored through and through" the *Carleton*. In the melee, Lieutenant Dacres was knocked unconscious and assumed dead; if not for the intervention of nineteen-year-old midshipman Edward Pellew, Dacres's seemingly lifeless body would have been thrown over the *Carleton*'s side, which was standard procedure in the midst of a naval battle. Within an hour, eight men had been killed and six wounded and there was more than two feet of water in the *Carleton*'s rapidly sinking hull.

General Guy Carleton in the *Maria* had just decided that his flagship must come to the support of the beleaguered schooner. At that moment, however, a cannonball fired from the American galley *Congress* (and undoubtedly aimed by Benedict Arnold) passed within a few inches of the heads of both Carleton and Dr. Knox, who were standing together on the quarterdeck. Without betraying the slightest agitation, Carleton turned to Knox and said, "Well, Doctor, how do you like a sea fight?" Carleton's composure, however, did not apparently translate into action, and the boats of the *Inflexible,* rather than those of the *Maria,* ultimately towed the *Carleton* to safety.

That left only the British gunboats—with names like *Dreadful, Blast, Infernal, Tartar, Thunderbolt, Furious,* and *Destruction*—to bear, one participant remembered, "the brunt of [the enemy's] whole fire." At this point, Pausch recounted, the "battle began to get very serious." Each gunboat had been equipped with eighty rounds, and by all accounts the artillery teams in each boat performed nobly—but so did the Americans. In a naval fight, cannonballs routinely skipped across the water's surface like flat stones, and these low-flying projectiles inflicted significant damage to both the Americans and the British, punching holes in the hulls and hurling deadly splinters across the vessels' crowded decks. As Pausch could later tell from the many "boards and stoppers" with which the British carpenters patched the gunboats, "the cannon of the rebels were well served." Despite Arnold's misgivings about the inexperience of his men, he had been able to instill the discipline and confidence required to face a well-trained force that might easily have overwhelmed them.

In the meantime, hundreds of native warriors allied with the British had taken up positions on both Valcour Island and the mainland and were firing on the vessels at either end of the American line. At some point in the midst of the battle, William Hay's wife ventured from their shoreside house with her two-year-old daughter in her arms to get some water from a nearby spring. "To her great amazement and terror," her daughter later recounted, she found herself in the midst of a large group of Indians, who were waiting in ambush, "prepared to receive the American crews, if they should attempt to effect an escape by landing." Clutching her baby to her breast, Mrs. Hay began to cry. But instead of attacking the young mother and her child, the warriors allowed them to return to their home unharmed.

The Americans had killed or wounded a significant number of the enemy, but they were suffering considerable casualties of their own. Rowboats went from vessel to vessel transporting the wounded to the fleet's hospital ship, the *Enterprise,* where Dr. Stephen McCrea and his assistant performed heroic service. Jahiel Stewart was stationed aboard the schooner and watched as "they brought the wounded aboard [and] the doctors cut off [a] great many legs and arm[s]." Over the course of the nearly eight-hour battle, Stewart saw no fewer than seven dead bodies thrown over the *Enterprise's* side.

As the battle raged into the late afternoon, an American cannonball hit the powder magazine of a British gunboat with a German artillery crew. At that moment, several hundred yards away, George Pausch was taking careful aim with his own cannon when his sergeant called his attention to the explosion on the other end of the line. "At first I could not tell what men were on board," he wrote, "but . . . after the smoke had cleared away, I recognized the men by the cords around their hats." Since they were fellow Germans, Pausch quickly rowed over to the burning gunboat, which in addition to being on fire was sinking beneath its crew. Soon there were a total of forty-eight soldiers and sailors on Pausch's boat. "What a predicament I was in!" he wrote. "Every moment I was in danger of drowning with all on board . . . [including] those I had just rescued and who had been already half lost!"

Then, around 5:00 p.m., as Pausch struggled to keep his overloaded gunboat from capsizing, the *Inflexible* sailed into the bay. The awesome sight of this big ship using the spring line on her anchor cable to bring her cannons into position seems to have had a cooling effect on the American fire, and after only a few volleys from her eighteen-pounders the battle came to a virtual standstill. Adding to the impact of the *Inflexible*'s arrival was the fact that she almost immediately succeeded in sinking the gondola *Philadelphia*. (More than 150 years later, a group of salvagers discovered the wreck on the bottom of the lake with her mast still standing and a cannonball wedged between the timbers of her bow. Today the *Philadelphia* is the centerpiece of the Smithsonian National Museum of American History.)

The arrival of the *Inflexible* gave the British gunboats the opportunity to fall back to about six hundred yards from the Americans—beyond the deadly reach of the rebel grapeshot but still within the gunboats' firing range. As darkness approached, General Carleton and Captain Pringle decided to eliminate any danger of the rebels retaking the *Royal Savage* and ordered the schooner burned. Around sundown, the vessel's gunpowder magazine exploded, and the canted wreck lay burning for the rest of the night.

By nightfall all firing had ceased as Pringle arranged his fleet into a semicircle designed to prevent the Americans from escaping to the south, and Arnold held an impromptu council of war with Waterbury and Wigglesworth. Sixty of their officers and men had been killed or wounded.

Three-quarters of their ammunition had been expended. Arnold's galley, the *Congress,* had sustained "seven shot between wind and water" and had been hit below the waterline at least a dozen times. The *Washington's* mast had been shot in two, and she was taking on dangerous amounts of water. The gondola *New York* had lost all her officers except her captain, and then, of course, there was the burning wreck of the *Royal Savage* and the *Philadelphia* at the bottom of the lake. By the morning, they would undoubtedly be in range of the enemy's entire fleet. Given the damage the Americans had sustained, another confrontation was not in their best interests. They must, it was agreed, find a way to retreat down the lake.

The question was how to do it. The brisk northerly wind had diminished to a gentle breeze, and as the air temperature began to drop, a thick fog formed over the surface of the lake. One of Arnold's officers—very likely it was General Waterbury—proposed that since the British had sealed off the southern entrance to Valcour Bay, they go the other way by "hauling round the island, through the narrow pass" across the rocky shoals to the north. Once again Arnold disagreed with his second-in-command. Thanks to the fog, the night was going to be exceptionally dark. Also in their favor was the fact that Carleton had ordered the destruction of the *Royal Savage,* which still burned brightly at the south tip of Valcour Island. As anyone who had looked out the window of a well-lit house at night could attest, the British sentries must be virtually blind to anything beyond the glow of the blazing hulk. Another factor in the Americans' favor was that after eight hours of firing cannons, both armies were more than a little deaf. If they muffled their oars, the British were unlikely to hear them rowing past. They would do exactly what the British least expected: sail and row their way through the enemy lines and escape to the south.

For the risk-averse Waterbury, it must have been both frustrating and more than a little terrifying to know that their fate was tied to a leader who always seemed to go for the most spectacular and dangerous stroke. There was also a coldness about Arnold—an insensitivity to the cost of what he demanded of others. During the retreat from Canada back in June, with the British army bearing down on them from the north, he had insisted that his aide shoot his horse before they boarded the last boat out of St. Johns. The aide thought this unnecessarily cruel, but for Arnold the sacrifice of both his aide's and his own horse was what the cause of liberty required, especially if it added luster to the swashbuckling tale of his flight from Canada.

With Arnold it was always difficult to draw the line between acceptable risk and self-serving derring-do, and the retreat from Valcour Bay was to be no exception. They had just spent the last eight hours fighting a bloody and desperate battle. They had certainly sent a message of defiance to the British, but at what cost? Their fleet was in a shambles; dozens of men had been killed. Was this Arnold's idea of a "defensive war"? And now, rather than taking the safe and sure route around the island, Arnold insisted that they sail *through* the enemy.

Colonel Wigglesworth in the *Trumbull* was the first to leave. With hardly enough sail set to give the galley steerage and with a lantern suspended under her stern that could be seen only by those directly behind, the *Trumbull* set out into the night, hugging the western shore where there appeared to be a gap in the British line. "The rest of the squadron followed in succession at intervals of two hundred and three hundred yards," remembered James Cushing, the sergeant of marines aboard Arnold's galley, the *Congress*. Taking up the rear was Arnold himself. "Strict silence and stillness were enjoined," remembered Cushing, "and we passed the enemy's line without seeing one of his vessels or being ourselves perceived." Once again, Arnold had pulled it off.

By the early morning, the vessels of the American fleet began to arrive at Schuyler Island, about seven and a half miles to the south, where they "refreshed" themselves and made what repairs they could. That morning, Arnold wrote Gates an account of what became known as the Battle of Valcour Island. He was clearly proud of how his men had performed in the engagement and was hopeful that his fleet would now "make the utmost dispatch" toward Ticonderoga. "I think we have had a very fortunate escape," he wrote, "and have great reason to return our humble and hearty thanks to Almighty God for preserving and delivering so many of us from our more than savage enemies." But as he also noted in his letter, there'd been an ominous change in the wind.

With the arrival of daybreak on the morning of October 12, a thick mist still lay over the lake, and it took some time before the British realized that the American fleet had disappeared. "To our great mortification," Carleton recounted, "we perceived . . . that they had found means to escape." Pringle attributed the Americans' miraculous retreat to "the extreme obscurity of the night," but Carleton acknowledged "the great diligence used by the enemy in getting away from us."

According to another account, Carleton was in such "a rage" upon realizing the enemy had eluded his grasp that he set off in pursuit without giving orders to the rest of the fleet. Eventually realizing his mistake, he sheepishly returned to Valcour, after which a stiff southerly breeze prevented the British from effectively continuing the chase.

Throughout the day on October 12, neither fleet was able to make any significant progress down the lake against the adverse wind. By the early morning hours of October 13, however, the wind began to die and shift. A northerly breeze gradually worked its way down the lake, and the British set off in pursuit, with the *Maria, Carleton,* and *Inflexible* leading the chase. For the Americans to the south, it was the worst possible development. As their enemies flew down the lake in the building northwesterly, they lay becalmed on a windless sheet of water. They could do nothing but row as the British bore down on them with frightening speed. By the time the new breeze finally reached the Americans, the British were just five miles away.

Arnold had no choice but to prepare for exactly the scenario he had spent the last two and a half months attempting to avoid—a fight on the open lake against vessels representing the greatest naval power in the world. His fleet had become dangerously spread out, with Wigglesworth in the *Trumbull* well ahead and Waterbury in the *Washington* lagging behind. Just before them was one of the narrowest points of the lake at Split Rock, which had served for generations as the dividing line between the warring Abenakis to the north and Mohawks to the south. Here, at this ancient line of battle, he might be able to replicate the circumstances that had worked so well at Valcour.

Using his yawl to transmit messages to the various vessels under his command, he attempted to gather the fleet together at Split Rock. Waterbury, however, asked to be allowed to run his leaky galley up onto the shore—which two heavily damaged gondolas had already been forced to do the day before—so that he and his crew could proceed to Fort

Ticonderoga on foot. Arnold would have none of it. "I received for an answer," Waterbury later wrote, "by no means to run her ashore, but to push forward to Split Rock, where he would draw the fleet in a line, and engage them again."

The one exception was the hospital ship *Enterprise,* which must get back to Ticonderoga as quickly as possible. Jahiel Stewart recorded that "the general's boat came up and ordered us to make all speed we could to Ty [short for Ticonderoga], and all the other ships to stop." But as the British bore down on them from the north, Wigglesworth in the *Trumbull* and several of the other American vessels at the front of the fleet proved reluctant to backtrack and meet the enemy, requiring that Arnold ultimately abandon any hope of making a stand at Split Rock. "When I came to Split Rock," Waterbury later complained, "the whole fleet was making their escape as fast as they could and left me in the rear to fall into the enemy's hands."

As soon as the vanguard of the British fleet caught up to the *Washington* a few miles below Split Rock, Waterbury struck, or lowered, his flag without firing a shot. Arnold never officially criticized Waterbury, but Sergeant James Cushing on board the *Congress* clearly felt that Waterbury had abandoned *them* to the British, labeling the *Washington*'s surrender a "dastardly act." Compounding Arnold's frustration was the response of the *Trumbull* to Waterbury's capitulation. Wigglesworth claimed that once he saw that the *Washington* had been taken, he "thought it my duty to make sail and endeavor to save the *Trumbull* galley if possible." Double-manning the oars and throwing his ballast stones over the side, Wigglesworth soon disappeared down the lake.

Arnold in the galley *Congress,* with four gondolas hovering beside him like frightened ducklings, must face the British alone.

The *Maria* might not have been the biggest vessel in the British fleet, but she was the fastest. This, it turned out, put Captain Pringle in a difficult position since he had no interest in taking on Arnold all by himself. So he lowered his topgallant sails to allow the *Carleton* and *Inflexible* to catch up before he reached the enemy. Throughout the fighting ahead, the *Maria,* several British officers grumbled, "kept at a greater distance . . . than any officer inspired with true courage . . . would have done." This apparently did not hold true for the other two British vessels, which were soon within what Arnold described as "musket shot" and blasting away at the *Congress*.

For the next two hours, Arnold fought off the enemy vessels, "two under our stern and one on our broadside," as the crews of the gondolas, which were next to useless in a sea fight, could do little more than provide moral encouragement. Arnold later recounted how the British warships "kept up an incessant fire . . . with round and grapeshot, which we returned as briskly. The sails, rigging, and hull of the *Congress* were shattered and torn in pieces. The first lieutenant and three men killed." The *Congress* was now in danger of sinking. The time had come, he decided, to run their vessels onto the shore and destroy them before they were taken by the British.

Up ahead Arnold saw a familiar spot: the cove on the eastern shore where he had entertained his officers back in August near the home of Peter Ferris. By this time the wind had shifted into a more easterly direction, meaning that the cove was now almost directly upwind from their present position. Arnold ordered his men to row for Ferris Bay.

For the British it was a frustratingly familiar scenario. As the *Congress* and the four gondolas used their "sweeps" to propel themselves into the wind, the enemy's larger ship and schooners were stymied by the adverse and land-blocked breeze. Pringle later complained of how the Americans had been "greatly favored by the wind being off shore," but once again, Arnold had used both the wind and his knowledge of the topography of Lake Champlain to his advantage.

Once they'd run all five vessels up onto the shore, Arnold insisted that their flags with thirteen horizontal stripes and the Union Jack in the corner remain flying from the mastheads. Unlike Waterbury, he was not about to surrender to the British. He then directed the vessels' marines to jump overboard with their packs and muskets and climb the twenty-five-foot bank overlooking the beach, where they would, Sergeant Cushing recounted, "form a line for the defense of their vessels and flags against the enemy."

Watching in terrorized fascination from his family's house was fourteen-year-old Squire Ferris, who later recounted what he saw that day on the east shore of Lake Champlain. As the British fired at the American fleet, Arnold ordered his gunner to blow up the galley's powder magazine—but not until the gunner had made sure all the wounded had been taken ashore. Arnold assumed his orders had been followed only to discover after the fuse had been lit that a man still remained aboard the *Congress*. Lieutenant Ephraim Goldsmith had been severely wounded in the thigh by grapeshot during the Battle of Valcour, and there he was—lying helplessly on the deck. When Goldsmith realized what was about to happen, he, in Squire Ferris's words, "begged to be thrown overboard." Arnold had no alternative but to watch in horror as the *Congress* exploded and Goldsmith's body was "blown into the air."

Arnold, by this point, had been awake for almost three days. He had also had very little to eat and was, in his own words, "exceedingly fatigued and unwell." He'd seen twenty-three of the seventy-three men aboard the *Congress* killed or wounded—casualties that he seems to have accepted, like the lives of the two horses he'd ordered shot at St. Johns, as part of the ugly reality of war. But the death of Lieutenant Goldsmith was different. Sixty-nine years later, by which time Arnold was long dead and regarded by all good American citizens as evil incarnate, Squire Ferris recalled how on that afternoon in October 1776 the general "showed the greatest feelings . . . and threatened to run the gunner through on the spot." Only after Goldsmith's body had been "taken up and buried on shore," Ferris remembered, did Arnold allow them to begin the long march through the woods toward Fort Ticonderoga.

Arnold did not reach the American fort until four in the morning of October 14. The next day, Gates wrote to General Philip Schuyler in Albany that "few men ever met with so many hairbreadth escapes in so short a space of time." Some faulted Arnold for being "fiery, hot and impetuous . . . without discretion" and for the unnecessary destruction of more than two-thirds of the American fleet. But two weeks later, when Carleton ordered his troops back up the lake to St. Johns for the winter, Arnold could take consolation in knowing that no matter what the cost, he had done it—he had prevented the British from taking Fort Ticonderoga and continuing to Albany and, eventually, to New York. And perhaps just as important, while Washington's army to the south continued to suffer setback after setback, Arnold had shown that it was possible to stand up and *fight*.

If Arnold remained a controversial and, as a consequence, underappreciated figure in his own army, his British opponents, who did not have to contend with his often imperious and self-dramatizing manner, were more generous with their praise. Lieutenant Digby wrote of his "remarkable coolness and bravery," while Secretary of State Germain lauded Arnold as "the most enterprising man among the rebels."

Indeed, from General Carleton's perspective, Arnold seemed to have been ubiquitous—from the taking of Fort Ticonderoga at the very beginning of the rebellion, to the attack on Quebec, to the American retreat from Canada, and now this irritatingly difficult and bloody naval battle. Prior to ordering the British fleet back up the lake, Carleton had led a small reconnaissance mission to Fort Ticonderoga, and there, once again, had been Arnold, this time in a rowboat boldly examining *them*.

The British immediately attempted to surround Arnold, who soon realized that the enemy boats were about to cut him off. They must, he announced to his men, start rowing back to the fort as quickly as possible. The sudden appearance of the British had put a panic into Arnold's crew, who fell into such confusion that they were in danger of being captured. Demonstrating the winning manner that served him so well in battle but seemed to desert him outside the theater of war, Arnold assured his men that those were not British boats chasing them but their fellow Americans. Sure enough, the crewmen began to settle down, especially when Arnold promised "a bottle of rum for each if they gained the shore first," even as he unbuckled the stiff piece of ornamental velvet (known as a "stock") around his neck and took up one of the oars himself. Only after they'd reached land did Arnold reveal that, in truth, those *were* British boats pursuing them, and they had better run for their lives.

Midshipman Edward Pellew was in the British boat right behind Arnold's. The American general had escaped, but in his haste he had left behind his stock and buckle, which Pellew took as a keepsake. Years later, by which time Pellew had become the much-decorated admiral Viscount Exmouth, he could not help but wonder how differently the War of Independence might have turned out if on that cold autumn day near the southern tip of Lake Champlain he had captured Benedict Arnold.

CHAPTER THREE

A Cabinet of Fortitude

S oon after General Carleton and the British army headed north back to Canada, Benedict Arnold headed south with General Horatio Gates and several battalions of New Englanders. Now that his mission on Lake Champlain had ended, he needed a new assignment. He also hoped for a promotion to major general.

In Albany, Arnold met up with his former aide Major James Wilkinson of Maryland. (Wilkinson was the one who had so reluctantly shot his horse before jumping aboard the boat that Arnold pushed from the shores of St. Johns.) The two officers no longer shared the easy familiarity that had once characterized their relationship. Wilkinson was just nineteen, with a plump lower lip and sparkling eyes. He had a remarkable talent for winning the trust of a superior, then using that superior as a stepping-stone to an even more powerful and potentially helpful mentor. When Wilkinson first arrived in Boston in the summer of 1775, he had attached himself to General Nathanael Greene. By spring of the following year, when he found himself leading a company of New Hampshire men into Canada, he set his sights on "an officer who had at that period acquired great celebrity," none other than Benedict Arnold. And by the summer of 1776—as Arnold prepared to sail up Lake Champlain to meet the British— Wilkinson had come to the attention of Arnold's superior officer, Major General Horatio Gates.

Up until that point, Gates and Arnold had had nothing but the best of professional and personal relationships, despite the fact that they could not have been more different. Arnold was a dashing risk taker who relished combat. Gates, more than a decade older, was so nearsighted that without his glasses, which were a seeming fixture on his long and narrow nose, he was essentially blind. Arnold gloried in his appearance; Gates, on the other hand, was as careless a dresser as the most slovenly New England militiaman, and with his long thinning hair resembled, a British officer claimed, a bespectacled midwife. Well-read and a noted storyteller, Gates could keep a room full of officers and politicians amused for hours. Arnold, although a more than credible writer, was famously inarticulate. Benjamin Rush, a doctor from Philadelphia, described the American Hannibal as "well made and his face handsome. His conversation [however] was uninteresting and sometimes indelicate. His language was ungrammatical and his pronunciation vulgar." A fellow army officer claimed that "the fighter did not combine . . . any intellectual qualities with his physical prowess. Instead of engaging an interesting argument, he shouted and pounded the table."

Arnold might not have been much of a conversationalist, but that apparently did not prevent him from talking about his many sexual conquests since becoming a widower—what he described in a letter to another officer as "scenes of sensual gratification incident to a man of nervous constitution." While stationed at Crown Point on Lake Champlain he had become involved with a woman who, a fellow officer reported, "intended to have call'd her son Arnold." During the Siege of Quebec, he had risked venturing behind enemy lines at night, a sentry remembered, "woman hunting." High-strung and libidinous, he had little patience with anything beyond the here and now. When it came time to send his two older boys away to school, he wrote their instructor that he wanted their education to be "useful rather than learned. Life is too short and uncertain to throw away in speculations upon subjects that perhaps only one man in ten thousand has a genius to make a figure in."

When not animated by some overpowering emotion, Arnold could be, one suspects, deadly dull. Dull was not something the quick-witted James Wilkinson could long tolerate, and by December 1776 he had thrown in his lot with General Gates.

Gates might not have been the flashiest of dressers or a firebrand on the battlefield, but he had the highest of ambitions. He wanted an independent command, something best secured in the halls of the Continental Congress. His nominal purpose in marching south with five hundred soldiers from New England was to support Washington's army as it retreated across New Jersey toward the Delaware River. But as became increasingly apparent to the young Wilkinson, Gates had an agenda of his own.

From its beginnings as a loosely organized group of locally based militia companies in the days after Lexington and Concord in April 1775, the American army had evolved gradually and, on occasion, spasmodically into three region-based entities: the southern army in Georgia, South Carolina, and North Carolina, which in June 1776 had successfully repulsed General Clinton's attempt to take Charleston; the northern army under Philip Schuyler that had, thanks to Arnold's recent heroics, repulsed the British attempt to take Fort Ticonderoga; and what came to be known as the "Grand Army" under Washington, made up of soldiers from as far north as New Hampshire and as far south as Virginia, and that by November 1776 was retreating across New Jersey toward Pennsylvania.

The vast majority of the soldiers in those three American armies had committed to serve for no more than a single year, and as had occurred in Boston in December 1775, many of the soldiers currently serving under Washington were approaching the end of their terms of service. Washington had already convinced Congress of the necessity of recruiting soldiers whose enlistments would extend to the end of the war, and in the year to come he would begin to forge an army that had at its heart a group of battle-seasoned veterans. But that was still in the future.

In the late fall of 1776, Washington, the supposed commander in chief of the American forces, had, in fact, surprisingly little actual authority. The leadership and disposition of the northern and southern armies were determined by Congress. Even the soldiers in Washington's own army were, to a remarkable extent, beyond his control. Those who had not already deserted after the setbacks in New York and New Jersey were, in most cases, planning to return home when their enlistments expired in a matter of weeks. And then there were the officers like Horatio Gates, who, as events soon proved, were more interested in advancing their own careers than in assisting their commander in his hour of most profound need.

• • •

By the middle of December, Washington had established his headquarters just to the west of the Delaware River in Newtown, Pennsylvania. The retreat across New Jersey had been long and humiliating, made all the more mortifying by the fact that General Howe was obviously toying with the ever-diminishing remnants of the Continental army. At first the Hessian officer Johann Ewald had been baffled by the slow pace of Howe's pursuit. "It became clearly evident," he wrote, "that the march took place so slowly for no other reason than to permit Washington to cross the Delaware safely and peacefully."

From General Howe's perspective, there was no need to engage the Americans, since the war had already been, for all practical purposes, won. In just three months, the British had taken 4,500 prisoners and almost 3,000 muskets along with close to 250 cannons and 17,000 cannonballs. By December, Washington had lost by death, injury, and desertion more than three-quarters of the soldiers under his command in the main army. The offer of a pardon to the citizens of New Jersey in late November had resulted in thousands of former patriots' declaring their loyalty to the king. "Our affairs are in a very bad situation," Washington admitted. "The game is pretty near up—owing in a great measure to the insidious arts of the enemy."

Compounding Washington's anguish was the knowledge that his once trusted adjutant general Joseph Reed had lost faith in him. Reed had been away from headquarters when a letter arrived from the Continental army's second-ranking officer, Major General Charles Lee. Assuming the letter related to official business, Washington promptly broke the seal. He soon discovered that Reed had established his own line of communication with Lee and that the primary topic of their correspondence was the failings of their commander in chief. "I received your most obliging, flattering letter," Lee wrote, "[and] lament with you that fatal indecision of mind which in war is a much greater disqualification than stupidity or even want of personal courage. . . . Eternal defeat and miscarriage must attend the man of the best parts if cursed with indecision." Washington was as aware as anyone of what he called "that warfare in my mind." Caught between the opposing desires of the Continental Congress and his staff, he had failed to overrule Nathanael Greene's determination to defend Fort Washington, even though Washington's own instincts had told him that the fortress must be abandoned. Yes, he had been, in that instance, fatally indecisive, but did that justify Reed's going behind his back? Rather than truthfully declaring his misgivings, Reed had, much like the opportunistic James Wilkinson, chosen to cultivate the good graces of another officer, even suggesting that Lee "go to Congress and form the plan of the new army."

Washington could have angrily confronted his adjutant general; instead he forwarded Lee's letter to Reed with a note of apology. "Having no idea of its being a private letter," he explained, "much less suspecting the tendency of the correspondence, I opened it, as I had done all other letters to you [relating to] the business of your office. . . . This, as it is the truth, must be my excuse for seeing the contents of a letter which neither inclination *or* intention would have prompted me to." Leaving Reed to twist in the icy emptiness of his withheld wrath, Washington refused to even mention the contents of Lee's letter. Not until more than six months later did Washington finally respond to Reed's repeated attempts to explain himself. "I was hurt," Washington admitted, "not because I thought my judgment wronged by the expressions contained in [the letter], but because the same sentiments were not communicated immediately to myself." Reed would continue as adjutant general for the duration of the campaign, but as Washington's brilliantly executed act of passive aggression had made clear, their former intimacy had ended.

And so, knowing that his own adjutant and the number two general in the Continental army had been gossiping about his shortcomings, Washington oversaw the long and dismal retreat across New Jersey. Lieutenant James Monroe, the future president of the United States, never forgot the example set by the commander in chief during that march. "A deportment so firm, so dignified," he wrote, "but yet so modest and composed I have never seen in any other person."

About a year before, Thomas Paine had written *Common Sense,* the tract that dared to say the once unspeakable truth that had been on all their minds—that the time had come to break away from the mother country. Now Paine was a volunteer with Washington's army, and whenever he had a spare minute during the march across New Jersey he scribbled the notes (using, according to legend, the head of a drum for a desk) that became *The Crisis.* "These are the times that try men's souls," he wrote. "The summer soldier and the sunshine patriot will, in this crisis, shrink from the service of their country; but he that stands it *now* deserves the love and thanks of man and woman." As if he were speaking with Washington's duplicitous adjutant general in mind, he insisted that difficult epochs like these were "the touchstones of sincerity and hypocrisy, and bring things and men to light which might otherwise have lain forever undiscovered. . . . They sift out the hidden thoughts of man and hold them up in public to the world." A relative few, Paine continued, possess a "natural firmness . . . which cannot be unlocked by trifles, but which, when unlocked, discovers a cabinet of fortitude." Such a man was Washington. "God hath blessed him with uninterrupted health," Paine wrote, "and given him a mind that can even flourish upon care."

There was the example of Washington, but there was also Major General Nathanael Greene, who should have, by all rights, been dismissed after the disaster at Fort Washington. Perhaps sensing that an act of forgiveness might forge a bond of loyalty that would serve him well in the future, Washington had chosen to stand by the former Quaker who walked with a limp. In the days ahead Greene's well-reasoned letters to Congress helped convince the delegates of that body to grant Washington the sweeping powers he needed to rebuild the army. And then there was the example of the twenty-one-year-old artillery captain from New York named Alexander Hamilton, "marching," a fellow soldier later remembered, "with a cocked hat pulled down over his eyes apparently lost in thought, with his hand resting on the cannon, and every now and then patting it . . . as if it were a favorite horse or a pet plaything." An undergraduate at what is now Columbia University, Hamilton was about to become one of Washington's most trusted subordinates.

These men were not panicking; they were quietly preparing for whatever the future held. As Washington would write in a few weeks' time to the Philadelphia financier Robert Morris, "It is vain to ruminate upon, or even reflect upon the authors or causes of our present misfortunes. We should rather exert ourselves and look forward with hopes that some lucky chance may yet turn up in our favor." This was not the same man who just a few months before had raged indignantly about the inadequacies of his army even as he ached to end it all in battle. This was a leader who had determined to make the best of events that were ultimately beyond his control.

By December 8 the American army had successfully reached the Pennsylvania side of the Delaware River. Rendered virtually uncrossable by

Washington's foresighted determination to sweep the eastern length of the river clean of boats, the Delaware provided a much-needed barrier between the American army and the British. At about two o'clock that afternoon, William Howe and General Charles Cornwallis, along with three other officers, resplendent in their gold-laced uniforms, arrived at the riverside town of Trenton to examine the enemy line.

With winter approaching, Howe had resolved to maintain his head-quarters in New York City, leaving the Hessians to occupy a series of strategically placed towns in western New Jersey. When the Delaware froze in January, Howe's army would be able to march across the river, and, if the British leader so chose, take Philadelphia. Recognizing the danger of their situation in Philadelphia, the delegates of the Continental Congress had relocated a hundred miles southwest to Baltimore, Mary-land. Until the day the Delaware went from being a moat to being a bridge, there was nothing much for Howe to do but wait in his comfort-able headquarters in New York, where his mistress, the blond and beauti-ful Elizabeth Lloyd Loring of Boston, was waiting for him. The season was on his side.

Almost as soon as Howe and his entourage arrived at the bank of the Delaware for their inspection, an American battery of thirty-seven can-nons mounted on the opposite side of the river opened up on the British officers. Exhibiting the same sangfroid he had demonstrated during the Battle of Bunker Hill, Howe refused to take cover. "Wherever we turned," a German officer wrote in awe, "the cannonballs hit the ground, and I can hardly understand, even now, why all five of us were not killed." Even if Howe had done his best to ignore it, he had clearly not expected the rebel barrage. As it turned out, this was just the first in an ever-lengthening series of unpleasant surprises for the British commander in chief.

As Howe was about to discover to his regret, he had squandered his one and only chance to crush Washington's army. Never again would he have the advantages he had enjoyed for a few brief months in New York. The British army that had loomed so large that summer was rapidly being swallowed up by the immensity of the American countryside. Now that the fighting had expanded beyond New York into New Jersey and Penn-sylvania, Howe simply did not have enough soldiers to occupy what land he had so far secured *and* wage a proper war against the Americans.

Contributing to the difficulties Howe faced were the demands of his

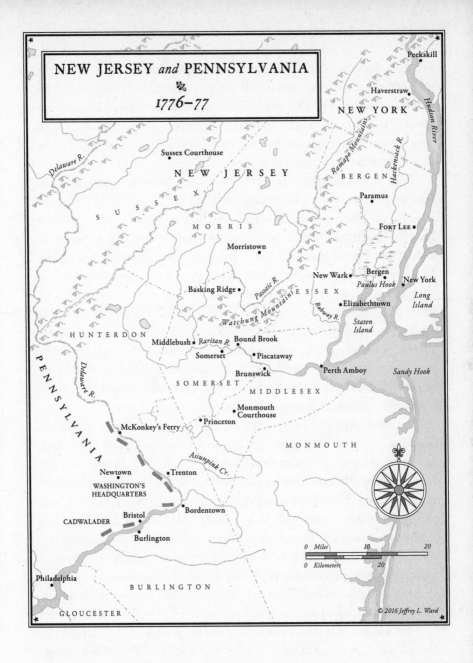

NEW JERSEY *and* PENNSYLVANIA

1776–77

Peekskill

Haverstraw

NEW YORK

Hudson River

Delaware R.

Sussex Courthouse

N E W   J E R S E Y

S U S S E X

Ramapo Mountains

B E R G E N

Hackensack R.

Paramus

M O R R I S

FORT LEE

Morristown

New Wark

Bergen

New York

Basking Ridge

Passaic R.

E S S E X

Paulus Hook

Long
Island

Watchung Mountains

Rahway R.

Elizabethtown

H U N T E R D O N

Middlebush

Raritan R.

Bound Brook

Staten
Island

Somerset

Piscataway

Sandy Hook

Brunswick

Perth Amboy

S O M E R S E T

M I D D L E S E X

P E N N S Y L V A N I A

Delaware R.

Monmouth
Courthouse

M O N M O U T H

McKonkey's Ferry

Princeton

Assunpink Cr.

Newtown

Trenton

WASHINGTON'S
HEADQUARTERS

Bordentown

CADWALADER

Bristol

Burlington

| 0 | Miles | | 10 | | 20 |
| 0 | Kilometers | | | 20 | |

Philadelphia

B U R L I N G T O N

GLOUCESTER

© 2016 Jeffrey L. Ward

brother. New York Harbor, Admiral Howe determined, was not a safe
year-round anchorage for his fleet. And so General Henry Clinton and
seven thousand troops were dispatched to Rhode Island to provide the
British navy with a safe winter haven at Newport. Without enough troops
available to him in New Jersey, Howe was forced to establish far fewer

outposts than he would have liked, meaning that the Hessian soldiers he assigned to these posts, especially the ones along the Delaware, were dangerously isolated. On December 20 he wrote to Secretary of State Germain, "The chain, I own, is rather too extensive." He could only hope that there were enough loyalists in New Jersey to keep his thinly distributed troops "in perfect security."

But that did not prove to be the case. Even before they entered New Jersey, his army had established a horrifying reputation for literally raping and pillaging its way through Westchester County to the north of New York. Stephen Kemble was a deputy adjutant to William Howe and a native of New Brunswick, New Jersey. During the march to White Plains in October, many of the soldiers had proved impossible to control—"outrageously licentious and cruel to such a degree as to threaten with death all such as dare obstruct them in their depredations"—and Kemble could only "shudder for Jersey, the army being thought to move there shortly." Instead of being surrounded by thankful loyalists, the Hessians that Howe had left to man the outposts across the breadth of New Jersey found themselves besieged by local inhabitants who would do almost anything to get them out of their state.

The Hessians were, they soon realized, in the New Jersey equivalent of Indian country. "The rascal peasants meet our men alone or in small unarmed groups," a Hessian officer complained. "They have their rifles hidden in the bushes or ditches and the like. When they believe they are sure of success and they see one or several men belonging to our army, they shoot them in the head, then quickly hide their rifles and pretend they know nothing." When Colonel Johann Rall, the commander of the Hessian force stationed at Trenton, New Jersey, tried to send a letter to Princeton, just twelve miles away, one of the two messengers was killed and the other wounded, ultimately requiring him to send an escort of more than a hundred men to ensure the delivery of the correspondence.

Rall was a tough and courageous professional soldier; he had led the charge that was largely responsible for the taking of Fort Washington. But even he was driven to distraction by the near-constant harassment his outpost suffered not only from the locals but from the same Continental battery on the opposite bank of the Delaware that had nearly killed General Howe. On the rare occasion his men were able to sleep, they were forced to remain in uniform with their weapons by their sides. When one of his officers suggested that they build a redoubt to help defend one of the entrances into town, he erupted, "Scheiszer bey Scheisz [Shit on shit]! Let them come. . . . We will get them with the bayonets." For as Rall knew full well (and Washington came to appreciate), Trenton's open street plan was virtually impossible to defend from attack.

As early as December 14, Washington began to think about a way to capitalize on the overextension of the British forces in New Jersey, writing to Connecticut governor Jonathan Trumbull that he hoped "to attempt a stroke upon the forces of the enemy, who lay a good deal scattered and to all appearance in a state of security. A lucky blow in this quarter would be fatal to them and would most certainly raise the spirits of the people, which are quite sunk by our late misfortunes."

Before he could begin to formulate a possible plan, Washington received startling news from a different quarter: General Charles Lee was now a prisoner of the British army.

By the second week in December, Gates and his men were working their way south across war-torn New Jersey. Unsure of where Washington's army was located, Gates sent ahead the man he was grooming to be his next adjutant, Major James Wilkinson, to secure instructions as to how he should proceed.

Wilkinson didn't find Washington, but after several days of searching, he did find Charles Lee, who had spent the night with a prostitute in a house in Basking Ridge, New Jersey, several miles from his army. Lee was doing his best to ignore Washington's repeated requests that he march as quickly as possible across New Jersey and join him in Pennsylvania. Wilkinson was convinced that Lee intended to launch his own attack on the poorly defended British post at Princeton—an attack that might have made Lee instead of Washington the new American hero of the Revolution. But it never happened. As Lee, still in his nightshirt and slippers, penned a letter for Wilkinson to deliver to Horatio Gates ("Entre nous," the letter read, "a certain great man is most damnably deficient"), a pounding was heard at the front door. The house, they soon learned, had been surrounded by British dragoons. Within a few minutes, Lee was being carried most ignominiously away by the enemy, and Wilkinson, who somehow pulled off a miraculous escape, was on his way back to General Gates.

The news of Lee's capture so rattled Gates that he temporarily left his army under the command of Benedict Arnold so that he and Wilkinson and "a light guard" could proceed west as fast as possible to the safety of Pennsylvania. If not exactly a courageous response to Lee's misfortune, it had at least served to get Gates across the Delaware River.

Washington was more irritated than alarmed by Lee's misfortune. He did not say it outright, but he must also have been relieved. Freed of a troubling distraction, he could now direct his undivided attention to taking advantage of the opportunity General Howe had given him.

No matter how much Washington aspired to be a great general in the European mold, he was at heart a backwoodsman. Most of his formative years had been spent as either a surveyor in the wilds of Virginia or a soldier fighting the French and Indians in what is now western Pennsylvania. He might be, as Thomas Jefferson remarked, "the most graceful figure that could be seen on horseback," but once he dismounted, he moved with the unmistakable toe-to-heel gait of a native warrior—a "peculiar walk" that his step-grandson attributed to his "long service on the frontier." Washington had been indelibly imprinted by his time in the American wilderness, and it would be the hit-and-run style of the native way of war that remained his forte even as he worked tirelessly in the years ahead to rebuild the Continental army into a European-style force.

As had been demonstrated at Long Island and New York, Washington was not a good battlefield thinker. Howe (with the help of Henry Clinton) consistently outgeneraled him. Washington's gifts were more physical and improvisational. When dire necessity forced him to ad-lib, when the scale of the fighting was contained enough that he was able to project his own extraordinary charisma upon those around him, there was no better leader of men. Instead of a diminutive Napoleon who scrutinized his battle plans from the sanctity of his headquarters tent, Washington—as commanding a physical presence as ever led an army— exuded the dignified grace of an Indian sachem. And in the days ahead, events would play to those personal strengths.

Howe had done Washington a favor by forcing him to abandon the coast and take up residence along an inland river, where his relatively small force could attack the overextended British outposts almost at will.

Washington had lost most of his original army, but he could seek temporary assistance from militiamen in New Jersey and Pennsylvania. Howe had no such local advantage. Since there were three thousand miles of ocean between his army and home, every man the British commander lost was, at least in the short term, irreplaceable.

Howe had also lost the benefit of the naval superiority he had enjoyed at New York. Washington, on the other hand, currently controlled a more than forty-mile stretch of the Delaware thanks to the fleet of river craft his men had collected as well as the thirteen row galleys of the Pennsylvania navy stationed at Philadelphia. With the Delaware and the state militia at his disposal, Washington possessed a window of genuine opportunity until the river froze in January.

Even Howe's own officers recognized the perilous position their army was in. On a night in late December, Lieutenant Colonel Charles Mawhood, stationed in Princeton, told a Dutch doctor that "if he was in General Washington's place he would make an attack on several of the principal posts at the same time; that they were all so weak that he might certainly cut them off and be in possession of Jersey in a few days."

Sure enough, during the week preceding Christmas, Washington started to put into place a plan to attack the outpost at Trenton, a plan he had begun to consider as early as December 14, when he first mentioned the possibility to Governor Trumbull. And then, on December 22, his estranged adjutant general Joseph Reed, who was rarely seen at Washington's headquarters in Newtown, had the temerity to propose by letter from Bristol, Pennsylvania (approximately fourteen miles to the south), the supposedly original idea of making "a diversion or something more at or about Trenton." "Our affairs are hastening fast to ruin," Reed melodramatically wrote, "if we do not retrieve them by some happy event. Delay with us is now equal to a total defeat." Up until that point, Reed had wandered sullenly up and down the Delaware, complaining to congressional delegate Benjamin Rush and others that it appeared evident that they "had begun an opposition to Great Britain which we have not strength to finish." Now, at this belated hour, Reed was attempting to claim as his own a plan that Washington had set into motion at least a week before. In his letter to Washington, Reed, who had already betrayed the confidence of his commander in chief, was posing for the historical record, and many of his fellow officers had come to regard him as, in the words of the historian George Bancroft, "a vacillating trimmer." One can detect the annoyance in Washington's December 23 reply, in which he informed Reed "that Christmas day at night, one hour before day is the time fixed upon for our attempt on Trenton. For heaven's sake keep this to yourself."

By the middle of December, Horatio Gates had arrived at the American camp beside the Delaware. From the beginning, Gates was reluctant to serve under Washington. Even though His Excellency requested that he accompany him on the mission to Trenton, Gates demurred, claiming that ill health required him to go to Philadelphia for medical attention. When Washington then requested that he at least stop in Bristol to settle the "uneasiness of command" that had arisen between the Continental soldiers and militiamen stationed there, he once again equivocated. Gates was taking up where Charles Lee had left off when it came to an almost insubordinate disregard for the wishes of his commander in chief.

No such tensions appear to have existed between Washington and Benedict Arnold. We have no record of their meeting, but with Reed, Lee, and now Gates positioning themselves to take advantage of what they saw as Washington's imminent downfall, it must have been a relief to meet with an officer who would rather fight than play politics. Arnold's most recent contribution to the cause had been twofold. Not only had he stopped the British advance; by convincing Carleton to return to Canada, he'd made possible the addition of more than five hundred veteran soldiers to Washington's army from the north. Included in this group were two officers who were destined to make important if not critical contributions in the days ahead—the grizzled New Hampshire veteran Colonel John Stark and Brigadier General Arthur St. Clair of Pennsylvania. It is tempting to speculate about what might have happened if Arnold had been at Washington's side during the raid on Trenton, but by then he had already received orders to report to Rhode Island. With the British now in Newport, Washington needed an officer he could trust to bolster the defenses in that state, and soon Arnold was headed north.

On December 23 Horatio Gates decided that even though he was very ill, he somehow had the stamina required to ride not just to Philadelphia but the extra hundred miles to the new temporary home of the Continental Congress in Baltimore. On top of that, he wanted his new favorite, Major James Wilkinson, to accompany him. Since Wilkinson was currently serving on General Arthur St. Clair's staff, he needed to first apply for leave, which St. Clair reluctantly granted.

During the ride to Philadelphia the next day, Gates "appeared," Wilkinson remembered, "much depressed in mind, and frequently expressed the opinion that while General Washington was watching the enemy above Trenton, [the British] would privately construct bateaux, pass the Delaware in his rear, and take possession of Philadelphia before he was aware of the movement." Instead of boldly attacking one of the British outposts, Gates felt that Washington should retreat to the south of the Susquehanna River and build himself a new army. Convinced that whatever Washington attempted to do along the Delaware was doomed to fail, he intended to "propose this measure to Congress at Baltimore, and urged me to accompany him to that place."

After a night at the City Tavern in Philadelphia, during which Gates got into an "unpleasant altercation" with some loyalists, Wilkinson decided that "duty forbade" his continuing on to Baltimore, and that he must return to St. Clair. Before the two parted, Gates dashed off a letter to Washington for Wilkinson to take back with him to Newtown.

When he arrived at the general's headquarters around two in the afternoon of December 25, Wilkinson was surprised to learn that Washington had marched with his troops to McKonkey's Ferry on the west bank of the Delaware River, about ten miles above Trenton. Their route was easily "traced," he remembered, "as there was a little snow on the ground, which was tinged here and there with blood from the feet of the men who wore broken shoes." About dusk, he found Washington "alone with his whip in his hand, prepared to mount his horse." Washington was about to lead the operation that could either make or break not only his own military career but perhaps the future of the United States, and Wilkinson must now deliver what was likely to be a most unwelcome message. It was as uncomfortable a situation as he ever experienced, and in his memoirs Wilkinson provided a detailed account of his conversation with Washington after he had handed him Gates's letter.

Obviously distracted, Washington looked up at the young major and said with what Wilkinson described as "solemnity," "What a time is this to hand me letters!"

Wilkinson explained that he had been "charged with it by General Gates."

"By General Gates! Where is he?"

"I left him this morning in Philadelphia."

"What was he doing there?"

"I understood him that he was on his way to Congress."

"On his way to Congress!"

Washington now knew for a certainty that if the attack on Trenton should miscarry, Gates, safely removed from any connection to the failure, had positioned himself to become his successor. Washington broke the seal and began to read. Wilkinson bowed and left to join General St. Clair on the bank of the Delaware.

Sixteen-year-old John Greenwood was much like Joseph Plumb Martin, the teenager from Connecticut who had witnessed the British landing at Kips Bay, New York, back in September. Like Martin, Greenwood had joined the army more out of a boyish desire for adventure than in the service of high-minded ideals. On that frigid Christmas night he had every reason to regret the decision as he, along with more than two thousand others, waited his turn to be rowed and poled across the ice-choked river. High-sided vessels used for transporting iron ore known as Durham boats carried the soldiers, who remained standing throughout the passage, while wider ferries transported the horses and fieldpieces. At first, a freezing rain soaked them to the skin; then it started to hail. By the time they arrived on the New Jersey bank it was blowing "a perfect hurricane" and had begun to snow.

Making matters even worse, Greenwood was suffering from the dreaded "itch"—a highly contagious bacterial infection that had afflicted him and many of the others since leaving Fort Ticonderoga back in November. Also known as impetigo, the itch first appeared between the soldier's fingers, creating vesicles that when ruptured spread the infection to other parts of the body as a malodorous crust formed across the soldier's ulcerated skin. "I had the itch then so bad," Greenwood remembered, "that my breeches stuck to my thighs, all the skin being off, and there were hundreds of vermin upon me."

But that night on the Delaware, the extreme cold was what most concerned the young soldier. Once he and his compatriots had been delivered to land by the same sailors from Marblehead who had rescued Washington's army during the retreat across the East River, they made a huge bonfire out of some fence rails. Turning himself like a turkey on a spit, Greenwood "kept [himself] from perishing before the large bonfire."

They had no idea what lay before them. They were wet and freezing and, in Greenwood's case, literally crawling with pus-encrusted lice, and yet they were, for reasons that were difficult to explain, enjoying themselves. "The noise of the soldiers coming over and clearing away the ice," Greenwood recounted, "the rattling of the cannon wheels on the frozen ground, and the cheerfulness of my fellow comrades encouraged me beyond expression, and big coward as I acknowledge myself to be, I felt great pleasure."

Their commander in chief, however, did not share in the good spirits. Once ashore, Washington wrapped himself in a cloak, and sitting on a box that had formerly served as a beehive, he contemplated what to do next. He had hoped to get his army of twenty-four hundred soldiers across the Delaware by midnight. Given the miserable weather and ice, it would be three in the morning by the time the last cannon and soldier reached the New Jersey shore. His army had a punishing twelve-mile march ahead of it through the sleet and snow. He had originally planned to reach Trenton well before dawn for a surprise attack, but that was now impossible. Could he, in good conscience, ask these men to march into a village defended by professional Hessian soldiers in broad daylight? "As I was certain there was no making a retreat without being discovered . . . I determined to push on at all events," he later wrote.

With the snow blowing in their faces, the men marched into the storm. In the beginning, the pace was frustratingly slow—no faster, Greenwood remembered, "than a child ten years old could walk." During a particularly long halt, he became so "benumbed with cold that I wanted to go to sleep," and he sat down on a nearby stump. "Had I been passed unnoticed," he remembered, "I should have frozen to death without knowing it; but as good luck always attended me, Sergeant Madden came and, rousing me up, made me walk about."

To help illuminate their path, the artillerymen lit the saltpeter-soaked cords of rope used to fire the cannons (known as slow match), and Elisha Bostwick from Connecticut remembered how the makeshift torches "sparkled and blazed in the storm all night." At one point as they approached a creek crossing, the rear legs of Washington's horse slid out from underneath it on what Bostwick called "the slanting slippery bank." In the flickering snow-filled light, Bostwick watched as Washington "seized his horse's mane and the horse recovered"—an astonishing act of strength and control that confirmed the general's reputation as the greatest horseman of his generation. Bostwick also remembered how his commander exhorted them "in a deep and solemn voice [to] keep by your officers. For God's sake keep by your officers."

Well before they reached Trenton, Washington divided his force into two wings, with General John Sullivan leading the division along the river road while Washington and Greene took the inland route with the intention of attacking the village simultaneously from opposite ends. Seizing a small village currently occupied by fifteen hundred Hessians was unlikely to serve as anything more than a symbolic victory, especially since there were several other enemy outposts throughout New Jersey that would undoubtedly respond to an American attack. This meant that even if Washington somehow succeeded in taking Trenton, he must withdraw his army as quickly as possible back across the Delaware before other, more powerful Hessian detachments in the vicinity had a chance to exact what would likely be brutal revenge on the exhausted and freezing Americans.

Daylight had begun to creep into the clouded sky when those leading the advance came upon a strange sight. There, looking at them warily from a nearby field, was a group of soldiers—not Hessians but Americans. Who were these people?

General Adam Stephen of Virginia was in command of a brigade that had been stationed downriver of Washington's headquarters before joining the current expedition against the Hessians at Trenton. A few days before, one of Stephen's men had been picked off by the Hessians on the opposite bank of the Delaware. Without consulting Washington, who had been a bitter military and political rival of Stephen's since the French and Indian War, he sent over a raiding party across the river to avenge the American soldier's death. That night they had attacked one of the guardhouses outside Trenton and wounded several of the enemy.

Washington immediately called up General Stephen from the back of the column and asked whether the men's story was true. It was. "You sir," he shouted, "may have ruined all my plans by having put [the enemy] on their guard." One soldier remembered that "he never saw Washington exhibit so much anger." As it turned out, however, Stephen's retaliatory expedition had actually worked to the Americans' benefit.

The previous day, Colonel Rall had received a warning from British headquarters that according to a well-placed spy, an American assault was imminent. When Stephen's men opened fire that night, Rall assumed that this was the anticipated attack, and once the Americans had fled into the darkness, the Hessians inevitably began to relax, particularly given the appalling weather. As a consequence, despite having arrived several hours behind schedule, Washington—thanks to Stephen's premature and largely ineffective strike—was able to catch the Hessians by surprise.

And yet, even if the majority of the Hessians were literally caught napping that morning, they responded to the American attack with remarkable speed. The battle that followed did not last long, but it was nonetheless savagely fought, and for John Greenwood it unfolded in a wild, almost hallucinatory rush. "The first intimation I received of our going to fight was the firing of a six-pound cannon at us, the ball from which struck the fore horse that was dragging our only piece of artillery, a three-pounder. The animal, which was near me as I was in the second division on the left, was struck in its belly and knocked over on its back. While it lay there kicking, the cannon was stopped, and I did not see it again after we had passed on." About two hundred yards ahead appeared several hundred Hessians, "two deep in a straight line," with Colonel Rall on horseback beside them. The Hessians fired but did little damage. Unfortunately, the Americans' weapons were so wet that they would not fire. An officer shouted, "Charge bayonets and rush on!" They only had, Greenwood remembered, "one bayonet to five men," but "rush on we did." The Hessians fired once, and before they had a chance to reload, the Americans were within three feet of them. "They broke in an instant," Greenwood remembered, "and ran like so many frightened devils into the town, . . . we after them pell-mell."

For many of Washington's officers and men, this was their first taste of hand-to-hand combat. "Here succeeded," the artillery commander Henry Knox wrote to his wife, Lucy, "a scene of war of which I had often conceived but never saw before. The hurry, fright, and confusion of the enemy was not unlike that which will be when the last trump shall sound." The Americans' muskets might have been ineffective, but not

Knox's fieldpieces, which, although relatively small, were more mobile than the Hessians' larger cannons. Knox had also instructed a group of his artillery officers and men to rush upon the Hessian fieldpieces with the intention of capturing the cannons and turning them against the enemy, which quickly had a demoralizing effect on the Germans. After several valiant countercharges, Colonel Rall was mortally wounded by a musket ball to the abdomen, and in less than a half hour all the Hessians who hadn't escaped or been killed had surrendered.

Toward the end of the fighting, General St. Clair sent Wilkinson to find Washington for orders. "I . . . rode up to him at the moment Colonel Rall, supported by a file of sergeants, was presenting his sword," he wrote. "On my approach [Washington] took me by the hand and observed, 'Major Wilkinson, this is a glorious day for our country,' his countenance beaming with complacency; whilst . . . Rall, who the day before would not have changed fortunes with him, now pale, bleeding and covered with blood, in broken accents seemed to implore those attentions. . . . How awful the contrast."

The American soldiers had been taught to loathe the Hessians as cold-blooded mercenaries. With their boot-blacked mustaches, brass combat caps, and hair pulled back into grease-stiffened queues, they appeared to be nearly identical automatons of war. But Greenwood and his friends now realized that the Hessian prisoners were actually terrified young men much like themselves. "Some of the poor fellows," he wrote, "were so cold that their underjaws quivered like an aspen leaf. . . . Seeing [that] some of our men were much pleased with the brass caps which they had taken from the dead Hessians, our prisoners, who were besides exceedingly frightened, pulled off those that they were wearing and giving them away put on the hats which they carried tied behind their packs."

Some later claimed that the Hessians had been hopelessly drunk after the Christmas celebrations of the night before, but as Greenwood and others testified, this was not the case. If any side indulged in alcohol, it was the Americans, who broke into the Hessian liquor supply and became raucously inebriated. Greenwood remembered how with the Hessian caps on their heads, the drunk American soldiers "would strut . . . with their elbows out and some without a collar to their half-a-shirt, no shoes, etc."

Washington and his officers briefly considered continuing what they had started in New Jersey and attacking the equally understaffed outpost in Princeton before the British stationed there received word of the American attack on Trenton. It soon became apparent, however, that the drunkenness of their own men gave them no choice but to return across the Delaware.

During the passage back, Colonel Glover's mariners from Marblehead requested that the Hessian prisoners help them free the ice from the sides of the boat by jumping in unison. Elisha Bostwick long remembered how the queues of the Hessians' hair, which he compared to "the handle of an iron skillet," began "flying up and down" as the prisoners "all set to jumping . . . [and] soon shook off the ice from the boats." They came from two different cultures and were supposedly each other's enemy, but for a brief while on the icy Delaware, the Americans and Hessians were, literally and figuratively, all in the same boat.

By the following morning, Washington's army of approximately twenty-four hundred soldiers and their nine hundred Hessian prisoners had returned to the Pennsylvania side of the river. Soon after dispatching the prisoners to the care of militiamen stationed in Philadelphia, Washington received word that General John Cadwalader's Pennsylvania militiamen stationed to the south in Bristol had crossed over to the Jersey side of the river. The original plan had been for them to assist in the previous night's attack, but due to the severity of the ice, which had a tendency to pile into an impassable chaos of jagged chunks below the falls at Trenton, they had remained stuck in Bristol. That had not prevented them, however, from attempting to cross the next day. Once on the Jersey side, they reported that the British forces along the river had all fled back toward New York. What should they do next? Return across the river or wait for Washington's force to join them?

Washington had already succeeded beyond his (or anyone else's) wildest dreams. The British traveler Nicholas Cresswell was in Virginia when he heard the news about Trenton. "Their late successes have turned the scale and now they are all liberty mad again," he wrote. According to Wilkinson, "Trenton reanimated the timid friends of the Revolution and invigorated the confidence of the resolute. . . . The American community began to feel and act like a nation determined to be free." Could Washington justifiably hazard throwing this all away by attempting yet another military adventure in New Jersey?

During a council of war on December 27, several of his generals argued that he must order Cadwalader and the militia back into Pennsylvania. But that was not what His Excellency wanted to do, and gradually the majority of the generals came around to his way of thinking. If they did nothing to capitalize on what had been achieved at Trenton, there was a danger that once the Delaware froze solid in January, the British would simply march across the river and take Philadelphia. To ensure that this did not happen, they must attempt to drive the British out of southwestern New Jersey.

Given the ultimate course of events, there has been a tendency to accept Washington's decision to recross the Delaware as a sound one. But take away the benefit of hindsight, and one can begin to appreciate the enormous risks Washington assumed by returning to New Jersey. If Howe responded to the attack on Trenton with a significant show of force, the Continentals would soon find themselves in what one of Washington's officers described as a "cul de sac," with the ice-clogged Delaware at their backs and a far superior force at their front. The only alternative would be to fight, and if past experience had taught them anything, this was exactly the scenario to avoid.

But Washington would have none of it. Goaded by Cadwalader's militia and inspired by his most recent success, he allowed his naturally aggressive inclinations to overrule his better judgment. Knowing full well that a defeat would leave his country in an even worse position than it had been in just a week before, Washington elected to jeopardize everything he had so far accomplished in hopes of pushing the British back toward New York.

Part of Washington's motivation was the upcoming expiration of the Continental army's term of duty at the end of the year. If he had them all together on the opposite shore with the British ahead and the river behind, the soldiers might be more willing to reenlist, especially if offered a bonus. To a limited degree, this proved to be the case. Once they had returned to New Jersey, he did succeed in getting at least a portion of the army to remain with him for the next six weeks. (Not included in this group was John Greenwood, who when told he was about to be promoted to ensign replied that he "would not stay to be a colonel.") And then, just a day later, word reached Washington in his new headquarters in downtown Trenton that General Cornwallis and an estimated eight thousand British soldiers were preparing to head his way.

On January 1 Washington called a council of war attended by the newly promoted Brigadier General Henry Knox, as well as Generals Greene, Sullivan, and St. Clair, and his adjutant general Joseph Reed. Reed had kept his distance from the commander in chief throughout most of December, but now he had something useful to offer. He'd just returned from a scouting mission to Princeton, where he and a company of gentlemen dragoons from Philadelphia had secured several British prisoners who provided intelligence about the impending attack. It was not exactly a rapprochement, but Reed had returned to being a valued member of Washington's staff.

They were, it was agreed, "in a critical situation." Given the state of the ice, they couldn't retreat across the Delaware before the British were upon them. And besides, Wilkinson (who received his information from St. Clair) wrote, "if [the retreat] could be effected at all it would depreciate the influence of antecedent successes and check the rising spirit of the community." On the other hand, "to give battle under the circumstances. . . . hazard[ed] the annihilation of the Grand Army."

One option was to fall back to where Cadwalader's militiamen were currently stationed in Crosswicks, New Jersey, about seven miles to the southeast on a tributary of the Delaware. The other possibility was to order Cadwalader to join them and make a stand at Trenton. The problem was that, as the Hessians had learned, Trenton's open street plan made it a difficult town to defend. At that point, Reed made his most significant contribution of the war. Having grown up in this area, he knew that on the other side of Assunpink Creek, which flowed into the Delaware along the southern edge of the town, was a section of high ground bounded by the Delaware on one side and a swamp on the other. If Washington relocated the American army to the south bank of the Assunpink, they would be in a much more defensible position. Assuming Cornwallis marched into Trenton along the main road from Princeton, the British would have to cross a single and very narrow stone bridge to attack the Americans. That settled it. Instead of retreating back to Crosswicks, they would immediately order Cadwalader to join them in Trenton.

• • •

The Hessian captain Johann Ewald was astonished by the effect of Washington's attack on Trenton. "Thus had the times changed!" he wrote. "The Americans had constantly run before us. Four weeks ago we expected to end the war . . . and now we had to render Washington the honor of thinking about our defense. . . . Since we had thus far underestimated our enemy, from this unhappy day onward we saw everything through the magnifying glass."

No one was more shocked than William Howe, who immediately summoned Cornwallis from the vessel that was about to take him home to England, where his sick wife anxiously awaited his return. The Howes' entire premise—that America could be won back through a combination of coercion and negotiation—was dependent on the British army's completely controlling the momentum of the war. If something was not done to reverse the fiasco at Trenton, all of the British victories leading up to this point might be for naught.

Up until now, William Howe's hopes for reconciliation had prevented him from destroying Washington's army when he had the chance. In his conversation with Cornwallis he made it plain that circumstances had changed. He must make the Americans regret that they had ever ventured back across the Delaware by inflicting the devastating defeat that the British had so far refused to deliver.

Cornwallis arrived in Princeton on January 1. During the council of war with his officers, he announced "his intention to advance toward Trenton in the morning." Colonel Carl Emilius von Donop, whose Hessians had been assigned to the New Jersey outposts and who was therefore familiar with the terrain, suggested that Cornwallis take the precaution of dividing his force into two columns, with one column marching into Trenton as the other performed a flanking movement similar to what had won the Battle of Long Island. Cornwallis would have none of it. Like Howe before him at the Battle of Bunker Hill, he would attack the Americans head-on. "The enemy was despised," Captain Ewald wrote, "and as usual we [Hessians] had to pay for it."

The British prisoners taken over the course of the last few days had assured the Americans that the enemy would soon be headed toward Trenton. Realizing that his army needed all the time it could get to prepare for the British attack, Washington sent out a thousand soldiers along with Captain Thomas Forrest's artillery regiment of six fieldpieces to delay the enemy as best they could. As the morning turned to afternoon, Forrest and the others performed brilliantly, firing on the British and then falling back at regular intervals until they'd retreated to within sight of the American forces in Trenton. At that point, Washington, along with Generals Greene and Knox, rode out to thank Forrest and his fellow officers for everything they had so far done. Then came the real reason for their visit. Forrest and the others were to make "as obstinate a stand as [possible]" at their current position. Not until they were in danger of "hazarding the [field]pieces" should they finally retreat across the Assunpink.

James Wilkinson had a "fair flank view of this little combat" from the opposite side of the river. By that time the sun had set, and Wilkinson "could distinguish the flame from the muzzles of our muskets." Soon the American advance corps was in danger of being overwhelmed by the enemy

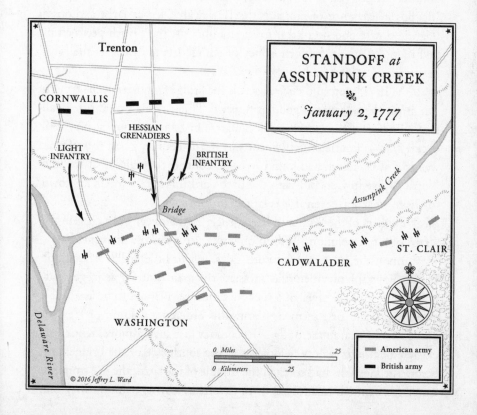

onslaught and had begun to run for the bridge. One of those soldiers was John Howland of Providence, Rhode Island. "The bridge was narrow," he remembered, "and our platoons in passing it were crowded into a dense and solid mass." There, at the west rail of the bridge, was His Excellency George Washington astride a "noble horse." "The firm, composed, and majestic countenance of the general inspired confidence and assurance in a moment so important and critical," Howland remembered. "I was pressed against the shoulder of the general's horse and in contact with the general's boot. The horse stood as firm as the rider, and seemed to understand that he was not to quit his post and station."

Once the American soldiers had succeeded in joining their comrades on the bank of the Assunpink, the British took up positions about a thousand yards away, with the river and the town between the two armies. The American forces, which now amounted to close to seven thousand men, were spread out for almost a mile, with the soldiers standing about an arm's length apart. Ensign Robert Beale remembered that there was "no possible chance of crossing the [Delaware]; ice as large as houses floating down, and no retreat to the mountains, the British between us and them." Captain Stephen Olney of Rhode Island called it "the most desperate situation I had ever known."

If the British forced their way across the bridge and overran the American army, the war was as good as finished. Philadelphia would surely fall that winter, and the Continental Congress in Baltimore might very well decide that a negotiated settlement was in the country's best interests. It was as if Washington had found a way to conflate the standoff at the Old North Bridge in Concord with the Battle of Bunker Hill in Charlestown to create what was, even if it is largely unappreciated today, the make-or-break moment of the War of Independence. "If there ever was a crisis in the affairs of the Revolution," Wilkinson wrote, "this was the moment."

Cannons began to fire on both sides, but to little effect. After some British light infantrymen and Hessian riflemen (known as jaegers) attempted to ford the creek at a spot that did not turn out to be as vulnerable as it had at first seemed, Cornwallis ordered a column of Hessian grenadiers to charge the bridge. To counter just such a move, Knox had clustered close to twenty fieldpieces at the south side of the bridge, and before the Hessians had reached the middle of the span, the fire from the American cannons had forced them to retreat, leaving behind thirty-one killed and wounded while an almost equal number surrendered to the rebels on the south side of the bridge.

The British infantry were next. In this instance, the Americans held their fire until the enemy had, in the words of Sergeant Joseph White, "come on some ways." A signal was given and the resulting onslaught forced the British to retire. Two more times the grenadiers formed and resumed the charge only to be turned back in each instance. The third and final British retreat caused the entire American line to shout "as one man." But Cornwallis was not yet through.

This time he put together what was described as "a very heavy column." In anticipation of the charge, Washington ordered Cadwalader's militiamen to take up positions to the right of the bridge. Meanwhile the American artillerymen, according to Sergeant White, "loaded with canister shot [antipersonnel ammunition composed of iron balls smaller than grapeshot] and let them come nearer."

It was tragically ironic. All of General Howe's caution during the previous battles—during which he had vowed not to lose a single man's finger "wantonly"—had come down to this one terrifying confrontation. "We fired all together again," wrote Sergeant White, "and such destruction it made, you cannot conceive. The bridge looked red as blood, with their killed and wounded and their red coats." Adding to the horror of the scene was the eerie sound of the canister shot hurtling through the air—what White described as "a terrible squeaking." By the end of this one last attempt to cross the Assunpink, the Americans had suffered a mere 50 casualties while 365 British and Hessian soldiers had been killed, wounded, or captured—most occurring in the space of little over an hour.

"In this awful moment," Wilkinson wrote, "the guardian angel of our country admonished Lord Cornwallis that his own troops were fatigued and that the Americans were without retreat." Confident that the Americans were trapped between his army and the river, the British commander decided to cease the attack until morning. That night he was reputed to have assured his officers that "we've got the Old Fox safe now. We'll go over and bag him in the morning." One of Cornwallis's officers dared to disagree. "My Lord," Sir William Erskine warned, "if you trust those people tonight you will see nothing of them in the morning." Erskine, it turned out, was right.

• • •

At that night's council of war, Washington claimed that "a battle was certain if he kept his ground until the morning." Since this was likely to result in the defeat of the American army, several of his officers insisted that they start retreating along the shore of the Delaware; others wanted to stay their ground and, if necessary, go down fighting. St. Clair later told Wilkinson that Washington, "yielding to his natural propensities, favored the latter." But St. Clair, according to Wilkinson's account, proposed a third option.

He'd spent the day guarding the fords on the right of the American line, above the bridge. There he'd found a road that some locals told him led to the Quaker Bridge in the direction of Princeton. Why not secretly march out and around Cornwallis's army under the cover of night and hit the British the next morning where they least expected it—in their rear at Princeton? Joseph Reed had nothing but encouraging things to say about this as a possible escape route, and when the Virginian Hugh Mercer "forcibly pointed out its practicability and the advantages that would necessarily result from it," Washington began to voice his enthusiasm for the proposal, noting that "it would avoid the appearance of a retreat." It was agreed. As watch fires were stoked along the Assunpink to shield the activities behind the American line, Washington's army would attempt to elude disaster through a daring "ruse de guerre."

That night the temperature plummeted. "The roads which the day before had been mud, snow, and water," Stephen Olney wrote, "were congealed now and had become hard as a pavement." Instead of slowly slogging their way through the mire, Washington's army was able to move at a surprisingly fast speed over the rock-solid ground. In just five hours' time, they put nine miles between them and Cornwallis's army in Trenton. By dawn, they were approaching the outskirts of Princeton. "The morning was bright, serene, and extremely cold," Wilkinson remembered, "with a hoar frost which bespangled every object." At that point, a portion of Washington's army came upon a British force of three regiments and three troops of dragoons led by Lieutenant Colonel Charles Mawhood, the same officer who just a few days before had spoken of the likelihood of an American attack.

Mawhood and his troops were on their way to reinforce Cornwallis when some of his dragoons spotted the Americans. Thinking at first they'd come upon just a handful of the enemy, Mawhood prepared to attack, only belatedly realizing that he was up against a much larger force than he had anticipated. Both armies raced for the high ground in an open field beside Thomas Clarke's house, and after the Americans, led by the Virginian Hugh Mercer, unleashed a volley, the British responded with a volley of their own.

Wilkinson's view of the battle was blocked by the surrounding hills and trees, but he did see evidence of the confrontation. "I well recollect that the smoke from the discharge of the two lines mingled as it rose and went up in one beautiful cloud." On ground level, however, as Mawhood's soldiers charged into the midst of the American line with their bayonets fixed, the scene was anything but beautiful. The grass was covered by a layer of ice, much of it now smeared with the blood of dead and dying soldiers. As Mercer's men began to retreat, the American general was knocked down from his gray horse by the butt of a British musket. When one of the regulars cried out, "Call for quarters, you damn rebel," Mercer responded, "I am no rebel." Vainly attempting to defend himself with his sword, Mercer was bayoneted repeatedly before the regulars left him for dead.

By then Washington had ridden up from the rear and was attempting to bring some order to the retreating American line. With the arrival of reinforcements, there were now more than enough soldiers to begin to turn the tide of battle. Even though it put him in plain view of the enemy, Washington rode ahead of the American line and turned to address the soldiers behind him. "Parade with us, my brave fellows," he cried out. "There is but a handful of the enemy, and we will have them directly!" At that moment the British let loose a fearsome volley that instantly enveloped the field in powder smoke. One of Washington's aides was so convinced his commander had just been killed that he covered his eyes with his hat. But sure enough, Washington emerged from the roiling cloud unharmed.

Soon the Americans were advancing toward the British, who, now clearly overmatched, fled toward Princeton. "O, my Susan!" an American soldier wrote. "It was a glorious day, and I would not have been absent from it for all the money I ever expect to be worth . . . when I saw [General Washington] brave all the dangers of the field and his important life hanging as it were by a single hair with a thousand deaths flying around him."

As the British retreated, Washington called to those around him, "It is a fine fox chase, my boys!" and took off in pursuit. "Such was the impetuosity of the man's character," Wilkinson wrote, "when he gave reins to his sensibilities." For a general who had spent the last five months presiding over one miserable defeat after another, it must have been a refreshing release of emotion, and Wilkinson claimed that Washington pushed the chase of the retreating British to such an extent that his officers became concerned about his whereabouts.

Soon Princeton had been flushed of its British occupiers, some of whom attempted a halfhearted stand at the college's Nassau Hall before surrendering. Once again, Washington had a decision to make. Should they continue to Brunswick, which contained a large supply of military stores? Washington later claimed that if he had had six to eight hundred fresh troops, he could have marched to Brunswick and, in his own words, "put an end to the war."

By then, however, even Washington was beginning to feel the strain of the last eighteen hours of continual marching and combat. After having extricated himself from a seemingly impossible situation in Trenton, he finally began to think about consolidating the gains he had so far won. "The danger of losing the advantage . . . by aiming at too much induced me," he wrote, "by the advice of my officers, to relinquish the attempt."

Washington reluctantly led his army north, and on January 6, after a march of several days, they reached Morristown, a community amid the rugged Watchung Mountains. There his army could defend itself against a possible British attack while remaining close enough to New York to respond to any move Howe might make. But, as it turned out, Howe and especially Cornwallis, who did his best to dismiss Washington's march to Princeton as a mere stunt, had had enough for the winter.

The Battles of Trenton and Princeton are often looked to as the point at which Washington blossomed into the brilliant commander we revere today. But that is to ignore the next four years. At the Second Battle of Trenton Washington's natural aggressiveness had succeeded in turning a potential catastrophe of his own devising into an improbable triumph. But as he appears to have realized already, this was no way to win a war.

CHAPTER FOUR

The Year of the Hangman

I n the winter of 1777, Benedict Arnold fell in love.

After more than a month in Rhode Island devising schemes to dislodge the British army from Newport, Arnold traveled to Boston to recruit the troops he needed to make those plans a reality. He also had more personal business to attend to. If his expected promotion to major general were to come through, he would need to update his uniform. On March 1 he wrote to Paul Revere requesting that he assist him in securing a sword knot (an ornamental lanyard that an officer looped around his hand to prevent the weapon from being dropped to the ground), a sash (purple if he was shopping for a major general's), one dozen silk hose, and "two best appalits," or epaulets.

At some point during his stay in Boston, Arnold had the pleasure of meeting a young woman whom he described in a letter to Henry Knox's wife, Lucy, as "heavenly." Like Lucy, Elizabeth Deblois was the daughter of a wealthy Boston loyalist. Not only was she beautiful and well-off; she had a way about her. "She puckers her mouth a little," a smitten John Quincy Adams recorded in his diary more than a decade later, "and contracts her eyelids a little, to look very pretty; and is not wholly unsuccessful." In early March 1777, when Elizabeth was just sixteen, all this lip puckering and eye fluttering was, at least for the thirty-six-year-old widower Benedict Arnold, irresistible.

In hopes of winning her affection, Arnold had a trunk of gowns sent to Lucy Knox for delivery to the Deblois residence. He then requested that Lucy let him know how the offering was received. "I shall remain under the most anxious suspense until I have the favor of a line from you," he wrote. "Conceive the fond anxiety, the glowing hopes, and chilling fears that alternately possess the breast of . . . your obedient . . . servant, Benedict Arnold." He might be a soldier who had seen more than his share of hardship and death, but he clearly had a softer side—even if a trunk's worth of gowns (which might have come Arnold's way through one of the many privateers that sailed out of Boston) was not the most romantic of gifts.

Once back in Rhode Island, with the prospects of an assault on Newport looking increasingly remote, Arnold began to ponder his next professional move. While stationed the year before at Ticonderoga, he had befriended not only Horatio Gates, but Gates's commanding officer at the time, Philip Schuyler. Schuyler came from one of the leading families of New York; he had a beautiful home in Albany and a country estate in Saratoga, and it would not be long before Alexander Hamilton, who was now a member of Washington's staff, fell in love with one of Schuyler's three daughters. Schuyler's wealth and privilege represented everything Arnold aspired to one day have, while the more nakedly ambitious Horatio Gates had a background (his father had been a Thames waterman, his mother a housekeeper to a duke) that was closer to Arnold's own relatively modest origins. That winter Arnold wrote to both Schuyler and Gates with a proposal that addressed what had become for him (as well as for many of his fellow officers) one of the most vexatious problems of the war: how to support oneself in the Continental army.

The organization of the American army was based, in large part, on the British model, with one notable exception. Because they had to buy their commissions, British army officers tended to be financially independent products of the upper class; in fact, one of the reasons Horatio Gates had quit the British service was that his lack of social standing severely limited his potential rise through the ranks. American officers, on the other hand, although from the upper echelons of their communities, rarely possessed the personal wealth of their British counterparts. In the beginning of the war, these officers joined the army assuming that the conflict was going to be a brief and glorious struggle. By the winter of 1777, these same officers were finding themselves in increasingly straitened financial circumstances. Short of printing money (which was already starting to plummet in value), the Continental Congress had not yet found an effective way to pay for the war effort.

This reality does not appear to have altered Arnold's spendthrift ways. He had started the war with a significant personal "fortune" (at least that was what he claimed), but it wasn't long before that fortune was gone. Not only did he enjoy the luxuries of life; he was also exceedingly generous with his friends, especially when it came to helping them serve the cause of American liberty. Just a few weeks before, when he learned that his Connecticut friend Colonel John Lamb was unable to secure the government funds he needed to establish his own artillery regiment, Arnold instructed his sister Hannah to provide Lamb with one thousand pounds.

It went without saying that Arnold could not afford to give away this amount of money. However, by that winter he had hit upon a way by which he could serve his country *and* live in the style to which he had grown accustomed. As he proposed to both Schuyler and Gates in letters that contained a nearly identical paragraph, he wanted to continue along the line he had started during his remarkable performance on Lake Champlain. "I should be fond of being in the navy," he announced to the two superior officers to whom he had become the closest. As major military operations along the East Coast stagnated to a virtual standstill that winter, he felt that the best way to cripple Howe's army was by sea. And yet the American navy, "to our disgrace," was currently "rotting in port, when if properly stationed, might greatly distress if not entirely ruin the enemy's army by taking their provisions ships."

As he had proven at Valcour, Arnold was a natural-born mariner. He also had a personality that was ideally suited to the sea, where a captain was the monarch of the floating fiefdom of his ship. Arnold's impatience and abruptness, which always seemed to get him in trouble on dry land, were what was expected of a ship's captain. The long stints at sea would also keep him safely removed from the annoying backbiters who had plagued him during his almost two years as an army officer. But perhaps the best part of being a naval officer, from Arnold's perspective, was the prize money.

In the American navy, a ship's crew received half the total worth of a captured merchant vessel and the entire value of a man-of-war, with the lion's share going to the captain. As a successful naval officer, Arnold could fulfill all his Gates-like ambitions while living like the lordly Schuyler. This is the great what-if of Arnold's career. Had he been a commodore rather than a general, he might have outshined even John Paul Jones.

But before Arnold had a chance to explore the possibility of a move to the navy, he received some stunning news. Not only had the Continental Congress decided *not* to award him his expected promotion; it had promoted five brigadier generals past him to the rank of major general.

George Washington was commander in chief of the Continental army, but as we have already seen, his powers were quite limited. Not only did the Continental Congress control the northern and southern armies; it also reserved the authority to appoint generals to all three armies, including Washington's own, the Grand Army. This inherently political selection process had created a list of generals that even John Adams had to admit was of exceptionally inferior quality. It also placed Washington in the difficult position of having to appease those officers who felt that they had been unjustly overlooked.

In the past, Washington had remained amazingly respectful of the delegates' right to choose whomever they saw fit. But even he had difficulty believing that Congress had overlooked Benedict Arnold, who was, he wrote to the Virginia congressman Richard Henry Lee, one of the most "spirited and sensible" officers in the army. Washington was both embarrassed and appalled on Arnold's behalf. "We have lately had several promotions to the rank of major general," he wrote to Arnold on March 3, "and I am at a loss whether you have had a preceding appointment . . . or whether you have been omitted through some mistake. Should the latter be the case I beg you will not take any hasty steps in consequence of it, but allow proper time for recollection, which, I flatter myself, will remedy any error that may have been made. My endeavors to that end shall not be wanting."

Washington eventually learned that the promotions had been based on a newly instituted quota system by which each state was allotted two major generals. Since Connecticut already had two officers of that rank, the Continental Congress, in its wisdom, had determined that their top-ranking brigadier general, who also happened to have the best record in the army, should suffer the humiliation of watching five of his lesser peers move past him in the ranks. Henry Knox wrote to his brother that "this

most infallibly pushes [Arnold] out of the service." At Washington's repeated urgings, Arnold promised to do nothing rash but admitted that he
could not help but "view [the nonpromotion] as a very civil way of requesting my resignation."

While he attempted to maintain a brave face to Washington, Arnold
showed no such restraint in a March 25 letter to Horatio Gates. Even if
Washington was correct in saying that his own qualifications had nothing
to do with his having been overlooked for promotion, he remained convinced that the accusations made by Moses Hazen and others had influenced the actions of Congress. Most recently, John Brown, an officer from
Pittsfield, Massachusetts, whose hatred of Arnold went back to the taking
of Fort Ticonderoga in May 1775, had written a petition to Congress that
accused him of thirteen misdemeanors, ranging from the absurd (Arnold,
Brown insisted, had been responsible for infecting the army with smallpox
during its stay in Canada) to the more familiar (confiscating goods for his
own personal gain in Montreal). Echoing what he had written to Gates
the summer before on Lake Champlain, Arnold wrote, "I cannot . . . help
thinking it extremely cruel to be judged and condemned without an opportunity of being heard or even knowing my crime or accuser. I am conscious of committing no crime since in the public service that merits
disgrace. . . . When I received a commission of brigadier I did not expect
Congress had made me for their sport, or pastime, to displace, or disgrace
whenever they thought proper. . . . If this plan is pursued no gentleman
who has any regard for his reputation will risk it with a body of men who
seemed to be governed by *whim and caprice.*"

Many commentators have faulted Arnold for being hypersensitive to
a perceived slight. But Arnold was by no means alone in his frustrations
with Congress. In the months to come Nathanael Greene, Henry Knox,
and John Sullivan also threatened to resign when a French officer was
placed ahead of them, with Greene angrily insisting, "I would never give
any legislative body an opportunity to humiliate me but once." John
Stark of New Hampshire, a hero of the Battle of Bunker Hill and an important part of Washington's victory at Trenton, did, in fact, quit the
Continental army over his treatment by Congress. And as we shall see,
both Horatio Gates and Philip Schuyler would experience their own moments of torment and frustration. If anything, one has to marvel at the
restraint Arnold demonstrated given how, in his words to Gates, "surprised

and mortified" he felt by Congress's refusal to acknowledge his contribution to the war.

By the middle of April, Arnold had been given permission to leave his post in Rhode Island. He'd also learned that "the heavenly Miss Deblois" had rejected his trunk of gowns. "Miss Deblois has positively refused to listen to the general," Lucy Knox wrote her husband, "which with his other mortification will come very hard upon him."

Arnold decided that he had no choice but to argue his case before Congress, which by March had moved back to Philadelphia. But before he made his way to Philadelphia, he must visit his sister and his three sons in New Haven.

New York's royal governor, William Tryon, was exceedingly frustrated with the British commander in chief, William Howe. Tryon, forty-seven, was a man of action. As governor of North Carolina six years before, he had led colonial militiamen against the self-proclaimed "Regulators" who refused to pay the taxes Tryon had levied to help finance his new and very regal governor's mansion in New Bern. Tryon had been triumphant and several Regulator leaders had been hanged. Now he was governor of New York, and he could only wonder why Howe had so far refused to prosecute the current conflict with the zeal Tryon had demonstrated in the South. After the embarrassment of Trenton and Princeton, which had caused him, Tryon wrote Secretary of State Germain, "more real chagrin than any other circumstance this war," he was impatient for General Howe to strike back. But Howe, who appears to have spent most of the winter in New York drinking and gambling with the beautiful Mrs. Loring at his side, seemed reluctant to settle on a specific plan for the upcoming campaign.

At first Howe had talked about working cooperatively with British forces coming down from Canada. By the early summer of 1777, when General Carleton took up where he had left off by attacking Fort Ticonderoga, Howe and his brother would have launched an assault up the Hudson to Albany. Short of destroying Washington's army, securing the Hudson River corridor had the best chance of winning the war. But as word filtered back from England that General John Burgoyne was going to be the one to lead the campaign out of Canada, Howe's attention began to shift. Burgoyne was Howe's junior in rank and a notorious grandstander. If Howe assisted Burgoyne from New York, "Gentleman Johnny" would inevitably receive most of the credit for having driven a wedge between New England and New York. No, Howe, as leader of the British forces, was not about to serve in a subordinate role. Instead, he would seize Philadelphia and, assuming Washington gave him the opportunity, crush the Continental army. After the shock of Trenton and Princeton, the gloves were off. Let Burgoyne win his laurels on his own.

In the meantime, Howe seemed in no particular hurry to get the present campaign under way. Doing his best to conceal his frustration, Governor Tryon volunteered to lead an operation in Connecticut that resembled, to a remarkable degree, the assault on Concord, Massachusetts, that began the Revolution. British intelligence had recently learned that the rebels had accumulated a huge magazine of provisions and military stores in Danbury, almost twenty-five miles inland from Long Island Sound. Leading a force of approximately two thousand regulars and loyalists, Tryon would, after landing on the Connecticut coast, march to Danbury, destroy the stores, and return to the waiting transport vessels the following day.

Seventeen seventy-seven, it had been predicted, was destined to be the year the rebellion finally came to an end. The date's three sevens looked like the gallows from which all the traitors would swing. What better way to begin what the loyalists liked to call "the year of the hangman" than with a devastating lightning strike into the New England interior?

On the evening of April 25, Tryon, assisted by Sir William Erskine (the same officer who had warned Cornwallis that Washington would escape from Trenton if given the opportunity), landed with his men on the east side of the Saugatuck River at Cedar Point in modern Westport, Connecticut. After a night of sleeping on their arms in the rain, Tryon and his troops began the march toward Danbury.

Thirty miles up the Connecticut coast, Benedict Arnold was attempting to enjoy his time in New Haven. Back in January, when he had stopped by on his way from Washington's headquarters on the Delaware to his assignment in Rhode Island, the citizens of New Haven had hailed him as a conquering hero. For the son of a bankrupt alcoholic, it had been a heady time.

This visit, however, was different. His recent humiliations—in both love and war—were the talk of the town. The unfinished mansion on the

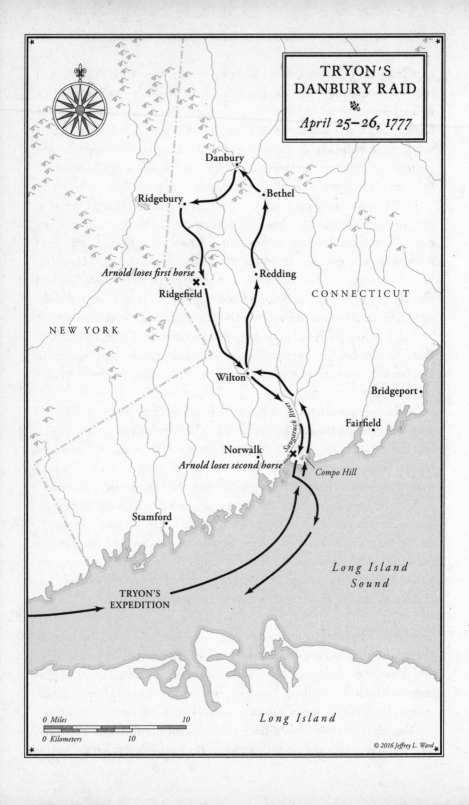

TRYON'S
DANBURY RAID

April 25–26, 1777

Danbury

Ridgebury

Bethel

Arnold loses first horse

Redding

Ridgefield

CONNECTICUT

NEW YORK

Wilton

Bridgeport

Saugatuck River

Fairfield

Norwalk

Arnold loses second horse

Compo Hill

Stamford

Long Island
Sound

TRYON'S
EXPEDITION

0 Miles   10

0 Kilometers   10

Long Island

© 2016 Jeffrey L. Ward

New Haven waterfront that he'd begun building prior to the Revolution—paneled with mahogany from Honduras, with stables for twelve horses and an orchard of a hundred fruit trees—had become a sadly dilapidated monument to his declining fortunes.

And then, on the afternoon of April 26, just as he prepared to begin the long trek to Philadelphia, Arnold received word that the British were headed to Danbury.

By the night of April 26, Tryon's men had marched almost completely unopposed to Danbury, where they proceeded to destroy 1,700 tents, 5,000 pairs of shoes, 60 hogsheads of rum, 20 hogsheads of wine, 4,000 barrels of beef, and 5,000 barrels of flour, as well as putting the torch to more than forty houses. The town's meetinghouse, it was discovered, was also "full of stores," and that too was consigned to the flames.

Later that night, after an almost thirty-mile ride in the rain, Arnold rendezvoused with Generals David Wooster and Gold Silliman and about six hundred militiamen in the town of Redding, about eight miles to the south of Danbury. Knowing that Tryon's path back to his ships at the mouth of the Saugatuck River would likely take him through Ridgefield, Arnold and Silliman resolved to march to that town with four hundred men while Wooster and a smaller force harassed the rear of the retreating British. The hope was that Wooster could delay the enemy long enough to allow Arnold and Silliman the time to prepare a proper reception.

At a narrow point in the road through Ridgefield, bounded by a steep rocky ledge on one side and a farmhouse on the other, Arnold oversaw the construction of a breastwork made of wagons, rocks, and mounds of earth. Around eleven in the morning, Wooster, sixty-six years old and a veteran of the French and Indian War who had had his differences with Arnold while in Canada, bravely led his men against the enemy's rear. A British officer later remarked that the elderly general "opposed us with more obstinacy than skill." Before Wooster had a chance to fall back, he received a musket ball in the groin. His son rushed to his aid, and when a regular bore down on the two of them, the younger Wooster refused to ask for quarter and, according to a British officer, "died by the bayonet" at his mortally wounded father's side.

In the meantime, Arnold hastened to prepare his tiny force of less than five hundred militiamen, instructing them to hold their fire until the British were well within range. As Tryon approached at the head of a column that extended for more than a half mile behind him, he realized that "Arnold had taken post very advantageously." The American general might have a much smaller force of mere militiamen, but dislodging them was not going to be easy. At that point, Tryon requested that the more experienced William Erskine, whom Tryon regarded as "the first general [in the British army] without exception," assume command.

Erskine was not about to repeat the mistake Cornwallis had committed at the bridge over the Assunpink Creek in Trenton. Instead of assaulting Arnold's well-prepared force head-on, he sent out flanking parties that worked their way far enough to the edges of the breastwork that they were able to fire directly on the militiamen. With nothing between them and the enemy's musket balls, the militiamen began to retreat. All the while, Arnold continued to ride his horse back and forth along the fragmenting American line in an attempt to form a rear guard that might protect the men as they fell back.

Arnold once claimed that "he was a coward till he was fifteen years of age" and that "his courage was acquired." The son of a devout Congregationalist mother who frequently harangued him about the inevitability of death, he appears to have become convinced that he was somehow immune to the perils that had claimed four of his siblings and left only himself and his sister Hannah to grow into adulthood. The year before, when he lay in a makeshift hospital bed in Quebec with his left leg in a splint and with two pistols at his side in the event of a surprise attack by the enemy, he had insisted in a letter to Hannah that the "Providence which has carried me through so many dangers is still my protection. I am in the way of my duty and know no fear."

As had been proven at Valcour Island and now at the little town of Ridgefield, this was no idle boast. His men were fleeing all around him, but Arnold refused to yield. His horse was ultimately hit by nine different musket balls before the stricken animal collapsed to the ground. His legs ensnared in the stirrups, Arnold struggled to untangle himself as a well-known Connecticut loyalist rushed toward him with a fixed bayonet. "Surrender!" the loyalist cried. "You are a prisoner!" Reaching for the two pistols in the holsters of his saddle, Arnold was reputed to have said, "Not yet," before shooting the loyalist dead. He soon extricated himself from the stirrups and escaped into the nearby swamp.

Tryon, with Erskine's help, had easily defeated the Americans. His soldiers, however, were exhausted, leaving him no choice but to encamp near Ridgefield and continue the march the next morning. That night Arnold conducted a quick council of war and with Silliman's help prepared to lay another trap for the enemy.

By delaying the enemy at Ridgefield, Arnold had given his Connecticut countrymen the time required to descend upon the British invaders. "The militia began to harass us early . . . and increased every mile, galling us from their houses and fences," a British officer wrote. "Several instances of astonishing temerity marked the rebels in this route. Four men, from one house, fired on the army and persisted in defending it till they perished in its flames. One man on horseback rode up within fifteen yards of our advanced guard, fired his piece and had the good fortune to escape unhurt."

By that time, Arnold had been joined by his friend John Lamb and his artillery regiment, the corps that Arnold had helped finance with the loan of a thousand pounds back in February. Now that he had three fieldpieces at his disposal, Arnold found a section of high ground about two miles north of Norwalk that commanded a fork in the road through which Tryon must pass. According to a witness, Arnold had "made the best disposition possible of his little army." Unfortunately, a loyalist became aware of Arnold's position and, knowing of a place on the Saugatuck River that was fordable, led Tryon's soldiers across the river just to the north of the roadblock.

Momentarily foiled, Arnold led the attack on the rear of the fleeing British, who had by the late afternoon reached the relative safety of Compo Hill overlooking Long Island Sound, where the fleet of warships and transports awaited. Throughout the day, Arnold had been his usual daredevil self. "[He] exposed himself almost to a fault," a witness wrote, "[and] exhibited the greatest marks of bravery, coolness, and fortitude."

Once the regulars had been reinforced with some fresh troops from the transports, Tryon and Erskine determined to disperse Arnold's militiamen before they began loading their soldiers onto the ships. It was then, a British officer recalled, that Major Charles Stuart "gained immortal honor." What Stuart realized was that Lamb and his friend Eleazer Oswald—both of whom had been with Arnold at Quebec—had nearly completed a makeshift battery for their three six-pounders. They must attack before the cannons could begin firing. With a vanguard of just a dozen men, Stuart led a bayonet charge of more than four hundred regulars that quickly overran the rebel position. Lamb and Oswald did their best—the British officer commented that the fieldpieces "were well served"—but when Lamb, who'd already lost an eye during the assault on Quebec, was hit in the side by a round of grapeshot, the Americans began to retreat.

Once again, Arnold showed no qualms about putting himself in harm's way and, according to a witness, "rode up to our front line and [ignoring] the enemy's fire of musketry and grapeshot [exhorted us] by the love of themselves, posterity, and all that's sacred not to desert him, but . . . all to no purpose." For the second time in as many days, Arnold had a horse shot out from underneath him while a musket ball creased the collar of his coat. Even the British were impressed. "The enemy opposed with great bravery," an officer marveled, "many opening their breasts to the bayonets with great fury and our ammunition began to be very scarce."

Having successfully dispersed the rebels and captured their field-pieces, Tryon could now embark his exhausted soldiers onto the trans-ports. From a British perspective, the raid had been an astounding success. "This coup by Governor Tryon may go nigh to carry the defec-tion of Connecticut and Rhode Island . . . from the rebel cause" was the hopeful assessment of one British officer.

For his part, Arnold was deeply troubled by the fact that his native state had "suffered such an insult without resistance or proper revenge." That was overstating the case. Yes, this had not been Connecticut's finest hour, but many militiamen had demonstrated commendable courage. And then, of course, there had been the example of Benedict Arnold, who had proven once again that he was, as Washington had already acknowl-edged, one of the bravest officers in the Continental army.

On May 2 the Continental Congress learned of the raid on Danbury, during which one of the brigadier generals whom they had passed over for promotion had led the militia against an overwhelmingly superior force while getting two horses shot out from underneath him. John Adams had proclaimed earlier in Congress that "I have no fears from the resignation of officers if junior officers are preferred to them. If they have virtue they will continue with us." However, when he considered this new evidence in light of all Arnold's other accomplishments, from the taking of Fort Ticonderoga to the March to Quebec and the Battle of Valcour Island, even Adams began to think twice about the delegates' treatment of the brigadier from Connecticut.

That day a congressman suggested that the army might, in fact, profit from another major general. "The ballots being taken," the record reads, "Brigadier General Benedict Arnold was promoted to the rank of major general." A week later, in a letter to Nathanael Greene, John Adams even suggested that Congress might strike a medal for the hero of Ridgefield. On one side there would be "a platoon firing at General Arnold, on horseback, his horse falling dead under him." On the other side would be a scene from the skirmish at Compo Hill, showing Arnold "on a fresh horse, receiving another discharge of musketry. . . . This picture alone, which as I am informed is true history, if Arnold did not unfortunately belong to Connecticut, would be sufficient to make his fortune for life. I believe there have been few such scenes in the world."

As his caveat about Arnold's place of residence suggested, Adams— despite his obvious appreciation of Arnold's bravery—was only willing to go so far. Arnold might now be a major general, but Congress was not about to restore him to his original level of seniority. This meant that if Arnold should find himself serving with any of the five generals who had been promoted past him back in February, he would still be considered their inferior.

This was not, as far as Arnold was concerned, acceptable. He must do as he had originally intended. He must take his case to Congress. But before he traveled all the way to Philadelphia, he would stop at Morristown, New Jersey, and meet with His Excellency George Washington.

Congress had placed Washington in an impossible position. He was expected to prosecute the war to the best of his abilities, and yet Congress was unwilling to allow him to choose the officers on whom he depended the most. Washington could have refused to abide such seemingly arbitrary restraints. Indeed, it could be argued that he owed it to his officer corps to demand that they be treated with appropriate fairness and respect. But that would have, in all likelihood, forced a showdown with Congress at a time when he had much more pressing matters to attend to.

Washington appears to have instinctively recognized that the limitations imposed by a seemingly petty and wrong-minded Congress were one of the necessary evils of being the commander in chief of an army fighting to create a new republic.

John Adams and the rest of the Massachusetts delegates, none of whom had any significant military experience, certainly had a self-serving and unrealistic view of how to conduct the war. Washington, fortunately, wore no such blinders. What is truly remarkable is his ability, both on a military and on a personal level, to look beyond the frustrations of the moment and somehow convince his officers (most of them, anyway) to do what was right for the future of their country, despite the shortsightedness of the overlords in Congress. He also used his communications with his disgruntled officers as an opportunity to give them some practical advice.

Arnold was a case in point. He was one of Washington's best generals, but he had his failings. Like Washington himself, he had an inordinate appetite for risk. But as Washington was only now beginning to realize—especially after having almost lost his entire army at the Second Battle of Trenton—aggression could be carried too far. It was time, Washington decided, to adopt a deliberately defensive-minded policy that he came to call a "War of Posts." Instead of looking to fight the British on the battlefield in "a general action," he must do everything in his power to avoid the climactic struggle that might result in the destruction of his army. That winter, he sent Nathanael Greene to Congress to explain this strategy, which, Greene reported, "appeared to be new to them. However, they readily admitted the probability from the reasons offered."

Having so recently had to deny his own deepest impulses, Washington took it upon himself to counsel Arnold. Back in March, when Washington first learned that Arnold had not received his promotion, he had chosen to begin the letter informing him of the bad news with a tactfully delivered suggestion. Arnold must be wary of attacking the British at Newport. "Unless your strength and circumstances be such, that you can reasonably promise yourself a *moral certainty* of succeeding," Washington wrote, "I would have you by all means to relinquish the undertaking, and confine yourself in the main to a defensive opposition." Only after he had imparted this bit of hard-won advice did Washington take up the topic of the promotion.

When Arnold arrived at his headquarters in Morristown on May 12, Washington greeted him by appealing to his considerable vanity. According to a recent intelligence report, the British had assigned Arnold "the character of a devilish fighting fellow." Arnold had brought with him a handbill recently published by John Brown, whom Arnold termed "as infamous a gallows' bird as ever escaped." In addition to listing all of Arnold's transgressions (none of which have ever been substantiated), Brown made a claim that possibly hit a little too close to home. "Money is this man's god," the handbill read, "and to get enough of it, he would sacrifice his country."

Washington knew better than anyone what it was like to be placed in an unfair and difficult position. But Washington was unusual in his ability to withstand a seemingly confounding host of troubles. As Joseph Reed remarked in the letter with which he attempted to reestablish his former friendship with Washington, he regretted that "I did not avail myself of your example of patience and silence under evils which . . . are too deeply rooted to admit of a total cure." Like Reed, Arnold was constitutionally unable to maintain Washington's "patience and silence under evils." He must, he told Washington, insist that Congress clear his sullied name and address the issue of his seniority within his rank.

But as Arnold quickly discovered on his arrival in Philadelphia on May 16, Congress was already embroiled in issues involving the Continental army, specifically what to do with its northern army currently headquartered in Albany, New York. By the spring of 1777, the excitement and unanimity that had made possible the passage of the Declaration of Independence had long since subsided. Although never formalized into political parties, two distinct factions had begun to emerge within Congress. On one side were the New England radicals like John and Samuel Adams who had led the push for independence, with their native Massachusetts distinguishing itself as, in John Adams's words, "the barometer at which every other [state] looks." The members of this faction tended to distrust the military and in the tradition of their Puritan forefathers insisted that the war could only be won if the American people exhibited a high level of public "virtue" by sacrificing their personal concerns for the good of their country. To this group, a standing army represented a dangerous threat to the viability of the republic. Citing the examples of Caesar and Oliver Cromwell, both of whom had used their armies to seize control of the civil government, they viewed Washington's increase in popularity in the wake of Trenton and Princeton with concern. Instead of a standing army, they favored the use of the states' militias as a safer, less expensive, and inherently more republican way to fight the war. The radicals turned a deaf ear to Washington's insistence that creating a disciplined standing army was the only way to defeat the professionals of the British army, and they had little enthusiasm for finding a way to finance it. For a variety of political and personal reasons, the New England delegates forged an informal alliance with certain key delegates from the South and were determined supporters of Horatio Gates when it came to who should command the northern army.

On the other side were the states from the middle portion of the country, with New York being to this more conservative group what Massachusetts was to the radicals. New York's wealthy merchants and landowners had been considerably less enthusiastic about the push for independence and were not about to let the New Englanders' self-righteous insistence on sacrifice interfere with their ability to profit from the war effort. They tended to support Washington's push for a standing army and were resolute in championing their own Philip Schuyler as commander of the northern army.

Schuyler had spent much of the winter and spring in Philadelphia addressing a series of complaints and accusations that the New Englanders hoped would prompt his resignation. However, after a committee had cleared his name of any wrongdoing, the delegates decided by a single vote to retain Schuyler as head of the northern army, requiring Gates, who had assumed that with the backing of the New Englanders the command was his, to surrender the position to his hated rival. Freshly bruised by the debates associated with this vote, Congress had little patience with Arnold's concerns about his seniority. Even the normally tactless and bullheaded Arnold realized that it was in his best interests to delay the question of his rank until another day. Instead, he requested that a committee of the Board of War look into the accusations made by Brown and the others. In a surprisingly short time the committee expressed its "entire satisfaction . . . concerning the general's character and conduct, so cruelly and groundlessly aspersed."

But that, it turned out, was not all. Congress might not be willing to address the issue of seniority, but it *was* willing to express its appreciation for Arnold's recent exploits by presenting him with . . . a horse! Like Arnold's gift to Miss Deblois of a trunk of gowns, a horse was not perhaps the most appropriate way for Congress to demonstrate its high regard for the hero of Ridgefield, but at least the present had a certain utility.

Being a friend of both Schuyler's and Gates's, Arnold could not be claimed by either side in the sectional rift that was currently dividing Congress. On the morning of May 22, John Adams wrote his wife, Abigail, a letter that spoke to the tortured ambivalence of Congress's attitude toward Arnold: "I spent last evening at the war office with General Arnold. . . . He has been basely slandered and libeled. The regulars say, 'he fought like Julius Caesar.' I am wearied to death with the wrangles between military officers, high and low. They quarrel like cats and dogs. They worry one another like mastiffs, scrambling for rank and pay like apes for nuts." Lost in this farrago of news and opinion is any sense of the human cost of being a soldier capable of fighting "like Julius Caesar." Arnold, in Adams's view, although extraordinarily brave, must ultimately remain a casualty of Congress's insistence that Washington's generals be selected by the country's civil government, no matter how removed that government might be from the realities of fighting a war.

And then, on May 29, the focus shifted from the halls of Congress to the mountains of New Jersey. After months of waiting for Howe to make his move, Washington had decided to move first.

Morristown had been good to Washington's army. Nestled amid the Watchung Mountains, this small and relatively isolated community of farmers and merchants was close enough to New York to allow Washington to monitor Howe's every move even as the surrounding terrain protected his army from a possible British attack. The winter in Morristown had also given the American commander in chief the opportunity to inoculate his army for smallpox, the disease that had so far killed many more American soldiers than the muskets and fieldpieces of the British.

But perhaps the best thing to come out of the stay amid the mountains was the beginning of a new and rejuvenated army. Finally, as winter turned to spring and the fresh surge of optimism inspired by the victories at Trenton and Princeton had had a chance to ripple across the full length and breadth of the United States, recruitment efforts began to yield significant numbers of soldiers. Thanks, in part, to Howe's seeming indolence, the Continental army had been given the time to rebound from a low of barely a thousand men in the winter of 1777 to almost nine thousand soldiers, and on May 29, Washington moved twenty miles south to Middlebrook, where he had a commanding view of the countryside between Perth Amboy and New Brunswick. He was now close enough to the British that he could respond quickly to a possible move on Philadelphia, especially since he had also stationed several thousand troops under John Sullivan in Princeton.

On June 13 Howe sent a total of eighteen thousand troops—twice the size of the opposing American force—in two columns to the towns of Somerset and Middlebush, teasingly close to Washington's position and threatening to cut off Sullivan from a possible retreat to the north. Based on Washington's behavior the previous year, Howe had every reason to expect that the American general would take the bait and engage him in battle. But this was not the Washington of 1776. Having finally committed himself to fighting a defensive war, he refused to assume the type of risk that had almost destroyed his army several times before. He also had better intelligence. Howe, he learned, had left his army's heavy baggage back on Staten Island. He was "marching light" and clearly had no intention of continuing on to Philadelphia anytime soon. The best thing Washington could do was to not be drawn into battle.

Washington had finally hit upon a way to win this seemingly unwinnable war—not through military brilliance but by slowly and relentlessly wearing the enemy down. Throughout the month of June, Washington displayed a cool resolve that was in stark contrast to the fiery pugnacity of just a few months before. Not everyone was sure they approved of Washington's unwillingness to engage the enemy. Some in his own army dismissed what they called Washington's "Fabian" strategy (in reference to Fabius Maximus, the Roman leader who defeated Hannibal through a war of attrition) as unnecessarily cautious. But Washington remained resolute. "We have some among us, and I dare say generals," he wrote to Joseph Reed on June 23, "who . . . think the cause is not to be advanced otherwise than by fighting. . . . But as I have one great end in view, I shall maugre all the strokes of this kind, steadily pursue the means which, in my judgment, leads to the accomplishment of it, not doubting but that the candid part of mankind, if they are convinced of my integrity, will make proper allowances for my inexperience and frailties."

Over the course of the next few weeks, the British army performed several exhausting and time-consuming maneuvers, but none of them succeeded in instigating a significant confrontation. Finally, on July 1, after one last failed attempt to catch a portion of Washington's army unaware, Howe withdrew his forces entirely out of New Jersey and began loading his army onto transports waiting in the Narrows.

Washington initially assumed that the ships were about to head up the Hudson River to assist in yet another British advance out of Canada. It was the only move that made any strategic sense. But as he'd learned over the course of the previous year, William Howe rarely adhered to conventional military strategy.

On June 19, as Washington shadowed Howe's baffling series of moves back and forth across the New Jersey countryside, Horatio Gates arrived in Philadelphia. Even though just about every officer stationed in or near Philadelphia was preoccupied with the tense and complex dance between British and American forces in New Jersey (Arnold had left the city to take over command of some militiamen in Trenton), Gates proceeded straight to the State House (today's Independence Hall). From his perspective, the enemy within his own army was far worse than the enemy without.

Back in March he had assumed that he had finally wrested control of the northern army from Philip Schuyler only to learn in early June that Schuyler had outfoxed *him*. This was not to be tolerated. He must present his case to the Continental Congress. Under the pretense that he had some vital news to deliver, Gates was allowed to speak before the assembled delegates. Almost as soon as he had sat down in what a disapproving delegate from New York termed "a very easy cavalier posture in an elbow chair," it became apparent that Gates did not, in fact, have anything of essential importance to communicate. What he wanted to talk about was himself. Reading from some prepared notes, he announced that "it is impossible that so wise, so honorable and so just an assembly can have treated one of the first officers in the American army with such unmerited contempt."

Under normal circumstances Gates was known as an articulate and enjoyable conversationalist. "He possessed some learning, a great deal of reading, and talents for extensive and accurate observation," remembered

Benjamin Rush. This, however, was not to be his finest hour. According to the New York delegate William Duer, "His manner was ungracious, . . . his delivery incoherent and interrupted with frequent chasms, in which he was poring over his scattered notes." At one point, Gates lashed out at the New York delegate James Duane, claiming that he was "the author of his disgrace." Duane immediately took to his feet and, addressing President John Hancock, expressed the hope that "the general would observe order and cease any personal applications." Other delegates joined in what became a growing chorus of criticism as Gates "stood upon the floor and interposed several times in the debates which arose on this subject." Soon the "general clamor in the house" reached the point that Gates had no choice but to leave, even though "his eastern [or New England] friends rose and endeavored to palliate his conduct and to oppose his withdrawing."

It was an outrageous violation of the supposed sanctity of Congress. If Arnold, Schuyler, or even Washington had dared to behave in a similar manner, the powerful delegates from New England would have showed no mercy. But Gates was so beloved that the New Englanders refused to criticize him for such shocking disregard for the primacy of civil authority.

Adams liked to think that he and his fellow Massachusetts delegates were motivated solely by higher principles, but partisan interests were clearly driving their unswerving support of Horatio Gates. In fact, William Duer claimed that the New Englanders had "brought [Gates] in with an intention to browbeat the New York members" into backing away from their support of Schuyler. Whatever the case may be, Gates was allowed to remain in Philadelphia with no apparent military responsibility for the next several weeks. Not until July 8 did Congress finally instruct him "to repair to headquarters and follow the directions of General Washington." Once again Gates refused to play a subordinate role to the commander in chief and departed instead for his home in Virginia.

A few days later, Congress refused to restore Benedict Arnold's seniority, and on July 11 he submitted his resignation. For Arnold, it had been a very long and exasperating two months in Philadelphia. Not only had the matter of his rank been left unresolved, but he had also failed to secure compensation for his considerable personal expenses during the campaign in Canada. Adding insult to injury, Miss Deblois's rejected trunk had ended up with Lucy Knox, who wanted to know if she could have one of the scarves; Nathanael Greene's wife, Caty, also in Boston, expressed interest in a gown.

And then, on the very same day that Arnold tendered his resignation, Congress received an express communication from Washington. His Excellency had just been handed a garbled report that the British general John Burgoyne had achieved a startling victory in the north. No one, as of yet, knew what Howe intended to do with the regulars he had loaded onto the transports off Staten Island, but it now seemed almost certain that Burgoyne was headed for Albany. "There is now an absolute necessity . . . to check General Burgoyne's progress," Washington wrote. What he needed was "an active, spirited officer" to be immediately sent to the northern army. What he needed was Benedict Arnold. "If General Arnold has settled his affairs and can be spared from Philadelphia," he wrote, "I would recommend him for this business. . . . He is active, judicious, and brave . . . and I have no doubt of his adding much to the honors he has already acquired."

That afternoon Congress decided not to accept Arnold's resignation and ordered him to report to Washington's headquarters in Morristown.

CHAPTER FIVE

The Dark Eagle

On the morning of July 6, 1777, the British general John Burgoyne awoke to astonishing news. Almost without firing a shot, his army had taken Fort Ticonderoga and the neighboring fortification at Mount Independence.

He had spent the winter and spring in England, meeting with King George III, Secretary of State George Germain, and other officials in an effort to promote himself as the potential savior of the British war effort. The previous fall he had been a disgruntled witness to General Carleton's failed campaign to take the American-held fortress at the southern end of Lake Champlain. Without overtly suggesting that Carleton lacked the fortitude and creativity to lead a second attempt, he presented his own carefully crafted plan describing how he would assail Fort Ticonderoga with an overwhelming artillery barrage and then proceed down nearby Lake George to the Hudson River and then to Albany, where he would link up with Howe's forces coming up the Hudson from New York. Burgoyne, self-assured to the point of being brash, had been optimistic about his chances of conquering Fort Ticonderoga, but not even he had thought it could be done so quickly.

A little over a mile to the southwest of the American fort was Sugar Loaf Hill (known today as Mount Defiance), with an elevation of more than 850 feet. The Americans were aware that cannons placed atop this peak would command both the lake and the fort. However, no general—including both Generals Schuyler and Gates—had chosen to do anything

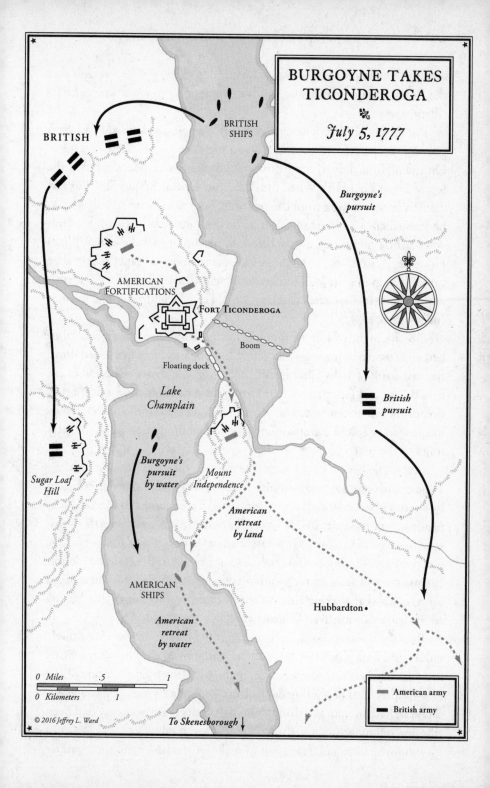

BURGOYNE TAKES
TICONDEROGA

July 5, 1777

BRITISH SHIPS

BRITISH

Burgoyne's pursuit

AMERICAN FORTIFICATIONS

Fort Ticonderoga

Boom

Floating dock

British pursuit

Lake Champlain

Burgoyne's pursuit by water

Mount Independence

American retreat by land

Sugar Loaf Hill

AMERICAN SHIPS

American retreat by water

Hubbardton •

0 Miles .5 1
0 Kilometers 1

© 2016 Jeffrey L. Ward

To Skenesborough ↓

American army
British army

about it. The hope was that Sugar Loaf Hill was steep-sided enough that the British would be discouraged from attempting to place a piece of artillery atop it.

But as one of Burgoyne's artillery officers had proclaimed, "Where a goat can go, a man can go, and where a man can go, he can drag a gun." On the night of July 4, the British placed two twelve-pounders near the top of Sugar Loaf Hill. When the American general Arthur St. Clair saw cannon barrels jutting from the top of this supposedly inaccessible peak, he immediately realized that Burgoyne had succeeded in doing to him what a little more than a year before Washington had done to William Howe in Boston when the American commander in chief had placed cannons atop unguarded Dorchester Heights. Like Howe, St. Clair realized he had to evacuate his army from Fort Ticonderoga and Mount Independence.

On the night of July 6, the Americans abandoned the fortress they had once touted as impregnable. Most of St. Clair's army fled south down the east bank of Lake Champlain, and Burgoyne sent a thousand of his best British and German soldiers in pursuit. But another significant portion of the American force had escaped by water down the narrow, river-like thread of Lake Champlain toward Skenesborough, more than thirty miles to the south.

Before the British could begin the pursuit, they had yet another challenge to surmount. A bridge composed of twenty-two sunken piers linked by a series of floating docks now connected Ticonderoga to Mount Independence on the east side of Lake Champlain. Just to the north of this structure was what Burgoyne described as "a boom made of very large pieces of round timber fastened together by riveted bolts and double chains made of iron an inch-and-a-half square." The rebels had worked for nearly a year making this system of chain-enforced logs the floating equivalent of an impassable breastwork.

But like the fort, both the boom and the bridge proved surprisingly vulnerable. In a matter of minutes the cannons of the British gunboats had blasted their way through the chain and dispensed with one of the fifty-foot sections of floating dock. Thus, Burgoyne wrote, "a passage was found in half an hour . . . through impediments that the enemy had been laboring ten months altogether to make impenetrable."

Burgoyne now had a decision to make. As he had written the winter before in the proposal that had won him command of Britain's second effort to invade America from Canada, the best way to transport an army from Lake Champlain to the Hudson River was via Lake George, just a three-and-a-half-mile portage away from Fort Ticonderoga. After a thirty-two-mile boat ride to the southern tip of the lake, his army would have been within easy reach of the Hudson, with a well-established road leading to the river.

Following the Americans to Skenesborough, on the other hand, made absolutely no strategic sense. Twenty-four miles of swampy wilderness lay between that settlement and the Hudson, the only route through it being a rudimentary pathway that followed the marshy edges of Wood Creek toward the river. As he'd foreseen in his "Plan of the Campaign from the Side of Canada," taking the Skenesborough route would provide the rebels with the opportunity to delay his march "by felling trees, breaking bridges, and other obvious impediments."

One of Burgoyne's loyalist advisers was the fifty-two-year-old former army officer Philip Skene. Being the founder of Skenesborough, he undoubtedly spoke enthusiastically about the prospect of building a road from the hamlet that bore his name to the Hudson. But Burgoyne was too aware of the potential pitfalls and too headstrong to be swayed by the siren song of a self-interested loyalist.

What seems to have captured Burgoyne's imagination that morning on Lake Champlain was the chance to succeed where his predecessor Guy Carleton had failed. The year before, he had stood by in frustration as Carleton had let the battered remnants of Benedict Arnold's Mosquito Fleet escape down the lake and then had given up altogether on the planned assault on Ticonderoga. Now that Burgoyne had taken the fort and had the American army on the run, he could finally put an end to the American navy at the place where it had been born, in Skenesborough. What's more, he'd have the satisfaction of witnessing this historic event from the quarterdeck of his massive new flagship, the 113-foot, twenty-six-gun *Royal George*.

That did not change the fact that he belonged not in Skenesborough, but here at Fort Ticonderoga overseeing the transfer of his army from Lake Champlain to Lake George. He could easily have delegated the pursuit of the American navy to a subordinate. But in the end, Burgoyne, a notorious gambler, could not help himself. Caught up in the ecstatic

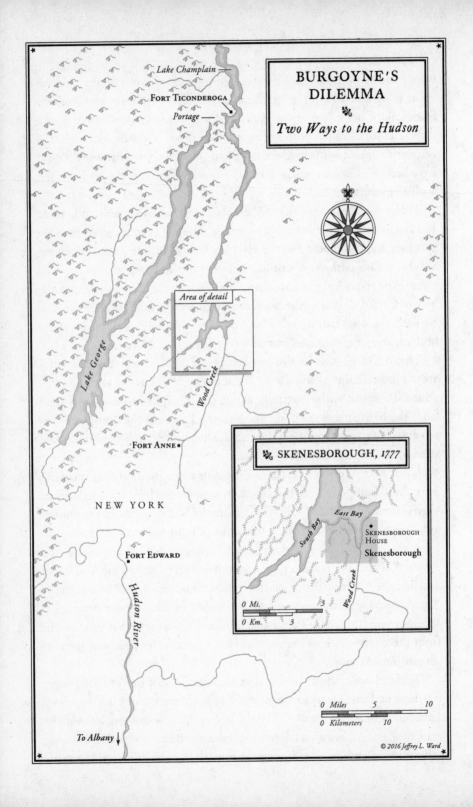

BURGOYNE'S
DILEMMA

Two Ways to the Hudson

Lake Champlain

FORT TICONDEROGA

Portage

Area of detail

Lake George

Wood Creek

FORT ANNE ∎

NEW YORK

FORT EDWARD ∎

Hudson River

SKENESBOROUGH, *1777*

East Bay

South Bay

SKENESBOROUGH
HOUSE

Skenesborough

Wood Creek

0 Mi.   3
0 Km.   3

0 Miles   5   10
0 Kilometers   10

To Albany ↓

© 2016 Jeffrey L. Ward

rush of seeing the first part of his carefully thought-out plan come to almost instant fruition, he made the mistake of his life. He sailed to Skenesborough.

James Thacher, a young doctor from Plymouth, Massachusetts, serving in the Continental army, had been roused from his bed at midnight. Fort Ticonderoga was being abandoned, he was told, and he must "immediately . . . collect the sick and wounded and as much of the hospital stores as possible and assist in embarking them on board the bateaux and boats at the shore." And so, at three in the morning on July 6, the voyage to Skenesborough had begun.

Their fleet consisted of about two hundred bateaux and the brave survivors of the Mosquito Fleet: two galleys, two schooners, a sloop, and a solitary gondola. The vessels were, Thacher remembered, "deeply laden with cannon, tents, provisions, invalids, and women" and accompanied by a guard of six hundred men commanded by Colonel Pierse Long of New Hampshire.

"The night was moonlit and pleasant," Thacher recorded in his journal, "the sun burst forth in the morning with uncommon luster, the day was fine, the water's surface serene and unruffled. The shore on each side exhibited a variegated view of huge rocks, caverns, and cliffs, and the whole was bounded by a thick, impenetrable wilderness." At several points the lake's passage through the surrounding hills grew so narrow that their view of the sky was almost completely blocked by "the precipices which overhung them."

Although they were apprehensive of what the future held, they were confident that "the bridge, boom, and chain, which cost our people such immense labor," were sufficient to hold back, at least for now, the British fleet. So they, in Thacher's words, "availed ourselves . . . of the means of enlivening our spirits." As a fife and drum played some of their favorite tunes, Thacher found a large quantity of wine bottles amid the hospital stores, and they "cheered [their] hearts with the nectareous contents."

At three in the afternoon, their "enchantingly sublime" voyage through the forest terminated at the roughly triangular body of water that served as Skenesborough's harbor. Bounded by tree-covered hills of almost mountainous proportions, with the falls of Wood Creek to the south, the little hamlet that had once been dominated by the stone manor house and barn built by Philip Skene now included a large fort and barracks constructed by the American army the year before. Before they could follow Wood Creek to Fort Anne, about halfway to the Hudson, the bateaux had to be carried and dragged over a three-hundred-yard portage.

Suddenly the boom of a cannon erupted from the north. "Here we were," Thacher wrote, "unsuspicious of danger. But behold! Burgoyne himself was at our heels." The Battle of Skenesborough was about to begin.

The British gunboats were the first to arrive, but perhaps most intimidating of all was the sight of the 384-ton *Royal George* approaching from behind them, her immense yards almost touching the rocky bluffs on either side before she glided into the harbor. Only two American vessels were able to put up anything of a fight, the galley *Trumbull* and the schooner *Liberty*, but after exchanging just a few volleys their commanders struck their colors and surrendered as the crews of the *Gates, Revenge,* and *Enterprise* made preparations to blow up their vessels' powder magazines. Even before the arrival of the gunboats, the British had disembarked several regiments that had surreptitiously climbed over the mountain to the west and were now, the Americans discovered, attempting to surround them.

Giving up on any attempt at an organized retreat, Colonel Long's soldiers "were seen to fly in every direction for personal safety." "In this desperate condition," Thacher wrote, "I perceived our officers scampering for their baggage. I ran to the bateau, seized my chest, carried it a short distance, took from it a few articles and instantly followed in the train of our retreating party."

Miraculously, most of the American forces were able to escape Skenesborough before the British could cut them off. As fire from the exploding American vessels spread along the line of abandoned bateaux (many of which also carried their own supplies of gunpowder), just about every building in Skenesborough, including the sawmill that had cut the planks out of which Arnold's fleet had been constructed, was engulfed in flames. One of the British officers claimed that he had never seen "so tremendous a sight; for exclusive of the shipping, building, etc., the trees all up the side of the hanging rock had caught fire, as well as at the top of a very lofty hill. The element appeared to threaten universal destruction."

Meanwhile the Americans fled south as quickly as possible. "We took the route . . . through a narrow defile in the woods," Thacher wrote, "and were so closely pressed by the pursuing enemy that we frequently heard calls from the rear to 'march on, the Indians are at our heels.'" But they needn't have worried. Burgoyne had his hands full back in Skenesborough.

It must have been an awesome and potentially terrifying spectacle as Burgoyne watched the conflagration from the *Royal George.* Fortunately, from the general's point of view, there was one exception to the seemingly universal destruction: Philip Skene's stone manor house, which was set apart from the rest of the hamlet, was left untouched, and in the days ahead, this imposing, yet still-unfinished structure became his headquarters.

Five days later, when he wrote to Secretary of State Germain from what he called "Skenesborough House," Burgoyne did not betray the slightest unease about his decision to remain in this fire-scorched settlement in the woods. Not only had he taken Ticonderoga and destroyed the pitiful remnants of the American fleet (in fact the two masts of a sunken rebel schooner could be seen poking out of the harbor just outside his window), his army had defeated the Americans at Hubbardton to the east and, most recently, at Fort Anne, to the south. "I am confident of fulfilling the object of my orders," he proclaimed. In fact, he was so sure of his ultimate success that he had already begun to look ahead to next winter.

"Should I appear to have any [merit]," he wrote, "I ask as reward your lordship's support with the king for a discretionary leave to return to England in the winter. . . . My constitution is not fitted for an American winter and I flatter myself I shall not be suspected tardy in my return." Left unsaid was the fact that while in London on Christmas Day of the previous year Burgoyne had bet a friend fifty guineas that he would return the following Christmas a hero, and he needed to be in England if he was to collect his winnings. The man whom Horace Walpole had dubbed "General Swagger . . . who promises to cross America in a hop, step, and a jump," was acting true to form. For Secretary of State Germain, it was not a good sign.

George Washington had been led to believe as recently as that spring that Fort Ticonderoga "can never be carried, without much loss of blood." When he learned that the fortress had been surrendered in a single day, he was outraged. The sudden and inexplicable loss of Ticonderoga meant that Albany might be taken before the northern army received the reinforcements required to stop Burgoyne's powerful and well-equipped force. "The evacuation of Ticonderoga . . . is an event of chagrin and surprise not apprehended, nor within the compass of my reasoning," he wrote Philip Schuyler on July 15. "This stroke is severe indeed and has distressed us much."

Washington's response was mild, however, compared with that of the New England delegates in the Continental Congress, who were convinced that Schuyler and particularly Major General Arthur St. Clair must be punished for this astonishing and inexplicable loss, with John Adams insisting that "we shall never be able to defend a post until we shoot a general."

According to a rumor circulated among the New Englanders in the northern army (and darkly referred to by Samuel Adams in the Continental Congress), both Schuyler and St. Clair were, in fact, traitors. James Thacher recorded in his journal what he termed the "extravagantly ridiculous" claim that the two generals had been compensated by the enemy for surrendering the fort without a fight. According to the rumor, "they were paid . . . in *silver balls*, shot from Burgoyne's guns into our camp and that they were collected by order of General St. Clair and divided between him and General Schuyler."

Any objective person familiar with the situation at Ticonderoga would realize that St. Clair had actually done his country a great service by evacuating his army with such efficiency. Not only had he saved the northern army from capture, he had actually set the stage for the enemy's undoing. "It is predicted by some of our well informed and respectable characters," Thacher wrote on July 14 from Fort Edward on the eastern bank of the Hudson, "that this event, apparently so calamitous, will ultimately prove advantageous by drawing the British army into the heart of our country and thereby place them more immediately within our power."

Even Washington, once he'd had a chance to vent his initial displeasure, recognized that Burgoyne was, in essence, marching into a largely self-created trap. Washington had served his military apprenticeship amid the forests of western Pennsylvania during the French and Indian War. As a result, he had a much more realistic understanding of what was required to advance an army through the wilderness than a British general who had gained his renown leading dragoons in Portugal. "[The British] can never think of advancing without securing their rear," Washington wrote Schuyler on July 24, "and the force with which they can act against you will be greatly reduced by the detachments necessary for that purpose . . . ; this circumstance with the encumbrance they must feel in their baggage, stores, etc., will inevitably . . . be fatal to them." Burgoyne was about to learn firsthand that unless an army, whether it be British or American, had a navigable lake or river at its disposal, travel through what one of his German officers referred to as "this evil, mountainous, and watery continent" was too difficult to be sustained for even the shortest of distances.

Burgoyne could have backtracked the thirty or more miles to Ticonderoga and proceeded with his original plan of transporting his army down the length of Lake George. But as he explained to Germain, "wishing to prevent the effect which a retrograde motion often has to abate the panic of the enemy," he had decided to remain in Skenesborough, where there were twenty-four miles of marshy forest between him and Fort Edward on the Hudson.

If Burgoyne had been able to begin marching south immediately, he might have covered the distance in a reasonable amount of time. But now that he had taken Ticonderoga, his first priority, as Washington had predicted, was to establish a supply line from Canada; otherwise his army would begin to starve. As Burgoyne attended to logistical necessities in the weeks that followed, Schuyler had the opportunity to make the already wretched road to Fort Edward—particularly the eighteen-mile stretch beginning at Fort Anne—impassable. That Burgoyne had foreseen exactly this scenario the winter before does not seem to have prompted him to make any constructive attempts to prevent Schuyler's axe-wielding New Englanders from doing everything in their power to delay his army.

Burgoyne later claimed that the remarkable efficiency with which his men cleared the road and rebuilt the bridges "justified my perseverance" in pushing on from Skenesborough. In reality, however, the British army ultimately lost several precious weeks as it was forced to hack its way south through the soggy snarl of tree trunks and branches created by the

Americans. "The country being a wilderness in almost every part of the passage," Burgoyne wrote, "the enemy took the means of cutting large timber trees on both sides of the road so as to fall across and lengthways with the branches interwoven. The troops had not only layers of these to remove in places where it was impossible to take any other direction, but also they had above forty bridges to construct and others to repair, one of which was of logwork over a morass two miles in extent."

As if this were not enough, the forty-three cannons Burgoyne had decided to bring with him to Albany (of an original train of 138 guns) were simply too heavy to be lugged over a freshly cut dirt road. Burgoyne had no choice but to transport the artillery down Lake George—a process that was made much more complicated than it otherwise had to be, since his army was now divided between Skenesborough and Ticonderoga. Not until July 31 would the bulk of the British army finally reach the Hudson.

But when Burgoyne wrote to Germain on July 30, he was still upbeat. "Nothing has happened since I had the honor to write last to change my sentiments of the campaign," he insisted. It was true that in addition to felling trees and plugging creeks, Schuyler's men were stripping the surrounding countryside of crops and livestock. But even this he dismissed with what began to sound like an increasingly hollow bravado. "The perseverance of the enemy in driving both people and cattle before them as they retreat seems to me an act of desperation or folly," he claimed. "It cannot finally injure me."

Underlying Burgoyne's continued confidence in the ultimate success of the campaign was the knowledge that while he worked his way south toward the Hudson, Lieutenant Colonel Barry St. Leger was launching a second, diversionary campaign from Lake Ontario in the west. Once St. Leger and his army had taken Fort Stanwix at the headwaters of the Mohawk River, they would follow that waterway to a junction with Burgoyne in Albany. With two British armies approaching from opposite sides of the Hudson, the Americans would be forced to divide their already undermanned army, thus increasing the likelihood that Burgoyne would take Albany with the same ease with which he had conquered Ticonderoga.

But Burgoyne, ever the gambler, had yet another ace up his sleeve. Even though he had not yet heard anything from the south—despite having sent ten different messengers—he assumed that William Howe's army based in New York was also working its way toward Albany. Not only would Howe inevitably draw away many of the American forces that might otherwise have opposed Burgoyne; even more critically, Howe would help him establish a second supply line from New York. But all that, of course, went without saying. Or did it?

General Henry Clinton arrived in New York on July 5. Having come up with the strategy that had won the Battle of Long Island for William Howe—and having received none of the credit—the ever-contentious Clinton had grown weary of his subordinate role in New York, and had spent the winter in England attempting to tender his resignation. But Germain and the king had showered their touchy general with praise and even awarded him the Order of the Bath—the same distinction that Howe had earned for his part in the Battle of Long Island. Now back in America, Clinton knew that Germain and the king were hopeful that Burgoyne's thrust from Canada would be the stroke that put an end to the war. When Clinton learned that Howe had no intention of cooperating with Burgoyne, and was, in fact, preparing to load his eighteen-thousand-man army onto a fleet of 267 ships and sail instead for Philadelphia, he was dumbfounded.

Over the course of the next week, the two generals met three different times as Clinton attempted to convince Howe that he must send his fleet not to Philadelphia but up the Hudson toward Albany; it was the only sensible move. But as had been true in the past, the fact that Clinton was the one offering the advice made it a near certainty that Howe would do the opposite.

Clinton left notes of their discussions, which sometimes became embarrassingly personal. After a recitation of their mutual frustrations with each other, which reached back all the way to the Battle of Bunker Hill when Howe had directed some "sharp expressions" at Clinton, they both agreed that "by some cursed fatality we could never draw together."

Clinton soon realized that Howe did not fully appreciate the importance the ministry placed on Burgoyne's expedition to Albany. In truth, Germain had not explicitly stated that Howe must work in concert with Burgoyne. When Howe had first introduced the idea of going to Philadelphia, Germain had made no objection to the proposal, apparently assuming that Howe's army would conquer Philadelphia in the spring and then turn its attention north in the summer.

But that was before Howe wasted the entire month of June playing a game of cat and mouse with Washington in New Jersey. Now that it was already July, there simply was not the time for Howe both to take Philadelphia and to assist Burgoyne. It was one or the other. When Clinton insisted that Burgoyne's army might fall into serious trouble if Howe did not offer his assistance, Howe simply responded that "he had sent home his plan, it was approved, and he would abide by it."

Since Howe committed very few of his thoughts to paper, his true motivations remain elusive. He may have been driven by a mixture of jealousy of Burgoyne, irritation with Clinton, and the buried, possibly unadmitted recognition that, having elected *not* to destroy Washington's army the year before, he had already missed his only opportunity to end the war. If he couldn't put a stop to the rebellion, he might as well have the satisfaction of beating Washington on the battlefield, and sailing for Philadelphia, where neither Clinton (who would remain in New York) nor Burgoyne could get in his way, provided the best chance of doing exactly that.

Going by sea avoided the potential challenge of marching to Philadelphia through enemy territory. It would also provide his brother, Admiral Howe, with the opportunity to demonstrate his unparalleled skill as a seaman and navigator. The rebels' jaws had dropped the previous fall when Admiral Howe had led a large number of square-rigged ships up the East River and through the infamous Hell Gate into Long Island Sound—a feat that many of New York's most experienced pilots had declared impossible. When it came to transporting the British army to Philadelphia, there were two possible water routes—either up the Delaware River or, more indirectly, up the Chesapeake Bay—and both presented untold challenges to even a seasoned mariner like Admiral Howe. Sailing for Philadelphia would allow the Howe brothers to share in whatever glory this campaign had to offer.

Still to be seen, however, was whether taking the rebel capital would have any significant impact on the outcome of the war. If Burgoyne should, as Clinton warned, fall into trouble during his march to Albany, Howe's apparent abandonment of a fellow British general to his fate would be difficult to explain.

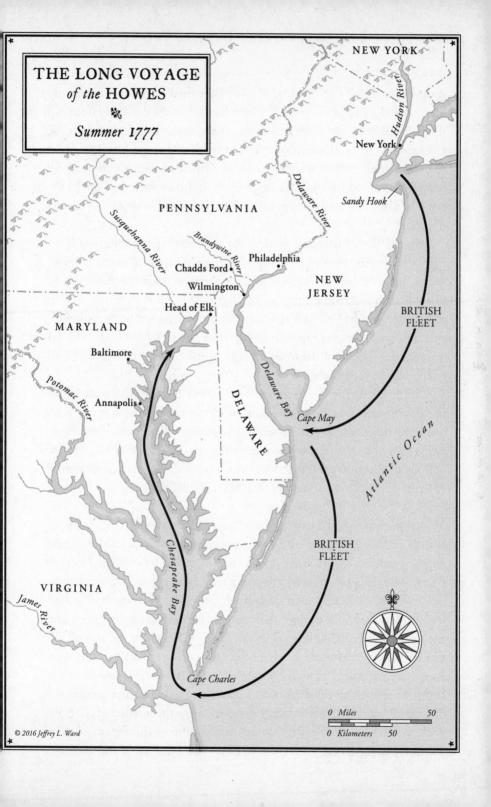

THE LONG VOYAGE
of the HOWES
❧
Summer 1777

NEW YORK

Hudson River

New York

Sandy Hook

PENNSYLVANIA

Delaware River

BRITISH
FLEET

Susquehanna River

Brandywine River

Chadds Ford

Philadelphia

Wilmington

NEW
JERSEY

Head of Elk

MARYLAND

Baltimore

Delaware Bay

DELAWARE

Cape May

Potomac River

Annapolis

Chesapeake Bay

Atlantic Ocean

BRITISH
FLEET

VIRGINIA

James River

Cape Charles

0   Miles   50
0   Kilometers   50

© 2016 Jeffrey L. Ward

Not until July 23, after more than two weeks of delays due to an uncooperative wind, did Admiral Howe's fleet finally set sail from Sandy Hook. By the end of the month, Howe had made the decision not to sail up the Delaware, but embark instead on the much longer voyage to the Chesapeake. Although the extra time at sea wouldn't get him any closer to Philadelphia, it had a greater chance of placing Washington's army between him and his ultimate destination and thus increased the likelihood of the battlefield confrontation that General Howe so desperately desired.

Already the soldiers and particularly the horses in the transport ships had been "tossed about exceedingly" and were suffering from the heat. When the men learned on July 30 that their confinement at sea would likely extend for several more weeks and take them even farther south, they were, Admiral Howe's secretary Ambrose Serle wrote, "struck with this business, every one apprehending the worst. . . . May GOD defend us from the fatality of the worst climate in America at this worst season of the year to experience it!"

But Serle's biggest fear was not for the army but for the reputation of its commander. Not only was General Howe refusing to support Burgoyne to the north, he had already wasted a good portion of the campaign season and was about to squander even more of it at sea. "What will my dear country think and say, too, when this news is carried home? *Horreo*. . . . I can write no more. My heart is full."

When Burgoyne had departed from Canada, his army of eight thousand British and German soldiers had been accompanied by several hundred native warriors. The majority of the Indians to the west of the Hudson River—with the notable exception of a few tribes of the Iroquois nation in New York—had elected to throw their lot in with the British, who had long since determined to limit the colonists' expansion into the west. The warriors accompanying Burgoyne had been promised the usual spoils of war, including enemy scalps. Even before the taking of Fort Ticonderoga, Burgoyne had issued a proclamation that promised "to give stretch to the Indian forces under my direction . . . to overtake the hardened enemies of Great Britain . . . wherever they may lurk." For the inhabitants of New York and New England, whose ancestors had suffered through more than a century of terrifying wilderness warfare with the French and Indians, this was no idle threat. And then on July 19, while still based in Skenes-borough, Burgoyne's army received an infusion of five hundred additional warriors, some of whom had traveled more than a thousand miles from the upper Great Lakes for the opportunity to fight on the side of Great Britain.

During an elaborate ceremony within "a large arbor" created in the woods outside the fire-blackened zone of destruction surrounding Skenes-borough, Burgoyne informed the warriors through an interpreter that while it was "permissible [to] scalp those whom you have killed in battle and treat them as you are wont," they were not allowed "to practice this on any prisoners or wounded." According to a German surgeon who witnessed the ceremony, the Indians responded with a tremendous war whoop, "emitting [the] sound with all their strength from their chests," and after dancing before the general settled down to the consumption of a barrel of British-provided rum. Two days later they were headed south toward the Americans.

Over the course of the next few weeks Burgoyne's warriors turned the forested outskirts of Fort Edward into a living nightmare for the American soldiers unfortunate enough to be stationed at the outpost. Of a thirty-four-man scouting party that set out from the fort on July 21, only twelve made it back alive. The following day a sentry was killed and another scalped, followed by what an American officer described as "a smart engagement" with the Indians during which eight militiamen were killed and fifteen wounded. Making these losses all the more traumatic were what the warriors did to the bodies, which were left to rot in the woods surrounding the fort. One officer was found with the soles of his feet sliced open; another had been drawn and quartered and left hanging from a tree. "This strikes a panic on our men," the newly arrived Brigadier General John Glover from Marblehead wrote, "which is not to be wondered at when we consider the hazard they run as scouts, by being fired at from all quarters (and the woods so thick they can't see three yards before them) and then to hear the cursed war hoop which makes the woods ring for miles. Our army at this post is weak and shattered, much confused, and the numbers by no means equal to the enemy."

Making things even worse, Fort Edward provided the American soldiers with little in the way of protection. "Nothing but the ruins of it [are] left," Schuyler reported, "and they are so totally defenseless that I have frequently galloped my horse in on one side and out of the other." Since the men had nothing to shelter them from the elements, except for what Schuyler described as "a little brush," the frequent downpours "wet the men to the skin." Terrified, disconsolate, and increasingly racked by disease, the militiamen began to desert.

By that time, Washington had moved his own army to the western bank of the Hudson, near the crossing at King's Ferry, about fifty miles above New York City, in anticipation of a possible move north by Howe. The British fleet had been seen at the mouth of the Delaware at the end of July and then disappeared from view, its ultimate destination a mystery. Washington was convinced that the jog to the south had been a feint and that Howe was about to reappear at Sandy Hook for a final charge up the Hudson. However, not until he was absolutely sure where the British fleet was headed would he begin his own march toward Albany.

In the meantime, he had taken steps to get Schuyler some much needed help. "Immediately upon the receipt of your first letter," Washington wrote on July 18, "conceiving the distress that you would labor under for want of the assistance of an active officer, . . . I wrote to Congress and desired them to send up General Arnold. . . . I need not enlarge upon the well-known activity, conduct, and bravery of General Arnold; the proofs he has given of all three have gained him the confidence of the public and of the army—the eastern troops in particular." Arnold had arrived at Washington's headquarters the night before and, "waiving for the present all dispute about rank," was now about to depart for Albany and ultimately Fort Edward.

Even before Arnold reached Fort Edward, he had stirred up some unnecessary controversy. While in Albany on July 21, he was heard to "publicly condemn the retreat from Ticonderoga and declared that some person must be sacrificed to an injured country." Soon after Arnold's arrival at Fort Edward the following day, his remarks made their way to General St. Clair, who as the former commander at Fort Ticonderoga was already suffering under what he described as "a heavy load of obloquy." As St. Clair complained to Washington, "The public prejudices ran high enough and did not need to be increased by the unasked opinion of an officer of his rank." When St. Clair confronted him about the remarks, Arnold claimed that "he could not recollect anything of the matter," and that if he had said anything, "it was only repeating the sentiments of the army and country or a few questions he had jestingly put to" another officer. "Cruel jesting," St. Clair wrote, "when a man's life and honor are both at stake!" Clearly Arnold had little sympathy for St. Clair, who was one of the brigadier generals who had been promoted past him. "If my elevation has raised the envy of some," St. Clair wrote Washington, "it was unsolicited on my part as it was unexpected, and surprised me as much as it did them."

Schuyler, for one, was now very happy to have the services of Arnold, whom he put in command of his left wing. With the British working their way toward Fort Edward, Schuyler decided he must move the majority of his troops several miles south to Moses Creek while Arnold with several brigades under his command was stationed at Snook Hill, a small outpost close enough to Fort Edward that he could keep a close watch on the progress of the British toward the Hudson. In a July 27 letter to Washington, Arnold reported that "the woods being so full of Indians . . . it is almost impossible for small parties [of our men] to escape them." After enumerating how they had been "daily insulted by the Indians," he described a particularly troubling event that had occurred the previous day.

"Yesterday morning our picket at Ft. Edward, where we have one hundred men advanced, was attacked by a large party of Indians and regulars." As Arnold's advance guard retreated to the main body of his troops, one lieutenant and five privates were killed and scalped and four wounded. But most disturbing of all was what the Indians did to a twenty-five-year-old woman named Jane McCrea. McCrea and an older companion named Sarah McNeil were attempting to join the British army—McNeil was related to one of Burgoyne's generals and McCrea was engaged to a loyalist who was then stationed at Fort Ticonderoga. They were hiding in a house near Fort Edward when they were discovered by two warriors, one of whom was a Wyandot (or Huron) named Panther. At some point the women were separated and McCrea was killed and scalped.

Panther later claimed that McCrea had actually been killed by the Americans who were firing on him as he attempted to take her to the British; according to another account, an argument among the warriors had led to the killing of McCrea. Whatever the case may be, Burgoyne was outraged to learn of the scalping of a female civilian and insisted that the offending warrior be punished. When it became clear that this would cause the immediate defection of the Indians, who might decide to revenge themselves on the British, Burgoyne relented, but the damage had been done. A young woman (who grew more beautiful and tragically innocent with each retelling) had been murdered and mutilated by Indians under the employ of the British.

In his own account, Arnold claimed that both women "were shot, scalped, stripped, and butchered in the most shocking manner, one of them a young lady of family who has a brother, an officer in the regular service." He hadn't gotten the facts entirely right, but Arnold's tone of horrified outrage was perfectly suited to helping make the death of Jane McCrea the sensation that, some have argued, helped change the course of the war.

In the days and years ahead, the death and scalping of Jane McCrea became a permanent fixture in the folklore of the Revolution. However, even without the scalping of McCrea, Burgoyne had already touched something deep within the collective psyche of the region. Well before the fall of Ticonderoga, Burgoyne's use of native warriors had angered and horrified New Englanders, whose fear of wilderness war reached back to the arrival of the Pilgrims in 1620. Throughout the summer of 1777, militiamen began to pour into the northern army from Massachusetts, Connecticut, and especially New Hampshire, where more than 10 percent of the eligible male population volunteered over the course of the summer. Even more than their love of liberty, the New Englanders' multigenerational fear of native peoples was what finally moved them to rise up and extirpate a British army that had dared to reawaken this ancient source of terror, despair, and guilt.

Arnold also had a suggestion for Washington. During his march to Quebec in the fall of 1775, he had commanded a regiment of Virginia riflemen under Colonel Daniel Morgan, who had an intimate understanding of wilderness warfare. "I wish Colonel Morgan's regiment would be spared to this department," he wrote Washington. "I think we should then be in a condition to see General Burgoyne with all his infernals on any ground they might choose. . . . We might [even] beat up his quarters at Skenesborough."

In the days ahead, Washington did as Arnold suggested. Even though

Morgan's regiment of sharpshooters was a valued part of his own army, which Washington would bitterly miss in the month to come, he decided that the Virginians might be, as Arnold advised, essential to turning the tide in the north. Both Schuyler and ultimately Gates thanked Washington for having sent them Morgan and his men, but the idea had originally been Arnold's.

By August 1, Arnold had received a letter from a Georgia delegate of the Continental Congress informing him "that it is not probable that he will be restored to his rank." Arnold, who was once again performing essential and dangerous service for his country, had reached the breaking point with Congress. Schuyler wrote to Washington explaining that Arnold "has asked my leave to retire. I have advised him to delay it for some time." Once again, Arnold laid aside his own hurt and anger and remained with Schuyler, whom he praised in a letter to Washington as having "done everything a man could do in his situation. I am sorry to hear his character has been so unjustly aspersed and calumniated."

As it so happened, the futures of both Schuyler and Arnold were about to be decided not on a battlefield, but at the State House in Philadelphia.

During the debates in Congress regarding who was to blame for the evacuation of Fort Ticonderoga, the Massachusetts delegates were determined to denigrate Schuyler, whom John Adams termed "the evil genius of the northern department," and extol Horatio Gates. "Gates is the man of my choice," Samuel Adams wrote to the Virginia delegate Richard Henry Lee; "he is *honest* and *true* and has the art of *gaining the love of his soldiers* principally because he is *always present* and shares with them in *fatigue and danger*"—this despite the fact that Gates had spent the winter of 1777 in his comfortable headquarters in Albany rather than with his men at Ticonderoga. On August 2 the New England delegates made their wishes explicit in a letter to George Washington: "We take the liberty to signify to your Excellency that in our opinion no man will be more likely to restore harmony, order, and discipline and retrieve our affairs in [the northern] quarter than Major General Gates."

Gates's more than yearlong quest to secure an independent command had inevitably created tensions between himself and Washington. As had happened with Charles Lee and Joseph Reed (who had recently declined an offer to lead the newly created Continental cavalry corps), a distance had developed between Gates and the commander in chief, whose own near-limitless ambitions required that his subordinates pay him the required deference and respect.

Washington responded to the delegates' request to endorse the candidate of their choosing by asking "to be excused from making the appointment." Claiming that Congress had historically considered the northern department "more peculiarly under their direction, and the officers commanding there always of their nomination," he would defer to them, especially since "the choice of an officer to the command may involve very interesting and important consequences." When, as expected, Congress appointed Gates the new head of the northern department, Washington tepidly congratulated his former adjutant general by "wishing you success and that you may speedily be able to restore the face of affairs in that quarter."

In the days that followed, Congress turned its attention to the matter of Benedict Arnold's rank. Arnold's current position as General Schuyler's trusted subordinate did not enamor him with the powerful delegates from Massachusetts, who had finally succeeded in placing Gates at the head of the northern army. On August 8, after two days of debate, the delegates voted on an amendment to adjust Arnold's seniority "on account of his extraordinary merit and former rank in the army." When the votes were finally tallied, the amendment had overwhelmingly failed (6 to 16) with the states whose generals had been promoted past Arnold in February all voting unanimously against him. Although Arnold's association with Schuyler may have been the deciding factor, the Massachusetts delegate James Lovell claimed it had actually come down to principle. "It was really a question between monarchical and republican principles put at a most critical time," he explained in a letter to the New Hampshire delegate William Whipple. So as to assert Congress's supremacy over the military, a sacrifice must be made, in Lovell's view, of Benedict Arnold.

Henry Laurens was a new delegate from South Carolina, and he was shocked at how the "old and valuable servant Major General Arnold" had been treated by Congress. "The reasoning upon this occasion was disgusting," he wrote. "[Arnold] was refused not because he was deficient in merit or that his demand was not well founded but because he asked for it and that granting at such instance would be derogatory to the honor of Congress." Laurens was fairly certain that the vote would "deprive us of that officer and may be attended by further ill effects in the army." In the meantime, other matters were demanding the attention of both Schuyler and Arnold.

With the abandonment of Ticonderoga, only one fort of any significant size in the region remained in American control: Fort Stanwix, a two-hundred-foot square of wood and sod strategically positioned at the headwaters of the Mohawk River in present-day Rome, New York. The fort's commander, Colonel Peter Gansevoort, came from a Dutch family that had lived in the region since the 1660s. Over six feet tall and just twenty-eight years old, Gansevoort had distinguished himself for his bravery and leadership during the disastrous retreat from Canada in 1776. In May 1777 he'd been put in command of Fort Stanwix, a dilapidated structure dating back to the French and Indian War, which despite having been rechristened Fort Schuyler was still commonly referred to by its original name.

Knowing that a possibly overwhelming British force was about to head their way from Lake Ontario to the west, Gansevoort and his men had worked frantically to rebuild the fortress's fifteen-foot-thick ramparts and two-foot-thick casemates, as well as the spear-shaped bastions that jutted out from each corner of the fort. On August 2 the last boatloads of provisions had just arrived when the vanguard of the British army under the command of Lieutenant Colonel Barry St. Leger descended upon them. Soon they were surrounded by an army of eight hundred British, German, and loyalist soldiers and eight hundred native warriors.

There were 750 of them crowded into a fort built for half that number. The nearest American outpost was more than thirty miles down the Mohawk River toward Albany. The pressures on the fort's commander were intense, particularly given the recent fate of Ticonderoga. Earlier in the summer Gansevoort's brother Leonard had sent him a letter. "I beg you and depend upon you and your regiment will not be a disgrace to the New York arms," he wrote. "Your father flatters himself that you will conquer or die."

Gansevoort decided that the Continental flag—red and white horizontal stripes with a Union Jack in the upper left-hand corner—must be

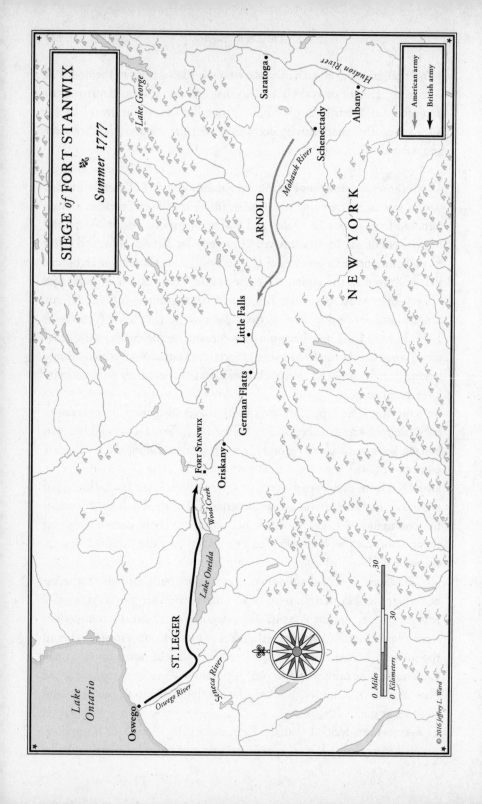

SIEGE *of* FORT STANWIX

Summer 1777

American army

British army

Lake Ontario

Oswego

Oswego River

ST. LEGER

Seneca River

Lake Oneida

Wood Creek

FORT STANWIX

Oriskany

German Flatts

Little Falls

ARNOLD

Mohawk River

Schenectady

Albany

Saratoga

Lake George

Hudson River

N E W   Y O R K

0 Miles   30

0 Kilometers   30

© 2016 Jeffrey L. Ward

seen flying above the fort. Unfortunately, he had not been provided with a flag. So he resolved to make one of his own. A cloak and some shirts provided the blue field in the flag's corner while the red and white stripes were made from what the second-in-command, Marinus Willett, described as "different pieces of stuff collected from sundry persons." On August 3, the day after the opening of the British siege, this makeshift standard was hoisted above Fort Stanwix. According to Willett, "The flag was sufficiently large and a general exhilaration of spirits appeared on beholding it wave."

On August 7 Gansevoort learned that a relief column of 750 New York militiamen had been ambushed by St. Leger's warriors at Oriskany, about twelve miles to the east. The American forces, which also included close to a hundred Oneidas (a subset of the Iroquois nation), suffered casualties of more than 50 percent, with 385 killed. The next day St. Leger sent Gansevoort a message: unless the Americans immediately surrendered, his Indians "would kill every man in the garrison." That night at one in the morning, Willett and another officer slipped out of the fort on a "secret expedition" to seek help. The next day Gansevoort responded to St. Leger: "It is my determined resolution . . . to defend this fort and garrison to the last extremity, in behalf of the United American States, who have placed me here to defend it against all their enemies."

On August 3 Burgoyne finally heard from William Howe. The letter had been folded inside a hollowed-out silver bullet that was to be swallowed if the messenger was captured—a necessary precaution, it turned out, since two of Burgoyne's messengers had already been hanged by the rebels. The letter contained distressing news. Howe was headed for Philadelphia and unable to help him. Clinton remained in New York, but with a force so small that there was little he could do. Normally confiding, Burgoyne decided to keep this latest bit of information to himself.

What made the message all the more difficult to take was the gradual realization that he was also not going to get any assistance from the north. Carleton, still angry about losing the command to Burgoyne, claimed that he did not have the men required to protect the supply line from Canada, which meant that Burgoyne had to leave behind nine hundred men at Ticonderoga.

And then he received what was, perhaps, the most demoralizing blow.

So far, his native warriors had served him exceedingly well, not only inspiring terror among the enemy but also providing him with the captives that gave him the intelligence he needed. "The Indians have done good service," he wrote Germain in early August. "Not a day passes without prisoners brought in, some from miles behind the enemy's camp. . . . My effort has been to keep up their terror and avoid their cruelty. I think I have in great measure succeeded. They attack very bravely, they scalp the dead only and spare the inhabitants." This, of course, was not entirely true. Burgoyne failed to mention the scalping of Jane McCrea, which had created a rift between Burgoyne and the warriors from the west, who increasingly resented his attempts to temper their behavior. On August 5 they announced that they were returning home. Burgoyne did his best to convince them to stay, but within a few days they had departed, leaving him with less than a hundred warriors.

It was extremely ironic. Just as the outrage over the death of Jane McCrea was reaching its peak throughout the region, Burgoyne lost the majority of his Indians. When this disappointment was combined with the news from the north and south, the British general was forced to face the terrifying realization that from here on in, he was on his own. On August 20 he informed Germain that "the prospect of the campaign . . . is far less prosperous than when I wrote last. . . . I little foresaw that I was to be left to pursue my way through such a tract of country and hosts of foes without any cooperation from New York. . . . I yet do not despond."

The wife of the German general Friedrich Adolph Baron von Riedesel (which many of the English pronounced as "Red Hazel") could attest to the truth of this last statement. As the army paused at Fort Edward to assemble the huge amount of provisions needed before crossing the river and marching on Albany, Burgoyne did not betray the least sign of despair. According to Baroness Riedesel, who along with her husband and their three children spent an idyllic three weeks in a tiny building near Fort Edward that they called the "Red House," Burgoyne "liked having a jolly time and spending half the night singing and drinking and amusing himself in the company of the wife of a commissary, who was his mistress and, like him, loved champagne."

And besides, he had at least one source of hope. On the Mohawk River to the west, Barry St. Leger had won a recent victory over the New York militia at Oriskany and still had Fort Stanwix under siege. With luck he would take that fortress, then soon be on his way to Albany. This made it imperative that Burgoyne do something to prevent the Americans from attempting to relieve Fort Stanwix. "Therefore," he explained to General Riedesel, "it was of the greatest importance that a detachment of the left wing should make a move and thus intimidate the enemy and prevent him from sending this force against St. Leger." In order to prevent Arnold (whom Burgoyne mistakenly believed to be now in command of the American forces) from marching west, he must send a detachment of his own to the east.

By August 16 Burgoyne had dispatched a total of fourteen hundred mostly German soldiers on a mission to secure provisions and horses in the countryside to the east. That morning, near the town of Bennington, they fell prey to the force of nature known as John Stark.

One of the heroes of Bunker Hill and also present at the Battle of Trenton, Stark had done what Arnold only threatened to do. Rather than dillydally with a capricious Congress, he had simply resigned once he learned that several junior officers had been promoted past him. He was then given an independent command by the New Hampshire General Court, and within six days had raised a brigade of fifteen hundred men. Beholden to no one—least of all Congress—Stark considered himself to be a kind of land-based freebooter. When Schuyler ordered him to join the Continental army stationed on the Hudson, he replied, "Stark chooses to command himself," and announced his determination to remain on Burgoyne's left. On August 16 he was perfectly positioned to defeat the extensive British foraging party led by Lieutenant Colonel Friedrich Baum in what Stark described as the "hottest" action he had ever seen. By the time the fighting had ended, Stark counted 207 enemy dead and 700 prisoners, meaning that Burgoyne had lost, in just one day, approximately 15 percent of his entire force.

By the second week in August, Schuyler's army had retreated even farther to the south toward Albany. Although he wanted Arnold with him on the Hudson, he reluctantly agreed to send the general on a rescue mission to Fort Stanwix. Marinus Willett had reached Schuyler's headquarters and explained just how desperate the situation at the besieged fort had become. Soon Arnold was on his way up the Mohawk.

By August 21 he had traveled more than eighty miles to the town of German Flatts. Several friendly Oneida Iroquois who had recently been to Fort Stanwix reported that given the large number of British regulars and warriors that St. Leger had at his disposal, Arnold must wait for reinforcements before he continued west—otherwise a massacre similar to what had happened at Oriskany would be the inevitable result. While waiting at German Flatts, Arnold hit upon a way to raise the Siege of Fort Stanwix without risking a single man.

During the march through the wilderness of Maine in the fall of 1775, Arnold had been accompanied by a group of Abenakis that included Natanis, who along with his brother Sabatis had been there during the storming of Quebec. According to a tradition not recorded until the 1870s, Natanis prophesied that Arnold, whom he called "the Dark Eagle," would ultimately fail in accomplishing his overly ambitious objectives. Although the account of the prophecy is probably apocryphal, Arnold had nonetheless extensive experience working with native peoples by the time he led the rescue mission up the Mohawk River. While in German Flatts, he began to realize that the Iroquois might hold the key to saving the Americans at Fort Stanwix.

The six tribes of the Iroquois nation were the Mohawk, Oneida, Onondaga, Cayuga, Seneca, and Tuscarora, whose territories stretched from the Hudson River and Champlain Valley into western Pennsylvania. The Iroquois had enjoyed centuries of peace within their own nation and developed a highly sophisticated culture and political structure that some have argued contributed to the Americans' evolving ideas of how thirteen English colonies might become a single nation. But the Revolution had changed everything. Most of the tribes of the Iroquois had sided with Great Britain, but the Oneida, due in part to their proximity to the American settlements along the Mohawk River and the influence of the Presbyterian missionary Samuel Kirkland, had sided with the United States. With the unity of the Iroquois broken, Arnold recognized an opportunity.

His soldiers had recently arrested several New York loyalists, including a resident of the nearby town of Little Falls named Hanjost Schuyler. Married to an Oneida woman and regarded by many to be "as much native as white," Hanjost was well known by the Iroquois throughout the region, including the Mohawks who had aligned themselves with the

British. One of Arnold's officers, Lieutenant Colonel John Brooks, proposed that they pretend to condemn Hanjost to hang for treason and see whether, in exchange for a conditional pardon, he might be willing to assist them in convincing St. Leger's native allies to abandon the siege. Arnold immediately approved of the plan, and with his brother serving as a hostage, Hanjost soon departed for Fort Stanwix.

By August 20 the British siege lines had progressed to within 150 yards of the fort. Knowing that their young commander had no intention of surrendering and that the British commander had vowed to look the other way as his warriors massacred them all, Gansevoort's men became increasingly restive. That night, three of them deserted. Fearing that the desertions might become impossible to control, Gansevoort resolved that if help did not come within the next few days, he must mount a nighttime breakout attempt through the British lines.

On August 21 Hanjost arrived at the siege lines surrounding Fort Stanwix, where he breathlessly claimed that he had just escaped from Benedict Arnold, who was now marching toward them with more than a thousand soldiers. For good measure, Hanjost had shot his coat full of bullet holes to prove how narrowly he had escaped from the Americans. Soon after, an Oneida arrived telling pretty much the same story, except that Arnold now had two thousand soldiers. Not long after that, a second Oneida ran into the British camp claiming that Arnold's army was now up to three thousand soldiers.

St. Leger's native allies had already grown impatient with the Siege of Fort Stanwix. They'd also suffered many more casualties than they had anticipated during the fighting at Oriskany. Not only had this been an especially brutal battle—one young Seneca warrior claimed that "blood was shed in a stream running down the descending ground"—they had been required to take up arms against their own people. Already disgruntled with the slow pace of the campaign and traumatized by the fact that the American Revolution had launched them into a terrifying civil war, the Mohawks, Senecas, and other Iroquois under St. Leger decided to quit the nineteen-day Siege of Fort Stanwix.

For Lieutenant Colonel Barry St. Leger, it all came to an end in a baffling and ultimately maddening rush. Just as the fort was about to fall into his hands, his warriors—goaded on by Hanjost Schuyler and the Oneidas—abandoned him. He had no idea whether Arnold was really about to attack (as it turned out, the American relief column was forty miles away), but having lost the support of his Indian allies, he had no choice but to quit as well. By the next day, he and his men were on their way back to Lake Ontario.

For the fort's commander, it was a miraculous turn of events that made him, especially among the citizens of northern New York, a hero for life. Even that most distrusting of New Englanders John Adams praised Gansevoort for having proven "that it is possible to hold a post." But as the more than seven hundred American soldiers who had endured the Siege of Fort Stanwix would readily have admitted, in the end they owed their lives to Benedict Arnold.

On August 30, after a thirty-eight-day voyage, William Howe's army finally arrived at Head of Elk, Maryland, at the northern extreme of Chesapeake Bay. As predicted, the passage had been blisteringly hot, killing 27 men and 170 horses. At night, violent thunderstorms had pummeled the fleet with rain, and several ships suffered direct lightning strikes that had set at least one vessel on fire. After a week onshore restoring the health of the men and horses, the British began the almost fifty-mile march toward Philadelphia. By then, Washington had assembled an army of close to fifteen thousand men and positioned them between the enemy and their ultimate destination.

On September 1 Washington received word that Arnold had broken the Siege of Fort Stanwix. "I flatter myself that we shall have nothing more to apprehend in that quarter this campaign," he wrote to John Hancock, "and that the disgrace and disappointment they have met with will produce a favorable change in the dispositions of the Indians." The victories at Fort Stanwix and Bennington left Washington in an upbeat mood, especially since Howe must now realize that he had made a monumental blunder by abandoning Burgoyne to the north. Inspired by and perhaps even envious of the American victories to the north, Washington resolved to oppose the British on the battlefield in eastern Pennsylvania.

On September 5 he issued General Orders calling for "one bold stroke" that stood in stark contrast to the defensive strategy he had employed in New Jersey back in June. "In every other quarter the American arms have, of late, been rapidly successful," he announced. "Who can forbear to emulate their noble spirit? Who is there without ambition to

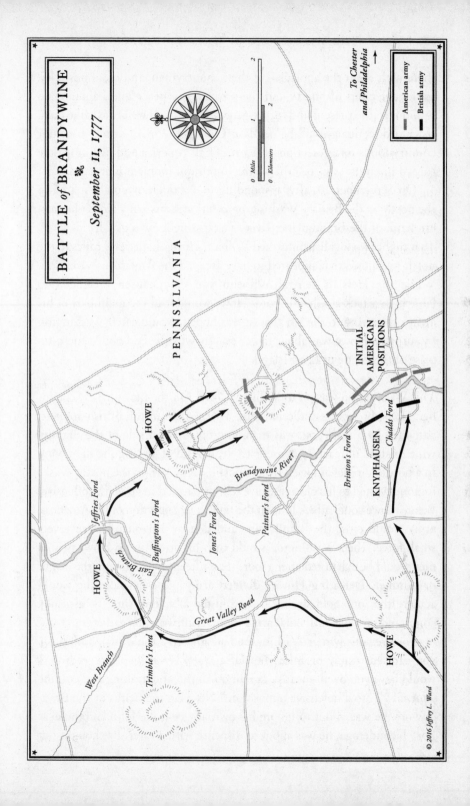

BATTLE *of* BRANDYWINE

September 11, 1777

To Chester and Philadelphia

American army
British army

PENNSYLVANIA

INITIAL AMERICAN POSITIONS

HOWE

HOWE

HOWE

HOWE

KNYPHAUSEN

Jeffries Ford

Buffington's Ford

Jones's Ford

Painter's Ford

Brinton's Ford

Chadds Ford

Brandywine River

East Branch

West Branch

Trimble's Ford

Great Valley Road

© 2016 Jeffrey L. Ward

share with them the applauses of their countrymen, and of all posterity, as the defenders of liberty and the procurers of peace and happiness to millions in the present and future generations? . . . If we behave like men, this third campaign will be our last. Ours is the main army; to us our country looks for protection. The eyes of all America and of Europe are turned upon us. . . . The critical, the important moment is at hand."

On September 10, after responding to a sudden overnight march to the north by the British, Washington positioned his army along the eastern bank of the Brandywine River at a crossing known as Chadds Ford. That night two loyalists informed William Howe that twelve miles to the north was a ford that appeared to have escaped the Americans' attention. While the Hessian general Wilhelm von Knyphausen pretended to launch an attack at Chadds Ford, Howe would lead the main part of his army on a swing to the left that, it was hoped, would catch Washington by surprise. Howe was about to get exactly what he had hoped for: a reprise of the Battle of Long Island.

But Washington was on to William Howe. On the morning of September 11, early reports indicated that a large column of British soldiers, shrouded by a thick fog, was marching up the west side of the Brandywine. Instead of reacting conservatively, instead of placing the right wing in a position to defend itself from a possible attack from the north, Washington reverted to his old aggressive self: he decided to go on the offensive. Before Howe could attack him on the right, a large portion of the American army would cross the Brandywine and destroy Knyphausen's relatively small force. Then Washington would turn his attention to Howe, whose men would be exhausted after a more than fifteen-mile march in the height of summer. Defeating Howe's divided army piece by piece, he would achieve the "one bold stroke" he had lusted after ever since he assumed command of the Continental army more than two years earlier.

The previous winter Washington had advised Arnold that "unless . . . you can reasonably promise yourself a *moral certainty* of succeeding, I would have you by all means . . . relinquish the undertaking and confine yourself . . . to a defensive opposition." Now, on the banks of the Brandywine, he was about to ignore his own advice. Like John Burgoyne at Fort Ticonderoga, he was about to dispense with a carefully thought-out plan (the War of Posts) and roll the proverbial dice. Risking everything, Washington decided to attack.

Almost as soon as Washington initiated the assault on Knyphausen around 11:00 a.m. by sending the approximately four thousand soldiers under the commands of Generals Greene and Sullivan across the river, he began to receive reports that Howe's column had mysteriously disappeared. Washington then became convinced that Howe hoped to fool him with a feint and that the force he'd just sent across the Brandywine was about to face the entire British army. Reversing himself, he ordered his men back to the eastern shore of the Brandywine. Despite receiving a report that a column of British soldiers was indeed attempting to flank him on the right, Washington and his staff remained so confident that they had penetrated to the bottom of Howe's plan that they, according to the soldier who delivered the message, "laughed at my intelligence and sent me back . . . without an answer." But as it turned out, Howe had, in fact, crossed the Brandywine to the north and was now about to attack the Americans' ill-prepared force on the right. Washington had been outgeneraled once again.

General John Sullivan had the unenviable task of attempting to stop the British advance on the American right. Despite not having the time to properly position his force, his officers and men still put an astonishing number of cannon- and musket balls in the air, and the sound of the great guns was heard as far away as Philadelphia. A British officer wrote, "There was a most infernal fire of cannon and musketry. . . . The balls plowing up the ground. The trees cracking over one's head. The branches riven by the artillery. The leaves falling as in autumn by the grapeshot." Making the catastrophe that had become the Battle of Brandywine all the more galling to Washington was the realization that had he held to his earlier determination to remain on the defensive, his army would have been positioned to deliver the British a potentially crushing blow. Just as had happened at the Battle of Long Island, Washington's lack of generalship had denied his army the opportunity to meet the British in a fair fight.

During the latter portion of the fighting, as the British threatened to overrun the American right, a new addition to Washington's military family, the twenty-year-old Marquis de Lafayette, was wounded in the leg by a musket ball. By the time the French officer had been taken off the battlefield, the Continental army was in full retreat. As Washington and his staff followed the stream of soldiers in the deepening dusk, the American commander turned to his new adjutant general Timothy Pickering and said, "Why, 'tis a perfect rout."

CHAPTER SIX

Saratoga

On August 30 Benedict Arnold reported to the headquarters of the northern army on an island at the confluence of the Mohawk and Hudson Rivers. By then he'd learned that Congress had voted against restoring his seniority. But instead of being angry, Arnold appears to have become increasingly confident that, as he'd done at the Battle of Ridgefield in the spring, he was about to convince Congress of the error of its ways. He had just come to the rescue of the Americans at Fort Stanwix and eliminated the British threat from the west without firing a shot. Combine that with the prominent role he would surely play in the impending battle with Burgoyne's army to the north, and Congress would have no choice but to set things right.

During the two and a half weeks he'd spent on the Mohawk, the northern army stationed on the west side of the Hudson had been transformed. Not only had the victory at Bennington helped boost American morale, but a steady influx of militiamen from New England, as well as Continental troops from the South, had made this a new army. And there to reap the rewards of events that had been months in the making was the army's newly appointed commander, Horatio Gates.

For his predecessor, Philip Schuyler, it was the worst of all possible fates. For more than a year he and Gates had been contending with each other for command of the northern army. As of the spring, it looked as if Schuyler had finally become the army's undisputed leader. But then came the humiliating loss of Fort Ticonderoga. Even though he had spent the last month and a half since then laying the groundwork for what was likely to be the decisive battle of the war, Congress had recalled him to Philadelphia. "I have done all that could be done . . . ," he wrote to Gates, "but the palm of victory is denied me, and it is left to you, general, to reap the fruits of my labors."

As an officer who had served happily under Schuyler, Arnold was immediately placed in a difficult position by the arrival of Gates. And yet there was reason for hope. He and Gates had worked well together the year before on Lake Champlain. Indeed, without Gates, Arnold might never have fought the Battle of Valcour Island. When he repeatedly insulted the officers presiding over the court-martial of Moses Hazen, it had been Gates who refused to act on the board's insistence that Arnold be arrested. In the weeks prior to Valcour, Gates exhibited extraordinary patience in his responses to Arnold's often demanding and querulous letters as he nervously awaited the British onslaught. After the battle, when there were many who criticized Arnold for losing the majority of his fleet, Gates staunchly supported his subordinate even though Arnold had ignored his orders to fight only a defensive action against the British. By all rights, Arnold should have been thankful and pleased to have Gates back as his commander.

Certainly the rest of the northern army seemed happy about the change in leadership. Schuyler, a New York aristocrat, had never been willing to cultivate the affections of the New Englanders. Like Washington, he disliked having to rely on the militiamen, whose brief terms of enlistment made them notoriously unreliable. Gates, on the other hand, had been singing the militiamen's praises since the Siege of Boston, referring to them fondly as "my Yankees." Not surprisingly, he was received with open arms by the many New Englanders in the northern army. One officer credited him with putting "a new face upon our affairs"; another claimed that since the arrival of Gates, "it is the happiest camp I ever was in: the officers and soldiers put the greatest confidence in the general."

Arnold, however, would have none of it. Whether it was out of a genuine loyalty to Schuyler or a surly orneriness prompted by Congress's ill treatment, he appointed two officers to his staff, Henry Brockholst Livingston and Richard Varick, with strong ties to Gates's predecessor—a move that was almost guaranteed to offend his new commander. Arnold and Gates were two very different men, and part of the reason they had worked so well together the previous year was that they had been separated by the length of Lake Champlain. Arnold was too emotionally obtuse, too aggressive and impulsive to work closely with a commander whose greatest strengths were administrative and who had never commanded an army in battle.

For his part, Gates knew from previous experience that Arnold was likely to be a difficult officer to control. He also knew that the victories at Fort Stanwix and Bennington were none of his doing and that the downfall of Burgoyne was beginning to look like a fait accompli. Gates was predisposed to view Arnold as a dangerous holdover from Schuyler who might attempt to seize the glory that was properly his.

But in the beginning, at least, all seemed to be going quite well. Like Schuyler before him, Gates placed Arnold in command of the army's left wing, which now included a veteran of the march to Quebec, Colonel Daniel Morgan and his corps of Virginia riflemen. The rifle's grooved barrel imparted a spin to the bullet that, like the spiral of a football, gave the projectile much greater accuracy and range than a ball fired from a smoothbore musket. Although known for its deadly accuracy, the rifle was time-consuming to reload and could not be equipped with a bayonet, making Morgan's corps vulnerable to a British bayonet charge. Early on, it was decided, perhaps at Arnold's urging, to augment Morgan's force with 250 handpicked light infantrymen under the command of Major Henry Dearborn, another veteran of the Quebec campaign. With the addition of Dearborn's musket-equipped soldiers, what was already the elite unit of the northern army was turned into a much more flexible and powerful force.

By September 14 Burgoyne's army had crossed the Hudson on a temporary bridge of boats to the western bank, near the hamlet of Saratoga. The defeat at Bennington had taken its toll as had the disappointing news from Fort Stanwix, but in the end, the land itself turned out to be Burgoyne's greatest adversary. As he was just discovering, no army, no matter how well organized and prepared, could hurl itself into the deciduous jungle of the American wilderness and expect to emerge intact. Stripped of most of their native allies, down to a month's provisions, and with little to no hope of support from the north, south, or west, Burgoyne's soldiers were marooned in this country of towering trees and insect-breeding swamps, all the while knowing that militiamen from New England and riflemen from Virginia were gathering in the surrounding forest like flocks of predatory birds. They must fight their way to Albany and to civilization.

Without native scouts to infiltrate the woods ahead of them, the British were virtually blind. With no clear idea as to the enemy's location, they were forced to feel their way down the road to Albany, repairing bridges and clearing away downed trees, their fleet of provision-packed boats following them along the river's west bank. (In addition to serving as floating wagons, these bateaux provided the army with a possible exit strategy should it become necessary to retire across the Hudson.) Not until September 18, when they established camp at a clearing near the edge of what came to be known as the Great Ravine—a deep, tree-filled gash in the countryside through which a stream ran to the Hudson—did they finally make contact with the enemy.

By then the Americans had begun to entrench themselves on a flat-topped minimountain beside the Hudson known as Bemis Heights, approximately three miles south of the Great Ravine. By placing his army here, on this hundred-foot-high bluff, Gates had reduced Burgoyne's options to two: either force his way down the road to Albany, which was crowded against the river by the looming high ground of Bemis Heights, or plunge into the forest that surrounded the grassy plateau of the American position and attempt a difficult frontal assault. Instead of attacking the British, Gates wanted the enemy to come to him now that the high ground gave his army a decided advantage.

Arnold, ever restless, was incapable of simply waiting it out, and on the morning of September 18, Gates granted him permission to lead a probe to the north with three thousand men. Bemis Heights overlooked a wide plain of recently cultivated farmland, still dotted with tree stumps and intercut by forested ravines, with the Hudson to the east and wooded hills to the west. Arnold's column had emerged from one of the dense patches of woodland when they came upon a group of people digging for potatoes in a farmer's abandoned field. With provisions tight, the British were desperate for food, and this was a foraging party made up of soldiers and female camp followers. Even though the foragers were unarmed, Arnold's soldiers opened fire, killing and wounding fourteen and taking several prisoners before a British relief column forced the Americans to retreat to their camp on Bemis Heights.

By the third week in September, through an influx of Continental soldiers from the South and militiamen from New England and New York, the northern army had grown to more than nine thousand men. They were still entrenching their newly occupied high ground, ultimately creating a U-shaped, three-quarter-mile-long breastwork behind which Arnold occupied a small red farmhouse on the left with Gates in yet another farmhouse in the center. On the morning of September 18, the renegade John Stark finally arrived from the east with his little army of New Hampshire militiamen. Even though a battle was imminent, Stark claimed that with his men's terms of enlistment about to expire, he was within his rights to abandon the northern army to whatever fate had in store.

That night, the New Hampshire men stood around the campfires with their possessions still on their backs, whispering to one another as they mulled over whether Gates's offer of a bounty was enough to convince them to stay. Apparently not. At five minutes after midnight, Stark and his men headed out into the darkness. One of Gates's officers later remembered that Stark's brigade must have heard the sound of the fighting the next day, "yet not a man returned."

By the morning of September 19, Gates knew that Burgoyne's army was moving in his direction. American scouts posted in the trees on the eastern side of the Hudson had reported that they could see several columns of the enemy emerging from the wooded fringes of the Great Ravine. But Gates was reluctant to attack. His army was well posted and well supplied on its plateau beside the river; Burgoyne was running out of provisions. The best strategy, from Gates's perspective, was to wait for as long as possible to engage the British. Once again, however, Arnold was impatient to know more about the enemy's position, and at his suggestion Gates agreed to send out Daniel Morgan's corps of riflemen to see what the British were up to.

Peering out from the edge of the trees bordering the southern side of a farm owned by the loyalist John Freeman, Morgan discovered that a British regiment under Major Gordon Forbes had been deployed around the farm's abandoned home and outbuildings. Concealed behind the trees, Morgan instructed his men to pick out the enemy's officers, who were completely unaware of the riflemen's presence and could be distinguished by the glinting silver gorgets around their throats. Once the

Americans had their targets in view, Morgan, who always commanded from the rear, ordered them to fire. Every single British officer in Forbes's regiment was either killed or wounded, and soon the survivors were sprinting for the trees behind them. Convinced that they had encountered an isolated advance party of the British, Morgan's men took off in pursuit, only to discover as they neared the opposite side of the field that the nearly sixteen hundred British soldiers constituting the center column of Burgoyne's army were waiting for them behind the trees.

A mad scramble ensued as the Americans, outnumbered almost three to one, fled from the field in disorder. Major Robert Morris, who had been leading the overly impetuous charge on his horse, was so taken by surprise that he had no choice but to ride *through* the British lines. Somehow he came out the other side unscathed and eventually made his way back through the woods to the American side of Freeman's Farm, where over the course of the next hour, Morgan attempted to re-form his dispersed battalion by issuing his trademark turkey call.

That might have been the end of it. If Gates had had his way, Morgan would have continued to watch and harass the British but would have refused to engage them in battle, thereby letting Burgoyne take up the positions from which he planned to initiate an attack on the American left the next day. But thanks, in large part, to Arnold, another scenario was about to unfold.

Colonel James Wilkinson, Arnold's former adjutant during the withdrawal from Canada in the spring of 1776 and now a member of Gates's staff, called it the "accidental" battle. Neither commander was looking for a fight that day, but once Morgan's men had blundered into the center of Burgoyne's army, an unanticipated dynamic started to take hold. With Arnold standing beside him at what Wilkinson described as "in front of the center of the camp, listening to the peal of small arms," Gates begrudgingly allowed his second-in-command to keep feeding additional portions of his left wing into the fighting at Freeman's Farm—fighting that Gates and Arnold could not even *see* from Bemis Heights. With each new group of American reinforcements, the clamor increased until by day's end one of the fiercest struggles of the Revolution was in full swing.

It was certainly an unusual way to conduct a battle. By requiring that his senior officers remain with him atop Bemis Heights (Wilkinson

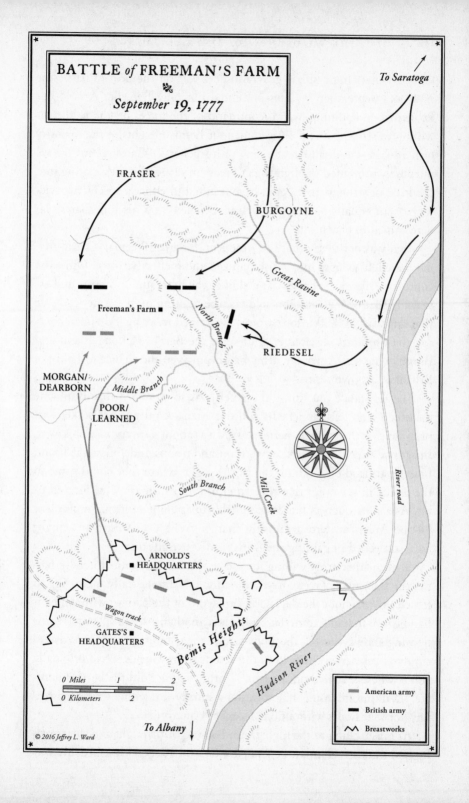

BATTLE of FREEMAN'S FARM

✤

September 19, 1777

To Saratoga

FRASER

BURGOYNE

Great Ravine

Freeman's Farm ■

North Branch

RIEDESEL

MORGAN/
DEARBORN

Middle Branch

POOR/
LEARNED

South Branch

Mill Creek

River road

ARNOLD'S
■ HEADQUARTERS

Wagon track

GATES'S
■ HEADQUARTERS

Bemis Heights

Hudson River

0 Miles   1   2

0 Kilometers   2

To Albany ↓

American army

British army

Breastworks

© 2016 Jeffrey L. Ward

reported that "not a single general officer was on the field of battle the 19th [of] September"), Gates prevented not only Benedict Arnold but *anyone* from assuming overall command of the forces on the field. Unwilling to strip his main encampment at Bemis Heights of the majority of his soldiers and, apparently, any of his generals, Gates seems to have purposely prevented the fighting at Freeman's Farm from escalating into the kind of struggle that could have resulted in either a spectacular victory or an equally spectacular defeat. Perched atop his hill, Gates was determined to play it safe.

That was not to say that the American forces at Freeman's Farm that day were left to lapse into a disorganized and ineffective force. Quite the contrary. Due to the bravery and skill of the more junior officers and especially that of the common soldiers, the fighting on the American side that day was, in Wilkinson's words, "sustained more by individual courage than military discipline." Unlike in the Battles of Long Island and Brandywine, the American army had been given the chance to fight the British on its own terms.

The resistance put up by the rebels was so stubborn that Burgoyne believed Gates had launched a full-out attack. Under the mistaken impression that the entire American army was about to overwhelm his own, Burgoyne elected to keep the two thousand troops under General Simon Fraser stationed on a hill on the British right, where they could come to the rescue in the event that the center of the British army ran into trouble. As a consequence, Fraser was unable to attempt a turning movement on the American left, a measure that, in Wilkinson's estimate, might have succeeded in gaining the British a decisive advantage.

With neither army willing to engage the majority of its forces in battle, the fighting at Freeman's Farm, although dramatically increasing in ferocity throughout the day, never broke out of the pattern with which it had begun: first one frontal assault, then another, as each side took turns fighting its way across the body-strewn field only to be repulsed and thrown back across the field to the woods from whence it had originally come, where it rallied once again. "In this manner did the battle fluctuate," Wilkinson wrote, "like waves of a stormy sea, with alternate advantage for four hours without one moment's intermission."

As Fraser clung to the high ground on the British right and the army's highest-ranking German general, Baron von Riedesel, pushed his way down the road to Albany on the left, Burgoyne in the center with sixteen hundred men confronted almost the entire American force on the field, which by the end of the day had grown to three thousand soldiers. "Few actions have been characterized by more obstinacy in attack or defense," Burgoyne later wrote. The British sergeant Roger Lamb described it as "a constant blaze of fire . . . both armies seemed to be determined on death or victory." Burgoyne commented on the American sharpshooters who "placed themselves in high trees in the rear of their own line, and there was seldom a minute's interval of smoke, in any part of our line without officers being taken off by [a] single shot." Amid all this raging furor, Burgoyne remained an inspiration. "General Burgoyne was everywhere," Lieutenant William Digby wrote, "and did everything [that] could be expected from a brave officer."

Gates, on the other hand, never strayed from the safety of the American encampment on Bemis Heights (one officer claimed he even spent some of the battle gossiping in another officer's tent), all the while insisting that Arnold stay with him. It would be difficult to imagine a more cruel form of torture for a man of Arnold's temperament than to require him to remain within hearing but out of sight of a battle involving his own men. Finally, Arnold simply couldn't take it anymore.

Toward evening, as Gates and Arnold stood together in front of the American camp, Colonel Morgan Lewis, the army's deputy quartermaster general, returned from the field of battle. Wilkinson was there to witness what happened next. "Being questioned by the general, [Lewis] reported the undecisive progress of the action; at which Arnold exclaimed, 'by God I will soon put an end to it,' and clapping spurs to his horse, galloped off at full speed. Colonel Lewis immediately observed to General Gates, 'you had better order him back, the action is going well, he may by some rash act do mischief.' I was instantly dispatched, overtook, and remanded Arnold to camp." For Arnold, this was undoubtedly one of the most infuriating and humiliating moments of his life, especially since it was Wilkinson, his former adjutant, who had called him back.

Almost no trustworthy firsthand accounts of the battle mention Arnold's participation in the fighting on September 19, but there is one exception. Enoch Poor of New Hampshire was the officer whose promotion to brigadier general had convinced John Stark to resign from the Continental army. A year before, Poor had been the president of the court-martial board that had exonerated Moses Hazen and called for Arnold's arrest. Now he was a part of Arnold's left wing. The day after the battle he wrote a letter. "Arnold rushed into the thickest of the fight with his usual recklessness," he reported, "and at times acted like a madman. I did not see him once, but S [probably Colonel Alexander Scammell, who was in the thick of the fighting] told [me] this morning that [Arnold] did not seem inclined to lead alone, but as a prominent object among the enemy should present itself, he would seize the rifle-gun and take deliberate aim."

Although it is impossible to say with any certainty when Arnold made his appearance on the battlefield, this may have been after his encounter with Wilkinson. Too late to make much of a difference, unhinged by having been excluded from the field, he vented his frustrations by ripping rifles out of the hands of nearby sharpshooters and taking potshots at the enemy. More pathetic than heroic, it was a disturbing harbinger of things to come.

Around dusk, just as it looked like the British center might finally be overwhelmed, General von Riedesel, in response to a message from Burgoyne, swept in from the British left and forced the Americans to retreat. With night coming on, the battle was essentially over. Although Burgoyne claimed victory, since he still remained on the field, his army had been dealt a potentially mortal blow—700 British killed, wounded, and captured to the Americans' 150. And as everyone in the American army knew, the blow had been inflicted, almost exclusively, by the soldiers under Arnold's command.

A thick fog shrouded the banks of the Hudson the next morning, and around 7:00 a.m. a British deserter, his face still blackened with powder from the previous day's battle, was escorted through the American lines to General Gates. A soldier in the eighteenth century started loading his musket by biting off the end of a paper cartridge and pouring the powder down the weapon's barrel. By the end of a battle, one side of the soldier's face—the right side if he was right-handed—was so smeared with powder that it was virtually black. According to Wilkinson, the powder-stained deserter informed Gates that Burgoyne's "whole army was under arms and orders had been given for the attack of our lines."

Gates liked to think of his position on Bemis Heights as unassailable, but in reality the American army was highly vulnerable on the morning of September 20. The right side might be, as Burgoyne later described it, "unattackable," but this was not the case on the left. The breastwork in that portion of the camp was far from complete. The men stationed on the camp's left side, almost all of whom had fought long and hard the day before, were exhausted. Due to what Wilkinson termed "the defects of our organization," they had not yet drawn their ammunition. Most of the men were without bayonets. Due to the fog, it was impossible to see anything more than twenty yards away, providing the British with just the opportunity to launch an overwhelming bayonet charge.

Gates put his men on the alert, and for the next hour, they stood at the lines, staring into the swirling mist. Wilkinson called it "an hour of awful expectation and suspense, during which hope, fear, and anxiety played on the imagination; many could hear the movement of the enemy and others could discern . . . the advance of their column, but between eight and nine o'clock the sun dispersed the vapor and we had no enemy in view."

Wilkinson later learned from one of Burgoyne's officers that the British had, in fact, planned to launch an attack that morning. However, when Fraser pointed out that the grenadiers and light infantry who were to lead the charge "appeared fatigued by the duty of the preceding day," Burgoyne delayed the action until the next morning. And then, at dawn of September 21, a spy came into the British camp with a coded letter from General Clinton in New York. Clinton didn't have enough men to attack Albany, but he was capable of making "a push" up the Hudson as far as Fort Montgomery, about fifty-five miles north of New York. It was a far cry from the support Burgoyne had expected from Howe, but perhaps Clinton's attack on Fort Montgomery would force Gates to draw some of his soldiers south. Even if this did not really change much of anything, Burgoyne decided to postpone his own attack until he heard back from Clinton. And thus, what Wilkinson called the British army's "golden, glorious opportunity" was lost.

Five days earlier and 250 miles to the south in Pennsylvania, George Washington was preparing for his second confrontation with the British in less than a week. Although Brandywine had not turned out as he had hoped, his men's morale remained remarkably high. If given another opportunity, his army would prevail—he was sure of it—especially given the importance of protecting Philadelphia from the British.

A few days earlier he had moved his army across the Schuylkill River, the shallow but fast-moving waterway that Howe must cross if he were to take Philadelphia. Then, "with a firm intent of giving the enemy battle wherever I should meet them," Washington decided to go, once again, on the offensive and ordered his men to march back across the river.

Howe had been in no hurry to pursue the Americans after the Battle of Brandywine. But now he was eager to attack. Washington had an army of twelve thousand men; Howe's stood at eighteen thousand. Washington's army must be footsore and exhausted after marching back and forth across the Schuylkill. As Howe sent Cornwallis in pursuit on September 16, Washington attempted to position his men along the crest of South Valley Hill and block the British advance toward the river.

Before any fighting took place, Washington realized that his men did not have the time required to form a proper line of battle and ordered a sudden withdrawal into the valley behind them. The valley might have offered what his adjutant Timothy Pickering claimed was "a most favorable position," but one had to wonder whether another Brandywine was in the making.

All this time the sky had been growing increasingly dark as the already brisk wind built into a gale. And then, about 5:00 p.m., as hand-to-hand fighting began to break out between the Americans and the British advance guard of jaegers under Colonel Johann Ewald, what Ewald described as "an extraordinary thunderstorm" suddenly unleashed "the heaviest downpour in the world." Instead of individual raindrops, a solid mass of water seemed to fall out of the sky. Almost instantly the roads were transformed into quagmires. The civilian guide James Parker called it "a mud deluge, the roads so deep there was no bringing on the artillery." Given the volume of water, fighting became impossible as the soldiers' weapons refused to fire.

Howe took refuge in the nearby Boot Tavern. Washington, on the other hand, had no choice but to order a retreat. His officers reported that the downpour had ruined almost all the men's reserves of gunpowder. With what Henry Knox estimated to be a staggering four hundred thousand musket cartridges rendered useless, Washington needed to put a significant amount of distance between himself and the British, whose double-flap leather ammunition boxes had succeeded in keeping their powder dry. Washington ultimately sent his army all the way to Yellow Springs on a grueling six-mile march that took nearly fourteen hours to complete. So ended what came to be known as the Battle of the Clouds.

In the days after the Battle of Freeman's Farm, there were several prominent officers in the northern army who claimed that whatever glory had been won by the Americans on September 19 was owing to the efforts of Benedict Arnold. He may not have spent any significant time on the battlefield, but he had been the one who issued the orders and directed the troop movements. In fact, if Gates had allowed Arnold to lead the left wing in the field as he had so ardently wished to do, the day might have ended with an overwhelming American victory.

But there was another way to view the Battle of Freeman's Farm. Gates's reluctance to engage the enemy had combined with Arnold's natural aggressiveness to achieve what was, in actuality, an extraordinary result. It may have forever scarred both of them, but a highly successful form of collaboration had occurred between Gates and Arnold that day atop Bemis Heights.

Without putting the principal part of the northern army at risk, the defensive-minded Gates had reluctantly allowed Arnold's left wing to inflict a wound upon Burgoyne's army that ranked with that suffered by William Howe during the Battle of Bunker Hill. It was a lesson in balancing the competing demands of caution and aggression that George Washington had yet to learn. The fact of the matter remained, however, that Gates and Arnold were two entirely different types of leaders who had come to resent the other's interference even if that interference may have been exactly what each of them needed. Although, in essence, a major American victory, the Battle of Freeman's Farm had irrevocably damaged the once happy relationship between Gates and Arnold.

It might be termed the battle of the underlings. In Arnold's corner were his aides Richard Varick and Henry Livingston. Both men would go on to have highly successful careers (Varick later served as Washington's private secretary and as mayor of New York; Livingston became an associate justice on the U.S. Supreme Court). But in September 1777 they were young, excitable protégés of Philip Schuyler, who despised Horatio Gates.

Spurred on by Schuyler back in Albany (who told them to destroy his letters), they took clear delight in watching relations between Gates and Arnold deteriorate and inevitably encouraged Arnold's worst tendencies.

In Gates's corner was James Wilkinson. Having formerly served as Arnold's adjutant, Wilkinson knew that the general's passionate nature made him an easy man to anger. In the days after the Battle of Freeman's Farm, he instigated several administrative changes clearly aimed at antagonizing the commander of the left wing. Even before the battle, Wilkinson took it upon himself to assign some newly arrived militiamen to the right wing even though Gates had promised Arnold they would go to the left—a move that caused what Varick gleefully referred to as "a little spurt . . . between Gates and Arnold." And then, immediately on the heels of the battle, Wilkinson came up with the idea of modifying the army's command structure so that instead of reporting to Arnold on the left wing, Morgan and his riflemen reported directly to Gates.

To make matters even worse, the official account of the battle, which Wilkinson almost surely had a hand in, made no mention of Arnold or his left wing, claiming that "to discriminate in praise of the officers would be injustice, as they all deserve the honor and applause of Congress." Arnold became convinced that Gates, at Wilkinson's urging, had robbed him not only of the credit he deserved (and needed if he were ever to win his proper seniority as a major general) but also of the most prized corps under his command. Arnold was predictably furious, and that night he confronted Gates in his quarters.

By all accounts the meeting devolved into a profanity-laced shouting match. When Arnold claimed that Morgan's riflemen were properly under his command, Gates responded by questioning whether Arnold had any legitimate rank at all in the northern army given that he had offered his resignation to Congress back in July. Arnold, according to Wilkinson, responded with "high words and gross language," and demanded a pass to Philadelphia. Assuming Gates valued his military skills too highly to permit him to leave, Arnold appears to have expected him to back down. Instead, Gates readily agreed to the proposal.

But he didn't stop there. Benjamin Lincoln was one of the officers who had been promoted past Arnold in February. During the Battle of Freeman's Farm on September 19, Gates had issued an order for Lincoln, who was then on detached service on the east side of the Hudson, to rejoin the northern army as soon as possible. When that occurred in the next day or so, Lincoln, not Arnold, would be the army's second-in-command, and Arnold would be free to leave. This may have been when Arnold first learned that Lincoln was about to join the army, and incandescent with rage and hurt, he returned to his quarters.

Besides being very angry, Arnold appears to have been genuinely mystified by the treatment he had received, and that night he wrote Gates a letter. "Conscious of no offense or neglect of duty," he could not understand why "I have been received with the greatest coolness at headquarters, and often huffed in such a manner as must mortify a person with less pride than I have and in my station in the army." Since Gates no longer wanted him, he hoped "to join General Washington, and may possibly have it in my power to serve my country although I am thought of no consequence in this department."

While Arnold poured out his heart to his commander, Gates spent the night writing an equally revealing letter to his wife. "The fatigue of body, and mind, which I continually undergo," he complained, "is too much for my age and constitution. . . . A general of an American army must be everything, and that is being more than one man can long sustain." This is the lament of a man overwhelmed by his responsibilities. There is nothing angry or defiant about this letter; he is simply exhausted. Never mentioning Arnold, he frankly admits that he is not up to the task. One cannot help but wonder whether Gates was as much a victim of Wilkinson's scheming as Arnold. Certainly Arnold's aide Richard Varick believed this was the case and claimed in a letter to Philip Schuyler that Wilkinson "is at [the] bottom of the dispute between Arnold and Gates."

When word began to circulate around the camp that Arnold intended to leave, many officers voiced their support for the unhappy general. Brigadier General Poor even proposed that his fellow officers present an address to Arnold thanking him "for his conduct in the late action" and asking him to remain with the army. Making this demonstration of support all the more unexpected was the fact that a year earlier at Fort Ticonderoga Poor had called for Arnold's arrest. But when efforts were made to translate this new support into a formal statement, "the matter was hushed," Livingston reported to Schuyler, "some through jealousy, others for fear of offending Gates. . . . They all wish [Arnold] to stay, but are too pusillanimous to declare their sentiments."

Soon after, the Connecticut militia officer Major Leonard Chester approached Wilkinson about the possibility of effecting a reconciliation. It had become obvious that Arnold's aides, who made no effort to conceal their hatred of Gates, had become a liability. If Arnold agreed to rid himself of Livingston (who as a volunteer was presumably the more expendable of the two), Wilkinson assured Chester that it would "open a way for an accommodation." But when Chester made the proposal to Arnold, he erupted into a fury, claiming that "his judgment had never been influenced by any man, and that he would not sacrifice a friend to please the 'Face of Clay.'" Unable to admit that the appointment of two former Schuyler aides to his staff had been a mistake from the start, Arnold rejected out of hand this final attempt at reaching a compromise. Prickly and hotheaded, Arnold had, in effect, sealed his fate, a fate that had been stage-managed from the start by James Wilkinson.

Both Livingston and Varick eventually decided that they had no choice but to leave the northern army. For his part, Arnold determined to stay. Despite everything he had so far endured, he was not going to do as John Stark and the New Hampshire militiamen had done and abandon the army on the eve of battle.

By the end of September, Gates had received an infusion of four thousand new soldiers, many of them militiamen from New England. At thirteen thousand men, the American army was close to double that of the British. Just as important was the arrival of a group of Oneidas, who proved invaluable in providing the Americans with prisoners and intelligence. In the meantime, progress continued on the fortifications surrounding Bemis Heights, which by the beginning of October were virtually impregnable.

By that time, Burgoyne had elected to fortify his own position along the southern edge of the Great Ravine, building a series of redoubts and breastworks that extended for as many as two and a half miles. With an eye on his supplies and only the vague promise that "other powerful armies of the king" were about to come to their rescue, Burgoyne reduced his men's daily rations by half.

Everything appeared to be moving in the Americans' favor, and Gates was content to simply wait it out, knowing that the passage of each day reduced the prospects of the British and increased his own. By then, Gates had taken over Arnold's left wing and put Lincoln in charge of the right. "Removed from command and excluded from headquarters," Wilkinson wrote, "General Arnold experienced the keenest mortification. . . . In this awkward situation, he hung about the camp, . . . murmuring discontent and scattering sedition."

On October 1 Arnold wrote the letter that concluded his correspondence with the commander of the northern army: "I think it my duty . . . to acquaint you [that the soldiers of] the army are clamorous for action. The militia who compose a great part of the army are already threatening to go home. . . . I have reason to think, from intelligence since received, that had we improved the 20th of September it might have ruined the enemy. That is past. Let me entreat you to improve the present time. . . . I hope you will not impute this hint to a wish to command the army, or to outshine you, when I assure you it proceeds from my zeal for the cause of my country in which I expect to rise or fall."

What Arnold expected to achieve by this tactless, tone-deaf plea is difficult to determine, and the letter never received a reply. If Arnold was to have a role in the fighting to come—indeed, if there was to *be* any fighting to come—he must take matters into his own hands.

By the third week of September, with the British general William Howe's army hovering outside Philadelphia, the delegates of the Continental Congress had fled the city and were making their way to Lancaster, Pennsylvania, about eighty miles to the west. Washington and the main portion of the Continental army remained on the north side of the Schuylkill with the intention of blocking Howe's army from entering Philadelphia. The Schuylkill was fordable in only a handful of places, and the challenge was to keep his army between the British and the city. Complicating matters was the existence of a large collection of vital stores to the northwest in Reading, Pennsylvania. After making several marches to the west, Howe was showing what Washington described as "a violent inclination" to turn the right flank of the American army and head for the supply depot, the loss of which would have been even more catastrophic than the capture of Philadelphia.

By then the American army had received yet another setback. On the night of September 20, a detachment to the south led by General Anthony Wayne camped for the night near a tavern named for the Corsican patriot

Paoli, where they suffered a surprise bayonet attack that left hundreds dead, wounded, and captured. And then, just as Washington prepared to respond to yet another move west by the British, Howe suddenly turned his army in the opposite direction and slipped across the Schuylkill at a ford on the American army's left. Having caught Washington flat-footed, Lord Cornwallis and his grenadiers marched unopposed into Philadelphia on September 26. On that same day, the rest of the British army took up quarters in Germantown, about five miles north of Philadelphia.

Howe was convinced that Washington's exhausted army had nothing left to give. While Gates to the north enjoyed a large influx of militiamen, Washington had received scant support from the local populace. Unlike the New England colonies, which for more than a hundred years had required that each town have its own company of militia, citizen soldiers were not a tradition in Pennsylvania, a colony founded by pacifist Quakers. Pennsylvania was also much more culturally diverse than New England, and there was not the unanimity of militant patriot sentiment that existed to the north. As a result, Washington's army, despite being in what was considered friendly territory, was looked on with apathy if not outright hostility by many of the locals. According to the Massachusetts congressional delegate James Lovell, "the Philadelphians themselves say it would not be so in New England [where] every stone wall would rattle about [the enemy's] ears." With little prospect of local assistance; after reversals at Brandywine, the Battle of the Clouds, Paoli; and now, after losing Philadelphia without a fight, surely Washington had learned that his best policy was to avoid another humiliating encounter with the British army.

Washington, however, refused to see it that way. From his perspective, his army had repeatedly been on the brink of victory only to have circumstances turn tragically against them. Rather than dwell on his own role in those sudden reversals of fortune, he was determined to mount another comeback along the lines of Trenton and Princeton.

Howe had divided his army between Germantown and Philadelphia. Whether it was out of arrogance or carelessness, he had provided the Americans with an opportunity more than equal to the one Washington had tried to capitalize on at Brandywine. By attacking and destroying the segment of the British army in Germantown on the morning of October 4, Washington hoped to transform Howe's decision to occupy Philadelphia into the blunder that would lose Great Britain the war.

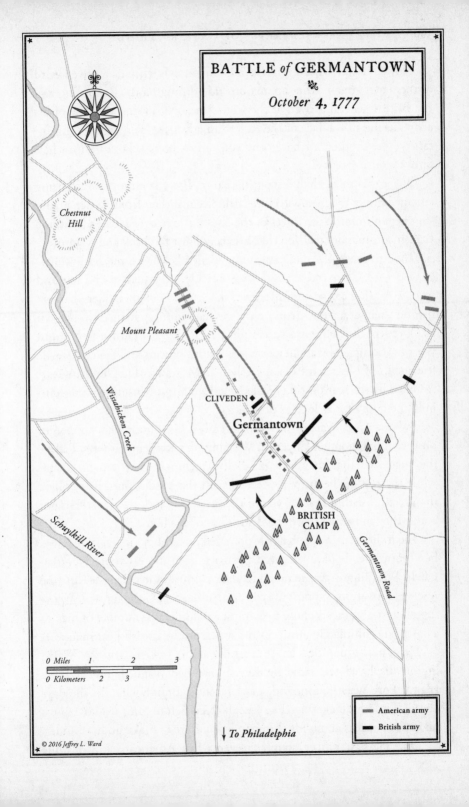

BATTLE *of* GERMANTOWN

October 4, 1777

Chestnut Hill

Mount Pleasant

Wissahickon Creek

CLIVEDEN

Germantown

BRITISH CAMP

Germantown Road

Schuylkill River

0 Miles 1 2 3

0 Kilometers 2 3

American army

British army

↓ *To Philadelphia*

© 2016 Jeffrey L. Ward

Howe was at his headquarters in Germantown when he received word of the dawn attack. After an anxious ride through a thick morning fog, the British general arrived at the front lines only to find the elite of his army fleeing in the face of the American advance. "For shame, light infantry!" he shouted. "I never saw you retreat before. Form! Form! It is only a scouting party."

But it was more than a scouting party. Three columns of the enemy emerged out of the mist with three fieldpieces at their front. When grapeshot began to rattle the leaves of the chestnut tree over Howe's head, the British commander realized that his army must fall back and re-form.

The first wave of Americans under Generals Wayne and Sullivan advanced into Germantown but were quickly separated in the fog and smoke. Adding to the confusion was the eruption of an artillery barrage behind them at a stone mansion on the road into Germantown. Known as Cliveden, the house was the summer residence of a loyalist family and was now occupied by about a hundred British officers and men under the leadership of Lieutenant Colonel Thomas Musgrave. Despite being surrounded by the rear portion of the American army, Musgrave resolved to hold the house for as long as possible.

By that time, Washington and several of his officers had stopped to observe the standoff at Cliveden. Washington's adjutant Timothy Pickering suggested that they leave a small detachment to guard the house while the rest of the army proceeded with the attack. But Henry Knox disagreed, insisting that "it would be unmilitary to leave a castle in our rear." They must first drive the British out of the house.

The military principle Knox expounded certainly sounded impressive, but the former bookseller could not have been more wrong. Unfortunately, Washington was tempted to believe him. Rather than sending the reserves forward to support Wayne and Sullivan in Germantown, Washington and his officers chose to commit a considerable number of men to a costly and ultimately unsuccessful attack on the British-held mansion.

Here, in this pointless pause at a stone house in Germantown, Washington displayed the same indecision that had plagued him at Long Island, Fort Washington, and, most recently, Brandywine. In the days ahead, Timothy Pickering (like Joseph Reed before him) would express his own concerns about his commander's failure to make up his mind.

One Hessian officer counted seventy-five Americans killed while trying to storm the mansion. Some of Knox's cannonballs sailed through the house's front windows and out through the back, only to fall among the American soldiers advancing on the other side of the house. The resulting confusion gave Howe the chance to counterattack, and soon the British had the Americans on the run.

On the afternoon of October 7, three days after the Battle of Germantown and eighteen days after the Battle of Freeman's Farm, the British general John Burgoyne finally made his move—and a curious move it was. By that point he'd given up on receiving any help from Henry Clinton in New York. Rejecting advice to retreat to the north, he decided to mount one last attempt at turning the American left. But, instead of beginning at dawn with the fury of a lion, Burgoyne and a force of about fifteen hundred men waited until 1:00 p.m. before they occupied a small cabin to the south of Freeman's Farm.

At that moment Gates and his officers were gathered around a table enjoying what was in the eighteenth century the main meal of the day. "At the dinner at Gates's that day," Lieutenant Colonel John Brooks remembered, "the chief point of discussion among the officers was whether we should commence the attack or receive General Burgoyne behind our breastwork at the lines, should he attempt to advance."

Even though Arnold no longer had an official role in the northern army, he was in attendance that afternoon and showed no qualms about joining the discussion. "Arnold," Brooks remembered, insisted "that the assailant had the advantage: for he can always take his own time, and choose the point of attack; and if repulsed, he has only to retreat behind his own lines and form again." But Gates, Brooks remembered, disagreed, claiming that "if undisciplined militia were repulsed in the open field and the enemy pressed upon them in their retreat, it would be difficult to form them again, even behind their own breastworks; for if they were under a panic, they would keep on retreating, even after they had passed their own lines." Gates, despite claiming that he "never desired to see better soldiers than the New England men made," ultimately had little faith in their fighting abilities.

Brooks remembered that as Gates and Arnold argued about how to conduct the impending battle, they heard firing from the Americans' advanced pickets near the river. "The firing increasing," he recalled, "we all rose from table; and General Arnold, addressing General Gates said,

'Shall I go out and see what is the matter?' General Gates made no reply, but upon being pressed, said, 'I am afraid to trust you, Arnold.' To which Arnold answered, 'Pray, let me go: I will be careful and if our advance does not need support I will promise not to commit you.' Gates then told him he might go and see what the firing meant."

To prevent him from doing anything reckless, Gates made sure that Arnold was accompanied by the northern army's new second-in-command, Benjamin Lincoln. Whereas Arnold was a testy gamecock of a man, Lincoln projected an aura of affable equanimity. An apparent narcoleptic, he had a habit of falling asleep during councils of war and may have entirely missed the argument between Arnold and Gates. While stationed on the east bank of the Hudson, Lincoln had been placed in the unenviable position of convincing the irascible John Stark to at least listen to the commander of the northern army. Now he must find a way to control Benedict Arnold.

After riding "with great speed toward the enemy's lines," the two major generals stopped to look out from the edge of a tree-covered hill, where they could see Burgoyne and several of his officers standing on the roof of a cabin surrounded by an army of more than a thousand men. The British had occupied what was known as the Barber Farm set amid a field of uncut wheat. Wilkinson had also ventured to the edge of the American lines and left this account of what he saw: "After entering the field, [the British troops] displayed, formed the line, and sat down in double ranks with their [muskets] between their legs. Foragers then proceeded to cut the wheat or standing straw, and I soon after observed several officers mounted on the top of a cabin . . . from whence with their glasses they were endeavoring to reconnoiter our left, which was concealed from their view by intervening woods." Even though firing could still be heard near the river, both Arnold and Lincoln realized that the British were preparing to attack the American left.

By the time Arnold and Lincoln had returned to the top of Bemis Heights, Gates had moved from his headquarters to the forward edge of the American lines. "General Gates," Lincoln said, "the firing at the river is merely a feint. Their object is your left. A strong force of 1,500 men are marching circuitously, to plant themselves on yonder height. That point must be defended, or your camp is in danger."

It must have been quite a scene: Gates, his glasses perched on the bridge of his nose, with Arnold, Lincoln, Wilkinson, and others, either mounted or standing beside their horses, gathered around him. Technically, Arnold was no longer an officer in the northern army, but that did not prevent him from suggesting that he have a role in the fighting ahead. "It is late in the day," Nathaniel Bachellor heard him say, "but let me have some men and we will have some fun with them before sunset." Gates seems to have done his best to ignore Arnold's suggestion. Turning to his adjutant James Wilkinson, Gates said, "Well then, order on Morgan to begin the game."

For Gates, who had earlier announced his commitment to letting the British attack first, this was an unusually aggressive move—indeed it was exactly what Arnold had proposed to do back on September 19. But for Arnold on October 7, it wasn't enough. "That is nothing," he blurted. "You must send a strong force."

"General Arnold," Gates replied, "I have nothing for you to do. You have no business here."

Swearing loudly, Arnold turned his horse and rode back to his quarters in the little red farmhouse on the northwest corner of Bemis Heights.

It was left to Lincoln to convince Gates to do as Arnold had suggested. Coaxing where Arnold had criticized, Lincoln was able to persuade Gates to deploy a host of regiments under Enoch Poor, Ebenezer Learned, and others until by the late afternoon there were at least eight thousand Americans engaged in what came to be known as the Battle of Bemis Heights, the second engagement in what today is collectively referred to as the Battle of Saratoga.

As the fighting raged amid the fields and forests below, Arnold raged in his farmhouse on the hill. Some said he drank to excess during that awful period of confinement; others said he stoked himself on opium—a not improbable scenario given that he had undoubtedly taken the drug after suffering his debilitating leg injury at Quebec. At some point, he emerged from the house and, according to Wilkinson, "rode about the camp betraying great agitation and wrath."

His friend Leonard Chester, the same Connecticut man who had attempted to broker a reconciliation with Gates the week before, had lent him a dark-brown, almost black horse named Warren for the fallen hero

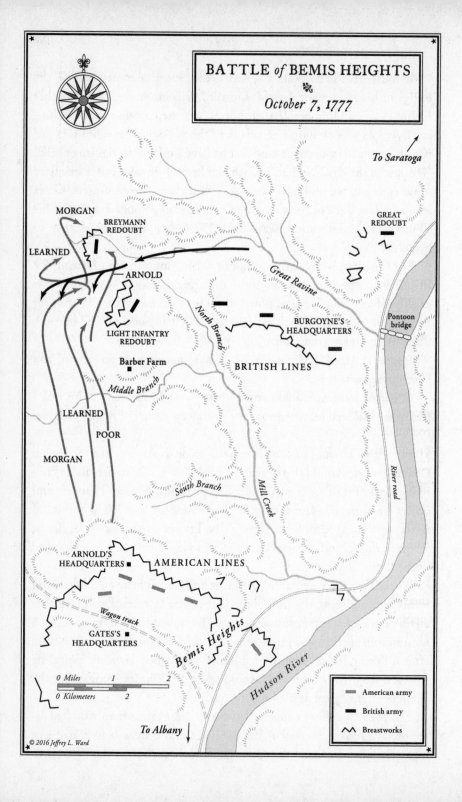

BATTLE of BEMIS HEIGHTS

October 7, 1777

To Saratoga

MORGAN

BREYMANN
REDOUBT

LEARNED

ARNOLD

GREAT
REDOUBT

Great Ravine

Pontoon
bridge

LIGHT INFANTRY
REDOUBT

BURGOYNE'S
HEADQUARTERS

North Branch

BRITISH LINES

Barber Farm

Middle Branch

LEARNED

POOR

MORGAN

Mill Creek

South Branch

River road

ARNOLD'S
HEADQUARTERS

AMERICAN LINES

Wagon track

GATES'S
HEADQUARTERS

Bemis Heights

Hudson River

0 Miles   1   2

0 Kilometers   2

American army

British army

Breastworks

To Albany

© 2016 Jeffrey L. Ward

of Bunker Hill. After pausing at an open hogshead of rum, where he drank an entire "dipperful," Arnold "wheeled his horse," according to Dr. Edmund Chadwick, "and dashed into the fight."

When Horatio Gates learned that Arnold had been sighted riding toward the scene of action, he sent out Major John Armstrong to order him back. Having suffered the same indignity at the hands of James Wilkinson, Arnold was not about to endure it once again, and when he saw Armstrong approaching he put the spurs to his horse and disappeared into the smoke-filled chaos of the battlefield.

It was later said that Arnold rode about the field that day "more like a madman than a cool and discreet officer . . . at a full gallop back and forth." His seemingly erratic behavior did not prevent him, however, from recognizing a key vulnerability in the enemy line. Arnold might be vain, overly sensitive to a slight, and difficult to work with, but there were few officers in either the American or British army who possessed his talent for almost instantly assessing the strengths and weaknesses of the enemy.

Early on he realized that an officer on a gray horse was playing a prominent role in maintaining the integrity of the British right. Arnold rode over to Colonel Morgan on the American left and requested that he order a sharpshooter to aim at the British officer. It took three shots, but eventually the Indian fighter Tim Murphy placed a rifle ball into the gut of General Simon Fraser, the Scotsman who was Burgoyne's intimate friend and the commander of the British right. The Americans had already begun to overwhelm the enemy, but the felling of Fraser by an American sniper appears to have precipitated the collapse of the British line. Lieutenant William Digby claimed that the loss of Fraser "helped to turn the fate of the day." Soon the British were in retreat, abandoning their fieldpieces and taking refuge behind the two timber redoubts that guarded the right end of their encampment.

The Americans had done it. They had succeeded in driving the enemy from the field. But Arnold in his angry furor was not finished. He would drive the British from their barricades and claim the victory that Gates had denied him on September 19.

That afternoon as the sound of musketry and artillery echoed amid the autumn-tinged trees below Bemis Heights, Horatio Gates remained in

his quarters at the rear of the American camp, doing his apparent best to
ignore the course of the battle. The British officer Sir Francis Clerke had
been wounded and captured while carrying a critical message from Burgoyne. Now he was laid out on Gates's bed and "engaged," Wilkinson
remembered, "in a warm dispute on the merits of the Revolution" with
the American commander.

It was certainly an unusual time to conduct a conversation about the
legitimacy of the American Revolution. But for Gates, a former British
officer who had taken up the colonists' cause, the debate spoke to the very
essence of deciding who he was: a freedom fighter or a traitor.

Sir Francis admitted, Wilkinson remembered, "that every procedure
on [the colonies'] part, short of the Declaration of Independence, was
warranted by the conduct of the British administration . . . , but that the
sudden act of severance convinced him the contest had originated in a
premeditated view to independence." The assertion outraged Gates, who
"contended that the idea of disunion had never entered into the head of
any American" until the actions of the British government gave the colonists no other choice. According to Wilkinson, Gates "became quite in-
censed, and calling me out of the room asked me if I had ever heard so
impudent a son of a b[itch]." Within the week, Clerke would be dead and
Gates would be the hero of the Battle of Saratoga.

The sun had begun to set by the time Arnold saw a way to end it. Although he no longer had any official standing in the northern army, he
remained an immensely charismatic presence on the battlefield, and
more than a few American officers and their men were willing to follow
him just about anywhere.

He had just led a futile and bloody charge into what was referred to as
the Light Infantry Redoubt, a massive wall of timbers that proved impossible to storm. Arnold sat conspicuously on his horse waving his sword
with such abandon that he slashed the head of an American officer without realizing it. And then, out of the corner of his eye, he saw that the
enemy's redoubt on the far left—a smaller structure manned primarily by
German soldiers under the command of Heinrich Breymann—was accessible through a sally port from the rear. It would require him to ride
diagonally across the battlefield and place him between two lines of fire,
but if he was able to enter the redoubt from behind as American forces

led by Morgan attacked from the front, they might succeed in dislodging the Germans from a position that was critical to the enemy's overall defense.

On he rushed through deepening twilight on a horse named for the dead hero who had given him the commission with which his military career had begun. Now, two and a half years later, with a trail of fifteen to twenty riflemen following in his wake, he was in the midst of his own quest for immortality. He burst through the sally port and, with his horse turned sideways to the redoubt's German defenders, demanded their surrender. One of the soldiers raised his musket and fired, the ball smashing into the thigh bone of Arnold's left leg and killing his horse. The animal collapsed, pinning him to the ground as he shouted for the riflemen behind to "Rush on!"

American soldiers swarmed into the redoubt from all sides, and those Germans who were not captured, killed, or wounded fled into the night. Henry Dearborn had been with Arnold when he'd been injured at Quebec, and he was one of the first to reach him as he lay beneath his dead horse in the Breymann Redoubt.

Dearborn asked if he had been badly wounded. "In the same leg," Arnold replied. "I wish it had passed [through] my heart."

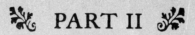

PART II

Secret Motives

* AND *

Designs

How can we draw the line and say at what
precise point [treachery begins] . . . when the
treachery is in progress of execution, or . . .
when the mind is still wavering upon it? In
short, how loose and slippery becomes the
ground . . . if . . . we stray forth in quest of
secret motives and designs!

~Lord Mahon, *History of England,*
vol. 7, 1854

CHAPTER SEVEN

The Bite of a Rattlesnake

A rnold had been hit in the left femur, just above the knee. Since the femur is the strongest bone in the human body, it offers the greatest resistance to the passage of a bullet, which fractures the bone into splinters that can do more damage than the bullet itself as they scatter like shrapnel throughout the muscle and blood vessels of the thigh. Given the likelihood of infection, military doctors in the eighteenth century routinely resorted to amputation when faced with a fracture as serious as Arnold's. But by the time he'd been delivered to the hospital in Albany on October 11, four days after the Battle of Bemis Heights, Arnold had made it clear that he was keeping his leg.

Arnold had a history of recovering from a serious injury with remarkable speed. Less than six months after being felled by a ricocheted bullet at Quebec, he was strong enough to oversee the American retreat from Canada and leap aboard the last boat out of St. Johns. Three months after that he was bounding from cannon to cannon across the smoke-filled deck of a galley on Lake Champlain. For Arnold, the experience of war had always been profoundly physical, and he was not about to lose his left leg to the saw of an overly cautious army surgeon. "He is very . . . impatient under his misfortunes," Dr. James Thacher wearily recorded in his journal on the morning of October 12, "and required all my attention during the night."

Soon after Arnold's arrival in Albany, he was joined by his fellow major general Benjamin Lincoln, who had been shot in the ankle after having stumbled into the rear guard of the retreating enemy the day after the Battle of Bemis Heights. Lincoln had not even participated in the fighting at Saratoga. Now, thanks to a bullet he'd taken while fleeing for his life, he was being hailed for his bravery and courage.

From the medical staff's perspective, the contrast between the two generals could not have been more striking. Even during "the most painful operation by the surgeon," Lincoln cheerfully entertained those gathered around him with stories and anecdotes. "In [Lincoln's] character is united the resolution of the soldier; the politeness of the gentleman, the patient philosopher, and pious Christian," marveled Dr. James Browne.

Arnold, on the other hand, refused to submit stoically to his fate. Having been trained as an apothecary, he knew more than most about the practice of medicine in an age when bloodletting and a concoction made of cinchona bark were used to stave off gangrene, and he had little faith in his doctors. "His peevishness would degrade the most capricious of the fair sex," Browne wrote. "He abuses us for a set of ignorant pretenders and empirics."

On October 17 John Burgoyne's army finally laid down its arms. Horatio Gates—the commander in chief of the northern army—had never ventured onto the field of battle during two days of brutal fighting. He had so thoroughly bungled treaty negotiations prior to the British surrender that Congress was ultimately forced to renege on several of the agreement's overly generous terms. However, none of this altered the fact that the Battle of Saratoga had changed the course of the war. An entire army of British and German professional soldiers had been overwhelmed by a swarming mass of American patriots. This was big, extraordinary news, and the sheer magnitude of the victory guaranteed that Gates—no matter how imperfect his performance may have been—was about to become a national hero.

By October 23 news of the British surrender had reached the eastern seaboard, where celebratory cannons were fired in towns stretching from Boston to Portsmouth, New Hampshire. Two days later, Washington learned of the surrender, not from Gates, but from General Israel Putnam, stationed on the Hudson River. On December 2 the word of Burgoyne's defeat reached King George III, who reportedly "fell into agonies on hearing this account." And then, two days later, on December 4, a Boston merchant who had been dispatched to France with the news arrived at the door of Benjamin Franklin. According to the messenger, the effect was "electrical." As Gates basked in the praise of the nation and the world, Arnold lay on a hospital bed with his wounded leg immobilized in a wooden box.

The leg that ultimately emerged from the fracture box would be two inches shorter than it had once been. That, however, was several months in the future. Throughout the fall and winter of 1777–78, Arnold's movements were so restricted and the pain was so severe that he could not even write a letter. The one bit of good news was that on November 29 Congress voted to restore his proper seniority as a major general.

Unfortunately, Washington did not inform him of the fact until almost two months later, on January 20. As anyone who has waited for a long-anticipated letter knows, delays of this kind are not good for the soul. The anger and outrage that had once fueled Arnold's bravery in battle turned inward as his hatred of Gates (whom he termed "the greatest poltroon in the world") became an all-consuming passion.

That winter, one of Gates's aides caught a glimpse of the injured general, who was still confined to his bed. "The malice of this man is so bitter," the aide reported on February 19, "[that he] reminds one of a taper, sinking in its socket, which emits a feeble gleam just before it expires." The warrior who had once been touted as gallant and intrepid—an American Hannibal—was now being compared to a guttering candle.

By the last week in October, General William Howe had achieved just about everything he had set out to accomplish. He had bested Washington on the battlefield and now his army occupied the rebel capital of Philadelphia. And yet, despite all these triumphs, Howe's army was dangerously close to suffering the same fate as Burgoyne's.

Howe possessed Philadelphia, but it did him little good since he had no way, as of yet, to get his brother's fleet of ships—and all the provisions and supplies they contained—to the city's waterfront. About a mile down the river from Philadelphia, where the Schuylkill flowed into the Delaware to create a swirl of mudflats, the Americans had planted a line of forty-foot-wide timber frames known as chevaux-de-frise. Topped by rows of metal-sheathed spikes designed to tear out the bottom of a wooden sailing vessel, the chevaux-de-frise were guarded by American forts on either side of the river as well as by the two dozen galleys of the Pennsylvania navy. Howe had conquered Philadelphia, but the Americans controlled the mile-long stretch of the Delaware between the chevaux-de-frise and the city. If British supply ships were to reach Philadelphia before Howe's soldiers began to starve, he and his brother must find a way to break the American blockade by the end of November. Otherwise the British would be forced to evacuate the city before winter sealed the river in ice.

By the end of October, Howe had withdrawn his troops from Germantown and consolidated his forces in Philadelphia so that he could devote as many soldiers as possible to attacking one of the forts guarding the chevaux-de-frise. On the west side of the river, on a tiny island of mud, was Fort Mifflin, which would require an amphibious assault. On the east side was Fort Mercer, which was accessible by land. That decided it: Colonel Carl von Donop, the same officer who had been in command of the Hessian forces in New Jersey the previous year, would lead a force of two thousand soldiers against Fort Mercer. Once the fort had been secured, the British could open a channel in the eastern side of the river that would enable ships to make their way to Philadelphia.

On October 16 the American soldiers stationed at Fort Mercer fired a salute to celebrate the Battle of Bemis Heights. Though Howe would not receive official word of Burgoyne's fate for several weeks to come, he could not help but begin to realize that all of the hard-won battles of the last few months had been for nothing. While he and his brother had concentrated on taking Philadelphia, they had left Burgoyne to suffer a defeat so catastrophic that it might tempt France to enter the war.

On the evening of October 22, Colonel Donop and his two thousand Hessians attacked Fort Mercer. By the end of the fighting, Donop was mortally wounded and the Germans had been repulsed. Making matters even worse, two British warships that had been squeezed through a narrow gap in the chevaux-de-frise so that they could offer assistance in the attack had run aground on a shoal within easy reach of the American navy. The next morning, the rebel galleys, painted black and yellow, descended on the stricken vessels like the hornets they so closely resembled, and in the midst of the fighting the *Augusta,* a huge, sixty-four-gun ship of the line, burst into flames. When the vessel's powder magazine exploded, the thunderous concussion rattled the windows of houses more than thirty miles away.

Thomas Paine was with a group of American soldiers near Germantown

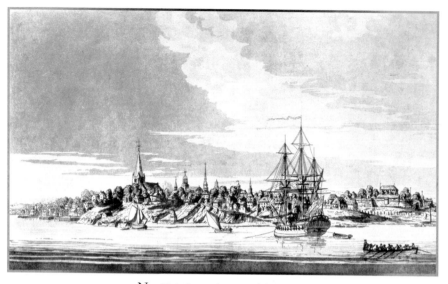

New York City at the time of the Revolution.

George Washington as painted in New York by Charles Willson Peale in July 1776. By the middle of the following month, more than four hundred British ships had gathered off the eastern shore of Staten Island.

General Henry Knox by Charles Willson Peale. Knox, the American artillery chief, held the Bible on which Benedict Arnold placed his hand when he pledged his allegiance to the United States in 1778.

Joseph Reed, Washington's adjutant general at the Battle of Long Island, by Charles Willson Peale. After his falling-out with Washington in the autumn of 1776, Reed became the controversial president of the Supreme Executive Council of Pennsylvania's state legislature.

Nathanael Greene by John Trumbull. Although Greene was largely responsible for the loss of Fort Washington and Fort Lee, he ultimately proved to be Washington's most trustworthy general.

General John Sullivan by Richard Morrell Staigg. Sullivan was captured at the Battle of Long Island, served throughout the Philadelphia campaign in 1777, and ended his career as a major general by leading the campaign against the Iroquois in 1780.

General Israel Putnam by Dominique Fabronius. Just days before the Battle of Long Island, Washington put Putnam in the unenviable position of commanding the American forces on the heights of Brooklyn.

General William Alexander, otherwise known as Lord Stirling, by Bass Otis. Prior to his capture by the British, Stirling fought heroically at the Battle of Long Island. The following year he alerted Washington to some of the initial intrigue associated with the Conway Cabal.

General William Howe, commander of the British forces on Long Island in 1776 and during the Philadelphia campaign in 1777.

Admiral Richard Howe by James Watson. The older brother of William Howe, Admiral Howe had high hopes of convincing the rebellious Americans to agree to a negotiated settlement in 1776.

George Germain by Nathaniel Hone. As secretary of state, Germain oversaw the British war effort throughout most of the Revolution.

A sketch by Archibald Robertson depicting the arrival of Admiral Howe's flagship, HMS *Eagle* (with sails set and approaching from the Narrows), at Staten Island in July 1776.

General Henry Clinton by John Smart. Clinton came up with the idea of the flanking movement that won the Battle of Long Island and ultimately assumed command of the British forces in 1778.

General Charles Cornwallis by Thomas Gainsborough. Cornwallis was outfoxed by Washington at the Second Battle of Trenton, then had the satisfaction of leading the British forces into Philadelphia in the fall of 1777.

A 1778 sketch of a British light infantryman by Philip James de Loutherbourg.

A Hessian miter cap taken during the American Revolution. Like the headgear worn by a British grenadier, the miter cap was intended to make a Hessian soldier appear taller and more forbidding to the enemy.

A Loutherbourg sketch of a British grenadier.

Archibald Robertson's sketch of Kips Bay (today's East Thirty-Fourth Street) about the time of the attack that launched the British invasion of Manhattan Island in September 1776.

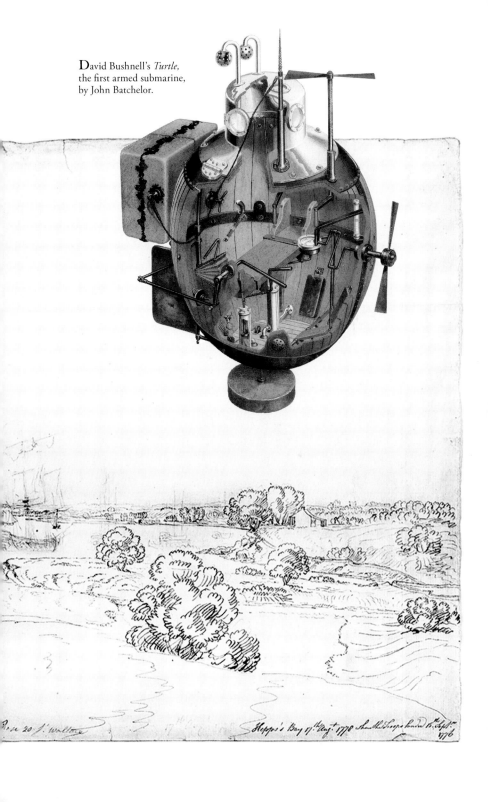

David Bushnell's *Turtle,* the first armed submarine, by John Batchelor.

A drawing by Charles Randle of the American fleet assembled
at Lake Champlain's Valcour Bay in the fall of 1776.

Randle's depiction of the British fleet at Valcour.

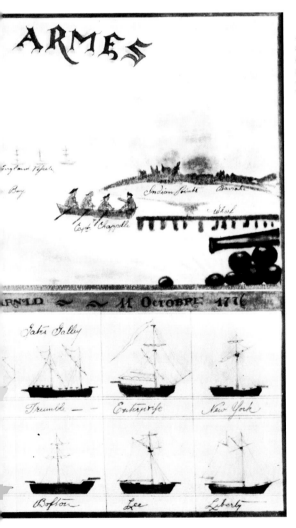

Another Randle drawing, showing silhouettes of Arnold and other American officers as well as line drawings of the American vessels that fought in the Battle of Valcour Island.

Benedict Arnold by
Pierre Eugène du Simitière.

This painting by A. Cassidy has
been tentatively identified as that of
Benedict Arnold. Certainly the nose
and the fleshy chin are similar to those
in the Du Simitière drawing. This is a
man who has never known self-doubt.

A drawing by Henry Gilder that shows how Arnold tucked the American
fleet inside Valcour Bay, thus forcing the British to approach from downwind.

General Guy Carleton by Mabel Messer. As commander of the British forces in Canada, Carleton led the unsuccessful attempt to take Fort Ticonderoga in 1776.

John Trumbull's sketch of Hessian colonel Johann Rall's surrender at the First Battle of Trenton. Washington and his officers are mounted on the left.

A caricature of Major General Charles Lee by A. H. Ritchie. Prior to his capture by the British in Basking Ridge, New Jersey, Lee had emerged as one of Washington's most vocal critics.

Trenton's Assunpink Bridge as it looked in 1789. The arch did not exist at the time of the standoff between Washington and Cornwallis during the Second Battle of Trenton.

An artist's rendering of Fort Stanwix near the headwaters
of the Mohawk River in present-day Rome, New York.

Although General Philip Schuyler did
much to set the stage for the Battle of
Saratoga, his nemesis Horatio Gates was
destined to, in Schuyler's words, "reap
the fruits of my labors."

Colonel Peter Gansevoort commanded
the American forces during the Siege of
Fort Stanwix.

General Horatio Gates by Charles Willson Peale. After his victory at the Battle of Saratoga, Gates became embroiled in the controversial Conway Cabal, then suffered defeat three years later at the Battle of Camden.

Major James Wilkinson by Charles Willson Peale. Wilkinson instigated the falling-out between Benedict Arnold and Horatio Gates during the Battle of Saratoga, then contributed to the intrigue associated with the Conway Cabal.

Richard Varick by Ralph Earl. After serving in Benedict Arnold's military family during the Battle of Saratoga, Varick rejoined Arnold in the summer of 1780, when he was given command at West Point.

Colonel Daniel Morgan by Charles Willson Peale. Morgan's Virginia riflemen fought alongside Benedict Arnold at both Quebec and Saratoga.

Benjamin Lincoln by Charles Willson Peale. Lincoln was one of the major generals who had been promoted past Benedict Arnold. Cooperative and well liked, he took over as second-in-command at the Battle of Bemis Heights and, like Arnold, suffered an injury to his leg.

British general John Burgoyne by Sir Joshua Reynolds. Burgoyne claimed that if not for the presence of Benedict Arnold, he would have won the Battle of Saratoga.

Philadelphia, then the largest city in the American colonies, in 1768, by George Heap.

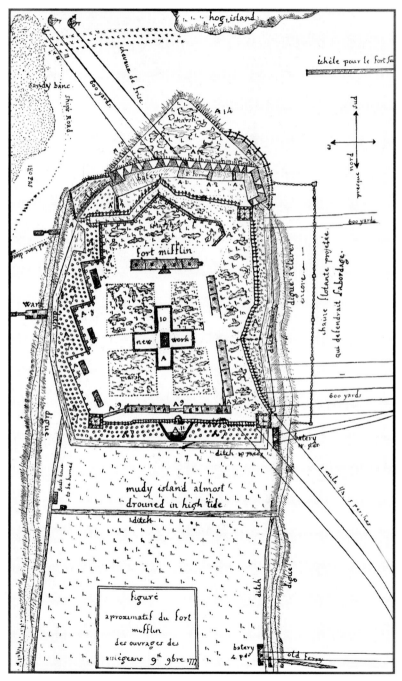

Map of Fort Mifflin near Philadelphia by François de Fleury, showing the positions of British batteries and warships as well as a line of chevaux-de-frise to the left.

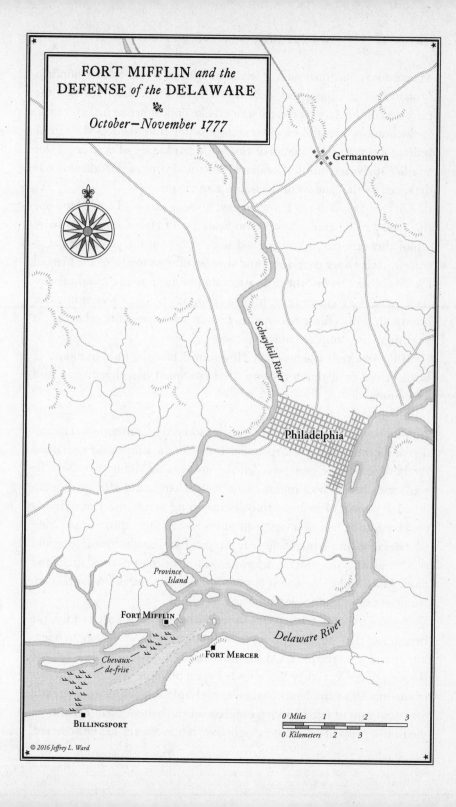

FORT MIFFLIN *and the* DEFENSE *of the* DELAWARE

October–November 1777

Germantown

Schuylkill River

Philadelphia

Province
Island

FORT MIFFLIN

*Chevaux-
de-frise*

FORT MERCER

Delaware River

BILLINGSPORT

0 Miles   1   2   3
0 Kilometers   2   3

© 2016 Jeffrey L. Ward

when he was "stunned with a report as loud as a peal from a hundred cannon at once." In a letter to Benjamin Franklin he described how the explosion of the *Augusta* created a cloud like none other he had ever seen: "a thick smoke rising like a pillar and spreading from the top like a tree." It did not become the symbol of a new and terrible age of destruction for another 168 years, but in the fall of 1777 the skyline of Philadelphia was darkened by the shadow of the mushroom cloud.

On that day, William Howe penned his resignation. "I am led to hope that I may be relieved," he wrote to Secretary of State George Germain, "from this very painful service wherein I have not the good fortune to enjoy the necessary confidence and support of my superiors." He blamed his lack of success on "the little attention . . . given to my recommendations since the commencement of my command," but Howe must have known that his failure had nothing to do with Germain, who had, if anything, given him too much latitude.

Still to be seen was whether Howe must face the final indignity of being forced to abandon the city whose conquest had already cost him his command.

Sixteen-year-old Joseph Plumb Martin had been a Connecticut state soldier at Kips Bay when on September 15, 1776, the British had unleashed the horrific barrage that preceded the invasion of Manhattan. Now he was a member of Washington's Continental army, and after having endured a month of near-continuous marching across the Pennsylvania countryside, he had been assigned to Fort Mifflin on aptly named Mud Island. Here, on a bank of silt that was just four hundred yards long and two hundred yards wide, in a fort made, for the most part, of sticks and mud, Martin was about to suffer hardships that were, in his estimation, "sufficient to kill half a dozen horses."

By November 3, when Martin's regiment arrived at Fort Mifflin, the British had decided that this tiny, ill-equipped fort was the key to opening a passage up the river. On the other side of a thin channel of water to the west of the fort, they had already begun building a series of batteries in the mucky swamplands of the Pennsylvania shore. Due to a week of torrential rain in late October, progress on the batteries had been, from the British perspective, excruciatingly slow, but as Martin soon discovered, the enemy already had enough cannons in place to make life inside Fort Mifflin a sleepless, mud-soaked struggle for survival.

Except for what Martin called a "zigzag" of granite along its eastern wall, the entire fort was made of nothing stouter than earth and wood. This meant that the five hundred American soldiers had almost nowhere to hide whenever a barrage of British cannonballs, known as round shot, came hurtling their way. First, a sentinel with his eyes trained on the British cannons saw the muzzle flash and cried out, "A shot!" Then, Martin remembered, "everyone endeavored to take care of himself." Inevitably, "in spite of all our precautions," there were casualties. In one instance, Martin saw five members of an American cannon crew "cut down by a single shot." In another, he saw "men who were stooping to be protected by the works, but not stooping low enough, split like fish to be broiled."

In addition to round shot, the British fired exploding shells that, when they weren't knocking down the log palisades that lined the western side of the fort or blasting the wooden barracks into rubble, regularly created fifty-foot geysers of mud within the fort's interior. Sometimes the shells buried themselves so deep in the fort's mud floor that, Martin remembered, "their report could not be heard when they burst, and I could only feel a tremulous motion of the earth."

After a day spent dodging shells and shot and trying to return the enemy's fire, the Americans were put to work rebuilding what was left of their fort. "The British batteries in the course of the day would nearly level our works," Martin remembered, "and we were, like the beaver, obliged to repair our dams in the night." Under such conditions, sleep became a virtual impossibility, especially since the fort's barracks were vulnerable to the enemy. "Sometimes some of the men, when overcome with fatigue . . . would slip away into the barracks to catch a nap of sleep," Martin remembered, "but it seldom happened that they all came out again alive. I was in this place a fortnight and can say in sincerity that I never lay down to sleep a minute in all that time."

Here, on this lonely outpost at the muddy confluence of the Schuylkill and the Delaware, Martin and his five hundred compatriots had become the Continental army's last hope. If somehow they could hold out until the end of November, the British would be forced to abandon Philadelphia and head back to New York to prepare for winter quarters.

• • •

Washington's headquarters was at Whitemarsh, Pennsylvania, about sixteen miles to the north of Philadelphia. On the morning of November 5, he and his staff rode south to Germantown, where they hoped to catch a glimpse of the Siege of Fort Mifflin. Washington was painfully aware of the tremendous importance this pitiful little fortress had assumed. "Nothing in the course of this campaign has taken up so much of the attention and consideration of myself and all the general officers," he wrote to Henry Laurens, the new president of the Continental Congress. Since Fort Mifflin could not contain any more men, the only way that Washington could provide assistance was for his army to attack the British gun emplacements on the Pennsylvania shore—a tremendously risky move given the presence of Howe's army in nearby Philadelphia. If he had any hope of coming to Fort Mifflin's relief, Washington needed to augment his army with reinforcements from Gates's army to the north.

Washington had entered one of the most difficult and frustrating periods of his life. While Gates had enjoyed success at Saratoga, he had endured the string of disappointments that culminated in the loss of Philadelphia. Making matters even worse, Gates had not yet delivered official word of Burgoyne's surrender to either Washington or Congress. Apparently enjoying the fact that the powers that be were being kept in suspense as to the specifics of the treaty (a treaty that he may already have begun to regret), Gates was allowing the news of his victory to spread across the United States. By the time Congress and Washington had the chance to examine the treaty (which to appease the British commander's pride had been termed a "convention"), Gates would already be famous throughout the nation as the conqueror of Burgoyne.

By the end of October, Washington had heard enough unofficial reports of the British surrender to believe that Gates had, in fact, been victorious. Desperate for reinforcements from the north to support the defense of Fort Mifflin and yet with no official word from Gates, Washington was reduced to sending his twenty-two-year-old aide Alexander Hamilton on a mission "to lay before [General Gates] the state of this army and the situation of the enemy and to point out to him the many happy consequences that will accrue from an immediate reinforcement being sent from the northern army."

Hamilton took less than a week to make the grueling three-hundred-mile trip to Albany. Upon reporting to Gates's headquarters, he discovered that the commander of the northern army was in no mood to comply with Washington's request for additional troops. "I found insuperable inconveniences in acting diametrically opposite to the opinion of a gentleman whose successes have raised him to the highest importance," Hamilton reported. Although Gates eventually sent more brigades south, he deeply resented the fact that Washington had given a mere aide "dictatorial power."

By that time, Gates had sent an emissary of his own, his adjutant James Wilkinson, to deliver the news of Saratoga to Congress. (To Washington's considerable annoyance, Gates did not feel it necessary to send *him* official word of his victory.) Whereas Hamilton had made the trip in a week, Wilkinson, who had taken such delight in orchestrating Benedict Arnold's downfall after the Battle of Freeman's Farm, took more than twice that long to cover the same distance. In the aftermath of the Battle of Saratoga, Wilkinson had grown giddy with his own seemingly limitless prospects. If Congress did as Gates had requested, he would be granted the brevet rank of brigadier general for the honor of having delivered the news of Saratoga—quite a leap for a twenty-year-old major.

He had just arrived in Reading, Pennsylvania, about sixty miles to the northeast of Congress's new temporary quarters in York. Wilkinson could have pushed on the next morning to deliver official word of Saratoga to an anxiously waiting Congress. Instead, he decided to accept the invitation offered by General Thomas Mifflin, the namesake of Fort Mifflin, to have tea with him in Reading.

Like Joseph Reed, Mifflin had once served as one of Washington's closest associates and was now one of his harshest critics. Although officially the Continental army's quartermaster, most of his efforts in the fall of 1777 appear to have been channeled toward creating a shadowy kind of exploratory committee to investigate the possibility of replacing Washington with Horatio Gates. Needless to say, Wilkinson was just the man Mifflin wanted to talk to.

The next morning, Mifflin and Wilkinson were joined by two congressmen from Massachusetts who had made a special trip from York to speak with Horatio Gates's adjutant before his much-anticipated arrival at Congress. (Wilkinson did not name them in his *Memoirs,* but we do know that the delegates Samuel Adams and James Lovell were two of Gates's staunchest supporters.) "I was minutely questioned by them,"

Wilkinson remembered, "respecting the military operations in the north. General Washington's misfortunes were strictured severely by them." Mifflin and his companions were also interested in a letter that an Irish-born brigadier general from France named Thomas Conway had written to General Gates. Conway had served at both Brandywine and German-town and had nothing good to say about Washington. Wilkinson knew the piece of correspondence well. Gates had read and commented on the letter with great relish, and had especially enjoyed the part in which Conway enumerated the "thirteen reasons for the loss of the Battle of Brandywine."

As Wilkinson later admitted, "a state of revolution is the most seduc-ing on earth." By the end of his conversation with Mifflin and the two delegates, Wilkinson must have been positively euphoric about the pos-sibilities ahead. With rain making travel difficult, he decided to spend another day in Reading and accepted a request from Major General Lord Stirling "to take a potluck dinner with him."

Stirling was in Reading recovering from a fall from his horse and spent most of that long drunken night recounting his exploits at the Bat-tle of Long Island. At some point Wilkinson fell into conversation with one of Stirling's aides and mentioned the letter from Conway to Gates. Ill advisedly, it turned out, Wilkinson took the liberty of quoting one of the letter's juicier passages from memory: "Heaven has been determined to save your country; or a weak general and bad counselors would have ruined it."

What Wilkinson apparently did not know was that Stirling despised Thomas Conway, who had mockingly referred to him as "my Lord" in the days prior to the Battle of Brandywine. Soon after Wilkinson's departure, Stirling wrote to Washington about what Gates's adjutant had said con-cerning the French officer's letter to Horatio Gates. "Such wicked duplic-ity of conduct," Stirling wrote, "I shall always think it my duty to detect."

By the time Washington received Stirling's letter, he was already familiar with what he described as Conway's "intriguing disposition." Several weeks before, when informed that certain members of Congress wanted to promote the French brigadier to the rank of major general, he had in-sisted in an unusually strident letter that Conway's "importance in this army exists more in his own imagination than in reality."

Much as he'd done the year before when he became aware of Joseph Reed's clandestine correspondence with Charles Lee, Washington decided to respond quickly to Stirling's revelation. He had received Stirling's letter on the evening of November 4. By the following morning, prior to setting out from his headquarters in Whitemarsh for Germantown, Washington had penned Conway this note:

> A letter which I received last night contained the following paragraph: "In a letter from General Conway to General Gates he says—'Heaven has been determined to save your country; or a weak general and bad counselors would have ruined it.'" I am, sir, your humble servant, George Washington.

Forceful yet understated, the note gave no indication as to who was Washington's source. Given the purposeful ambiguity of the language, it was easy to jump to the conclusion that he possessed an actual copy of Conway's letter. Washington had put what historians have subsequently called the Conway Cabal on notice that he knew exactly what they were up to.

Washington's visit to Germantown on the morning of November 5 may have marked his first time back to the scene of the battle that after such a promising start had gone so disastrously wrong. Since the shattered shell of Cliveden occupied the highest point in Germantown, Washington climbed to the roof of the house. There, atop the building that had been the focus of the misguided assault that may have cost Washington a victory, he looked through his spyglass toward Fort Mifflin. "We could discover nothing more than thick clouds of smoke and the masts of two vessels," an aide wrote, "the weather being very hazy."

For now, Washington's hands were tied when it came to supporting the defenders of Fort Mifflin. But that had not prevented him from launching the first salvo in the political battle that was to establish him as the undisputed leader of not only an army but a nation.

Ten days later, on the morning of November 15, the Howe brothers mounted their final and most desperate attempt to take Fort Mifflin. For the last five days the recently completed British batteries on the Pennsylvania shore, one of which was only five hundred yards from Fort Mifflin's west wall, had been pounding away at the fortress. On November 11 the fort's commander, Colonel Samuel Smith, had been attempting to dash off a letter to Washington when a cannonball slammed into the chimney he'd been leaning against and buried him beneath a pile of bricks and mortar. Once Smith had been transported across the Delaware for medical attention at Fort Mercer, the twenty-eight-year-old French engineer François de Fleury became the de facto leader of the American forces at Fort Mifflin.

Over the course of the next three days, Fleury's courage and ornery endurance were an inspiration to his men. Even Joseph Plumb Martin, who rarely had anything good to say about a commanding officer, was impressed. The only safe place on Mud Island was behind the stone wall on the eastern side of the fort, where the men built a small fire with splinters from the broken palisades. Each night, as Fleury oversaw the rebuilding of the fort's earthworks and palisades, the soldiers under his command began to disappear. "We used to . . . run into this place for a minute or two's respite from fatigue and cold," Martin remembered. "When [Fleury] found that the workmen began to grow scarce, he would come to the entrance and call us out. He had always his cane in his hand, and woe betided him he could get a stroke at."

Although Colonel Smith had written Washington that the time had come to abandon Fort Mifflin, Fleury was convinced that "the fire of the enemy will never take the fort. It may kill us men, but this is the fortune of war." But by November 15 even Fleury had begun to have second thoughts.

That morning Admiral Howe succeeded in getting more than half a dozen warships through the gap in the chevaux-de-frise. Two of the vessels worked their way into the channel on the west side of Mud Island. The largest, the *Vigilant,* had been specially modified so that she floated several feet higher in the water than normal. When she finally anchored beside the island, the warship was so close to the fort that the British marines in the vessel's crosstrees were able to lob grenades into the fort's interior as riflemen on the topmast picked off any American who attempted to fire a cannon. In the meantime, several larger British ships took up positions on the east side of the island, where they placed the fort and its defenders in a lethal cross fire.

In one twenty-minute period on the morning of November 15, the British estimated that a stunning 1,030 cannonballs were fired at the hapless fort. By midday, Martin remembered, "nearly every gun in the fort was silenced. . . . Our men were cut up like cornstalks. . . . When the firing had in some measure subsided and I could look about me, I found the fort exhibited a picture of desolation; the whole area of the fort was completely ploughed as a field; the buildings of every kind hanging in broken fragments and the guns all dismounted. . . . If ever destruction was complete, it was here."

That night the decision was made to abandon the fort. Before climbing into one of the waiting boats, Martin went to look for the soldier who had become his best friend in the army. "I found him, indeed," he sadly remembered, "but lying in a long line of dead men who had been brought out of the fort to be conveyed to the main. . . . Poor young man!"

As what was left of the fort burned behind them, Martin and his fellow survivors were rowed to the New Jersey shore and marched to a grove of pitch pines for the night. Wrapping himself in a blanket, Martin lay down on the ground and didn't wake up until noon of the next day.

Only later did they learn how close they had come to forcing the British to abandon Philadelphia. "Just before the reduction of the forts," a reliable source maintained, "the enemy balanced exactly upon the point of quitting the city, and a straw would have turned in either scale." Thomas Paine was so inspired by the heroism displayed at Fort Mifflin that he published an open letter to William Howe. "The garrison with scarce anything to cover them but their bravery," he wrote, "survived in the midst of mud, shot, and shells, and were at last obliged to give it up more to the powers of time and gunpowder than to the military superiority of the besiegers. . . . You are fighting for what you can never obtain, and we are defending what we never mean to part with."

What Martin and his fellow defenders had done was inspirational, but it had come at a considerable cost. All was not right with Joseph Plumb Martin. After two weeks of constant shelling and having lost "the most intimate associate I had in the army," he appears to have experienced the eighteenth-century equivalent of post-traumatic stress syndrome. "When I awoke," he remembered, "I was as crazy as a goose shot through the head."

Martin eventually recovered enough to continue to serve in the army, but he never succeeded in leaving those two weeks at Fort Mifflin behind him. By the end of his military career he had participated in most of the great battles of the Revolution. He had been at the Battle of Long Island

and five years after that would be at Yorktown. But all those engagements were but "the sting of a bee" compared to what he had suffered at Fort Mifflin, which he likened to "the bite of a rattlesnake."

In the years after the War of Independence, historians paid scant attention to the Siege of Fort Mifflin, primarily because, Martin believed, "there was no Washington, Putnam, or Wayne there." "Had there been," he conjectured, "the affair would have been extolled to the skies." As Martin and the five hundred defenders of Fort Mifflin had learned first-hand, "great men get great praise, little men nothing."

It took another week for the British to pull up the chevaux-de-frise and destroy what remained of the Pennsylvania navy, but on November 24 the first of Howe's transport ships began to head up the Delaware. "To our joy," a Hessian officer exulted, "some thirty large vessels arrived at Philadelphia laden with all kinds of merchandise and provisions, through which the army was suddenly delivered from its wants."

Now that the British were in Philadelphia to stay, Washington pondered what to do next. A delegation from Congress made it clear that they expected him to conduct "a winter's campaign with vigor and success." By then Gates had gained the reputation among his supporters in Congress as the general who, unlike Washington, dared to engage the enemy and attack. Of course, Gates's newfound image as a warrior was based largely on what Benedict Arnold had been able to initiate offensively in spite of Gates's preference for a purely defensive mode of war. That, however, was lost on the Washington skeptics in Congress who accused the commander in chief of having, in the words of the Massachusetts delegate James Lovell, "fabiused [our affairs] into a very disagreeable posture," a reference to the Roman general Fabius Maximus, whose name became a byword for caution and delay in warfare.

To a certain extent, Washington had only himself to blame. The previous spring he had sent Nathanael Greene to Philadelphia to introduce his plan for pursuing his War of Posts, a defensive strategy that made perfect sense in the abstract but which he had repeatedly violated by assuming the offensive at Brandywine and then at Germantown. Despite his best intentions, Washington had been unable to shed his naturally aggressive instincts, and the result had been a mishmash of bellicosity and indecision that had ill served both himself and his army.

That December Washington appealed to his generals for advice. Should he, as Congress wanted, attack the British in Philadelphia? As always, that was what he *wanted* to do. But was it the *right* thing to do? Of all the letters of advice he received that fall, the most useful came from the general who knew him the best, Nathanael Greene.

> We must not be governed . . . by our wishes . . . [Greene counseled]. Let us not flatter ourselves from the heat of our zeal that men can do more than they can. . . . The successes of last winter [at Trenton and Princeton] were brilliant and attended with the most happy consequences in changing the complexion of the times, but if the bills of mortality were to be consulted, I fancy it would be found we were no great gainers by those operations. . . . An attack upon the city of Philadelphia appear[s] to me like forming a crisis for American liberty which if unsuccessful I fear will prove her grave.

This, it turned out, was exactly what Washington needed to hear. When Howe emerged from Philadelphia in early December and attempted to lure him into another battlefield encounter, Washington refused to be drawn into an engagement he could not afford to lose. After several days of cautious sparring, Howe returned in frustration to Philadelphia for the winter.

Finally, after nearly three years of halfheartedly attempting to suppress his naturally aggressive instincts, Washington had internalized the lesson that he had first professed to have learned the spring before. From here on in, he would do what was best for his army and his country, no matter what the critics (as well as his inner demons) might say.

About twenty miles from Philadelphia—close enough to monitor the enemy and far enough away for his depleted army to regroup—Washington established his winter quarters at Valley Forge. "To see men without clothes to cover their nakedness," he wrote of that march up the Schuylkill, "without blankets to lay on, without shoes by which their marches might be traced by the blood from their feet, and almost as often without provisions as with; marching through frost and snow and at Christmas taking up their winter quarters within a day's march of the enemy, without a

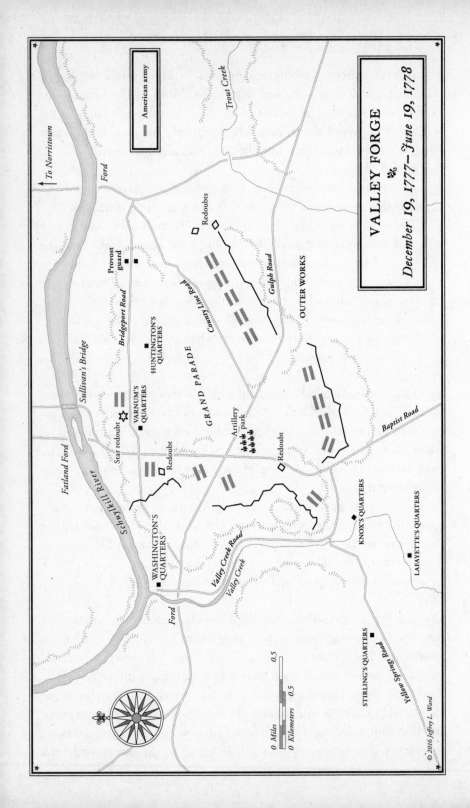

VALLEY FORGE

December 19, 1777 – June 19, 1778

American army

To Norristown

Trout Creek

Ford

Sullivan's Bridge

Provost guard

Bridgeport Road

County Line Road

Gulph Road

OUTER WORKS

Redoubts

Fatland Ford

Schuylkill River

Star redoubt

VARNUM'S QUARTERS

HUNTINGTON'S QUARTERS

GRAND PARADE

Redoubt

Artillery Park

Redoubt

Baptist Road

WASHINGTON'S QUARTERS

Ford

Valley Creek Road

Valley Creek

KNOX'S QUARTERS

LAFAYETTE'S QUARTERS

STIRLING'S QUARTERS

Yellow Springs Road

0 Miles   0.5
0 Kilometers   0.5

© 2016 Jeffrey L. Ward

house or hut to cover them till they could be built, and submitting to it without a murmur is a mark of patience and obedience which in my opinion can scarce be paralleled."

By that winter, the famed "Spirit of 1776" had long since passed. Now that the Revolution had become a long-term war, most American males had decided to leave the job of fighting for their nation's liberty to others. A quota system had been instituted by which each of the states was responsible for providing a designated number of soldiers to the Continental army. In Connecticut, for example, the militiamen in a community were divided into groups (known as squads) according to how much taxable property they owned, with each squad responsible for providing a soldier to the army. A very rich person might have a squad of his own while three less wealthy citizens might make up another squad. If, as was usually the case, no one in the squad was willing to serve in the army, they hired a substitute, which was how Joseph Plumb Martin ended up back in the army.

As it turned out, Martin, having been born in America, was the exception. After the Battle of Brandywine, a British officer listed the nationality of the rebel prisoners. If this list is any indication, most of the soldiers in Washington's army had been born not in America but in England, Ireland, and Germany, with only 82 of the 315 prisoners (approximately 25 percent) listed as native born. This meant that while the vast majority of the country's citizens stayed at home, the War for Independence was being waged, in large part, by newly arrived immigrants. Those native-born Americans who by mid-1777 were serving in the army tended to be either African Americans, Native Americans, or what one historian has called "free white men on the move," such as Joseph Plumb Martin.

They did not have the education and social standing of the zealous patriots who had served during the early years of the Revolution, but they would become the battle-hardened backbone of the Continental army. They would also earn their commander's unwavering respect and even affection. Like Washington, they were in this war until the end.

On December 18 Washington ordered his army to begin building "soldiers' huts" in the hill-surrounded hollow of Valley Forge. Just sixteen by fourteen feet, with log walls that were six feet high and with a single wooden fireplace in the back, each structure was to house twelve men. But building accommodations was the least of his army's problems. By the end of December, Washington had no way to feed his men. "Unless some great and capital change suddenly takes place," he wrote, his army of approximately twelve thousand men "must inevitably be reduced to one or other of these three things: starve, dissolve, or disperse."

Due, in large part, to the neglect of Congress (not to mention the apathetic performance of the outgoing quartermaster, Thomas Mifflin), the army's support system had been allowed to collapse. The steady supply of meat and other provisions that was to have flowed into Valley Forge on a daily basis had stopped almost completely. Regiment after regiment took up the call of "NO MEAT! NO MEAT!" as officers worried that they might soon have a full-scale mutiny on their hands.

The needless suffering of the army at Valley Forge prompted Washington to address Congress with uncharacteristic candor and emotion. "I can assure those gentlemen," he wrote to President Henry Laurens, "that it is a much easier and less distressing thing to draw remonstrances in a comfortable room by a good fireside than to occupy a cold bleak hill and sleep under frost and snow. . . . Although they seem to have little feeling for the naked and distressed soldier, I feel superabundantly for them, and from my soul pity those miseries, which it is neither in my power to relieve or prevent."

Having reconciled himself to conducting a defensive war against the British, he had decided to take the offensive in his dealings with Congress. Washington, it turned out, had finally found his element. Where he had so often faltered and equivocated on the battlefield, he entered the political fray in the winter of 1777–78 with a forceful and almost ruthless relish that few could have anticipated—especially Thomas Conway, Horatio Gates, and Thomas Mifflin.

By December Gates had learned that a copy of the letter to him from Thomas Conway had apparently made its way to Washington. Unaware that his own adjutant was the source of the Conway quote, Gates immediately assumed that Hamilton had made copies of his private correspondence while visiting his Albany headquarters in early November. He decided to write directly to Congress with the claim that his "letters have been stealingly copied." His apparent hope was that the revelation and eventual scandal would add to the host of troubles that Congress had already inflicted upon the commander in chief.

It was hardly necessary. In addition to ignoring Washington's objections and promoting Conway to major general, Congress had determined that Conway should be inspector general of the newly reconstituted Board of War, the body that was to oversee the reorganization of the Continental army. But that was not all. Horatio Gates was to serve as the board's president while James Wilkinson (who had been awarded, as requested, the brevet rank of brigadier general) was to become the board's secretary. According to Washington's friend and physician Dr. James Craik, the strategy of the pro-Gates faction in Congress was now obvious. Although "they dare not appear openly as your enemy," they hoped to "throw such obstacles and difficulties in your way as to force you to resign."

What the Gates faction did not know was that Washington had an extremely well-placed spy. One of the commander in chief's aides was a twenty-three-year-old South Carolinian named John Laurens, whose father, Henry, happened to be the new president of the Continental Congress. John had been educated at the finest schools in France, Switzerland, and England. He had returned to America to join the Continental army, and had been wounded at both Brandywine and Germantown. Throughout the winter of 1777–78, John and his father, whom John called his "dearest friend," carried on a secret correspondence that did more to save America, it could be argued, than any of the much-heralded spy rings of the latter stages of the Revolution.

Henry Laurens, like his son, was well educated; he was also one of the wealthiest plantation owners in South Carolina. One of the reasons he had been elected president after John Hancock's resignation was that he had so far refused to align himself with any faction; he also kept his own counsel when it came to the relative merits of the army's commander in chief. But as Laurens made clear to his son, he was convinced that Washington was essential to holding the country together, especially since in the winter of 1778, Congress, through a combination of indifference, self-interest, and factionalism, had almost ceased to function.

"Our whole frame is shattered," Henry warned his son on January 8, 1778. "We are tottering and without the immediate exertions of wisdom and fortitude we must fall flat down." The states, and by extension the American people, appeared to have lost interest in supporting their national government. That winter in York, attendance in Congress hovered at around seventeen delegates (less than a third of a full roster), bottoming out, on occasion, at a paltry thirteen members. Gone were the times when men like Franklin, Jefferson, and Adams had worked together to create historic documents like the Declaration of Independence, which, as a point of comparison, had been signed by fifty-six members of Congress.

The most immediate danger, however, came from the pro-Gates faction's attempts to undermine Washington, which John Laurens reported had "affect[ed] the general very sensibly." In truth, there was little Washington's critics could do without publicly declaring that they wanted to replace him with Gates, and no one in the winter of 1778, with the exception of Thomas Conway, was willing to go that far. Rather than an outright ouster attempt, the Conway Cabal was more of a trial balloon—an act of passive aggression that tested Washington's ability to withstand the criticism that went with being the principal personage of the war. "In all such juntos," Henry Laurens reported, "there are prompters and actors, accommodators, candlesnuffers, shifters of scenes and mutes." If this group had a leader, it was Thomas Mifflin, whom Laurens described as "the pivot upon which the late mischiefs have turned," and for whom "patriotism [is] the stalking horse to [his] private interests."

The Conway Cabal was too loosely organized to be a significant threat, but that did not prevent "the junto" from being a frustratingly persistent irritation throughout the winter of 1778. "To break the combination is a work not to be easily, nor suddenly, performed," Laurens counseled his son. "There is no other measure so likely to defeat the projects against your friend as a steady perseverance in duty." In other words, Washington should go about his business as best he could, and the cabal would eventually die a natural death.

In a matter of months, the twenty-year-old Marquis de Lafayette had become one of Washington's favorite officers. Not only was he brave (according to Nathanael Greene, "the Marquis is determined to be in the way of danger"), he was loyal, and on December 30 he wrote the letter that sealed their friendship. According to Lafayette, the commander in chief's congressional critics were "stupid men who without knowing a single word about war undertake to judge you, to make ridiculous comparisons. They are infatuated with Gates without thinking of the different circumstances, and believe that attacking is the only thing necessary to conquer. . . . If you were lost for America, there is nobody who could keep the army and the Revolution [together] for [another] six months." From here on in, Lafayette promised, "I am . . . fixed to your fate, and I shall follow it and sustain it as well by my sword as by all means in my power."

The next day Washington responded in kind, declaring that "it will ever constitute part of my happiness to know that I stand well in your opinion. . . . We must not in so great a contest, expect to meet with nothing but sunshine. I have no doubt but that everything happens so for the best; that we shall triumph over all our misfortunes, and shall, in the end, be ultimately happy; when, my dear marquis, if you will give me your company in Virginia, we will laugh at our past difficulties and the folly of others." With the emotional support of a young French officer whom he came to regard as a surrogate son and with the just as vital political support of the president of Congress, Washington directed his attention to saving his army from ruin.

On January 25, Rhode Island colonel Israel Angell ordered a coffin to be built for a soldier who had died the night before in the icy encampment at Valley Forge. In his journal Angell described the men under his command as "poor naked souls destitute of money and every necessity of life," who were being "struck off on the list of time, one, two, and three in the space of twenty-four hours."

Amid this sad and poignant scene of human suffering, Washington and his aides worked to ensure that the Continental army never again experienced the hardships that had been thrust upon it by a Congress that remained infuriatingly distrustful of its very existence. Over the course of the next few months, Valley Forge acquired the look of a surprisingly formidable fortress. A series of earthen walls and redoubts provided protection to the east and south, while the Schuylkill River served as a buffer to the north and the cliffs of Valley Creek formed a natural barrier to the west. At the extreme northwest corner of the triangular-shaped encampment, at the confluence of Valley Creek and the Schuylkill, Washington had established his headquarters in a forge owner's summerhouse of fieldstone.

At this stone house, where on February 8 he was joined by his wife,

Martha, Washington created a kind of think tank composed of young and brilliant men who were, through a combination of audacity and naïveté, willing to think creatively about the fundamental questions of military and civil governance. Working together in a sixteen-foot-square room heated by a single fireplace, Washington and his aides labored day and night to produce the immense, incredibly detailed, and eloquently written document (which takes up thirty pages of dense type in Washington's collected works) that was to serve as the blueprint by which Congress might reorganize the army. From creating the equivalent of a lifetime pension plan for the officers to finding a way to provide a steady and dependable stream of provisions and clothing for the common soldiers, the document succeeded brilliantly in addressing what were termed "the numerous defects in our present military establishment."

Originally, the Board of War was to have tackled the stupendous task of remaking the army, but realizing that the current political squabble made it impossible for Washington and Gates to work effectively together, Congress selected a committee of delegates specifically chosen to travel to Valley Forge and eventually make the appropriate recommendations after being presented with Washington's imposing dossier. Even those members not predisposed to view Washington's proposals in a positive light, such as Massachusetts's Francis Dana, came away deeply impressed by the integrity and immense amount of labor Washington had applied to the task. As Henry Laurens had advised, Washington was slowly but surely proving that he, more than any other individual, was essential to the successful prosecution of the war, even as his soldiers—due to no fault of his own—were literally dying around him.

At the center of the talented group of young men who constituted Washington's military family were John Laurens and Alexander Hamilton. Hamilton had grown up in poverty on the Caribbean island of St. Kitts. Laurens had grown up on his father's rice plantation near Charleston, South Carolina. Both men were intimately familiar with African slavery and both believed that it was incompatible with the ideals of liberty and freedom for which they were fighting. For America to be truly free, slavery must come to an end, and Laurens believed he knew how it could one day come about.

On January 14, as he and his fellow aides prepared for the arrival of the delegation from Congress, he wrote to his father with a proposal:

"Cede me a number of your able bodied men slaves instead of leaving me a fortune." With these men, John proposed to create a company of black soldiers that would test the efficacy of a bold new plan he had devised: to eradicate the institution of slavery by offering the promise of freedom to any enslaved man who was willing to serve in the Continental army for the duration of the war. "I would bring about a two-fold good," he wrote. "First, I would advance those who are unjustly deprived of the rights of mankind to a state which would be a proper gradation between abject slavery and perfect liberty, and besides I would reinforce the defenders of liberty with a number of gallant soldiers."

His father immediately wanted to know what Washington thought of the proposal. Washington, John claimed, had not dismissed it out of hand. Although in the days ahead, his father's doubts and the rush of events moved him to set the plan aside, John was not finished with the proposal and would ultimately take it all the way to the South Carolina legislature, where, as his father had predicted, it went nowhere. This did not change the fact that in the winter of 1778, at one of the lowest points of the war, something extraordinary was happening at Washington's headquarters in Valley Forge.

In the meantime, as Henry Laurens had also predicted, the pro-Gates faction began to show signs of internal discord. In a letter to Washington in late December, Conway dared to mock the commander in chief by referring to him as "the Great Washington." A copy of the letter made its way to Congress, and soon even Conway's proponents began to question his judgment. In January, in response to a series of increasingly acrimonious letters from Gates, Washington finally revealed that the general's own adjutant and secretary to the Board of War, James Wilkinson, had been the source of the leak about the Conway letter. What Washington later referred to as "the most absurd contradictions" of Gates's response must have been roundly enjoyed by the commander in chief and his staff. Wilkinson subsequently learned that Gates had "denounced me as the betrayer of Conway's letter . . . in the grossest language," and in February Wilkinson challenged his once-beloved general to a duel. But before pistols had been raised in a graveyard in York, the two former intimates tearfully embraced and were, at least for the moment, reconciled.

On February 19 Gates raised the white flag, solemnly proclaiming in a letter to Washington "that I am of no faction" and pleading with him not to "spend another moment upon this subject." By that point a virtual squadron of Washington loyalists were making it known to anyone they suspected of infidelity to His Excellency that treachery would not be tolerated. Lafayette, whom the Board of War had attempted to woo with the promise of a wintertime campaign into Canada that never materialized, gleefully forced Gates and Conway into toasting Washington's health. Henry Knox ventured all the way to John Adams's home in Braintree, where it became apparent to Adams that "the design of his visit was . . . to sound me in relation to General Washington." Adams passed the test by declaring him "the center of our Union." The Virginian Daniel Morgan, just back from Saratoga, so forcefully badgered Board of War member Richard Peters that Peters feared for his life. In Virginia, a host of Washington supporters teamed up to give the delegate Richard Henry Lee a similar treatment while Patrick Henry passed along an unsigned letter he had received that was critical of Washington. Washington's aides determined that the letter's handwriting revealed it to have come from the pen of the Philadelphia doctor Benjamin Rush, who may also have been behind an anonymous account of Washington's many blunders that had been left on the steps of Congress.

It had been a difficult and trying four months, but Washington was now confident that "the machinations of this junto will recoil upon their own heads." Five days after receiving Gates's plea to end the controversy, he replied that he was willing to bury their past differences "in silence, and as far as future events will permit, oblivion."

As the Conway Cabal raged and the soldiers at Valley Forge suffered from disease and a lack of food, the inventor David Bushnell prepared to have one more go at the British. Having failed to sink Admiral Howe's flagship in New York Harbor with an explosive device transported by the one-man submersible *Turtle*, Bushnell had decided to simplify his approach. Eliminating the submarine entirely, he had developed a large floating keg filled with gunpowder that was designed to explode when it struck against the side of an enemy ship. The plan was to release fifty of these hundred-pound kegs upriver of the British fleet, which had been secured along the Philadelphia waterfront for the winter, and hope that the current carried the kegs to their target.

On the morning of January 6, a work detail under General Sullivan launched Bushnell's kegs into the river. If just one of these kegs exploded against the side of an enemy ship, it might initiate a chain reaction along the tightly packed line of vessels that would soon engulf the Philadelphia waterfront in a maelstrom of fire and smoke. Judging by the explosion of the *Augusta,* the collective destructive power contained in the powder magazines of the British fleet was enough to potentially level a good portion of the city.

What Bushnell had not taken into account was the perimeter of logs that the British had laid around their ships to protect them from the ice floes that floated up and down the river with the tide. The kegs' progress down the river also proved to be much slower than he'd expected, and the sun had begun to rise by the time the first of the explosive devices arrived at the waterfront. Curious as to what the kegs contained, a Philadelphia bargeman hauled one of them out of the water only to have it explode in his arms, killing him and the onlookers who had gathered around him.

Panic soon erupted in the city, with someone starting the rumor that the kegs contained American soldiers, who much like the Greeks in the Trojan horse, were about to emerge from their little boats and fall upon the city. Clearer heads soon prevailed, and British marksmen began firing on the kegs, which burst harmlessly in the middle of the Delaware. A Hessian officer commented that "the sight of some fifty of these little machines exploding one by one was as beautiful as the enemy's designs were destructive." Thus ended what was later dubbed the Battle of the Kegs.

In the January 20 letter accompanying Benedict Arnold's new commission as major general, Washington attributed the communication's delay to "the situation of my papers and the want of blank commissions." It was not the most convincing of excuses, but the letter also contained a paragraph of genuine concern and admiration. "May I venture to ask whether you are upon your legs again," Washington wrote, "and if you are not, may I flatter myself that you will be soon? There is none who wishes more sincerely for this event than I do, or who will receive the information with more pleasure. . . . As soon as your situation will permit, I request that you will repair to this army, it being my earnest wish to have your services in the ensuing campaign. In hopes of this, I have set you down in an arrangement now under consideration, and for a command, which, I trust, will be agreeable to yourself and of great advantage to the public."

Not until March 12, by which time he'd been transported from Albany to Middletown, Connecticut, where his sons attended school, did Arnold reply. He would have answered earlier, he wrote, "had the situation of my wounds permitted my forming any judgment when I should be able to take the field." As it turned out, he had suffered a setback. Although his fractured leg was healing quite nicely, some previously undetected bone splinters created by the bullet on October 7 had begun to work their way through his reopened leg wound. If he was ever to walk again, the splinters had to be extracted. "This my surgeon assures me will be a work of time," he wrote, "perhaps two and possibly five or six months." Wishing Washington all success, Arnold promised that "as soon as my wounds will permit . . . I will immediately repair to headquarters."

Disappointed not only by the slow progress of his wounded leg but by the prospect of missing the coming campaign, Arnold returned to an old obsession: "the heavenly Miss Deblois." Even though she had rebuffed him in no uncertain terms the year before, he wrote to her on April 8:

> Twenty times have I taken my pen to write to you, and as often has my trembling hand refused to obey the dictates of my heart. A heart which has often been calm and serene amidst the clashing of arms and all the din and horrors of war trembles with diffidence and the fear of giving offense when it attempts to address you on a subject so important to its happiness. . . . Neither time, absence, misfortunes, nor your cruel indifference have been able to efface the deep impression your charms have made, and will you doom a heart so true, so faithful, to languish in despair . . . ? Dear Betsey, suffer that heavenly bosom (which surely cannot know itself the cause of misfortune without a sympathetic pang) to expand with friendship at last and let me know my fate.

By April 26 "dear Betsey" had once again made it clear that Arnold should look elsewhere for the love and support for which he so desperately yearned. That did not prevent him from writing one more time, claiming that "if fame allows me any share of merit, I am in a great measure indebted for it to the pure and exalted passion your charms have inspired me with." Just to prove that he would not take no for an answer, he included a letter addressed "to your Mama for your Papa," with which he hoped to "request his sanction to my addresses." It was an embarrassing display that underlined the miserable depths to which Arnold had sunk. Even though his leg was months away from being anywhere close to serviceable, he could no longer remain an uninvolved spectator. He must head south and rejoin Washington's army.

In early February the already grim conditions in the American camp at Valley Forge had only worsened. By the end of the month more than a thousand Continental soldiers had died of disease, cold, and malnutrition. Although the soldiers displayed extraordinary fortitude and endurance, there had been several near revolts, and Washington realized that he needed to find some way to provide his men with immediate relief. It was the last thing Nathanael Greene wanted to do, but begrudgingly he agreed to assume the role of quartermaster.

The countryside had been almost stripped of provisions by the British, but Greene was able to establish at least a trickle of supplies into Valley Forge. "The inhabitants cry out and beset me from all quarters," Greene wrote to Washington on February 15, "but like Pharaoh I harden my heart." By March, with the onset of spring, fresh supplies could be more easily secured, and the crisis began to pass. Washington could begin to rebuild. That did not prevent Congress from calling for an investigation of Mifflin's role as quartermaster, which meant that the former "pivot" of the Conway Cabal soon found himself embroiled in the same kind of controversy that he had once directed at the commander in chief.

That winter there had been a new and much-anticipated arrival at Valley Forge. Friedrich Wilhelm von Steuben, a forty-seven-year-old Prussian-born army officer who claimed to be a baron and an intimate of Frederick the Great, had volunteered to be what Thomas Conway should have been: the army's inspector general. Having been prepped by Benjamin Franklin in Paris, the baron knew exactly how to sell himself to Washington and his staff. Since John Laurens was fluent in French, he served as Steuben's interpreter and was soon providing his father with enthusiastic reports. "I think he would be the properest man we could choose for the office of inspector general," he wrote. "He seems to be perfectly aware of the disadvantages under which our army has labored from short enlistments and frequent changes; seems to understand what our soldiers are capable of, and is not so staunch a systematist as to be averse from adapting established forms to stubborn circumstances."

Incredibly, this overweight Prussian fraud, who had lied about almost all his qualifications, proved to be exactly what the soldiers of Washington's army needed. On March 25 Laurens wrote, "The baron discovers the greatest zeal, and an activity which is hardly to be expected at his years." A week later: "Baron Steuben is making a sensible progress with our soldiers. The officers seem to have a high opinion of him." Three weeks after that, on April 18, Steuben was still, according to Laurens, "exerting himself like a lieutenant anxious for promotion, and the good effects of his labor are visible." For his part, Joseph Plumb Martin remembered the spring at Valley Forge "as a continual drill."

On April 30 Washington learned of the treaty with France. The news of the British defeat at Saratoga had proven, once and for all, that the Americans were capable of winning the War of Independence. Recognizing a chance to revenge, if not recoup, their losses during the previous war in North America, France had decided that the time had come to form an alliance with the United States. On May 2 the agreement was read before Congress, and it was officially ratified on May 4. On May 6 a celebration was held at Valley Forge.

> Yesterday we celebrated the new alliance with as much splendor as the short notice would allow [John Laurens wrote to his father]. Divine service preceded the rejoicing. After a proper pause, the several brigades marched by their right to their posts in order of battle, and the line was formed with admirable rapidity and precision. Three salutes of artillery, thirteen each, and three general discharges of a running fire by the musketry, were given in honor of the king of France, the friendly European powers, and the United American States. Loud huzzas! The order with which the whole was conducted, the beautiful effect of the running fire, which was executed to perfection, the martial appearance of the troops, gave sensible pleasure to everyone present.

After a winter that had come dangerously close to destroying Washington and his army, the celebration marked a truly extraordinary turnaround.

Indeed, the prospects for the future were so bright that Nathanael Greene asked Washington whether he should stop collecting provisions. Washington told him to keep at it. "There may still be business enough to call for our most strenuous efforts," he cautioned.

All the while, Benedict Arnold, a crutch by his side and no doubt wincing with every jolt, rode in a carriage toward Valley Forge.

CHAPTER EIGHT

The Knight of the Burning Mountain

S he was seventeen and beautiful. In keeping with the latest fashions from London, a billowing cloud of intricately coiffed hair surrounded her slender face. For the last eight months, she and her two older sisters had been caught up in the whirl of dances, plays, horse races, and teas by which the officers of the British army had transformed the normally staid Philadelphia social scene. But there was more to the character of Peggy Shippen than mere frivolity. A friend of the family later reported that "she had too much good sense to be vain," and that she was "particularly devoted to her father, making his comfort her leading thought, often preferring to remain with him when evening parties and amusements would attract her sisters."

That fortunate father, Edward Shippen, had spent the last three years attempting to avoid all political entanglements. A former judge of the royal government's vice admiralty court, he had been from the start suspected of loyalist leanings. In the early years of the Revolution he had moved his family to a country house on the Schuylkill, where he had remained under surveillance by the Pennsylvania authorities, particularly after his son joined the British army in New Jersey. Paraphrasing a line from Joseph Addison's play *Cato,* Judge Shippen insisted that "in these times I shall consider a private station as a post of honor." Careful, accommodating, and kind, Shippen remained devoted to his children, and after a winter in British-occupied Philadelphia, he feared that his daughters' enthusiasms for the entertainments offered by the army's officers might have forever branded them as loyalists.

On May 8, 1778, the frigate *Porcupine* arrived at Philadelphia with dispatches for William Howe's replacement as commander in chief, Sir Henry Clinton. Clinton must abandon the city that his predecessor had devoted almost half a year to conquering. Five thousand British troops were to be dispatched from America that summer for an operation against French St. Lucia. Soon to become a skeleton of its former self, the British army in North America must be consolidated in New York.

Now that France had recognized the United States, what had previously been a colonial rebellion had become a world war. In the months ahead, Britain would find itself besieged on fronts as far away as India and as close to home as the English Channel as the focus of the conflict shifted from North America to the sugar-rich islands of the West Indies. As difficult as it may be to believe today, Britain's islands in the Caribbean were of considerably more economic importance in the eighteenth century than all thirteen American colonies combined.

There was nowhere in the world where money could be made at such a staggering clip as the Caribbean. In 1776 the British West Indies generated 4.25 million pounds of trade, almost three times what had been made by Great Britain's East India Company. France was just as dependent on her Caribbean possessions, which accounted for more than a third of all her overseas trade. If Britain could scoop up a few more of these precious islands from the French, it might provide a way to pay for what had so far been a financially ruinous war. Britain was even considering giving up entirely on its American possessions so that it could concentrate what resources it still had left to fighting the French. For Philadelphia's loyalists, it was almost beyond comprehension: after a mere eight-month British occupation, they were about to suffer the same reversal of fortune that their counterparts in New Jersey and Boston had already experienced and get handed back to the patriots.

On May 18, just before this devastating news became public knowledge, the British army staged what its organizer, a twenty-eight-year-old captain with a poet's heart named John André, described as "the most splendid entertainment . . . ever given by an army to their general." It might be true that William Howe was leaving Philadelphia under less than auspicious circumstances. But that did not change the fact that he had, according to André, "universally endeared himself to those under his command."

Beginning with a regatta on the Delaware River and ending thirteen hours later with a dance in a hall lined with eighty-five mirrors, the meticulously choreographed celebration created by André included a lavish dinner served by thirty-five enslaved Africans (each with a silver collar around his neck), a midnight fireworks display, and on a square section of grass near the Philadelphia waterfront, a medieval jousting match.

For an impressionable seventeen-year-old girl, who had shared in her father's anxious attempts to trim his sails to the ever-shifting political winds, the pageantry and excess of André's Mischianza (Italian for medley or mixture) appears to have offered Peggy Shippen a captivating refuge from the troubling uncertainties of the real world. Prior to the arrival of the British, a new state constitution had created the most radical form of government in the United States: a unicameral state legislature that enabled Pennsylvania's farmers and tradespeople to challenge the wealthy merchants and landowners who had previously dominated the politics of the colony.

But as quickly became clear in Philadelphia, a revolution aimed at freeing a country from political and economic oppression had the potential to create a new form of tyranny. In this case, a purely democratic form of government, unhindered by any checks and balances, allowed the majority to run roughshod over the liberties of the minority. Whether they be the once privileged members of Philadelphia's upper class, like the Shippens, or the city's pacifist Quakers, who for religious reasons refused to sign the state's loyalty oath, anyone suspected of "an equivocal neutrality" or, even worse, outright "Toryism" was put under careful watch and in several cases exiled from the state. Now, with the British about to evacuate the city, the radical patriots were about to return to power with a vengeance. If the past few years in Philadelphia were any indication, a shrill insistence on conformity was about to descend upon the city. With that prospect looming over the festivities, Peggy could not be faulted for allowing herself to indulge, if just for a day, in the collective fantasy presented by the Mischianza.

Along with her two sisters, she had been given a starring role in the marvelous nonsense surrounding a "tilting tournament" between the Knights of the Blended Rose and the Knights of the Burning Mountain. Dressed in a scandalous Turkish costume, she was to be championed by a knight whose shield depicted a bay leaf and the motto "Unchangeable."

Shippen family tradition claimed that at the last minute Peggy's father prevented his three daughters from participating in the Mischianza. André's own account of the festivities, however, suggests that the Shippen sisters were there. Whether or not Peggy Shippen watched from the stands as two British officers dressed in satin and silk battled to a courteous draw is ultimately irrelevant. In a matter of months she was to meet the real-life equivalent of the Knight of the Burning Mountain: a major general with an injured leg whose love of finery and impatience with civil authority was about to set him on a crash course with the radicals of Philadelphia.

The passage of the Declaration of Independence had forced Americans to make a choice—either side with the newly created United States or declare their continued loyalty to the British king. Many, if not most, American citizens were politically apathetic—their highest priority was their own and their family's welfare. All they wanted was to be allowed to lead the contented and peaceful lives they had enjoyed prior to the Revolution. But now they had to declare which side they were on. Although the Continental army's loyalty should have been self-evident, Congress determined that the time had come for its officers to take a formal oath of allegiance.

On May 30, at the artillery park of Valley Forge, Henry Knox administered the oath to Benedict Arnold. By then Arnold had received the gift of a new pair of epaulets and a sword knot from Washington "as a testimony of my sincere regard and approbation of your conduct." In the letter accompanying the gift, Washington had urged Arnold not to endanger his recovery "by coming out too soon." But there was no stopping Benedict Arnold. Even though his leg was not even close to being fully healed and it would be another two years before he could ride a horse, he had joined the rejuvenated Continental army in Valley Forge. Now Washington had to figure out what to do with a fighting general who could not fight.

And so, perhaps with the two new epaulets gracing his shoulders, Arnold laid his hand on the Bible and vowed to "support, maintain, and defend the . . . United States against . . . King George the Third . . . and will serve the said United States in the office . . . which I now hold, with fidelity, according to the best of my skill and understanding." He was attended by two aides. Matthew Clarkson, just nineteen, had been with him at Saratoga. David Salisbury Franks, thirty-eight, had been living in Montreal when he first met Arnold and became paymaster of the Continental army during its retreat from Canada. He had since spent several years in Philadelphia. Loyal and sometimes as volatile as his general, Franks had an excellent education and, like Clarkson, who came from a leading New York family, brought a decidedly aristocratic flair to Arnold's official family.

By early June it had become obvious that the British were preparing to evacuate Philadelphia. Having been there during the evacuation of Montreal, Arnold and Franks (who had both dedicated a considerable amount of their own money to the American cause in Canada) knew that an army's leave-taking created not only chaos and dislocation but a considerable amount of economic opportunity. Since not just the British army but all those who considered themselves British subjects were about to leave Philadelphia, a host of traders were desperate to get their merchandise out of the city before the goods were confiscated by the returning Continental army. A shortage of transports meant that almost all available space had been taken up by the three thousand loyalists whom Clinton had promised to transport by water to New York. (Because of the lack of ships, Clinton had no choice but to delay sending the five thousand troops to the Caribbean until they had marched across New Jersey to New York.) Unable to take their goods with them, many merchants who had spent the winter in Philadelphia decided to venture out to Valley Forge, where they hoped to convince any Continental officer who would listen that their "true allegiance" was to the United States and that they needed a pass to ensure that their goods were not confiscated by suspicious American authorities once the British had withdrawn from the city.

One of the more stubborn supplicants was James Seagrove. The first time Seagrove had appeared at Valley Forge to plead his case, Baron von Steuben had ordered that he be physically ejected from camp. By early June he was back and appealing directly to Benedict Arnold. Seagrove and several partners had shares in a schooner that was loaded with an assortment of valuable trade goods. Seagrove was one of a large number of Americans whose loyalties shifted with whatever side happened to hold sway. He had been in New York during the Continental army's panicked retreat to Harlem after the British assault at Kips Bay, and Alexander Hamilton later testified that Seagrove had provided helpful advice about how Hamilton and his men might avoid the enemy. However, Seagrove had elected to spend the winter of 1778 in Philadelphia, and despite previous service in the Pennsylvania militia, he and his fellow investors had attempted to capitalize on the financial prospects created by the presence of the British army. Now, with the British about to leave, he hoped to sail his schooner out of Philadelphia with a pass that would allow the vessel to take shelter in an American port without running afoul of Continental officials.

By this point in his life, Arnold appears to have decided that after losing both his health and his fortune to his country, he must reclaim, as best he could, what was owed him. Arnold was not contemplating anything treasonous; he was simply attempting to recoup the considerable personal wealth he had devoted to a country that had not yet found a way to compensate him for his losses. In this, Arnold was by no means alone. Virtually every officer in the Continental army had reached the point where he had begun to wonder whether all the lost income and personal suffering had been worth it. Those who hadn't already resigned were often forced to pursue private economic opportunities, many of them ethically if not legally dubious, to make ends meet.

No one had a greater appreciation of the unhappy dilemma faced by an officer in the Continental army than Washington. In his memo to the congressional committee sent to Valley Forge back in January, he had challenged the commonly held view in Congress that a truly patriotic officer should be expected to put his own concerns aside when it came to serving his country. "Few men are capable of making a continual sacrifice of all views of private interest, or advantage, to the common good," Washington insisted. "It is in vain to exclaim against the depravity of human nature on this account—the fact is so, the experience of every age and nation has proved it, and we must in a great measure change the constitution of man before we can make it otherwise. No institution, not built on the presumptive truth of these maxims, can succeed." Washington then went on to describe what had been, in essence, Benedict Arnold's experience during the first three years of the Revolution.

> At the commencement of the dispute—in the first effusions of
> their zeal, and looking upon the service to be only temporary,
> they entered into it, without paying any regard to pecuniary, or

selfish considerations. But finding its duration to be much longer than they at first suspected, and that instead of deriving any advantage from the hardships and dangers, to which they were exposed, they on the contrary were losers by their patriotism and fell far short even of a competency to supply their wants, they have gradually abated in their ardor; and with many, an entire disinclination to the service under its present circumstances has taken place. . . . There can be no sufficient tie upon men, possessing such sentiments.

Arnold was not unique in having suffered financially during the war. But unlike many of his fellow officers, he was going to do something about it. After Congress's repeated refusals to grant him his proper rank; after being treated with such diabolical cunning by Gates and Wilkinson at Saratoga; and after almost losing his left leg to an enemy musket ball, he felt justified in taking advantage of whatever economic opportunities came his way.

On June 4 he granted James Seagrove his pass, a pass that appears to have given Arnold a stake in Seagrove's schooner the *Charming Nancy*. It was just one in an ever-growing number of get-rich schemes that Arnold embarked on in the months ahead, all of them assisted by the fact that on June 18, with the British about to leave Philadelphia, Washington named him military governor of Philadelphia. For someone of Arnold's proclivities, it was the perfect opportunity to engineer a series of insider deals— all of them as secret as possible—that took advantage of his status as the most powerful military figure in Philadelphia. Even before entering the city, Arnold drew up an agreement with his aide David Franks, instructing him to "purchase European and East India goods in the city of Philadelphia to any amount" with funds provided by Arnold and "not to make known to his most intimate acquaintance that the writer was concerned in the proposed purchase." Although as governor Arnold was supposed to control and, in the beginning at least, prohibit such purchases by others, he obviously did not feel such strictures should apply to himself.

Like many American mariners and merchants, Arnold's early revolutionary beliefs had been nurtured in the smuggling trade. For men like John Hancock in Boston and Arnold in New Haven, finding a way around the stifling economic restrictions imposed by the British government had been not only a financial necessity but an expression of patriotism, a finger in the eye of the British regime. Now that the Continental Congress in Philadelphia had proven to be, if anything, even more dysfunctional and unjust than the ministry in London, Arnold saw nothing disloyal in doing what Americans had always done: profit as best they could from whatever commercial circumstances presented themselves.

Even Quartermaster Nathanael Greene, who received a 1 percent commission on the transactions in his department that earned him, according to one estimate, a total of $175,000 during the Revolution, had his own secret agreements with investors. In one such contract, Greene stated that "it is my wish that no mortal should be acquainted with the persons forming the company except us three," since he thought it "prudent to appear as little in trade as possible. For however just and upright our conduct may be, the world will have suspicions to our disadvantage." Greene was discreet enough to keep such transactions secret. Discretion, however, had never been Arnold's strong suit.

During the last days of the British occupation, the Swiss artist Pierre Eugène du Simitière stopped by Captain John André's temporary residence in Philadelphia. Besides packing up his own belongings, André had decided that it was within his rights to include some objects from the considerable collection of the absent owner of the house, Benjamin Franklin. In addition to musical instruments, an account book, an electrical apparatus, and a set of china, André took the portrait of the venerable sage who had helped to negotiate the treaty with France. When Du Simitière objected, André simply smiled and continued about his business.

André had been educated in the finest schools in Europe. In addition to being handsome and well-read, he was a brilliant conversationalist who had socialized regularly with the Shippen girls and their extensive circle of friends. But as his confiscation of Benjamin Franklin's belongings might suggest, there was an edgier, even ruthless side to the British captain. Much like James Wilkinson, André had a talent for ingratiating himself with whoever happened to be in the best position to advance his career. The portrait of Franklin would find its way into the collection of André's commanding officer, General Charles Grey. (Not until the following century would the portrait be returned to the United States; it is now part of the presidential collection in the White House.) The Mischianza had been a ploy to express his high regard for William Howe. Although he and General Grey had several interesting years ahead of them, André would, perhaps inevitably, begin to find his way into the good graces of the new British commander in chief, Henry Clinton.

On the morning of June 18, Elizabeth Drinker, a mother of four and a lifelong member of the Society of Friends, awoke to discover that the British were gone. "Last night it was said there was 9,000 of the British troops . . . in town," she recorded in her diary. "This morning when we arose, there was not one red-coat to be seen. . . . [They] had not been gone a quarter of an hour before the American light horse entered the city. . . . The few [Americans] that came in today had drawn swords in their hands [and] galloped about the streets in a great hurry. Many were much frightened at their appearance."

That evening, Arnold set out in a carriage from Valley Forge with orders from Washington to "proceed to Philadelphia and take the command of the troops there." Arnold was to "preserve tranquility and order in the city, and give security to individuals of every class and description." In other words, he must make sure that the newly returned patriots did not take out their frustrations on the Philadelphians who had chosen to remain in the city even though it had been under enemy control.

Congress had not made it easy for the new military governor. As mandated by what was guaranteed to be an unpopular edict, Arnold must "prevent the removal, transfer, or sale of any goods, wares, or merchandise in possession of the inhabitants of the city" until Clothier General James Mease could determine what loyalist goods should be confiscated for use by the Continental army and what goods should be put up for sale. By June 23 Arnold had entered into a secret agreement with Mease and his deputy William West that those goods that didn't go to the army should be purchased by themselves (undoubtedly at a bargain price) and subsequently "sold for the joint equal benefit of the subscribers."

With the entry of France, the British had become desperate to end the war, even sending a peace commission with General Clinton to offer the Americans everything they could possibly want short of independence. Given that the British army was about to evacuate Philadelphia and begin a ninety-mile journey across New Jersey to Sandy Hook before being loaded onto transports and delivered back to New York, the Continental Congress saw no reason to accept the British offer.

For Clinton and his officers, it was a demeaning turn of events. Not only must they flee back to New York; if the French navy appeared in force that summer, they might even be required to abandon America altogether for the safety of Halifax, Nova Scotia. All of this had been unthinkable two years before when the British had hounded Washington and his broken army across New Jersey. Now the British were the ones who must retreat across the state, with Washington and his resurgent army hounding *them* as they struggled across what Clinton described as "a devoured country, inimical almost to man."

Since his soldiers were not going to be able to live off the land, they needed to bring their provisions. The resulting twelve-mile-long baggage train was, in Clinton's estimation, "wantonly enormous." Clinton divided his ten-thousand-man army into three groups, each of them large enough to hold off a sizable enemy attack force until assisted by one of the other groups. The Hessian general Knyphausen and four thousand men were to lead the column while Cornwallis commanded a two-thousand-man rear guard, leaving Clinton and four thousand men in the middle.

On the morning of June 19, Washington's army of thirteen thousand soldiers marched from Valley Forge. Many of his officers felt that they had one of the best opportunities of the war. Without placing their own army at unnecessary risk, they could attack a relatively isolated portion of Clinton's divided army. Others claimed that Washington's best policy was to let Clinton's army march across New Jersey as quickly as possible in anticipation of the British evacuating New York upon the arrival of the French fleet.

That was what Major General Charles Lee thought Washington should do, and in a council of war in Hopewell, New Jersey, on June 24, he advised the commander in chief to hold back. Until his recent release in a prisoner exchange, Lee had spent the last year and a half in confinement in New York. Sardonic, profane, and opinionated, Lee had been one of Washington's most outspoken critics at the time of his capture in December 1776. After having endured the machinations of the Conway Cabal during the winter of 1777–78, Washington might have been expected to greet the arrival of Charles Lee with a certain amount of caution and even distrust.

Instead, he had welcomed the returning general with what appeared to be genuine pleasure and had subsequently responded to Lee's frequent quibbles and complaints with commendable restraint. Thanking Lee for being a "fountain of candor," Washington claimed that "no man can be more sensible of the defects of our present arrangement than I am." At the council of war in Hopewell, the commander in chief seemed, from General Nathanael Greene's perspective, dangerously close to following Lee's advice.

The previous fall, Greene had been the one who had reminded Washington of the importance of not risking his army unnecessarily. But this, Greene insisted, was the exception to the rule. "If we suffer the enemy to pass through the Jerseys without attempting anything upon them," he wrote soon after the council of war, "I think we shall ever regret it. I cannot help thinking we magnify our difficulties beyond realities. . . . People expect something from us and our strength demands it. I am by no means for rash measures, but we must preserve our reputation. I think we can make a very serious impression without any great risk, and if it should amount to a general action I think the chance is greatly in our favor." Soon after receiving Greene's letter, Washington decided to attack.

Since Lee was the highest ranking of Washington's generals, he was the natural choice to lead the division that was to engage the rear of Clinton's column. But when presented with the opportunity, Lee deferred, claiming the command was "the more proper business of a young volunteering general," such as Lafayette, "than of the second in command in the army." But once Washington had drawn up plans for Lafayette to lead a small army of five thousand soldiers, Lee changed his mind. "My ceding it," he decided, "would . . . have an odd appearance." He now wanted the command.

Many generals might have responded to Lee's change of heart with irritation and even anger. Washington, however, remained remarkably unperturbed. "Your uneasiness . . . fills me with concern," he admitted, "as it is not in my power, fully, to remove it without wounding the feelings of the Marquis de Lafayette." But he had a solution. Lee would get the command and Lafayette would "proceed as if no change had happened," with Lee providing "every assistance and countenance in your power."

By reining in his own not-inconsiderable temper to a seemingly impossible degree, Washington had succeeded in calling an erratic and self-important general's bluff. When the attack began on the morning of June 28, all eyes would be on Charles Lee.

After his horrendous two weeks at Fort Mifflin in November, Joseph Plumb Martin had spent much of the winter on foraging duty in the Pennsylvania countryside. Now he was part of a group of light infantry who had spent the last few days shadowing the rear of the British column. By the time they reached Englishtown, New Jersey, the bulk of the Continental army had caught up with them. That morning Martin and his comrades set out toward Monmouth. Martin's brigade was to act in support of the division commanded by Charles Lee once Lee had launched his attack against the rear of the British column.

Between ten and eleven in the morning, Martin emerged from a narrow, tree-covered valley into an open field. The temperature was in the nineties, and he claimed that "the mouth of a heated oven seemed to me to be but a trifle hotter than this ploughed field; it was almost impossible to breathe." Up ahead he could hear "a few reports of cannon," but nothing to indicate that any significant fighting was taking place.

Suddenly Martin's brigade was ordered to fall back. Soon they were surrounded by retreating American soldiers from Lee's division. They had entered a wooded valley and had sat down in the shade alongside the road to let Lee's artillery pass by when Washington and his aides "crossed the road just where we were sitting." Washington asked one of Martin's officers "by whose order the troops were retreating." When he was told "by General Lee's," Washington was heard to say, "Damn him." It was, Martin remembered, "certainly very unlike him, but he seemed at the instant to be in a great passion; his looks if not his words seemed to indicate as much."

A year and a half before, Martin had been present when Washington erupted into an impotent fury as he attempted to stop the retreat of the Connecticut soldiers after the British assault on Kips Bay. This time, in the scorching heat of a New Jersey summer, it was going to be different.

Washington soon found Charles Lee and, according to John Laurens, "expressed his astonishment at the unaccountable retreat." The army's second-in-command was without a good answer. "Mr. Lee indecently replied that the attack was contrary to his advice and opinion in council." After pointing out that if he hadn't believed in the operation he should

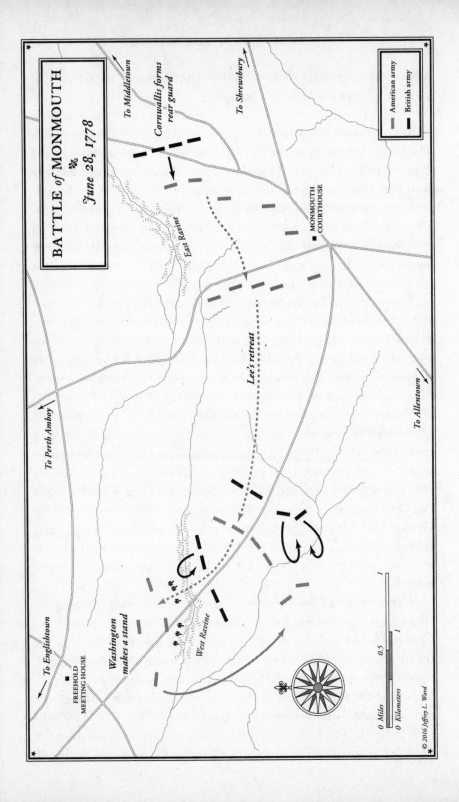

BATTLE *of* MONMOUTH
June 28, 1778

To Middletown

To Shrewsbury

Cornwallis forms
rear guard

East Ravine

MONMOUTH
COURTHOUSE

Lee's retreat

To Perth Amboy

To Allentown

To Englishtown

FREEHOLD
MEETING HOUSE

Washington
makes a stand

West Ravine

American army
British army

0 Miles   0.5   1
0 Kilometers   1

© 2016 Jeffry L. Ward

never have insisted on leading it, Washington set about turning the battle around.

Washington, it soon became clear, was in his element. "The commander in chief was everywhere," Greene wrote. "His presence gave spirit and confidence and his command and authority soon brought everything into order and regularity." Lafayette claimed that "never had I beheld so superb a man."

On a section of elevated ground bounded by a swamp on one side and a hill on the other, he prepared his army to meet the British onslaught. "In this spot," John Laurens wrote, "the action was hottest and there was considerable slaughter of British grenadiers." Try as they might, the British could not break through the stubborn American resistance. Thanks to Baron von Steuben, this was not the same army the British had fought at Brandywine and Germantown; they were now nearly as obstinate and well disciplined as their British and German opponents. Making the fighting all the more hellacious was the intense heat. "Fighting is hot work in cool weather," Martin wrote; "how much more so in such weather as it was on the 28th of June, 1778." Henry Clinton, who had by this point joined his grenadiers and artillery on a hillside overlooking the American position, later admitted that he was "near going raving mad with heat."

In the midst of the cannonade, Martin noticed that one of the American artillery crews included a husband-and-wife team. The woman was reaching for a cartridge when "a cannon shot from the enemy passed directly between her legs without doing any other damage than carrying away all the lower part of her petticoat." In the years to come, the woman artillerist whom Martin had seen on a hillside near the Monmouth Courthouse became the basis of the legend of Molly Pitcher.

Martin and his cohorts eventually had the satisfaction of forcing the British to retreat to the other side of a large ravine. They were tempted to continue the pursuit but found it impossible in the stifling heat. "We then laid ourselves down under the fences and bushes to take breath," he remembered, "for we had need of it."

From Clinton's perspective, what the Americans later touted as the Battle of Monmouth was a minor rearguard action that had virtually no impact on his army's march to Sandy Hook, during which he lost not a single wagon. The Americans, of course, had a very different view of what had transpired that day. John Laurens proudly proclaimed that at Monmouth, "the standards of liberty were planted in triumph on the field of battle."

Washington's real victory had been not over the British, but over Charles Lee. In the flurry of letters that followed the battle, Lee had the temerity to insist that "the success of the day was entirely owing" to the fact that he had ordered a retreat. Otherwise, "this whole army and the interests of America would have risked being sacrificed." A court-martial soon followed, and after being suspended from the army for a year, Lee attempted to lure Washington into a public war of words. But by then, even Washington's former enemies had to admit that His Excellency was now the Continental army's undisputed leader.

As if to emphasize the point, in early July, General John Cadwalader of Philadelphia, who had played an important role in the Second Battle of Trenton, challenged Washington's earlier nemesis Thomas Conway to a duel. A few weeks later, while still recovering from the bullet wound he had suffered through the cheek, Conway felt compelled to write Washington a letter of farewell: "My career will soon be over, therefore justice and truth prompt me to declare my last sentiments. You are in my eyes the great and the good man. May you long enjoy the love, veneration and esteem of these states whose liberties you have asserted by your virtues."

On the night after the Battle of Monmouth, Washington wrapped himself in his cloak and lay down under a tree amid his men. He had no way of knowing it then, but this was to be his last battlefield encounter until the Siege of Yorktown, more than three years in the future. The war was about to undergo a startling transformation as America's alliance with France created a whole new series of challenges and frustrations. On that night in Monmouth, Washington may already have begun to anticipate this dramatic shift.

Around midnight an officer approached. Fearful that he might wake the general, the officer hesitated, but Washington told him to come forward. "I laid here *to think*," he explained, "and not to sleep."

Arnold appears to have initially believed that his new role as military governor of Philadelphia would allow him to focus on both his physical and financial recovery. Almost immediately, however, he realized that governing this violently divided city was no easy sinecure.

The city was a shambles. The British had used the State House as a prison, and the floors of its once immaculate rooms were heaped with human waste. The newly returned delegates of the Continental Congress had to meet temporarily in nearby College Hall until the filth could be removed. Other public buildings and "genteel houses" had been used for stables by the British, who cut holes in the floors so that the dung could be shoveled into the cellars. According to the New Hampshire delegate Josiah Bartlett, "The country northward of the city for several miles is one common waste, the houses burnt, the fruit trees and others cut down and carried off, fences carried away, gardens, and orchards destroyed."

Over the course of the next few weeks, thousands of citizens who had spent the winter outside Philadelphia flooded back into the ravaged city. Not unexpectedly, they had little sympathy for anyone who had fraternized with the enemy. During the Independence Day celebrations on July 4, the revelers directed their outrage at a woman whose hairstyle identified her as a British collaborator. The Quaker Elizabeth Drinker recorded in her journal that "a very high headdress was exhibited through the streets this afternoon on a dirty woman with a mob after her, with drums, etc., by way of ridiculing that very foolish fashion."

Even for the most tactful and respectful of officers, the post of military governor of Philadelphia would have been a challenge. In addition to suffering in the convulsive aftermath of British occupation, the city was soon the scene of frequent clashes between the Continental Congress and the Supreme Executive Council of the state's legislature as these two political bodies vied for dominance. For Arnold, who knew no other mode than full-out attack, it was an entirely hopeless situation, especially given his weakened physical condition. Not only was his leg a concern, he was soon afflicted by what his aide David Franks described as "a violent oppression in the stomach."

The army officer Elias Boudinot called on Arnold several times during his first days in Philadelphia. He found him, he later remembered, "in a state of health, which I thought rendered him unequal to the fatigue of his then station. He was much crowded with business and I ventured to warn him of ill consequences of so much attention to it." In mid-July, Arnold made one of several missteps when he hosted a ball for the citizens of the city but failed to invite the many Continental army officers then in Philadelphia. "I hear General Arnold has rendered himself not a little

unpopular," Nathanael Greene reported. "I am very sorry for this circumstance, as it will render his situation disagreeable, owing to the
clamor and cabal of those who conceive themselves injured."

Seeking to alleviate the immense and unwelcome pressures of his current station, Arnold returned to an idea he had first proposed to both
Horatio Gates and Philip Schuyler a year and a half earlier. On July 19 he
wrote Washington to find out what he thought about his taking on "a
command in the navy." Here, once again, is the great what-if of Arnold's
career. Had he at this pivotal stage been allowed to free himself from the
hell that had become his life in Philadelphia, had he applied his talents to
a pursuit that while fulfilling his desire to serve his country also lined his
pockets, he might have become one of the immortal heroes of the
Revolution.

As he eventually proposed to Congress, he hoped to lead a naval expedition to Barbados and Bermuda. In a variation of John Laurens's earlier plan, Arnold described how he would free the islands' slaves and
enlist them on American privateers that used the islands as bases against
the enemy. It was an ambitious and fascinating proposal, but Congress
was ultimately unwilling to sanction the mission, especially since Washington, who admitted that his knowledge of the sea was limited, had little enthusiasm for it.

But by then Arnold had decided that Philadelphia wasn't that bad
after all. Once again, he had fallen in love.

On July 14 Washington received a letter from the French vice admiral
Charles Hector, Comte d'Estaing, who had just arrived at the mouth of
the Delaware River with a fleet of twelve ships of the line and five frigates.
It was, in Washington's words, "a great and striking event" that had instantly given France—and by extension, the United States—naval superiority in North America. But already an unsurpassed opportunity had
been squandered. For reasons that were not entirely clear, d'Estaing had
taken an outrageously long eighty-seven days to navigate the Atlantic—
more than twice the duration of even a relatively slow passage. If the
French had succeeded in completing anything close to a normal crossing,
they might have bottled up the British in Philadelphia and forced the
Howe brothers to surrender. Speed, however, was not to be d'Estaing's
strong suit.

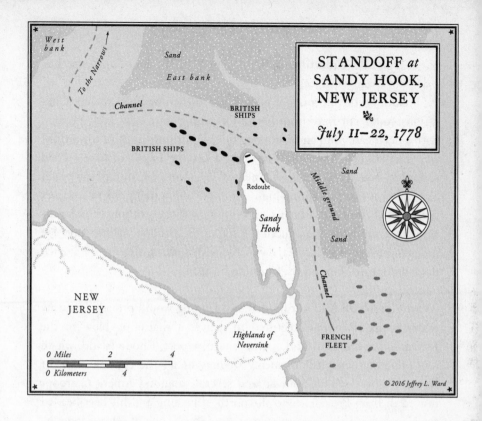

On the evening of July 11, d'Estaing arrived at Sandy Hook, the out-
cropping of barrier beach where ships about to sail into New York Harbor
waited for a favorable combination of wind and tide. By that time, Clinton had succeeded in getting his army to New York City while Admiral
Howe, who had delayed his return to England, worked feverishly to prepare his relatively small fleet for the anticipated French attack. Howe had
decided to anchor what warships he had in a defensive line along the
channel that led from the Hook to the Narrows. D'Estaing's huge ships
outgunned the British fleet by 850 to 534. But they would have to work
their way one by one past the forbidding line of British vessels that Howe
had converted into what were essentially floating batteries.

For the next ten days, the French fleet lay at anchor just outside Sandy
Hook while d'Estaing resupplied his ships and pondered what to do next.
Before he could confront the British, his ships must work their way over
the sandbar that extended from the tip of Sandy Hook. D'Estaing's
American pilots could only guarantee twenty-two feet of water over the

bar at high tide. Unfortunately his flagship, the 196-foot *Languedoc,* had a draft of twenty-five feet.

Finally, on the morning of July 22, the French weighed anchor. Conditions could not have been better for sailing into New York Harbor, with a northeast wind and incoming tide all pushing his ships toward the city. But as they approached the bar, d'Estaing began to have second thoughts. The depth of the channel was a concern (Admiral Howe later claimed that due to a spring high tide there was actually thirty feet over the bar), but it may have been a close-up view of the awaiting British warships that ultimately convinced d'Estaing to abandon the attempt. He ordered the *Languedoc* to bear away, and with dusk coming on, the French fleet disappeared behind the southern horizon.

Washington still held out hope that d'Estaing would provide his army with the naval support required to deliver a shattering blow to the British—if not at New York, perhaps at Newport, Rhode Island, which was presently occupied by enemy soldiers under the command of Sir Robert Pigot. As John Sullivan and several thousand American troops moved in from Providence to the north, d'Estaing and his fleet headed for Newport on the western side of Aquidneck, one of several large islands contained within the southern reaches of Narragansett Bay. The French had just entered the bay and begun cooperative operations with the Americans when Admiral Howe suddenly appeared to the south with a fleet of thirty-one ships, most of them much smaller than the French vessels. Rather than risk being trapped in the harbor, d'Estaing decided to engage Howe in the naval battle that might win or lose the war.

On the morning of August 10, the French sailed out of Newport to meet the British. For a day and a night, the two enemy fleets cautiously pursued one another as each admiral attempted to establish the same "weather gage" that Benedict Arnold had used to his advantage at Valcour Island. By the following day, after making a dramatic turn to the north, Howe seemed on the verge of gaining the longed-for upwind position when the wind began to build to gale force. By the end of the day, rain squalls had reduced visibility to almost nothing. D'Estaing ordered his fleet to sail south in search of sea room, and by night it was blowing so hard that both fleets were thinking only of their own survival.

What was later called "the Great Storm" wreaked tremendous havoc on both fleets, but no vessel suffered greater damage than d'Estaing's flagship, the ninety-gun *Languedoc*. By 4:00 a.m. on August 12, she had lost her bowsprit and all her masts when her rudder snapped. The immense ship wallowed so violently in the towering seas that several cannonballs shook loose and began to roll wildly across the deck. After several sailors were hurled over the side, lines were strung across the deck to provide the crew with something to cling to as the vessel threatened to tear itself apart. And then, in the late afternoon hours of August 13, they saw an enemy ship.

Around 6:00 p.m., as the *Languedoc* tossed helplessly in the waves, the forty-four-gun *Renown* approached from astern and fired a broadside into the French ship's transom. Cannonballs crashed through the windows of d'Estaing's stateroom and, after traveling the full length of the ship, buried themselves in the timbers of the bow. The French moved two cannons into the admiral's quarters, and after exchanging gunfire for several hours, the British captain decided to hold off until morning. When at dawn two French ships appeared on the horizon, the *Renown* gave up the attack.

A week later, when the *Languedoc* limped into Newport, d'Estaing was in no mood to continue the siege. Washington's aide John Laurens acted as an interpreter. "Imagine the cruel situation of the count," he wrote, "to see his ship thus insulted after having arrived in the midst of the English squadron and preparing for combat in which victory was inevitably his; but a most dreadful storm of which he had no idea dispersed everything."

Abandoning Sullivan's now overmatched army, which was forced to make a desperate but ultimately well-executed retreat off Aquidneck Island, d'Estaing and his fleet sailed to Boston for repairs. By November they were on their way to the Caribbean for the winter. Having wasted two opportunities to do battle with the smaller British fleet, the French had turned their attention south. It did not bode well for the future of the French-American alliance.

Washington spent the rest of the summer in White Plains, where he could keep a close eye on Clinton's army in New York. Although obviously disappointed by d'Estaing's lack of success, he nonetheless took immense satisfaction in knowing that the British were now bottled up in

New York. "It is not a little pleasing, nor less wonderful to contemplate," he wrote, "that after two years maneuvering and undergoing the strangest vicissitudes that perhaps ever attended any one contest since the creation, both armies are brought back to the very point they set out from. . . . The hand of Providence has been so conspicuous in all this, that he must be worse than an infidel that lacks faith and more than wicked that has not gratitude enough to acknowledge his obligations."

But Washington also knew that the war was far from over. When a delegate from Congress dared to imply that the British must soon be forced to give up the fight, Washington countered by pointing out that the longer the war dragged on, the more it favored the enemy. "The true point . . . is not simply whether Great Britain can carry on the war," he wrote, "but whose finances (theirs or ours) is most likely to fail, which leads me to doubt *very much* the infallibility of [American success]." Washington's message was unmistakable: unless Congress found a way to bring some kind of financial stability to the new nation—Continental currency was now worth a fraction of its original value and falling fast— all Britain had to do was wait until the United States fell into complete economic ruin.

He also recognized that the alliance with France did not guarantee ultimate triumph. If her forces suffered many more of the kinds of setbacks that had plagued the Comte d'Estaing, France might decide that her interests no longer coincided with those of the United States. "I am heartily disposed to entertain the most favorable sentiments of our new ally," he wrote to President Henry Laurens, "and to cherish them in others to a reasonable degree, but it is a maxim founded on the universal experience of mankind that no nation is to be trusted farther than it is bound by its interest, and no prudent statesman or politician will venture to depart from it." If America's fortunes appeared, at least for the moment, to be on the rise in the war against the British, Washington refused to take anything—even the alliance with France—for granted.

With France's entry in the war, all the opponents began to feel the need for more reliable intelligence. Prior to leaving for the Caribbean, d'Estaing began to fear that the British might attack his ships while they were undergoing repairs in Boston. Insisting that "good spies must be the basis of all," he offered to help pay for whatever information the Americans could provide. Washington assured the French admiral that he had the means to obtain the required intelligence, but he soon realized that this simply was not the case. Without better information about the movements of the British fleet, the French would be unable to provide the Continental army with the necessary support. Washington needed to build a better spy network.

In an October 6 letter to Lord Stirling, he set forth the principle that would guide his increasingly sophisticated intelligence-gathering efforts. "As we are often obliged to reason the designs of the enemy from the appearances which come under our own observation and the information of our spies," Washington wrote, "we cannot be too attentive to these things which may afford us new light. Every minutia should have a place in our collection. For things of a seemingly trifling nature when conjoined with others of a more serious cast may lead to very valuable conclusions."

But as Washington was to learn to his great regret, sometimes what were to become "the designs of the enemy" were developing in plain sight.

It is impossible to say when the thirty-seven-year-old Benedict Arnold and eighteen-year-old Peggy Shippen first met, but we do know that on September 25 Arnold wrote her a love letter—much of it an exact copy of the letter he had sent to Betsey Deblois six months before. But if the overheated rhetoric was recycled ("Twenty times have I taken up my pen to write to you . . . ," the letter began), Arnold's passion was nonetheless genuine. Knowing of "the affection you bear your amiable and tender parents," he had also taken it upon himself to write to Peggy's loyalist-leaning father.

Arnold assured Edward Shippen that even if they were on opposite sides of the political fence, he did not see that as a problem. "Our difference in political sentiments," he wrote, "will, I hope, be no bar to my happiness. I flatter myself the time is at hand when our unhappy contest will be at an end, and peace and domestic happiness be restored to everyone." He also assured Peggy's father that he was wealthy enough "to make us both happy" and that he had no expectations of any kind of dowry.

Here in this letter to the father of his beloved are hints as to the motives behind Arnold's subsequent behavior. Prior to the Revolution, Arnold had been a colonial merchant on the make. While lacking the social connections of the Shippens, who were the equivalent of Philadelphia aristocracy, Arnold's prospects of accumulating a sizable personal fortune

had been good. Having lost that once significant wealth, he had embarked on a campaign to reestablish himself as a prosperous merchant.

In addition to his earlier Philadelphia-based financial schemes, Arnold had entered into plans to buy up goods in British-held New York in
anticipation of the enemy's withdrawal. But in September 1778 he did
not yet have the money he needed to maintain Peggy in the style to
which she was accustomed. There was also the matter of the Shippens'
politics. They might not be outright loyalists, but they had a decided
distaste for the patriots' undeclared war on Philadelphia's upper class.

The adoption of the new constitution in 1776 had turned the political
order of the state upside down. Pennsylvania's artisans, farmers, and me-
chanics (many of whom were Scotch-Irish Presbyterians) did not have the
financial wherewithal of the wealthy Quakers and Anglican landowners
who formerly ruled Pennsylvania, but they were now in control. Needless
to say, the conservatives who had been voted out of office (and who called
themselves Republicans) had nothing but contempt for the lowly radicals who in tribute to the document that had brought them to the fore
called themselves Constitutionalists.

A Republican tended to be well-to-do and had no qualms about enjoying the finer things in life. A Constitutionalist prided himself on his
patriotic austerity and zeal. Arnold had always favored the aristocratic
grace of a Philip Schuyler to the slovenly egalitarianism of a Horatio
Gates. Given his newfound interest in the daughter of Edward Shippen
and his lifelong desire to acquire the wealth his bankrupt father had denied him, it is perhaps not surprising that he embraced the cause of the
marginalized nobility of Philadelphia with a vengeance.

Thumbing his nose at the pious patriots who ruled the city, Arnold
purchased an ornate carriage and entertained extravagantly at his new
residence in the same grand house in which William Howe had formerly
lived. With his two elegant aides at his side, he attended the Southwark
Theatre, despite the fact that Congress had advised the states to ban all
such entertainments as "productive of idleness, dissipation, and general
depravity of principles and manners." He issued passes to suspected loyalists wanting to visit with friends and relatives in New York. He even
dared to appear at a ball in a scarlet uniform, which caused a young lady
whose father had been arrested for corresponding with the British to joy-
fully exclaim, "Heyday, I see certain animals will put on the lion's skin."

In perhaps his most ingenious ploy, he donated five hundred dollars to support the children of Dr. Joseph Warren, the fallen hero of Bunker Hill. Some of Arnold's most vociferous critics had been the delegates from Warren's home state. These same delegates had so far refused to support measures to pay for the support of the Warren children. By writing those same children a considerable check, Arnold was able to drape himself in the flag of patriotic charity even as he mischievously tweaked the skinflint zealots from Massachusetts. Oh, how he must have inwardly smiled when none other than that old Puritan and adamant supporter of Horatio Gates, Samuel Adams, was shamed into personally thanking him for the gift to the family of his fallen friend!

And then there was the case of the British merchant vessel *Active,* which had become the focus of a bitter dispute between the state of Pennsylvania and the Continental Congress. During a voyage from Jamaica to New York, four captured sailors from Connecticut had led a bloody mutiny against the ship's British crew. But before they could get the *Active* to safe haven in Connecticut, two American privateers, one of which was from Pennsylvania, forced them to sail to Philadelphia. The sailors from Connecticut claimed that they deserved all the prize money since they had successfully taken the ship before the arrival of the privateers. When the Pennsylvania authorities decided that the mutineers must split their take with the privateers, Arnold rushed to the aid of his "fellow countrymen" and used his influence to get the Continental Congress to overturn the verdict. What he chose not to reveal was that his help was contingent on his receiving half of whatever settlement came the Connecticut sailors' way.

All that fall, Arnold delighted in being the outrageous provocateur. In October, Timothy Matlack, secretary of Pennsylvania's Supreme Executive Council, complained that his son, a sergeant in the militia, had been treated disrespectfully by Arnold's aide David Franks. Instead of tactfully promising the high-ranking state official that Franks would make a proper apology, Arnold was unrepentant, insisting that "whenever necessity obliges the citizen to assume the character of a soldier, the former is entirely lost in the latter and the respect due to a citizen is by no means to be paid to the soldier, any farther than his rank entitles him to it." When Arnold learned that the schooner *Charming Nancy* (the same vessel for which he had granted a pass when he was still at Valley Forge) was trapped in Egg Harbor, New Jersey, he commandeered some army wagons and lugged her cargo of trade goods (of which he was now a part owner) to Philadelphia, where he supplied the city and also made a handsome profit.

But it was at the many social functions he either hosted or attended that Arnold, the famously wounded warrior, truly made his mark. Since standing was still difficult, he often held court from the confines of a chair, which only accentuated the impression he made. When the one-year-old granddaughter of Benjamin Franklin kissed him on the cheek with what her mother described as "an old fashion smack," Arnold responded that "he would give a good deal to have her for a schoolmistress to teach the young ladies how to kiss." With dark hair, gray eyes, and a sharp beak of a nose, he was glorious in his epaulets and sword, but his misshapen left leg, often propped up on a portable camp stool, was what garnered the most attention—particularly since the tight-fitting breeches and silk stockings of a gentleman left little to the imagination. Congressman James Duane of New York wrote a friend that he had overheard "two ladies of our acquaintance in deep debate about this same wounded leg." As Peggy Shippen could no doubt attest, the battle-scarred Benedict Arnold was *sexy*.

Arnold pursued Peggy with his characteristic intensity. "Cupid has given our little general . . . a more mortal wound than all the hosts of Britons could," Mary Morris reported to her financier husband Robert. Peggy's father wrote his own father that "my youngest daughter is much solicited by a certain general. . . . Whether [a marriage] will take place or not depends upon circumstances." What those circumstances were is uncertain, but they may have involved Arnold's war injury. "A lame leg is at present the only obstacle," Peggy's new brother-in-law, Edward Burd, wrote that winter. "But a lady who makes that the only objection and is firmly persuaded it will soon be well again, can never retract; however expressly conditional an engagement may have been made."

Arnold, as might be expected, was optimistic about the prospects of his ultimate recovery. "We have every reason to hope [the leg] will be well again," Burd continued, "though I am not so sanguine as he is with respect to the time. But the leg will be a couple of inches shorter than the other, and disfigured." By the middle of October, Arnold had begun to make his first, virtually unassisted steps since sustaining his injury.

According to one report, "with the assistance of a high heeled shoe and cane, he begins to hop about the floor and in great measure dispense with his crutches."

We are without Peggy's own account of her courtship, but according to family tradition, as well as what we know of her future behavior, she was exceedingly high-strung (one friend described her as having "great sensibility"). At some point her father apparently responded to Arnold's entreaties with an outright refusal. This seems to have triggered one of the histrionic displays of emotion for which Peggy later became well known and ultimately led, according to one account, to her father "reluctantly" giving his consent.

They were strikingly different in age and background, but Benedict Arnold and Peggy Shippen appear to have had more in common than one might expect. Passionate, excitable, and intelligent, they were kindred spirits in a world gone mad. And yet, one can see why Edward Shippen had reservations about his youngest daughter's suitor. Indeed, there was something deeply troubling about Arnold's behavior as governor of Philadelphia. In his frantic pursuit of wealth and his deliberately belligerent disregard for the city's radical establishment, he was, in effect, dancing on the edge of a precipice, and that winter Washington's former adjutant general, the Philadelphia lawyer Joseph Reed, pushed him over the edge.

CHAPTER NINE

Unmerciful Fangs

At first glance, Joseph Reed seemed an unlikely champion of Pennsylvania's radical Constitutionalists. A London-educated lawyer with an English wife, he had established a reputation as one of Philadelphia's finest and most ambitious attorneys prior to the Revolution. But the Reeds had not fit comfortably into the upper echelons of Philadelphia society. Reed's pious wife complained that one of Peggy Shippen's relatives had accused her of being "sly," claiming that "religion is often a cloak to hide bad actions."

Brilliant, mercurial, and outspoken, Reed had a habit of antagonizing even his closest friends and associates, and after his falling-out with Washington in the winter of 1776 over his clandestine correspondence with Charles Lee, he had served in a variety of official capacities, always restless, always the smartest, most judgmental person in the room. As William Gordon, a New England minister who had heard many complaints about Reed during his tenure as adjutant general, wrote to Washington, Reed was "more formed for dividing than uniting."

And then, in the fall of 1778, Reed stepped down as a Pennsylvania delegate to the Continental Congress to assist the state's attorney general in prosecuting twenty-three suspected loyalists for treason. For a man who believed that he and he alone possessed the capacity and righteousness to ferret out the sinners in what had come down to a war of good against evil, it was the perfect role. Since many of the accused collaborators came from Philadelphia's upper class, his position as prosecutor allowed him to menace the very group that had proven so unaccommodating to his wife. It also established him as one of the city's most zealous and unforgiving patriots.

The state, however, did not give Reed much evidence to work with, and he lost every case except for two against the well-to-do Quakers Abraham Carlisle and John Roberts. Both men were respected members of the community, and as several American soldiers testified, Roberts had bravely assisted the prisoners being held in Philadelphia during the British occupation. But as Reed had proven during their trials, they had also assisted the British army in a variety of ways, and they had been sentenced to death.

That these two men currently posed a threat to the security and liberties of the state was difficult to believe, and thousands of citizens signed petitions requesting that they be pardoned. But on November 4, 1778, Carlisle and Roberts were hanged on the common of Philadelphia—an event that Reed viewed with grim satisfaction. Unless an example was made of these men, he insisted in a letter to Nathanael Greene, the cause of American freedom was sure to suffer. "New characters are emerging from obscurity like insects after a storm," he wrote the day after the executions. "Treason, disaffection to the interests of America and even assistance to the British interest is called openly only error of judgment." As Reed also revealed in his letter to Greene, the real reason why these Quakers had to be hanged was that they were wealthy. In the class war that was about to tear the city apart, Reed had clearly determined which side he was going to be on.

Not surprisingly, many other rich Philadelphians, such as John Cadwalader, the general who had challenged Thomas Conway to a duel on the Fourth of July, favored a very different approach. Instead of mercilessly prosecuting the guilty, why not let the city's war-ravaged society start to heal? That this approach had considerable merit is suggested by the statement made by William Howe's secretary Ambrose Serle prior to the British evacuation: "The Congress," Serle maintained, "if they knew their business, had only one measure to take, which is to publish a General Amnesty, and they drive us from the Continent forever." If Serle was correct, patriot hard-liners like Joseph Reed were actually prolonging the war by forcing otherwise reluctant loyalists into the arms of the British.

For both Reed and Cadwalader, former friends who had grown to despise each other, Benedict Arnold was the litmus test. By daring to challenge the all-powerful radicals, Arnold was, according to Cadwalader, providing some much needed balance in Philadelphia. "Every man who has a liberal way of thinking highly approves his conduct," he insisted. But for Reed, Arnold was anathema. In an apparent act of protest against the hanging of the Quakers, Arnold had hosted what Reed called "a public entertainment the night before last of which not only Tory [or loyalist] ladies but the wives and daughters of persons proscribed by the state and now with the enemy at New York formed a very considerable number. The fact is literally true," he sputtered to Nathanael Greene. Perhaps contributing to Reed's ire was the fact that he and his wife had recently moved to the house next to Arnold's and had not been invited to the party.

By December Reed had become president of the state's Supreme Executive Council, making him the most powerful man in one of the most powerful states in the country. He had initially run for the position under the pretense of forming a coalition of radicals and conservatives but quickly made it clear that compromise of any kind was not to be tolerated. Conservative patriots such as Cadwalader, the wealthy merchant Robert Morris, and the Pennsylvania lawyer Robert Wilson (who had defended many of the loyalists whom Reed had prosecuted during the fall of 1778) were the enemy.

But so were, in Reed's view, the Continental Congress and the Continental army. As president of Pennsylvania's Supreme Executive Council, he insisted that his state prevail in any and all disputes with the country's national government, regardless of what was best for the United States as a whole. Philadelphia was at the vortex of an increasingly rancorous struggle involving almost all the seminal issues related to creating a functioning democratic republic, issues that would not begin to be resolved until the Constitutional Convention of 1787. Amid all this angst-ridden upheaval, Reed looked to the prosecution of Benedict Arnold, whose inability to recognize the consequences of his actions made him a surprisingly easy (if hardly innocent) target, as the pretext to flex his state's considerable political muscle. For Arnold it would be a bewildering and infuriating experience that made him come to doubt the cause to which he had given so much.

But for a little more than a month, before matters between Arnold and Reed had a chance to a boil over, the two antagonists were forced to put their differences aside and remain on their best behavior. George and Martha Washington had come to town.

By January 1779 Washington had reluctantly left his army's new winter quarters in Middlebrook, New Jersey, to take up temporary residence in Philadelphia, where he could meet with Congress about his plans for the coming campaign. Washington and Martha found themselves on a festive merry-go-round of social obligations sponsored by the embattled doyens of Philadelphia's upper class, who used the commander in chief's presence as an excuse to entertain with a lavishness that had not been seen in the city since John André's Mischianza. Washington was appalled by what he found in Philadelphia—not only in the excesses of the dinners and balls, in stark contrast to the lean conditions the army suffered, but, more important, in Congress's inability to grapple with the most pressing issues of the day. Without an executive branch and without the ability to collect taxes (a right that was reserved by the states), the American national government during the Revolution was unable to provide the leadership that the war effort required. Congressional delegates could debate and pass resolutions but were without the authority to effect significant change. Back in November 1777, Congress had finalized the Articles of Confederation, a document that established a system by which the nation's legislative body could more efficiently direct the war and conduct foreign diplomacy. Unfortunately, the articles would not be ratified by the states until early 1781, and Congress remained stuck in the old familiar rut of partisanship and indecision.

In a distressing throwback to the Gates-Schuyler schism of the previous year, the delegates had become embroiled in yet another factional dispute, this one involving two feuding American emissaries to France—Silas Deane of Connecticut and Arthur Lee of Virginia. One of the casualties of the controversy was President Henry Laurens, who stepped down in frustration and handed over the leadership role to the New Yorker John Jay.

"Party disputes and personal quarrels are the great business of the day," Washington complained to a friend in Virginia, "whilst the momentous concerns of an empire—a great and accumulated debt, ruined finances, depreciated money, and want of credit . . .—are but secondary considerations and postponed from day to day, from week to week as if our affairs wore the most promising aspect. . . . And yet an assembly, a concert, a dinner or supper that will cost three or four hundred pounds will not only take men off from acting in but even from thinking of this business while a great part of the officers of your army from absolute necessity are quitting the service and the more virtuous few . . . are sinking by sure degrees into beggary and want."

Washington had little sympathy for Arnold's increasingly tempestuous relations with state and national officials. When Arnold complained about his treatment by the Board of War, Washington responded, "I have never heard, nor is it my wish to be acquainted with the causes of the coolness between some gentlemen composing the Board of War and yourself. I most sincerely hope that they may never rise to such a height as to oblige either party to make a public matter of it as I am under more apprehensions on account of our own dissensions than of the efforts of the enemy."

How much Washington knew about Arnold's financial scheming is a matter of conjecture. But as Washington asserted to his friend in Virginia, he highly disapproved of just the kind of lifestyle Arnold had so passionately embraced. "Idleness, dissipation, and extravagance seem to have laid fast hold of most [of Philadelphia]," he wrote. "Speculation, peculation, and an insatiable thirst for riches seem to have got the better of every other consideration." Clearly there was more of Joseph Reed in Washington than Arnold would have liked.

By the time Washington returned to the army's headquarters in Middlebrook in late January, Arnold was making preparations to leave the military. Unlike Pennsylvania, New York was a state that held the hero of Valcour Island, Fort Stanwix, and Saratoga in high regard. Officials such as Philip Schuyler and John Jay had encouraged him to consider becoming a landowner on the scale of the loyalist Philip Skene, whose vast estate at Skenesborough at the southern tip of Lake Champlain had been confiscated by the state. So far Arnold's financial dealings in Philadelphia had failed to yield the anticipated returns. Exiting the army and becoming a land baron in New York might be the way for him to acquire the wealth and prestige that he had always craved and that Peggy and her family expected. It would also have the benefit of removing him from the increasingly unpleasant turmoil in Philadelphia.

By early February he had decided to embark on a journey to New York but not until after stopping to visit with Washington at his head-quarters in New Jersey. By then, Reed had launched an investigation into Arnold's conduct as military governor. Fearing that the general might escape to New York before he could be brought to justice for his sins in Philadelphia, Reed hurriedly put together a list of eight charges, most of them based on rumor rather than actual evidence. Given the pettiness of many of the charges (which included being ungracious to a militiaman and preferring loyalists to patriots), Reed appeared to be embarked on more of a smear campaign than a genuine attempt to bring a criminal to justice. That Arnold was, in fact, guilty of some of the more substantive charges (such as illegally purchasing goods upon his arrival in Philadel-phia and using his influence to secure a favorable result for the Con-necticut crew members of the *Active* in exchange for a portion of the take) did not change the fact that Reed did not have the evidence required to make a creditable case against him. Arnold knew as much, and he com-plained of his treatment to Washington and his family of officers.

Washington, much like Nathanael Greene, who corresponded regu-larly with both Reed and John Cadwalader, had refused to take sides in the dispute between Philadelphia's radicals and conservatives. Arnold's prior history of controversy was well known, and in retrospect Washing-ton should never have made him military governor, a position that re-quired personal skills that Arnold simply did not have. Washington also knew that Reed was hardly the steadfast patriot he currently claimed to be. For the last year, a disturbing rumor about Reed had been circulating among the officers of the Continental army. According to John Cad-walader, Reed had been in such despair over the state of the war in late December 1776 that he'd decided to spend the night of Washington's assault on Trenton at a home in Hessian-occupied New Jersey, where he'd been poised to defect to the British in the event of an American defeat. For Cadwalader, the fact that Reed, who had come so close to his own treason, now self-righteously prosecuted Quakers and other Philadel-phians for the same crime was hypocritical in the extreme. It's likely that Washington had heard at least some version of Cadwalader's claim and just as likely that he took the charges Reed had assembled against Arnold with a grain of salt. That did not change the fact that Reed's position as president of the Supreme Executive Council required Washington to treat his combustible former adjutant general with a greater degree of civility than he probably deserved.

On February 8, 1779, Arnold wrote to Peggy from the army's headquarters in Middlebrook. "I am treated with the greatest politeness by General Washington and the officers of the army," he assured her. "[They] bitterly execrate Mr. Reed and the council for their villainous attempt to injure me." Arnold claimed that the consensus at headquarters was that he should ignore the charges and continue with his journey to New York. Despite this advice, he had resolved to return to Philadelphia, not only to clear his name but because he was so desperately missing Peggy. "Six days' absence without hearing from my Dear Peggy is intolerable," he wrote. "Heavens! What must I have suffered had I continued my journey—the loss of happiness for a few dirty acres. I can almost bless the villainous . . . men who oblige me to return."

Arnold was confident that he would ultimately prevail, claiming that the "rude attacks . . . can do me no injury." But he also admitted to feeling a certain world-weariness. "I am heartily tired with my journey and almost so with human nature. I daily discover so much baseness and ingratitude among mankind that I almost blush at being of the same species, and could quit the stage without regret was it not for some few gentle, generous souls like my Dear Peggy, who still retain the lively impression of their Maker's image, and who with smiles of benignity and goodness, make all happy around them." In complete and utter denial regarding his own complicity in the trouble in which he now found himself, he was also deeply in love.

Once back in Philadelphia, Arnold was soon under near-ceaseless attack by Pennsylvania's Supreme Executive Council even as he moved ever closer to marriage. Before Congress had a chance to address the state's charges against Arnold, Reed accused the delegates of favoritism on Arnold's behalf. Since the council was unwilling to provide the required evidence—primarily because they did not have any—the congressional committee appointed to examine the charges had no choice but to find in Arnold's favor. This finding resulted in a volcanic outpouring of outrage on the part of the council accompanied by threats of withholding the state militia and the large number of state-owned wagons upon which Washington's army depended. This bare-knuckled act of political intimidation gave Congress no choice but to table the committee's report and turn the charges against Arnold over to Washington for a court-martial.

More than a few congressional delegates began to wonder what Reed was attempting to accomplish by this investigation. Arnold was no saint, but so far Reed had failed to produce anything close to the damning evidence he claimed to possess. There was at least one member of Congress who had come to suspect the worst of the Supreme Executive Council's president.

As a patriot and a Philadelphian, Congress's secretary, Charles Thomson, had once considered Reed a friend. No more. Reed's refusal to bring forward any legitimate evidence, combined with his continual assaults on the authority and integrity of Congress, made Thomson wonder whether his former friend was attempting to destroy the political body upon which the very existence of the country depended. Was Reed, in fact, the traitor?

The previous summer Reed had been contacted by a woman representing the British peace commission with an offer of ten thousand pounds if he would assist the commission's efforts with Congress. In a letter published in a Philadelphia newspaper, Reed claimed to have indignantly refused the overture. But had he really? Back in England, one of the commissioners had recently assured Parliament that secret efforts were under way to destabilize the government of the United States and that these "other means" might prove more effective in ending the war than military attempts to defeat Washington's army. Was this what Reed was up to?

> [A] question is started [Thomson wrote Reed on March 21]. Suppose it were possible to conceive that a president and council of one of the united states were the persons with whom those other means have been used—what would be the line of conduct they would probably pursue . . . ? Would it not be to divide the people by every means in their power; to lessen the reputation and consequently the weight and authority of the great council of the United States; to poison the minds of the people and prejudice them against Congress by misrepresentation of facts and publications calculated to deceive; to seize every occasion of quarreling with Congress, and endeavor to bring the other states and

particularly the legislature of their own into the dispute; to labor
to damn the reputation of . . . general officers of the army, not
sparing those of their own state whom they cannot hope to influence, especially such as are distinguished for their spirit and
bravery; and if they cannot effect their purpose to disparage their
past services, pour upon them a torrent of abuse with a gentle
salvo of "as it is reported and believed"; and to . . . alienate the
inhabitants of their own state from the service by representing
military discipline as degrading to freemen; . . . to leave the defenses of their country unguarded and unrepaired, that the
enemy may meet with no opposition, in case they think proper
to attack or invade it, etc.

There is no evidence that Reed was indeed bent on a treasonous effort
to bring down Congress, but as Thomson made so eloquently clear, his
zealous, verging on monomaniacal, pursuit of Arnold was threatening to
accomplish exactly that. Arnold eventually became a traitor of the highest order, and ultimately he alone was responsible for what he did. However, one cannot help but wonder whether he would have betrayed his
country without the merciless witch hunt conducted by Reed and his
Supreme Executive Council.

In the meantime, Arnold needed money and he needed it fast. His investment schemes had not come close to covering his ostentatious lifestyle. Now that he was embroiled in controversy and in the process of
resigning as military governor, he was no longer the attractive investment
partner he had once been. New business deals were proving difficult to
secure. Yet he had promised Edward Shippen that he would bestow "a
settlement" on his daughter prior to their marriage as proof that he possessed the financial resources Peggy's father required. And so in March,
Arnold took out a loan for twelve thousand pounds from the French shipping agent Jean Holker and with the help of a sizable mortgage bought
Mount Pleasant, a mansion on ninety-six acres beside the Schuylkill that
John Adams had once claimed was "the most elegant seat in Pennsylvania." There was one hitch, however. Although he had technically purchased Peggy a mansion, they were not going to be able to live in it, since

Arnold needed the rental payments from the house's current occupant to help pay off the mortgage.

Harassed by Reed, crushed beneath a frightening burden of debt, Arnold nonetheless had the satisfaction of finally winning Edward Shippen's consent, and on April 8, 1779, he and Peggy were married in a small ceremony at the Shippens' house. At last, Arnold had what he had always wanted: a young, beautiful, and adoring wife who was, he proudly reported the next morning to several of his friends, good in bed—at least that was the rumor the Marquis de Chastellux, a major general in the French army who was fluent in English, heard a year later when visiting Philadelphia.

That there was some basis to the story is suggested by the letter Arnold subsequently wrote to General Robert Howe. In that letter, Arnold admitted that as a widower he had "enjoyed a tolerable share of the dissipated joys of life." None of those "scenes of sensual gratification," he was pleased to report, could compare with what he had "since felt and still enjoyed" with Peggy. Arnold, it seems clear, wanted the world to know just how good it was to be, even after all the setbacks and frustrations he had so far suffered, Peggy Shippen's husband.

However, within just a few weeks of their marriage, Arnold was finding it difficult to lose himself in the delights of the connubial bed. Through a tortuous series of maneuverings and threats, Reed had not only forced a court-martial upon Arnold; he was now attempting to delay the proceedings so that he could gather more evidence. What's more, he had called one of Washington's former aides as a witness, an even more disturbing development since Arnold had no idea what the aide knew. With the prospect of a new and perhaps devastating disclosure about to come to light and with no apparent end to his sufferings in sight, Arnold began to realize that he was, in fact, in serious trouble.

Making matters even worse, his left leg was not healing as quickly as he had hoped. Major General Benjamin Lincoln, who had suffered his own leg injury at Saratoga, had long since returned to active duty and had been given command of the army's southern department. Arnold, in the meantime, had been thrown to the wolves in Philadelphia. As the pressures on him continued to mount (and his drinking no doubt increased) his right leg became racked by gout, making it impossible for him to walk. Arnold had been in tight spots before, but always in the past he had been able to *do* something to bring about a miraculous recovery. But now, besieged by debt and controversy, without the use of his legs, what was there left to do? Without a trace of Washington's patience, he was incapable of simply waiting it out. He must do what he had always done: attack his enemies and redeem himself through a single, extraordinary act. At some point in late April or early May, he began to consider a course of action that by its sheer audacity and risk made all his other stunning escapes and comebacks look tame by comparison.

If the last nine months had taught Arnold anything, it was that the country to which he had given everything but his life could easily fall apart. Since it had no taxing power, Congress was incapable of solving the current economic problems, and the country's currency was on its way to becoming worthless. Because of the resulting runaway inflation, price controls were now the order of the day among the radical Constitutionalists of Philadelphia, but those controls were a violation of the economic liberties that had inspired this revolution in the first place. Instead of a national government, Congress had become a powerless facade behind which thirteen largely autonomous states did whatever was best for each of them. Indeed, it might be argued that Pennsylvania president Joseph Reed was now more influential than all of Congress combined. Just look what he had been able to force the delegates into doing this winter and spring. And if men like Joseph Reed were going to be the new leaders of the United States, Arnold, for one, wanted no part of it.

What made all of this particularly galling to Arnold was the hostility that Reed and apparently most of the American people held toward the Continental army. Since no one wanted to pay for anything beyond their own state's borders, a standing national army was viewed with ever-increasing apathy and suspicion. Now that France had entered the conflict, the prevailing belief was that the war had already been won. Let the foreigners take care of it, and perhaps with the help of some state militiamen, everything would work out fine.

Indeed, Arnold's problems in Philadelphia were symptomatic of a national trend as more and more Americans regarded Continental army officers like Arnold as dangerous hirelings on the order of the Hessian mercenaries and British regulars while local militiamen were looked to as the embodiment of the true patriotic ideal. In reality, rather than fighting for freedom against the British, many of these militiamen were employed by community officials as thuggish enforcers to terrorize local citizens whose loyalties were suspect. In Philadelphia, for example, the state's militiamen had begun to serve as the strong arm of the Constitutionalists— evicting loyalists from their homes and interrupting meetings of the conservative Republican Party—while Continental army officers like Arnold and Cadwalader became, almost by default, the defenders of the wealthy minority. In this increasingly toxic and potentially explosive environment, issues of class threatened to transform a revolution that had once inspired a collective quest for national independence into a sordid and ultimately self-defeating civil war.

For Philadelphia was, by no means, the only place in the country where the War of Independence had devolved into an ugly internal struggle. To the north of British-occupied New York was what was known as the Neutral Ground—a twenty-mile-wide swath of territory along the Hudson River where gangs of patriots and loyalists, known as Skinners and Cowboys, respectively, turned Westchester County into a lawless wasteland.

The same held true in Connecticut, Long Island, and New Jersey, where a tidal version of the Neutral Ground existed along the bays and inlets of each state's coastline. Instead of gangs of Skinners and Cowboys, the unlucky towns along these shores were regularly ravaged by boatloads of patriot and loyalist refugees in a seemingly ceaseless cycle of Viking-like raids that historians have called the Whaleboat Wars.

Even worse were conditions along the frontiers of New York and Pennsylvania, where a series of recent Indian raids had moved Washington to plan a summer campaign led by General John Sullivan against the hostile tribes of the Iroquois. Washington's orders to Sullivan were shockingly straightforward: "the total destruction and devastation of their settlements and the capture of as many prisoners of every age and sex as possible." As Great Britain's focus shifted to the French and the islands of the West Indies, Americans were turning their attention to destroying one another.

By the spring of 1779, Arnold had begun to believe that the experiment in independence had failed. After four years of war, it was time to bring the British back and reestablish the ordered, peaceful, and free society the American colonies had once enjoyed. However, that assumed the British were in a position to win the war. Spain was poised to enter the conflict on the side of France, and that summer all of Great Britain would hold its collective breath as a combined French-Spanish armada gathered in the English Channel. The threatened invasion never occurred, but that did not change the fact that Henry Clinton's force in New York was significantly smaller than what Howe had possessed the year before and that Britain's leaders were too distracted by more immediate concerns to focus on the war in America. Like two punch-drunk fighters in the final rounds, both sides were staggering so badly that no one could predict who would still be standing when the war came to its eventual conclusion.

By late April Arnold had decided that he just might be the one to tip the scales. As far as he could tell, the British had a higher regard for his abilities than his own country did. At that time, John Burgoyne was in London defending himself before Parliament with the claim that if not for Arnold, his army would have defeated Gates at the Battle of Saratoga. That February, the New York–based *Royal Gazette* had referred sympathetically to his plight in Philadelphia: "General Arnold heretofore had been styled another Hannibal, but losing a leg in the service of the Congress, the latter considering him unfit for any further exercise of his military talents, permit him thus to fall into the unmerciful fangs of the executive council of Pennsylvania." Yes, perhaps the time was right for him to offer his services to the British.

Arnold is usually credited with coming up with the idea himself, but there are reasons to suspect that the decision to turn traitor originated with Peggy. Certainly the timing is suspect, following as it does so soon after their marriage. Arnold had grown embittered and distraught, but even he had to admit that the Revolution had catapulted him from the fringes of respectability in New Haven to the national and even international stage as one of the luminaries of the war. Peggy, on the other hand, had regarded the Revolution as a disaster from the start. Not only had it initially forced her family to flee from Philadelphia; it had reduced her beloved father to a cringing parody of his former self. How different life had been during those blessed months of the British occupation, when noble, kindhearted gentleman-officers like John André had danced with the belles of the city and dressed them up like scandalously clad dolls for the Mischianza. With her ever-growing emotional and physical attachment to Arnold fueling her outrage, she had come to despise the revolutionary government that had once again seized control of the city and was now attempting to destroy her husband.

Arnold had claimed during his troubles with Horatio Gates that "no man" could influence his judgment. But as his young aides at Saratoga had discovered, he was highly susceptible to the opinions of those around him. Indeed, many of his troubles in Philadelphia might be attributed to the fact that he had surrounded himself with such a strident group of disaffected conservatives. By marrying Peggy, Arnold had attached himself to a young, loyalist-leaning woman who, as her courtship with Arnold revealed, knew how to get what she wanted. When her father had initially refused to allow her to marry Arnold, she had used her seeming frailty—her fits, her hysteria, whatever you wanted to call it—to artfully manipulate him into agreeing to the engagement in fear that to do otherwise might cause his emotionally delicate daughter irreparable harm. Peggy had gotten her way with her father, and once she was married, she would get her way with her equally indulgent husband.

John Adams knew how difficult it was for a loving husband to act in opposition to his wife. He had watched as the Pennsylvania patriot John Dickinson had succumbed to his spouse's pressure to back away from the inevitability of independence. "If . . . my wife had expressed such sentiments to me," Adams wrote, "I was certain, that if they did not wholly unman me and make me an apostate, they would make me the most miserable man alive." Adams was lucky; his wife and virtually every member of his extended family supported his political positions. Arnold now found himself in an entirely different situation. Instead of appealing to the better angels of his patriotism, Peggy was calling forth the demons that had been whispering in his ear ever since his first troubles during the retreat from Montreal.

Given the ultimate course of Arnold's life, it is easy to assume that he had fully committed himself to treason by the time he sent out his first feelers to the British in early May 1779. But as subsequent events proved, that was not the case. Angered over his treatment by his own country and increasingly enticed by Peggy to turn traitor, he still nonetheless felt a genuine loyalty to Washington.

It all came to a head on May 5 when Arnold wrote the commander in chief what can only be described as a hysterical letter. The apparent reason for the communication was the delay of his court-martial from May to June 1. What the letter was really about was Arnold's fear that he might actually do as his wife suggested. "If your Excellency thinks me criminal," he wrote, "for heaven's sake, let me be immediately tried and if found guilty executed."

What Arnold wanted more than anything at this pivotal juncture was clarity. With the court-martial and his exoneration behind him, he might be able to fend off Peggy's tantalizing appeals. Joseph Reed, however, was bent on delaying the court-martial for as long as possible. In limbo like this, Arnold was dangerously susceptible to seeing treason not as a betrayal of all he had once held sacred but as a way to save his country from the revolutionary government that was threatening to destroy it. During the English Revolution a hundred years before, the defection of one of Cromwell's favorite officers, George Monck, had made possible the restoration of King Charles II, who in gratitude awarded Monck a host of preferments including the vast tract of territory in North America that eventually became North and South Carolina. Even as Arnold considered using "Monk" as his alias with the British—a name that would inevitably appeal to John André, the British officer to whom Peggy suggested he reach out—he still had trouble abandoning the cause to which he had given so much.

Through all Arnold's struggles, Washington had been a constant supporter, and in Arnold's outpouring of anguish on May 5, he offered His Excellency a warning. If this was happening to him, it could also happen to Washington. "Let me beg of you sir to consider that a set of artful unprincipled men in office may misinterpret the most innocent actions and by raising the public clamor against your Excellency place you in the same disagreeable situation I am in. Having made every sacrifice of fortune and blood, and become a cripple in the service of my country, I little expected to meet the ungrateful returns I have received of my countrymen, but as Congress have stamped ingratitude as a current coin I must take it. I wish your Excellency for your long and eminent services may not be paid of in the same coin."

In the reference to money, Arnold had unintentionally betrayed the real reason why he had been moved to consider this course. If he handled the negotiations correctly, turning traitor could be extremely lucrative. Not only would he be able to walk away from his current financial obligations, he might command a figure from the British that made him independently wealthy for life.

Prior to the Battle of Valcour Island, Arnold had complained to Horatio Gates about the injustice of the allegations concerning his conduct during the retreat from Canada. None of those charges had been proven, but now, during the spring of 1779, Arnold was on his way to turning one of the more outrageous claims into a chilling prophecy. "Money is this man's god," Colonel John Brown had insisted two years before, "and to get enough of it, he would sacrifice his country."

By reaching out to the British, Arnold was about to give his enemies the exquisite satisfaction of having been right all along. Like Robert E. Lee at the beginning of the American Civil War, Arnold could have declared his change of heart and simply shifted sides. But as he was about to make clear, he was doing this first and foremost for the money.

CHAPTER TEN

The Chasm

After three years of British occupation, New York City had become a blasted shell of its former self—a refuge for loyalists, a black market for profiteers, a squalid way station for the desperate and despairing, who clung to the lower tip of Manhattan Island like barnacles to a rock. Soon after the British took over New York in September 1776, fire destroyed a significant portion of the city, and in that charred swath of ruin many of the poorer residents lived within a haphazard collection of tents and shanties. Across the East River in Brooklyn's Wallabout Bay, a moored fleet of prison ships provided American captives with one of two options: a slow death amid the fetid confines of a floating hellhole or an opportunity to join the British navy. Prostitutes had always been in New York, but now with a large number of bored and unhappy soldiers based in the city, the profession flourished like never before.

The British might be the enemy, but their currency, unlike America's "Continental," held its value. What was known as the "London trade" soon came into being as, in a supreme irony, former patriot smugglers from New Jersey, Long Island, and Connecticut used their talents for avoiding the authorities to get their goods to British New York, where they were paid in pounds sterling. In Philadelphia an illicit lumber trade developed as ship captains and their crews set out down the Delaware bound for Boston only to be "captured" by the British. Once their confiscated cargoes had been sold in New York (and the captain and crew had been paid an appropriate commission), the British authorities proved surprisingly happy to offer the sailors their freedom in a prisoner exchange. Upon returning to Philadelphia, the American sailors were soon back at it. One captain had successfully completed five trips to New York before the Pennsylvania Supreme Executive Council realized that his repeated captures were more than a mere fluke.

Every day, a great seething wave of loyalists, patriots, freed slaves, deserters, merchants, and tradespeople washed in and out of the city. It was the perfect environment for espionage, and on May 10, 1779, a British-born purveyor of crockery and fine china from Philadelphia named Joseph Stansbury arrived at the door of Captain John André in downtown New York.

A few days before, Arnold had requested to meet with Stansbury, who in addition to being a shopkeeper to the wealthy liked to dabble in verse, much of it published anonymously and voicing his decidedly British loyalties. Stansbury was well known to the Shippens, and Peggy undoubtedly encouraged her husband to contact him about carrying a verbal message to John André.

Stansbury and Arnold probably met at the general's residence in Philadelphia, where he informed the crockery merchant that he wanted to explore the possibility of defecting to the British. But first Arnold needed to be assured of two things: Were the British in this war to stay? And how much were his services worth?

In the weeks ahead Stansbury, with the help of the loyalist chaplain and fellow poet Jonathan Odell and the messenger John Ratoon, established a line of communication with the British that stretched across New Jersey and into New York. Arnold's timing, it turned out, was quite good. André had just been put in charge of British intelligence operations, and he was eager to assure Arnold that the British were not about to give up their American colonies. "No thought is entertained of abandoning the point we have in view," André wrote Arnold. "On the contrary, powerful means are expected for accomplishing our end." He also wanted to assure Arnold of his country's "liberality" when it came to payment. If Arnold should, for example, help them "defeat a numerous body [of Continental soldiers], then would the generosity of the nation exceed even his own most sanguine hopes." If, however, "his manifest efforts be foiled and after every zealous attempt, flight be at length necessary, the cause in which he suffers will hold itself bound to indemnify him for his losses and receive him with the honor his conduct deserves."

After suggesting some of the ways Arnold might help them—from stealing dispatches to identifying the location of ammunition depots—André outlined the code that he was to use in future communications. First, Arnold needed to provide André with "a long book" for reference purposes. (*Blackstone's Commentaries on the Laws of England* was an early choice but was eventually replaced by Bailey's *Universal Etymological English Dictionary*, which had the advantage of listing the words alphabetically.) Each word in his message was to be keyed to the book with the help of three numbers: "the first is the page, the second the line, the third the word."

Another way to transmit secret messages was through the use of invisible ink, of which there were two options—one that was revealed by the application of a liquid chemical, the other by heat, each to be identified by a letter at the top of the page. "*F* is fire," André instructed, "*A*, acid." In order to mask the true topic of the communication, André advised pretending that "an old woman's health may be the subject." He also suggested that Peggy get into the act by writing him letters that "talk of the Mischianza and other nonsense" but also contained invisible writing between the lines.

Arnold appears to have been pleased by the interest André and, by extension, Henry Clinton had showed in him. But in typical fashion he immediately overstepped himself by making unreasonable, almost insulting demands of the British commander in chief. "As I esteem the interest of America and Great Britain inseparable," he wrote in his next message, "Sir Henry may depend on my exertions and intelligence." All of this was contingent, however, on Arnold's knowing what the British were up to. "It will be impossible to cooperate unless there is a mutual confidence," he insisted.

Arnold then went on to provide Clinton with a laundry list of information: Washington was planning on moving his army to the Hudson River as soon as the spring grass had sprouted for the horses. The American commander had so far been unable to provide General Lincoln at Charleston, South Carolina, with what he needed to defend the city: "They are in want of arms, ammunition and men. . . . Three or four thousand militia is the most that can be mustered to fight on any emergency." He also had news about d'Estaing, who had spent the winter in the West Indies: "The French fleet has conditional orders to return to this continent," he wrote. "They depend on great part of their provision from hence. A [French] transport originally a 64 and a foreign 28 guns are daily expected here for provision."

But Arnold had an additional condition. He needed more than vague assurances as to his compensation. "I will cooperate when an opportunity offers and as life and everything is at stake I will expect some certainty. My property here secure and a revenue equivalent to the risk and service done." Paraphrasing a passage from Addison's tragedy *Cato,* Arnold added a melodramatic rejoinder: "I cannot promise success; I will deserve it." He also wanted André to know that "Madam Arnold presents you her particular compliments." With this coded letter on its way to New York, Arnold began to make preparations for his court-martial at the Continental army's headquarters in Middlebrook.

Nathanael Greene had extended an invitation to Arnold to stay with him at his quarters. Upon his arrival, Arnold presented Greene with a letter from Silas Deane, the former emissary to France who had stirred up his own share of controversy that winter and who had spent much of the year living with Arnold at his house in Philadelphia. "This will be handed you by General Arnold," Deane wrote, "who tho' deprived of the use of either leg, and in constant pain, feels so much more sensibly the wound his character has received from base and envious men. . . . No arguments can dissuade him from attempting the journey tho' so weak and lame that he has not been able to walk one step for some time."

After railing against "the most unrelenting fury" of Arnold's treatment by Reed, Deane offered a touching testimonial: "In all his distresses which for ten months past I have been sympathizing witness, this country's good has ever appeared to be nearest his heart and first in his wishes."

Arnold undoubtedly knew the contents of Deane's letter. That he was willing to place that letter into the hands of Nathanael Greene within a few weeks of having disclosed precious military secrets to the British reveals the extent of Arnold's treachery. Not only had he betrayed his country; he had betrayed in that single act the trust of two of his closest friends.

Arnold, of course, did not see it that way. The same narcissistic arrogance that enabled him to face the gravest danger on the battlefield without a trace of fear had equipped him to be a first-rate traitor. Arnold had never worried about the consequences of his actions. Guilt was simply not a part of his makeup since everything he did was, to his own mind, at least, justifiable. Where others might have shown, if not remorse, at least hesitation or ambivalence, Arnold projected unwavering certitude. Whatever was best for him was, by definition, best for everyone else.

As Washington had made clear during their correspondence that spring, now that Arnold was about to be judged by a military tribunal, it was imperative that as commander in chief he view the proceedings with as much objectivity as possible. To do otherwise—to voice private sympathies in the context of an official proceeding—would require Washington to become, in his own words, "lost to my own character." Here, in this reference to character, Washington hit upon the essential difference between himself and Arnold. Washington's sense of right and wrong existed outside the impulsive demands of his own self-interest. Rules mattered to Washington. Even though Congress had made his life miserable for the last four years, he had found ways to do what he considered best for his army and his country without challenging the supremacy of civil authority. To do otherwise, to declare himself, like the seventeenth-century English revolutionary Oliver Cromwell, master of his army and his country, would require him to become "lost to my own character."

For Arnold, on the other hand, rules were made to be broken. He had done it as a pre-Revolutionary merchant and he had done it as military governor of Philadelphia. This did not make Arnold unusual. Many prominent Americans before and since have lived in the gray area between selfishness and altruism. What made Arnold unique was the godlike inviolability he attached to his actions. He had immense respect for a man like Washington, but Arnold was, in the end, the leading personage in the drama that was his life. Not lost *to* his own character, but lost *in* it, Arnold did whatever Arnold wanted, and upon arriving at Middlebrook he made what Washington described as a "self-invited" appearance at headquarters.

The commander in chief was not pleased. Ignoring warnings as to "the impropriety of his entering upon a justification of his conduct in my presence" even as he ranted about "those whom he denominated his persecutors," Arnold was ultimately dismissed with what Washington termed a "rebuke." For Arnold, it must have been a startling, perhaps pivotal, moment. Hidden beneath Washington's normally equable, understated exterior was a will that was more than equal to his own.

By the spring of 1779, the British commander Henry Clinton, still stuck in New York City, had begun to look longingly toward West Point, about sixty miles up the Hudson River. If he could gain control of the cluster of fortifications surrounding this S-shaped bend in the river while establishing a series of posts between there and New York, he would effectively seal off the flow of goods across the river upon which the Continental army depended. It might be a more practical way to accomplish what Burgoyne had hoped to do by marching down from Canada. If he could seize West Point, he might find a way to win the war.

A few weeks before, Arnold had told him that Washington was contemplating a move to the Hudson. Clinton did not have, as of yet, the troops and ships he needed to push all the way up the river to West Point, but now that he had some idea of Washington's timetable, he might as well anticipate the enemy's next move and capture the forts at Stony Point on the west side of the river and Verplanck's Point on the opposite shore, about fifty miles north of New York City and about eleven miles south of West Point. Here, at this relatively narrow portion of the river, was the King's Ferry, a crucial crossing point upon which trade between New England and the middle states depended. By capturing the forts that guarded the ferry, he would force the Americans to make an eleven-mile detour to the north. Once he'd established a British foothold at King's Ferry, he would be poised to make a run at West Point when his anticipated reinforcements arrived later in the summer.

On May 30 Clinton, with six thousand troops and a fleet of more than two hundred ships, started up the Hudson and without much trouble seized the undermanned fortress at Stony Point as well as the relatively insignificant redoubt at Verplanck's Point. Unfortunately, from Arnold's perspective, word of the British movement up the river arrived at Washington's headquarters on the very day his court-martial began. Washington had no choice but to call for a postponement and start moving his army into the region between the newly taken British positions and West Point.

Rather than returning to Philadelphia, Arnold decided to move to nearby Morristown, New Jersey, "to wait events." But as the summer

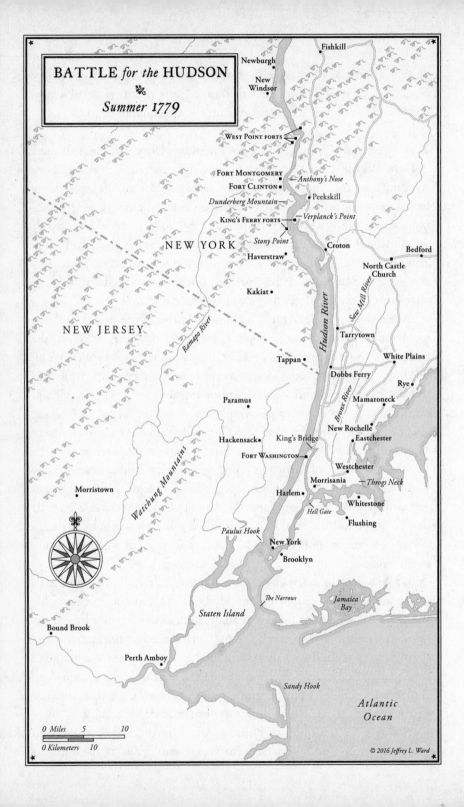

BATTLE *for the* HUDSON

Summer 1779

Fishkill

Newburgh

New
Windsor

WEST POINT FORTS

FORT MONTGOMERY — *Anthony's Nose*
FORT CLINTON
Dunderberg Mountain — Peekskill

KING'S FERRY FORTS — *Verplanck's Point*
Stony Point

NEW YORK

Croton

Bedford

Haverstraw

North Castle
Church

Kakiat

Hudson River

Saw Mill River

NEW JERSEY

Ramapo River

Tarrytown

White Plains

Tappan

Dobbs Ferry

Rye

Paramus

Bronx River

Mamaroneck

Hackensack

King's Bridge

New Rochelle

FORT WASHINGTON

Eastchester

Westchester

Morristown

Morrisania

— *Throgs Neck*

Watchung Mountains

Harlem

Whitestone

Hell Gate

Flushing

Paulus Hook

New York

Brooklyn

*Jamaica
Bay*

The Narrows

Staten Island

Bound Brook

Perth Amboy

Sandy Hook

*Atlantic
Ocean*

0 Miles   5   10
0 Kilometers   10

© 2016 Jeffrey L. Ward

campaign slowed to a stalemate on the Hudson and Washington turned his attention to supervising the transformation of the handful of fortifications at West Point into an impregnable complex of forts and redoubts, Arnold began to realize that the court-martial was not going to happen any time soon. He must return to Philadelphia and to Peggy.

By then he had received a second message from John André. Like Washington prior to Arnold's court-martial, Clinton was not pleased by Arnold's assumption that the two of them were equals, and he issued the equivalent of Washington's earlier rebuke. André informed Arnold that his commander "wishes to apprise you that he cannot reveal his intentions as to the present campaign, nor can he find the necessity of such a discovery or that a want of proper degree of confidence is to be inferred from his not making it." The onus at this point was not on the British but on Arnold, and it was up to him to find that "one shining stroke" by which they might "accelerate the ruin to which the usurped authority is verging and . . . put a speedy end to the miseries of our fellow creatures."

What Arnold needed to do, André insisted, was to secure a "conspicuous command" in Washington's army. If, for example, he was able to orchestrate the surrender of, say, five to six thousand soldiers, Clinton would be willing to reward him with "twice as many thousand guineas"—not a bad sum, even by Arnold's standards.

But as Clinton was well aware, Arnold's current injuries precluded him from active command. The American general was, whether he admitted it or not, damaged goods from the British perspective, and Clinton was not about to guarantee the rewards that Arnold clearly felt were his due. His well-publicized problems in Philadelphia further reduced his value. "Whatever merit this officer might have had," Clinton later wrote, "his situation . . . made him less an object of attention."

Arnold, ever thin-skinned, sensed as much, and on July 11 Stansbury reported that André's earlier letter was "not equal to his expectations" and that "he found by the laconic style and little attention paid to his request that the gentleman appeared very indifferent respecting the matter." Instead of sending along any additional information, Arnold provided Stansbury with a shopping list from Peggy for various types of cloth and ribbon. Was Arnold mocking André—the officer who had once made Peggy a dress?

Toward the end of July André sent a letter that was almost apologetic.

"I am sorry any hesitation should still remain," he wrote, "as I think we have said all that the prudence with which our liberality must be tempered will admit." In early August, Stansbury forwarded a verbal message from Arnold in which he insisted that although "he wished to serve his country in accelerating the settlement of this unhappy contest"—according to Arnold's self-referential logic, it was possible to serve his country by being a traitor to it—"yet he should hold himself unjust to his family to hazard his all on the occasion and part with a certainty (potentially at least) for an uncertainty." In other words, André had so far failed to meet Arnold's monetary requirements.

On August 16 André appealed directly to Peggy. "It would make me very happy to become useful to you here," he wrote. "You know the Mischianza made me a complete milliner. Should you not have received supplies for your fullest equipment for that department, I shall be glad to enter into the whole detail of capwire, needles, gauze, etc., [and] render you in these trifles service from which I hope you would infer a zeal to be further employed." Cloaked behind the elliptical vernacular of espionage was an awareness on André's part that if his correspondence with Arnold was ever going to yield results, Peggy had to be a part of it.

According to one account, Peggy later claimed that it was only "through great persuasion and unceasing perseverance" that she was ultimately able to steer her husband into treason. As she was no doubt learning, Arnold's sensitivity to a slight required that he be managed with considerable care. Before further negotiations could be constructively pursued, her husband needed to cool down.

Clinton's plan to attack West Point was contingent on the arrival of a fleet of reinforcements from England. But by July, the promised ships and soldiers had not yet arrived, and the season was getting dangerously late. If he was without the manpower to take West Point, perhaps he might succeed in luring at least a portion of Washington's army away from the Hudson River with a raid on the Connecticut coast led by the New York governor, William Tryon. Tryon's subsequent "war of desolation" shocked even Clinton with its violence, but Washington refused to take the bait. When his ever-expanding intelligence network informed him that Tryon's need of troops had drained the fortress at British-held Stony Point of a significant number of soldiers, Washington decided to act.

On July 16 the Pennsylvania general whose emotional outbursts earned him the nickname of "Mad Anthony" Wayne led a nighttime assault up the cliff-like walls of Stony Point. The first man inside the fort was Lieutenant Colonel François de Fleury, the same French engineer who had fought so courageously at Fort Mifflin two years before. That night at 2:00 a.m. Wayne sent Washington a brief but typically theatrical note. "The fort and garrison . . . are ours," he wrote. "Our officers and men behaved like men who are determined to be free."

A month later, the Virginian captain Henry "Light Horse Harry" Lee led an equally daring assault on the British outpost at Paulus Hook, New Jersey, just across the harbor from New York. Although of minimal strategic importance, both operations were proof that, much to Clinton's dismay, the Americans were still a force to be reckoned with. Compounding the British general's frustrations was the lack of promised support he had so far received from England. By the end of the summer, Clinton had become so rattled and depressed by his inability to make any significant progress against the enemy that he decided to tender his resignation. "He told me with tears in his eyes," one of his officers recounted, "that he was quite an altered man, that business oppressed him, that he felt himself incapable of his station." As Clinton despaired, Washington began to plan his boldest operation of the war. On September 13 he sent a proposal to the French commodore d'Estaing, who had begun to make his way north from the West Indies and who Washington hoped would support his army in a multipronged assault on New York City. This time the Americans would provide the French fleet with the harbor pilots they should have had the previous year, enabling them to "immediately enter the harbor" and attack the British at three strategic points: Staten Island, New York City, and the upper Hudson. In the meantime, the Continental army would attack Manhattan Island from the north. "I have taken the liberty to throw out these hints for Your Excellency's information," he wrote, "and permit me to entreat that you will favor me as soon as possible with an account of your Excellency's intentions." The French ambassador, Conrad-Alexandre Gérard, had already discouraged Washington from depending on the French fleet, but that had not prevented him from continuing to plan for a possible joint French-American assault on New York. By the beginning of October he had heard nothing from d'Estaing and yet kept pushing to assemble a large force that included an additional ten thousand militiamen, even though he had no concrete idea as to where the French fleet was currently located.

Washington obviously sensed that the British were vulnerable, and as he assembled the soldiers and supplies required for the operation, Clinton began to consolidate his army in New York by withdrawing his forces from both the Hudson River and Newport, Rhode Island. In reality, however, Washington had no justifiable basis to move forward with the operation. Still, as week followed week with no word from d'Estaing, Washington continued to hold out hope.

One can only wonder what was motivating this forlorn and entirely unrealistic expectation. The previous fall, Lafayette had departed for France, meaning that Washington had been almost a year without the companionship of the young general whom he regarded, he admitted to a French official that September, "as my own son." Later that month, Washington wrote Lafayette an uncharacteristically revealing letter in which he asked his friend to pass along a message to his wife, whom Washington had not yet met.

> Tell her . . . that I have a heart susceptible of the tenderest passion, and that it is already so strongly impressed with the most favorable ideas of her, that she must be cautious of putting love's torch to it; as you must be in fanning the flame. But here again me-thinks I hear you say, I am not apprehensive of danger. My wife is young; you are growing old and the Atlantic is between you. All this is true, but know my good friend that no distance can keep *anxious* lovers long asunder, and that the wonders of former ages may be revived in this. But alas! Will you not remark that amidst all the wonders recorded in holy writ no instance can be produced where a young woman from *real inclination* has preferred an old man. This is so much against me that I shall not be able *I fear* to contest the prize with you, yet, under the encouragement you have given me I shall enter the list for so inestimable a jewel.

Whether it was fantasizing about the wife of a young friend or the mi-raculous appearance of a French naval commander, Washington was clearly in need of some form of escape from the dreary reality of a war that was entering its fifth year.

Finally, by the middle of November, Washington had no choice but to abandon his hopes for a fall invasion of New York. By that time, he'd learned that d'Estaing was still off the coast of Georgia. "We have waited so long in anxious expectation of the French fleet at the Hook . . . since its first arrival at Georgia," he wrote his stepson, John Parke Custis, on November 10, "that we begin to fear that some great convulsion in the earth has caused a chasm between this and that state that cannot be passed. . . . There seems to be the strangest fatality, and the most unaccountable silence attending the operations to the southward that can be conceived."

And then, five days later, he learned that after assisting American forces under Benjamin Lincoln in a failed assault on British-held Savannah, d'Estaing was on his way back to France.

On October 4, 1779, the escalating tension between Philadelphia's radical Constitutionalists and conservative Republicans finally exploded into violence. That morning several hundred militiamen decided to round up the spouses and children of exiled loyalists, as well as any other "disaffected persons," and expel them from the city. Several political leaders, such as the artist Charles Willson Peale, who had become an ally of Joseph Reed's, attempted to dissuade this increasingly irate group of armed citizens from breaking into people's homes and dragging them out into the street, but the militiamen refused to listen. "To reason with a multitude of devoted patriots assembled on such an occasion," Peale wrote, "was in vain."

The militia began by seizing the Quaker Jonathan Drinker as he walked out of the Friends Yearly Meeting, and with Drinker and several others under guard, started marching through the streets of Philadelphia. For anyone who had been in Boston at the beginning of the Revolution, it was a familiar sight: a band of outraged citizenry had taken to the streets to demand justice. But instead of railing against the Crown, they were threatening their fellow citizens. A country born in a revolution was in danger of being destroyed by the same distrust of authority with which it had begun.

Word reached the lawyer James Wilson and several of his conservative friends that the militiamen were now headed in their direction. Soon Wilson and his friends, including a handful of Continental army officers, had barricaded themselves behind the doors of Wilson's house. Initially, it seemed that the expected confrontation might be avoided as the militiamen proceeded to march past the Wilson residence at the corner of Third and Walnut Streets. However, just as the last militiamen were filing past, Captain Robert Campbell opened an upper-story window. Words were exchanged between Campbell and some of the militiamen, a shot was fired—by whom is still in doubt—and in the hail of musketry that followed, Campbell was killed. Soon the militiamen had surrounded the house and begun to beat down the doors.

This was just the kind of dramatic encounter that seemed to demand Benedict Arnold's presence. Just as he had done at the Battle of Ridgefield, he might have led Wilson and the others in a stand that forced even his most vocal critics to acknowledge his irrefutable worth to the nation's cause. There have even been some Arnold biographers who have insisted that he was indeed there, leading the beleaguered conservatives in a heroic defense of their God-given rights against a mob of radical militiamen.

But instead of becoming the hero of what came to be known as the Battle of Fort Wilson, during which several militiamen were killed and many more wounded when they burst into the house, Arnold, who had long since resigned as military governor of Philadelphia, ended up playing a far more minor and ignoble role. By the time he approached the scene of the encounter in his carriage—hardly the most heroic way for a general to come to the rescue—it was too late. Joseph Reed, of all people, had already ridden into the crowd of militiamen on a horse and waving his pistol ordered them to disperse. When Arnold finally arrived, he had to be helped out of the carriage and, as he was being assisted into the house, exclaimed, "Your president has raised a mob and now he cannot quell it." Unfortunately, the crowd had indeed been quelled, and by the time he had limped his way to a second-story window and appeared with a pistol in each hand, there was nothing left for him to do.

Adding insult to injury, at some point Arnold's carriage was surrounded by a swarm of angry Philadelphians who pelted the vehicle with rocks and forced his coachman to beat a hasty retreat. The next day, Arnold complained to Congress that he'd been attacked by a "mob of lawless ruffians [who] threaten[ed] my life." Since there was "no protection to be expected from the authority of the state for an honest man," he demanded that Congress provide him with a guard of "twenty men and a good officer." In what was becoming the eighteenth-century equivalent of a broken record, Arnold made sure to remind the delegates of his past service: "This request I presume will not be denied to a man who has so often fought and bled in the defense of the liberties of his country." Far from providing protection, Congress berated him for casting aspersions against the integrity of the state of Pennsylvania and denied the request.

On October 13, a week after her husband's humiliating exchange with Congress, Peggy finally responded to John André's August 16 appeal. "Mrs. Arnold presents her best respects to Captain André," she wrote, "[and] is much obliged to him for his very polite and friendly offer of being serviceable to her." After an almost two-month silence, Arnold had apparently decided to reopen their correspondence. Just to make sure the British got the message, Peggy added, "Mrs. Arnold begs leave to assure Captain André that her friendship and esteem for him is not impaired by time or accident."

By waiting her husband out, Peggy had allowed the deteriorating conditions in Philadelphia to work to her advantage. Now that Continental soldiers and Pennsylvania militiamen were killing each other in the city's streets (deaths that Joseph Reed dismissed as the "casual overflowings of liberty"), Arnold had decided that his best bet was with the British.

On December 3 he provided Stansbury with a long list of information—Washington's army was about to take up winter quarters; Congress was looking to Holland for financial relief; the American force at Charleston was still woefully inadequate. Arnold also included a question in his message to the British: "Tell me if you wish to have a useful hand in their army, and to pay what you find his services merit?"

Arnold's court-martial had been rescheduled for later that month. If the trial did not go well, it was possible that he might suffer a fate similar to General Charles Lee's and be suspended or even cashiered from the army. Even if he was found guilty of just one of the charges, Washington might not be willing to award him the kind of command that would afford him the access and intelligence the British required of him.

A new sense of urgency entered Arnold's preparations for the court-martial. He must not only exonerate himself; he must emerge from the proceeding triumphant. His future as a traitor depended on it.

CHAPTER ELEVEN

The Pangs of a Dying Man

By December 1779 the Continental army had begun to take up winter quarters in Morristown, New Jersey, which had served as Washington's base of operations in the aftermath of the victories at Trenton and Princeton three years before. Surrounded by the Watchung Mountains as well as a marshy moat of wetlands, Morristown would prove to be the best of all possible refuges during the worst of all possible winters.

Valley Forge is often looked to as the archetypal survival story in the American Revolution, but in truth the winter of 1778 had been unusually mild. Not so the winter of 1780. It started in late November 1779 with a blizzard that left nine inches of snow on the ground, soon followed by another of equal magnitude in early December. That, it turned out, was just the beginning. Over a ten-day period starting on December 28 and ending on January 7, three major snowstorms pummeled the eastern seaboard with high winds and frigid temperatures. By the second week in January there were four feet of snow on the ground, with drifts of over eleven feet.

The month of January 1780 proved to be the coldest in the recorded meteorological history of the eastern United States. At Philadelphia, the Delaware River was frozen in by December 21 and did not reopen until March 4 after a seventy-five-day freeze; New York City was sealed in by ice for an unheard-of five weeks, allowing the British to travel to Brooklyn and Staten Island by sleigh. Although Washington had hopes of using the ice bridge to launch an attack, moving an army under these conditions was an impossibility.

And besides, his army was in no shape to fight. The conveniently ubiquitous Joseph Plumb Martin was one of the soldiers quartered in the more than eleven hundred log huts built in the Jockey Hollow section of Morristown. In this heavily forested, hill-humped basin on the road to Morristown, where each of eight brigades was assigned its own "mountain," the two brigades from Connecticut were given what was considered "the presumed place of convenience" near the mansion owned by the loyalist Peter Kemble.

January 1780 was, Martin remembered, "cold enough to cut a man in two." After four successive days of snow, the already underprovisioned army was left without means to secure any additional food. "Here was the keystone of the arch of starvation," he wrote. "We were absolutely, literally starved; I do solemnly declare that I did not put a single morsel of victuals into my mouth for four days and as many nights, except a little black birch bark which I gnawed off a stick of wood, if that can be called victuals. I saw several of the men roast their old shoes and eat them. . . . If this was not 'suffering,' I request to be informed what can pass under that name."

Back in June, Arnold's court-martial had been delayed due to the British advance up the Hudson. Only after Washington and his army had settled into their new quarters at Morristown did Arnold's trial recommence on December 23 at Dickerson's Tavern at the corner of Spring and Water Streets. Because of delays and adjournments during a month of almost apocalyptic weather, the court-martial did not reach its conclusion until January 21, when it finally became time for Arnold's summation.

A court-martial was a fairly routine occurrence in the life of an army. When an officer's conduct was called into question, the court-martial provided the means by which he could be exonerated or, if the proceedings did not go well, suffer the ignominy of a judgment against him. On January 21 Arnold was determined to clear himself of even a hint of wrongdoing, and on that cold winter day at Dickerson's Tavern, he was at his indignant, self-righteous best.

He began by describing how he had "sacrificed a great part of a handsome fortune" in the service of his country. "The part which I have acted in the American cause," he continued, "has been acknowledged by our friends and by our enemies to have been far from an indifferent one. My time, my fortune, and my person have been devoted to my country in this war." After reading several testimonials, including the letter from Washington that had accompanied the gift of the epaulets, he asked: "Is it probable that after having acquired some little reputation, and after having gained the favorable opinion of those whose favorable opinion it is an honor to gain, I should all at once sink into a course of conduct equally unworthy of the patriot and soldier?"

That, of course, is exactly what Arnold had done. And, indeed, now that he was providing the British with vital military information, he was guilty of crimes that were far blacker than anything brought forward in this trial. But that did not prevent him from launching into his defense with an eloquence and verve that was enough to take one's breath away at the sheer audacity of the man.

Almost none of the charges against him, he convincingly argued, were worthy of a trial. There was, however, one exception. If during his first days in Philadelphia as military governor he had prohibited others from making purchases while he went about buying goods for his own benefit then, yes, he had, in fact, sinned. "If this part of the charge is true," he maintained, "I stand confessed, in the presence of this honorable court, the vilest of men; I stand stigmatized with indelible disgrace, the disgrace of having abused an appointment of high trust and importance, to accomplish the meanest and most unworthy purposes: the blood I have spent in defense of my country will be insufficient to obliterate the stain." By so harshly condemning an act that paled beside what he had already done and planned to do, Arnold had become the oratorical equivalent of the berserker who had stormed the enemy redoubt at Saratoga. He was mocking not only his military judges but the gods, and like Satan he was magnificent in his fearless and pugnacious pride.

But Arnold was not through. In addition to insisting on his own unblemished innocence, he attacked the integrity of his accuser. Using the same tactics of innuendo and insinuation that Joseph Reed had used against him, Arnold invoked the rumor that John Cadwalader had been spreading about Reed for two years now. "When the affairs of America wore a gloomy aspect," Arnold proclaimed, "when our illustrious general was retreating through New Jersey, with a handful of men, I did not propose to my associates, basely to quit the general, and sacrifice the cause of my country to my personal safety by going over to the enemy, and making my peace. I can say I never basked in the sunshine of my general's favor and courted him to his face, when I was at the same time treating him with the greatest disrespect, and vilifying his character when absent. This is more than a ruling member of the council of the state of Pennsylvania can say, 'as it is alleged and believed.'"

In suggesting that Reed had been contemplating treason in the winter of 1776, Arnold ventured into a realm of hypocrisy that can only be described as sublime. Like Shakespeare's King Lear raging on the storm-blasted heath, Arnold had been "more sinned against than sinning," and in his delusional faith in his own honesty he felt justified in accusing his adversary of exactly the transgression he was about to commit.

Arnold's court-martial board was headed by the North Carolinian Robert Howe and included Henry Knox, the same general who had held the Bible on which Arnold had placed his hand when he pledged his allegiance to the United States at Valley Forge. The board did not completely vindicate him, but it came close, acquitting Arnold of all the charges except for issuing a pass to the *Charming Nancy*, which the board decided he had "no right to give." Although his use of government wagons was not technically illegal, the board judged it "imprudent and improper," and he was sentenced to a reprimand.

Arnold was predictably outraged by the fact that he had not been completely cleared of all the charges. "A reprimand," he complained to Silas Deane. "For what?" That did not prevent him, however, from asking Deane to translate the court's proceedings into French so that they could be published in Paris. He was proud of his summation and wanted the world to know how convincingly he had answered his critics.

In the meantime, public opinion in Philadelphia had started to swing in Arnold's favor. On February 3 the Pennsylvania Supreme Executive Council, the very body that had spent the last year pursuing him like a hunted animal, issued what might be interpreted as a retraction: "We do not think it proper to affect ignorance of what is the subject of public conversation, and the sentence of the court-martial tending to impose a mark of reprehension upon General Arnold. We find his sufferings for, and services to, his country so deeply impressed upon our minds as to obliterate every opposing sentiment, and therefore beg leave to request that Congress will be pleased to dispense with the part of the sentence which imposes a public censure, and may most affect the feelings of a brave and gallant officer."

For the last year, Arnold had served as the lightning rod through which much of the anger and frustration associated with the power struggle between the Continental Congress and Pennsylvania's Supreme Executive Council had flowed. By the conclusion of his trial, much of that rage had been expended, and even Joseph Reed appears to have recognized that the hero of Saratoga had been made to suffer unnecessarily for what was, in essence, a question of state's rights. Unfortunately, from Arnold's perspective, the Continental Congress was not willing to follow up on the council's plea for leniency.

Arnold had spent the months after the trial attempting to reach a settlement with Congress over how much he should be compensated for his expenses during his time in Canada after the march to Quebec. With his accustomed lack of discretion, he had accused just about any delegate unlucky enough to become involved in the process of "private resentment or undue influence." As he had done so often in his life, Arnold had picked a self-destructive quarrel with the very people upon whom his future welfare depended. When Arnold's sentence was taken up by Congress, the delegates voted overwhelmingly to allow the reprimand to stand.

In March, Peggy gave birth to a son. By then his household had expanded to include his sister Hannah and his youngest son from his prior marriage (the two older boys were now at school in Maryland), and with his expenses mounting, he was more desperate than he had ever been for money. An appeal to the chevalier de La Luzerne, the new French ambassador, for a loan resulted in a demeaning refusal that forced Arnold to move his family from their comfortable quarters in the Penn Mansion to a much smaller house owned by Peggy's father. As was now obvious, Arnold had grossly misrepresented his overall worth prior to their marriage.

Once again, Arnold's frustrations with his finances caused him to look to the sea. In March he sent several letters to Washington requesting his permission to command a naval expedition that was to depart from New London, Connecticut, with several hundred Continental soldiers. What he wanted to achieve by this expedition is difficult to determine. Did he plan on hijacking the ships under his command and surrendering them to the British? Or might the expedition have served as a last-ditch effort to reinvent himself as an American naval officer? Whatever the case may be, when Washington insisted that he did not have enough soldiers to support the expedition, the idea was dropped.

And then, on April 6, Washington finally issued the long-awaited reprimand. Arnold's providing a permit to the *Charming Nancy* was "peculiarly reprehensible, both in a civil and military view." The "affair of the wagons" was, to repeat the wording of the court-martial decision, "imprudent and improper." Given Congress's decision to uphold the reprimand, Washington had simply done what he had to do. What he did not have to do was write the private letter that accompanied the reprimand.

> Our profession is the purest of all [Washington wrote]. Even the shadow of a fault tarnishes the luster of our finest achievements. The least indiscretion may rob us of the public favor, so hard to be acquired. I reprimand you for having forgotten that, in proportion as you have rendered yourself formidable to our enemies; you should have been guarded and temperate in your deportment towards your fellow citizens. Exhibit anew those noble qualities, which have placed you on the list of our most valued commanders. I will myself furnish you, as far as it may be in my power, with the opportunities for regaining the esteem of your country.

This was undoubtedly sincere, heartfelt advice, but to suggest that Arnold become "guarded and temperate" was to ignore the essence of who Arnold was. Washington, as complex and highly controlled a human being as has ever lived, was capable of modulating his conduct to what the situation required. Not Arnold.

Washington had a blind spot when it came to his contentious major general with a wounded leg. Some of it may have been wishful thinking. More than ever before, he needed as many dynamic and capable generals as he could get. But he also seems to have liked and may even have envied Arnold, a general who was regularly performing the kinds of heroics that might have been Washington's destiny had he been a few years younger and not saddled with the crushing responsibility of commander in chief. In any event, the good news for Arnold was that Washington had virtually promised to award him whatever position was in his power. By late April Arnold knew what he wanted: command at West Point.

Washington had responded to Clinton's seizure of the fortifications at King's Ferry the previous summer by overseeing the expansion and re-finement of the works at West Point, about eleven miles up the Hudson River. By turning West Point into the largest, most important fortress in the United States, Washington had created, ironically, a vulnerability that the country had not previously possessed: a military stronghold so vital that should it fall into the hands of the enemy it might mean the end of the war. The major general who presided at West Point had under his command not only the complex of fortifications that served as the strate-gic "key" to both the Hudson River and Lake Champlain to the north but also the many smaller American posts between West Point and British-occupied New York to the south. With housing available in the surrounding countryside, Peggy and their infant son could be with Ar-nold when it came time to make his true allegiance known. Yes, West Point was the perfect posting for a traitor.

We don't know exactly when Arnold came up with the idea of surren-dering West Point to the British, but it must have been after he learned that he had not gotten the naval command. Initially, he had asked Wash-ington for a leave from the army, but by the middle of April he wanted back in. Philip Schuyler had been in Philadelphia for much of that win-ter, and at some point Arnold began to seek his help in securing the com-mand at West Point. Schuyler had been appointed chairman of a congressional committee that was to confer with Washington about the state of the army, and on April 28 he departed for headquarters in Mor-ristown with the promise that he would speak to the commander in chief on Arnold's behalf.

By late May, Arnold had heard nothing and was growing impatient. "I have not yet had the pleasure of receiving a line from you since you arrived at camp," he wrote to Schuyler on May 25, "and know not who is to have the command at the North [i.e., Hudson] River." Finally, Schuyler re-sponded on June 2. He had good news. For one thing, Washington still liked him. "He expressed a desire to do whatever was agreeable to you," Schuyler wrote, "dwelt on your abilities, your merits, your sufferings, and on the well-earned claims you have on your country and intimated that as soon as his arrangements for the campaign should take place that he would properly consider you. . . . If the command at West Point is offered, it will be honorable; if a division in the field, you must judge whether you can support the fatigues, circumstanced as you are." That was enough for Arnold. As far as he was concerned, the command at West Point was already his—at least that was what he decided to tell the British.

By May he had reestablished contact with the enemy in New York. Unfortunately, John André and Henry Clinton were more than 750 miles to the south at the Siege of Charleston. Clinton had left General Knyphausen in command of the forces in New York. The Hessian general was enthusiastic about Arnold's renewed interest in betraying his country; in fact, the news was of such importance that he felt he must defer making any concrete promises until after Clinton's return. The year before, this delay might have been enough to cause Arnold to quit in a huff; now he appeared perfectly willing to wait.

In early June he left Philadelphia on a trip to Connecticut, where he planned to attend to some personal business, not the least of which was the sale of his house in New Haven. But first he must stop at headquarters in Morristown. By that time he had adopted the new alias of "Mr. Moore" with the British, and on June 12, as he was about to depart for the north, Arnold wrote Knyphausen that "Mr. Moore expects to have the command of West Point offered him on his return."

Despite the confidence of the note, Arnold must have known that Washington was not in a position to guarantee him anything.

The late spring of 1780 had been, from the commander in chief's perspective, the worst months of the war. The winter had been bad enough, but May had marked the near collapse of the Continental army. All spring, the soldiers had been on virtual starvation rations, but on May 21 the supply of provisions stopped completely. "The men were now exasperated beyond endurance," Joseph Plumb Martin wrote. "They could not stand it any longer. They saw no other alternative but to starve to death or break up the army, give all up and go home. This was a hard matter for the soldiers to think upon. They were truly patriotic; they loved their country, and they had already suffered everything short of death in its cause; and now, after such extreme hardships to give up all was too much, but to starve to death was too much also. What was to be done?"

It was not as if the rest of the nation was suffering from extraordinary want. Throughout much of the United States, Americans were experiencing a war-related economic boom. These same citizens might be enjoying an unusual level of prosperity, but they were not about to share it with their struggling national government and their even more beleaguered army. Without an ability to raise its own taxes, the Continental Congress had been forced to rely on printing its own money to pay for the war. But after five years of churning out bills that had become almost worthless, even as it unsuccessfully attempted to convince the states to collect the taxes required to support the army, Congress was left with few options. By the spring of 1780, everything was beginning to grind to a terrible and tragic halt. As Congress bickered about how to restructure the Quartermaster's Department, the rank and file of the Continental army were starving to death.

In desperation, Washington reached out to Joseph Reed in hopes of convincing the president of Pennsylvania's Supreme Executive Council to help in some way. "I assure you, every idea you can form of our distresses will fall short of the reality," he wrote. "All our departments, all our operations, are at a stand; and unless a system, very different from that which has for a long time prevailed, be immediately adopted throughout the states, our affairs must soon become desperate beyond the possibility of recovery. If you were on the spot, my dear Sir, if you could see what difficulties surround us on every side, how unable we are to administer to the most ordinary calls of the service, you would be convinced, that these expressions are not too strong, and that we have everything to dread. Indeed, I have almost ceased to hope."

On May 25 the troops in Morristown reached the point of no return. "Here was the army starved and naked," Martin wrote, "and . . . their country sitting still and expecting the army to do notable things while fainting from sheer starvation. . . . We had borne as long as human nature could endure, and to bear longer we considered folly." That evening, the men from Martin's brigade, one of the two from Connecticut, lingered on the parade ground "growling like sore-headed dogs." Instead of retiring for the night after roll call, they marched over to the other Connecticut brigade and, with their fife and drums playing, encouraged their fellow New Englanders to join them. When all attempts to convince the men to retire to their quarters failed, Washington's officers realized that they had a mutiny on their hands.

By nightfall, the troops from Pennsylvania, whose quarters were near that of the Connecticut brigades, had been called out and positioned around the rebellious New Englanders. Although they called it the Continental army, the American force was, in actuality, a collection of regiments and brigades whose primary loyalties were not to their country but to the states they called home. Given the social and cultural differences between the various regions of the country, soldiers from New England viewed their counterparts from the middle states as strange and almost alien creatures. At one point while stationed at White Plains, New York, Martin and some of his Connecticut brethren found themselves serving with soldiers from Pennsylvania—"two sets of people," he wrote, "as opposite in manners and customs as light and darkness. Consequently there was not much cordiality subsisting between us."

That night on the parade ground at Morristown's Jockey Hollow, however, the troops from Connecticut and Pennsylvania began to realize that their suffering had given them a mutual bond. After asking "what was going on among the Yankees," the troops from Pennsylvania began to think about participating in rather than putting down the mutiny. "Let us join them," Martin remembered them saying. "They are good fellows, and have no notion of lying here like fools and starving."

At one point an officer from Pennsylvania addressed the Connecticut troops directly. All of them, their officers included, were suffering from hunger. "You Connecticut troops have won immortal honor to yourselves the winter past by your perseverance, patience, and bravery," he assured them, "and now you are shaking it off at your heels." Eventually, the officer was able to convince them to return to their quarters, and the food began to roll in. "Our stir did us some good in the end," Martin wrote, "for we had provisions directly after, so we had no great cause for complaint for some time."

A few days after the mutiny of the two Connecticut regiments, Washington admitted that the disturbance "has given me infinitely more concern than anything that has ever happened, and strikes me as the most important, because we have no means at this time, that I know of, for paying the troops, but in Continental money; and as it is evidently impracticable from the immense quantity it would require, to pay them . . . as much as would make up the depreciation. Every possible means in my power will be directed . . . to preserve order and promote the public service; but in such an accumulation of distresses, amidst such a variety of embarrassments, which surround us on all sides, this will be found at least extremely difficult."

Five days after the Connecticut mutiny, Washington received news of the most stunning defeat of the war. Charleston had fallen to the British. Rather than abandoning the city when he still had the chance, Benjamin Lincoln had allowed the pleas of local citizens to delay his exit until it was too late, and he and almost his entire army of fifty-five hundred soldiers had been captured. The following day, on May 31, Washington confessed to Joseph Jones, an attorney from Virginia who served in the Continental Congress, that he feared "our cause is lost."

A country that had begun the Revolution with surprising resolve and determination had lost its appetite for war. As the Continental army was left to wither and die, what had briefly been a country would soon be reduced to a quarreling collection of sovereign states, or as Washington said to Jones, "I see one head gradually changing into thirteen."

In the end, it had all come down to money. Unwilling to pay the taxes demanded by Great Britain, the American people had fomented a revolution; unwilling to pay for an army, they were about to default on the promise they had made to themselves in the Declaration of Independence.

Twenty-five-year-old Lieutenant Colonel Ebenezer Huntington was from Benedict Arnold's birthplace, Norwich, Connecticut. He had begun the war full of idealism and patriotic pride. Now he was, in his own words, "ashamed" to call himself an American.

> The rascally stupidity which now prevails in the country at large is beyond all descriptions . . . [he wrote to his brother back home in Connecticut]. Why do you suffer the enemy to have a foothold on the Continent? You can prevent it. Send your men to the field. Believe you are Americans. [Do] not suffer yourselves to be duped into the thought that the French will relieve you and fight your battles. . . . It is a reflection too much for a soldier. You don't deserve to be freemen unless you can believe it yourselves. . . . I despise my countrymen. I wish I could say I was not born in

America. . . . The insults and neglects which the army have met with from the country beggars all description. It must go no farther. They can endure it no longer. I have wrote in a passion; indeed I am scarce ever free from it. I am in rags . . . and only a junk of fresh beef and that without salt to dine on this day; received no pay since last December. Constituents [back home] complaining and all this for my cowardly countrymen who flinch at the very time when their exertions are wanted and hold their purse strings as though they would damn the world rather than part with a dollar to their army.

Benedict Arnold could not have agreed more, and in one of his communications to the British he compared the plight of America to "the pangs of a dying man, violent but of a short duration." Later in life, he insisted that he had taken the course he did because he had come to believe "our cause was hopeless; I thought we never could succeed, and I did it to save the shedding of blood." Arnold was in no position to insist on the altruism of his actions, but as the words of Ebenezer Huntington demonstrated, he was not the only Continental officer who had become disenchanted with the course of the Revolution.

On his way to Connecticut, Arnold decided to stop at West Point, a place that, he admitted to the British, he had never seen before. Except when it came to courting a woman, Arnold was not the sort to indulge in flights of poetical enthusiasm, but even someone of his matter-of-fact temperament must have been struck by the dramatic beauty of this portion of the Hudson. Much more than a mere waterway, the Hudson, which has been dubbed the "River of Mountains," is a cleft in the continent. A billion years ago, igneous and metamorphic rock formed the basis of the Hudson Highlands—a ridge of hills that extends north from Stony Point to include West Point more than eleven miles upriver. One million years ago, a glacier carved out a deeper and wider river channel even as it rounded the tops of the hills. When the ice retreated between eighteen and fourteen thousand years ago, the essential topography of the Hudson had been established.

In its majesty and echoing distances, the Hudson dwarfs any other river in the eastern United States. The Hudson's watershed extends for thirteen thousand square miles into New York, New Jersey, Connecticut, Massachusetts, and Vermont. The outflow of the river (as much as four hundred thousand gallons of water per second in the spring) creates its own ocean current that reaches south along the New Jersey shore for as many as 150 miles. But if the Hudson has an impact on the surrounding ocean, the ocean has its own implacable influence on the Hudson. For almost half of its 315-mile overall length, from New York Harbor to Troy, the Hudson is tidal, meaning that it flows south at ebb tide and north with the flood. A water-filled canyon amid the mountains, the Hudson Highlands is a place where ancient and unseen forces are in a constant tug of war, and at West Point, Washington and his engineers created a fortress to match the overwhelming scale of what is truly the gateway to an empire.

The craggy heights surrounding the S bend at West Point afforded a natural opportunity for building fortifications to guard the river, but they also presented a special challenge. The two forts on either side of the river—a series of redoubts on Constitution Island to the east and (appropriately enough) Fort Arnold to the west—commanded the river, but they, in turn, were commanded by the heights behind them, requiring that an interlocking series of fortifications be constructed that fit like puzzle pieces into the complexities of the surrounding hills. Remembering what had happened when the British had found a way to get a cannon to the top of a seemingly inaccessible height and taken Fort Ticonderoga in a single day, Washington insisted that his engineers leave nothing to chance, and behind Fort Putnam, which commanded Fort Arnold on the river's western shore, he ordered the construction of six additional redoubts, the highest of which was the fortification atop the peak of Rocky Hill (known as Redoubt Number 4), a dizzying eight hundred feet above the river.

As if this Anasazi-like colony of forts were not enough, the Americans had laid a five-hundred-yard-long chain across the river at the southernmost bend of the S curve. Composed of twelve hundred links forged from iron bars that were two and a quarter inches thick, the chain weighed sixty-five tons and was supported by a series of log rafts. Since the surrounding mountains transformed even a blustery breeze into a whirl of cat's-paws, a sailing ship attempting to navigate this portion of the river was already at a disadvantage as it approached this awesome impediment to navigation. As much a symbol as a reality, the linked barrier across the river sent an unmistakable message to the enemy: *You must stop here.*

But as Arnold's cold and pragmatic eye quickly detected, West Point had its flaws. On June 16, after a tour of the fortifications led by the current commander, General Robert Howe (who also happened to have been the president of his court-martial board), Arnold filed a report with the British. Recording his findings from an American officer's perspective (in case the letter should fall into the wrong hands), he described a fort that was already suffering from serious neglect within just nine months of Washington's efforts to make it impregnable. Arnold claimed to have been "greatly disappointed in both the works and garrison. There is only fifteen hundred soldiers, which will not half man the works." In addition, there was a key vulnerability at Redoubt Number 4. "I am told the English may land three miles below and have a good road to bring up heavy cannon to Rocky Hill. This redoubt is wretchedly executed, only seven or ten foot high and might be taken by assault by a handful of men." He also had little faith in the chain across the Hudson. "I am convinced the boom or chain thrown across the river to stop the shipping cannot be depended on. A single ship large and heavy-loaded with a strong wind and tide would break the chain."

Three years before, just as Burgoyne was about to suffer defeat at Saratoga, Henry Clinton had taken Fort Clinton, a fort between Stony Point and West Point, on the west bank of the Hudson, with commendable ease. He had done it out of a halfhearted attempt to relieve some of the pressure on Burgoyne to the north, and once he'd learned of that officer's fate, he had retreated back to New York. He had, however, gained valuable experience in the Hudson Highlands, and the potential line of attack Arnold described was very similar to what he had employed against Fort Clinton.

But before the British could take advantage of this unmatched opportunity, two things had to happen: Clinton needed to return from Charleston, and Arnold needed to get himself appointed commander at West Point.

As Arnold traveled to Hartford and then New Haven in an attempt to liquidate his holdings prior to his hoped-for coup on the Hudson, Peggy was holding up her end of their matrimonial bargain in Philadelphia. Robert Livingston was an influential congressional delegate from New York. A letter from Livingston might make the difference in convincing Washington to give Arnold the command at West Point.

By all accounts, men found Peggy immensely attractive. Years later, after she and Arnold had moved to London, a British officer known for his many affairs described her as "the handsomest woman in England." In 1780, during the weeks of Arnold's travels to West Point and Connecticut, Peggy made a point of paying Congressman Livingston more attention than Arnold's sister Hannah thought appropriate. In a letter to Arnold, Hannah reported that the two of them had spent the weeks of his absence in "frequent private assignations and . . . numberless billets-doux." Livingston was, according to Hannah, "a dangerous companion" for his wife.

Peggy was not being unfaithful; she was doing what had to be done to make sure that Livingston wrote in support of her husband. On June 22 Livingston sent a letter to Washington containing the dubious claim that the security of the state of New York depended on a change of commanders at West Point, and that Arnold was the officer to ensure the security of the undermanned fortress. Washington responded a week later by insisting that "I am under no apprehension now of danger to the post at West Point." Clearly baffled by Livingston's sudden interest in a post that was under no immediate threat from the enemy, Washington politely insisted that he had no reason, as of yet, to replace the fort's commander, Robert Howe. Now that Clinton was back from Charleston, Washington had more important things to worry about.

The triumph in Charleston had given Clinton hope that victory in America was now within his grasp. He was no longer interested in resigning, and as he and André sailed back to New York in early June, Clinton made plans to attack Washington's feeble army before it had a chance to leave Morristown. Unfortunately, General Knyphausen had already launched an assault on the Americans before the troops under Clinton's command had arrived from the South. Overwhelmed by an unexpected show of strength on the part of the New Jersey militia, Knyphausen ended up losing more men, André reported, than Clinton had lost during the entire Siege of Charleston.

Washington's unsuccessful attempt to take the British-occupied
stone mansion of Cliveden during the Battle of Germantown.

Washington's headquarters during the long winter at Valley Forge.

John Laurens, one of Washington's valued aides during the winter at Valley Forge.

Henry Laurens, president of the Continental Congress, by V. Green Mezzotinto. The correspondence between Laurens and his son John during the winter of 1778 provided Washington with the information and support he needed to weather the Conway Cabal.

Marquis de Lafayette by Charles Willson Peale. Just nineteen when he first met Washington, Lafayette would become a kind of surrogate son to the American commander in chief.

Alexander Hamilton by William Weaver. Soon after serving in the New York and New Jersey campaigns of 1776, Hamilton became an essential member of Washington's military family.

The Irish-born French general Thomas Conway, who found himself at the center of the cabal that bears his name.

General Thomas Mifflin and his wife by John Singleton Copley. Mifflin was, according to Henry Laurens, the "pivot" of the Conway Cabal during the winter of 1778.

David Bushnell's unsuccessful attempt to sink the British fleet at Philadelphia with fifty floating barrels of gunpowder was humorously referred to as the Battle of the Kegs.

The Battle of Monmouth by Alonzo Chappel. Fought in blistering heat during the summer of 1778, this engagement marked Washington's last battlefield appearance before the Siege of Yorktown in 1781.

Major John André made this sketch of Benedict Arnold's future wife, Peggy Shippen, during the British occupation of Philadelphia in 1777–78.

A sketch made by John André of three participants—including a knight often mistaken for a lady—in the Mischianza, an elaborate celebration held during the final weeks of the British occupation of Philadelphia.

I Benedict Arnold Major General
do acknowledge the UNITED STATES of AME-
RICA to be Free, Independent and Sovereign States, and
declare that the people thereof owe no allegiance or obedience to George the Third, King of Great-Britain; and I
renounce, refufe and abjure any allegiance or obedience to
him; and I do *Swear* that I will, to the ut-
moft of my power, fupport, maintain and defend the faid
United States againft the faid King George the Third, his
heirs and fucceffors, and his or their abettors, affiftants and
adherents, and will ferve the faid United States in the office of
Major General which I now hold, with
fidelity, according to the beft of my fkill and underftanding.

Sworn before me this *B Arnold*
30th May 1778 at the
Artillery Park Valley Forge Henry B Gibbs

Benedict Arnold's oath of allegiance,
signed on May 30, 1778, at Valley Forge.

Pierre Ozanne's sketch
of Comte d'Estaing's
French fleet outside
Sandy Hook, New
Jersey, during the
summer of 1778.
The line of British
ships anchored along
the channel to New
York can be seen in
the distance.

Major David Salisbury Franks, one of Benedict Arnold's aides when the general was stationed in Philadelphia and West Point.

General John Cadwalader served with Washington during the Second Battle of Trenton. A political conservative, he was a supporter of Benedict Arnold during the latter's embattled tenure as military governor of Philadelphia.

Right: An Ozanne sketch of d'Estaing's dismasted flagship, the *Languedoc,* being fired on by HMS *Renown* after the Great Storm of 1778.

A panoramic view of West Point on the Hudson River by Pierre Charles L'Enfant about the time of Benedict Arnold's treason.

Benedict Arnold's July 15, 1780, coded letter
offering to sell West Point to the British.

Inclosed in a cover addressed to Mr. Anderson.

Two days since I received a letter without date or signature, informing me that S. Henry —— was obliged to me for the intelligence communicated, and that he placed a full confidence in the sincerity of my intentions, &c. &c. —— On the 13th Instant I addressed a letter to you expressing my Sentiments and expectations, viz, that the following Preliminaries be settled previous to cooperating —— first, that S. Henry secure to me my property, valued at ten thousand pounds Sterling, to be paid to me or my Heirs in case of Loss; and, as soon as that ~~happens~~ shall happen, —— hundred pounds per annum to be secured to me for life, in lieu of the pay and emoluments I give up, for my Services as they shall deserve —— If I point out a plan of cooperation by which S.H. shall possess himself of West Point, the Garrison, &c. &c. &c. twenty thousand pounds Sterling I think will be a cheap purchase for an object of so much importance. At the same time I request a thousand pounds to be paid my Agent —— I expect a full and explicit answer —— the 20th I set off for West Point. A personal interview with an officer that you can confide in is absolutely necessary to plan matters. In the mean time I shall communicate to our mutual Friend S——y all the intelligence in my power, until I have the pleasure of your answer.

July 15th
                            Moore

To the line of my letter of the 13th
I did not add seven.

N.B. the postscript only relates to the manner of composing the Cypher in the letter referred to ——

The decoded July 15 letter.

The house built by Colonel Beverley Robinson that served as Benedict Arnold's headquarters when he was commander at West Point.

A sketch by Benson J. Lossing of the dining room in Robinson House where Benedict and Peggy Arnold entertained guests prior to the discovery of his treason in September 1780.

Beverley Robinson, who was with John André aboard the *Vulture* prior to André's meeting with Benedict Arnold.

Joshua Hett Smith's house overlooking Haverstraw Bay on the Hudson River. This was where Benedict Arnold and John André discussed plans for the surrender of West Point to the British.

William Smith Jr. by John Wollaston. Smith, the chief justice of New York, was the loyalist older brother of Joshua Hett Smith, who escorted John André through the Neutral Ground in Westchester County prior to his capture by three New York militiamen.

Major Benjamin Tallmadge by John Trumbull. Despite his success at creating the Culper Ring of spies, Tallmadge never suspected Benedict Arnold of treachery until it was almost too late.

John André's sketch of being rowed to his nighttime meeting with Benedict Arnold.

John André's self-portrait, sketched prior to his execution in Tappan, New York.

Benedict Arnold's effigy being paraded through the streets of Philadelphia on September 30, 1780.

The Saratoga National Historical Park's "Boot Monument," near where Arnold suffered the leg injury that initiated his descent into treason. Without mentioning the traitor by name, the monument describes Arnold as "the 'most brilliant soldier' of the Continental Army."

But as Clinton soon discovered, an even more attractive opportunity had presented itself. Arnold was once again interested in offering his services, and this time he had something concrete to offer: the fortress at West Point. But that was not all. D'Estaing had been replaced by the Comte de Rochambeau, who was headed for America with an army of four thousand soldiers and a fleet of warships under the command of Charles-Henri-Louis d'Arsac de Ternay. In his latest communication to the British, Arnold reported that the French fleet was headed to Newport. If Clinton could trap the newly arrived French force in Narragansett Bay, he might pull off his second stunning victory in as many months.

But first he needed to be absolutely sure that Arnold was, in fact, the one who was feeding them this information. André dispatched several spies who reported that just as Arnold had claimed in one of his messages, he was traveling throughout Connecticut. Confident that the information Arnold was providing could be trusted, Clinton readied an army of six thousand British soldiers for an assault on Newport.

Washington had first received word of Rochambeau's pending arrival from Lafayette, who reached Morristown on May 10. "Here I am, my dear general," Lafayette had exulted in his first letter to Washington since his return to America, "and in the midst of the joy I feel in finding myself again one of your loving soldiers." Then had come the mutiny of the Connecticut regiments and the loss of Charleston. But by the middle of June, Washington had rekindled dreams of a combined French-American attack on New York.

Once again, however, his optimism proved unwarranted. On his arrival at Newport, Rochambeau insisted that his army needed time to restore itself after the long transatlantic passage; like d'Estaing before him, the French admiral Ternay was reluctant to risk his fleet in an attack on New York, especially when the arrival of reinforcements from Britain gave the enemy fleet clear naval superiority. Making matters even worse, Rochambeau did not have the promised uniforms and equipment that the near-naked American army needed. And then, in the middle of July, Washington learned that Clinton was headed for Newport.

Washington might have responded with dread and even panic. His own army was on the west side of the Hudson River, starving and ill equipped; the French were about to be attacked in Rhode Island, and there was nothing he could do about it. It all might be over before the end of the summer. There was no way Washington was going to get his own army to Newport, but what if he attacked the British garrison in New York? Because of the move against Newport, the enemy army in the city was now reduced by six thousand men (Washington mistakenly believed the number was closer to eight thousand). With reinforcements from the militia, he would cross the Hudson at King's Ferry and march his army south for an attack on New York. Even if he did not succeed in taking the city, he might force Clinton to abandon his mission against the French in Newport.

If his assault on New York was to have any hope of success, it needed to be ably led. Nathanael Greene was to command the army's right wing. But what about the left? Even though Schuyler and Livingston, not to mention the general himself, had urged that Arnold be put in command at West Point, Washington had higher ambitions for the hero of Saratoga.

By the end of July, Arnold had staked everything on the West Point gambit. From what he could tell, Henry Clinton was enthusiastic about the idea. Unfortunately, Arnold's travels had made communication with the British difficult since the only way he could get a message to New York was through Joseph Stansbury in Philadelphia. Peggy became the conduit through which messages from Arnold and André flowed, and given the uncertainty of Arnold's whereabouts, Peggy often had no choice but to hold on to the messages for weeks at a time. The resulting, almost monthlong delay had been agonizing, and yet Washington had been just as difficult to pin down. By the end of July Arnold had not yet received definitive word from either the British or the American commander. That did not prevent him from barreling ahead under the assumption that he was about to replace Robert Howe as commander at West Point and that the British were going to pay him handsomely for his subsequent efforts on their behalf.

After a brief stop in Philadelphia, during which he informed Congress that he was about to return to active duty and therefore needed an advance of twenty-five thousand Continental dollars (which, surprisingly, he was duly paid), he was on his way to catch up with Washington in Kakiat, New York, on the west side of the Hudson River. If all went according to plan, Peggy and their infant son would soon be on their way to meet him at their new residence near the fortress at West Point.

On July 31 Arnold found Washington on a height of land overlooking the Hudson, watching his army being transported across the river to Verplanck's Point. The commander in chief's head was full of preparations for his assault on New York. That day he wrote Rochambeau that "the only way I can be useful to you is to menace New York, and even to attack it, if the force remaining there does not exceed what I have reason to believe. I am pressing my movements for that purpose with all the rapidity in our power." To Lafayette, who was acting as Washington's emissary to the French commander, he wrote, "I am exceedingly hurried in arranging and preparing a variety of matters."

Washington might have been preoccupied, but he was undoubtedly pleased to see Arnold, whose leg had at last healed to the point that he could now ride a horse. Washington later remembered that Arnold asked "if I had thought of anything for him." The American commander had what he believed to be very good news. Instead of wasting his talents at West Point, Arnold was to lead the army's left wing during the assault on New York—a position that Washington described as "a post of honor."

Arnold responded in a completely unexpected way. "Upon this information," Washington remembered, "his countenance changed, and he appeared to be quite fallen; and instead of thanking me, or expressing any pleasure at the appointment, never opened his mouth." Washington later admitted to having "a good opinion of Arnold before his treachery was brought to light." Rather than arousing any suspicions in the commander in chief, Arnold's unusual response seems to have provoked genuine concern. To Washington on that day on the Hudson, Arnold appeared to be a broken man who lacked the confidence to take advantage of the opportunity he had been offered. It never occurred to Washington to question Arnold's motives, and one can only wonder whether Arnold felt at least a modicum of shame as the man he admired as much as anyone suggested that he take some time to think it over. "I desired him to go on to my quarters," Washington remembered, "and get something to refresh himself, and I would meet him there soon."

Arnold did as his commander in chief suggested, and once at headquarters, he took Washington's trusted aide Tench Tilghman aside and expressed his "great uneasiness" with the prospect of commanding the left wing, claiming that "his leg . . . would not permit him to be long on horseback; and intimated a great desire to have the command at West Point."

Eventually Washington arrived at headquarters, and Tilghman told him of his conversation with Arnold. "I made no reply to it," he remembered, "but [Arnold's] behavior struck me as strange and unaccountable." Washington apparently decided that for both Arnold's and the army's benefit, Arnold should lay aside his misgivings and assume command of the left wing. Even with a leg that had been broken below the knee at Quebec and above the knee at Saratoga, he was one of the best generals Washington had. In the General Orders for August 1, Arnold was listed as commanding the left wing.

Several days later, 130 miles to the south in Philadelphia, Peggy Arnold was just finishing dinner at the home of the financier Robert Morris when a guest arrived with news from Washington's army. Her husband, the guest informed her, was not going to have the command at West Point; instead, he had been "appointed to a different but more honorable command."

Much like Arnold on the banks of the Hudson, Peggy did not react as might have been expected. According to one account, "The information affected her so much as to produce hysteric fits." By that time, Arnold's aide David Franks had grown accustomed to Peggy's "occasional paroxysms of physical indisposition, attended by nervous debility, during which she would give utterance to anything and everything on her mind." Years later she described these emotional outbursts to her father as "a confusion in my head resembling what I can suppose would be the sensations of anybody extremely drunk." To avoid these scenes, the members of Arnold's household and staff had become, according to Franks, "scrupulous of what we told her, or said in her hearing."

The interchange at the Morris residence, however, had been beyond Franks's ability to control, and all attempts to placate Peggy "produced no effect." After sixteen months of marriage, during which she had given birth to a child while managing her temperamental husband through the tense series of negotiations upon which their financial welfare increasingly appeared to depend, Peggy had reached the breaking point.

• • •

But Peggy need not have worried. Clinton ultimately failed to convince his counterpart in the British navy, Admiral Mariot Arbuthnot, that the projected expedition to Newport was worth his while. When he realized that he was not going to receive the required naval support, Clinton called off the operation. Having gotten only as far as Huntington, Long Island, Clinton and André were soon sailing back to New York with their six thousand troops. When Washington learned of the British army's return, he called off the attack.

In the General Orders for August 3 was a postscript: "Major General Arnold will take command of the garrison at West Point."

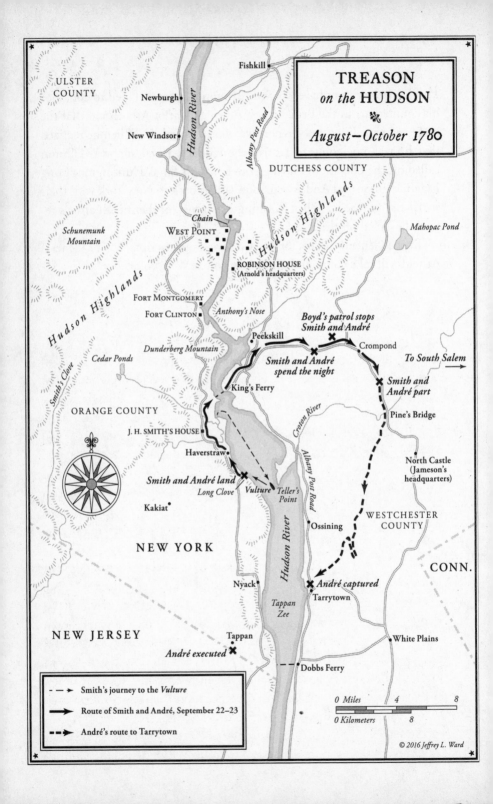

ULSTER
COUNTY

Newburgh

New Windsor

Fishkill

Hudson River

Albany Post Road

DUTCHESS COUNTY

Chain
WEST POINT

Hudson Highlands

Mahopac Pond

ROBINSON HOUSE
(Arnold's headquarters)

*Schunemunk
Mountain*

Hudson Highlands

FORT MONTGOMERY
FORT CLINTON

Anthony's Nose

Hudson Highlands

Peekskill

Boyd's patrol stops
Smith and André

Crompond

To South Salem

Dunderberg Mountain

Cedar Ponds

Smith and André
spend the night

Smith and
André part

Smith's Clove

King's Ferry

Croton River

Pine's Bridge

ORANGE COUNTY

J. H. SMITH'S HOUSE

Albany Post Road

North Castle
(Jameson's
headquarters)

Haverstraw

Smith and André land
Long Clove   Vulture   *Teller's
Point*

WESTCHESTER
COUNTY

Kakiat

Ossining

NEW YORK

Hudson River

CONN.

Nyack

*Tappan
Zee*

André captured
Tarrytown

White Plains

NEW JERSEY

Tappan

André executed ✗

Dobbs Ferry

TREASON
on the HUDSON

August – October 1780

- - - →   Smith's journey to the *Vulture*

——→   Route of Smith and André, September 22–23

▪▪▪►   André's route to Tarrytown

0 Miles   4   8

0 Kilometers   8

© 2016 Jeffrey L. Ward

CHAPTER TWELVE

The Crash

By the time Arnold arrived at his headquarters on the east bank of the Hudson, more than a mile down the river from West Point in present-day Garrison, New York, his injured left leg had healed to the extent that with the assistance of a special high-heeled red shoe he could walk without a cane. Walking any distance, however, was still impossible. Luckily, his new residence on the river was ideally suited for "an invalid," he wrote his predecessor at West Point, General Robert Howe. Situated on a steep bank and flanked by two high, tree-covered hills, the house, originally built by the loyalist Beverley Robinson, offered dramatic views of the Hudson and had its own dock. After a short ride on horseback down to the waterside, Arnold would stump his way to his awaiting barge powered by eight oarsmen and steered by a coxswain.

Once settled in his seat, Arnold enjoyed a combination of comfort and mobility that he had not known since his injury at Saratoga. Gliding across the glittering waters of the Hudson, with green, tree-covered mountains on either side, he now had the ability to travel up and down the river with amazing speed, especially when the current was behind him. Arnold's chief concern was the fortress at West Point, just a short hitch to the north, but he was also responsible for the series of much smaller riverside fortifications that extended more than thirty miles down the river to Dobbs Ferry on the river's eastern bank.

Arnold could travel easily within the American limits of the river, but he had no reliable way, as of yet, to send or receive messages to and from

British-occupied New York. This meant that even though he was now in command at West Point, he had not yet heard whether or not Henry Clinton had accepted his terms for surrendering the fortress. All evidence points to Arnold being in a lonely state of uncertainty during the first weeks of August. With Peggy in Philadelphia, there was no one in whom he could confide, meaning that he must remain on his guard at all times. In addition to several servants, he had two aides: David Franks, who had been with him in Philadelphia, and Richard Varick, the young New Yorker who had encouraged his sparring with Horatio Gates at Saratoga. While Franks had tolerated Arnold's suspicious behavior in Philadelphia, Varick proved to be much less open minded.

What Arnold needed at this immensely complicated point in his life was privacy to conduct his secret correspondence with the British, but privacy was almost impossible to find in the crowded confines of Robinson House. Due to the lack of space, Varick was forced to sleep in the room that served as Arnold's office, and the meddlesome aide was almost always close at hand. By the time Varick arrived at Arnold's headquarters, the general had already accumulated a large number of government stores that were kept in a locked room. Given how much Congress still owed him, Arnold felt justified in converting the provisions into cash. Varick, however, saw such activities as a betrayal of the government's trust, and in several instances interfered in Arnold's surreptitious efforts to sell the provisions. But it was in the general's attempts to establish a line of communication into New York that Varick proved the most troublesome.

One of Arnold's responsibilities as commander at West Point was, in the words of Washington's orders, "to obtain every intelligence of the enemy's motions." It was an order tailor-made for a traitor. If he could discover the identities of the spies Washington and other American officers had enlisted in New York, he would gain information of vital importance to the British. But when he questioned Generals Howe and Lafayette about their contacts in New York, both officers refused to share the contacts' identities—and with good reason. One of the principles of espionage was that the fewer people who knew the identity of a spy the better. By daring to inquire about the names of people whom their handlers had sworn never to divulge, Arnold, in his characteristically tactless and impertinent way, was asking for information he had no right to know. He must establish his own spy network, a process that in itself offered an excellent opportunity for masking his attempts to communicate with André and Clinton in New York.

One of the people Robert Howe did put him in contact with was Joshua Hett Smith, a thirty-one-year-old attorney of uncertain political affiliations whose older brother William had sided with the British and now served as chief justice of New York. With a host of family and friends in the city, the younger Smith had apparently been useful in some way to Arnold's predecessor. Smith was also strategically located in a house on the west bank of the river, just two miles to the south of King's Ferry, the vital east-west link between Stony and Verplanck's Points that was approximately halfway between West Point and Dobbs Ferry. Smith appears to have been more than a little star-struck by the hero of Saratoga (offering "to render any service to a gentleman whose character I revere") and might prove to be just the person Arnold needed as events unfolded in the weeks ahead. Unfortunately, Arnold's aide Richard Varick objected with increasing vehemence to his association with Smith, whose "moral and political character" was, Varick insisted, suspect. Making matters even worse, Varick and Franks quickly became fast friends, and Arnold must have heard his two aides whispering disapprovingly behind his back.

By the third week in August the cumulative pressures had begun to weigh heavily on Arnold. Although his official correspondence projected the aura of a take-charge officer doing his best to ensure the security of the river, those who dealt with him directly found him to be unaccountably distracted. According to Sebastian Bauman, who was in charge of the artillery at West Point, Arnold had "but a poor idea of this place, which I can assure you, after all his inquiry of its particular strength, and the weakest part of it. For his head appeared to me bewildered from the very first moment he took command here." As it always seemed to do in times of stress, his good leg became inflamed with gout, forcing him to curtail his daily visits to West Point. His letters to his sister Hannah were so peremptory and mean-spirited that she termed him "a perfect master of ill nature."

Finally, on August 24, Arnold received a packet of correspondence from Peggy in Philadelphia that included the much-anticipated letter from André. The British spy chief was happy to report that Clinton had agreed to his terms, especially if he could guarantee the capture of three thousand American soldiers during the fall of West Point. Instead of stripping the fortress of personnel, which had been his original objective, Arnold embarked on a twofold project: do as little as possible to complete the much-needed repairs and improvements to the fort's outer works while making sure the required number of soldiers were either in or near the fortress on the day of the British attack.

By early September, Arnold had learned of yet another stunning American defeat in the South. After the loss of Charleston, the Continental Congress had decided to appoint Horatio Gates as the new commander of the southern army. For Gates, whose reputation had suffered as a consequence of the infighting associated with the Conway Cabal, it was a chance to prove that the victory he claimed for himself at Saratoga was legitimately his.

On August 16 in Camden, South Carolina, Gates suffered one of the bloodiest and most humiliating defeats of the war. Nine hundred American soldiers were killed or wounded; a thousand were made prisoners as Gates abandoned the field in apparent panic and rode an estimated 180 miles before finally coming to a stop.

Arnold could hardly contain himself. "It is an unfortunate piece of business to that hero," he wrote Nathanael Greene, "and may possibly blot his escutcheon with indelible infamy. It may not be right to censure character at a distance, but I cannot avoid remarking that his conduct on this occasion has in no wise disappointed my expectations or predictions on frequent occasions."

Gates's debacle at Camden, coupled with Benjamin Lincoln's equally spectacular defeat at Charleston, gave Arnold the satisfaction of knowing that his two superior officers at Saratoga had so far proven unable to succeed without him. Thanks to Lincoln and Gates, America's military prospects had never been so bleak, and Arnold was poised to make the most of it.

Arnold never found a reliable way to get messages into New York, but by early September, he had convinced a Mrs. McCarthy to carry a sealed message into the city that eventually made its way to André. By that time, the British spy chief had been named Clinton's adjutant general. It was an astonishing rise for an officer who was only thirty years old. In a letter home to his family in England, André admitted that he could "hardly look back at the steep progress I have made without being giddy." Usually an adjutant general in the British army held the rank of lieutenant colonel, but André had only recently been named a major—a promotion that had caused considerable grumbling among officials in London due to André's young age and lack of social connections. For André, the taking of West Point would be a way to prove to the world that he was worthy of the trust that Clinton had so far placed in him. It might also be the way that he eliminated his own very Arnold-like concerns about money.

One of the few successes Admiral d'Estaing had enjoyed over the last year had been the taking of the Caribbean island of Grenada, a British possession upon which much of the André family's income depended. As a consequence, André's "mode of life" had been drastically altered, "and all my golden dreams vanished." If he played an indispensable role in the taking of West Point, however, he would most assuredly be awarded the kind of royal favor that would eliminate any future financial concerns.

André had the polished manners of a scholar and a gentleman, but within him lurked an ambition that was perhaps even more ruthless than Arnold's. Over the last year, he had developed a reputation as Clinton's essential right-hand man. Before that, however, he had been an enthusiastic participant in two of the most gruesome massacres of the war. He'd been there with General Charles "No Flint" Grey at Paoli, Pennsylvania, on the night of September 20, 1777, when the British had surprised the Americans commanded by Anthony Wayne and, in André's approving words, put "to the bayonet all they came up with and, overtaking the main herd of the fugitives, stabbed great numbers and pressed on their rear till it was thought prudent to order them to desist." "It was a most bloody piece of work," he bragged to his mother, "and, I believe, will alarm them very much."

A year later, at the town of Old Tappan, New Jersey, Grey and André succeeded in surprising the Virginian George Baylor's dragoons while they slept in several barns. As subsequent archaeological evidence confirmed, many of the dead were stabbed from above, indicating that they were most likely on their knees, pleading for their lives, when they were killed. Even local loyalists were shocked by the slaughter. According to the New York judge Thomas Jones, the massacre of Baylor's men was "inconsistent with the dignity or honor of a British General and disgraceful to the name of a soldier." In the weeks ahead, it became convenient to portray André as the unwitting victim of Arnold's conniving duplicity, but in many fundamental ways André and Arnold were two of a kind.

In his letter to André, Arnold had proposed that the British officer pose as a New Yorker named "John Anderson" whom Arnold had cultivated for intelligence purposes. Under this pretense, André would report to one of the American posts—in addition to the forts along the river, there were several advance posts at the northern edges of the Neutral Ground on the east side of the Hudson in Westchester County—where a meeting between André and Arnold could be arranged. In anticipation of this event, Arnold had written the American officers in command of these posts to expect a visit from a John Anderson of New York and to notify him of the informant's arrival.

Although the plan seemed straightforward to Arnold, it involved immense risks for André. Earlier in the war he'd spent more than a year as an American prisoner, much of it in Carlisle, Pennsylvania, during which he'd come to know more than a few American officers before winning his release through a prisoner exchange. There were also plenty of American officers who had served time as prisoners in New York and who had come to know André there. If he should be recognized and captured behind American lines, he would, in all likelihood, be executed as a spy. As a consequence, Clinton refused to allow his trusted adjutant to venture across American lines in disguise. If he was going to meet with Arnold, he could only do it dressed as a British officer.

The wearing of a uniform to designate a soldier's allegiance was an ancient convention of war. Another was the white flag of truce, often referred to simply as a flag. Under the protection of a flag, a uniformed enemy soldier could not be fired upon and was granted the opportunity to speak with a representative from the opposing side. Often the flag of truce was used to negotiate a surrender, but it also could provide the opportunity to discuss more private matters. For example, after the Battle of Saratoga, the wife of a British officer who had been badly wounded before his capture by the Americans was granted the right to cross the lines under a flag so that she could be with her husband.

A flag was not to be used to secure a military advantage over the enemy, but abuses occurred all the time. Prior to the Battle of Trenton, an American officer approached one of the Hessian outposts in New

Jersey, supposedly to explore the possibility of defecting to the British but really, the Hessian commander later insisted, to gain knowledge of the disposition of the enemy forces prior to an anticipated attack. It was a violation of the rules of war, but Clinton decided that the safest way to provide André and Arnold with the opportunity to discuss the upcoming British attack on West Point was to do it under the sanction of a flag.

Beverley Robinson, the builder of the house that served as Arnold's headquarters, was now serving as the colonel of a regiment of loyalists in New York. Claiming that he wanted to discuss concerns about his property on the Hudson (a ploy he had used earlier when attempting to discover whether General Israel Putnam might be interested in changing sides), Robinson would appear at Dobbs Ferry on the east bank of the Hudson, which was safely within the Neutral Ground, with a flag. Accompanying him would be none other than Major John André, not posing as the civilian John Anderson (as Arnold had wished), but (in accordance with Clinton's orders) as himself. The problem was how to communicate this change of plans to Arnold.

André decided to write directly to the commander of the most advanced American forces, Colonel Elisha Sheldon, stationed at North Castle, New York. The letter that he crafted was a masterwork of indirection and deception that was ultimately passed by Sheldon to Arnold. Writing as John Anderson, André explained that he would be unable to "assume a mysterious character . . . as friends [i.e., Arnold] have advised." Instead, at noon on Monday, September 11, a British officer, "between whom and myself no distinction need be made," would appear at Dobbs Ferry. In other words, Major John André, not John Anderson, would be at Dobbs Ferry on September 11.

Arnold didn't like it, protesting in a carefully worded response that "you must be sensible my situation will not permit my meeting or having any private intercourse with such an officer." That, however, did not prevent him from venturing toward Dobbs Ferry in his barge at the appointed time.

That morning, British gunboats similar to the ones he had faced at Valcour Island were prowling the edges of the river near Dobbs Ferry. The watery equivalent of the Neutral Ground on the east side of the river, this portion of the Hudson was the scene of near-constant skirmishing between British and Continental forces. Clearly, the commanders of the gunboats had not gotten word that several British officers wanted to meet with a noteworthy American general, and one of the gunboats fired on Arnold's barge. Barely escaping alive, he was forced to scurry to the safety of the west bank of the river. For the rest of the day, Arnold waited in the vain hope that André and Robinson, who were presumably waiting on the east bank of the river, would realize what had happened and venture across the river.

As it so happened, Private Joseph Plumb Martin (a participant just a few months before in the mutiny of the two Continental regiments from Connecticut) was now stationed at Dobbs Ferry. Having grown up not far from New Haven, Martin had encountered Arnold before the war, and he later claimed that he "never had too good an opinion of him." It may have been while Arnold was anxiously killing time on the west bank of the Hudson on September 11 that Martin stumbled across the American general. "I met him upon the road a little distance from Dobbs Ferry," he remembered. "He was then taking his observations and examining the roads. I thought that he was upon some deviltry. We met at a notch of the roads, and I observed he stopped, and sitting upon his horse, seemed minutely to examine each road. I could not help taking notice of him, and thought it strange to see him quite alone in such a lone place. He looked guilty, and well he might for Satan was in as full possession of him at that instant as ever he was of Judas."

By three o'clock in the afternoon, Arnold had given up on André and was headed back up the river to Robinson House. Arnold was a notorious risk taker, but after nearly getting blown out of the water he seems to have decided that it was now André's turn to put himself in harm's way. The next time they attempted a meeting, André would come to *him*.

On September 14 the British admiral George Rodney arrived at Sandy Hook, New Jersey, with a fleet of twelve ships of the line and four frigates. Unlike Admiral Arbuthnot, Rodney had a reputation for being a skillful and bold fighter, and he was eager to help Clinton follow up the recent British victories at Charleston and Camden with an even more pivotal success in New York.

Up until then, Clinton and André had kept their correspondence with Arnold a profound secret. They now decided to take Rodney into their confidence and set into motion the amphibious operation up the

Hudson that Clinton believed could bring the war to a dramatic close. As he'd already predicted—somewhat mysteriously—to Chief Justice William Smith of New York, "The rebellion would end suddenly in a crash."

"It became necessary at this instant," Clinton later wrote, "that the secret correspondence under feigned names which had been so long carried on [with Benedict Arnold] should be rendered into certainty." After two weeks of wary and halfhearted attempts to arrange a conference, the time had finally come for André and Arnold to meet.

On September 16 a fourteen-gun sloop of war named HMS *Vulture* anchored within sight of the home of Joshua Hett Smith on the Hudson River. Smith's house overlooked Haverstraw Bay, a wide tidal sea bound by King's Ferry to the north and Teller's Point to the south, and the *Vulture* had anchored on the west side of the Hudson, just off Teller's Point. Whether or not the young lawyer regarded the arrival of a vessel named for a bird that feeds on the bodies of the dead as an ill omen, he could not help but notice that the British ship had anchored provocatively close to his own residence.

Two days before, Smith had hosted Arnold and his wife, Peggy, who had just completed the journey from Philadelphia with their six-month-old son, Edward. The Arnolds' reunion at Smith's house must have made for an emotional scene, but that did not prevent Peggy's husband from getting down to business. By the time the Arnolds were on their way to Robinson House in the general's barge, Smith had agreed to make his house available for a secret meeting between Arnold and an informant from New York. As a consequence of this commitment, Smith was about to take his wife and their nephew to a friend's house in Fishkill, twenty-five miles up the Hudson, for a brief holiday. Once he'd delivered them to Fishkill, Smith would return to help facilitate Arnold's meeting with the shadowy figure from the city who was more than likely aboard the *Vulture*.

Smith, it seems clear, had no inkling of Arnold's treasonous intentions. As far as he was concerned, Arnold was doing what Robert Howe had done before him—cultivating contacts in New York. Still, one had to wonder how a man who styled himself a lawyer could be either so dimwitted or so gullible that his suspicions were not aroused by Arnold's increasingly problematic behavior. One of those blithe and oblivious individuals who contentedly believe whatever they are told, Smith was a character out of a Restoration comedy who was about to find himself in the midst of a Greek tragedy.

At midday on September 17, Arnold was at his headquarters entertaining a table full of guests when he received a message from Robinson House's original owner. Beverley Robinson was one of the passengers aboard the *Vulture,* and there were private matters he wanted to discuss with Arnold under the protection of a flag.

Arnold had no choice but to reveal the nature of the letter to those gathered around the table, and the concerns raised by his old Connecticut friend John Lamb, who now, conveniently enough, served as commandant at West Point, forced him to promise that he would consult Washington before contacting the loyalist colonel.

As it so happened, His Excellency was due to cross the Hudson at King's Ferry later that day on his way to a meeting with General Rochambeau and Admiral Ternay in Hartford, Connecticut. That afternoon, Arnold headed down the river to meet with Washington before the commander in chief continued on to Hartford. Since Arnold's proposed meeting with Robinson had nothing to do with military matters, Washington quite predictably insisted that he first consult New York state authorities before he met with the loyalist colonel. With the matter apparently settled, Washington and his entourage of fifty or so officers and men (which included Alexander Hamilton, Henry Knox, and Lafayette) departed for Hartford. Arnold and Washington had seen each other for the last time.

Once back at his headquarters, Arnold prepared a reply to Robinson. According to a French official, one of the documents later found among Arnold's papers was a long, undated letter from Robinson, probably written when Arnold was first exploring the possibility of defecting to the British. In order to put an end to the war, "it is necessary," Robinson wrote, "that a decisive advantage should put Britain in a condition to dictate the terms of reconciliation." It was also in the best interests of both sides that this be accomplished "without an unnecessary waste of . . . blood." According to Robinson, "There is no one but General Arnold who can surmount obstacles so great as these."

One might have thought that Arnold would try to hide the fact that he and Robinson had a prior relationship. But that did not prove to be the case. According to his disapproving aide Richard Varick, the original draft of the letter Arnold penned to Robinson "bore the complexion of one from a friend rather than one from an enemy." Only after Varick had rewritten the letter into a more stiffly formal document did he allow Arnold to send it.

What the aide did not know was that the packet ultimately sent to Robinson also included a second letter. "I shall send a person . . . on board the *Vulture*, Wednesday night the 20th instant," Arnold wrote, "and furnish him with a boat and a flag of truce. You may depend on his secrecy and honor, and that your business . . . shall be kept a profound secret. . . . I think it will be advisable for the *Vulture* to remain where she is until the time appointed."

But there was more. After crossing the Hudson on his way to Hartford, Washington had informed Arnold that on his return he planned to inspect the fortifications at West Point. In a postscript to his letter to Robinson, Arnold wrote, "I expect his Excellency General Washington to lodge here on Saturday night next, and will lay before him any matter you may wish to communicate." Arnold's meaning was unmistakable. If Clinton wanted to attack West Point when Washington was away (and unable to interfere with Arnold's surrender of the fortress), they needed to do it in the next few days. However, if they wanted a chance at capturing not only America's most important fortress but the Continental army's commander in chief, they should attack on the night of Saturday, September 23.

Arnold had hoped to meet with Beverley Robinson on the night of September 20, but Joshua Hett Smith, who had agreed to row out to the *Vulture*, wasn't able to secure a boat until the following evening. By then he'd found two brothers, Samuel and Joseph Cahoon, to man the boat's oars. Once they had rowed Smith out to the *Vulture* and picked up Robinson (who, Arnold claimed, wanted to see whether "he could obtain a pardon and his estate [be] restored to him"), they were to take the loyalist colonel to a prearranged meeting place on the west bank of the Hudson where Arnold would be waiting. Everything appeared to be in place, but as Smith and Arnold soon discovered, the Cahoon brothers were having second thoughts.

All suspicions aside—and certainly rowing out to a British vessel at night struck them as more than a little suspicious—they simply did not want to do it. Samuel had been up the night before riding to Robinson House and back with messages for Arnold and Smith, and he was exhausted. When his brother Joseph learned they were rowing to a British vessel, he said he feared being shot at by an American patrol boat. Even Samuel's wife got into the act and told the brothers they should not go. Despite the fact that the Cahoons were tenant farmers on his property, Smith was clearly hopeless when it came to convincing them to do much of anything. In a supreme irony, Arnold told the two brothers that if they refused to go, he would look upon them as "disaffected" persons. When that had no apparent effect, Arnold said that if they did not do what "was required for the good of [their] country and Congress," he would put them "under guard immediately."

The Cahoons were sitting morosely on the stoop to Smith's porch when the lawyer came out with two drams of rum. By now it was past eleven o'clock at night. Once the rum had had a chance to produce the desired effect, Arnold offered each brother fifty pounds of flour if they did as he requested. The deal was on.

With Smith at the rudder in the stern and with the Cahoon brothers pulling at the sheepskin-muffled oars, they headed out into the night. It was approaching twelve thirty when Smith hailed the lookout on the *Vulture*. Leaving the Cahoon brothers on the boat, Smith climbed up onto the ship's deck and was taken down below, where he soon found himself in the presence of three men: the *Vulture*'s captain, Andrew Sutherland; Colonel Beverley Robinson; and Major John André, his scarlet officer's coat covered by a blue-caped cloak and who was introduced to Smith as Mr. John Anderson.

Arnold had provided Smith with a letter for Robinson explaining that he would be conducted "to a place of safety" for their meeting. In addition to the letter, Arnold had given Smith passes for himself and the Cahoons as well as for "Gentleman Mr. John Anderson" and two servants, along with a scrap of paper on which Arnold had confirmed his identity by writing "Gustavus [one of his code names] to John Anderson." With these documents in hand, Robinson and André retired into another cabin to discuss what to do next.

Based on the letter alone, it seemed obvious that Arnold was expecting to meet with Robinson. But as André pointed out, the American general had provided a pass only for him. "Upon considering all these matters," Robinson later wrote, "Major André thought it was best for him to go alone as both our names was not mentioned in any one of the papers, and it appeared to him (as indeed it did to me) that Arnold wished to see him. I therefore submitted to be left behind, and Major André went off with Smith."

But as subsequently became clear to Smith, Arnold had hoped to meet not with André but with Robinson. By providing a pass for André/Anderson and neglecting to include a pass for Robinson, the American general had unintentionally introduced an element of ambiguity that allowed a young and ambitious officer to insert himself into negotiations that Arnold wanted to conduct with someone else.

Upon returning to the captain's cabin, Robinson explained to Smith that due to illness he could not go ashore, but that "Mr. Anderson would answer all purposes" and accompany him to the meeting with Arnold. As far as Smith was concerned, Anderson was a citizen just like himself with information of extreme interest for Arnold and the Continental army.

The tide had started to flow in by the time they began the row back to shore at about one in the morning. "Mr. Anderson, from his youthful appearance and the softness of his manners," Smith wrote, "did not seem to me qualified for a business of such moment; his nature seemed fraught with the milk of human kindness." Smith was the first of many in the days ahead who would find André to be an unusually sensitive and sympathetic figure. Having served in the military families of a wide variety of superior officers—from the warm and generous William Howe to the suspicious and often ill-tempered Henry Clinton—André had developed a chameleon-like talent for ingratiating himself with whoever might be useful to him. He had yet to meet, however, General Benedict Arnold.

Smith was the first one onshore, and when he explained that Anderson rather than Robinson was going to be meeting with him, Arnold appeared "much agitated and expressed chagrin at the disappointment of not seeing Colonel Robinson." André was Peggy's boyish former acquaintance, and Arnold may have felt that he lacked the gravitas for negotiations of such importance. Robinson, on the other hand, was a former friend of Washington's whom Arnold may have regarded as a kind of turncoat peer. Throughout that long night and into the next morning, Arnold, according to Smith, "had not recovered the trepidation into which he was thrown on Mr. Anderson's first landing." By insisting that he, not Robinson, meet with Arnold, André had initiated a series of events that would have disastrous consequences for all of them.

Arnold and André talked amid a grove of fir trees near where the Long Clove gap is bracketed by the jagged peaks of High and Low Tor on the west bank of the Hudson. Not only was it night, they were in the combined shadows of two mountains and the surrounding trees. It must have been so dark that they could barely make out each other's presence, only their white breeches and André's expensive, white-topped boots visible in the gloom. André spoke with the cultured accent of a British officer and intellectual; Arnold's speech was blunt and uncouth even to the ear of an American. They had much to talk about. But first things first: Arnold wanted to know what he would be paid if he failed to deliver West Point. In his original correspondence, he had insisted on ten thousand pounds, but Clinton had offered him only six thousand. Given the risks he was running, this was not enough. He must receive the higher sum. André explained that he was not in a position to make such a guarantee but promised to assure General Clinton that Arnold was deserving of the ten thousand should their plans go awry.

That was apparently enough for Arnold, and they began to discuss the details of how the British were to take West Point. Arnold would make every effort to render the three thousand soldiers inside the fortifications as ineffectual as possible by dividing them into detachments and then sending them out, supposedly to meet the enemy, but really to weaken the defenses to the point that they could easily be taken. They worked out the routes that the British should follow. André later claimed that he was to land on a section of tableland downriver of the fortress at the head of a large force and then, after marching into the hills, attack the fortress from above, perhaps using the highly vulnerable Redoubt Number 4 as the starting point.

After almost three hours of conversation, they were interrupted by Smith. Much to the lawyer's vexation, Arnold had insisted that he remain in the boat with the Cahoons. Over on the opposite bank of the river, he'd seen the light beginning to fill up the sky. Dawn was approaching; if Smith and the Cahoons were to return André to the *Vulture* before their movements could be observed by those looking out from either side of the Hudson, they must get him back now. Arnold told Smith to talk to the Cahoons, who were no doubt asleep in the boat. As the brothers must have pointed out, the flooding tide was running against them and would make the row to the *Vulture* a misery, especially since their government-issue boat was too big and heavy for just two oarsmen. They did not have enough time to make it there and back before sunrise.

When Smith informed Arnold and André of the Cahoons' reluctance to venture forth, neither officer appeared very disturbed. There was too much left to talk about to conclude the discussion just yet. And besides, Arnold had some papers he wanted to go over with André, which could only be examined in the light of day. They would ride to Smith's house, four miles to the north, where they could continue the conversation throughout the day, and André would be rowed back to the *Vulture* the following night.

As Smith and the Cahoons moved the boat up the river, Arnold and André rode on horseback to Smith's house. Soon after they had set out, apparently much to André's surprise, they came upon an American sentry. Arnold gave the password and the two riders entered the American lines. André, in the uniform of a British officer, was now in enemy territory.

By the time they reached Smith's house, the sun was about to appear over the eastern hills. Not long after their arrival, a cannon boom echoed out from the opposite shore of the Hudson, at the tip of Teller's Point. Colonel James Livingston, in command at King's Ferry, had grown increasingly irritated by the presence of a British sloop of war so close to his post. The night before, on his own initiative, he had a small cannon and perhaps a howitzer dragged to Teller's Point, where they were mounted behind some quickly thrown together fortifications. At dawn, the Americans began to fire on the British ship. At that moment, the incoming tide had just started to shift, meaning that there was virtually no current in the river. There was also no wind, and for the next two hours the *Vulture* was a sitting duck.

"Six shot hulled us," Beverley Robinson wrote, "one between wind and water, many others struck the sails and rigging and boats on deck.

Two shells hit us, one full on the quarterdeck and near the main shrouds."
Finally, the tide turned; the Hudson began to flow again toward the sea,
and the *Vulture* sailed out of range.

Back at Smith's house, Major André, probably by now at a second-
story window to get a better view, watched as the vessel that was to have
delivered him to safety and eventual glory disappeared down the river.

CHAPTER THIRTEEN

No Time for Remorse

I t took several hours for Smith and the Cahoon brothers to row the boat back to the creek near Smith's house. The current along the western shore of Haverstraw Bay fragments into back eddies, and even though the tide was coming in, they often found themselves fighting against the current. After "much labor and taking the circuit of the eddies," they were just arriving at the creek when the guns at Teller's Point opened up on the *Vulture,* which to Smith's eye looked as if it had been "set on fire." The unexpected cannonade appears to have deeply affected Smith. If he and the Cahoons had tried to deliver Arnold's informant back to the sloop of war that morning, they would have, in all likelihood, been blown to pieces by an American cannonball. Smith never admitted as much, but judging from his subsequent actions, he appears to have resolved not to venture out again by water.

By the time Smith and the Cahoons reached the house, Arnold had taken a break from his discussions with André and was on his way to the outhouse. "He walked lame," Joseph Cahoon remembered, "and had on a blue coat and white breeches." Smith found André upstairs. He'd taken off his cloak, thus revealing the uniform of a British officer. When Smith expressed his surprise, Arnold, using André's alias, claimed that Anderson was an American citizen from New York who had borrowed the uniform "from pride or vanity, from [a British] officer of his acquaintance." Most people might have found this explanation difficult to believe, but not, apparently, Smith.

The *Vulture,* it turned out, had sailed only a few miles down the river, where she anchored off Ossining, New York. The ship eventually returned to her original position at Teller's Point, but by then Arnold had introduced the possibility that André might have to return to New York by land. The safest route was to cross the river at King's Ferry (where, as the name suggests, there was regular ferry service) and then take the road south through the Neutral Ground on the east side of the Hudson to White Plains and, ultimately, Manhattan Island.

André later claimed that he had immediately objected to this proposal since it required him to change out of his uniform. As an adjutant general, André held too important an office to assume the role of a mere spy. Spies, like traitors, were hanged, and Clinton had expressly forbidden him from adopting the dress of a civilian during his face-to-face meeting with Arnold. However, André had already broken one of his commander's stipulations by agreeing to hide the documents Arnold had given him (which included plans of West Point and an inventory of the fortress's artillery and personnel) inside his white-topped boots, "between my stockings and my feet." Bit by bit, André was allowing himself to be forced into actions that he had known from the start were not in his best interests.

For his part, Arnold appears to have remained completely unsympathetic to the risks he was asking the young British officer to face. Like the horses Arnold had ordered shot before boarding the last boat out of St. Johns four years earlier, André was merely the means by which he was to achieve the glory that was to be his destiny. But, of course, from André's perspective, the same held true about Arnold. The difference was that in this test of wills André was no match for the imperious and uncaring American general. Rather than stand his ground and insist that he be rowed back to the *Vulture* in his uniform, André allowed himself to be manipulated into doing what just the night before would have been unthinkable.

Smith had an old claret-colored coat with gold-tinseled buttons that fit André perfectly. The brim of an equally old, round-topped, bowler-style beaver hat would keep his face in shadow. If the adjutant general must, in fact, set out by land, he had his disguise.

Around ten in the morning, Arnold announced that he needed to get back to Robinson House. His aides at headquarters were sure to object to his having spent the night at Smith's. Peggy, who was adored by both Franks and Varick, had assumed the role of buffer between her husband

and his aides, but that did not change the fact that he needed to head back up the river.

Arnold was still upset about having had to meet with André instead of Robinson. Eager to be rid of the man whom he regarded as a mere surrogate, he had no qualms about leaving André under the care of a person who had so far proven far from reliable. Never one for attention to detail, Arnold was being willfully careless just when he should have been making every effort to ensure the British spy chief's safe return to New York. Indeed, Arnold's behavior at this critical moment is so puzzling that one has to wonder whether jealousy was contributing to his need to put some distance between himself and Peggy's young and handsome friend.

To cover all contingencies, Arnold provided Smith and André with the documents they required no matter what route they took. If André should end up returning through the Neutral Ground and be stopped by an American sentry, the pass (which read: "Permit Mr. John Anderson to pass the guards to the White Plains, or below, if he chooses, he being on public business by my direction. B. Arnold, M. Genl.") guaranteed him safe passage. If he were stopped by the British, so much the better. From Arnold's perspective, the plan for the surrender of West Point was now in place, and as soon as André returned to New York, the British army, which had already been loaded onto transports, would be heading up the Hudson with the next flood tide.

Smith later insisted that illness kept him in bed most of the day and eventually made it impossible for him to take André by water to the *Vulture*. However, that same illness did not prevent him from ultimately accompanying André on the far more arduous overland route into the Neutral Ground. What really seems to have motivated Smith's decision to take André by land was (besides the fear of an American cannonball) the need to pick up his wife in Fishkill on the east side of the Hudson. Since he had to cross the river anyway, taking André by land was the easier of the two alternatives. It also eliminated the need for another infuriating round of negotiations with the reluctant Cahoon brothers.

André spent a long and unhappy day waiting for dark. "I endeavored to amuse him," Smith wrote, "by showing him the prospect from the upper part of my house, from where there was an extensive view over the capacious bay of Haverstraw, to the opposite shore; he cast an anxious look toward the *Vulture* and with a heavy sigh wished he was on board. I endeavored to console him by the hope of his being at White Plains or New York before her. . . . From this time he seemed shy and desirous to avoid much conversation and carefully avoided being seen by persons that came to the house."

Around dusk, Smith decided to head out for King's Ferry, about two miles to the north. An enslaved African American servant accompanied Smith and André, all of them mounted on horses. For someone who had supposedly spent most of the day sick in bed, Smith was in remarkably good spirits that night. As they approached Stony Point, he started to talk about how Anthony Wayne had taken the fortress from the British just the year before. "I found my fellow traveler very backward in giving any opinion or saying much about it," Smith observed. No wonder. Wayne had been the American officer in command of the soldiers massacred by Grey's and André's forces at Paoli. More recently, Wayne had been the subject of a humorous ballad by André called "The Cow Chase" that mocked Wayne's unsuccessful attempt to capture a group of British loyalists at Bull's Ferry, New Jersey. In a strange coincidence, the poem was due to be published the very next day in New York's loyalist newspaper, the *Royal Gazette*. One can only wonder whether Smith's mention of Anthony Wayne brought to André's mind the final stanza of that poem:

> And now I've closed my epic strain,
> I tremble as I show it,
> Lest this same warrior drover, Wayne,
> Should ever catch the poet.

As they rode down the hill toward King's Ferry, they came upon a well-lit tent, where several American officers were passing around a bowl of rum. Smith appears to have become somewhat infatuated with the idea that he was escorting a mysterious personage of immense importance to the American cause. Leaving André to continue toward the ferry with his servant, Smith climbed off his horse to share a drink with the soldiers. After requesting that the bowl be refilled with liquor, Smith enjoyed a long drink and turned to Captain William Cooley. "In three weeks' time," he predicted, "we shall all be in New York!" Somewhat bewildered by Smith's strangely enthusiastic pronouncement, Cooley demurred, "Sir, I don't know." "Let it be three months," Smith countered with a laugh, and after another drink, he was on his way to catch up with André at the steps down to the ferry.

Once they began crossing the river, the jocularity continued. Smith held court from the bow, joking with the boatmen and offering "to give them something to revive their spirits if they would row across soon," while André stood silently by himself in the aft portion of the ferry. Once they'd landed at Verplanck's Point (and Smith had given the ferrymen eight dollars), they came upon the tent of Colonel James Livingston, who had fired on the *Vulture* that morning from Teller's Point. Once again, Smith dismounted to talk as André continued on ahead. Livingston had served his law clerkship with Smith's brother and invited the two travelers to have supper with him, but hinting that he was on a mission of the highest importance for General Arnold, Smith said they must continue on.

Soon they were headed south into the troubled depths of the Neutral Ground, which might be more properly termed the "Contested Ground." Although they were still in what was considered American territory, they had reached the point where it was possible to come upon a detachment of soldiers from either side. Bands of lawless gangs—Skinners if they considered themselves patriots, Cowboys if they were loyalists—regularly plundered homes and farms until virtually all of Westchester County had been reduced to a haunted wasteland. After five years of war, many, if not most, residents, had fled to Connecticut to the east or toward Peekskill to the north. Those who insisted on remaining in their homes had been stripped of almost all human dignity by the bandits' unceasing depredations. "Fear was apparently [their] only passion," a traveler wrote. "The power of volition seemed to have deserted them." This was the rocky, heavily wooded country of Washington Irving's Rip Van Winkle and the Headless Horseman, and through this ghostly, terror-gripped land— where grass grew in the once well-tended fields and apples were left to rot in the trees—Major John André must pass.

They had traveled about eight miles when they were stopped by an American patrol party commanded by Captain Ebenezer Boyd. Boyd demanded to know why they were traveling at night. Where had they come from? Where were they headed? "I told him who I was and that we had passports from General Arnold . . . that we were on the public service on business of the highest import," Smith wrote. In order to read Smith's pass, Boyd told them to follow him to a nearby house where they could secure a light. "Mr. Anderson seemed very uneasy," Smith remembered, "but I cheered him by saying our papers would carry us to any part of the country to which they were directed."

Finding Smith's paperwork in order, Boyd became uncomfortably curious about what exactly they were up to, especially since it required them to travel by night. Fending off the officer's questions as best he could, but clearly enjoying the fact that he was involved in such a mysterious mission, Smith continued to talk with Boyd, who then told of a recent incursion by the Cowboys in the neighborhood toward which they were headed. He strongly advised them to backtrack to a house where they could find a place to spend the night.

Since being captured by the loyalist Cowboys might actually hasten his return to New York, André was eager to continue on. Smith, however, decided they should take the captain's advice. That night, the two men ended up sharing a single bed. "I was often disturbed with the restless motions and uneasiness of mind exhibited by my bed fellow," Smith remembered, "who on observing the first approach of day, summoned my servant to prepare the horses for our departure."

Once they'd begun riding through the foggy, predawn light, Smith could see by André's haggard appearance that he "had not slept an hour during the night." But with each step toward New York, the young man's spirits began to soar. "I now had reason to think my fellow traveler a different person," Smith remembered, "from the character I had at first formed of him."

Assuming it was only a matter of hours before he reached safety, André began to show off, regaling Smith with a dazzling display of erudition. "He had consulted the muses as well as Mars, for . . . music, painting, and poetry seemed to be his delight," Smith remembered. André betrayed the fact that he was a British officer by expressing the hope that the war would end, not in a clash with Washington's army, but with the French in a "fair open-field contest." By now there could have been little doubt in Smith's mind as to André's actual identity. Whether or not Smith decided that it was too late to make a fuss or he simply did not care all that much about which side ultimately prevailed in the war, he seems never to have voiced any misgivings in André's presence. To make sure his companion did not begin to regret having aided and abetted his escape to the south, André assured Smith "that measures were then in agitation" to bring about a negotiated peace between the two governments.

At some point in the midst of André's rhapsody, they came upon a solitary American officer riding up from the south. From Smith's perspective the meeting was of no consequence, and he failed to even mention the encounter in his subsequent account of their ride through the Neutral Ground. For André, however, the appearance of the officer came as a terrifying shock. He *knew* this man.

Colonel Samuel Blachley Webb was a former aide of Washington's who had been a prisoner in New York for more than a year and a half, and he was now on parole so that he could visit his family in Connecticut. There was absolutely no conceivable way that Webb was not going to recognize the British adjutant general. By this time, however, André was a far cry from the immaculate officer he had been in New York. He was dressed in shoddy clothes and hadn't bathed or shaved in several days; a thick stubble had sprouted on his cheeks. As an American officer later described him, André had the look of "a reduced gentleman." Webb stared into his face, said nothing, and kept on riding to the north.

André later admitted that the encounter "made his hair rise." Smith, however, hadn't the slightest idea that his companion's world had almost collapsed. If anything, the scare added to André's sense of relief and joy, and his discourse continued unabated.

"The pleasantry of converse and mildness of the weather so insensibly beguiled the time" that before Smith realized it, they were approaching the bridge across the Croton River that marked the southern limit of the American lines. Smith had already warned André that he was going to turn back before they crossed the bridge. Indeed, André's jubilant mood that morning probably had much to do with the prospect of leaving the scatterbrained Smith behind.

Just before the bridge, they came to the house of an old woman who had lost almost all her possessions in the recent Cowboy raid. The ruffians had left her with only a single cow, and with some fresh milk added to a gruel of cornmeal, the two travelers enjoyed their first meal since the previous morning.

Once back on their horses, it was time to part. Smith claimed that

André was so "affected" that he offered him his gold watch "in remembrance of him as a keepsake." Smith politely refused the gift, and the two men went their separate ways.

Smith had warned André to take the inland route to White Plains since the road along the river into Tarrytown was reputed to be rife with Cowboys. André, of course, did the opposite of what Smith advised. For André, the Cowboys were his friends.

He was galloping along the Old Post Road, just fifteen miles from the King's Bridge crossing into Manhattan. Up ahead a bridge crossed a small stream known as Clark's Kill. Beyond that, a huge tulip tree, 111 feet high and 24 feet in circumference, with sprawling, fantastically shaped branches, loomed over the road. Suddenly a very tall man dressed in the green, red-faced coat of a Hessian jaeger stepped out of the shadows. Raising his musket, the man told André to halt.

It was about time. Finally, André had encountered someone from his own side. He could now see that two others, also carrying muskets, were coming out from behind a rail fence on the right. "My lads," André said good-naturedly, "I hope you belong to our party."

"What party?" the Hessian asked.

"The lower," André said, meaning British-occupied New York.

"We do," the tall soldier assured him; "my dress shows that."

Relief flooded across André's face. "I am a British officer," he said, "have been up the country on particular business, and would not wish to be detained a minute." With that he held up the gold watch he had offered Joshua Smith. The big Hessian told him to dismount. "We are Americans," he said, no doubt with a smile.

As it turned out, André had stumbled onto three New York militiamen who had been assigned to watch the road for suspect persons such as himself. Only a few days before the giant in the Hessian coat, John Paulding by name, had escaped from a British prison in New York City. An American sympathizer had given him the German uniform as a disguise, and after making his way to the edge of the Hudson River, he had rowed a small boat to safety the following night. Now he was back with his company in the Neutral Ground. With Paulding that morning on the Old Post Road were Isaac Van Wart and Abraham Williams. A short distance away, another group of four New York militiamen were monitoring a road to the east.

André was a fair-to-middling poet and artist but not a good actor, and had always been relegated to minor roles in the amateur plays produced in Philadelphia and New York. A blush spreading across his cheeks, he let out a most unhappy laugh. "God bless my soul," he said, "a body must do anything to get along now-a-days," and with that he held out Arnold's pass. Paulding was the only one of the three militiamen who could read, and he examined the pass.

"You had best let me go, or you will bring yourselves into trouble," André warned, "for your stopping me will detain General Arnold's business. I am going to Dobbs Ferry, to meet a person there and get information for him."

Paulding told his compatriots the pass looked real. Why then, they wondered, had this John Anderson told them he was a British officer, and what was he doing with a gold watch—the kind of expensive accessory that only a few American officers were wealthy enough to own? They had better search him.

They took André into the thick woods on the west side of the road, carefully replacing the fence rails behind them so that passersby would not suspect that anything unusual was going on. As they demanded, André took off his outer clothes, which Williams carefully searched. André later complained that they greedily tore the lining out of his waistcoat in search of money. However, according to New York state law, militiamen such as Paulding, Williams, and Van Wart were allowed to keep whatever booty they might confiscate from a British or loyalist captive. Assuming André was the person who he'd originally said he was, they were completely within their rights. Unfortunately, Williams had not found anything to cast doubt on the legitimacy of the man's pass. That was, until they told him to take off his boots.

They found nothing in the boots, but according to Van Wart, the bottoms of the captive's two stockings sagged suspiciously. Tucked inside each of the two stockings were three unsealed letters. Paulding quickly scanned the papers, then cried out, "He's a spy!"

They marched André more than twelve miles to the headquarters of Lieutenant Colonel John Jameson, who had recently succeeded Colonel

Elisha Sheldon as commander of the advanced American posts along the borders of the Neutral Ground. Prior to setting out, André had attempted to bribe the three militiamen into letting him go, offering them "whatever sum of money you mention, or quantity of dry goods." "No, by God," Paulding replied, "if you would give us ten thousand [pounds], you should not stir a step." As André well knew, that was precisely the sum that Arnold had demanded two nights earlier should his plan to surrender West Point not succeed. As it was turning out, the failure of that plan had nothing to do with Arnold and everything to do with Major John André.

They arrived at Jameson's headquarters in North Castle around five thirty in the evening. Arnold had alerted the officers in the advanced posts to expect a John Anderson from New York. But according to the militiamen, Anderson had been captured while heading south *to* New York. That he had concealed documents related to the security of West Point was also troubling. But was this sufficient evidence to accuse Arnold, Jameson's superior officer, of being a traitor? Anderson might be a double agent, working both sides to his personal advantage. After consulting the other officers at his headquarters, Jameson decided to do what at the time seemed the safe thing: send Anderson under guard to Arnold with a letter of explanation while sending the confiscated documents to Washington, who was presumably on his way back from Hartford and probably in the neighborhood of Danbury. If Arnold was, in fact, a traitor, it should be a relatively simple matter to capture him as he made his way south toward the Neutral Ground. (It never occurred to Jameson, he later explained, that an armed British vessel might be within reach of Arnold's barge.)

How much André contributed to the discussion about where he should be sent is not known. Given how remarkably engaging he could be, one is tempted to speculate that his assurances that he and Arnold were pursuing America's best interests encouraged Jameson to send him to Robinson House. By that evening, André, accompanied by four Connecticut militiamen under the command of Lieutenant Solomon Allen, was headed to Arnold's headquarters.

Later that night, Major Benjamin Tallmadge of the Second Continental Light Dragoons arrived at Jameson's headquarters. Tallmadge and his men regularly battled with the British and loyalist Cowboys in the Neutral Ground and had just returned from a foray to White Plains. Unknown to just about everyone but Washington, Tallmadge, twenty-six, was also the head of the American spy network. Over the last year, he had done much to develop what is now known as the Culper Ring, which had already provided valuable information through agents stationed in New York and Long Island. Unlike Jameson, Tallmadge was schooled in the art of espionage, and when he heard about the capture of John Anderson, his suspicions were immediately aroused. He later hinted that he had proposed to Jameson that he and his dragoons immediately set out to Robinson House and place Arnold under arrest. Whether or not that conversation ever occurred, he did end up convincing Jameson that it was a mistake to send Anderson to Arnold's headquarters and that he should order the captive's return. In order not to cast any premature suspicion on Arnold's loyalty, they decided to claim that reports of Cowboy attacks in the region made it necessary to recall the prisoner to North Castle. They would then send out Lieutenant Allen once again with only the message to Arnold informing him of Anderson's capture. But could they intercept Anderson before he reached Robinson House?

Arnold was having a difficult time containing his two troublesome aides. The day before, Joshua Hett Smith had stopped at his headquarters after delivering John Anderson as far as the American lines in the Neutral Ground—news that gave Arnold, Smith later wrote, "much satisfaction." The Arnold household had been about to sit down to a midday dinner of salted cod, and Arnold asked Smith to join them. It did not go well.

In the midst of the meal, Peggy asked if there was more butter. When the servant told her that the butter was all gone, Arnold said, "Bless me, I had forgot the oil I bought in Philadelphia. It will do very well with salt fish."

When the servant delivered the oil to the table, Arnold commented that it had cost him eighty dollars. Smith snidely responded, "Eighty pence," suggesting that a Continental dollar was worth no more than a penny. Richard Varick shot back, "That is not true, Mr. Smith." Soon an argument was raging between Smith and Varick that quickly included Franks. Seeing that her husband was becoming "very angry," Peggy "begged that the dispute might be dropped as it gave her great pain."

Varick stomped out huffily from the room, and once dinner had ended and Smith was on his way to meet up with his wife in Fishkill, Arnold confronted his two aides in his office. "If I asked the Devil to dine with me," he said with seething menace, "the gentlemen of my family should be civil to him."

André and his guards had made it just past Peekskill when they were stopped by the messenger sent out by Jameson and Tallmadge and told to return to North Castle. By eight in the morning, André had been taken to another American post at South Salem, which was judged safer than North Castle. By that point, André, who had not slept for several days, was feeling as miserable as he looked. Now that he was being held under guard, he knew that the chances of his escape were essentially nil, especially since Washington would soon be receiving his packet of documents.

Making his agony all the worse was the knowledge that he had come within a whisker of pulling off the coup that might have ended the war. If he had not greeted the militiaman in the Hessian coat with the admission that he was a British soldier—a confession he had absolutely no reason to make—West Point would almost surely have fallen. It was not Arnold's fault the scheme had failed; it was André's.

André, no doubt, knew this—a realization that must have mortified him to the core. It then became his mission to paint himself not as the scheming spy he actually was, but as an honorable British officer who had been, like the American people, betrayed by Benedict Arnold. Playing upon the growing sense of outrage that was about to grip the officers with whom he was to spend the final days of his life, he portrayed himself as the youthful, almost-too-good-to-be-true victim. If he played his cards right, he might be able to establish enough sympathy with the impressionable, ill-tutored Americans (whom he had condescendingly referred to as "those dung-born tribes" in his recently published ballad) to win his ultimate release. In order to set this process in motion, André decided to write to George Washington.

That morning Lieutenant Joshua King, under whose charge André had been placed, ordered his barber to give the prisoner a much-needed shave and to dress his long black hair, which had been tied into a queue with a length of black ribbon. "When the ribbon was taken from his hair," King remembered, "I observed it full of powder." In the eighteenth century, what was called Cyprus powder, made from granulated and sweet-smelling reindeer moss, was often sprinkled into a gentleman's hair. King now knew that "I had no ordinary person in charge."

Once he'd been shaved and given some fresh clothes, André asked whether he might get some exercise in the yard outside his window and whether King would join him. Soon the two officers were pacing back and forth across the grass in the presence of several guards. At some point, King remembered, André turned to him and announced that "he must make a confidant of somebody, and he knew not a more proper person than myself as I had appeared to befriend a stranger in distress. After settling the point between us, he told me who he was and gave me a short account of himself."

Around three o'clock that afternoon, André asked for a pen and paper. Sitting in a slat-backed rocking chair, he began to write to His Excellency George Washington.

> What I have as yet said concerning myself was in the justifiable attempt to be extricated; I am too little accustomed to duplicity to have succeeded.
>
> I beg your Excellency will be persuaded that no alteration in the temper of my mind, or apprehension for my safety, induces me to take the step of addressing you; but that it is to rescue myself from an imputation of having assumed a mean character for treacherous purposes or self-interest; a conduct incompatible with the principles that actuate me, as well as with my condition in life.
>
> It is to vindicate my fame that I speak, and not to solicit security.
>
> The person in your possession is Major John André, Adjutant General to the British army.

André then went on to explain how he had "agreed to meet upon ground not within the posts of either army a person, who was to give me intelligence," and how at the insistence of Arnold (whom he never named) everything had gone very wrong. "Against my stipulation, my intention, and without my knowledge beforehand, I was conducted within one of your posts. Your Excellency may conceive my sensation on this occasion, and will imagine how much more must I have been affected by a refusal to reconduct me back the next night as I had been brought. Thus become a prisoner, I had to concert my escape." He then recounted the circumstances of his capture. "Thus . . . was I betrayed . . . into the vile condition of an enemy in disguise within your posts," he wrote.

He ended with an appeal to Washington.

> Having avowed myself a British officer, I have nothing to reveal but what relates to myself, which is true on the honor of an officer and a gentleman.
>
> The request I have to make to your Excellency, and I am conscious I address myself well, is that in any rigor policy may dictate, a decency of conduct towards me may mark that, though unfortunate, I am branded with nothing dishonorable, as no motive could be mine but the service of my King and as I was involuntarily an impostor.

It is an extraordinary rhetorical performance, particularly given the circumstances under which it was written. Alexander Hamilton later praised André's letter for having been "conceived in terms of dignity without insolence, and apology without meanness." By the time Hamilton made that comment, however, he was under André's alluring spell. What Hamilton failed to remember, or preferred to forget, was that the letter's coda included a reference to the American prisoners in Charleston, South Carolina: "I take the liberty to mention the condition of some gentlemen at Charleston who being either on parole or under protection were engaged in a conspiracy against us. Though their situation is not similar, they are objects who may be set in exchange for me or are persons whom the treatment I receive might affect." Here, in what amounts to a brazen threat, André betrays everything he has so far said. He might claim to be attempting to vindicate his honor, but he is really trying to save his life. From a military point of view, there was no reason to reveal his identity at this time. André's letter to Washington was, in actuality, a needlessly premature confession that was almost as embarrassingly misdirected as his earlier confession to the militiaman whom he had mistaken to be a Hessian.

What really irritated André was the fact that he had been undone by three American peasants. Just as had happened the day before with the Cahoon brothers, the three militiamen had refused to do as they'd been told by their social superiors. In this country, the lower orders apparently had minds of their own, no matter how little education they might have, and in the nation that was to emerge from this seemingly never-ending war, ordinary citizens would ultimately have, whether or not their betters chose to admit it, the last word.

Soon after writing his letter to Washington, André made a comic sketch that depicted his captors as ludicrous bumpkins. In the days ahead, he claimed that Paulding, Williams, and Van Wart were nothing but brigands who had really been after his money—a claim that his newest confidant, Benjamin Tallmadge, later repeated, despite the militiamen's own testimony. But Tallmadge had his own reasons for belittling what the three militiamen had accomplished.

The capture of John André had revealed a glaring gap in the spy network put together by Washington and Tallmadge. Despite the sophistication and reach of the Culper Ring, Arnold had succeeded in outfoxing Washington's spy chief, who later admitted that he had "no suspicion of [Arnold's] lack of patriotism or political integrity." Disparaging André's captors was an easy way for Tallmadge to lay the blame for the unraveling of Arnold's plot not on André but on the man who had insisted that he return by land. Casting aspersions on the lowly militiamen was also a way for Tallmadge to solidify his growing sense of spiritual kinship with André, who seemed to possess all the poise and dignity that a young American officer aspired to have. For Tallmadge, King, and a growing number of their peers, adulating André and reviling Arnold became the way to distance themselves from a traitorous officer whom they had once regarded as a hero.

The messenger sent to deliver the package of documents to Washington had been told that the commander in chief was returning from Hartford by the same way he had come—what was known as the lower road through Danbury. However, since Washington had decided to stop at West Point on his return trip, he had taken a different, more northerly route via Fishkill, New York, and the messenger had entirely missed his mark. After venturing to Danbury and finding no trace of Washington, the messenger eventually made his way back to the American post at

South Salem, where André's recently written letter was added to the packet. Soon, the messenger set out again—this time to Robinson House, where His Excellency was expected to meet with Arnold.

In the meantime, Lieutenant Colonel Jameson's message to Arnold, after being initially delayed by the return of André, had also not been delivered. Even though it had been more than two days since André's capture, word of that event had not yet reached either Arnold or Washington, both of whom were about to receive their messages within hours of each other on Monday, September 25.

Washington and his entourage left Fishkill very early that morning so that they could have breakfast at Arnold's headquarters. They were approaching the fortifications on Constitution Island on the east side of the Hudson, when Washington suddenly veered off on a road to the right. "General," Lafayette is claimed to have said, "you are going in a wrong direction. You know Mrs. Arnold is waiting breakfast for us and that road will take us out of our way." "Ah," Washington responded with a laugh, "I know you young men are all in love with Mrs. Arnold and wish to get where she is as soon as possible. You may go and take your breakfast with her, and tell her not to wait for me. I must ride down and examine the redoubts on this side of the river and will be there in a short time."

Despite Washington's offer, all his general officers felt obliged to accompany him on his tour of Constitution Island. A servant had already been dispatched to notify Arnold of their imminent arrival; to let him know of the delay, Washington sent two aides, Samuel Shaw and James McHenry, directly to Robinson House.

The aides and Washington's servant ended up arriving at Arnold's headquarters at the same time. Even though Peggy was still upstairs in their bedroom, Arnold urged them to begin breakfast. It is not known whether Arnold was with them at the table or somewhere else in the house when Lieutenant Allen, after two days of marching up and down the east side of the Hudson (first with André in his custody and now with only a message for Arnold), arrived at Robinson House. Arnold tore open the letter from Jameson and read. Soon he knew that André had been captured and that Washington either already had or was about to receive the packet of papers he had given André.

Arnold had always been at his best in the chaos of battle. But

this—the ruin of a plan that had promised him not only financial independence but eternal glory—was too much for even him. And yet, despite betraying "great confusion," he was careful to instruct Allen not to
speak to anyone about the message and to wait for his reply.

He found Peggy upstairs in their bedroom and told her what had happened. No one knows what transpired between them, but it must have
involved desperate tears and contingency plans. To give Arnold the time
required to reach the safety of British-held New York, he needed her help.
Washington was due to arrive for breakfast at any moment and then
proceed across the river to inspect West Point. Judging from the behavior
of Washington's aides, the commander in chief had no suspicion, as of
yet, of Arnold's treasonous activities. Peggy had to make sure it stayed
that way for as long as possible. She might never see her husband again,
but for at least the next hour she must do nothing to suggest that anything was wrong. Peggy's hysterical episodes had been a regular part of
the Arnold household for more than a year; as David Franks could attest,
they were a powerful, seemingly unrestrainable force. For the next hour,
however, she must find a way to contain herself. Her husband's life depended on it.

There was a knock on the bedroom door. It was Franks. Washington
was, in his aide's words, "nigh at hand." Arnold emerged from the bedroom, shaken and in a hurry. Franks should get his horse saddled. He was
to tell His Excellency that he was on his way to West Point to prepare for
his arrival "and would return in about an hour." Arnold climbed onto his
horse and rather than take the gradual, switchback path to the riverside,
"galloped almost down a precipice" to the dock, where his barge awaited.

He told the coxswain that he had a message that must be delivered to
Beverley Robinson aboard the *Vulture* under a flag. He needed to get
there and back as quickly as possible so that he could meet with Washington after his inspection of West Point. As he'd done four years before
on Lake Champlain when pursued by the British near Fort Ticonderoga,
he offered his men an incentive: two barrels of rum if they got him there
and back in a timely fashion.

On they rushed down the river—the mountains on either side just
beginning to take on the reds, yellows, and purples of autumn. He kept
scanning the water behind them, but there was no sign of pursuers. His
carefully constructed plan had fallen apart, but he still had, he assured

himself, much to offer the British, who would, no doubt, be very happy
to see him. It's unlikely he worried much about John André, who was, to
his mind, just another casualty of war. One can only wonder whether he
thought at all about how his brother officers and the country as a whole
would react to his treason. The entire premise of this undertaking had
been that the surrender of West Point would result in the collapse of the
Revolution and the happy reunification of the British Empire. For having
effected this magical transformation, Arnold would be hailed as the de-
liverer of his once divided country. But now, even if the British won the
war, Arnold would be forever branded a traitor.

Could he feel it—the vast upwelling of rage and indignation that was
about to explode over the country with the violence of a Hudson River
thunderstorm, obliterating any hint that he had once been America's bravest and fiercest battlefield general? He must have thought about Peggy and
their young son stranded deep in what was now enemy territory. If she
succeeded in convincing them that she had had nothing to do with his
actions, surely Washington would allow her to join him in New York.

Soon they were coming up alongside the *Vulture*. Arnold put the
handkerchief that had served as his flag into his pocket and climbed up
the ship's sides. Initially, at least, Robinson and Captain Sutherland *were*
happy to see him. But as Arnold explained that André had been captured
while taking the land route to New York, the British officers' relief turned
to concern and even anger. Why hadn't André returned to the *Vulture*
under the protection of the same flag with which he had left? Why had
he changed out of his uniform? What would Clinton say?

For the moment, however, Arnold must deal with his boat crew. His
coxswain was called into Sutherland's cabin, where Arnold announced
that he and his compatriots were now prisoners. Both Robinson and
Sutherland were horrified by the petty cruelty of Arnold's treatment of
his loyal boatmen, and on the *Vulture*'s return to New York all seven of
them were released on parole.

Treason, along with suicide, is the most self-centered of acts. Un-
moored from his past and without, as of yet, a future, Arnold was now
the loneliest man on God's earth.

Within a half hour of Arnold's departure, Washington arrived at Robinson House. After a quick breakfast, he and his officers, with the exception

of Hamilton, who remained at Arnold's headquarters (no doubt to catch up on Washington's correspondence), climbed into an awaiting barge to join Arnold at West Point.

But as the fortress's commandant, Colonel John Lamb, explained with considerable embarrassment (not knowing of His Excellency's impending arrival, he had failed to fire off the expected salute), Arnold had not been at West Point in two days. That did not prevent Washington from going through with his inspection, and not until four o'clock that afternoon did he finally return to Arnold's headquarters. Upon Washington's arrival at Robinson House, Hamilton informed him that a package of documents had recently arrived. Soon the papers, which in addition to the documents Arnold had given André included André's letter to Washington, were spread out before the commander in chief. Within minutes he knew the full extent of Arnold's treachery—that he had conspired to surrender West Point to the British, and that he had fled approximately six hours earlier down the river. Arnold was obviously on his way to New York, and Washington must at least try to apprehend him before he escaped to British territory.

Within minutes Hamilton had taken to his horse and was galloping to Verplanck's Point in the unlikely hope of arriving there before Arnold. Once Hamilton had gone, Washington called Henry Knox and Lafayette into the room and explained that the officer he had once regarded as one of his best generals had plotted to surrender West Point to the British. For someone of Washington's inherently trusting nature, what Arnold had done was inconceivable.

Being a republic, the country they were struggling to create was ruled not by a king or an emperor but by the mutual consent of the governed. Arnold had betrayed not just Washington but every American citizen he had pledged to protect. Since republics rely on the inherent virtue of the people, they are exceedingly fragile. All it takes is one well-placed person to destroy everything. Washington, his face betraying the sadness, anger, and shock of this most recent revelation, turned to Lafayette and asked, "Whom can we trust now?"

By then, after an apparently prearranged delay of several hours, Peggy Arnold had erupted into one of her hysterical episodes. According to Richard Varick, she emerged from her room "with her hair disheveled and flowing about her neck; her morning gown with few other clothes remained on her, too few to be seen even by a gentleman of the family, much less by many strangers."

Varick had been suffering from a high fever for several days and taken to his bed. "I heard a shriek to me," he wrote to his sister a few days later, "and sprang from my bed, ran upstairs and there met the miserable lady, raving distracted." Peggy grabbed him by the hand and with a "wild look" asked, "Colonel Varick, have you ordered my child to be killed?" She then fell to her knees and implored him "to spare her innocent babe." Soon David Franks and Dr. William Eustis, who had served as Arnold's physician and been a frequent guest at Robinson House, had arrived, and the three carried her to her bed, "raving mad." When Peggy insisted that "she had not a friend left here," Varick told her not to worry; in addition to the three of them, her husband would soon return from West Point. "No," she cried, "General Arnold will never return, he is gone; he is gone forever." Looking toward the ceiling, she claimed that spirits had carried him into the sky and "put hot irons in his head."

This theatrical display continued for more than an hour until it became apparent that Washington had returned to the house. Undoubtedly realizing that it was in her husband's best interests to distract the commander in chief at this critical juncture, she told Varick that "there was a hot iron on her head and no one but General Washington could take it off, and [that she] wanted to see the general."

Varick dutifully did as Peggy had requested and soon Washington, having just learned of her husband's treachery, was at her side. When Varick announced that the general was now before her, she said, "No, it is not." When Washington attempted to assure her of his presence, she insisted, "That is not General Washington; that is the man who was agoing to assist Colonel Varick in killing my child."

Peggy had apparently decided that insanity was her best defense. All that night and well into the following morning, she succeeded in convincing anyone who was brought into her presence that Arnold's treason had left her bereft of reason. It also meant that she did not have to answer any questions. Even the very bright and normally clearheaded Alexander Hamilton was completely taken in. "Her sufferings were so eloquent," he wrote his fiancée, "that I wished myself her brother, to have a right to become her defender."

When she finally seemed to come to her senses the following day, she was asked where she wanted to go next—to Arnold in New York or to her family in Philadelphia? Although we don't know the exact circumstances under which she was given this choice, she chose her family, and on September 27, two days after the revelation of her husband's betrayal, she, her baby, and David Franks headed for Philadelphia.

On the way home, they stopped at the residence of a woman in New Jersey who was a confirmed loyalist. Finally letting her guard down, Peggy was reputed to have admitted that "she was heartily tired of the theatrics she was exhibiting . . . that through great . . . and unceasing perseverance she had ultimately brought the general into an arrangement to surrender West Point." If this account is true (and there is no reason to suspect it is not), Peggy had devoted more than a year to convincing her husband to betray his country and then, as soon as the plan fell apart, left him to his fate in New York. Arnold, apparently, was not the only traitor in the family.

On the evening of September 25, Hamilton returned from Verplanck's Point. He had been too late to stop Arnold but had alerted Nathanael Greene to put the army on the west side of the Hudson under marching orders in the event that the British decided to go through with the attack. Washington received two letters that evening from the *Vulture,* which had already left for New York: one from Beverley Robinson, the other from Benedict Arnold.

Arnold was unapologetic to the last. "The heart which is conscious of its own rectitude," he wrote, "cannot attempt to palliate a step which the world may censure as wrong. I have ever acted from a principle of love to my country, since the commencement of the present unhappy contest between Great Britain and the colonies. The same principle of love to my country actuates my present conduct, however it may appear inconsistent to the world, who very seldom judge right of any man's actions." It was a sham defense. In the month prior to his desertion, Arnold had written to Nathanael Greene and others concerning attempts to petition Congress about its refusal to properly compensate the army's officers. Arnold had proposed that a thousand of them march on Philadelphia and present "a spirited but decent memorial setting forth their claims and requesting immediate justice. . . . If justice is not done to the army, their necessities will occasion them to disband, and the country will of course be left to the ravages of the enemy." From Arnold's perspective, Congress was the source of America's current woes, and something must be done to rescue the country. To his mind, treason, like the proposed march on Philadelphia, was a form of protest that was completely justified given the mess Congress had created. It wasn't his fault if the public failed to appreciate the essential altruism of what might seem like an egocentric act.

Arnold was not looking for any favors for himself ("I have too often experienced the ingratitude of my country to attempt it," he wrote), but there was the matter of his wife. "From the known humanity of your Excellency, I am induced to ask your protection for Mrs. Arnold from every insult and injury that a mistaken vengeance of my country may expose her to. It ought to fall only on me; she is as good and as innocent as an angel, and is incapable of doing wrong." In a postscript, he insisted that his aides, as well as Joshua Smith, "are totally ignorant of any transactions of mine that they had reason to believe were injurious to the public."

Robinson's letter to Washington concerned the fate of Major André, who after spending some time under guard at Robinson House was transported to the prison at West Point and ultimately to army headquarters in Tappan, New York, thirty-four miles to the south. Colonel Robinson informed Washington that, according to Arnold, André had left the *Vulture* under the protection of a flag. Disregarding the fact that this was a blatant misuse of a hallowed military convention, Robinson established the defense that was later argued by Henry Clinton: given the circumstances under which André had left the *Vulture,* he "cannot be detained by you without the greatest violation of flags, and contrary to the custom and usages of all nations."

What Robinson and Clinton did not know was that in his own letter to Washington, André had made a completely different argument: since Benedict Arnold had taken him across enemy lines, André had become, technically, a prisoner of war and had been justified in doing anything he could—including changing out of his uniform—to effect his escape. In other words, since it was all Arnold's fault, André should go free, which was an even more ludicrous defense than the argument made by Robinson and Clinton. André did even further damage to his case a few days later when, after being transported to Tappan, he admitted to a board of inquiry headed by Nathanael Greene "that it was impossible for him to suppose he came on shore under the sanction of a flag."

They were in the midst of a violent conflict that had resulted in the deaths of thousands of British and American soldiers. For a few brief days in the autumn of 1780, however, the War of Independence had come down to an argument over the niceties of military protocol—all to save the life of an officer who seemed bent on becoming a sacrifice to everything an honor-bound British gentleman held as true.

Through several different channels, Washington informed Clinton that the only way he would release André was in exchange for Arnold. No matter how sorely tempted he may have been on a personal level to do exactly that, Clinton acknowledged to his staff that "a deserter is never given up." Washington had no choice, in the end, but to execute Major André.

Arnold had his freedom and a commission as a British brigadier, but that did not prevent him from becoming an increasingly isolated and pathetic figure. André, imprisoned in Tappan, was now surrounded by a coterie of adoring American officers, and for a handful of days in October he became the leader of a cult of his own devising. Officer after officer made the pilgrimage to the little stone house that served as his jail to pay homage to the beautiful, sleek-haired boy with dark eyes and ivory skin who had been sentenced to die for the sins of Benedict Arnold. "To an excellent understanding well improved by education and travel, he united a peculiar elegance of mind and manners, and the advantage of a pleasing person," Hamilton wrote his friend John Laurens. "His sentiments were elevated and inspired esteem, they had a softness that conciliated affection." At one point in his conversations with Hamilton, André broke down in tears when he described the debt he owed his commander in chief. "Clinton has been too good to me," he said; "he has been lavish of his kindness. I am bound to him by too many obligations and love him too well to bear the thought that he should reproach himself." Soon after, André wrote a letter to Clinton, expressing these same sentiments while insisting that "misfortune, not guilt," had led to his capture.

When André realized that all hope for release had been extinguished, he wrote once again to Washington, this time concerning the form of

execution. A soldier was executed by a firing squad; a spy, however, suffered the disgrace of being hanged by the neck until dead. André held out
hope that Washington would allow him to die with as much dignity (and
as little pain) as possible. "Buoyed above the terror of death by the con-
sciousness of a life devoted to honorable pursuits, and stained with no
action that can give me remorse," he wrote, "I trust that the request I
make to your Excellency at this serious period, and which is to soften my
last moments, will not be rejected. Sympathy towards a soldier will surely
induce your Excellency and a military tribunal to adapt the mode of my
death to the feelings of a man of honor."

But Washington, who had made sure *not* to meet André, refused to
yield. What Arnold had done had rocked the country to its already shaky
foundations. The times required an act of unbending firmness to drive
home the point that treason in this new, half-formed country was not to
be tolerated. It almost cost him Hamilton, who regarded the decision as
an unnecessarily "hard hearted policy," but in the end Washington realized that he could not grant the prisoner his wish.

Joseph Plumb Martin saw André at Tappan and described him as "an
interesting character." He also realized, unlike the many American officers who'd taken up André's cause, that the adjutant general was something less than a martyred saint, particularly given the precedent
established by the British four years before during the invasion of New
York. "There has been a great deal said about [André]," Martin wrote, "but
he was but a man, and no better, nor had he better qualifications than the
brave Captain [Nathan] Hale, whom the British commander caused to be
executed as a spy . . . without the shadow of a trial, denying him the use
of a Bible or the assistance [of] a clergyman in his last moments. . . . André
had every indulgence allowed him that could be granted with propriety."
Washington, to Martin's mind, was completely justified in sentencing
André to be hanged.

The execution had originally been scheduled for October 1, but the exchange of last-minute correspondence with Clinton required that it be
delayed until the following day at noon. When on the morning of October 2 André received word of the timing of his death, he was, according
to Dr. James Thacher, who had attended Benedict Arnold in Albany after
the Battle of Saratoga and was there that day in Tappan, "without

emotion." André had determined that he was going to exit this world with the grace and self-possession that his many American acolytes had come to expect.

By that time, André's servant Peter had arrived from New York with his master's regimental uniform. When he entered the room that morning to dress him, the servant was in tears. "Leave me till you can show yourself more manly," André insisted and proceeded to shave and dress himself unassisted. After eating his breakfast, he placed his hat on the table before him and announced, "I am ready at any moment, gentlemen, to wait on you."

Thacher described the scene once André emerged from his prison. "A large detachment of troops was paraded and an immense concourse of people assembled; almost all our general and field officers, excepting his Excellency and his staff, were present on horseback; melancholy and gloom pervaded all ranks, and the scene was affecting and awful."

All eyes were on André, who walked arm and arm with the officers on either side of him. According to Thacher, André "appeared as if conscious of the dignified deportment which he displayed, . . . retained a complacent smile on his countenance, and politely bowed to several gentlemen whom he knew, which was respectfully returned."

The procession, stepping to the beat of the death march, turned up a hill, and André saw, for the first time, the gallows: two immense forked timbers supporting an equally large crosspiece. Washington had determined that it was best not to tell André beforehand what his decision had been concerning his punishment. Suddenly realizing he was about to be hanged, André, in Thacher's words, "involuntarily started backward and made a pause." "Why this emotion, sir?" one of his attendants asked. "I am reconciled to my death," André explained, "but I detest the mode." As André paused near the gallows, Thacher noticed that he'd placed his foot on a round stone and, rolling it back and forth, noticeably gagged, "as if attempting to swallow."

A wagon containing a black coffin was moved into place under the gibbet. But when André attempted to step up into the wagon, his legs buckled; grabbing the tailboard, he was able to pull himself in. "At this moment he appeared to shrink," Thacher observed, "but instantly elevating his head with firmness, he said, 'It will be but a momentary pang.'" André took a white handkerchief from his pocket and, after taking off his hat, tied the silk piece of cloth over his eyes with, Thacher wrote, "perfect firmness, which melted the hearts and moistened the cheeks not only of his servant but of the throng of spectators."

An imprisoned loyalist had agreed to serve as André's executioner on the condition that he be granted his freedom. So as to mask his identity, he had blackened his face with soot, and he attempted to slip the noose over André's head. But André, seeing that the executioner's hands were besmirched with soot, objected, telling him to "take off your black hands." André would do it himself. "He slipped the noose over his head," Thacher wrote, "and adjusted it to his neck without the assistance of the awkward executioner." The provost announced that he had an opportunity to speak, if he desired. André pulled the handkerchief from his eyes and said, "I pray you to bear me witness that I meet my fate like a brave man."

Those gathered there that day were deeply impressed by these words. There were some, however, who remembered what the American Nathan Hale had said under similar circumstances: "I only regret that I have but one life to give for my country." Hale had expressed his loyalty to the United States; André thought only of his own honor.

With the handkerchief back in place around his eyes, and with his arms tied at the elbows behind him, the order was given for the horses to pull the wagon out from underneath him. The sudden movement of the wagon, combined with the slack in the rope, imparted what one witness described as "a most tremendous swing." Thacher claimed André died almost instantly. Another doctor present at the scene saw it differently. "André was a small man," he wrote, "and seemed hardly to stretch the rope, and his legs dangled so much that the hangman was ordered to take hold of them and keep them straight."

A half hour later, André's body was cut down from the scaffold and prepared for burial in a nearby grave. A witness remembered that André's "head was very much on one side, in consequence of the manner in which the halter drew upon his neck. His face appeared to be greatly swollen, and very black, much resembling a high degree of mortification. It was indeed a shocking sight to behold."

That afternoon, probably about the same time that André was executed, Washington received a packet from Henry Clinton with several letters representing his final attempt to change Washington's mind. Included among the correspondence was another letter from Benedict Arnold. By that point, it had become clear to Arnold that the young British major whom he'd formerly dismissed as just another underling (and an incompetent one at that) had stolen all of the attention he had expected to receive in New York. André, it turned out, was beloved by Clinton, who had difficulty hiding his antipathy for the traitor who had left his cherished protégé behind. As Clinton and others worked round the clock for André's release, Arnold realized that it was in his own best interests to contribute to the chorus of support. So he'd written Washington this letter.

In addition to making all the usual arguments about André being under the protection of a flag, he added a very personal threat. If André should suffer death, "I shall think myself bound by every tie of duty and honor to retaliate on such unhappy persons of your army as may fall within my power, that the respect due to flags, and to the law of nations, may be better understood and observed. If this warning should be disregarded, and [André] suffer, I call Heaven and earth to witness that your Excellency will be justly answerable for the torrent of blood that may be spilt in consequence." It was difficult to determine upon whom, exactly, he was going to direct his wrath, but if André should die, Arnold promised to unleash a retaliatory killing spree of epic proportions.

Marooned in New York, with only his bottomless pride to console him, Arnold had grown as hysterical in his own violent way as his wife. Washington, on the other hand, had managed to rise above the fury of rage and suspicion that Arnold's treason had unleashed among so many American officers. "How black, how despised," Nathanael Greene thundered, "loved by none, and hated by all. Once his country's idol, now her horror." "We were all in astonishment," Alexander Scammell remembered, "each peeping at his next neighbor to see if any treason was hanging about him: nay, we descended to a critical examination of ourselves." Or as Henry Knox admitted to his friend Greene, "I cannot get Arnold out of my head."

Washington no doubt felt all of these things and more. However, in the course of the last four years since his disastrous, emotionally ragged performance at the Battle of Long Island, he had learned to take the longest of views. Nothing of consequence, he now knew, could be decided in a single battle, no matter how brilliantly fought. Winning a war and

creating a new nation took time. The betrayal of Benedict Arnold had
been a shock, of course, but the United States, despite having no money,
no order, and no solidarity, had so far survived five years of bitter conflict.
"This is an event that occasions me equal regret and mortification," he
wrote his French counterpart Count Rochambeau. "But traitors are the
growth of every country and in a revolution of the present nature, it is
more to be wondered at, that the catalogue is so small than that there
have been found a few."

Washington also had no illusions about Benedict Arnold. Soon after
André's execution, John Laurens wrote to Washington insisting that the
traitor must now be racked by "a mental hell." Washington disagreed.
The intensity of Arnold's self-absorption meant that he was incapable of
regret, or as Washington wrote in response to Laurens, "He wants
feeling! . . . While his faculties will enable him to continue his sordid
pursuits, there will be no time for remorse."

It had been revealed to him dangerously late, but Washington now
knew his man.

EPILOGUE

A Nation of Traitors

For the citizens of Philadelphia, Benedict Arnold's betrayal was a personal affront. Joseph Reed, it turned out, had been right all along, and as president of Pennsylvania's Supreme Executive Council he took great delight in calling for the seizure of Arnold's papers and possessions. "Though no direct proof of his treachery was found," the *Pennsylvania Packet* reported, "the papers disclose such a scene of baseness and prostitution of office and character as it is hoped this new world cannot parallel."

On September 30 the Philadelphia artist Charles Willson Peale helped create the spectacle that was to be the patriot answer to André's Mischianza. Perched on the seat of a cart pulled by two horses was a life-size effigy of Arnold featuring a two-faced rotating head. In one hand he held a letter from the devil telling him he could now hang himself; in another he held a black mask. Looming over the two-faced Arnold was Beelzebub himself with a bag of gold and a pitchfork. Militiamen and Continental troops with candles in the muzzles of their muskets escorted the cart through the city streets to the tune of the "Rogue's March." The night ended with Arnold's effigy being consumed in fire.

As a warrior at Valcour Island and Saratoga, Benedict Arnold had been an inspiration. But it was as a traitor that he succeeded in galvanizing a nation. Just as the American people appeared to be sliding into apathy and despair, Arnold's treason awakened them to the realization that the War of Independence was theirs to lose.

• • •

The United States had been created through an act of disloyalty. No matter how eloquently the Declaration of Independence had attempted to justify the American rebellion, a residual guilt hovered over the circumstances of the country's founding. Arnold changed all that. By threatening to destroy the newly created republic through, ironically, his own betrayal, Arnold gave this nation of traitors the greatest of gifts: a myth of creation. The American people had come to revere George Washington, but a hero alone was not sufficient to bring them together. Now they had the despised villain Benedict Arnold. They knew both what they were fighting for—and against. The story of America's genesis could finally move beyond the break with the mother country and start to focus on the process by which thirteen former colonies could become a nation.

As Arnold had demonstrated, the real enemy was not Great Britain, but those Americans who sought to undercut their fellow citizens' commitment to one another. Whether it was Joseph Reed's willingness to promote his state's interests at the expense of what was best for the country as a whole or Arnold's decision to sell his loyalty to the highest bidder, the greatest danger to America's future came from self-serving opportunism masquerading as patriotism. At this fragile stage in the country's development, a way had to be found to strengthen rather than destroy the existing framework of government. The Continental Congress was far from perfect, but it offered a start to what could one day be a great nation. By turning traitor, Arnold had alerted the American people to how close they had all come to betraying the Revolution by putting their own interests ahead of their newborn country's. Already the name Benedict Arnold was becoming a byword for that most hateful of crimes: treason against the people of the United States.

Dissent had created America, but, as had been proven by Arnold (who claimed in an address published soon after his treason, "the private judgment of any individual citizen of this country is . . . free from all conventional restraints"), dissent could also destroy it. For the American experiment to work, a way must be found to balance political freedom with the need for political stability.

But to get to that point, the War of Independence must first be won. In the months ahead, the voices dominating Congress began to echo less the radicals' cry for moral purity and sacrifice and shift to a more pragmatic, fiscally minded effort to provide Washington with the resources he needed to defeat the British. Already in Pennsylvania the change had begun. Less than two weeks after Arnold's effigy had been burned to cinders, many of the Constitutionalists in the legislature were voted out of office, giving the Republicans increasing control of state government. The radicals may have been right about Arnold, but they had been unable to make government work. Whether or not the Republicans were going to be any better at solving rather than exacerbating the state's problems remained to be seen.

Peggy Arnold was not welcome in Philadelphia. Among her husband's papers was a letter (in which she spoke disparagingly of the French ambassador La Luzerne and several female members of Philadelphia society) that earned her little sympathy. There was also John André's letter in which he offered himself to Peggy as the "complete milliner." Insisting that Peggy's continued presence in Philadelphia posed a risk to the city and the nation, the Pennsylvania Supreme Executive Council demanded that she be exiled to New York.

By that time, Peggy's hysteria had lapsed into what her brother-in-law Edward "Neddy" Burd described as "a kind of stupor from which she is not yet recovered and has not shed a tear for six days past. . . . She keeps [to] her room and is almost continually on the bed. Her peace of mind seems to me entirely destroyed." Peggy's father feared that her return to Arnold would cause her to "be debased, and her welfare, even in another world, endangered, by his example." But in the end, Shippen had no choice but to accompany his daughter to Paulus Hook, New Jersey, where she was transported to New York and her awaiting husband. Within a few weeks, Peggy was pregnant with their second child.

In his new role in the British army, Arnold proved to be a still dangerous opponent. Within the year he would make good on his threat to Washington, and in a bloodbath comparable to the massacres at Paoli and Old Tappan, Arnold would—it might be said—avenge the death of Major John André.

By the fall of 1780, Joseph Plumb Martin's life in the Continental army had changed for the better. He had been chosen for the newly created Corps of Sappers and Miners under the command of David Bushnell, the inventor of the military submarine *Turtle*. Washington had decided that if he should ever succeed in trapping the British at the southern tip of

Manhattan, the Continental army must be schooled in the complex art of conducting a siege. The men of Bushnell's corps were to master the engineering skills involved in digging trenches, building roads, laying and removing explosives, and other technical duties. "All the officers were required to be acquainted with the sciences," Martin remembered, "and it was desirable to have as intelligent young men as could be procured to compose it, although some of us fell considerably short of perfection."

As Martin soon discovered, Bushnell's quirkiness made him a difficult leader. In the months ahead, Martin found himself having to settle the frequent disputes between Bushnell and his men. For Martin, it was a different, more intellectual challenge than he had previously faced. Although he initially "had some doubts in my own mind . . . whether I was altogether qualified," that did not prevent him from doing his absolute best.

Unlike Benedict Arnold, Martin had long since resigned himself to the necessity of fulfilling his obligations to his country even though "she failed in fulfilling hers with me." In the end, Martin decided, "The case was much like that of a loyal and faithful husband and a light-heeled wanton of a wife. But I forgive her and hope she will do better in [the] future."

Arnold's aides Richard Varick and David Franks were cleared of having any knowledge of their commander's treasonous activities as was the remarkably naive Joshua Hett Smith. That did not prevent New York state authorities from imprisoning Smith, who eventually escaped and fled to England.

Once it became clear that Arnold had acted more or less alone, Washington determined to "make a public example of him." Working with the cavalry officer Henry Lee, who was stationed in New Jersey, he set into motion a secret plan to kidnap Arnold at his home in New York and transport him across the Hudson. It was imperative, Washington insisted, that Arnold be taken alive.

With the help of Justice William Smith, Arnold published an address to the American people in which he attributed his treason to his frustrations with Congress and his misgivings about the alliance with France, a country that he accused of "fraudulently avowing an affection for the liberties of mankind while she holds her native sons in vassalage and chains." Arnold may have had a point about the injustices of French society, but the address appears to have had the opposite of the intended effect on the American people. In the meantime, Arnold's attempts to recruit a regiment of loyalists were not going well. Rather than let him languish in New York, Clinton decided that Arnold should lead an expedition to Virginia.

One of Arnold's new recruits was a deserter named John Champe, who claimed that the general's example had inspired his own decision to join the British. What Arnold did not realize was that Champe was a secret agent who had been recruited by Lee to effect the general's abduction. Champe had spent several weeks shadowing Arnold and knew that every night, around midnight, he strolled the grounds of his home and after a visit to the outhouse retired to bed.

By the morning of December 11, Champe had dislodged a board on the fence surrounding Arnold's yard in anticipation of subduing him that night and dragging him to a boat waiting onshore. Unfortunately, December 11 proved to be the day that Arnold's regiment was mobilized for the operation in Virginia. Soon Champe and Arnold, the latter unaware that he had almost joined André on the gallows, were headed south toward what had become the major theater of the war.

After its disastrous flirtation with Horatio Gates, Congress decided to nominate the general whom Washington regarded as his most talented subordinate to command the southern department of the Continental army. Nathanael Greene's military career had almost ended four years before with the disastrous surrender of Fort Washington. A year later he served with spirit and even brilliance during the retreat at Brandywine, preventing that botched battle from becoming the catastrophe it might otherwise have been. When the Continental army was starving at Valley Forge, he had agreed to take the thankless job of quartermaster. He was creative and reliable, but unlike Lafayette he had not succeeded in becoming the commander in chief's intimate friend. Washington could be a demanding superior, and at one point two years before, feeling underappreciated and overworked, Greene had threatened to resign. Now, however, he was being given the chance he had always wanted.

The times, however, were anything but auspicious. Arnold's treason had had a riveting effect—government leaders were at long last beginning to focus on providing Washington with the support he needed to fight the war—but there was a genuine danger that all would be lost before the country could save itself. Lord Cornwallis had capitalized on the victories at Charleston and Camden and was threatening to subdue the entire South. As Henry Lee, who had been chosen to serve under Greene, realized, his new commander had been placed in an almost impossible position. America was just one defeat away from disaster. In the event of another ruinous loss, "the country south of the James River . . . would be ground to dust and ashes," Lee predicted. "Such misery, without hope, could not long be endured . . . [requiring] re-annexation to the mother country." The situation was so dire that Washington refused Greene's request for a brief leave to say good-bye to his wife, Caty, and their children.

Greene had overseen the trial of John André and was then serving as Arnold's replacement as commander at West Point. On the morning of October 21, after writing a letter of farewell to Caty, Nathanael Greene began the long journey south.

ACKNOWLEDGMENTS

O
ne of my biggest debts is to my mother, the late Marianne D. Philbrick, whose lifelong fascination with Benedict Arnold made the writing of this book seem like an inevitability. Dr. Samuel Forman, author of *Dr. Joseph Warren*, provided early insights and suggestions regarding the research on the medical issues associated with Benedict Arnold's injury at the Battle of Saratoga. Erick Tichonuk, then the executive director of the Lake Champlain Maritime Museum in Vergennes, Vermont, was immensely helpful in guiding my exploration of Lake Champlain and Valcour Island. In 2014 I was lucky enough to attend Bruce Venter's Third Annual Conference on the American Revolution, at Colonial Williamsburg, and profited by presentations given by Edward G. Lengel, James Kirby Martin, Andrew O'Shaughnessy, Glenn Williams, Todd Andrlik, Don Hagist, David Mattern, and James L. Nelson. Peter Malinowski, aquaculture program director of the New York Harbor School and director of the Billion Oyster Project, took my family on a revelatory exploration of New York Harbor that included circumnavigations of both Staten and Manhattan Islands; many thanks to Brad Burnham for providing the boat. My appreciation of the role New York and Brooklyn played in the Revolution was greatly enhanced by a month-and-a-half stay in Brooklyn Heights; thanks to my granddaughter Lydia Philbrick McArdle, who was born at NYU Langone Medical Center in the Kips Bay neighborhood of Manhattan the day before the anniversary of the Battle of Long Island, for providing not only the impetus to spend time in Brooklyn but also a panoramic view of the East River from her hospital room. Many thanks to Harry Carpenter, Dillard Kirby, and especially Finn Wentworth for making my research trip to Morristown, New Jersey, so instructive and illuminating; thanks also to the staffs of three important Morristown historical sites: Washington's Headquarters Museum, the Schuyler-Hamilton House, and the Jockey Hollow Encampment. Thanks to Curt Viebranz and Douglas Bradburn for facilitating my visit to George Washington's Mount Vernon and the Fred W. Smith National Library. At the William L. Clements

Library in Ann Arbor, Michigan, J. Kevin Graffagnino, Brian Dunnigan, and Cheney Schopieray helped me navigate the Henry Clinton Papers as well as a host of other resources. Jeff Flannery gave me an unforgettable tour of the treasures contained in the stacks of the Library of Congress Manuscript Reading Room, and Valerie Paley was most helpful at the New-York Historical Society. Thanks also to the staffs of the New York Public Library, the Pennsylvania State Archives, the New Haven Museum, the Massachusetts Historical Society, and the West Point Museum, as well as those of the following historical sites: Valley Forge; Fort Mifflin, Fort Ticonderoga, the Saratoga Battlefield; the Brandywine Battlefield; and the Paoli Battlefield.

For reading and commenting on the manuscript, I am indebted to Art Cohn, Richard Duncan, Peter Gow, Jennifer Philbrick McArdle, Thomas McGuire, James Kirby Martin, Bruce Miller, James L. Nelson, Samuel Philbrick, Thomas Philbrick, and Barnet Schecter. Many thanks to my son, Ethan Philbrick, and his husband, Will DeWitt, for listening to and commenting on an early draft of the first chapter.

As he was for my four preceding books, my researcher, Michael Hill, has been an immense help throughout the last three years of researching and writing. Jenny Pouech was a huge help when it came to securing permissions for the images that are in this book. Jeffrey Ward did his usual stellar job with the maps.

At Viking, I have been privileged once again to work with the incomparable Wendy Wolf and am already looking forward to what will be our seventh book together. Many thanks also to Brian Tart, Andrea Schulz, Amy Hill, Carolyn Coleburn, Lindsay Prevette, Kristin Matzen, Bruce Giffords, Georgia Bodnar, Kate Stark, Lydia Hirt, and Mary Stone. Thanks as well to Kathryn Court, John Fagan, Patrick Nolan, and Louise Braverman at Penguin. Thanks to Jason Ramirez for the jacket design.

I have been with my agent, Stuart Krichevsky, for seventeen years and am extraordinarily lucky to count him as both a friend and a literary adviser. Thanks also to his coworkers Shana Cohen, Ross Harris, and David Gore. Thanks to Rich Green at ICM Partners for his enthusiasm and insight. Many thanks to Meghan Walker of Tandem Literary for keeping me connected to my readers through my Web site and social media.

Finally, a special thanks to my wife, Melissa, and to all our family members for their patience and support.

NOTES

ABBREVIATIONS

AA5——*American Archives*, 5th series, edited by Peter Force

COS——*Campaign of 1776*, edited by Henry Johnston

DAR——*Documents of the American Revolution*, edited by K. G. Davies

JCC——*Journals of the Continental Congress*, edited by Worthington Chauncey Ford et al.

LCJR——*Life and Correspondence of Joseph Reed*, edited by W. B. Reed

LDC——*Letters of Delegates to Congress*, edited by Paul Smith

LOC——Library of Congress

MHS——Massachusetts Historical Society

NA——National Archives

NDAR——*Naval Documents of the American Revolution*, edited by William Bell Clark

NEHGR—*New England Historical and Genealogical Register*

NYHS——New-York Historical Society

NYPL——New York Public Library

PGW——*The Papers of George Washington: Revolutionary War Series*, edited by Philander Chase et al.

PNG——*Papers of General Nathanael Greene*, edited by Richard Showman and Dennis M. Conrad

WGW——*Writings of George Washington*, edited by John Fitzpatrick

WMQ——*William and Mary Quarterly*

I have adjusted the spelling and punctuation of quotations to make them more accessible to a modern audience—something that has already been done by the editors of several collections cited below.

PREFACE: THE FAULT LINE

As John Shy writes in *People Numerous and Armed,* "the bedrock facts of the American Revolutionary struggle, especially after the euphoric first year, are not pretty" (p. 23). Charles Patrick Neimeyer in *America Goes to War* speaks of the "later generations of historians who celebrated a mythified sort of fighting man" (p. 26). For information on Charles Thomson's unpublished account of the activities of the Continental Congress, I have relied on Boyd Stanley Schlenther's biography *Charles Thomson: A Patriot's Pursuit,* which includes John Jay's claim that "no person in the world is so perfectly acquainted with . . . the American Revolution as yourself," as well as Thomson's decision "not to tear away the veil" (pp. 202–5). My thanks to David Mattern for bringing this resource to my attention.

CHAPTER ONE: DEMONS OF FEAR AND DISORDER

For information on Washington's Life Guard, as well as the description of their being "handsomely and well made," I have looked to Carlos Godfrey's *Commander-in-Chief's Guard,* p. 19. In my discussion of Thomas Hickey's trial and execution I am indebted to Brian Carso's *"Whom Can We Trust Now?,"* in which he details how the Continental Congress responded to the issues raised by the plot involving Thomas Hickey by passing resolutions that "defined treason as disloyalty to the colonies," and in so doing created "a *de facto* declaration of independence some two weeks before the formal Declaration was adopted" (pp. 58–59). Daniel McCurtin's account of the arrival of the British fleet is in Douglas Freeman's *Washington,* 4:127, which also includes a discussion of the signal flags flown from the heights of Staten Island. Henry Knox tells of how he and Lucy watched the approach of the British fleet in a July 11, 1776, letter to his brother William, in Francis Drake's *Life and Correspondence of Henry Knox,* p. 28. Joseph Reed writes of how the British fleet seemed to have "dropped from the clouds" and of his amazement at the "prodigious fleet" in an Aug. 9, 1776, letter to his wife, in *LCJR,* 1:215, 216. On the importance of the Hessians to the British army, see David Hackett Fischer's *Washington's Crossing,* pp. 51–65. Howe's reference to his "utter amazement at the decisive and masterly strokes" implemented by Germain are in Piers Mackesy's *War for America,* p. 70. Edward Gibbon's claim that Germain "hopes to reconquer Germany in America" is in Andrew O'Shaughnessy's *Men Who Lost America,* p. 175, as is Germain's assumption that Howe would deliver "one decisive blow [and] finish this rebellion in one campaign" (p. 177). Benjamin Franklin's letter to Admiral Howe in which he refers to the "fine and noble china vase, the British Empire" is quoted in David Syrett's *Admiral Lord Howe,* p. 52.

　　Charles Willson Peale's 1776 portrait of Washington is at the Brooklyn Museum of Art. Joseph Reed writes of Washington's "point of honor" in an Aug. 4, 1776, letter to Mr. Pettit in *LCJR,* 1:213. Benjamin Rush's claim that Washington had the "unmistakable look of a soldier" is in Richard Brookhiser's *Founding Father,* p. 114. My thanks to Barnet Schecter for directing my attention to Washington's bold July 12, 1776, proposal to launch a preemptive strike against the British on Staten Island; see Schecter's *George Washington's America,* pp. 133–35. Washington's July 10, 1776, letter to John Hancock, in which he refers to the "melancholy and mournful victory," is in *PGW,* 5:258–61. The reference to Nathanael Greene's "raging fever" is in his Aug. 15, 1776, letter to Washington in *PGW,* 6:30.

Philip Fithian's description of the alarm guns' "Crack! Crack!" is in his *Journal*, Aug. 22, 1776, p. 215. Ambrose Serle describes the beauty of the scene during the invasion of Long Island in his *Journal*, pp. 71–73. Horace Walpole's remarks about the silence of the Howe brothers appear in O'Shaughnessy's *Men Who Lost America*, p. 88. Henry Clinton's reference to himself as a "shy bitch" is in William Willcox's *Portrait of a General*, p. 44. Fischer in *Washington's Crossing* discusses the court-martial that kept Smallwood and other American officers in New York during the Battle of Brooklyn as well as the reorganization of the Continental army that led to Sullivan's account of the troops "wandering about western Long Island" (pp. 91–93). Washington's Aug. 25, 1776, letter to Putnam, in which he talks about "the distinction between a well-regulated army, and a mob," is in *PGW*, 6:126–28. Clinton describes how he came up with the battle plan for the Battle of Long Island and how he tried to sell it to General Howe in his account of the American Revolution at the William L. Clements Library in Ann Arbor, Michigan, and published as *American Rebellion*, edited by William Willcox, pp. 40–44. My account of Stirling's standoff with Grant draws upon works cited in *COS*, p. 168. See Michael Stephenson's *Patriot Battles* on the losses suffered by Stirling's Marylanders, p. 239. In a Sept. 3, 1776, letter in *History of Lancaster County, Pennsylvania*, by Franklin Ellis and Samuel Evans, Lieutenant Colonel James Chambers claims that Stirling fought "like a wolf" (p. 47). Washington's mournful reference to the loss of the "brave fellows" under Stirling is in George Scheer and Hugh Rankin's *Rebels and Redcoats*, p. 168. Howe makes the claim that his soldiers "would have carried the redoubt" in a Sept. 3, 1776, letter to Germain, in Thomas Field's *Battle of Long Island*, p. 380. Putnam's observation that "General Howe is either our friend or no general" is in Joseph Ellis's *Revolutionary Summer*, p. 119.

Alexander Graydon's reference to "a pitiless pelting" is in *COS*, p. 210. My account of how Washington came to the decision to retreat across the East River and how the retreat was effected is based largely on *COS*, pp. 212–24. Schecter in *Battle for New York* refers to Washington's threat to sink an overcrowded boat, p. 165. Tallmadge's description of the fog is in *COS*, pp. 222–24. The account of Fithian's reluctance to believe that the army was retreating is in his *Journal*, Aug. 30, 1776, p. 221. Greene's description of the retreat as "the best effected . . . I ever read or heard of" is in *COS*, p. 224.

Washington writes of being "entirely unfit" to write in an Aug. 31, 1776, letter to John Hancock, in *PGW*, 6:177. Washington refers to the Connecticut militia as "dismayed, intractable, and impatient to return" and predicts that without a standing army "our liberties must of necessity be greatly hazarded, if not entirely lost," in his Sept. 2, 1776, letter to John Hancock in *PGW*, 6:199. Daniel Brodhead's angry claim that "less generalship never was shown in any army since the art of war was understood" is in *COS*, p. 65, as is John Haslet's claim that Washington "has too heavy a task, assisted mostly by beardless boys," p. 52. According to Dave Palmer in *George Washington's Military Genius*, "Washington's one great strategic blunder of the war was his decision to defend [New York] with his whole army." Palmer also discusses how "political pressure" contributed to the decision (p. 131). Joseph Reed writes of being "cooped up . . . on this tongue of land" in a Sept. 2, 1776, letter to his wife; he writes about the "sacrifice of us" in a Sept. 6, 1776, letter, also to his wife, in *LCJR*, 1:230, 231. Ellis in *Revolutionary Summer* quotes Joseph Reed's Sept. 6, 1776, letter to his wife and claims that "at this tense and crowded moment, Washington was preparing to make himself into a martyr" (p. 139). Washington's Sept. 30, 1776, letter to Lund Washington, in which he writes of being in "an unhappy, divided state" while detailing renovations to Mount Vernon, is in *PGW*, 6:440–43. Although written two weeks after the evacuation of New York, the letter clearly exhibits the same despairing yet pugnacious state of mind he was feeling in the aftermath of the Battle of Long Island.

John Adams's whispered words to Benjamin Rush are quoted in Thomas McGuire's *Stop the Revolution*, as are Adams's labeling of Sullivan as a "decoy duck" (pp. 130–31) and his assessment of Admiral Howe's "Machiavellian maneuvers" (p. 139). My account of the *Turtle*'s unsuccessful attempt to blow up Admiral Howe's flagship is based on Phelps Stokes's *Iconography of Manhattan Island*, 5:997–98, and Lincoln Diamant's *Chaining the Hudson*, pp. 20–30. On a third-rate ship of the line in the British navy, see Patrick O'Brian's *Men-of-War*, pp. 13–28. I have based my account of Admiral Howe's cabin aboard the *Eagle* partly on Friedrich von Muenchhausen's description of William Howe's quarters on the vessel *Britannia*, in *At General Howe's Side*, p. 21. John Adams describes Admiral Howe's interchange with Franklin in his *Autobiography* in *Diary and Autobiography of John Adams*, 3:422. Ambrose Serle's terse description of the conference is in his *Journal*, p. 106. Nathanael Greene's Sept. 5, 1777, letter to Washington is in *PGW*, 6:222–24. Washington refers to New York as "the key to the northern country" in his Sept. 8, 1777, letter to John Hancock, in which he also talks about "the establishing of strong posts at Mount Washington . . . and on the Jersey side opposite to it with the assistance of the obstructions already made," in *PGW*, 6:249–50.

Joseph Plumb Martin's account of the British attack at Kips Bay is in *Ordinary Courage*, subsequently referred to as his *Narrative*, pp. 23–24. Ambrose Serle writes of the "incessant . . . roar of guns" in his *Journal*, p. 104. Benjamin Trumbull's account of the attack is in his *Journal*, pp. 193–95. Philip Fithian records his friend Stephen Ranney's description of how "the grape-shot struck round him thick as though a person . . . had thrown his hand full of small stones" in his *Journal*, p. 235. As proof that Joseph Plumb Martin was not the only American soldier with an interest in alcohol, there is the testimony of the British lieutenant Loftus Cliffe, who reported that after the Battle of Long Island "every one of the enemies killed and wounded stunk infamously of rum" and elaborated that "their canteens still contained the remains of sheer spirits, even their officers were in this manner urged on," in a typescript of his journal at the William L. Clements Library in Ann Arbor, Michigan. Stokes in *Iconography of Manhattan Island* includes an account of how General Howe hoped to invade New York on the anniversary of the Battle of Quebec (5:1010). Loftus Cliffe refers to Howe's determination "not to lose the finger of a single man wantonly" in his journal at the Clements Library.

Washington describes how he rode toward Kips Bay with the "utmost dispatch" in a Sept. 16, 1776, letter to John Hancock in *PGW*, 6:313–14. Samuel Parson's testimony that Washington called out "Take the walls!" and "Take the cornfield!" is in *COS*, part 2, p. 93. Joseph Plumb Martin's mention of the "demons of fear and disorder" is in his *Narrative*, p. 25. Stokes in *Iconography of Manhattan Island* includes William Heath's account of Washington crying out, "Are these the men with which I am to defend America?" as well as Nathanael Greene's claim that Washington "sought death" and James Thacher's description of Washington's horse being led away by "one of his attendants" (5:1014). Ron Chernow sites testimony from Thomas Jefferson and Gouverneur Morris concerning the strength of Washington's passions and his attempts to control them, in *Washington*, p. xix. Henry Knox's description of Washington's imposing "supernatural" presence before James Paterson is in a July 22, 1776, letter to Lucy Knox at the NYHS. For a balanced account of Howe's stop at the home of Robert Murray, see Schecter's *Battle for New York*, pp. 189–90.

CHAPTER TWO: THE MOSQUITO FLEET

By following Benedict Arnold's correspondence with Horatio Gates during the summer and fall of 1776 (in *NDAR*, vol. 6), it's possible to track his fleet's progress up and down Lake Champlain. Since the lake flows north into the Richelieu River and ultimately into the St. Lawrence, to sail north is technically to sail down the lake, but given the obvious confusions this would have introduced (given that most of us think of north as the "up" direction), I will refer to sailing north as going up the lake and south as going down. William Digby describes the disturbing sounds of wolves preying on deer and the "great flocks of wild pigeons" in his *Journal*, in *British Invasion from the North*, edited by James Baxter, p. 154. In a Sept. 7, 1776, letter to Horatio Gates, Arnold tells of how some of his men "went on shore contrary to orders before the others were ready . . . [and] were attacked by a party of savages," who killed three and wounded six men, in *NDAR*, 6:734. On the American boatbuilding effort in Skenesborough see Neil Stout's "Birth of the United States Navy"; William Fowler's *Rebels under Sail*, pp. 166–74; and James Nelson's *Benedict Arnold's Navy*, pp. 227–56. When it comes to the vessels in both the American and British fleets I have also relied on John Millar's *American Ships of the Colonial and Revolutionary Periods*. Paul Nelson in "Guy Carleton versus Benedict Arnold" writes of how on Sept. 6, 1776, Carleton decided to build the *Inflexible* shortly after learning of the strength of the American fleet (p. 355). Adding to the challenges faced by the British were the falls at Chambly on the Richelieu River, which required them to lug all their vessels' frames and timbers overland for assembly at St. Johns. On what Arnold did to make his fleet strength known to the enemy, see Bayze Wells's *Journal* entries for Sept. 4–6, 1776, in which he describes how Arnold ordered his fleet into a "line of battle" across the lake and then two days later ordered the fleet to salute the arrival of the gondola *New Jersey* and sloop *Lee* with a cannonade that was "done in order and good discipline" (pp. 275–76). Edward Osler in "Battle of Valcour Island" describes how in building the *Inflexible*, "Trees growing in the forest in the morning would form a part of the ship before night" (p. 164). In a Sept. 23, 1776, letter, Captain Charles Douglas writes of how the *Inflexible* "will give us dominion of Lake Champlain" (*NDAR*, 6:951). Arnold writes of the approach of "the blowing season" in a Sept. 18, 1776, letter to Gates in *NDAR*, 6:884. John Greenwood, who was stationed at Ticonderoga during the summer and fall of 1776, refers to "the Mosquito Fleet, as it was called," in *Revolutionary Services of John Greenwood*, p. 37.

   John Bell in a July 26, 2013, posting in his blog *Boston 1775* titled "How Tall Was Benedict Arnold?" cites Samuel Downing's observation concerning no "wasted timber in him," as well as the claim by the Reverend Leake's father that he was a most "accomplished and graceful skater" (http://boston1775.blogspot.com/2013/07/how-tall-was-benedict-arnold.html). My account of Arnold's early civilian life and pre–Valcour Island Revolutionary War experience is based primarily on Clare Brandt's *Man in the Mirror*, pp. 9–85; James Kirby Martin's *Benedict Arnold*, pp. 11–222; and James Nelson's *Benedict Arnold's Navy*, pp. 3–226. Brandt quotes Arnold's outraged words about the Boston Massacre (p. 15); Nelson cites Arnold's kicking James Easton (p. 60) and his letter to Silas Deane, in which he refers to burying his sorrow over the death of his wife in "the public calamity" (p. 72).

James Wilkinson tells of how Arnold insisted on being the last American to leave St. Johns in his *Memoirs*, 1:55. Russell Bellico in *Sails and Steam in the Mountains* cites Horatio Gates's belief that Arnold would give "life and spirit to our dock yard" (p. 139). James Wilkinson refers to Arnold as "intrepid, generous, friendly, upright, honest" in an Aug. 5, 1776, letter to Richard Varick in *NDAR*, 6:61. In the same letter, he has this to say about Arnold's critics: "Is it for men who can boast more than an easy enjoyment of the Continental provision to blast the reputation of him who having encountered the greatest perils surmounted extremest hardships, fought and bled in a cause which they have only encumbered?" Wilkinson is here providing a stunningly accurate prediction of what he would subsequently become at the Battle of Saratoga when he decided that his future was better served by attaching himself to Arnold's new archenemy Horatio Gates and thus became one of Arnold's sharpest critics. James Kirby Martin cites Dr. Lewis Beebe's wish that "some person would . . . make the sun shine through [Arnold's] head with an ounce ball" in *Benedict Arnold*, p. 230. In his *Memoirs*, James Wilkinson provides a detailed description of the Moses Hazen court-martial, which quotes directly from the recorded testimony; he also cites Gates's Sept. 2, 1776, letter to John Hancock, in which he euphemistically refers to how Arnold's "temper might possibly lead him a little farther than is marked by the precise line of decorum" (1:70–74). Bayze Wells tells of the "most genteel feast of a roast pig" that was enjoyed by Arnold's officers on the eastern shore of the lake just to the north of Ferris Bay at Buttonmould Bay in the Aug. 29, 1776, entry in his *Journal*, p. 272.

Hannah Arnold's Aug. 5, 1776, and Sept. 1, 1776, letters, in which she refers to Arnold's youngest son, Hale, and his sunk trading vessel, as well as the fact that he is now "a broken merchant," are part of the correspondence that Arnold left aboard his former flagship the *Royal Savage*, which ultimately fell into the enemy's hands. To this day the documents are still in archives in Quebec, Canada, and were published in "Documents sur la Révolution américaine," *Revue de l'Université Laval, Québec* 2, no. 7 (Mar. 1948): 644, 746. James Kirby Martin cites Samuel Chase's letter to Arnold in which he writes, "Your best friends are not your countrymen," in *Benedict Arnold*, p. 233. For information on Horatio Gates, I have looked to Paul Nelson's *General Horatio Gates*, pp. 3–6. Gates's comments regarding the New England militiamen are in my *Bunker Hill*, p. 242. On the Gates-Schuyler controversy, see Nelson, pp. 58–73, and Jonathan Rossie's *Politics of Command in the American Revolution*, pp. 101–34.

Arnold writes of how "extremely cruel" it is to be accused of being "a robber and thief at a time . . . when I have it not in my power to be heard in my own defense" in a Sept. 7, 1776, letter to Gates in *NDAR*, 6:735. Gates refers to "the foul stream of that poisonous fountain, detraction" in a Sept. 11, 1776, letter to Philip Schuyler, in *AA5*, 2:294–95. Gates's Aug. 7, 1776, orders to Arnold, in which he insists that "it is a defensive war we are carrying on," are in *NDAR*, 3:95. Gates writes of "the draught of the lake as you desire" in a Sept. 5, 1776, letter to Arnold, in "Documents sur la Révolution américaine," *Revue de l'Université Laval, Québec* 2, no. 4 (Dec. 1947): 839. Arnold tells Gates that "I design making a remove to the island Valcour" in a Sept. 15, 1776, letter in *NDAR*, 6:837. Winslow Watson visited the site of William Hay's house overlooking Valcour Bay in the nineteenth century and interviewed Hay's surviving daughter, by then known as Mrs. Elmore, who had been two years old at the time of the battle, in Watson's "Fortresses of Crown Point and Ticonderoga," pp. 199–200. According to Oscar Bredenberg in "American

Champlain Fleet, 1775–1777," p. 253, Arnold had visited Hay's house opposite Valcour Island back in 1775 on his way to St. Johns, so clearly the area was already known to him. Arnold's Sept. 21, 1776, letter to Gates, in which he speaks of sending two boats to sound around Valcour, as well as how he is training the men in "the exercise of their guns," is in *NDAR,* 6:926. Gates assures Arnold that "no man alive could be more anxious for the welfare of you and your fleet" in a Sept. 23, 1776, letter in *NDAR,* 6:962. Bayze Wells writes of seeing "snow on the mountains" in an Oct. 1, 1776, entry in his *Journal,* p. 282. Arnold responds to the news of the taking of New York in an Oct. 7, 1776, letter to Gates in *NDAR,* 6:1117. Arnold's Oct. 10, 1776, letter to Gates, in which he expresses his fears that the British fleet will be "formidable," is in *NDAR,* 6:1197; Gates's Oct. 12, 1776, letter to Arnold referring to his "armada" is in *NDAR,* 6:1237.

Lieutenant Digby writes of how "noble a sight" it was to see a three-masted ship "in the very heart of the continent," in an Oct. 7, 1776, entry in his *Journal,* p. 153. Digby writes of the criticisms of Carleton for "hazarding himself on an element so much out of his line" in an Oct. 10, 1776, entry, p. 157. George Pausch writes of the "splendid and auspicious wind" in an Oct. 11, 1776, entry in his *Journal,* p. 82. Dr. Robert Knox's reference to first seeing one of the boats in Arnold's fleet is in J. Robert Maguire's "Dr. Robert Knox's Account of the Battle of Valcour" (subsequently referred to as "Knox's Narrative"), p. 148. John Bratten in *Gondola* Philadelphia *and the Battle of Lake Champlain* estimates that the British fleet was "already in midchannel, two miles beyond the southern end of Valcour Island, before the crews detected the concealed American fleet" (p. 58). David Waterbury speaks of his meeting with Arnold prior to the battle in an Oct. 24, 1776, letter to John Hancock in *AA5,* 2:1224. Oscar Bredenberg in "Royal Savage" cites the American crewman's exclamation "Lord have mercy . . . there's a three-masted ship," as well as Arnold's lament that "they are all navy people" (pp. 147–48). Bellico in *Sails and Steam in the Mountains* writes that Arnold had five hundred "greenhands" in the American fleet (p. 150).

Arnold speaks of the *Royal Savage*'s "bad management" in the account of the battle he wrote in an Oct. 12, 1776, letter to Gates in *NDAR,* 6:1235. George Pausch writes of how the battle quickly became "very animated" once the gunboats had taken up their positions to leeward of the American line in the Oct. 11, 1776, entry in his *Journal,* p. 82. In a Sept. 7, 1776, letter to Gates, Arnold writes how he has prepared "fascines to fix on the bows and sides of the gondolas to prevent the enemy's boarding and to keep off small shot" in *NDAR,* 6:734. Pausch describes how the American boats would disappear behind the cloud of powder smoke "to get a breath" in the Oct. 11, 1776, entry in his *Journal,* p. 82. Arnold writes of how he aimed the guns aboard the *Congress* with "good execution" in his Oct. 12, 1776, letter to Gates in *NDAR,* 6:1235. In "Open Letter to Captain Pringle," John Schank, John Starke, and Edward Longcroft, who commanded the *Inflexible,* the *Maria,* and the *Loyal Convert,* respectively, accused Pringle of showing "no inclination to fight" (p. 18). My account of the *Carleton*'s mauling at the hands of the American fleet is based largely on Edward Osler's "Battle of Valcour," p. 164, and Alfred Thayer Mahan's "Naval Campaign of 1776 on Lake Champlain," p. 154. Jahiel Stewart writes of how American cannonballs "bored through and through" the *Carleton* in an Oct. 11, 1776, entry in his "Journal" in Donald Wickman's "Most Unsettled Time on Lake Champlain," p. 92. Dr. Robert Knox describes his exchange with General Carleton after an American cannonball flew over their heads in "Knox's Narrative," p. 148. Bellico lists the names of the British gunboats and provides a good description of them in *Sails and Steam in the Mountains,* p. 143.

Lieutenant John Enys comments on how the gunboats "bore the brunt of [the enemy's] whole fire" in his *Journal*, p. 19. Pausch writes of how the fighting became "very serious" after the *Carleton* episode and how "the cannon of the rebels were well served" in an Oct. 11, 1776, entry in his *Journal*, pp. 82–83. For a detailed account of the British and German gunboats' role in the battle, see Douglas Cubbison's *"Artillery Never Gained More Honour,"* pp. 54–65. Arnold writes of how the fire of the native warriors on Valcour Island and on the western shore was "incessant" in his Oct. 12, 1776, letter to Gates in *NDAR*, 6:1235. Winslow Watson (who spoke with Mrs. Hay's grown daughter many years later) writes of the encounter between the young mother and the warriors in "Fortresses of Crown Point and Ticonderoga," pp. 199–200. Jahiel Stewart writes of how the American doctors "cut off [a] great many legs and arm[s]," in an Oct. 11, 1776, entry in his "Journal" in Wickman's "Most Unsettled Time on Lake Champlain," p. 92. Pausch describes the blowing up of the British gunboat and how he rescued the majority of its crew in his *Journal*, pp. 83–84. Mahan describes how the *Inflexible* effectively ended the battle toward evening "when five broadsides silenced their whole line" in "Naval Campaign of 1776 on Lake Champlain," p. 155. Bellico writes of how "a 24-pound ball was found lodged in the outside planking" of the *Philadelphia*'s bow, in *Sails and Steam in the Mountains*, p. 153. For an excellent account of how the *Philadelphia* was salvaged and eventually became the centerpiece of the Smithsonian National Museum of American History, as well as the basis of a reproduction at the Lake Champlain Maritime Museum, see Bratten's *Gondola* Philadelphia, pp. 74–164.

Arnold writes of the damage sustained by his fleet in the battle in his Oct. 12, 1776, letter to Gates in *NDAR*, 6:1235. James Wilkinson's account of the battle is based on his interview with James Cushing, the sergeant of marines on the *Congress*, who reported that during the council of war after the battle "some . . . were for hauling round the island, through the narrow pass, but Arnold decided on attempting a passage through the enemy's line," in Wilkinson's *Memoirs*, 1:90, where he also describes the fleet's nighttime retreat. Wilkinson served as Arnold's aide during the retreat from Canada and describes how Arnold insisted that Wilkinson shoot his horse before boarding the boat out of St. Johns (*Memoirs*, 1:55). Arnold writes of his fleet's "fortunate escape" in his Oct. 12, 1776, letter to Gates in *NDAR*, 6:1235. Carleton writes of the "great mortification" he felt on realizing that the enemy had escaped while acknowledging their "great diligence" in a letter to John Burgoyne written between Oct. 12 and 15, 1776, in *NDAR*, 6:1272. Pringle recounts the "extreme obscurity of the night" in an Oct. 15, 1776, letter to Secretary of the Admiralty Philip Stephens in *AA5*, 2:1070. General Riedesel's account of the battle and Carleton's indignant response to Arnold's escape came to him secondhand from a British officer who served during the battle; see Riedesel's *Memoirs*, pp. 71–72. According to a traditional account retold by Watson in "Fortresses of Crown Point and Ticonderoga," p. 199, mist still covered the lake when Carleton first set out after discovering Arnold's escape on the morning of Oct. 12. To the east, just below the southern tip of Grand Isle, Carleton saw what looked to be one of the enemy's vessels, and he ordered his men aboard the *Maria* to fire on what proved to be a tree-covered collection of rocks. Whether or not this actually happened, there is today a tiny island in South Hero, Vermont, called "Carleton's Prize."

Bellico in *Sails and Steam in the Mountains* cites Wigglesworth's account of how he was told by Arnold "to lie by for the fleet," as well as how Wigglesworth decided that it was "my duty to make sail and endeavor to save the *Trumbull* galley if possible" (p. 155).

Jahiel Stewart writes of how Arnold ordered the hospital ship *Enterprise* to "make all speed we could to Ty" in an Oct. 13, 1776, entry in his "Journal" in Wickman's "Most Unsettled Time on Lake Champlain," p. 94. Waterbury's account of his surrender is in his Oct. 24, 1776, letter to John Hancock in *AA5*, 2:1224. James Wilkinson relates Sergeant Cushing's reference to Waterbury's surrender as a "dastardly act," in his *Memoirs*, 1:91. In their "Open Letter to Captain Pringle," Schank, Starke, and Longcroft recount how Pringle shortened sail to slow his approach to the *Congress* and also accused him of keeping "a greater distance . . . than any officer inspired with true courage . . . would have done" (p. 19). Arnold writes of what was, in effect, the *Congress*'s last stand in an Oct. 15, 1776, letter to Philip Schuyler in *NDAR*, 6:1276. Pringle writes of Arnold being "greatly favored by the wind being off shore" in his Oct. 15, 1776, letter to Secretary Stephens in *AA5*, 2:1070.

Sergeant Cushing's account of how Arnold ordered the marines to take the high ground overlooking the beached boats is in Wilkinson's *Memoirs*, 1:91. We owe Squire Ferris's account of the heart-wrenching death of Lieutenant Goldsmith to Art Cohn, founder of the Lake Champlain Maritime Museum, who unearthed the account and published it in 1987 in "Incident Not Known to History," pp. 109–10. Up until the publication of Cohn's article, we only had the account of Dr. Robert Knox, who, watching from the *Maria*, reported that Arnold had "set fire to [the five vessels], burning the wounded and sick in them," in "Knox's Narrative," p. 148, which obviously placed Arnold in a decidedly negative light. Arnold writes of being "exceedingly fatigued and unwell" in an Oct. 15, 1776, letter to Schuyler in *NDAR*, 6:1275. Gates speaks of Arnold's "many hairbreadth escapes" in an Oct. 15, 1776, letter to Schuyler in *NDAR*, 6:1277. John Bratten cites Richard Henry Lee's description of Arnold as "fiery, hot and impetuous" in *Gondola* Philadelphia, p. 73. Digby writes of Arnold's "remarkable coolness and bravery" in his *Journal*, p. 164. James Kirby Martin cites Germain's description of Arnold as "the most enterprising man among the rebels" in *Benedict Arnold*, p. 244. Osler in "Battle of Valcour Island" recounts Pellew's attempt to capture Arnold and how he took his "stock and buckle" as a memento (p. 166). The *Oxford English Dictionary* describes a stock as "a kind of stiff close-fitting neckcloth," citing an 1806 definition of a stock being "part of an officer's dress which consists generally of black silk or velvet and is worn round the neck." According to Osler, the outcome of the Battle of Saratoga, to which Arnold's "skill and courage so materially contributed," might have been reversed "had the fortune of the chase been different," adding that at the time of his writing in 1835, Arnold's stock and buckle was "still preserved by Mr. Pellew's elder brother, to whom Arnold's son, not many years ago, confirmed the particulars of his father's escape" (p. 166).

CHAPTER THREE: A CABINET OF FORTITUDE

The reference to Benedict Arnold's "great celebrity" is cited in Andro Linklater's *Artist in Treason*, p. 20. Since Wilkinson is a thoroughly despicable character, who was, after his death, revealed to have carried on a traitorous correspondence with the Spanish government, there is always the question of his reliability. Admittedly, Wilkinson's *Memoirs* must be used with considerable caution, but any historian of the Revolution who dismisses his account out of hand is missing an essential resource. I would argue that Wilkinson's very deviousness makes him an especially useful witness. Since his relationships with both Arnold and Gates ended badly, his memories of the men are not tainted by the least vestige of hero worship; even when it comes to George Washington, he wasn't afraid to point to what he considered occasional lapses in His Excellency's judgment, which makes him almost unique among those writing about the Revolution in the nineteenth century. See Linklater's *Artist in Treason* for an excellent account of Wilkinson's value as a historical source: "Both as soldier and spy, Wilkinson always hungered for intelligence. It gave him a sense of power. He did not care about the source—gossip, maps, and explorers were equally acceptable. . . . As a result, he possessed an exceptionally well-informed, clear-eyed view of the rapidly changing era in which he lived, and of the advantages to be wrung from it" (p. 6).

Benjamin Rush writes of Arnold's "uninteresting and sometimes indelicate" conversation in his *Autobiography,* p. 158. Barry Wilson cites Alexander Hamilton's description of how Arnold "shouted and pounded the table" in *Benedict Arnold,* p. 10. Arnold writes of his sexual conquests in a Sept. 12, 1780, letter to Robert Howe in the Washington Papers at LOC. Thomas Hartley writes of Arnold's relationship with a woman at Crown Point who, had she lived, "intended to have call'd her son Arnold," in a Sept. 23, 1776, letter to Arnold in "Documents sur la Révolution américaine," *Revue de l'Université Laval, Québec* 2, no. 10 (June 1948): 928. In an 1832 pension application, Josiah Sabin recounts how "while at Quebec" Arnold went "out woman hunting beyond the line of sentinels," in *Revolution Remembered,* edited by John Dann, p. 21. Arnold's May 25, 1779, letter to the teacher Bartholomew Booth at the Hardwood School near Hagerstown, Maryland, about the practical education he wishes for his sons is in *NEHGR* 35 (Apr. 1881): 154. Paul David Nelson in *General Horatio Gates* cites John Burgoyne's comparison of Gates to an "old midwife" (p. 6). On the evolution of the American army from 1775 to 1776, see Robert Wright's *Continental Army,* pp. 3–90.

Johann Ewald writes "that the march took place so slowly for no other reason than to permit Washington to cross the Delaware safely and peacefully" in *Diary of the American War,* p. 30. Andrew O'Shaughnessy cites the statistics about specific American losses of men and equipment to the British after July 1776 in *Men Who Lost America,* p. 96. David Hackett Fischer claims that Washington had lost 90 percent of his army by Dec. 1776 in *Washington's Crossing,* p. 365. Washington writes that "the game is pretty near up" in a Dec. 18, 1776, letter to Samuel Washington in *PGW,* 7:369–71. General Charles Lee's Nov. 24, 1776, letter to Joseph Reed, in which he refers to "that fatal indecision of mind," is in *Charles Lee Papers,* 2:305–6. Michael Stephenson in *Patriot Battles,* p. 249, cites Washington's reference to "that warfare in my mind," which Washington used in his Aug. 22, 1779, letter to Joseph Reed, in which he attempted to counter Reed's, as well as Charles Lee's, suggestion that the loss of Fort Washington was due solely to him. Joseph Reed suggests that Charles Lee "go to Congress and form the plan of the new army" in his Nov. 21, 1776, letter to Lee in *Charles Lee Papers,* 2:293–94. Washington's Nov. 30, 1776, letter to Reed, in which he explains how he came to open Lee's Nov. 24 letter to Reed, is in *PGW,* 7:237. Ron Chernow cites Washington's June 11, 1777, letter to Reed, in which he admits "that I was hurt," in *Washington,* p. 266. Arthur Lefkowitz in *Long Retreat* cites James Monroe's memory of Washington's "deportment so firm, so dignified" (p. 82). Thomas Paine's *Crisis* is in *Spirit of 'Seventy-Six,* edited by Henry Steele Commager and Robert Wilson, pp. 505–7. On Washington's decision not to fire Nathanael Greene after the loss of Fort Washington, see Terry Golway's *Washington's General,* pp. 102–3; on how, in Golway's words, "Washington's loyalty to Greene was repaid a hundred times over" through Greene's Dec. 21, 1776, letter to John Hancock, in which he urged the Congress to give Washington "greater powers over the conduct of the war," see p. 109. Lefkowitz cites the description of Alexander Hamilton patting his cannon "as if it were a favorite horse" in *Long Retreat*, p. 102. Washington writes that "it is vain to ruminate upon, or even reflect upon the authors of our present misfortunes" in a Dec. 25, 1776, letter to Robert Morris in *PGW*, 7:439–40.

Fischer writes of the "ritual of European honor" enacted by Howe and the other officers on the banks of the Delaware and quotes Captain Muenchhausen's account of the American cannon barrage in *Washington's Crossing*, p. 135. Lefkowitz cites Howe's admission on Dec. 20, 1776, that "the chain, I own, is rather too extensive" in *Long Retreat*, p. 126. Stephen Kemble's account of the "licentious and cruel" conduct of the British army and his fears for the people of New Jersey is in the Nov. 7, 1776, entry of his *Journal*, p. 98. Lefkowitz in *Long Retreat* quotes the Hessian officer's reference to "the rascal peasants," as well as Colonel Rall's having to send more than a hundred men to protect a courier traveling from Trenton to Princeton (pp. 142–43). Stephenson in *Patriot Battles* cites Rall's frustrated response to the proposal to build a fortification to defend Trenton (p. 254). Washington's Dec. 14, 1776, letter to Connecticut governor Trumbull, in which he speaks of attempting "a stroke upon the forces of the enemy," is in *PGW*, 7:340–41. James Wilkinson's account of how he was present during the capture of Charles Lee is in his *Memoirs*, 1:103–12.

Chernow cites Thomas Jefferson's reference to Washington as "the most graceful figure that could be seen on horseback" in *Washington*, p. 124. George Custis in *Recollections and Private Memoirs of Washington* writes of Washington's "peculiar walk, that had the light elastic tread acquired by his long service on the frontier, and was a matter of much observation, especially to foreigners," p. 39; elsewhere Custis speaks of Washington's "mode of placing and taking up his feet, [which] resembled the step of precision and care, so remarkable in the aboriginal children of the forest" (p. 11). O'Shaughnessy in *Men Who Lost America* writes of Howe losing half his army during the winter of 1776–77, adding that "more troops were killed in minor forays than in battles" (p. 103). On the fleet of galleys that gave Washington control of the Delaware, see John Jackson's *Pennsylvania Navy*, pp. 74–78. Fischer in *Washington's Crossing* cites Charles Mawhood's statement that if he were in Washington's place "he would make an attack on several of the principal posts . . . ; that they were all so weak that he might certainly cut them off" (p. 326). For Joseph Reed's Dec. 22, 1776, letter to Washington, in which he proclaims, "Our affairs are hastening fast to ruin," see *PGW*, 7:414–16. Although George Bancroft overstated the case concerning Joseph Reed's strange and suspicious behavior prior to the attack on Trenton, much of what he says in *Joseph Reed: A Historical Essay* has merit. As Bancroft points out, even before Washington saw the suspicious letter from Charles Lee, Reed had attempted to resign just when his commander in chief needed him the most (p. 22); Bancroft also cites Reed's statement to Benjamin Rush that he feared that the American people "have not strength to finish" what had been started with the Revolution (p. 30). As for Reed's Dec. 22 letter to Washington, Bancroft writes, "It is impossible that Reed should not have known [of Washington's plans], for nothing was kept secret but the hour at which it was to take place. On the 22nd he writes a letter . . . , very skillfully drawn, [that] advises [Washington] to do what [Reed] must have known Washington was preparing to do, and makes his letter such as he might be able to show for his justification under any possible contingency" (p. 30). As William Stryker points out in *Reed Controversy,* Bancroft's evidence that Reed was secretly arranging to defect is based largely on his having confused him with another Colonel Reed from the Pennsylvania militia; however, several of Reed's contemporaries, including Benjamin Rush and John Cadwalader, later questioned the appropriateness of his behavior during this difficult period and would undoubtedly have agreed with Bancroft's description of Reed as "a vacillating trimmer" (p. 38). According to Joseph Trumbull, the army's commissary general, Reed was "universally hated and despised" by his fellow officers; see Lefkowitz, *Long Retreat,* p. 60.

After the fact, perhaps in an attempt to justify what many considered to be his highly suspicious behavior in the weeks before and after the Trenton mission (in which he did not participate), Reed drew up an extremely self-serving time line of events titled "Narrative of the Movements of the American Army in the Neighborhood of Trenton in the Winter of 1776–77" that was later used by his grandson to write a chapter in his hagiographic biography of his grandfather. Bancroft subsequently took issue with William Reed's account of his grandfather, sparking a minor pamphlet war between the two. Although self-serving (as all first-person accounts inevitably tend to be), Reed's "Narrative" is an extremely useful document, which I have drawn upon in this chapter. Washington's Dec. 23, 1776, letter to Reed, in which he informs him of the time of the attack on Trenton and adds, "For heaven's sake keep this to yourself," is in *PGW,* 7:423–24. In a Dec. 23, 1776, letter to Gates, Washington writes that "I shall not object to your going to Philadelphia on account of your health, but wish it would have permitted you to have gone to Bristol," where he says there is "some little uneasiness about command" (p. 418). On Gates's straying "to the edge of insubordination," see Fischer's *Washington's Crossing,* pp. 211–12. James Wilkinson's account of his trip to Philadelphia with Gates and his conversation with Washington when he handed him Gates's letter is in his *Memoirs,* 1:126–28.

John Greenwood's account of his participation in the Battle of Trenton (including his sufferings with "the itch") is in *Revolutionary Services of John Greenwood,* edited by his grandson Isaac, pp. 38–44. My account of "the itch" comes from C. Keith Wilbur's *Revolutionary Medicine,* p. 18. The only known remedy was the application of an ointment made of hog's lard accompanied by baths in sulfur-impregnated water. Fischer in *Washington's Crossing,* p. 219, tells of Washington sitting on the New Jersey side of the Delaware pondering the fate of his army. Washington writes of his decision "to push on at all events" in a Dec. 27, 1776, letter to John Hancock in *PGW,* 7:454. Elisha Bostwick describes how the makeshift "torches" on the fieldpieces "sparkled and blazed," as well as how Washington prevented his horse from falling on the "slanting slippery bank" and how he exhorted the soldiers in a "deep and solemn voice," in "Connecticut Soldier under Washington," p. 102. Washington's angry response to learning of General Stephen's independent expedition to Trenton the day before is described in "Memorandum Relating to Captain Richard Clough Anderson," in William Stryker's *Battles of Trenton and Princeton,* p. 374. According to Joseph Reed in his "Narrative," "an accident truly casual or rather providential baffled [Rall's] vigilance. A scout party returning from the Jerseys to Pennsylvania fell in with the advanced picket and gave an alarm about two hours before the real attack which being mistaken for that mentioned in Grant's letter [which warned Rall of an impending American attack] threw them into a state of greater security than ever—the storm also induced them to get under cover and lay aside their arms especially as the day was considerably advanced before the attack began" (pp. 398–99). See also Harry Ward's *Major General Adam*

Stephen and the Cause of American Liberty, p. 151, and Fischer's *Washington's Crossing*, pp. 231–33.

Henry Knox's Dec. 28, 1776, letter to Lucy Knox, in which he describes "a scene of war of which I had often conceived but never saw before," is in Stryker's *Battles of Trenton and Princeton*, p. 371. Washington's Dec. 25, 1776, "General Orders," which describes "a detachment of the artillery without cannon provided with spikes and hammers to spike up the enemy's cannon in case of necessity or to bring them off if it can be effected," is in *PGW*, 7:434. Wilkinson tells of how Washington proclaimed "this is a glorious day for our country" in his *Memoirs*, 1:131. Joseph Reed writes that one of the reasons Washington decided to return across the Delaware after the attack on Trenton was that "the soldiers drank too freely to admit of discipline or defense in case of attack," in his "Narratives," p. 391. Elisha Bostwick compares the Hessians' queues to "the handle of an iron skillet" and tells how they were "flying up and down" as the soldiers stomped the ice off the sides of the boats in "Connecticut Soldier under Washington," pp. 102–3.

Joseph Reed describes the circumstances under which the American soldiers stationed in Bristol crossed the Delaware the day after the attack on Trenton in his "Narrative," p. 395. Nicholas Cresswell's Jan. 5, 1777, account of how the news of Trenton made the American people "liberty mad again" is in his *Journal*, p. 179. Wilkinson writes of how "Trenton reanimated the timid friends of the Revolution and invigorated the confidence of the resolute" in his *Memoirs*, 1:132. Joseph Reed did not attend Washington's Dec. 27, 1776, council of war (for which there are no minutes) but nonetheless records what he heard about it in his "Narrative," claiming that "some of the members . . . disapproved the enterprise [and] advised the sending [of] orders to the militia to return, but the general and some others declared that though they would not have advised the movement yet being done it ought to be supported and the orders were accordingly issued for the troops to prepare to cross the river" (p. 397). Wilkinson provides an unusually clear-eyed assessment of Washington's decision to recross the Delaware in his *Memoirs*, 1:132–33: "At this eventful epoch the masterly judgment of General Washington seems to have been beguiled by his good fortune . . . [and he was] certainly infected by a chivalrous spirit. . . . By this step he threw himself into a cul de sac with a corps numerically inferior to that of the enemy in his front . . . yet under the guidance and protection of that god in whom he placed his trust, he extricated himself from this desperate situation, by converting his fault into a ruse de guerre." On Washington's naturally aggressive instincts, see Stephenson's *Patriot Battles:* "The aura of composure, rationality, almost detachment that surrounds Washington like a slightly saintly penumbra can be misleading when it comes to Washington the general. His natural bent as a commander . . . was highly aggressive—sometimes to the point of recklessness. He was by nature a fighter and an opportunist and, when cornered by circumstances as he now was, would almost always elect to roll the dice" (p. 255).

Joseph Reed writes that one of the reasons Cadwalader elected not to immediately return to the Pennsylvania side once he learned that Washington's army was no longer in New Jersey was that "if they should again return without attempting anything a general desertion might be apprehended," a motivation that surely contributed to Washington's decision to follow Cadwalader back to New Jersey, given that his Continentals' term of enlistment was due to expire (p. 395). However, emotional accounts of how Washington convinced his reluctant troops to reenlist (which I have elected not to emphasize) mask the fact that most of those troops were like John Greenwood and decided to quit. Greenwood recounts his decision not to reenlist in *Revolutionary Services*, p. 44. Wilkinson speaks of Reed's reconnoitering mission to Princeton and provides an account of Washington's Jan. 1 council of war in his *Memoirs*, 1:133–34. Joseph Reed in his "Narrative" provides his own account of these events, adding that when it came to the decision to take up a position to the south of the Assunpink, "as I was perfectly acquainted with the country I suggested to the general . . . to fix upon that as the ground where he would meet the enemy if they advanced" (p. 401).

Johan Ewald writes of how "the times changed" after Washington's attack on Trenton in *Diary of the American War*, p. 44; Ewald also writes of how "Colonel Donop suggested to Lord Cornwallis that he march in two columns [to Trenton]. . . . But the enemy was despised, and as usual we had to pay for it" (p. 50). Wilkinson tells of how Washington gave orders "for as obstinate a stand as could be made" and how he could "distinguish the flame from the muzzles of our muskets" in his *Memoirs*, 1:138. John Howland describes the crush of retreating soldiers at the stone bridge and how Washington and his horse were waiting for them on the west rail in *Life and Recollections of John Howland*, p. 73. Fischer in *Washington's Crossing* cites Robert Beale's account of "ice as large as houses floating down [the Delaware]" (p. 303). Stephen Olney calls it "the most desperate situation I had ever known" in "Life of Captain Stephen Olney," p. 193. Wilkinson calls the standoff at the bridge a "crisis in the affairs of the Revolution" in his *Memoirs*, 1:138. Sergeant Joseph White speaks of how they let the enemy "come on some ways" across the bridge before they fired; he also recounts how canister shot "made a terrible squeaking noise" and how the bridge "looked red as blood with their killed and wounded and their red coats" in his "Narration," in Stryker's *Battles of Trenton and Princeton*, pp. 478–80. Wilkinson writes of how "the guardian angel of our country admonished Lord Cornwallis" and refers to William Erskine's prediction that "you will see nothing of them in the morning" in his *Memoirs*, 1:130. Fischer cites Cornwallis's insistence that "we've got the Old Fox safe now" in *Washington's Crossing*, p. 313.

Wilkinson describes the American council of war in which General St. Clair proposed that they escape the British by taking the road on the American right in his *Memoirs*, 1:139–40, as does St. Clair himself in a passage cited by Douglas Freeman in *George Washington*, 4:345, in which he recounts how Mercer "immediately fell in with it." Washington writes of how the idea appealed to him because "it would avoid the appearance of a retreat" in a Jan. 5, 1777, letter to John Hancock in *PGW*, 7:521. Stephen Olney tells how the extreme cold made the once muddy roads "hard as pavement" in "Life of Captain Stephen Olney," p. 196. Wilkinson describes how "a hoar frost . . . bespangled every object" in his *Memoirs*, 1:141; he also tells how the smoke from the two lines of fire "mingled as it rose and went up in one beautiful cloud" (1:143). Fischer in *Washington's Crossing*, p. 333, tells of General Mercer's encounter with the British regulars. Sgt. R— in "Battle of Princeton" recounts how "the ground was frozen and all the blood which was shed remained on the surface," as well as how Washington exhorted the soldiers to "parade with us my brave fellows" (pp. 517–18). Freeman in *George Washington*, 4:354, cites G. W. P. Custis's account of how one of Washington's staff officers was so fearful he would be killed in the volley that he hid his eyes with his hat. The officer's description of Washington's life "hanging as it were by a single hair" is in George Scheer and Hugh Rankin's *Rebels and Redcoats*, p. 249. Wilkinson tells how Washington exclaimed, "It is a fine fox chase, my boys!" in his *Memoirs*, 1:145. Washington writes of his belief that with eight hundred fresh men he could have taken

Brunswick and "put an end to the war" in his Jan. 5, 1777, letter to John Hancock in *PGW*, 7:523; he also writes of the "danger of losing the advantage . . . by aiming at too much."

CHAPTER FOUR: THE YEAR OF THE HANGMAN

Benedict Arnold's Mar. 1, 1777, letter to Paul Revere is in the Benedict Arnold Papers at the MHS and is cited by James Kirby Martin in *Benedict Arnold*, p. 302, as well as by Charles Coleman Sellers in *Benedict Arnold, the Proud Warrior*, p. 141. Sellers also cites John Quincy Adams's diary description of Elizabeth Deblois (p. 141). Arnold's Mar. 4, 1777, letter to Lucy Knox is in the *Historical Magazine*, p. 305. Clare Brandt in *Man in the Mirror* writes of Gates being Arnold's "kindred spirit," while Schuyler was "a model of the secure and self-assured gentleman Arnold wished to be" (p. 92). On the straitened financial circumstances of American army officers such as Arnold, see Charles Royster's *Revolutionary People at War*, pp. 266–68, in which he refers to American military officers as "demi-gentry." Arnold's Mar. 8, 1777, letter to Horatio Gates, in which he speaks of his interest in the navy, is at the NYHS; Arnold's Mar. 8, 1777, letter to Philip Schuyler is at the NYPL, with the passage about the navy cited by Willard Sterne Randall in *Benedict Arnold*, p. 329. John Lamb tells how Arnold "offered the loan of one thousand pounds" and how Hannah Arnold "advanced with alacrity the money" in his *Memoir*, pp. 152–53. Nathan Miller discusses the issue of prize money in the Revolutionary American navy in *Sea of Glory*, p. 125.

Washington's Mar. 6, 1777, letter to Richard Henry Lee, in which he describes Arnold as "spirited and sensible," is in *PGW*, 8:523. Washington's Mar. 3, 1777, letter to Arnold, in which he asks him not to take any "hasty steps," is in *PGW*, 8:493. Martin cites Henry Knox's Mar. 23, 1777, letter to his brother William at the MHS, in which he says that "this most infallibly pushes him out of the service," in *Benedict Arnold*, p. 505. Arnold's Mar. 11, 1777, letter to Washington, in which he describes Congress's actions "as a very civil way of requesting my resignation," is in *PGW*, 8:552. Arnold's emotional Mar. 25, 1777, letter to Horatio Gates is at NYHS. Charles Coleman Sellers cites Nathanael Greene's vow that he would never give Congress "an opportunity to humiliate me but once" in *Benedict Arnold, the Proud Warrior*, p. 144. Willard Sterne Randall cites Lucy Knox's Apr. 30, 1777, letter to her husband, in which she refers to the news that "Miss Deblois has positively refused to listen to the general," in *Benedict Arnold*, p. 331.

On Governor William Tryon's time in North Carolina fighting the Regulators, see Paul David Nelson's *William Tryon and the Course of Empire*, pp. 54–89; Nelson cites Tryon's letter to Germain in which he talks about the "more real chagrin" he felt over the news of Trenton and Princeton (p. 148). Andrew O'Shaughnessy writes of how British strategy in 1777 threw "the apple of discord" among Howe, Burgoyne, and Clinton, in *Men Who Lost America*: "Howe was the commander in chief but he was given a subordinate role in the plan for the junction at Albany, whereas his modified plan to take Philadelphia offered him the opportunity to shine as much as Burgoyne" (p. 113). Richard Ketchum writes of how 1777 became known as "the year of the hangman" in *Saratoga*, p. 79. On Arnold's unfinished waterfront mansion, see Barry Wilson's *Benedict Arnold*, p. 12. On the American losses at Danbury, see "British Officer's Account of Danbury Raid" in *NDAR*, 8:456, and Martin, *Benedict Arnold*, p. 317. The references to Wooster fighting "with more obstinacy than skill," his son's death "by the bayonet," and Arnold's having "taken post very advantageously" are in the "British Officer's Account," in *NDAR*, 8:456. Nelson in *William Tryon*, p. 152, cites Tryon's reference to Erskine as "the first general without exception."

Benjamin Rush overheard Arnold talk about his being a "coward till he was fifteen" in Rush's *Autobiography*, p. 158. Arnold's Jan. 6, 1776, letter to his sister Hannah, in which he claims that he "know[s] no fear," is cited by Wilson in *Benedict Arnold*, p. 5. Christopher Ward in *War of the Revolution*, 2:494, describes Arnold's shooting of the Tory. The reference to the "astonishing temerity" of the militiamen is in the "British Officer's Account" in *NDAR*, 8:456. Martin in *Benedict Arnold* cites the claim that Arnold had "made the best disposition possible of his little army" (p. 320); Martin also cites the reference to Arnold having "exposed himself almost to a fault" (p. 320). The references to Major Stuart's role in taking the American fieldpieces, as well as to the militiamen's "great bravery," are all made in the "British Officer's Account" in *NDAR*, 8:456. Martin cites the reference to Arnold exhorting the militiamen "not to desert him" in *Benedict Arnold*, pp. 320–21. The "British Officer's Account" in *NDAR*, 8:457, contains the reference to "this coup by Governor Tryon." Arnold's complaint that Connecticut "suffered such an insult without resistance or proper revenge" is in Thomas Burke's May 2, 1777, letter to Richard Caswell in *LDC*, 7:13.

Congress's promotion of Arnold to major general on May 2, 1777, is in *JCC*, 7:323. John Adams's claims to have "no fears" about the resignation of officers who had been overlooked for promotion in a speech before Congress is recorded in "Benjamin Rush's Notes of Debates," Feb. 19, 1777, in *LDC*, 6:323–25. John Adams's May 9, 1777, letter to Nathanael Greene, in which he describes the design of a possible medal for Arnold, is in *LDC*, 7:49. Washington makes the case for a defensive "War of Posts" in a Sept. 8, 1776, letter to John Hancock in *PGW*, 6:249. However, it would not be until the winter of 1777 that Washington appears to have fully committed himself to this strategy. According to Joseph Ellis in *His Excellency George Washington*, Trenton and Princeton "served as defiant gestures by Washington . . . that fight was still in him. Having made that point . . . he never again felt it necessary to risk his entire army in one battle. It was as if he had successfully answered the challenge to a duel, and now could afford to adopt a more defensive strategy without worrying about his personal honor and reputation. He also began to realize that the way to win the war was not to lose it" (p. 99). Nathanael Greene's Mar. 24, 1777, letter to Washington, in which he describes Congress's response to "your Excellency's ideas of the next campaign. It appeared to be new to them," is in *PGW*, 8:627. Washington's Mar. 3, 1777, letter to Arnold, in which he advises Arnold not to attack Newport unless he has "a *moral certainty* of succeeding," is in *PGW*, 8:493. Martin in *Benedict Arnold* tells of Washington's citing the British intelligence report describing Arnold as "a devilish fighting fellow" (p. 323); Martin also cites John Brown's claim that "money is this man's god" (p. 324). Joseph Reed's June 4, 1777, letter to Washington, in which he speaks of Washington's "patience and silence under evils," is in *PGW*, 9:606.

On the Gates-Schuyler divide and its relationship to the rise of two distinct factions in Congress, see H. James Henderson's *Party Politics in the Continental Congress*, pp. 113–16; Henderson cites John Adams's boast that "our state is the barometer at which every other looks" (p. 110). Jonathan Rossie also writes probingly about the Gates-Schuyler divide in *Politics of Command*, pp. 135–53. In a May 12, 1777, letter to John Hancock, Washington describes Arnold as "a judicious, brave officer of great activity, enterprise, and perseverance" in *PGW,* 9:396–97. The Board of War's May 23, 1777, committee report clearing Arnold's "character and conduct, so cruelly and groundlessly aspersed" is cited in Martin's *Benedict Arnold,* p. 327. Congress's May 20, 1777, resolution that Arnold be presented with a horse "properly caparisoned . . . as a token of their approbation of his gallant conduct in the action against the enemy in their late enterprise to Danbury" is in *JCC,* 7:372–73. John Adams's May 22, 1777, letter to his wife, Abigail, in which he claims that Arnold "has been basely slandered and libeled," even as he complains that the "military officers . . . quarrel like cats and dogs," is in *LDC,* 7:103.

Ward in *War of the Revolution,* 1:319–23, provides an excellent account of the Continental army's winter in Morristown; Ward also details Washington's and Howe's moves back and forth across New Jersey during the month of June 1777 (1:325–29). Washington's June 23, 1777, letter to Joseph Reed, in which he speaks of having "one great end in view," is in *PGW,* 10:113–14. Reed had once again disappointed Washington by refusing an appointment to lead the Continental army's cavalry, and in this same letter Washington informs Reed that his refusal has left him "a good deal disconcerted" (p. 114). The text of "Horatio Gates's Notes for a Speech to Congress, June 18," in which he complains of having been treated with "unmerited contempt," is in *LDC,* 7:213. Benjamin Rush in his *Autobiography* writes of Gates's "talents for extensive and accurate observation" (p. 156). William Duer's June 19, 1777, letter to Schuyler, in which he describes Gates's testimony before Congress as "incoherent and interrupted with frequent chasms," is in *LDC,* 7:228–29, as is James Duane's June 18, 1777, letter to Schuyler, in which he recounts how Gates singled him out as "the author of his disgrace" (p. 225). William Duer writes of the New Englanders' attempt to "browbeat" the rest of the delegates into naming Gates the head of the northern department in his June 19, 1777, letter to Schuyler in *LDC,* 7:229. Martin in *Benedict Arnold,* p. 339, cites Congress's July 8, 1777, order to Gates to report to Washington's headquarters and recounts how he instead went to his home in Virginia.

Nancy Rubin Stuart in *Defiant Brides,* p. 31, writes of Lucy Knox's and Caty Greene's interest in some of the contents of Arnold's trunk of gowns. Washington's July 10, 1777, letter to John Hancock, in which he requests that Arnold "immediately set out for the Northern Department," is in *PGW,* 10:240. Hancock's July 12, 1777, letter to Arnold, in which he directs him "to repair immediately to headquarters," is in *LDC,* 7:338.

CHAPTER FIVE: THE DARK EAGLE

The danger of an enemy emplacement atop Sugar Loaf Hill had been openly acknowledged among the Americans as early as the previous fall, when the young John Trumbull "ventured to advance the new and heretical opinion that our position [at Ticonderoga] was bad and untenable, as being overlooked in all its parts" during a meeting with Horatio Gates and his "principal officers," who "ridiculed" Trumbull "for advancing such an extravagant idea." The next day, in order to prove his point, Trumbull along with Generals Anthony Wayne and Benedict Arnold climbed that peak where it became "obvious to all that there could be no difficulty in driving up a loaded carriage" (Trumbull's *Autobiography,* p. 29). Others would make the claim, but without the manpower to do much about it, Sugar Loaf Hill (later known as Mount Defiance) was left unsecured.

Burgoyne describes the boom and bridge connecting Fort Ticonderoga to Mount Independence in a July 11, 1777, letter to Germain in *DAR*, 14:136. Burgoyne's "Plan of the Campaign from the Side of Canada" is in Edward Barrington de Fonblanque's *Political and Military Episodes*, pp. 483–86. On Philip Skene's role in Burgoyne's decision to go to the Hudson via Skenesborough rather than Lake George, see Doris Begor Morton's *Philip Skene of Skenesborough*, pp. 53–55, as well as Richard Ketchum's *Saratoga*, pp. 239–42. For information on the *Royal George*, which dwarfed the behemoth of just a year before, the *Inflexible*, see John Millar's *American Ships of the Colonial and Revolutionary Periods*, pp. 248–49. James Thacher describes the voyage from Fort Ticonderoga to Skenesborough in his *Military Journal*, pp. 83–84. Morton writes about the Battle of Skenesborough in *Philip Skene of Skenesborough*, pp. 52–54; she also provides an excellent description of what the hamlet looked like in the summer of 1777 (pp. 28–30). Russell Bellico touches on the battle in *Sails and Steam in the Mountains*, pp. 172–73. James Hadden writes of how the yards of the *Royal George* "almost touched the precipices which overhung them" in his *Journal*, p. 89. Thacher, in his *Military Journal*, p. 84, describes how he collected what he could of his medical equipment and fled. Thomas Anburey was told of how the fire "threatened universal destruction" by "an officer who came up at the time" and recorded his account in a July 14, 1777, letter in *Travels through the Interior Parts of America*, p. 347. The German surgeon J. F. Wasmus describes in a July 8 entry in his *Journal* how an American "2-masted ship . . . had sunk but the masts could still be seen" (p. 60). Burgoyne describes the brief battle between British and American forces in Skenesborough in his July 11, 1777, letter to Germain in *DAR*, 14:137; in another private July 11 letter to Germain he writes of being "confident of fulfilling the object of my orders," as well as requesting that he be allowed to return to England during the upcoming winter (14:142). Ketchum tells of how Burgoyne bet a friend the previous Christmas that he would return to England a hero in a year in *Saratoga*, p. 79. Andrew O'Shaughnessy cites Horace Walpole's reference to Burgoyne as "General Swagger" in *Men Who Lost America*, p. 132.

Rupert Furneaux in *Battle of Saratoga* cites Anthony Wayne's claim that Fort Ticonderoga "can never be carried" (p. 58). Washington's July 15, 1777, letter to Philip Schuyler is in *PGW*, 10:290. Ketchum cites John Adams's claim that "we shall never be able to defend a post until we shoot a general" in *Saratoga*, p. 219. In an Aug. 7, 1777, letter to John Langdon, Samuel Adams writes that he couldn't account for the loss of Fort Ticonderoga "even upon the principle of cowardice. There seems to me to be the evident marks of designs," in *LDC*, 7:435. James Thacher relates the "extravagantly ridiculous" claim that St. Clair and Schuyler had been paid by the enemy with silver cannonballs, as well as the prediction that Burgoyne's taking of Fort Ticonderoga will "ultimately prove advantageous," in his *Military Journal*, p. 86. Washington's July 24, 1777, letter to Schuyler, in which he predicts that British delays due to logistical concerns will "inevitably . . . be fatal to them," is in *PGW*, 10:397. The German officer's reference to "this evil, mountainous, and watery continent" is cited by Tom Lewis in *Hudson River*, p. 133.

Burgoyne writes of the Americans' extraordinary efforts to block his path from Skenesborough to the Hudson, as well as his theory that "a retrograde motion" back to Fort Ticonderoga would have abated "the panic of the enemy," in a July 30, 1777, letter to Germain in *DAR*, 14:153. John Luzader has an excellent discussion of Burgoyne's route options in *Saratoga*, pp. 76–80. As Luzader points out, Burgoyne did not have enough boats to transport both his soldiers and the artillery down Lake George at the same time; however, since it took several weeks for him to get the cannons over the carrying place, he would have had plenty of time to transport his soldiers by water before getting the guns to Lake George. Luzader also writes of Burgoyne's army's transporting 43 of the original 138 pieces of artillery brought down from Canada (p. 83). Burgoyne claims that the Americans "cannot finally injure me" in a second, private letter written to Germain on July 30, 1777, in *DAR,* 14:154.

Henry Clinton's reference to the "cursed fatality" that existed between himself and Howe is in "Clinton's Minutes of a Conversation with Sir William Howe in John Smith's Hand" in the Clinton Papers at the William L. Clements Library in Ann Arbor, Michigan. William Willcox refers to Howe's insistence that "he had sent home his plan . . . and he would abide it" in "Too Many Cooks," p. 70. On the extraordinary seamanship demonstrated by Admiral Howe on sailing through Hell Gate in a fog on Oct. 12, 1776, see Barnet Schecter's *Battle for New York,* pp. 221–22. Ambrose Serle writes of the dread he felt following William Howe's decision to approach Philadelphia via the Chesapeake Bay rather than the Delaware River in his *American Journal,* p. 241.

Burgoyne's proclamation, in which he threatens "to give stretch to the Indian forces under my direction," is in Fonblanque's *Political and Military Episodes,* pp. 490–92. Wasmus writes of Burgoyne's meeting with the newly arrived warriors from the west in "a large arbor" in Skenesborough in a July 19, 1777, entry in his *Journal,* p. 63. For the devastation Burgoyne's native warriors wreaked upon the Americans at Fort Edward, as well as Glover's letter describing his soldiers as "shattered, much confused," see Ketchum, *Saratoga,* pp. 279–80. Schuyler writes of the condition of Fort Edward and the sufferings of the soldiers in a July 14, 1777, letter to Washington, as well as in a July 26–27, 1777, letter, in *PGW,* 10:279–81, 431. Washington's July 18, 1777, letter to Schuyler, in which he informs him that Arnold is on his way, is in *PGW,* 10:323. St. Clair's July 25, 1777, letter to Washington, in which he refers to Arnold's having "publicly condemn[ed] the retreat from Ticonderoga," is in *PGW,* 10:418–19.

Arnold's July 27, 1777, letter to Washington describing the circumstances surrounding the death and scalping of Jane McCrea is in *PGW,* 10:434. William Stone cites an account of the death of Jane McCrea passed on by a "Judge Hay" that claims she was killed by American friendly fire, in *Campaign of Lieut. Gen. John Burgoyne,* pp. 304–5; for an alternative account that claims McCrea was the victim of an argument among the warriors, see Luzader's *Saratoga,* pp. 86–92. Ketchum in *Saratoga,* p. 287, writes of how 10 percent of eligible males in New Hampshire volunteered for the militia in the wake of the fall of Ticonderoga and the death of Jane McCrea. As Luzader points out, many of these new recruits had joined the militia well before the death of Jane McCrea; this does not change the fact that the atrocities attributed to native warriors, which began even before the fall of Ticonderoga, contributed to the sense of outrage that fueled enlistments in the militia. In addition to suggesting that Daniel Morgan be sent to the northern army, Arnold details "the most shocking manner" in which "a young lady of family" was "shot, scalped, stripped, and butchered" in his July 27, 1777, letter to Washington in *PGW,* 10:434. Schuyler tells Washington that Arnold has just received a letter "advising him that it is not probable that he will be restored to his rank" in an Aug. 1, 1777, letter in *PGW,* 10:483. Arnold praises Schuyler for having "done everything a man could do in his situation" in his July 27, 1777, letter to Washington in *PGW,* 10:434.

John Adams's reference to Schuyler as "the evil genius of the northern department" is in "Charles Thomson's Notes of Debate over Motion to Send Gates to Command

Northern Dept" in *LDC,* 7:383. Samuel Adams's July 15, 1777, letter to Richard Henry Lee, in which he refers to Gates as being "the man of my choice," is in *LDC,* 7:344. The New England delegates' Aug. 2, 1777, communication with Washington, in which they express their desire to have Gates named to the head of the northern army, is in *LDC,* 7:405. Washington's Aug. 3, 1777, letter to John Hancock, in which he asks "to be excused from making the appointment," is in *PGW,* 10:492-93, as is Washington's Aug. 4, 1777, letter to Gates "wishing you success" (10:499). James Lovell's Aug. 8, 1777, letter to William Whipple, in which he refers to "a new motion to restore [Arnold's] rank" and that "it was really a question between monarchical and republican principles," is in *LDC,* 7:443. Henry Laurens refers to Arnold as "an old and valuable servant" in an Aug. 9, 1777, letter to Robert Howe; he speaks of Congress's actions toward Arnold as "disgusting" in an Aug. 12, 1777, letter to John Rutledge, both in *LDC,* 7:446, 469.

On Peter Gansevoort and the Siege of Fort Stanwix/Fort Schuyler, I have looked to Gavin Watt's *Rebellion in the Mohawk Valley;* on Gansevoort's background and personality, see pp. 60-62. On the dimensions and rebuilding of Fort Stanwix, see John Luzader's *Fort Stanwix,* pp. 7-22, 26-37. Stone in *Campaign of Lieut. Gen. John Burgoyne,* p. 219, makes the observation that even Americans "have always preferred calling" Fort Schuyler by its original name of Fort Stanwix. Leonard Gansevoort's letter to his brother Peter, in which he passes on their father's request that he "conquer or die," is cited in Watt's *Rebellion in the Mohawk Valley,* p. 120. Watt describes how Gansevoort's men made themselves a flag and cites Marinus Willett's account of the "exhilaration of spirits" it evoked among the Americans (p. 127). In the nineteenth century, the claim was made that this flag was actually the first instance of the Stars and Stripes being flown over a military installation, but as Luzader convincingly argues in *Fort Stanwix,* pp. 73-78, this flag was undoubtedly a "continental" flag, with the Union Jack in the upper left. Ensign William Colbrath of the Third New York Regiment kept a journal during the Siege of Fort Stanwix that provides an excellent account of the tense back-and-forth between Gansevoort and St. Leger after the Battle of Oriskany, which includes Gansevoort's determination to defend the fort "against all their enemies"; see *Days of Siege,* edited by Larry Lowenthal, pp. 36-37. See also Watt's *Rebellion in the Mohawk Valley,* pp. 205-12.

Wasmus in his *Journal* writes of Burgoyne's receiving a message from Howe in a hollowed-out silver bullet (p. 67). As Piers Mackesy writes in *War for America,* when it came to Carleton's refusal to assist Burgoyne, "Burgoyne's insistence on having his own way had recoiled on him. . . . The general whom he had elbowed out had denied him help" (p. 135). Burgoyne's Aug. 6, 1777, letter to Germain, in which he describes how he has tried "to keep up [the warriors'] terror and avoid their cruelty," is in *DAR,* 14:156. Burgoyne writes of the prospect of his campaign being "far less prosperous than when I wrote last" in an Aug. 20, 1777, letter to Germain in *DAR,* 14:166. On the pronunciation of Riedesel as "Red Hazel," see Stone's *Campaign of Lieut. Gen. John Burgoyne,* p. 370. Baroness Riedesel's reference to Burgoyne's carousing and her reminiscences about the time her family spent at the "Red House" near Fort Edward are in *Baroness von Riedesel and the American Revolution,* edited by Marvin Brown, pp. 44-45, 55-56. Riedesel tells of Burgoyne's hope that the expedition he has sent out on his left would prevent Arnold "from sending this force against St. Leger" in his *Memoirs, and Letters and Journals,* edited by Max von Eelking, 1:128. Ketchum in *Saratoga* recounts how Stark decided to resign when Enoch Poor and others were promoted past him, as well as Stark's insistence that "Stark chooses to command himself" (pp. 287–89). My account of Stark owes much to James Nelson's *Benedict Arnold's Navy*, in which Stark is described as "the military equivalent of a privateer captain who sometimes cooperates with federal authority, sometimes not, depending on whim" (p. 346). James Wilkinson reprints John Stark's Aug. 22, 1777, letter to Schuyler, in which he describes the action at the Battle of Bennington as "the hottest" he'd ever seen (quite a comment coming from a veteran of the Battle of Bunker Hill), in his *Memoirs*, 1:210–12.

Watt in *Rebellion in the Mohawk Valley*, pp. 221–23, cites Schuyler's Aug. 13, 1777, letter to Arnold ordering him to lead a relief party to Fort Stanwix. As Steve Darley explains in "Dark Eagle: How Fiction Became Historical Fact," there appears to be no historical basis for the oft-repeated claim that the Abenaki warrior Natanis (who actually did accompany Arnold's expedition to Quebec) referred to him as the Dark Eagle. The first reference to Arnold as the Dark Eagle that Darley could locate was in George Lippard's highly fictionalized *Legends of the American Revolution 1776*, published in 1876. Bruce Johansen in *Forgotten Founders*, pp. 56–118, argues that the Iroquois Covenant Chain influenced Benjamin Franklin and others when it came to the writing of the Declaration of Independence and ultimately the U.S. Constitution. James Thacher details how the idea to use Hanjost Schuyler in a ruse to lift the Siege of Fort Stanwix was originally conceived by John Brooks in his *Military Journal*, pp. 89–90. Watt details Gansevoort's desperation on Aug. 20–21, 1777, as well as how Hanjost Schuyler convinced the Iroquois under the British to abandon the siege, in *Rebellion in the Mohawk Valley*, pp. 246–61. Barbara Graymont writes of how "for the Six Nations, Oriskany was a battle of enormous significance because it marked the beginning of a civil war" in *Iroquois in the American Revolution*, p. 142; see also Joseph Glatthaar and James Kirby Martin's *Forgotten Allies*, pp. 160–69. The Seneca warrior's description of a stream of blood is in *Chainbreaker's War*, edited by Jeanne Winston Adler, p. 68. St. Leger's Aug. 27, 1777, letter to Carleton describing how Arnold "artfully caused messengers to come in one after the other with accounts of the nearer approaches of the rebels" is in *DAR*, 14:171. John Adams praises Gansevoort for proving "that it is possible to hold a post" in a Sept. 2, 1777, letter to his wife, Abigail, in *LDC*, 7:589. On Oct. 5, 1777, John Hancock in his capacity as president of the Continental Congress informed Gansevoort that "in consideration of your gallant behavior the Congress have been pleased to appoint you Colonel Commandant of the fort," in *LDC*, 8:53.

Adjutant General Major Carl Leopold Baurmeister writes of the loss of 27 men and 170 horses during the voyage to Head of Elk in a July 20–Oct. 17 letter in *Revolution in America*, p. 98. Washington's Sept. 1 letter to John Hancock, in which he expresses his hope that "we shall have nothing more to apprehend in that quarter this campaign" after the lifting of the Siege of Fort Stanwix, is in *PGW*, 11:110, as are his Sept. 5, 1777, General Orders calling for "one bold stroke" (11:147–48). On Howe's movements prior to the Battle of Brandywine, I have looked to three sources: Thomas McGuire's *Philadelphia Campaign*, 1:167–200; Samuel Smith's *Battle of Brandywine*, pp. 9–15; and Stephen Taaffe's *Philadelphia Campaign*, pp. 50–69. My account of the battle itself also owes much to McGuire, 1:167–260, Smith, pp. 9–23, and Taaffe, pp. 64–80, as well as Edward Lengel's *General George Washington*, pp. 227–42. According to Lengel, "The lightning successes at Trenton and Princeton apparently led Washington to underestimate the enemy, and to overestimate his own and his troops' ability to perform miracles on the battlefield" (p. 231). Smith cites Major John Skey Eustace's account of how Washington and his staff "laughed at my intelligence" (p. 13). The British officer's account of "a most infernal fire of cannon and musketry" is in Taaffe, p. 73. McGuire cites Pickering's memory of Washington telling him "'tis a perfect rout" (1:260).

CHAPTER SIX: SARATOGA

As can be seen in the bibliography, much has been written about the Battle of Saratoga. Of this vast literature, I have found two works particularly helpful: Richard Ketchum's *Saratoga,* which provides a rich and varied context to the battle, and John Luzader's *Saratoga,* a military history that dissects the Battles of Freeman's Farm and Bemis Heights with a steady and precise hand. All citations to "Ketchum" and "Luzader" in this chapter are to these two works unless otherwise noted.

Isaac Arnold in *Life of Benedict Arnold* writes of Arnold's "fixed determination to extort from Congress his proper rank, or die on the field" (p. 164). Willard Sterne Randall cites Schuyler's letter to Gates claiming that "it is left to you, general, to reap the fruits of my labors" in *Benedict Arnold,* p. 351. Gates's Oct. 20, 1777, letter to his wife and son after the Battle of Saratoga, in which he refers to "me and my Yankees," is at the NYHS. Ketchum cites Dearborn's claim that Gates had put "a new face upon our affairs" as well as Timothy Bigelow's description of the northern army as "the happiest camp I ever was in" (p. 347). Luzader writes of how Arnold's decision to appoint Varick and Livingston as his aides jeopardized his relationship with Gates (pp. 211–14). James Wilkinson writes of how the addition of Dearborn's light infantry increased "the weight and effect of [Morgan's] corps, which formed the elite of the army," in his *Memoirs,* 1:230. Luzader describes Gates's decision to entrench his army on Bemis Heights as "a strategic coup for the Americans," claiming that "any option Burgoyne chose forced him to act on Gates' terms" (p. 205). Andrew O'Shaughnessy in *Men Who Lost America* writes of how Burgoyne faced "an invidious choice of either running a gauntlet of enemy fire or launching a frontal attack against a well-entrenched enemy" (p. 154).

My account of how Burgoyne's army had been overwhelmed by the combined effects of the wilderness and the American militia owes much to the British sergeant Roger Lamb's Oct. 11, 1777, entry in his *Journal,* in which he describes how "the Americans . . . swarmed around the little adverse army like birds of prey" (p. 166). Burgoyne writes of how his army was weakened by "the total defection of the Indians" in an Oct. 20, 1777, letter to Germain in *DAR,* 14:229. In that same letter he claims that "the peremptory tenor of my orders and the season of the year admitted no alternative" than to attack the Americans at Bemis Heights and describes how with thirty days of provisions, he crossed the Hudson on "the bridge of boats" on Sept. 13 and 14, 1777 (14:229). Luzader describes the encounter between Arnold's division and the British foraging party on Sept. 18, 1777 (p. 216). Wilkinson describes in his *Memoirs,* 1:249, how Stark's men left Bemis Heights at 12:05 a.m. and how they could not "have been beyond the sound of the action when it began yet not a man returned."

In his *Memoirs,* 1:236, Wilkinson claims that he received the report that "the enemy had struck the chief part of their tents . . . [and] had crossed the gully at the gorge of the great ravine, and were ascending the heights in a direction towards our left," at 8:00 a.m. on Sept. 19, 1777. Luzader discusses the contrasting perspectives between Gates's defensive approach and Arnold's "more aggressive alternative" (pp. 231–34). In a Sept. 22, 1777, letter to Gates, Arnold writes, "On the 19th inst., when advice was received that the enemy were approaching, I took the liberty to give it as my opinion that we ought to march out and attack them. You desired me to send Colonel Morgan and the light infantry and support them; I obeyed your orders and before the action was over I found it necessary to send out the whole of my division to support the attack," reprinted in Wilkinson's *Memoirs*, 1:255. Wilkinson, who arrived on the scene shortly after Morgan's overly impetuous charge across Freeman's Farm, spoke with Major Morris as well as Morgan, who he claimed was so upset by the resultant melee that "he burst into tears, and exclaimed, 'I am ruined by God! Major Morris ran on so rapidly with the front, that they were beaten before I could get up with the *rear*, and my men are scattered God knows where,'" 1:237–38. Ketchum describes how Morgan's riflemen used the British officer's "identifying silver gorgets at their throats" to help them aim (p. 362).

Luzader writes that "by his decision to support Morgan with the New Hampshire regiments, he adopted Arnold's more aggressive tactical option . . . [and] thus converted Morgan's harassing action into the prelude to a pitched battle" (p. 236). Wilkinson's description of the battle as "perfectly accidental" and his comparison to "waves of a stormy sea," as well as all the other remarks attributed to him regarding the action at Freeman's Farm, are in his *Memoirs*, 1:239–48. Burgoyne describes the "obstinacy" of the action in his Oct. 20, 1777, letter to Germain in *DAR*, 14:330. Roger Lamb writes of "a constant blaze of fire" in his *Journal*, p. 159. Burgoyne's description of the devastating effect of American snipers on the British officer corps is in his *State of the Expedition*, p. 122. Lieutenant William Digby writes of Burgoyne's bravery in his *Journal*, p. 274. In a Sept. 22, 1777, letter, Richard Varick claimed that during the fighting on Sept. 19, Arnold "was ordering our troops [into the battle] while the other [Gates] was in Dr. Potts' tent backbiting his neighbors. . . . I further know that he asked where the troops were going when Scammell's battalion marched and upon being answered, he declared no more should go, he would not suffer the camp to be exposed," cited by Luzader, p. 265.

Wilkinson's account of how Gates ordered him to bring Arnold back to camp is in his *Memoirs*, 1:245–46. Although many historians are convinced that Arnold spent a significant amount of time on the field during the Battle of Freeman's Farm (see Willard Wallace's appendix "Was Arnold at the Battle of Freeman's Farm?" in *Traitorous Hero*, pp. 326–32), the evidence is based primarily on accounts that, in my estimation, confuse the fighting of Sept. 19 with that of Oct. 7, 1777. For an excellent examination of the evidence and the citation of the vital Sept. 20, 1777, letter from Enoch Poor, describing how Arnold "at times acted like a madman," see the appendix "Arnold, Gates, and Freeman's Farm" in Luzader, pp. 380–93. Wilkinson's account of how Burgoyne lost the "golden, glorious opportunity" on Sept. 20–21, 1777, which was based largely on his conversation with the British major general William Phillips after the battle, is in his *Memoirs*, 1:250–53. In his Oct. 20, 1777, letter to Germain, Burgoyne describes the right side of the American works atop Bemis Heights as "unattackable" and tells how he received a coded letter from Clinton on Sept. 21, 1777, "informing me of his intention to attack Ft. Montgomery in about ten days," in *DAR*, 14:231.

In a Sept. 23, 1777, letter to John Hancock, Washington writes of how he recrossed the Schuylkill "with a firm intent of giving the enemy battle wherever I should meet them" in *PGW*, 11:301. My account of the Battle of the Clouds is based largely on Thomas McGuire's *Philadelphia Campaign*, vol. 1, in which he cites Parker's and Ewald's descriptions of the intense rain as well as Knox's estimates as to the loss of American gunpowder; McGuire also describes how the leather double-flap cartridge boxes of the British prevented the rain from penetrating their powder (290–93). On Oct. 13, 1777, Washington wrote to John Hancock outlining how the American cartridge boxes should be modified: "Much care should be used in choosing the leather. . . . Each box should have a small inner flap for the greater security of the cartridges against rain and moist weather" (*PGW*, 10:498–99).

On the Gates-Arnold feud, see Paul David Nelson's two articles "Gates-Arnold Quarrel, September 1777" and "Legacy of Controversy: Gates, Schuyler, and Arnold at Saratoga, 1777," as well as Luzader, pp. 257–73, in which he cites Schuyler's Sept. 20, 1777, letter to Varick asking that he destroy his letters "lest an accident should [put] them into hands I do not wish they should fall into I mean the person you mention [Gates]." According to Jared Sparks, who spoke with many veterans of the battle, the falling-out between Gates and Arnold was "owing to the officious interference of Wilkinson, who was adjutant general to the army, and who insisted on the returns of a part of Arnold's division being made directly to him and influenced Gates to sustain his demand, which was done in general orders, without giving notice to Arnold" (*Life and Treason of Benedict Arnold*, pp. 114–15). Luzader cites Varick's Sept. 21, 1777, letter to Schuyler about the "little spurt" between Arnold and Gates (p. 258). Wilkinson discusses his role in the Arnold-Gates feud in his *Memoirs* and cites Gates's official account of the battle (in which neither Arnold nor his left wing is mentioned) as well as Arnold's Sept. 22, 1777, letter to Gates complaining of his having been received "with the greatest coolness at headquarters" (1:253–59). Luzader cites Livingston's Sept. 23, 1777, letter to Schuyler, in which he describes how Gates responded to Arnold's threat to leave with the reply that "Genl. Lincoln would be here in a day or two, that he should then have no occasion for him; and would give him a pass to go to Philadelphia, whenever he chose it" (p. 261). James Kirby Martin in *Benedict Arnold*, p. 386, cites Gates's Sept. 19, 1777, letter to Lincoln ordering him to join the northern army. Gates's Sept. 22, 1777, letter to his wife, Elizabeth, in which he complains that "a general of an American army must be everything, and that is being more than one man can long sustain," is at the NYHS.

Luzader cites Livingston's Sept. 25, 1777, letter describing the unsuccessful attempt by Poor and other generals to effect a reconciliation between Arnold and Gates as well as Livingston's Sept. 26, 1777, letter describing Arnold's rejecting a second attempt at compromise presented by Leonard Chester (which involved Livingston leaving the army) with the angry assertion that "he would not sacrifice a friend to please the 'Face of Clay'" (pp. 269–70). In his *Memoirs*, Wilkinson recounts how the arrival of "a band of Oneida Indians . . . [turned] upon the enemy the vengeance which they had prepared to inflict upon us" (1:253); he also describes how after being removed from command "Arnold experienced the keenest mortification" (1:260), and reprints Arnold's Oct. 1, 1777, letter to Gates informing him that the men are "clamorous for action" (1:260).

Washington complains of Howe's "violent inclination" to turn his right flank in a Sept. 15, 1777, letter to John Hancock in *PGW*, 11:237; in a Sept. 23, 1777, letter to Hancock he writes of how the British have "induced me to believe that they had two objects in view, one to get round the right of the army, the other perhaps to detach parties to Reading where we had considerable quantities of military stores," and how this "variety of perplexing maneuvers" enabled them "to pass the Schuylkill last night at the Flat Land and other fords in the neighborhood of it" (*PGW*, 11:301–2). James Lovell writes of the lack of local militia support for the American army in Pennsylvania in a Sept. 24 letter to Robert Treat Paine in *LDC*, 8:15. McGuire in *Philadelphia Campaign*,

2:76, cites Lieutenant Martin Hunter's description of Howe's berating the light infantry at Germantown for retreating before a mere "scouting party." In the notes to *PGW*, 10:398, the editors cite Timothy Pickering's account of how Henry Knox insisted that "it would be unmilitary to leave a castle in our rear," as well as Johann Ewald's estimation that seventy-five Americans were killed during the assault on Cliveden. In an Oct. 5, 1777, letter to Benjamin Harrison, Washington attributes the reversal suffered at Germantown to "a hazy atmosphere without a breath of air, so that the smoke of our artillery and small arms often prevented us from seeing thirty yards" in *PGW*, 11:401. McGuire provides an excellent account of the fatal pause at Cliveden and how Knox's cannonballs sailed through the house and onto American soldiers advancing on the other side in *Philadelphia Campaign*, 2:81–99.

In "Colonel Brooks and Colonel Bancroft at Saratoga," John Brooks, who would ultimately serve as governor of Massachusetts and was the officer who gave Arnold the idea of using Hanjost Schuyler to lift the Siege of Fort Stanwix, describes the debate between Gates and Arnold prior to the Battle of Bemis Heights on Oct. 7, 1777, as well as the interchange between the two officers once firing had been heard from the advance pickets, which participant Ebenezer Mattoon, in an Oct. 7, 1835, letter to the son of Philip Schuyler reprinted in William Leete Stone's *Campaign of Lieut. Gen. John Burgoyne*, identifies as "on the left of the British army" (p. 371). Mattoon describes how Lincoln and Arnold then rode together to investigate the British movement and the subsequent exchange involving Lincoln, Gates, and Arnold, whose response to Gates's dismissal is described as "reproachful and severe" (p. 371). Wilkinson claims, in typically self-serving fashion, that *he* was the one who informed Gates of the British movement on the American left, and quotes Gates as saying, "Well, then, order on Morgan to begin the game," in his *Memoirs*, 1:268. Providing a new light on what occurred between Gates and Arnold prior to the outbreak of the battle is a recently discovered letter written by Nathaniel Bachellor to his wife on Oct. 9, 1777, that includes Arnold's plea to 'let me have men and we will have fun with them before sunset.' As Bachellor makes clear, Gates had moved from his headquarters in the rear of the American camp to the front of the lines when he spoke with Arnold and the others prior to the beginning of the battle. My thanks to Eric Schnitzer of the Saratoga National Historical Park for providing a transcription of the letter, which is in the 'Nathaniel Bachellor' file in the Historian Files at Saratoga NHP. On Benjamin Lincoln's narcolepsy, see David Mattern's *Benjamin Lincoln and the American Revolution;* according to Mattern, "A contemporary wrote that, 'in the midst of conversation, at table, and when driving himself in a chaise, [Lincoln] would fall into a sound sleep'" (p. 13). Luzader describes Lincoln as "an honest broker between the Continental Army and John Stark" (p. 217). Mattoon describes how Lincoln took up after Arnold's dismissal by insisting that Gates "send a strong force to support Morgan and Dearborn, at least three regiments," in Stone's *Campaign of Lieut. Gen. John Burgoyne*, p. 372.

Ketchum recounts how after being dismissed by Gates, Arnold retired to his quarters, where he lingered, "drinking heavily" (pp. 398–99). According to Jared Sparks in *Life and Treason of Benedict Arnold*, p. 119, "Some persons ascribed [Arnold's] wild temerity to intoxication, but Major Armstrong, who assisted in removing him from the field, was satisfied that this was not true. Others said he took opium. . . . His vagaries may perhaps be sufficiently explained by the extraordinary circumstances of wounded pride, anger, and desperation, in which he was placed." Wilkinson describes Arnold's "great agitation and wrath" in his *Memoirs*, 1:273; Wilkinson identifies Arnold's mount as "a black or dark brown horse, the property of Mr. Leonard Chester" (p. 274). J. T. Headley in *Washington and His Generals,* originally published in 1813, when many battle participants were still alive, describes Arnold's horse as "a beautiful dark Spanish mare, named Warren, after the hero of Bunker Hill" (p. 158). Edmund Chadwick's account of Arnold drinking a "dipperful of . . . rum" is in William Leete Stone's *Visits to the Saratoga Battle-Grounds,* p. 227. Jared Sparks in *Life and Treason of Benedict Arnold,* p. 117, and Benson Lossing in *Pictorial Field-Book of the Revolution,* 1:61, describe Armstrong's futile pursuit of Arnold. Samuel Woodruff's description of Arnold as "more like a madman than a cool and discreet officer" is in Stone's *Visits to the Saratoga Battle-Grounds,* p. 226. Woodruff also testified that Arnold, "knowing the military character and efficiency of Gen. Fraser, and observing his motions in leading and conducting the attack, said to Morgan, 'that officer upon a grey horse . . . must be disposed of'" (pp. 225–26). Lossing in *Pictorial Field-Book,* p. 62, identifies the rifleman who killed Fraser as Timothy Murphy; according to Lossing, "Just previous to being hit by the fatal bullet, the crupper of [Fraser's] horse was cut by a rifle-ball, and immediately afterward another passed through the horse's mane, a little back of his ears. The aide of Fraser noticed this, and said, 'It is evident that you are marked out for particular aim; would it not be prudent for you to retire from this place?' Fraser replied, 'My duty forbids me to fly from danger,' and the next moment he fell"; Lossing also relates that "Fraser told his friends before he died that he saw the man who shot him, and that he was in a tree" (p. 62). William Digby's claim that Fraser's death "helped to turn the fate of the day" is in his *Journal,* p. 287.

Wilkinson describes the conversation between Gates and Clerke in his *Memoirs,* 1:269. Wilkinson also tells how Arnold unintentionally swiped the head of an American officer as well as how he "dashed to the left through the fire of the two lines and escaped unhurt; he then turned the right of the enemy . . . and [with a collection] of 15 or 20 riflemen threw himself with this party into the rear of the enemy" (1:273). Ebenezer Mattoon tells of how after having his horse shot out from under him, Arnold cried out, "Rush on, my brave boys," in Stone's *Campaign of Lieut. Gen. Burgoyne,* p. 375. Henry Dearborn in "Narrative of the Saratoga Campaign," p. 8, recounts how when Arnold entered the Breymann Redoubt through the sally port, "he ordered the enemy to lay down their arms." Dearborn also relates Arnold's wish that the enemy's musket ball had "passed [through] my heart" (p. 9).

CHAPTER SEVEN: THE BITE OF A RATTLESNAKE

According to William Stevenson's *Wounds in War,* "The large vessels of a limb, in a gunshot fracture case, are far more likely to be lacerated by splinters of bone driven outwards by the bullet, than they are to be wounded by the bullet itself" (p. 247). James Thacher's Oct. 12, 1777, description of Arnold being "very . . . impatient under his misfortunes" is in his *Military Journal,* p. 103. David Mattern in *Benjamin Lincoln and the Revolution,* p. 50, cites the aide's description of Lincoln's entertaining those gathered around him during "the most painful operation by the surgeon." Dr. James Browne praises Lincoln's stoicism in a Dec. 24, 1777, letter, in *NEHGR* 18 (1864): 34–35. According to the American surgeon John Jones in *Plain Concise Practical Remarks, on the Treatment of Wounds and Fractures,* published in 1776, when the two pieces of broken bone "lap over each other . . . the deformity which is frequently the consequence of broken bones is not owing to the exuberance of the uniting medium [known as a callus] but the ignorance or neglect of the surgeon, who is ever ready to conceal his want of knowledge or attention, under the cloak of luxuriant callus" (pp. 38–39). In a Mar. 12, 1778, letter to Washington, Arnold stated that "the callous is strongly formed in my leg" in *PGW,* 14:154. Louis Meier in *Healing of the Army,* p. 17, refers to cinchona bark and bloodletting as a treatment for gangrene in the eighteenth century. The reference to Arnold's "peevishness" is in Browne's Dec. 24, 1777, letter, in *NEHGR* 18 (1864): 35.

Richard Ketchum details how Gates bungled treaty negotiations by "ignoring Burgoyne's proposals and responding with demands of his own" that ultimately forced him "to accept Burgoyne's terms or reject them outright" in *Saratoga,* p. 420. Congress managed to get out of the terms Gates had agreed to (which would have allowed Burgoyne's army to return to England, and would have allowed the British to replace them with a whole new army in America) by insisting that Burgoyne had not shown good faith by attempting to retain some of his soldiers' weapons and ammunition. This resulted in Burgoyne's army being transported to Boston and ultimately Virginia, where they were treated as prisoners of war for the duration of the conflict; see Ketchum, *Saratoga,* pp. 435–36. Ketchum also tells of how the news of the British surrender was spread across America and to England and cites the king's "agonies" (pp. 443–45). Jonathan Loring Austin's account of informing Franklin of the victory at Saratoga and his claim that "the effect was electrical" is in "Account of Jonathan Loring Austin's Mission to France," p. 234. Lafayette quotes Arnold as referring to Horatio Gates as "the greatest poltroon in the world" in a Feb. 18, 1778, letter to Henry Laurens, in *Lafayette in the Age of the American Revolution,* edited by Stanley Idzerda, 2:296. Clare Brandt cites the Feb. 19, 1778, letter referring to Arnold as "a taper, sinking in its socket" in *Man in the Mirror,* p. 142.

John Tilley in *British Navy and the American Revolution,* pp. 106–14, provides an excellent description of the chevaux-de-frise, as well as the challenges facing the Howes in breaking the American blockade of the Delaware. Thomas McGuire in *Philadelphia Campaign,* 2:174, cites Thomas Paine's letter to Benjamin Franklin in which he compares the column of smoke that arose after the explosion of the *Augusta* to "a pillar and spreading from the top like a tree." William Howe's Oct. 22, 1777, letter to Germain, in which he asks to be "relieved from this very painful service," is in *DAR,* 14:243. Joseph Plumb Martin's account of the Siege of Fort Mifflin is in his *Narrative,* pp. 56–61. Washington writes of the "attention and consideration" he has given Fort Mifflin in a Nov. 17–18, 1777, letter to Henry Laurens in *PGW,* 12:292.

Washington's Oct. 30, 1777, letter to Alexander Hamilton, in which he instructs his aide to convince Gates of "the many happy consequences that will accrue from an immediate reinforcement being sent from the northern army," is in *PGW,* 12:60. Hamilton writes of the "insuperable inconveniences" he encountered during his conversation with Gates in a Nov. 6, 1777, letter to Washington in *PGW,* 12:141. Gates complains of the "dictatorial power" Washington had invested in Hamilton in a draft of a Nov. 7, 1777, letter to Washington in *PGW,* 12:154. James Wilkinson describes his long trip from Albany to York in his *Memoirs,* 1:330–32. Wilkinson cites Gates's Oct. 18, 1777, letter to John Hancock, in which he recommends "this gallant officer, in the warmest manner, to Congress; and entreat that he may be continued in his present office with the brevet of a brigadier general," in his *Memoirs,* 1:324. Although Wilkinson blamed the weather for the delays, there was also the unmentioned fact that his future wife was then staying in Reading. Wilkinson writes that "a state of revolution is the most seducing on earth" in his *Memoirs,* 1:351, where he also describes how he was "minutely questioned" by Thomas Mifflin and two congressional delegates in Reading (1:331).

Wilkinson cites Conway's reference to the "thirteen reasons for the loss of the Battle of Brandywine" in his *Memoirs,* 1:330; he also refers to his "potluck dinner" with Lord Stirling (1:331). Lord Stirling writes of Wilkinson's reference to a Conway letter describing Washington as "a weak general" in a Nov. 3, 1777, letter to Washington in *PGW,* 12:111. Stirling complains to Washington of Conway's having insubordinately informed his messenger to "tell my Lord I do refuse him the guard" in an undated letter written in late Aug. or early Sept. 1777, in *PGW,* 11:105. Washington refers to Conway's "intriguing disposition" in a Jan. 4, 1778, letter to Gates in *PGW,* 13:138. Washington makes the claim that Conway's merit is more in his "own imagination" than in reality in an Oct. 16, 1777, letter to Richard Henry Lee in *PGW,* 11:529. Washington's Nov. 5, 1777, letter to Conway, in which he refers to "a letter which I received last night" containing Conway's disparaging reference, is in *PGW,* 12:129. John Laurens tells of Washington's visit to Cliveden with his staff in a Nov. 5, 1777, letter to his father, Henry, in his *Army Correspondence,* p. 63.

Colonel Samuel Smith describes how "a ball came through the chimney and struck me on the hip so forcibly that I remained senseless for some time" in a Nov. 12, 1777, letter to Washington, in *PGW,* 12:231. Martin writes of how Fleury would search out the workers who had retreated behind the zigzag wall in his *Narrative,* p. 59. Fleury makes the claim that "the fire of the enemy will never take the fort" in a Nov. 14, 1777, entry in his "Journal" in *NDAR,* 10:490. John Jackson in *Pennsylvania Navy,* p. 255, refers to 1,030 cannon shots being fired by the British during one twenty-minute period on Nov. 15, 1777. Martin refers to the American soldiers being "cut up like cornstalks" as well as the complete "desolation" of the fort in his *Narrative,* p. 61; he also writes of finding his best friend dead (p. 62). Gouverneur Morris in a Feb. 1, 1778, letter written to John Jay from Valley Forge refers to how close the British had come to "quitting the city" in *LDC,* 9:4. McGuire in *Philadelphia Campaign,* 2:212, cites Thomas Paine's letter to William Howe in which he praises the bravery of the defenders of Fort Mifflin. Martin writes of how after his experience at Fort Mifflin he was "as crazy as a goose shot through the head"; he also refers to "the bite of a rattlesnake" and the lack of attention the episode received by historians in his *Narrative,* p. 63. Johann Ewald in *Diary of the American War,* p. 105, writes of the arrival of thirty British vessels at the Philadelphia waterfront on Nov. 24, 1777.

The appointment of a congressional committee on Nov. 28 to speak to Washington about pursuing a winter campaign with "vigor and success" is referred to in *LDC,* 8:329, as is James Lovell's Nov. 27, 1777, letter to Gates, in which he refers to Washington's having "fabiused [our affairs] into a very disagreeable posture." Nathanael Greene's Dec. 3, 1777, letter to Washington, in which he warns of "a crisis for American liberty" if the Americans attempt to attack the British in Philadelphia, is in *PGW,* 12:518–22. Washington's description of his army's "uncommon hardships" during the march to Valley Forge is in his Apr. 21, 1778, letter to John Banister in *PGW,* 14:577–78.

Joseph Plumb Martin's description of how his community in Connecticut was divided into "squads," each of which was responsible for providing a soldier for the Continental army, is in his *Narrative,* pp. 39–41. The list containing the nationality of American prisoners taken at the Battle of Brandywine is cited in McGuire's *Philadelphia Campaign,* 1:279. Charles Patrick Neimeyer cites the phrase "free white men on the move" in *America Goes to War,* p. 160. The dimensions of the "soldiers' huts" at Valley

Forge are given in the General Orders for Dec. 18, 1777, in *PGW,* 12:627–28. Washington makes the claim that his army is about to "starve, dissolve, or disperse," while also expressing how he feels "superabundantly" for the soldiers of his army, in a Dec. 23, 1777, letter to Henry Laurens in *PGW,* 13:683–84. Thomas Fleming writes of the soldiers' sufferings and the collective cry of "NO MEAT!" in *Washington's Secret War,* p. 25.

The Dec. 8, 1777, letter that Gates sent to both Washington and Congress, in which he refers to his letters having been "stealingly copied," is in *PGW,* 13:577. James Wilkinson claimed that when he returned to Albany after delivering word of Saratoga to Congress, Gates complained that "I have had a spy in my camp since you left me," and that he was confident that "he had adopted a plan, which would compel General Washington to give [Hamilton] up and that the receiver and the thief would be alike disgraced," in his *Memoirs,* 1:372–73. James Craik's Jan. 6, 1778, letter informing Washington of the attempt to "force you to resign" is in *PGW,* 13:160. Henry Laurens's Jan. 8, 1778, letter to his son, in which he makes the claim that "our whole frame is shattered," is in *LDC,* 8:545. Henry Laurens opened up his secret line of communication with his son John on Oct. 16, 1777, with a letter in which he refers to his distress at overhearing delegates speaking disparagingly of Washington and then requests that his son keep him informed of developments on his end within Washington's family: "All that I have said is between us. I will only add that your continued and particular advices consistent with that honor by which you are more strongly bound than you are by even duty to a father will oblige me and many distant friends" (*LDC,* 8:126). In a Jan. 3, 1777, letter, John refers to "the pernicious junto" and assures his father that "I have succeeded so far with secrecy" in *Army Correspondence,* p. 104.

In a Mar. 15, 1777, letter to John, Henry Laurens despairs of the condition of Congress: "a senate of 13 members, seldom above 17" (*LDC,* 9:296). Henry Laurens refers to Thomas Mifflin and others using the claim of patriotism as a "stalking horse to their private interests," and his belief that Washington's "steady perseverance in duty" is the best way to ride out the current difficulties, in a Jan. 8, 1778, letter to John in *LDC,* 8:545–46. John Laurens refers to the cabal's machinations having "affect[ed] the general very sensibly" in a Jan. 3, 1777, letter to his father in *Army Correspondence,* p. 103. Nathanael Greene asserts that Lafayette was "determined to be in the way of danger" in a Nov. 26, 1777, letter to Washington, in which he speaks of an incident from the night before, when the French general with five hundred militiamen and a portion of the rifle corps drove back the British pickets, in *PGW,* 12:409. Lafayette refers to the Gates faction in Congress as "stupid men" in a Dec. 30, 1777, letter to Washington, in which he also claims to have been "fixed to your fate" (*PGW,* 13:68–70). Washington's Dec. 31, 1777, response to Lafayette, in which he looks forward to the time in the future when they will "laugh at our past difficulties and the folly of others," is in *PGW,* 13:83–84.

Fleming in *Washington's Secret War,* p. 137, cites Israel Angell's diary entry describing the suffering and deaths of his men at Valley Forge. My thanks to Thomas McGuire for providing details about the Continental army's encampment at Valley Forge in the winter of 1778. The Jan. 29, 1778, document drawn up by Washington and his staff, which addresses "the numerous defects in our present military establishment," is in *PGW,* 13:376–404. For an excellent discussion of Washington's interaction with the congressional committee at Valley Forge, see Fleming's *Washington's Secret War,* pp. 166–205. On the friendship between John Laurens and Alexander Hamilton, see Ron Chernow's *Alexander Hamilton,* pp. 94–97, and Gregory Massey's *John Laurens and the American Revolution,* pp. 80–81. John Laurens's Jan. 14, 1778, letter to his father about his plan to create an African American corps of soldiers is in *Army Correspondence,* p. 108. In a Feb. 2, 1778, letter to his father about his proposal, John Laurens writes, "You ask, what is the general's opinion, upon this subject? He is convinced that the numerous tribes of blacks in the southern part of the continent offer a resource to us that should not be neglected. With respect to my particular plan, he only objects to it, with the arguments of pity for a man who would be less rich than he might be" (*Army Correspondence,* pp. 117–18).

Conway's Dec. 31, 1777, letter to Washington, in which he refers to "the Great Washington in this continent," is in *PGW,* 13:78. In a Jan. 4, 1778, letter to Gates, Washington writes, "I am to inform you then that Col. Wilkinson, [on] his way to Congress in the month of October last, fell in with Lord Stirling at Reading; and not in confidence that I ever understood, informed his aide de camp . . . that Gen. Conway had written thus to you, 'Heaven has been determined to save your country; or a weak general and bad counselors would have ruined it" (*PGW,* 13:138). Washington refers to "the most absurd contradictions" of Gates's attempt to explain himself in a Feb. 28, 1777, letter to John Fitzgerald in *PGW,* 13:694. Wilkinson writes of how Gates "denounced me as the betrayer of Conway's letter . . . in the grossest language" in his *Memoirs,* 1:384. Wilkinson describes how he "demanded satisfaction of Major Gen Gates for injuries . . . offered me" in an enclosure included in a Mar. 28, 1778, letter to Washington in *PGW,* 14:344–45. Wilkinson provides another account of the aborted duel in his *Memoirs,* 1:388.

Gates's Feb. 19, 1778, letter to Washington, in which he insists that "I am of no faction," is in *PGW,* 13:590. Fleming describes how Lafayette demanded that Gates and the members of the Board of War offer a toast to Washington in Jan. 1778, in *Washington's Secret War,* pp. 171–72. The letter in which John Adams recounts Henry Knox's visit to his home in Braintree to establish his loyalty to Washington is cited in *PGW,* 13:686. Don Higginbotham writes of Daniel Morgan's indignant encounter with Board of War member Richard Peters in *Daniel Morgan,* p. 83. Lund Washington's Feb. 18, 1778, letter to Washington, in which he reports that Richard Henry Lee was suspected of being a part of "the cabal against you," is in *PGW,* 13:587; in a Mar. 18 letter to Washington, Lund writes that John Parke Custis "had pushed RHL very close several times and that he had declared in the most solemn manner his innocence" (*PGW,* 14:221). Patrick Henry's Feb. 20, 1778, letter accompanying the unsigned letter critical of Washington that was sent to Henry from Benjamin Rush is in *PGW,* 13:609–10. In *Washington's Secret War,* pp. 169–70, Fleming gives an account of the appearance on the steps of Congress of the unsigned manuscript denouncing Washington. In a Feb. 28, 1778, letter to John Fitzgerald, Washington declares that "the machinations of this junto will recoil upon their own heads" (*PGW,* 13:106). Washington's Feb. 24, 1778, letter to Gates agreeing to bury "any offensive views . . . in silence and as far as future events will permit, oblivion," is in *PGW,* 13:655.

James Thacher in his *Military Journal* describes David Bushnell's activities after the *Turtle*'s unsuccessful attempt to blow up the *Eagle* in Sept. 1776, which included an unsuccessful attempt to blow up the *Cerberus* (the same ship that had brought Howe, Burgoyne, and Clinton to America in 1775) in New London Harbor. Thacher's description of the Battle of the Kegs also includes a humorous poem by that name written by Francis Hopkinson, pp. 122–24, 361–62. Washington's General Orders for Jan. 5, 1778, sending fifty men to report to General Sullivan at the Fatland Ford to help launch the kegs, is in *PGW,* 13:143. Harry Tinckom in "Revolutionary City, 1765–1783,"

p. 137, describes the incident with the bargeman as well as the rumor that the kegs contained soldiers. The Hessian major Baurmeister describes the "little machines exploding one by one," in *Revolution in America,* p. 151.

Washington's Jan. 20, 1778, letter to Arnold, in which he asks "whether you are upon your legs again," is in *PGW,* 13:288. Arnold's Mar. 12, 1778, reply is in *PGW,* 14:154. Arnold's two 1778 letters to Betsey Deblois are reprinted in full in Malcolm Decker's *Benedict Arnold,* pp. 285–88.

Nathanael Greene's Feb. 15, 1778, letter to Washington, in which he claims that "like Pharaoh I harden my heart," is in *PGW,* 13:546. For information on Steuben, I am indebted to Paul Lockhart's *Drillmaster of Valley Forge,* pp. 23–125. John Laurens's Feb. 28, 1778, letter to his father, describing Steuben as "the properest man we could choose for the office of inspector general," is in *Army Correspondence,* p. 132, as are the letters of Mar. 9, Mar. 25, Apr. 1, Apr. 5, and Apr. 18, 1778, pp. 132, 147, 152, 154, 160. Joseph Plumb Martin describes the spring at Valley Forge as a "continual drill" in his *Narrative,* p. 77. John Laurens's May 7, 1778, letter to his father describing the celebration of the alliance with France is in *Army Correspondence,* p. 169. Washington's May 5, 1778, response to Greene's query regarding whether he should continue to gather provisions is in *PGW,* 15:41.

CHAPTER EIGHT: THE KNIGHT OF THE BURNING MOUNTAIN

A Mrs. Gibson makes the claim that Peggy Shippen "had too much good sense to be vain," in Lewis Burd Walker's "Life of Margaret Shippen, Wife of Benedict Arnold," p. 414. Edward Shippen writes that he considers "a private station . . . a post of honor" in a Mar. 11, 1775, letter cited in Walker, "Life of Margaret Shippen," 24: 422. Piers Mackesy in *War for America,* pp. 183–84, gives the statistics as to the economic importance of the West Indies to both Britain and France. John André provides a detailed account of the Mischianza (which was also spelled Meschianza) in "Particulars of the Meschianza," pp. 353–57.

For an account of the convulsive political scene in Philadelphia prior to and after the British occupation, see Robert Brunhouse's *Counter-Revolution in Pennsylvania, 1776–1790,* pp. 18–68, as well as Owen Ireland's "Ethnic-Religious Dimension of Pennsylvania Politics, 1778–1779," pp. 423–48; as Ireland points out, there was a profoundly religious dimension to the split within Pennsylvania, with "the Scotch-Irish Presbyterians and their Calvinist allies . . . in charge of the state. Once in power, they defended the unicameral legislature which formed the basis of their power, enacted loyalty oaths to disable political and religious neutrals and opponents of the patriot movement, and replaced the Anglican-oriented College of Philadelphia with their own Presbyterian-dominated University of Pennsylvania" (p. 425). On the opposing, more conservative side were "a heterogeneous coalition of English Anglicans, Scotch Anglicans, English Quakers, and German Baptists" (p. 427). On the use of the term "an equivocal neutrality," see Richard M. Jellison's *Society, Freedom, and Conscience,* p. 140.

According to Walker in "Life of Margaret Shippen," 24: 427–28, Edward Shippen was visited by "prominent members of the Society of Friends, who persuaded him that it would be by no means seemly that his daughters should appear in public in the Turkish dresses designed for the occasion. Consequently, although they are said to have been in a *dancing fury,* they were obliged to stay away."

Washington's May 7, 1778, letter to Arnold that accompanied his gift of epaulets and a sword knot is in *PGW*, 15:74. Arnold's signed May 30, 1778, "Oath of Allegiance" is at the NA in Washington, D.C. Arnold's aide Matthew Clarkson would go on to become a long-serving president of the Bank of New York; on his other aide, David Salisbury Franks, see Oscar Straus's "New Light on the Career of Colonel David S. Franks," pp. 101–8, and James Flexner's *Traitor and the Spy*, pp. 221–22. For Washington's Jan. 29, 1778, report to the Continental Congress Camp Committee, in which he describes the financial suffering of the officers in the Continental army, see *PGW*, 13:377. On Arnold's involvement with James Seagrove and the *Charming Nancy*, see Richard Murdock's "Benedict Arnold and the Wonders of the *Charming Nancy*," pp. 22–26. Arnold's secret agreement with David Franks is paraphrased by Colonel John Fitzgerald in the transcript of Arnold's *Court Martial*, p. 21. On the influence of the smuggling culture of the American colonies on the Revolution, see John Tyler's *Smugglers and Patriots*, pp. 139–71. Terry Golway in *Washington's General*, pp. 203–4, discusses Nathanael Greene's various business schemes and quotes his secret business agreement.

Flexner in *Traitor and the Spy*, p. 215, recounts the encounter between Du Simitière and André in the home of Benjamin Franklin prior to the British evacuation. Elizabeth Drinker writes of the evacuation of the British and the arrival of the American army on June 18, 1778, in her *Diary*, 1:77. Washington's orders to Arnold about his priorities upon taking over as military governor of Philadelphia (in which he quotes Congress's resolution concerning halting the sale of goods) are in *PGW*, 15:472. Carl Van Doren in *Secret History of the American Revolution*, p. 169, quotes Arnold's agreement with Mease and West.

Henry Clinton's description of war-ravaged New Jersey and his "wantonly enormous" baggage train is in William Willcox's *Portrait of a General*, p. 232. Washington's June 15, 1778, letter to Charles Lee, in which he refers to him as a "fountain of candor," is in *PGW*, 15:406. Greene's June 24, 1778, letter to Washington, in which he urges him to make an attack on the British, is in *PGW*, 15:525–26. Charles Lee's June 25, 1778, letter to Washington, in which he announces his wish to take command of the operation against the British that he at first declined, is in *PGW*, 15:541. Washington's June 26, 1778, response, in which he suggests a compromise solution involving both Lee and Lafayette, is in *PGW*, 15:556. Joseph Plumb Martin's description of his experiences at the Battle of Monmouth are in his *Narrative*, pp. 81–88. John Laurens's June 30, 1778, letter describing Washington's confrontation with Lee is in his *Army Correspondence*, p. 197. Greene's July 2, 1778, letter describing Washington as being "everywhere" during the battle is in *PNG*, 2:451. Lafayette's assertion that he never saw "so superb a man" as Washington at Monmouth is in George Custis's *Private Recollections and Private Memoirs of Washington*, p. 27. John Laurens's description of the high point of the battle is in his *Army Correspondence*, p. 197. Willcox in *Portrait of a General*, p. 236, quotes Clinton's claim that he was going "raving mad with heat." Laurens describes the planting of the "standards of liberty" at Monmouth in his *Army Correspondence*, p. 198. Charles Lee's claim in a June 30, 1778, letter to Washington that the victory at Monmouth was "entirely owing" to his decision to retreat is in *PGW*, 15:595. Thomas Conway's July 23, 1778, letter to Washington, in which he claims that his career "will soon be over," is in *PGW*, 16:140. Custis quotes Washington as claiming that he had lain down on the night after the Battle of Monmouth to think instead of sleep in his *Recollections and Private Memoirs of Washington*, p. 80.

Josiah Bartlett's July 13, 1778, letter, in which he describes how badly Philadelphia had been treated by the British, is in *LDC,* 10:268. Elizabeth Drinker describes the woman with a "very high headdress" being harassed by a Philadelphia mob on July 4, 1778, in her *Diary,* 1:78. David Salisbury Franks speaks of Arnold's "violent oppression in the stomach" in a July 4, 1778, letter to Washington in *PGW,* 16:21. Elias Boudinot's account of finding Arnold both unwell and overworked during his first days as military governor of Philadelphia is in the testimony contained in Arnold's *Proceedings of a General Court Martial of Major General Arnold,* p. 78. Greene's July 25, 1778, letter, in which he describes how Arnold had alienated the army officers in Philadelphia by not inviting them to a ball he sponsored for the citizens of the city, is in *PNG,* 2:470. Arnold's July 19, 1778, letter to Washington, in which he expresses his interest in a naval command, is in *PGW,* 16:105. A description of Arnold's Sept. 8, 1778, proposal for a "West Indian Expedition," is in *LDC,* 10:602.

D'Estaing's July 8, 1778, letter to Washington is in *PGW,* 16:38; Washington describes the French fleet's arrival as "a great and striking event" in an Aug. 20, 1778, letter to Thomas Nelson Jr. in *PGW,* 16:341. My description of d'Estaing's encounter with Howe at Sandy Hook owes much to John Tilley's *British Navy and the American Revolution,* pp. 142–45; Tilley also writes insightfully about their second encounter off Newport (pp. 147–52). Christian McBurney's *Rhode Island Campaign,* pp. 126–28, contains an excellent account of the "Great Storm" and the ordeal of the *Languedoc.* John Laurens describes d'Estaing's "cruel situation" in an Aug. 22, 1778, letter in his *Army Correspondence,* pp. 220–21. Washington marvels about the "strangest vicissitudes" of the last two years of the war in an Aug. 20, 1778, letter to Thomas Nelson Jr. in *PGW,* 16:341. Washington discusses the fact that the enemy's financial strength may allow Britain to outlast America in the war in an Oct. 4, 1778, letter to Gouverneur Morris in *PGW,* 17:254. Washington argues that "no nation is to be trusted farther than it is bound by its interest" in a Nov. 14, 1778, letter to Henry Laurens in *PGW,* 18:250–51. Admiral d'Estaing insists that "good spies must be the basis of all" and extends "offers of money to gain this important end" in a Sept. 8, 1778, letter to Washington in *PGW,* 16:541. Washington insists that "every minutia should have a place in our collection" in an Oct. 6, 1778, letter to Lord Stirling, *PGW,* 17:267.

Arnold's Sept. 25, 1778, letter to Peggy Shippen is in Walker's "Life of Margaret Shippen," 25: 30–31. Carl Van Doren cites Arnold's letter to Edward Shippen of the same date in *Secret History of the American Revolution,* p. 186; Van Doren also cites Congress's condemnation of the theaters as promoting a "general depravity of principles" (p. 185). The Dec. 1, 1778, *Philadelphia Packet* published the article about an "American officer of great merit" daring to wear a scarlet uniform and the Tory lady's delighted response; also cited by Van Doren, p. 180. Isaac Arnold cites Arnold's July 15, 1778, letter to Mercy Scollay accompanying five hundred dollars toward the support of Joseph Warren's eldest son, as well as Samuel Adams's Dec. 20, 1779, letter to Elbridge Gerry, in which Adams recounts how he personally thanked Arnold "for his kindness" to the Warren children, in *Life of Arnold,* pp. 216–17. On Arnold's support of the Connecticut sailors aboard the *Active,* see H. L. Carson's "Case of the Sloop 'Active,'" p. 16. Arnold's Oct. 6, 1778, letter to Timothy Matlack, in which he claims that "the respect due to a citizen is by no means to be paid to the soldier," is cited in Arnold's *Court Martial,* pp. 26–27. On Arnold's involvement with the *Charming Nancy,* see Richard Murdock's "Benedict Arnold and the Wonders of the *Charming Nancy,*" pp. 22–26. Carl Van Doren in *Secret History of the American Revolution,* pp. 186–87, cites Sarah Franklin Bache's Oct. 22, 1778, letter to her father, Benjamin Franklin, describing

Arnold's provocative comments after receiving "an old fashion smack" from Bache's one-year-old daughter. In a Jan. 3, 1779, letter to Philip Schuyler, James Duane talks about the interest Arnold's leg had attracted among the ladies of Philadelphia, comparing it to Laurence Sterne's hilarious depiction of a widow's interest in "Uncle Toby's groin" (which was also injured in battle) in *Tristram Shandy*, in *LDC*, 11:405. Van Doren cites Mary Morris's letter describing Arnold's infatuation with Peggy Shippen in *Secret History of the American Revolution*, p. 187. Edward Shippen's Dec. 21, 1778, letter to his father, in which he writes that "my youngest daughter is much solicited by a certain general," is in Walker's "Life of Margaret Shippen," 25:33. Edward Burd's Jan. 3, 1779, letter, in which he writes that "a lame leg is at present the only obstacle," is also in Walker, 25:36. Elizabeth Tilghman's Mar. 13, 1779, letter, in which she describes Peggy as a woman of "great sensibility," is in Walker as well, 25:39. Walker asserts that Peggy's father "reluctantly gave his consent" after she reacted so strongly to his earlier refusal (p. 32). Flexner in *Traitor and the Spy*, p. 236, cites the description of how Arnold had begun "to hop about the floor."

CHAPTER NINE: UNMERCIFUL FANGS

For background on Joseph Reed, I have consulted *Life and Correspondence of Joseph Reed* (*LCJR*) written and compiled by his grandson W. B. Reed; John Roche's *Joseph Reed: A Moderate in the American Revolution;* George Bancroft's *Joseph Reed: A Historical Essay;* and William Stryker's *Reed Controversy: Further Facts with Reference to the Character of Joseph Reed.* The acrimonious exchange of letters between Reed and John Cadwalader after the Revolution in *Reprint of the Reed and Cadwalader Pamphlets* provides a fascinating look at Reed's behavior both as an adjutant general and as president of Pennsylvania's Supreme Executive Council. James Flexner in *Traitor and the Spy*, p. 237, cites the letter in which Reed's wife complains that Mrs. William Shippen had said that "I was sly, and that religion is often a cloak to hide bad actions."

William Gordon makes the claim that Reed "is more formed for dividing than uniting" in a Mar. 2–5, 1778, letter to Washington in *PGW*, 14:29; Gordon also describes Reed as a "treacherous person" and a "thorough paced lawyer." Joseph Plumb Martin in his *Narrative*, pp. 31–32, recounts how Reed's behavior during the Battle of Harlem Heights almost incited a rebellion among the troops from Connecticut after he unjustly accused a sergeant of cowardice. In a Dec. 14, 1777, letter to Washington, Lieutenant Colonel Isaac Sherman accused Reed "of giving orders entirely counter to mine" and putting his regiment "into confusion" and then proceeding to leave "the regiment and field with precipitation" during a skirmish outside Philadelphia (*PGW*, 12:610). Peter Messer in "'A Species of Treason and Not the Least Dangerous Kind,'" p. 326, recounts the testimony claiming that Roberts assisted several American prisoners during the British occupation. In a Nov. 5, 1778, letter to Nathanael Greene, Joseph Reed complains of Benedict Arnold's "public entertainment" the night before the hanging of the Quakers for treason and also explains why it was necessary to hang the two Quakers for treason: "being rich and powerful (both Quakers) we could not for shame have made an example of a poor rogue after forgiving the rich" (*Charles Lee Papers*, 3:250–52).

Ambrose Searle records his belief that if the Continental Congress granted "a General Amnesty" they would "drive us from this Continent forever" in the May 23, 1778, entry in his *Journal*, p. 296. John Cadwalader writes of how "every man who has a liberal way of thinking highly approves" of Arnold's conduct in a Dec. 5, 1778, letter to Nathanael Greene in the *Charles Lee Papers,* 3:270–71. Clare Brandt in *Man in the Mirror,* p. 161, writes of Reed's having moved next door to Arnold shortly before the hanging of the Quakers. Robert Brunhouse in *Counter-Revolution in Pennsylvania, 1776–1790,* writes of the political battles in Philadelphia in 1778–79 and how "everything [Arnold] did poured oil on the political fire and increased the gulf between the Constitutionalists and the conservatives" (p. 64).

On the Articles of Confederation and the Deane-Lee controversy and other infighting in Congress, see H. James Henderson's *Party Politics in the Continental Congress,* pp. 130–241, and Jack Rakove's *Beginnings of National Politics,* pp. 243–74. Washington's Dec. 18–30, 1778, letter to Benjamin Harrison, in which he complains of "party disputes and personal quarrels" dominating Congress, is in *PGW,* 18:449–50. Washington's Dec. 13, 1778, letter to Arnold, in which he expresses his wish not "to be acquainted with the causes of the coolness" between him and members of the Board of War, is in *PGW,* 18:399. Washington complains of how "idleness, dissipation, and extravagance" have taken over Philadelphia in his Dec. 18–30, 1778, letter to Benjamin Harrison in *PGW,* 18:449–50. In a Jan. 26, 1779, letter to Governor George Clinton, the New York congressional delegate Gouverneur Morris recommends Arnold "for the purpose of serving in some degree our western frontier and consequently enriching the intermediate country" (*LDC,* 11:520). The Pennsylvania Supreme Executive Council's eight charges against Arnold appear in *LDC,* 12:27. The escalating tensions between the council and Congress can be traced in the exchange of letters between the two bodies in *LDC,* 12:27–180.

Cadwalader's claim that Joseph Reed contemplated going over to the British in the days prior to the Battle of Trenton is detailed in a Sept. 3, 1782, letter under the name of Brutus that appeared in the *Independent Gazetteer* and is reprinted in *Reprint of the Reed and Cadwalader Pamphlets,* pp. 7–8. In an appendix to the *Reprint,* p. 4, is an extract from the journal of Margaret Morris, who lived in Burlington, New Jersey, at the time of the Battle of Trenton, in which she describes a conversation she had with a woman who lodged in the same room in which Reed and Colonel John Cox stayed the night of the battle. According to Morris's source, Reed and Cox "laid awake all night consulting together about the best means of securing themselves and that they came to the determination of setting off [the] next day as soon as it was light to the British camp, and joining them with all the men under their command. But when the morning came an express arrived with an account that the Americans had gained a great victory. . . . This report put the rebel general and colonel in high spirits and they concluded to remain firm to the cause of America."

Arnold's Feb. 8, 1779, letter to Peggy Shippen, in which he claims that "Washington and the officers of the army . . . bitterly execrate Mr. Reed and the council for their villainous attempt to injure me," is reprinted in Russell Lea's useful compilation of Arnold correspondence, *Hero and a Spy,* pp. 316–17. Roche in *Joseph Reed,* pp. 140–42, describes the circumstances under which Reed was offered ten thousand pounds if he would assist the efforts of the British peace commissioners, as well as Reed's attempts more than a year later, once this came to light, at damage control. Charles Thomson's Mar. 21, 1779, letter to Joseph Reed, in which he questions Reed's motives in attempting "to lessen the reputation and consequently the weight and authority of the great council of the United States," is in *LDC,* 12:219–22.

Flexner in *Traitor and the Spy,* p. 252, details the circumstances under which Arnold purchased Mount Pleasant and cites John Adams's description of it as "the most elegant seat in Pennsylvania." The Marquis de Chastellux's claims that Arnold "made the mysteries of the nuptial bed the subject of his coarse ribaldry to his companions the day after his marriage" are in his *Travels*, p. 114. Benedict Arnold's Sept. 12, 1780, letter to Robert Howe, in which he talks of Peggy in reference to "scenes of sensual gratification," is in the Washington Papers at LOC.

For a provocative analysis of how the country's increasingly bleak prospects influenced Arnold's decision to turn traitor, in particular the effects of "civilian ingratitude," see James Kirby Martin's "Benedict Arnold's Treason as Political Protest," p. 71. In a July 27, 1779, letter to his brother Simeon, Silas Deane describes the explosive political situation in Philadelphia: "The contest is between the respectable citizens of fortune and character, opposed to the Constitution of this state, and people in lower circumstances and reputation, headed by leaders well qualified for their business and supposed to be secretly supported by the President and Council. However things may end, it may at this instant be truly said there are few unhappier cities on the globe than Philadelphia, the reverse of its name, in its present character, which I hope will not be its situation for any time," in *Pennsylvania Magazine of History and Biography* 17, no. 1 (Apr. 1893): 348–49. John Shy writes of how the militia provided "the mechanism of [the American people's] political conversion" in *People Numerous and Armed*, p. 219. Sung Bok Kim writes about the Neutral Ground in Westchester County in "Limits of Politicization in the American Revolution," pp. 868–89. James Collins writes about the maritime version of the Neutral Ground in "Whaleboat Warfare on Long Island Sound," pp. 195–201. Washington writes of "the total destruction and devastation" of the Iroquois settlements in his May 31, 1779, orders to John Sullivan in *PGW*, 20:716–19.

Carl Van Doren cites the article in the *Royal Gazette* describing Arnold as a victim of the "unmerciful fangs" of the Pennsylvania legislature in *Secret History of the American Revolution*, p. 193. Burgoyne makes the claim that Arnold won the Battle of Bemis Heights in spite of Gates's preference for remaining on the defensive in *State of the Expedition from Canada*, p. 17. John Adams's claim that if he had had a wife and in-laws who, like John Dickinson's, were against independence "that if they did not wholly unman me and make me an apostate, they would make me the most miserable man alive" is in his *Autobiography* in *Diary and Autobiography of John Adams*, 3:316. Arnold's May 5, 1779, letter to Washington, in which he writes, "If your Excellency thinks me criminal for heaven's sake let me be immediately tried and if found guilty executed," is in *PGW*, 20:328. James Kirby Martin cites John Brown's claim that "money is this man's god" in *Benedict Arnold*, p. 324.

CHAPTER TEN: THE CHASM

Barnet Schecter writes of life in New York City upon the return of the British army from Philadelphia in *Battle for New York*, pp. 319–20, 325–26. Charles Royster details the "extensive trade with the enemy in New York City" in *Revolutionary People at War*, p. 272. Carl Van Doren describes the illegal lumber trade between Philadelphia and New York in *Secret History of the American Revolution*, p. 278, where he also tells how Arnold established his line of communication with André through John Stansbury and others as well as his use of codes and invisible ink (pp. 196–201). André's May 10, 1779, letter to Arnold is reprinted in the appendix to Van Doren's *Secret History*, pp. 439–40, as is Arnold's May 23, 1779, reply (pp. 441–42). Silas Deane's May 29, 1779, letter to

Nathanael Greene is at the NYHS. Washington writes of how he "could not be so lost to my own character as to become a partisan at the moment I was called upon" prior to Arnold's court-martial and how he gave Arnold a "rebuke" in a Nov. 20, 1780, letter to Joseph Reed in *WGW*, 20:370.

For a helpful account of American-British operations on the Hudson in the summer of 1779, see Michael Schellhammer's *George Washington and the Final British Campaign for the Hudson River, 1779*, pp. 77–87. In a June 2, 1779, letter to Timothy Matlack, Washington informs him that Arnold has gone to Morristown after the delay of his court-martial "to wait events" (*PGW*, 21:20). André's mid-June 1779 reply to Arnold is in Van Doren's *Secret History*, p. 448. Clinton writes of Arnold being "less an object of attention" after his troubles in Philadelphia in an Oct. 11, 1780, letter to George Germain in his own *American Rebellion*, p. 462. Stansbury's July 11, 1779, letter to André informing him that his previous communication was "not equal to his expectations" is in Van Doren's *Secret History*, pp. 449–50, as are Arnold's shopping list for Peggy, pp. 451–52; André's late-July response to Arnold, p. 453; Stansbury's late-July letter to André, pp. 453–54; and André's Aug. 16, 1779, letter to Peggy, p. 454. Peggy's reference to the "great persuasion and unceasing perseverance" it took to convince her husband to turn traitor is in *Memoirs of Aaron Burr*, edited by Matthew L. Davis, 1:219–20. See Schellhammer's *George Washington and the Final British Campaign for the Hudson River, 1779*, for accounts of Anthony Wayne's attack on Stony Point and Henry Lee's attack on Paulus Hook (pp. 142–55, 165–80). Clinton's tearful confession that he was "quite an altered man" after the disappointing campaign on the Hudson in the summer of 1779 is in William Willcox's *Portrait of a General*, p. 279. Washington's Sept. 13, 1779, letter to d'Estaing, in which he provides "hints" as to a possible joint French-American attack on New York, is in *PGW*, 22:409–10. The editors of *PGW* provide a detailed account of Washington's plan to attack New York in the fall of 1779 (22:594–623). Washington's Sept. 30, 1779, letter to Lafayette is in *PGW*, 22:562. Washington's Nov. 10, 1779, letter to John Parke Custis, in which he describes the apparent "chasm" between New York and Georgia, is in *WGW*, 17:90–91.

My account of the Battle of Fort Wilson has been drawn from "Charles Willson Peale's Account" in the appendix of *LCJR*, 2:424, in which he claims that "to reason with a multitude of devoted patriots assembled on such an occasion was in vain"; "Philip Hagner's Narrative" (also in *LCJR*), which includes Arnold's claim that "your president has raised a mob and now he cannot quell it" (2:427); and John Alexander's "Fort Wilson Incident of 1779: A Case Study of the Revolutionary Crowd," which cites Joseph Reed's dismissive description of the deaths of the militiamen and army officer as "the casual overflowings of liberty" (p. 608). Van Doren in *Secret History*, p. 252, cites Arnold's Oct. 6, 1779, letter to Congress asking for a guard to protect him from a "mob of lawless ruffians." Peggy Arnold's Oct. 13, 1779, letter to John André is also in *Secret History*, p. 455, as is Arnold's Dec. 3, 1779, communication with André (pp. 455–56).

CHAPTER ELEVEN: THE PANGS OF A DYING MAN

My description of Morristown is based largely on John Cunningham's *Uncertain Revolution*, pp. 13–15. On the hard winter of 1779–80 in Morristown, see David Ludlum's *Early American Winters, 1604–1820*, pp. 111–17. Cunningham writes about the "Contours at Jockey Hollow" and "the presumed place of convenience" where the

Connecticut brigades were stationed in *Uncertain Revolution*, pp. 98–99. Joseph Plumb Martin describes the extreme cold and speaks of "the keystone of the arch of starvation" in his *Narrative*, pp. 112–13.

Arnold's summation is in the *Proceedings of a General Court Martial for the Trial of Major General Arnold*, pp. 102–33. Arnold complains of the injustice of his reprimand in a Mar. 22, 1780, letter to Silas Deane in Carl Van Doren's *Secret History of the American Revolution*, pp. 250–51. During his post-Revolutionary pamphlet war with Joseph Reed, John Cadwalader revealed that after Arnold referred to the rumor about Reed's contemplated treason prior to the Battle of Trenton in his summation, he "apologized to me for inserting it in his defense, without my permission; I remarked that an apology was unnecessary from the public manner in which I had mentioned it," in *Reprint of the Reed and Cadwalader Pamphlets*, p. 36; Cadwalader also claimed that during Arnold's trial, Reed, "with a half shamed face seemed to apologize for being his prosecutor, and became his fulsome panegyrist" (p. 36). Isaac Arnold in *Life of Benedict Arnold* cites the Pennsylvania Supreme Executive Council's Feb. 3, 1780, recommendation that "Congress will be pleased to dispense with the part of the sentence which imposes a public censure" with the speculation that it "seems to have been extorted from [Arnold's] prosecutors by the indignation of the army and the people at the sentence" (pp. 262–63). Arnold's accusation that the treasury commissioners who were determining how much he should be compensated for his expenses in Canada were guilty of "private resentment or undue influence" is cited by Van Doren in *Secret History*, p. 251.

Arnold's Mar. 20, 1780, letter to Washington, in which he proposes yet another possible naval expedition, is in Russell Lea's compilation *Hero and a Spy* as are Washington's two Apr. 6, 1780, letters concerning his reprimand (pp. 384, 386–87). On the fortifications at West Point, I have looked to an excellent overview of what was done during the summer and fall of 1779 in *PGW*, 21:189–94, and Dave Palmer's *River and the Rock*, pp. 203–17. Van Doren in *Secret History*, p. 258, cites Arnold's May 25, 1780, letter to Philip Schuyler complaining that he had not yet heard from him about his promised conversation with Washington about him. William Reed reprints Schuyler's June 2, 1780, letter to Arnold, in which he conveys Washington's high regard for him, in *LCJR*, 2:276–77. Arnold's June 12, 1780, letter to the British, in which he assured them that he "expects to have the command of West Point offered him," is in Van Doren, *Secret History*, p. 460.

Joseph Plumb Martin describes the mutiny of the Connecticut brigades at Morristown in his *Narrative*, pp. 118–22. Charles Royster in *Revolutionary People at War*, p. 270, discusses the "enormous economic boom" created by the war. Washington's May 28, 1780, letter to Joseph Reed is cited by Douglas Freeman in *George Washington*, 5:166–67. Washington's May 27, 1780, letter to the president of Congress, in which he admits that the mutiny "has given me infinitely more concern than anything that has ever happened," is in *WGW*, 18:431, as is his May 31, 1780, letter to Joseph Jones, in which he expresses the fear that "our cause is lost," and that he sees "one head gradually changing into thirteen" (18:453). Ebenezer Huntington's July 7, 1780, letter to his brother Andrew, in which he complains of the "rascally stupidity which now prevails in the country," is in *Letters Written by Ebenezer Huntington during the American Revolution*, pp. 86–87. Arnold's July 12, 1780, letter to André, in which he claims that the "present struggles are like the pangs of a dying man," is in Van Doren's *Secret History*, p. 463. Arnold's claim that he "believed our cause was hopeless" is in Isaac Arnold's *Life of Benedict Arnold*, p. 287.

Tom Lewis in *Hudson River,* p. 138, writes of the waterway being the "River of Mountains." Eric Sanderson in *Manhattan,* p. 87, provides the statistics about the Hudson. Douglas Cubbison provides a detailed analysis of the many smaller fortifications associated with Revolutionary West Point in *Historic Structures Report: The Redoubts of West Point.* Lincoln Diamant in *Chaining the Hudson* writes extensively about the fortifications and especially the chain at West Point (pp. 121–22, 129, 141–56). Arnold's June 16, 1780, letter to the British describing the condition of the fortress at West Point is in Van Doren's *Secret History,* pp. 460–61.

The playboy Banastre Tarleton was the British officer who reportedly described Peggy Arnold as "the handsomest woman in England" in Mark Jacob and Stephen Case's *Treacherous Beauty,* p. 197. Hannah Arnold passes along her suspicions about Peggy's relationship with Robert Livingston in a Sept. 4, 1780, letter to Arnold cited in Van Doren's *Secret History,* pp. 303–4. Livingston's June 22, 1780, letter to Washington is in Lea's *Hero and a Spy,* pp. 395–96, as is Washington's June 29, 1780, response (pp. 396–97). Arnold's July 12, 1780, letter to André, in which he informs him of the arrival of the French at Newport, is in Van Doren's *Secret History,* pp. 462–63. Douglas Freeman cites Lafayette's Apr. 27, 1780, letter announcing his return to America in *George Washington,* 5:161. Washington's July 31, 1780, letter to Rochambeau, in which he writes that "the only way I can be useful to you is to menace New York," is in Jared Sparks's *Writings of George Washington,* as is Washington's July 31 letter to Lafayette, in which he writes of being "exceedingly hurried" (7:126–27, 128–29). Richard Rush recorded Washington's memory of Arnold's unusual behavior when told that he was to lead the left wing of the army rather than command at West Point in *Washington in Domestic Life,* pp. 77–81. The reference to Peggy's breaking into "hysteric fits" on hearing that Arnold had been placed in command of the left wing instead of West Point is in *Memoirs of Aaron Burr,* edited by Matthew L. Davis, 1:105. Isaac Arnold in *Life of Benedict Arnold,* p. 319, cites Mrs. James Gibson's account of Franks's testimony about Peggy in which he claimed that "she was subject to occasional paroxysms," and that as a consequence Arnold's aides had become "scrupulous of what we told her." Mark Jacob and Stephen Case in *Treacherous Beauty,* p. 127, cite Peggy's 1801 letter to her father at the Historical Society of Pennsylvania, in which she describes the occasional "confusion in my head." Washington's General Orders for Aug. 3, 1780, are in Lea's *Hero and a Spy,* pp. 407–8.

CHAPTER TWELVE: THE CRASH

In an 1832 pension application, Alpheus Parkhurst describes Arnold as wearing "a large red shoe" on his left foot, in *Revolution Remembered,* edited by John C. Dann, p. 57. Arnold's Aug. 5, 1780, letter to Robert Howe, in which he says his new headquarters at Robinson House is "the most convenient for an invalid" is in Russell Lea's *Hero and a Spy,* p. 411. After Arnold's treason was revealed, his aide Richard Varick successfully cleared his (and in the process, his fellow aide Franks's) reputation through a court of inquiry, the transcript of which provides much useful information about life at Robinson House in Aug. and Sept. 1780. Mrs. Martin, a housekeeper at Arnold's headquarters, testified that the general "kept his stores in his own private room and afterwards in a room appointed for the purpose, to which no person had access except himself," in *Varick Court of Inquiry,* p. 158. According to Varick, Arnold claimed that "he had

10,000 rations due to him since 1775, 1776 and 1777, for which he could not get an adequate compensation, and that he would in future draw all his rations"; Varick also testified that he "prevented any intercourse between" Arnold and a Captain Robinson, to whom Arnold wanted "to sell some rum" (pp. 134, 135).

Washington's Aug. 3, 1780, letter to Arnold, in which he orders him to "obtain every intelligence of the enemy's motions," is in Lea, *Hero and a Spy*, p. 408. Carl Van Doren in *Secret History of the American Revolution*, pp. 287–88, describes Arnold's attempts to learn the identities of the spies used by Howe and Lafayette. For information on Joshua Hett Smith, I have relied on Richard Koke's *Accomplice in Treason*, pp. 3–69. Smith's Aug. 13, 1780, letter to Arnold, whom, he unctuously claims, is "a gentleman whose character I revere," is in Lea, *Hero and a Spy*, p. 418. In an Aug. 24, 1780, letter to Robert Benson, aide-de-camp to New York's governor Clinton, Varick inquired into Smith's "moral and political character"; Benson answered on Sept. 19, 1780, that "from the conduct of his connections and his own loose character, I cannot persuade myself to think him entitled to the fullest confidence," in *Varick Court of Inquiry*, pp. 92–98. James Flexner in *Traitor and the Spy*, p. 321, cites Sebastian Bauman's claim that Arnold was "bewildered from the very first moment he took command" at West Point; Flexner also cites Hannah Arnold's accusation that her brother was "a perfect master of ill nature" (p. 321).

Arnold's Aug. 30, 1780, letter to André, in which he refers to receiving André's earlier letter on Aug. 24 and that he has "no doubt when he has conferenced with you that you will close with [his proposal]," is in Van Doren, *Secret History*, p. 470. Arnold's Sept. 12, 1780, letter to Nathanael Greene, in which he gleefully refers to Gates's loss at Camden as "an unfortunate piece of business to that hero," is in Lea, *Hero and a Spy*, p. 436. André's letter to his family describing his "steep progress" in the British army is in Robert McConnell Hatch's *Major John André*, pp. 214–15. My description of André's darker side owes much to John Evangelist Walsh's *The Execution of Major André*, which also refers to the British officer's involvement in the massacres at Paoli and Old Tappan (p. 21). André's description of the bayoneting of the fleeing American soldiers at Paoli is in the Sept. 20 entry of his *Journal*, p. 50. Flexner in *Traitor and the Spy*, p. 155, cites André's letter to his mother about Paoli. Thomas Demarest writes about the archaeological work performed at Old Tappan in "Baylor Massacre," pp. 70–76. Thomas Jones's condemnation of the Baylor Massacre as "an act inconsistent with the dignity or honor of a British General" is in his *History of New York during the Revolutionary War*, 1:286. Flexner cites André's letter referring to how d'Estaing's seizure of Grenada meant that "all my golden dreams vanished," in *Traitor and the Spy*, p. 295.

André's Sept. 7, 1780, communication with Arnold, in which he refers to the officer "between whom and myself no distinction need be made," is in Van Doren, *Secret History*, as is Arnold's Sept. 10 response in which he insists "my situation will not permit my meeting or having any private intercourse with such an officer" (p. 471). Joseph Plumb Martin writes of his seeing Arnold "in the vicinity of Dobbs Ferry" in his *Narrative*, pp. 129–30. Henry Clinton recounts how he brought Admiral Rodney into his confidence about his dealings with Arnold and how it became necessary for a face-to-face meeting with Arnold in his *American Rebellion*, p. 463. William Smith's memory of his conversation with Clinton, in which he predicted the Revolution would end "in a crash," is in the Sept. 26, 1780, entry to his *Memoirs*, 2:334.

Winthrop Sargent in *Life and Career of Major John André* reprints the letter from Beverley Robinson that was supposedly found among Arnold's papers after his defection, pp. 447–49. Varick testified that he insisted that Arnold rewrite his letter to Robinson because it "bore the complexion of one from a friend rather than one from an enemy," in *Varick Court of Inquiry*, p. 134. Arnold's two Sept. 18, 1780, letters to Beverley Robinson, in which he sets the stage for the rendezvous with André on the *Vulture* and refers to Washington's return from Hartford, are in Lea, *Hero and a Spy*, p. 448.

Much of what we know about the nights of Sept. 20 and 21, as well as events associated with Smith and André's journey into the Neutral Ground, comes from *Record of the Trial of Joshua Hett Smith* and Smith's subsequent (and less reliable) *Authentic Narrative of the Causes Which Led to the Death of Major André*. Smith testified that he had rowed out to the *Vulture* in expectation of picking up Beverley Robinson, who, Arnold had claimed, wanted to know if "he could obtain a pardon and his estate be restored to him" (pp. 73–74). Both Cahoon brothers testified to their testy exchange with Arnold about rowing out to the *Vulture* (pp. 6–14). Smith's account of how he ended up with André instead of Robinson is also in *Trial of Joshua Hett Smith*, pp. 74–80. In a Sept. 24, 1780, letter to Clinton, Robinson describes the circumstances under which André instead of himself ended up accompanying Smith to the meeting with Arnold, in Van Doren, *Secret History*, pp. 474–75. Smith speaks of André's "youthful appearance and the softness of his manners" in his *Narrative*, p. 20, as well as the "chagrin" and "trepidation" Arnold displayed at learning that he was meeting André instead of Robinson (pp. 21–22).

My account of the conversation between Arnold and André is necessarily conjectural; however, clues to what was said exist. After André's death, Arnold had the audacity to write Clinton claiming that André had assured him that he'd do everything he could to make sure Arnold received the full ten thousand pounds in the event he failed to deliver West Point; after his capture, André spoke extensively with Benjamin Tallmadge about how the British were to have taken West Point, information that Tallmadge then passed along to the Harvard historian Jared Sparks, who subsequently included the account in *Life and Treason of Benedict Arnold*. According to Sparks, once the British attacked West Point, Arnold was to send out "parties . . . from the garrison to the gorges in the hills and other distant points, under pretense of meeting the enemy as they approached; and here they were to remain, while the British troops landed and marched to the garrison through different routes in which they would meet no opposition. . . . The general principle . . . was that the troops should be so scattered and divided into such small detachments that they could not act in force, and would be obliged to surrender without any effectual resistance. By previous movements Arnold had in fact prepared the way for this scheme" (p. 208). Robinson's Sept. 24, 1780, letter to Clinton, in which he describes the pounding the *Vulture* took from the American battery off Teller's Point, is in Van Doren, *Secret History*, p. 475.

CHAPTER THIRTEEN: NO TIME FOR REMORSE

Joshua Hett Smith describes how he and the Cahoons rowed against the back eddies while getting the boat up the river and then provides his own perspective on the firing on the *Vulture* in his *Narrative*, pp. 21–22. Joseph Cahoon tells of Arnold's visit to the "necessary house" and his lame walk in *Trial of Joshua Hett Smith*, p. 16. Arnold's rather dubious explanation that André/Anderson had worn a British officer's uniform out of "pride or vanity" is in Smith's *Narrative*, p. 23. The best description of André's disguise is in the testimony of the New York militiaman John Paulding in *Trial of Joshua Hett Smith*, p. 55.

Smith describes André's fretful waiting at the second-story window of his house with a view of the *Vulture*, as well as his unsuccessful attempts to draw his companion into conversation about the taking of Stony Point, in his *Narrative*, pp. 23–24. Robert Hatch quotes extensively from André's "The Cow Chase" in *Major John André*, pp. 209–11. William Jameson and William Cooley tell about their conversation with Smith at the army tent at King's Ferry in *Trial of Joshua Hett Smith*, pp. 39–42. The ferrymen Cornelius Lambert, Lambert Lambert, and William Van Wart testify about the crossing with Smith and André in *Trial of Joshua Hett Smith*, pp. 34–39. Sung Bok Kim in "Limits of Politicization in the American Revolution," p. 882, cites Timothy Dwight's account of what the Revolution had done to the county's residents. Smith describes how he and André were stopped and questioned by the patrol party led by Captain Boyd in his *Narrative*, pp. 25–26, in which he also describes how they both slept in a single bed and continued their journey the next day (pp. 27–30). William Abbatt in *Crisis of the Revolution*, p. 22, describes the encounter with Samuel Webb and how it made André's "hair rise"; Abbatt also reprints Joshua King's account of his time with André in which he describes the British captive as looking like "a reduced gentleman" (p. 39). Smith details his parting with André in his *Narrative*, pp. 29–30.

John Romer in *Historic Sketches of the Neutral Ground*, p. 23, tells of the huge tulip tree near where André was taken by the three militiamen. In *Trial of Joshua Hett Smith*, pp. 52–60, John Paulding and Abraham (referred to as David in the transcript) Williams provide detailed testimony as to what was said during the capture of André. Abbatt in *Crisis of the Revolution*, p. 29, tells of Paulding's capture by the British and how he came to wear a Hessian jacket. Paulding claimed that he had responded to André's attempts to bribe them by asserting, "No, by God, if you would give us ten thousand guineas, you should not stir a step," in *Trial of Joshua Hett Smith*, p. 54. In a letter to Jared Sparks written thirty-three years later, Benjamin Tallmadge hinted that, if left to his own devices, he would have seized Arnold before the traitor learned of André's capture, claiming that "I suggested to [Lieutenant Colonel Jameson] a plan which I wished to pursue, offering to take the entire responsibility on myself, and which, as he deemed it too perilous to permit, I will not further disclose," in Morton Pennypacker's *General Washington's Spies*, p. 169. Suggesting that this may have been more a question of wishful thinking and hindsight than reality is the letter that Jameson wrote to Washington soon after Arnold's flight to the British, in which he explained that only after consulting with Tallmadge and "some others of the field officers," all of whom "were clearly of opinion that it would be right until I could hear from your Excellency," did he send the letter about the capture of Anderson to Arnold, in Van Doren's *Secret History*, p. 341.

Joshua Hett Smith claims that Arnold responded to the news that Smith had accompanied André as far as the American lines of the Neutral Ground with "much satisfaction" in his *Narrative*, p. 30. John Lamb provides a detailed description of the interchange around Arnold's table involving Varick, Smith, and others in *Varick Court of Inquiry*, pp. 149–51. Varick tells of Arnold's angry insistence that "if he asked the Devil to dine with him, the gentlemen of his family should be civil to him," in *Varick Court of Inquiry*, pp. 174–75. Van Doren cites André's reference to Americans as "dung-born tribes" in *Secret History*, p. 321. My account of André's conduct is in line with Brian Carso's judgment in *"Whom Can We Trust Now?"*: "A persuasive argument can be made . . . that André's inept facilitation of Arnold's offer to turn over West Point frustrated what might have otherwise led to a British victory in the Revolution" (p. 160). Joshua King's description of how he came to realize André was "no ordinary person" and how he became his eager confidant is in Abbatt's *Crisis of the Revolution,* p. 39.

Jared Sparks reprints André's Sept. 24, 1780, letter to Washington in *Life and Treason of Benedict Arnold,* pp. 235–38. Abbatt in *Crisis of the Revolution* includes a photograph of the rocking chair in which André reputedly wrote his letter to Washington; Abbatt also cites Hamilton's description of André's letter to Washington as "conceived in terms of dignity without insolence, and apology without meanness" (p. 40). John Evangelist Walsh in *The Execution of Major André,* pp. 152–71, recounts how in later life Tallmadge attempted to discredit André's captors. As Morton Pennypacker points out in *General Washington's Spies,* pp. 164–65, Tallmadge's later hostility toward the three militiamen may have been influenced by Paulding's participation two and a half years later in a raid on the loyalist DeLancey's home in Westchester County of which Tallmadge had not approved. In a letter to the historian Jared Sparks that is quoted in Pennypacker's *General Washington's Spies,* p. 171, Tallmadge freely admits that despite being Washington's spy chief, "Until the papers were found on Anderson, I had no suspicion of [Arnold's] lack of patriotism or political integrity."

Sparks quotes the exchange between Lafayette and Washington in which the commander in chief claimed that "you young men are all in love with Mrs. Arnold," in *Life and Treason of Benedict Arnold,* p. 240. James Flexner in *Traitor and the Spy,* p. 366, quotes the account of Arnold being thrown "into great confusion" by the message delivered by Lieutenant Allen. Franks describes how he informed Arnold that Washington was "nigh at hand," as well as how Arnold ordered him to tell Washington that he'd be back from West Point "in about an hour," in *Varick Court of Inquiry,* p. 130. Flexner in *Traitor and the Spy,* p. 367, cites the description of how Arnold "galloped almost down a precipice." In *Life and Treason of Benedict Arnold,* pp. 242–43, Sparks describes how Arnold fled down the river and once aboard the *Vulture* placed his boat crew under arrest. According to Sparks, "Sir Henry Clinton, holding in just contempt such a wanton act of meanness, set them all at liberty" (p. 243); Sparks also describes how Washington asked Knox and Lafayette, "Whom can we trust now?" (p. 247). Washington's own account of Arnold's flight down the Hudson, which the commander in chief apparently received from the barge's crew, whom he described as "very clever fellows and some of the better sort of soldiery," was recorded by his secretary Tobias Lear in 1796, and is quoted by Pennypacker in *General Washington's Spies,* pp. 177–79. For a probing analysis of the issues surrounding treason and a republic, see Brian Carso's *"Whom Can We Trust Now?,"* p. 240; Carso cites Benjamin Franklin's response to the news of Arnold's treason: "Judas sold only one man, Arnold three millions. Judas got for his one man 30 pieces of silver, Arnold got not a halfpenny a head. A miserable bargain!" (p. 154).

An Oct. 5, 1780, letter from Peggy Arnold's brother-in-law Edward Burd to his friend Jasper Yeates in the *Pennsylvania Magazine of History and Biography* provides evidence as to how Peggy delayed her delirious outburst until after her husband had safely escaped down the river: "General Arnold came up to her before he went off and told her that an accident had happened which obliged him to go into New York. She instantly sunk motionless on the bed where he left her. She continued without any signs of life for an hour and a half and people coming into her room brought her to herself. She then fell into hysterick fits in which she continued for a long time" (40:380–81). Richard Varick provides a detailed account of Peggy's apparent hysteria in an Oct. 1,

1780, letter to his sister Jane in *Varick Court of Inquiry,* pp. 189–93. Van Doren cites Hamilton's letter to his fiancée in which he writes that Peggy's "sufferings were so elo-quent that I wished myself her brother" in *Secret History,* p. 350. Peggy's reference to the "great persuasion and unceasing perseverance" it took to convince her husband to turn traitor is in the *Memoirs of Aaron Burr,* edited by Matthew L. Davis, 1:219–20.

Arnold's Sept. 25, 1780, letter to Washington is reprinted in *Minutes of a Court of Inquiry upon the Case of Major John André,* p. 18. Arnold's Aug. 23, 1780, letter to Na-thanael Greene about the potential march on Congress is in Russell Lea, *Hero and a Spy,* p. 424. In an Oct. 5, 1780, letter to Jasper Yeates, Edward Burd writes that "when General Washington received Arnold's impudent letter he threw it from him with indignation saying, 'Wretch, did he think I would treat Mrs. Arnold with humanity for his sake? No, she is far above him and every tenderness in my power shall be shown to her'" (*Pennsylva-nia Magazine of History and Biography* 40:381). Beverley Robinson's Sept. 25, 1780, letter of the same date to Washington is cited in Sparks's *Life and Treason of Benedict Arnold,* p. 250. Washington's Sept. 30, 1780, letter to Clinton, in which he quotes André as saying that it was "impossible for him to suppose he came on shore under the sanction of a flag," is in *WGW,* 20:104. Flexner in *Traitor and the Spy,* p. 388, quotes Henry Clinton as saying "a deserter is never given up." Hamilton writes of André in an Oct. 11, 1780, letter to John Laurens, in which he also cites André as writing to Clinton that "misfortune, not guilt, has brought it upon me," in *Papers of Alexander Hamilton,* 2:466–68.

In *Life and Treason of Benedict Arnold,* pp. 278–79, Sparks reprints André's Oct. 1, 1780, letter to Washington in which he requests to be shot rather than hanged. J. E. Mor-purgo in *Treason at West Point,* p. 137, cites Hamilton's criticism of Washington's decision to hang André as "hard hearted policy." Joseph Plumb Martin compares the deaths of André and Nathan Hale in his *Narrative,* p. 130. James Thacher's account of the death of André is in his *Military Journal,* pp. 222–23. Abbatt in *Crisis of the Revolution,* p. 75, tells of André's exhorting the face-blackened executioner to "take off your black hands"; Ab-batt also quotes a witness as recounting the "most tremendous swing" of André's body on the gallows (p. 76). Nathaniel Husted in *Centennial Souvenir of the Monument Association of the Capture of André,* p. 167, quotes a doctor who was present that day as saying that André's "legs dangled so much that the hangman was ordered to take hold of them and keep them straight." Walsh in *Execution of Major André,* p. 146, quotes the witness who remembered that André's "face appeared to be greatly swollen, and very black."

According to Douglas Freeman in *George Washington,* 5:222, Washington received the packet including Arnold's threatening letter about an hour after André's execution. Sparks in *Life and Treason of Benedict Arnold,* pp. 273–74, quotes Arnold's letter to Washington. Charles Royster in "'Nature of Treason,'" pp. 186–87, cites Knox's, Greene's, and Scammell's emotional reactions to Arnold's treason. Washington's Sept. 27, 1780, letter to Rochambeau, in which he writes that "traitors are the growth of every country," is in *WGW,* 20:97. Washington's Oct. 13, 1780, letter to John Laurens, in which he claims that Arnold "wants feeling," is in *WGW,* 20:173.

EPILOGUE: A NATION OF TRAITORS

The reference to Arnold's recently seized papers revealing "a scene of baseness and pros-titution of office and character as it is hoped this new world cannot parallel" is in the

Sept. 30, 1780, *Philadelphia Packet*. A detailed description of Charles Willson Peale's life-size effigy of Arnold with a rotating head is in the Oct. 3, 1780, edition of the *Philadelphia Packet*. Benjamin Irvin provides a suggestive analysis of Philadelphia's response to Arnold's treason in *Clothed in Robes of Sovereignty*, pp. 251–60. Dave Palmer in *George Washington and Benedict Arnold*, p. 174, writes of how in the aftermath of Arnold's treason "a spirit reminiscent of that of 1776 walked the land again," adding that "it is an irony among ironies that Benedict Arnold managed to do what no one else had. He revitalized the Revolution." Brian Carso in *"Whom Can We Trust Now?"* claims that Arnold's treachery became "part of the American creation myth": "Not only had Arnold betrayed his country, he had done so at the moment of creation, when its ideals and principles were taking their first gasps of breath" (p. 172). Arnold's Oct. 7, 1780, "Address to the American People," in which he claims "the private judgment of any individual citizen of this country is . . . free from all conventional restraints," is in Russell Lea's *Hero and a Spy*, pp. 544–46. According to Carso in *"Whom Can We Trust Now?,"* "The very premise of treason—an act of disloyalty against the sovereign—is modified when the system of government embraces political argument, debate, and inevitable discord among the sovereign citizenry. At what point dissension crosses over into treason is a difficult question" (p. 1).

H. James Henderson in *Party Politics in the Continental Congress* describes how a "different mood" came to Congress in the months and years after Arnold's treason in which the "era of the Party of the Revolution had passed and day of the technician had come. . . . Fiscal affairs were to be established on the pragmatic base of commercial expertise and even self-interest rather than patriotic denial" (p. 247). Irvin in *Clothed in Robes of Sovereignty*, pp. 259–60, writes of how less than two weeks after Peale's effigy of Arnold was paraded through the streets of Philadelphia, "Pennsylvanians turned Constitutionalist incumbents out of office in favor of fiscal modernizers such as Robert Morris. In Philadelphia, an erstwhile radical stronghold, Republicans enjoyed a three-to-one margin of victory. Not for four more years would the Constitutionalists mount a significant challenge to the Republican administration."

Edward Burd in an Oct. 5, 1780, letter to Jasper Yeates writes of how Peggy's "peace of mind seems . . . entirely destroyed"; he also tells of the recently seized letter she wrote to Arnold prior to his treason in which she describes "being at a concert of the ministers in which she is free in her observations upon several of the ladies there and which has given them much offense" (*Pennsylvania Magazine of History and Biography* 40:381). Edward Shippen's Oct. 5, 1780, letter to William Moore, in which he expresses his concern that his daughter's "welfare, even in another world" would be "endangered" if she returned to Arnold is cited by Clare Brandt in *Man in the Mirror*, p. 239. Concerning Peggy and Arnold's reunion in New York, Brandt writes: "Could he ever forgive her for deserting him when he needed her most? Perhaps he sympathized to some degree with her present turmoil . . . finally, one must remember the strong physical attraction between these two" (p. 239). In an Oct. 17, 1780, letter to Nathanael Greene, Thomas Paine insists that "the best thing that [Peggy Arnold] can do will be to sue for a divorce, which she is fairly entitled to as the man [her husband] is dead in law," in *PNG*, 6:404.

Joseph Plumb Martin writes of being assigned to the Corps of Sappers and Miners and describes his country as "a light-heeled wanton of a wife" in his *Narrative*, pp. 216–17. Washington writes of his intention to "make a public example of [Arnold]" in an Oct. 20, 1780, letter to Henry Lee in *WGW*, 20:223. Arnold's Oct. 7, 1780,

"Address to the American People," in which he accuses France of "fraudulently avowing an affection for the liberties of mankind," is in Lea's *Hero and a Spy,* pp. 544–46. In an Oct. 15, 1780, letter to the president of Congress, Washington writes of Arnold's address: "I am at a loss which to admire most, the confidence of Arnold in publishing, or the folly of the enemy in supposing that a production signed by so infamous a character will have any weight with the people of these states" (*WGW,* 20:189). Sergeant John Champe tells the story of how he almost succeeded in capturing Arnold in New York in Wilbur Hall's "Sergeant Champe's Adventure," pp. 339–40. Terry Golway in *Washington's General,* p. 233, cites Henry Lee's despairing assessment of conditions in the South in the fall of 1780. Nathanael Greene's preparations for assuming command of the southern army can be traced in the correspondence in *PNG,* 6:385–403.

BIBLIOGRAPHY

Abbatt, William. *The Crisis of the Revolution; Being the Story of Arnold and André.* New York: William Abbatt, 1899.

Abbott, Wilbur C. *New York in the American Revolution.* Port Washington, N.Y.: Ira Friedman, 1962.

"Account of Jonathan Loring Austin's Mission to France." In *Papers of Benjamin Franklin*, edited by William Willcox et al., 25: 234–35. New Haven, Conn.: Yale University Press, 1986.

Acland, Lady Harriet. *The Acland Journal: Lady Harriet Acland and the American War.* Edited by Jennifer D. Thorp. Winchester, U.K.: Hampshire County Council, 1994.

Adair, Douglass. *Fame and the Founding Fathers.* Indianapolis: Liberty Fund/Norton, 1974.

Adams, John. *Diary and Autobiography of John Adams.* Vols. 1–4. Edited by L. H. Butterfield et al. New York: Atheneum, 1964.

Adelson, Bruce. *William Howe: British General.* Philadelphia: Chelsea House, 2002.

Adler, Jeanne Winston. *Chainbreaker's War: A Seneca Chief Remembers the American Revolution.* Delmar, N.Y.: Black Dome Press, 2002.

Adlum, John. *Memoirs of the Life of John Adlum in the Revolutionary War.* Edited by Howard Peckham. Chicago: Caxton Club, 1968.

Alden, John Richard. *General Charles Lee: Traitor or Patriot?* Baton Rouge: Louisiana State University Press, 1951.

Alderman, Clifford L. *The Dark Eagle: The Story of Benedict Arnold.* New York: Macmillan, 1976.

Alexander, John K. "The Fort Wilson Incident of 1779: A Case Study of the Revolutionary Crowd." *WMQ*, 3rd ser., 31, no. 4 (Oct. 1974): 589–612.

Allen, Thomas. *Tories: Fighting for the King in America's First Civil War.* New York: HarperCollins, 2010.

Amory, Thomas. *John Sullivan.* Boston: Wiggin and Lunt, 1868.

Anburey, Thomas. *Travels through the Interior Parts of America. In a Series of Letters. By an Officer.* London: William Lane, 1789.

Anderson, Troyer Steele. *The Command of the Howe Brothers during the American Revolution.* 1936. Reprint, Cranbury, N.J.: Scholar's Bookshelf, 2005.

André, John. *Major André's Journal: Operations of the British Army under Lieutenant Generals Sir William Howe and Sir Henry Clinton, June 1777 to November 1778.* Tarrytown, N.Y.: William Abbatt, 1930.

———. "Particulars of the Meschianza." *Gentleman's Magazine* 48 (1778): 353–57.

Andrlik, Todd. *Reporting the Revolutionary War.* Naperville, Ill.: Sourcebooks, 2012.

Armitage, David, and Michael J. Braddick, eds. *The British Atlantic World, 1500–1800.* New York: Palgrave, 2002.

Arnold, Benedict. Account Book. MSS 106. New Haven Museum and Historical Society, New Haven, Conn.

———. "Benedict Arnold's Oath of Allegiance." May 30, 1778. War Department Collection of Revolutionary War Records, 1709–1939, NA.

———. *Daybook of Financial Transactions, 1777–1779.* Revolutionary Government Papers. Division of Archives and Manuscripts. Pennsylvania Historical and Museum Commission, Harrisburg, Pa.

———. Letter to Bartholomew Booth, May 25, 1779. *NEHGR* 35 (Apr. 1881): 154.

———. Letter to Lucy Knox, Watertown, Mar. 4, 1777. *Historical Magazine,* 2nd ser., 2 (1867): 305.

———. Letter to Robert Howe, Aug. 1780. George Washington Papers, LOC.

———. Letter to Robert Howe, Sept. 12, 1780. George Washington Papers, LOC.

———. *Proceedings of a General Court Martial for the Trial of Major General Arnold.* New York: privately printed, 1865.

Arnold, Isaac N. *The Life of Benedict Arnold: His Patriotism and His Treason.* Chicago: A. C. McClurg, 1905.

Avery, David. "A Chaplain of the American Revolution." *American Monthly Magazine* 17 (1900): 342–47.

Baack, Ben. "Forging a Nation State: The Continental Congress and the Financing of the War of American Independence." *Economic History Review,* n.s., 54, no. 4 (Nov. 2001): 639–56.

Bakeless, John. *Traitors, Turncoats, and Heroes: Espionage in the American Revolution.* New York: Da Capo Press, 1998.

Balderston, Marion, and David Syrett, eds. *The Lost War: Letters from British Officers during the American Revolution.* New York: Horizon Press, 1975.

Baldwin, Jeduthan. *The Revolutionary Journal of Col. Jeduthan Baldwin, 1775–78.* Edited by Thomas Williams Baldwin. Bangor, Maine: DeBurian, 1906.

Bamford, William. "Bamford's Diary." *Maryland Historical Magazine* 27 (Sept. 1932): 240–314.

Bancroft, George. *Joseph Reed: A Historical Essay.* New York: W. J. Widdleton, 1867.

Bangs, Isaac. *Journal of Lieutenant Isaac Bangs, April 1–July 29, 1776.* Edited by Edward Bangs. Cambridge, Mass.: John Wilson and Son, 1890.

Barbé-Marbois, François, Marquis de. *Complot d'Arnold et de Sir Henry Clinton.* Paris: Chez P. Didot, l'aîné, 1816.

———. *Our Revolutionary Forefathers: Letters of François, Marquis de Barbé-Marbois . . . 1779–1785.* Edited and translated by Eugene Parker Chase. New York: Duffield, 1929.

Barck, Dorothy C., ed. *Minutes of the Committee and the First Commission for Detecting and Defeating Conspiracies in the State of New York. Collections of the New-York Historical Society* 57–58 (1924–25).

Barck, Oscar T. *New York City during the War for Independence.* New York: Columbia University Press, 1931.

Barker, Thomas M., and Paul R. Huey. *The 1776–1777 Northern Campaigns of the*

American War for Independence and Their Sequel: Contemporary Maps of Mainly German Origin. New York: Purple Mountain Press, 2010.

Barnum, H. L. *The Spy Unmasked; or, Memoirs of Enoch Crosby, Alias Harvey Birch, the Hero of Mr. Cooper's Tale of the Neutral Ground.* New York: Harper, 1828.

Barrow, Thomas C. "American Revolution as a Colonial War for Independence." *WMQ,* 3rd ser., 25 (1968): 452–64.

Baurmeister, Carl Leopold. *Revolution in America: Confidential Letters and Journals, 1776–1784, of Adjutant General Major Baurmeister of the Hessian Forces.* Edited by Bernhard A. Uhlendorf. New Brunswick, N.J.: Rutgers University Press, 1957.

Becker, Carl. "John Jay and Peter Van Schaak." *Quarterly Journal of the New York State Historical Association* 1, no. 1 (Oct. 1919): 1–12.

Becker, John. *The Sexagenary; or, Reminiscences of the American Revolution.* Albany, N.Y.: J. Munsell, 1866.

Bellico, Russell P. *Sails and Steam in the Mountains: A Maritime and Military History of Lake George and Lake Champlain.* New York: Purple Mountain Press, 1992.

Berthoff, Rowland. *An Unsettled People: Social Order and Disorder in American History.* New York: Harper and Row, 1971.

Biddle, C. "The Case of Major André." *Memoirs of the Historical Society of Pennsylvania* 6 (1858): 319–416.

Bilharz, Joy. *Oriskany: A Place of Great Sadness—A Mohawk Valley Battlefield Ethnography.* Boston: Northeastern Region Ethnography Program, 2009.

Billias, George Athan. *General John Glover and His Marblehead Mariners.* New York: Holt, Rinehart and Winston, 1960.

———, ed. *George Washington's Generals and Opponents.* New York: William Morrow, 1969.

Bird, Harrison. *March to Saratoga: General Burgoyne and the American Campaign 1777.* New York: Oxford University Press, 1963.

———. *Navies in the Mountains: The Battles on the Waters of Lake Champlain and Lake George, 1609–1814.* New York: Oxford University Press, 1963.

Black, Jeremy. *War for America: The Fight for Independence, 1775–1783.* New York: St. Martin's, 1991.

Bliven, Bruce, Jr. *Battle for Manhattan.* New York: Holt, 1955.

Bloomfield, Joseph. *Citizen-Soldier: The Revolutionary War Journal of Joseph Bloomfield.* Edited by Mark E. Lender and James Kirby Martin. Newark: New Jersey Historical Society, 1982.

Boardman, Oliver. *Journal of Oliver Boardman of Middletown 1777. Burgoyne's Surrender.* In *Collections of the Connecticut Historical Society* 7:221–38. Hartford, 1899.

Bobrick, Benson. *Angel in the Whirlwind.* New York: Penguin, 1997.

Bodle, Wayne K. "'This Tory Labyrinth': Community, Conflict, and Military Strategy during the Valley Forge Winter." In *Friends and Neighbors: Group Life in America's First Plural Society,* edited by Michael Zuckerman, pp. 222–50. Philadelphia: Temple University Press, 1982.

———. *The Valley Forge Winter: Civilians and Soldiers in War.* University Park: Pennsylvania State University Press, 2002.

Bolton, Charles K. *The Private Soldier under Washington.* London: Kessinger, 2006.

Bonk, David. *Trenton and Princeton, 1776–1777: Washington Crosses the Delaware.* Oxford: Osprey, 2009.

Bostwick, Elisha. "A Connecticut Soldier under Washington: Elisha Bostwick's Memoirs of the First Years of the Revolution." Edited by William S. Powell. *WMQ,* 3rd ser., 6 (1949): 94–107.

Bowler, R. Arthur. *Logistics and Failure of the British Army in America.* Princeton, N.J.: Princeton University Press, 1975.

———. "Sir Guy Carleton and the Campaign of 1776 in Canada." *Canadian Historical Review* 55, no. 2 (June 1974): 131–44.

Boyd, Julian P. "Connecticut's Experiment in Expansion: The Susquehanna Company, 1753–1803." *Journal of Economic and Business History* 4 (1932): 38–69.

Boyd, Thomas A. *Mad Anthony Wayne.* New York: Scribner, 1929.

Boylan, Brian Richard. *Benedict Arnold: The Dark Eagle.* New York: Norton, 2003.

Boyle, Joseph Lee, ed. *Their Distress Is Almost Intolerable: The Elias Boudinot Letterbook, 1777–1778.* Baltimore: Heritage Books, 2002.

Boynton, Edward C. *History of West Point.* New York: Van Nostrand, 1871.

Bradford, Gamaliel. "The Wife of the Traitor." *Harper's Magazine* (June 1925): 23–33.

Braisted, Todd W. "The Black Pioneers and Others: The Military Role of Black Loyalists in the American War of Independence." In *Moving On: Black Loyalists in the Afro-Atlantic World,* edited by John W. Pulis, pp. 3–37. New York: Garland, 1999.

Brandt, Clare. *The Man in the Mirror: A Life of Benedict Arnold.* New York: Random House, 1994.

Bratten, John R. *The Gondola* Philadelphia *and the Battle of Lake Champlain.* College Station: Texas A&M University Press, 2002.

Bredenberg, Oscar E. "The American Champlain Fleet, 1775–1777." *Bulletin of the Fort Ticonderoga Museum* 12, no. 4 (Sept. 1968): 249–63.

———. "The Royal Savage." *Bulletin of the Fort Ticonderoga Museum* 12, no. 2 (Sept. 1966): 128–49.

Brewer, John. *The Sinews of Power: War, Money and the English State, 1688–1783.* Cambridge, Mass.: Harvard University Press, 1988.

Brookhiser, Richard. *Founding Father: Rediscovering George Washington.* New York: Free Press, 1997.

———, ed. *George Washington's Rules of Civility.* New York: Free Press, 1997.

Brooks, John. "Colonel Brooks and Colonel Bancroft at Saratoga." *MHS Proceedings* 3 (1855–58): 271–77.

Brooks, Noah. *Henry Knox.* New York: Putnam, 1900.

Brown, John. "Petition Addressed to the Honorable Horatio Gates, from John Brown." Albany, Dec. 1, 1776. *AA5,* 3:1158–59.

Brown, M. L. *Firearms in Colonial America.* Washington, D.C.: Smithsonian Institution, 1980.

Brown, Wallace. *The Good Americans: The Loyalists in the American Revolution.* New York: Morrow, 1969.

———. *The King's Friends: The Composition and Motives of the American Loyalist Claimants.* Providence, R.I.: Brown University Press, 1965.

Browne, Dr. J. Letter of Dec. 24, 1777. *NEHGR* 18 (1864): 34–35.

Brumwell, Stephen. *Redcoats: The British Soldier and War in the Americas, 1755–1763.* Cambridge, Mass.: Harvard University Press, 2002.

Brunhouse, Robert L. *The Counter-Revolution in Pennsylvania, 1776–1790*. Harrisburg: Pennsylvania Historical and Museum Commission, 1971.

Buel, Richard, Jr. *Dear Liberty: Connecticut's Mobilization for the Revolutionary War.* Middletown, Conn.: Wesleyan University Press, 1980.

———. *In Irons: Britain's Naval Supremacy and the American Revolutionary Economy.* New Haven, Conn.: Yale University Press, 1998.

Burd, Edward. Letter to Col. James Burd, Nov. 10, 1780. *Historical Magazine* 8 (1846): 363.

———. Letter to Jasper Yeates, Oct. 5, 1780. In "Notes and Queries." *Pennsylvania Magazine of History and Biography* 40 (1916): 380–81.

Burgoyne, Bruce, ed. *An Anonymous Hessian Diary, Probably the Diary of Lieutenant Johann Heinrich von Bardeleben of the Hesse-Cassel von Donop Regiment.* Bowie, Md.: Heritage Books, 1998.

Burgoyne, Bruce, and Marie Burgoyne, eds. *Revolutionary War Letters Written by Hessian Officers.* Westminster, Md.: Heritage Books, 2005.

Burgoyne, John. *A State of the Expedition from Canada.* London: J. Almon, 1780.

Burnett, Edmund C. *The Continental Congress.* New York: Norton, 1964.

Burr, Aaron. *Memoirs of Aaron Burr.* Edited by Matthew L. Davis. 2 vols. New York: Harper and Brothers, 1836.

Burr, William Hanford. "The Invasion of Connecticut by the British." *Connecticut Magazine* 10 (1906): 139–52.

Burrows, Edwin G., and Mike Wallace. *Gotham: A History of New York City to 1898.* New York: Oxford, 2000.

Burstein, Andrew. *Sentimental Democracy: The Evolution of America's Romantic Self-Image.* New York: Hill and Wang, 1999.

Burt, A. L. "The Quarrel between Germain and Carleton: An Inverted Story." *Canadian Historical Review* 11 (1930): 202–22.

Calhoon, Robert M. *The Loyalists in Revolutionary America, 1760–1781.* New York: Harcourt Brace, 1973.

Callahan, North. *Henry Knox: General Washington's General.* New York: Rinehart, 1958.

Calloway, Colin. *The American Revolution in Indian Country: Crisis and Diversity in Native American Communities.* New York: Cambridge University Press, 1995.

Campbell, William W. *Annals of Tryon County; or, the Border Warfare of New-York during the Revolution.* New York: J. & J. Harper, 1831.

Carbone, Gerald M. *Nathanael Greene: A Biography of the American Revolution.* New York: Palgrave Macmillan, 2009.

Carleton, Sir Guy, Capt. James Douglas, and Capt. Thomas Pringle. "An Account of the Expedition of the British Fleet on Lake Champlain . . . on the 11 and 13 of October 1776." Crown Point, 15 Oct. 1776. MS #AT7003, Box 1:95. New York State Library, Albany.

Carp, Benjamin. *Rebels Rising: Cities and the American Revolution.* New York: Oxford University Press, 2007.

Carp, E. Wayne. *To Starve the Army at Pleasure: Continental Army Administration and American Political Culture, 1775–1783.* Chapel Hill: University of North Carolina Press, 1984.

Carso, Brian F. *"Whom Can We Trust Now?": The Meaning of Treason in the United States, from the Revolution through the Civil War.* Lanham, Md.: Lexington Books, 2006.

Carson, H. L. "The Case of the Sloop 'Active.'" *Pennsylvania Magazine of History and Biography* 16 (1892): 385–98.

Case, James R. *An Account of Tryon's Raid on Danbury*. Danbury, Conn.: Danbury Printing Co., 1927.

Chadwick, Bruce. *George Washington's War: The Forging of a Revolutionary Leader and the American Presidency*. Naperville, Ill.: Sourcebooks, 2005.

Chapman, C. Richard, and Jonathan Gavrin. "Suffering: The Contributions of Persistent Pain." *Lancet* 353, no. 9171 (June 26, 1999): 2233–37.

Chastellux, Marquis de. *Travels in North America*. Translated by Basil Hall. 1828. Reprint, Carlisle, Mass.: Applewood Books, 2009.

Chernow, Ron. *Alexander Hamilton*. New York: Penguin, 2004.

———. *Washington: A Life*. New York: Penguin Press, 2010.

Chopra, Ruma. *Unnatural Rebellion: Loyalists in New York City during the Revolution*. Charlottesville: University of Virginia Press, 2011.

Christie, Ian R. *Crisis of Empire: Great Britain and the American Colonies, 1754–1783*. New York: Norton, 1966.

Clark, Jane. "Responsibility for the Failure of the Burgoyne Campaign." *American Historical Review* 35, no. 3 (Apr. 1930): 542–59.

Clark, William Bell, ed. *Naval Documents of the American Revolution*. Vols. 5–6. Washington, D.C.: U.S. Office of Naval Operations, 1964.

Clary, David A. *Adopted Son: Washington, Lafayette, and the Friendship That Saved the Revolution*. New York: Bantam Dell, 2007.

Clement, Justin, and Douglas R. Cubbison. "The British and German Artillery Gunboats at the Battle of Valcour Island." *Society for the Journal of Army Historical Studies* 85, no. 343 (Autumn 2007): 247–56.

Clinton, Henry. *The American Rebellion: Sir Henry Clinton's Narrative of His Campaigns, 1775–1782*. Edited by William B. Willcox. New Haven, Conn.: Yale University Press, 1954.

Cohen, Eliot A. *Conquered into Liberty: Two Centuries of Battles along the Great Warpath That Made the American Way of War*. New York: Free Press, 2011.

Cohen, Sheldon S. "Lieutenant John Starke and the Defense of Quebec." *Dalhousie Review* 47, no. 1 (Spring 1967): 57–64.

Cohn, Art. "An Incident Not Known to History: Squire Ferris and Benedict Arnold at Ferris Bay, October 13, 1776." *Vermont History* 55, no. 2 (Spring 1987): 97–112.

Colbrath, William. *Days of Siege: A Journal of the Siege of Fort Stanwix in 1777*. Edited by Larry Lowenthal. Fort Washington, Pa.: Eastern National, 1983.

Colles, Christopher. *A Survey of the Roads of the United States of America*. Edited by Walter Ristow. Cambridge, Mass.: Harvard University Press, 1961.

Collier, Sir George. "Admiral Sir George Collier's Observations on the Battle of Long Island." Edited by Louis Tucker. *New-York Historical Society Quarterly* 48, no. 4 (Oct. 1964): 293–305.

Collins, James F. "Whaleboat Warfare on Long Island Sound." *New York History* 25 (1944): 195–201.

Commager, Henry Steele, and Richard B. Morris, eds. *The Spirit of 'Seventy-Six: The Story of the American Revolution as Told by Its Participants*. Edison, N.J.: Castle Books, 2002.

Conway, Stephen. "British Army Officers and the American War for Independence." *WMQ*, 3rd ser., 41 (1984): 265–76.

——. *The British Isles and the War of American Independence.* New York: Oxford University Press, 2000.

——. "'The Great Mischief Complain'd Of': Reflections on the Misconduct of British Soldiers in the Revolutionary War." *WMQ,* 3rd ser., 47 (1990): 370–90.

——. "To Subdue America: British Army Officers and the Conduct of the Revolutionary War." *WMQ,* 3rd ser., 43 (1986): 381–407.

Cook, Fred J. *What Manner of Men: Forgotten Heroes of the American Revolution.* New York: William Morrow, 1959.

Corbett, Theodore. *No Turning Point: The Saratoga Campaign in Perspective.* Norman: University of Oklahoma Press, 2012.

Cornwallis, Charles. *Correspondence of Charles, First Marquis Cornwallis.* Vol. 1. Edited by Charles Ross. London: John Murray, 1859.

"Correspondence re Sept.–Oct. 1776 Campaign." *Bulletin of the Fort Ticonderoga Museum* 4, no. 25 (July 1938): 18–55.

Countryman, Edward. *A People in Revolution: The American Revolution and Political Society in New York, 1760–1790.* Baltimore: Johns Hopkins University Press, 1982.

Crary, Catherine S. "Guerrilla Activities of James DeLancey's Cowboys in Westchester County: Conventional Warfare or Self-Interested Freebooting." In *The Loyalist Americans: A Focus on Greater New York,* edited by Robert A. East and Jacob Judd, pp. 14–21. Tarrytown, N.Y.: Sleepy Hollow Restorations and the New York State American Revolution Bicentennial Commission, 1973.

——. *The Price of Loyalty: Tory Writings from the Revolutionary Era.* New York: McGraw-Hill, 1973.

——. "The Tory and the Spy: The Double Life of James Rivington." *WMQ,* 3rd ser., 16 (1959): 61–72.

Cray, Robert E., Jr. "The John André Memorial: The Politics of Memory in Gilded Age New York." *New York History* 7, no. 1 (Jan. 1996): 4–32.

——. "Major John André and the Three Captors: Class Dynamics and Revolutionary Memory Wars in the Early Republic, 1780–1831." *Journal of the Early Republic* 17, no. 3 (Autumn 1997): 371–97.

Cress, Lawrence Delbert. *Citizens in Arms: The Army and the Militia in American Society to the War of 1812.* Chapel Hill: University of North Carolina Press, 1982.

Cresswell, Nicholas. *Journal of Nicholas Cresswell.* London: Jonathan Cape, 1925.

Cubbison, Douglas R. *"The Artillery Never Gained More Honour": The British Artillery in the 1776 Valcour Island and 1777 Saratoga Campaigns.* Fleischmanns, N.Y.: Purple Mountain Press, 2007.

——. *Burgoyne and the Saratoga Campaign: His Papers.* Norman, Okla.: Arthur H. Clark, 2012.

——. *Historic Structures Report: The Redoubts of West Point.* http://www.hudsonriver valley.org/library/pdfs/articles_books_essays/historicstructuresrprt_westpt defenses_cubbison.pdf.

Cumming, John N. Letter to Dr. Nathaniel Scudder, Oct. 25, 1776. *Bulletin of the Fort Ticonderoga Museum* 5, no. 26 (Jan. 1939): 19–20.

Cunningham, John T. *The Uncertain Revolution: Washington and the Continental Army at Morristown.* West Creek, N.J.: Cormorant, 2007.

Cushman, Paul. *Richard Varick: A Forgotten Founding Father.* Amherst, Mass.: Modern Memoirs, 2010.

Custis, George W. P. *Recollections and Private Memoirs of Washington*. Washington, D.C.: William Moore, 1859.

Cutter, William. *The Life of Israel Putnam, Major-General in the Army of the American Revolution*. New York: George F. Cooledge & Brother, 1847.

Daigler, Kenneth A. *Spies, Patriots, and Traitors: American Intelligence in the Revolutionary War*. Washington, D.C.: George Washington Press, 2014.

Dann, John C., ed. *The Revolution Remembered*. Chicago: University of Chicago Press, 1980.

Darley, Stephen. *The Battle of Valcour Island: The Participants and Vessels of Benedict Arnold's 1776 Defense of Lake Champlain*. Seattle: Createspace, 2014.

———. "The Dark Eagle: How Fiction Became Historical Fact." *Early America Review* 10, no. 1 (Winter/Spring 2006). http://www.earlyamerica.com/dark-eagle -fiction-became-historical-fact/.

———. *Voices from a Wilderness Expedition: The Journals and Men of Benedict Arnold's Expedition to Quebec in 1775*. Bloomington, Ind.: AuthorHouse, 2011.

Darnton, Robert. *George Washington's False Teeth: An Unconventional Guide to the Eighteenth Century*. New York: Norton, 2003.

Daughan, George. *If by Sea: The Forging of the American Navy*. New York: Basic Books, 2008.

Davidson, Philip. *Propaganda and the American Revolution, 1763–1783*. Chapel Hill: University of North Carolina Press, 1941.

Davies, K. G., ed. *Documents of the American Revolution*. Vols. 12–17. Shannon, Ireland: Irish University Press, 1972–76.

Davies, Wallace Evan. "Privateering around Long Island during the Revolution." *New York History* 20 (1939): 283–94.

Davis, Robert P. *"Where a Man Can Go": Major General William Phillips, British Royal Artillery, 1731–1781*. Westport, Conn.: Greenwood Press, 1999.

Deane, Silas. Letter to Simeon Deane, July 27, 1779. *Pennsylvania Magazine of History and Biography* 17, no. 1 (Apr. 1893): 348–49.

Dearborn, Henry. "Narrative of the Saratoga Campaign." *Bulletin of the Fort Ticonderoga Museum* 1, no. 3 (Jan. 1929): 2–12.

———. *Revolutionary War Journals of Henry Dearborn, 1775–1783*. Edited by Lloyd A. Brown and Howard H. Peckham. New York: Da Capo Press, 1971.

Decker, Malcolm. *Benedict Arnold: Son of the Havens*. New York: Antiquarian Press, 1932.

Demarest, Thomas. "The Baylor Massacre—Some Assorted Notes and Information." Annual, *Bergen County History* (1971): 21–93.

De Pauw, Linda Grant. "Women in Combat: The Revolutionary War Experience." *Armed Forces and Society* 7 (1981): 209–26.

Desjardin, Thomas A. *Through a Howling Wilderness: Benedict Arnold's March to Quebec, 1775*. New York: St. Martin's Press, 2006.

Desmarais, Norman. "Arnold's Treason: The French Connection." 2005. Paper 28, Library Faculty and Staff Papers, Digital Commons. http://digitalcommons .providence.edu/facstaff_pubs/28.

Diamant, Lincoln. *Chaining the Hudson: The Fight for the River in the American Revolution*. New York: Fordham University Press, 2004.

Dickinson, H. T., ed. *Britain and the American Revolution*. London: Longmann, 1998.

Digby, William. *The Journal of Lieut. William Digby*. In *The British Invasion from the*

North: The Campaigns of Generals Carleton and Burgoyne from Canada, 1776–1777, edited by James Phinney Baxter, pp. 79–361. Albany, N.Y.: Joel Munsell's Sons, 1887.

Doblin, Helga, trans. *The Specht Journal: A Military Journal of the Burgoyne Campaign.* Westport, Conn.: Greenwood Press, 1995.

"Documents sur la Révolution américane." *Revue de l'Université Laval, Québec* 2, no. 4 (Dec. 1947): 344–49; 2, no. 7 (Mar. 1948): 642–48; 2, no. 8 (Apr. 1948): 742–48; 2, no. 9 (May 1948): 838–46; 2, no. 10 (June 1948): 926–43.

Douglas, William. "Letters Written during the Revolutionary War by Col. William Douglas to His Wife Covering the Period July 19, 1775, to Dec. 5, 1776." *New-York Historical Society Quarterly* 12–14 (1928–29): 149–54.

Drake, Francis Samuel. *Life and Correspondence of Henry Knox.* Cambridge, Mass.: Wilson and Son, 1873.

Drimmer, H. "Major André's Captors: The Changing Perspective of History." *Westchester Historian* 5, no. 75 (Spring 1999): 136–60.

Drinker, Elizabeth. *The Diary of Elizabeth Drinker, 1758–1795.* Vol. 1. Edited by Elaine F. Crane. Boston: Northeastern University Press, 1991.

Duffy, Christopher. *Fire and Stone: The Science of Fortress Warfare: 1660–1860.* Edison, N.J.: Castle Books, 2006.

Duncan, Captain Henry. "Journals." In *The Naval Miscellany,* edited by John K. Laughton. *Publications of the Navy Records Society* 20, no. 1 (1902): 105–219.

Dwight, Timothy. *Travels in New England and New York.* Vol. 3. Cambridge, Mass.: Harvard University Press, 1969.

Dwyer, William. *The Day Is Ours: November 1776–January 1777: An Inside View of the Battles of Trenton and Princeton.* New York: Viking, 1983.

Dykman, J. "The Last Twelve Days of Major André." *Magazine of American History* 21, no. 6 (May–July 1889): 493–98; 22, no. 6 (July–Dec. 1889): 49–57.

Ekirch, Arthur A. "The Idea of a Citizen Army." *Military Affairs* 17, no. 1 (Spring 1953): 30–36.

Ellis, Franklin, and Samuel Evans. *History of Lancaster County, Pennsylvania.* Philadelphia: Everts and Peck, 1893.

Ellis, Joseph J. *His Excellency George Washington.* New York: Vintage, 2005.

———. *Revolutionary Summer: The Birth of American Independence.* New York: Knopf, 2013.

Elting, J. R. *The Battles of Saratoga.* Monmouth Beach, N.J.: Philip Freneau, 1977.

Endy, Melvin B., Jr. "Just War, Holy War, and Millennialism in Revolutionary America." *WMQ,* 3rd ser., 42 (1985): 3–25.

Enys, John. *The American Journals of Lt. John Enys.* Edited by Elizabeth Cometti. Syracuse, N.Y.: Syracuse University Press, 1976.

Eulogies and Orations on the Life and Death of General George Washington. Boston: Manning and Loring, 1800.

Eustis, William. Letter to David Townsend, June 1776. *NEHGR* 23 (1869): 205–9.

Evelyn, Captain W. Glanville. *Memoir and Letters.* Edited by G. D. Scull. Oxford: James Parker, 1879.

Ewald, Johann. *Diary of the American War: A Hessian Journal.* Edited by Joseph Tustin. New Haven, Conn.: Yale University Press, 1979.

Fabing, Howard D. "On Going Berserk: A Neurochemical Inquiry." *Scientific Monthly* 83 (Nov. 1956): 232–37.

Ferguson, E. James. *The Power of the Purse: A History of American Public Finance, 1775–1790.* Chapel Hill: University of North Carolina Press, 1961.

Ferling, John. *The Ascent of George Washington: The Hidden Political Genius of an American Icon.* New York: Bloomsbury Press, 2009.

———. *First of Men: A Life of George Washington.* New York: Oxford University Press, 2010.

Field, Thomas. *Battle of Long Island.* Brooklyn: Long Island Historical Society, 1869.

Fine, Gary Alan. *Difficult Reputations: Collective Memories of the Evil, Inept, and Controversial.* Chicago: University of Chicago Press, 2001.

Fischer, David Hackett. *Liberty and Freedom: A Visual History of America's Founding Ideas.* New York: Oxford University Press, 2005.

———. *Washington's Crossing.* New York: Oxford University Press, 2006.

Fischer, Joseph R. *A Well-Executed Failure: The Sullivan Campaign against the Iroquois, July–September 1779.* Columbia: University of South Carolina Press, 1997.

Fisher, Darlene Emmert. "Social Life in Philadelphia during the British Occupation." *Pennsylvania History* 37, no. 3 (July 1970): 237–60.

Fitch, Jabez. *The New York Diary of Lieutenant Jabez Fitch of the 17th (Connecticut) Regiment from August 2, 1776, to December 15, 1777.* Edited by W. H. Sabine. New York: Colburn and Tegg, 1954.

Fithian, Philip Vickers. *Journal, 1775–1776, Written on the Virginia-Pennsylvania Frontier and in the Army around New York.* Edited by Robert Greenhalgh Albion and Leonidas Dodson. Princeton, N.J.: Princeton University Press, 1934.

Flavell, Julie, and Stephen Conway, eds. *When Britain and America Go to War: The Impact of War and Warfare in Anglo-America.* Gainesville: University Press of Florida, 2004.

Fleming, Thomas. *1776: Year of Illusions.* New York: Norton, 1975.

———. *Washington's Secret War: The Hidden History of Valley Forge.* New York: HarperCollins/Smithsonian Books, 2006.

Flexner, James Thomas. *George Washington in the American Revolution, 1775–1783.* Boston: Little, Brown, 1967.

———. *The Traitor and the Spy: Benedict Arnold and John André.* Syracuse, N.Y.: Syracuse University Press, 1991.

Fonblanque, Edward Barrington de. *Political and Military Episodes in the Latter Half of the Eighteenth Century. Derived from the Life and Correspondence of the Right Hon. John Burgoyne, General, Statesman, Dramatist.* London: Macmillan, 1876.

Foner, Eric. *Tom Paine and Revolutionary America.* New York: Oxford University Press, 1976.

Ford, Paul Leicester. "Henry Knox—Bookseller." *MHS Proceedings* 6 (1927–28): 227–303.

———. "Lord Howe's Commission to Pacify the Colonies." *Atlantic Monthly* 77 (1896): 758.

———. "Stray Leaves from a Traitor's Life." *Cosmopolitan Magazine* 28, no. 6 (Apr. 1900): 693–705.

Ford, Worthington Chauncey, et al., eds. *Journals of the Continental Congress, 1774–1789.* 34 vols. Washington, D.C.: U.S. Government Printing Office, 1904–37. http://lcweb2.loc.gov/ammem/amlaw/lwjc.html.

Forman, Sidney. *West Point: A History of the United States Military Academy.* New York: Columbia University Press, 1950.

Fortescue, John E. *The War of Independence: The British Army in North America, 1775–1783*. Mechanicsburg, Pa.: Stackpole Books, 2001.

Fowler, William M. *Rebels under Sail*. New York: Scribner's, 1976.

Freeman, Douglas Southall. *George Washington: A Biography*. 7 vols. New York: Scribner's, 1948–57.

Freeman, Joanne B. *Affairs of Honor: National Politics in the New Republic*. New Haven, Conn.: Yale University Press, 2001.

French, Alvah P. *History of Westchester County, New York*. Vol. 1. New York: Lewis Historical Publishing Company, 1925.

Frey, Sylvia. *Water from the Rock: Black Resistance in a Revolutionary Age*. Princeton, N.J.: Princeton University Press, 1991.

Furneaux, Rupert. *The Battle of Saratoga*. New York: Stein and Day, 1971.

Gaines, James R. *For Liberty and Glory: Washington, Lafayette, and Their Revolutions*. New York: Norton, 2007.

Gale, R. R. *"A Soldier-Like Way": The Material Culture of the British Infantry, 1751–1768*. Elk River, Minn.: Track of the Wolf, 2007.

Gérard, Conrad Alexandre. *Despatches and Instructions of Conrad Alexandre Gérard, 1778–1780*. Edited by John Meng. Baltimore: Johns Hopkins Press, 1939.

Gerlach, Don R. *Proud Patriot: Philip Schuyler and the War of Independence, 1775–1783*. Syracuse, N.Y.: Syracuse University Press, 1987.

Glanville, William Evelyn. *Memoir and Letters*. 1879. Reprint, Bedford, Mass.: Applewood Books, 2010.

Glatthaar, Joseph, and James Kirby Martin. *Forgotten Allies: The Oneida Indians and the American Revolution*. New York: Hill and Wang, 2006.

Glover, Michael. *Burgoyne in Canada and America: Scapegoat for a System*. New York: Atheneum, 1976.

Godfrey, Carlos E. *The Commander-in-Chief's Guard, Revolutionary War*. Washington, D.C.: Stevenson-Smith, 1904.

Golway, Terry. *Washington's General: Nathanael Greene and the Triumph of the American Revolution*. New York: Henry Holt, 2005.

Gooding, S. James. *An Introduction to British Artillery in North America*. Bloomfield, Ontario: Museum Restoration Service, 1980.

Gottschalk, Louis R. *Lafayette Comes to America*. Chicago: University of Chicago Press, 1935.

———. *Lafayette Joins the American Army*. Chicago: University of Chicago Press, 1937.

———, ed. *Letters of Lafayette to Washington*. N.p.: privately printed by Helen Fahnestock Hubbard, 1944.

Graham, Robert E. "The Taverns of Colonial Philadelphia." *Transactions of the American Philosophical Society*, n.s., 43, no. 1 (1953): 318–25.

Graymont, Barbara. *The Iroquois in the American Revolution*. Syracuse, N.Y.: Syracuse University Press, 1972.

Greene, George Washington. *The Life of Nathanael Greene*. New York: Putnam, 1867.

Greene, Nathanael. *Papers of General Nathanael Greene*. Edited by Richard Showman and Dennis M. Conrad. 13 vols. Chapel Hill: University of North Carolina Press, 1976–2005.

Greenwood, John. *The Revolutionary Services of John Greenwood of Boston and New York, 1775–1783*. Edited by Isaac J. Greenwood. New York: De Vinne Press, 1922.

Griswold, Rufus Wilmot, ed. *Washington and the Generals of the American Revolution.* 2 vols. Philadelphia: Carey and Hart, 1847.

Gruber, Ira. *The Howe Brothers and the American Revolution.* New York: Norton, 1975.

Hadden, Lieutenant James M. *Hadden's Journal and Orderly Books.* Edited by H. Rogers. Albany, N.Y.: Joel Munsell's Sons, 1884.

Hagist, Don. *British Soldiers, American War: Voices of the American Revolution.* Philadelphia: Westholme, 2012.

Hall, Charles S. *Benjamin Tallmadge: Revolutionary Soldier and American Businessman.* New York: Columbia University Press, 1943.

Hall, Wilbur C. "Sergeant Champe's Adventure." *WMQ,* 2nd ser., 18, no. 3 (July 1938): 322–42.

Hamilton, Alexander. Letter from a Gentleman at Camp. *Pennsylvania Packet,* Oct. 14 and 17, 1780.

———. *The Papers of Alexander Hamilton.* Vol. 2. Edited by Harold C. Syrett. New York: Columbia University Press, 1961.

Hamilton, Edward P. *Fort Ticonderoga: Key to a Continent.* Ticonderoga, N.Y.: Fort Ticonderoga, 1995.

Harcourt, Diana. "Body Image and Disfigurement: Issues and Interventions." *Body Image* 1 (2004): 83–97.

Haslewood, Captain William. "A Journal of a British Officer during the American Revolution." *Mississippi Valley Historical Review* 7 (June 1920–Mar. 1921): 51–58.

Hatch, Robert McConnell. *Major John André: A Gallant in Spy's Clothing.* Boston: Houghton Mifflin, 1986.

Hay, Thomas Robson. *The Admirable Trumpeter. A Biography of General James Wilkinson.* Garden City, N.Y.: Doubleday, Doran, 1941.

Headley, J. T. *Washington and His Generals.* 1813. Reprint, Yorklyn, Del.: Academy Honor Press, 1998.

Heath, William. *Memoirs of Major-General Heath.* Boston: Thomas and Andres, 1798.

Henderson, H. James. "Congressional Factionalism and the Attempt to Recall Benjamin Franklin." *WMQ,* 3rd ser., 27 (1970): 246–67.

———. "Constitutionalists and Republicans in the Continental Congress, 1778–86." *Pennsylvania History* 36 (1969): 119–44.

———. *Party Politics in the Continental Congress.* New York: McGraw-Hill, 1974.

Henriques, Peter. *Realistic Visionary: A Portrait of George Washington.* Charlottesville: University of Virginia Press, 2008.

Herrera, Ricardo A. "Self-Governance and the American Citizen as Soldier, 1775–1861." *Journal of Military History* 65, no. 1 (Jan. 2001): 21–52.

Hibbert, Christopher. *Redcoats and Rebels: The American Revolution through British Eyes.* New York: Norton, 2002.

Higginbotham, Don. *Daniel Morgan: Revolutionary Rifleman.* Chapel Hill: University of North Carolina Press, 1961.

———. "The Early American Way of War: Reconnaissance and Appraisal." *WMQ,* 3rd ser., 44 (Apr. 1987): 230–73.

———. *George Washington: Uniting a Nation.* Lanham, Md.: Rowman and Littlefield, 2004.

———, ed. *Reconsiderations on the Revolutionary War: Selected Essays.* Westport, Conn.: Greenwood Press, 1978.

——. *The War of American Independence: Military Attitudes, Policies, and Practice, 1763–1789*. Boston: Northeastern University Press, 1983.

——. *Washington and the American Military Tradition*. Athens: University of Georgia Press, 1985.

Hill, George Canning. *Benedict Arnold*. Philadelphia: J. B. Lippincott, 1865.

Hodges, Graham Russell. *Root and Branch: African Americans in New York and East Jersey, 1613–1863*. Chapel Hill: University of North Carolina Press, 1999.

Hoffman, Ronald, and Peter J. Albert. *Arms and Independence: The Military Character of the American Revolution*. Charlottesville: University of Virginia Press, 1984.

——, eds. *The Transforming Hand of Revolution*. Charlottesville: University Press of Virginia, 1995.

——, eds. *Women in the Age of the American Revolution*. Charlottesville: University Press of Virginia, 1992.

Houlding, J. A., and G. Kenneth Yates. "Corporal Fox's Memoir of Service, 1766–1783: Quebec, Saratoga, and the Convention Army." *Journal of the Society for Army Historical Research* 68, no. 275 (Autumn 1990): 146–68.

Howe, Archibald. *Colonel John Brown, of Pittsfield, Massachusetts, the Brave Accuser of Benedict Arnold*. Boston: W. B. Clarke, 1908.

Howland, John. *The Life and Recollections of John Howland*. Edited by Edwin M. Stone. Providence, R.I.: G. H. Whitney, 1857.

Howson, Gerald. *Burgoyne of Saratoga*. New York: Times Books, 1979.

Huber, Patricia. *Major Philip Ulmer: Hero of the American Revolution*. Charleston, S.C.: History Press, 2014.

Huddleston, F. J. *Gentleman Johnny Burgoyne: Misadventures of an English General in the Revolution*. Garden City, N.Y.: Garden City Publishing, 1927.

Hufeland, Otto. *Westchester County during the American Revolution, 1775–1783*. Harrison, N.Y.: Harbor Hill Books, 1974.

Hughes, J. M. "Notes Relative to the Campaign against Burgoyne." *MHS Proceedings* 3 (1855–58): 278–80.

Huntington, Ebenezer. *Letters Written by Ebenezer Huntington during the American Revolution*. New York: Charles Heartman, 1914.

Husted, Nathaniel C. *Centennial Souvenir of the Monument Association of the Capture of André*. New York: privately printed, 1880.

Ireland, Owen S. "The Ethnic-Religious Dimension of Pennsylvania Politics, 1778–1779." *WMQ*, 3rd ser., 18 (Jan. 1961): 35–53.

——. *Religion, Ethnicity, and Politics: Ratifying the Constitution in Pennsylvania*. University Park: Pennsylvania State University Press, 1995.

Irvin, Benjamin H. *Clothed in Robes of Sovereignty: The Continental Congress and the People Out of Doors*. New York: Oxford University Press, 2011.

Jackson, John W. *The Pennsylvania Navy, 1775–1781*. New Brunswick, N.J.: Rutgers University Press, 1974.

——. *With the British Army in Philadelphia, 1777–1778*. San Rafael, Calif.: Presidio Press, 1979.

Jacob, Mark, and Stephen H. Case. *Treacherous Beauty: Peggy Shippen, the Woman behind Benedict Arnold's Plot to Betray America*. Guilford, Conn.: Lyons Press, 2012.

Jacobs, James Ripley. *Tarnished Warrior: Major-General James Wilkinson*. New York: Macmillan, 1938.

Jameson, J. Franklin. *The American Revolution Considered as a Social Movement.* Princeton, N.J.: Princeton University Press, 1940.

Jellison, Richard M., ed. *Society, Freedom, and Conscience: The American Revolution in Virginia, Massachusetts, and New York.* New York: Norton, 1976.

Johansen, Bruce. *Forgotten Founders: How the American Indian Helped Shape Democracy.* Boston: Harvard Common Press, 1982.

Johnson, Clifton. *The Picturesque Hudson.* New York: Macmillan, 1915.

Johnson, James, et al., eds. *Key to the Northern Country: The Hudson River Valley in the American Revolution.* Albany: State University of New York Press, 2013.

Johnston, Henry P. *The Battle of Harlem Heights, September 16, 1776.* New York: Macmillan, 1897.

———. *The Campaign of 1776 around New York.* 1878. Reprint, Cranberry, N.J.: Scholar's Bookshelf, 2005.

———. *Nathan Hale, 1776.* New Haven, Conn.: Yale University Press, 1914.

———. *The Storming of Stony Point on the Hudson, Midnight, July 15, 1779.* 1900. Reprint, New York: Da Capo Press, 1971.

Jones, John, M.D. *Plain Concise Practical Remarks, on the Treatment of Wounds and Fractures. . . .* Philadelphia: Robert Bell, 1776.

Jones, Thomas. *History of New York during the Revolutionary War.* New York: NYHS, 1879.

"A Journal of the Carleton and Burgoyne Campaigns." *Bulletin of the Fort Ticonderoga Museum* 11, no. 5 (Dec. 1964): 234–69 (Apr. 20, 1776–June 22, 1777); 11, no. 6 (Sept. 1965): 307–35 (June 24, 1777–Aug. 17, 1777).

Kaplan, Roger. "The Hidden War: British Intelligence Operations during the American Revolution." *WMQ,* 3rd ser., 47, no. 1 (1990): 115–38.

Keegan, John. *Fields of Battle: The Wars for North America.* New York: Vintage, 1997.

Kelly, Alfred, et al. *Leadership in the American Revolution.* Washington, D.C.: Library of Congress, 1974.

Kelsay, Isabel T. *Joseph Brant: Man of Two Worlds.* Syracuse, N.Y.: Syracuse University Press, 1984.

Kemble, Lieutenant Colonel Stephen. *Journals of Lieutenant-Colonel Stephen Kemble, 1773–1789.* Boston: Gregg Press, 1972.

Kennett, Lee. *The French Forces in America, 1780–1783.* Westport, Conn.: Greenwood Press, 1977.

Kerber, Linda. *Women of the Republic: Intellect and Ideology in Revolutionary America.* New York: Norton, 1986.

Kerr, Lowell. "Benedict Arnold and the Warrens." *Americana* 30, no. 2 (Apr. 1936): 324–34.

Ketchum, Richard M. *Divided Loyalties: How the American Revolution Came to New York.* New York: Henry Holt, 2002.

———. *Saratoga: Turning Point of America's Revolutionary War.* New York: Holt, 1999.

———. *The Winter Soldiers.* Garden City, N.Y.: Doubleday, 1973.

Kilmeade, Brian, and Don Yaeger. *George Washington's Secret Six: The Spy Ring That Saved the American Revolution.* New York: Sentinel, 2013.

Kim, Sung Bok. "The Limits of Politicization in the American Revolution: The Experience of Westchester County, New York." *Journal of American History* 80 (1993): 868–89.

King, Lester. *The Medical World of the Eighteenth Century*. Chicago: University of Chicago Press, 1958.

Knollenberg, Bernhard, ed. "Correspondence of John Adams and Horatio Gates." *MHS Proceedings* 67 (Oct. 1941–May 1944): 135–51.

———. *Washington and the Revolution, a Reappraisal: Gates, Conway, and the Continental Congress*. New York: Macmillan, 1940.

Knott, Sara. *Sensibility and the American Revolution*. Chapel Hill: University of North Carolina Press, 2009.

Knox, Dudley W. *The Naval Genius of George Washington*. Boston: Houghton Mifflin, 1932.

Koke, Richard J. *Accomplice in Treason: Joshua Hett Smith and the Arnold Conspiracy*. New York: NYHS, 1973.

Krueger, John W. "Troop Life at the Champlain Valley Forts during the American Revolution." *Bulletin of the Fort Ticonderoga Museum* 14, no. 3 (Summer 1982): 158–64; 14, no. 5 (Summer 1984): 277–310.

Kurtz, Stephen G., and James H. Hutson, eds. *Essays on the American Revolution*. Chapel Hill: University of North Carolina Press, 1973.

Kwasny, Mark V. *Washington's Partisan War, 1775–1783*. Kent, Ohio: Kent State University Press, 1996.

Labaree, Leonard W. *Conservatism in Early American History*. New York: New York University Press, 1948.

Lafayette, Marie Joseph Paul Yves Roch Gilbert du Motier. *Lafayette in the Age of the American Revolution: Selected Letters and Papers, 1776–1790*. Edited by Stanley J. Idzerda et al. 5 vols. Ithaca, N.Y.: Cornell University Press, 1977–83.

Lamb, John. *Memoir of the Life and Times of General John Lamb*. Edited by Isaac Leake. Albany, N.Y.: Munsell, 1850.

Lamb, Roger. *An Original and Authentic Journal of Occurrences during the Late American War: From Its Commencement to the Year 1783*. Dublin: Wilkinson and Courtney, 1809.

Laramie, Michael. *By Wind and Iron: Naval Campaigns in the Champlain Valley, 1665–1815*. Yardley, Pa.: Westholme, 2015.

Laurens, John. *The Army Correspondence of Colonel John Laurens in the Years 1777–8*. With a Memoir by William Gilmore Simms. New York: Bradford Club, 1867.

Lea, Russell M. *A Hero and a Spy: The Revolutionary War Correspondence of Benedict Arnold*. Westminster, Md.: Heritage Books, 2008.

Lee, Charles. *Charles Lee Papers*. Vols. 2–4. New York: NYHS, 1872–74.

Lee, Richard Henry. *Life of Arthur Lee*. Boston: Wells and Lilly, 1829.

Lefkowitz, Arthur S. *The American Submarine* Turtle. Gretna, La.: Pelican, 2012.

———. *The Long Retreat: The Calamitous American Defense of New Jersey, 1776*. Metuchen, N.J.: Upland Press, 1998.

Leiby, Adrian C. *The Revolutionary War in the Hackensack Valley: The Jersey Dutch and the Neutral Ground, 1775–1783*. New Brunswick, N.J.: Rutgers University Press, 1962.

Lengel, Edward G. *General George Washington: A Military Life*. New York: Random House, 2007.

———. *This Glorious Struggle: George Washington's Revolutionary War Letters*. New York: HarperCollins, 2008.

Lewis, Tom. *The Hudson River: A History*. New Haven, Conn.: Yale University Press, 2005.

Linklater, Andro. *An Artist in Treason: The Extraordinary Double Life of General James Wilkinson.* New York: Walker, 2009.

"A List of Ships in the American and British Fleets. . . ." *Bulletin of the Fort Ticonderoga Museum* 1, no. 4 (July 1928): 13.

Livingston, William Farrand. *Israel Putnam: Pioneer, Ranger, and Major-General, 1718–1790.* New York: Putnam's, 1901.

Lockhart, Paul Douglas. *The Drillmaster of Valley Forge: The Baron de Steuben and the Making of the American Army.* New York: HarperCollins, 2008.

Logusz, Michael. *With Musket and Tomahawk: The Saratoga Campaign and the Wilderness War of 1777.* Havertown, Pa.: Casemate, 2010

Longmore, Paul. *The Invention of George Washington.* Charlottesville: University of Virginia Press, 1999.

Lossing, Benson John. *The Pictorial Field-Book of the Revolution.* 2 vols. Harper & Brothers, 1855.

———. "The Treason of Benedict Arnold." *Harper's New Monthly Magazine* 3 (1851): 451–61.

Lowenthal, Larry. *Hell on the East River: British Prison Ships in the American Revolution.* Fleischmanns, N.Y.: Purple Mountain Press, 2009.

Ludlum, David M. *Early American Winters, 1604–1820.* Boston: American Meteorological Association, 1966.

Lundin, Leonard. *Cockpit of the Revolution: The War for Independence in New Jersey.* Princeton, N.J.: Princeton University Press, 1940.

Lunt, J. *John Burgoyne of Saratoga.* London: Macdonald and Jane's, 1976.

Luzader, John F. *Decision on the Hudson: The Battles of Saratoga.* Fort Washington, Pa.: Eastern National, 2002.

———. *Fort Stanwix: Construction and Military History.* Fort Washington, Pa.: Eastern National, 2010.

———. *Saratoga: A Military History of the Decisive Campaign of the American Revolution.* New York: Savas Beatie, 2010.

Lydenberg, Harry Miller, ed. *Archibald Robertson: His Diaries and Sketches in America, 1762–1780.* New York: NYPL and Arno Press, 1971.

McAfee, Michael L. "Artillery of the American Revolution, 1775–1783." Washington, D.C.: American Defense Preparedness Association, 1974.

McBurney, Christian. *The Rhode Island Campaign: The First French and American Operation in the Revolutionary War.* Philadelphia: Westholme, 2011.

McCullough, David. *John Adams.* New York: Simon and Schuster, 2001.

———. *1776.* New York: Simon and Schuster, 2005.

McDevitt, Robert. *Connecticut Attacked, a British Viewpoint: Tryon's Raid on Danbury.* Chester, Conn.: Pequot Press, 1974.

McDougall, Walter A. *Freedom Just Around the Corner: A New American History, 1585–1828.* New York: Perennial, 2004.

McGuire, Thomas. *The Philadelphia Campaign.* Vols. 1–2. Mechanicsburg, Pa.: Stackpole Books, 2006–7.

———. *Stop the Revolution: America in the Summer of Independence and the Conference for Peace.* Mechanicsburg, Pa.: Stackpole Books, 2011.

Mackesy, Piers. *The War for America, 1775–1783.* Lincoln: University of Nebraska Press, 1992.

McLean, David. *Timothy Pickering and the Age of the American Revolution*. New York: Arno Press, 1982.

MacMillan, Margaret Burnham. *The War Governors in the American Revolution*. New York: Columbia University Press, 1943.

Maguire, J. Robert. "Dr. Robert Knox's Account of the Battle of Valcour, October 11–13, 1776." *Vermont History* 46, no. 3 (Summer 1978): 141–50.

Mahan, Alfred Thayer. *The Influence of Sea Power upon History, 1660–1783*. Boston: Little, Brown, 1918.

———. *The Major Operations of the Navies in the War of American Independence*. Cambridge, Mass.: Harvard University Press, 1913.

———. "The Naval Campaign of 1776 on Lake Champlain." *Scribner's Magazine* 23 (Feb. 1898): 147–60.

Manders, Eric. *The Battle of Long Island*. Monmouth, N.J.: Freneau Press, 1978.

Manifesto and Proclamation of the Commissioners, October 8, 1778. In *Proceedings of the British Commissioners at Philadelphia, 1778–9: Partly in Ferguson's Hand*, edited by Yasuo Amoh, Darren Lingley, and Hiro Aoki, pp. 146–47. Kyoto: Kakenhi Supplemental Project Research Report, Kyoto University, 2007.

Manucy, Albert. *Artillery through the Ages*. Washington, D.C.: U.S. Government Printing Office, 1955.

Martin, James Kirby. *Benedict Arnold: Revolutionary Hero; An American Warrior Reconsidered*. New York: New York University Press, 1997.

———. "Benedict Arnold's Treason as Political Protest." *Parameters* 11 (1981): 63–74.

Martin, James Kirby, and Mark Edward Lender. *A Respectable Army: The Military Origins of the Republic, 1763–1789*. Wheeling, Ill.: Harlan Davidson, 2006.

Martin, Joseph Plumb. *Ordinary Courage: The Revolutionary War Adventures of Joseph Plumb Martin*. Edited by James Kirby Martin. Chichester, West Sussex, U.K.: Wiley-Blackwell, 2012.

Massey, Gregory. *John Laurens and the American Revolution*. Columbia: University of South Carolina Press, 2000.

Mather, F. G. *The Refugees of 1776 from Long Island to Connecticut*. Albany, N.Y.: J. B. Lyon, 1913.

Mattern, David B. *Benjamin Lincoln and the American Revolution*. Columbia: University of South Carolina Press, 1995.

Mayer, Holly. *Belonging to the Army: Camp Followers and Community during the American Revolution*. Columbia: University of South Carolina Press, 1999.

Mazzagetti, Dominick. *Charles Lee: Self before Country*. New Brunswick, N.J.: Rutgers University Press, 2013.

Meier, Louis A. *The Healing of an Army, 1777–1778*. Norristown, Pa.: Historical Society of Montgomery County, 1991.

Merrill, Lindsay. *The New England Gun*. New Haven, Conn.: Yale University Press, 1975.

Messer, Peter C. "'A Species of Treason and Not the Least Dangerous Kind': The Treason Trials of Abraham Carlisle and John Roberts." *Pennsylvania Magazine of History and Biography* 123, no. 4 (Oct. 1999): 303–32.

Middlebrook, L. F. *Maritime Connecticut during the American Revolution*. Salem, Mass.: Essex Institute, 1925.

Middlekauff, Robert. *The Glorious Cause: The American Revolution, 1763–1789*. New York: Oxford University Press, 2005.

————. "Why Men Fought in the American Revolution." *Huntington Library Quarterly* 43 (Spring 1980): 143–44, 148.

Millar, John F. *American Ships of the Colonial and Revolutionary Periods*. New York: Norton, 1978.

Miller, Lillian B., ed. *The Peale Family: Creation of a Legacy, 1770–1870*. New York: Abbeville Press, 1996.

Miller, Nathan. *Sea of Glory: The Continental Navy Fights for Independence, 1775–1783*. New York: McKay, 1974.

Millis, Wade. "A Spy under the Common Law of War." *American Bar Association Journal* 11, no. 183 (1925): 183–88.

Mintz, Max M. *The Generals of Saratoga: John Burgoyne and Horatio Gates*. New Haven, Conn.: Yale University Press, 1990.

————. *Gouverneur Morris and the American Revolution*. Norman: University of Oklahoma Press, 1970.

Minutes of a Court of Inquiry upon the Case of Major John André. Albany, N.Y.: J. Munsell, 1865.

Mishoff, Willard O. "Business in Philadelphia during the British Occupation, 1777–1778." *Pennsylvania Magazine of History and Biography* 61, no. 2 (Apr. 1937): 165–81.

Mitchell, Broadus. *The Price of Independence: A Realistic View of the American Revolution*. New York: Oxford University Press, 1974.

Montresor, Captain John. *The Montresor Journals*. Edited by G. D. Scull. *Collections of the New-York Historical Society for the Year 1881*. New York, 1882.

Moore, Frank. *Diary of the American Revolution*. Vols. 1–2. New York: Scribner, 1859.

————. *Songs and Ballads of the American Revolution*. New York: D. Appleton, 1855.

Moore, Warren. *Weapons of the American Revolution and Accoutrements*. New York: Promontory Press, 1967.

Morgan, Edmund S. *American Heroes: Profiles of Men and Women Who Shaped Early America*. New York: Norton, 2009.

————. *The Birth of the Republic 1763–1789*. 3rd ed. Chicago: University of Chicago Press, 1992.

————. *Inventing the People: The Rise of Popular Sovereignty in England and America*. New York: Norton, 1988.

Morpurgo, J. E. *Treason at West Point: The Arnold-André Conspiracy*. New York: Mason/Charter, 1975.

Morris, Margaret. *Her Journal with Biographical Sketches and Notes*. Edited by John W. Jackson. 1836. Reprint, New York: Arno Press, 1969.

Morrissey, Brendan. *Saratoga 1777: Turning Point of a Revolution*. Oxford: Osprey, 2000.

Morton, Doris Begor. *Philip Skene of Skenesborough*. Granville, N.Y.: Grastorf Press, 1959.

Muenchhausen, Friedrich von. *At General Howe's Side, 1776–1778: The Diary of General William Howe's Aide de Camp, Captain Friedrich von Muenchhausen*. Translated by Ernest Kipping. Monmouth Beach, N.J.: Freneau Press, 1974.

Muller, John. *The Attack and Defense of Fortified Places, 1757*. Edited by David Manthey. Woodbridge, Va.: Invisible College Press, 2004.

Murdoch, David. H., ed. *Rebellion in America: A Contemporary British Viewpoint, 1769–1783*. Santa Barbara, Calif.: Clio Books, 1979.

Murdock, Richard K. "Benedict Arnold and the Wonders of the *Charming Nancy*." *Pennsylvania Magazine of History and Biography* 84 (1960): 22–26.

Murphy, Jim. *The Real Benedict Arnold*. New York: Houghton Mifflin, 2007.

Murray, Eleanor M. "The American Fleet on Lake Champlain, 1776." *Bulletin of the Fort Ticonderoga Museum* 5, no. 5–6 (July 1940): 138–39.

Nagy, John. *Invisible Ink: Spycraft of the American Revolution*. Yardley, Pa.: Westholme, 2011.

———. *Mutinies in the Ranks: Mutinies of the American Revolution*. Yardley, Pa.: Westholme, 2007.

———. *Spies in the Continental Capital: Espionage across Pennsylvania during the American Revolution*. Yardley, Pa.: Westholme, 2011.

Nash, Gary. *The Unknown American Revolution*. New York: Penguin, 2006.

Nebanzahl, Kenneth, and Don Higginbotham. *Atlas of the American Revolution*. Chicago: Rand McNally, 1974.

Neilson, Charles. *Burgoyne's Campaigns*. Albany: New York State Library, 1841.

Neimeyer, Charles Patrick. *America Goes to War: A Social History of the Continental Army*. New York: New York University Press, 1996.

Nelson, Craig. *Thomas Paine: Enlightenment, Revolution, and the Birth of Modern Nations*. New York: Penguin, 2006.

Nelson, Eric. *The Royalist Revolution*. Cambridge, Mass.: Harvard University Press, 2014.

Nelson, James. *Benedict Arnold's Navy: The Ragtag Fleet That Lost the Battle for Lake Champlain but Won the American Revolution*. New York: McGraw-Hill, 2007.

———. *George Washington's Great Gamble and the Sea Battle That Won the American Revolution*. New York: McGraw-Hill, 2010.

———. *George Washington's Secret Navy: How the American Revolution Went to Sea*. New York: McGraw-Hill, 2008.

Nelson, Paul David. *Anthony Wayne: Soldier of the Early Republic*. Bloomington: Indiana University Press, 1985.

———. "Citizen Soldiers or Regulars: The Views of American General Officers on the Military Establishment, 1775–1781." *Military Affairs* 43, no. 3 (Oct. 1979): 126–32.

———. *Francis Rawdon-Hastings, Marquess of Hastings: Soldier, Peer of the Realm, Governor-General of India*. Madison, N.J.: Farleigh Dickinson University Press, 2005.

———. "The Gates-Arnold Quarrel, September 1777." *New-York Historical Society Quarterly* 55 (July 1971): 235–52.

———. *General Guy Carleton, Lord Dorchester: Soldier-Statesman of Early British Canada*. Madison, N.J.: Fairleigh Dickinson University Press, 2000.

———. *General Horatio Gates: A Biography*. Baton Rouge: Louisiana State University Press, 1976.

———. "Guy Carleton versus Benedict Arnold: The Campaign of 1776 in Canada and on Lake Champlain." *New York History* 57 (July 1976): 339–66.

———. "Legacy of Controversy: Gates, Schuyler, and Arnold at Saratoga, 1777." *Military Affairs* 37, no. 2 (Autumn 1953): 41–47.

———. *William Tryon and the Course of Empire*. Chapel Hill: University of North Carolina Press, 1990.

Nelson, William. *The American Tory*. New York: Oxford University Press, 1961.

Nester, William. *The Frontier War for American Independence*. Mechanicsburg, Pa.: Stackpole Books, 2004.

Nickerson, Hoffman. "New York in the Strategy of the Revolution." In *History of the State of New York*, edited by Alexander C. Flick, 4:78–83. New York: Columbia University Press, 1934.

———. *The Turning Point of the Revolution; or, Burgoyne in America*. 1928. Reprint, Cranbury, N.J.: Scholar's Bookshelf, 2005.

Norton, Mary Beth. *The British-Americans: The Loyalist Exiles in England, 1774–1789*. Boston: Little, Brown, 1972.

———. "Eighteenth Century American Women in Peace and War: The Case of the Loyalists." *WMQ*, 3rd ser., 33 (1976): 386–409.

———. *Liberty's Daughters: The Revolutionary Experience of American Women, 1750–1800*. Ithaca, N.Y.: Cornell University Press, 1996.

O'Brian, Patrick. *Men-of-War: Life in Nelson's Navy*. New York: Norton, 1995.

Olasky, Marvin. *Fighting for Liberty and Virtue: Political and Cultural Wars in Eighteenth-Century America*. Washington, D.C.: Regnery, 1995.

Olney, Stephen. "Life of Captain Stephen Olney." In *Biography of Revolutionary Heroes; Containing the Life of Brigadier Gen. William Barton, and also of Captain Stephen Olney*, edited by Mrs. Catharine Williams, pp. 193–99. Providence, R.I.: published by the author, 1839.

O'Shaughnessy, Andrew. *An Empire Divided: The American Revolution and the British Caribbean*. Philadelphia: University of Pennsylvania Press, 2000.

———. "'If Others Will Not Be Active, I Must Drive': George III and the American Revolution." *Early American Studies* 2, no. 1 (Spring 2004): 1–47.

———. *The Men Who Lost America: British Leadership, the American Revolution, and the Fate of the Empire*. New Haven, Conn.: Yale University Press, 2013.

Osler, Edward. "The Battle of Valcour Island." *Bulletin of the Fort Ticonderoga Museum* 2, no. 5 (Jan. 1932): 163-70.

Ousterhout, Anne. "Controlling the Opposition in Pennsylvania during the American Revolution." *Pennsylvania Magazine of History and Biography* 105 (1981): 3–35.

Palmer, Dave R. *George Washington and Benedict Arnold*. Washington, D.C.: Regency, 2006.

———. *George Washington's Military Genius*. Washington, D.C.: Regency, 2012.

———. *The River and the Rock: The History of the Fortress West Point, 1775–1783*. New York: Hippocrene Books, 1991.

Palmer, John. *General von Steuben*. New Haven, Conn.: Yale University Press, 1937.

Palmer, Peter. *History of Lake Champlain, 1609–1814*. Fleischmanns, N.Y.: Purple Mountain Press, 1992.

Pancake, John. *1777: The Year of the Hangman*. University: University of Alabama Press, 1977.

Papas, Phillip. *Renegade Revolutionary: The Life of Charles Lee*. New York: New York University Press, 2014.

———. *That Ever Loyal Island: Staten Island and the American Revolution*. New York: New York University Press, 2007.

Parker, Matthew. *The Sugar Barons: Family, Corruption, Empire, and War in the West Indies*. New York: Walker, 2011.

Partridge, Bellamy. *Sir Billy Howe*. London: Longmans, Green, 1932.

Patterson, Samuel White. *Horatio Gates: Defender of American Liberties.* 1941. Reprint, New York: AMS Press, 1966.

———. *Knight Errant of Liberty: The Triumph and Tragedy of General Charles Lee.* New York: Lantern Press, 1958.

Pausch, George. *Journal of Captain Pausch.* Translated by William L. Stone. Albany, N.Y.: Joel Munsell's Sons, 1886.

Pavlovsky, Arnold M. "Between Hawk and Buzzard: Congress as Perceived by Its Members, 1775–1783." *Pennsylvania Magazine of History and Biography* 101 (July 1977): 349–64.

Pearson, Michael. *Those Damned Rebels: The American Revolution as Seen through British Eyes.* New York: Putnam, 1972.

Peckham, Howard H. *The Toll of Independence.* Chicago: University of Chicago Press, 1974.

Pell, Joshua, Jr. "Diary, April 1776–13 October 1777." *Bulletin of the Fort Ticonderoga Museum* 1, no. 6 (July 1929): 2–14.

Pennypacker, Morton. *George Washington's Spies on Long Island and in New York.* Brooklyn, N.Y.: Long Island Historical Society, 1939.

Philbrick, Nathaniel. *Bunker Hill: A City, a Siege, a Revolution.* New York: Penguin, 2013.

Philbrick, Thomas. "The American Revolution as a Literary Event." In *Columbia Literary History of the United States,* edited by Emory Elliott, pp. 139–55. New York: Columbia University Press, 1988.

Phillips, Leon. *The Fantastic Breed: Americans in King George's War.* Garden City, N.Y.: Doubleday, 1968.

Pickering, James H. "Enoch Crosby, Secret Agent of the Neutral Ground: His Own Story." *New York History* 47 (1966): 61–73.

———. "Shube Merrit: Freebooter of the Neutral Ground." *New York Folklore Quarterly* 21 (1965): 31–39.

Pickering, Octavius. *The Life of Timothy Pickering.* Boston: Little, Brown, 1873.

"Proceedings of a General Court Martial of the Line Held at Head Quarters in the City of New York, by Warrant of His Excellency George Washington Esq. . . . for the Trial of Thomas Hickey & Others, June 26, 1776." Washington Papers, vol. 29, June 26, 1776, Library of Congress.

Proceedings of the Supreme Executive Council of the State of Pennsylvania in the Case of Major General Arnold. New York: Munsell, 1865.

Pula, James S. *Thaddeus Kościuszko: The Purest Son of Liberty.* New York: Hippocrene Books, 1999.

Puls, Mark. *Henry Knox: Visionary General of the American Revolution.* New York: Palgrave Macmillan, 2008.

Purcell, Sarah J. *Sealed with Blood: War, Sacrifice, and Memory in Revolutionary America.* Philadelphia: University of Pennsylvania Press, 2002.

Quarles, Benjamin. *The Negro in the American Revolution.* Chapel Hill: University of North Carolina Press, 1996.

Radbill, Kenneth A. "Quaker Patriots: The Leadership of Owen Biddle and John Lacey." *Pennsylvania History* 45, no. 1 (Jan. 1978): 47–60.

Rakove, Jack. *The Beginnings of National Politics: An Interpretive History of the Continental Congress.* New York: Knopf, 1979.

——. *Revolutionaries: A New History of the Invention of America.* Boston: Houghton Mifflin, 2010.

Randall, Willard Sterne. *Benedict Arnold: Patriot and Traitor.* New York: William Morrow, 1990.

Raphael, Ray. *Founders: The People Who Brought You a Nation.* New York: New Press, 2009.

Rappleye, Charles. *Robert Morris: Financier of the American Revolution.* New York: Simon and Schuster, 2010.

Reed, John F. *Campaign to Valley Forge, July 1, 1777 to December 19, 1777.* Philadelphia: University of Pennsylvania Press, 1963.

Reed, Joseph. "General Joseph Reed's Narrative of the Movements of the American Army in the Neighborhood of Trenton in the Winter of 1776–77." *Pennsylvania Magazine of History and Biography* 8 (1884): 391–402.

Reed, William B. *Life and Correspondence of Joseph Reed.* 2 vols. Philadelphia: Lindsay and Blakiston, 1847.

——. *A Reprint of the Reed and Cadwalader Pamphlets.* Philadelphia, 1863.

Resch, John, and Walter Sargent, eds. *War and Society in the American Revolution: Mobilization and Home Fronts.* DeKalb: Northern Illinois University Press, 2007.

Reynolds, Paul R. *Guy Carleton: A Biography.* New York: William Morrow, 1980.

Richard, Carl J. *The Founders and the Classics: Greece, Rome, and the American Enlightenment.* Cambridge, Mass.: Harvard University Press, 1994.

Richter, Daniel. *Beyond the Covenant Chain: The Iroquois and Their Neighbors in Indian North America, 1600–1800.* University Park: Pennsylvania State University Press, 2003.

——. *The Ordeal of the Longhouse: The Peoples of the Iroquois League in the Era of European Colonization.* Chapel Hill: University of North Carolina Press, 1992.

Riedesel, Baroness von. *Baroness von Riedesel and the American Revolution: Journal and Correspondence of a Tour of Duty, 1776–1783.* Translated and edited by Marvin L. Brown Jr. Chapel Hill: University of North Carolina Press, 1965.

Riedesel, Major General. *Memoirs, and Letters and Journals, of Major General Riedesel during His Residence in America.* Edited by Max Eelking. Translated by William L. Stone. 2 vols. Albany, N.Y.: J. Munsell, 1868.

Risse, Guenter B. "Hysteria at the Edinburgh Infirmary: The Construction and Treatment of a Disease, 1770–1800." *Medical History* 32, no. 1 (1988): 1–22.

Roche, John F. *Joseph Reed: A Moderate in the American Revolution.* New York: Columbia University Press, 1957.

Rogers, N. A. M. *The Wooden World: An Anatomy of the Georgian Navy.* New York: Norton, 1996.

Romer, John L. *Historic Sketches of the Neutral Ground.* Buffalo, N.Y.: William Gay, 1917.

Rose, Alex. *Washington's Spies: The Story of America's First Spy Ring.* New York: Bantam, 2007.

Rose, Ben Z. *John Stark: Maverick General.* Waverly, Mass.: Treeline Press, 2007.

Rosenbach, Abraham S. Wolf. "Documents Relative to Major David S. Franks while aide-de-camp to General Arnold." *Publications of the American Jewish Historical Society* 5 (1897): 157–89.

Rosenberg, Bruce A. *The Neutral Ground: The André Affair and the Background of Cooper's* The Spy. Westport, Conn.: Greenwood Press, 1994.

Rossie, Jonathan G. *The Politics of Command in the American Revolution.* Syracuse, N.Y.: Syracuse University Press, 1975.

Royster, Charles. *Light-Horse Harry Lee and the Legacy of the American Revolution.* New York: Knopf, 1981.

———. "'The Nature of Treason': Revolutionary Virtue and American Reactions to Benedict Arnold." *WMQ,* 3rd ser., 36, no. 2 (Apr. 1979): 163–93.

———. *A Revolutionary People at War: The Continental Army and American Character, 1775–1783.* Chapel Hill: University of North Carolina, 1979.

Rush, Benjamin. *Autobiography.* Edited by George W. Corner. Princeton, N.J.: Princeton University Press, 1948.

———. *Letters of Benjamin Rush.* Edited by L. H. Butterfield, 1:182–85; 2:1197–208. Princeton, N.J.: Published for the American Philosophical Society by Princeton University Press, 1951.

Rush, Richard. *Washington in Domestic Life.* Philadelphia: J. B. Lippincott, 1857.

Ryerson, Richard Alan. *The Revolution Is Now Begun: The Radical Committees of Philadelphia, 1765–1776.* Philadelphia: University of Pennsylvania Press, 1978.

Saffron, Morris. H. "The Northern Medical Department, 1776–1777." *Bulletin of the Fort Ticonderoga Museum* 14, no. 2 (1982): 81–120.

Sanderson, Eric. *Manhattan: A Natural History of New York City.* New York: Abrams, 2009.

Sargent, Winthrop. *The Life and Career of Major John André, Adjutant-General of the British Army in America.* Boston: Ticknor and Fields, 1861.

Schaffel, Kenneth. "The American Board of War, 1776–1781." *Military Affairs* 50, no. 4 (Oct. 1986): 185–89.

Schecter, Barnet. *The Battle for New York: The City at the Heart of the America Revolution.* New York: Walker, 2002.

———. *George Washington's America: A Biography through His Maps.* New York: Walker, 2010.

Scheer, George F., and Hugh F. Rankin, eds. *Rebels and Redcoats.* 1957. Reprint, New York: Da Capo Press, 1987.

Schellhammer, Michael. *George Washington and the Final British Campaign for the Hudson River, 1779.* Jefferson, N.C.: McFarland, 2012.

Schiff, Stacy. *A Great Improvisation: Franklin, France, and the Birth of America.* New York: Henry Holt, 2006.

Schlenther, Boyd Stanley. *Charles Thomson: A Patriot's Pursuit.* Newark: University of Delaware Press, 1990.

Schulz, Emily L., and Laura B. Simon. *George Washington and His Generals.* Mount Vernon, Va.: Mount Vernon Ladies' Association, 2009.

Scott, A. J. *Fort Stanwix and Oriskany.* Rome, N.Y.: Rome Sentinel Company, 1927.

Selesky, Harold. *War and Society in Colonial Connecticut.* New Haven, Conn.: Yale University Press, 1990.

Sellers, Charles Coleman. *Benedict Arnold, the Proud Warrior.* New York: Minton, Balch, 1930.

———. *Charles Willson Peale.* 2 vols. Philadelphia, 1947.

Sergeant R—. "The Battle of Princeton." *Pennsylvania Magazine of History and Biography*

20 (1896): 515–19 (originally published in the *Phenix,* Mar. 24, 1832, at Wellsborough, Pa.).

Serle, Ambrose. *The American Journal of Ambrose Serle, Secretary to Lord Howe, 1776–1778.* Edited by Edward H. Tatum. San Marino, Calif.: Huntington Library, 1940.

Shy, John. *A People Numerous and Armed: Reflections on the Military Struggle for American Independence.* New York: Oxford University Press, 1976.

Silver, Peter. *Our Savage Neighbors: How Indian War Transformed Early America.* New York: Norton, 2008.

Silverman, Kenneth. *A Cultural History of the American Revolution.* New York: Thomas Crowell, 1976.

Smith, Joshua Hett. *Authentic Narrative of the Causes Which Led to the Death of Major André.* New York: Evert Duyckinck, 1809.

———. *Record of the Trial of Joshua Hett Smith, Esq., for Alleged Complicity in the Treason of Benedict Arnold, 1780.* Edited by H. B. Dawson. Morrisania, N.Y., 1866.

Smith, Joshua M. *Borderland Smuggling: Patriots, Loyalists, and Illicit Trade in the Northeast, 1783–1820.* Gainesville: University of Florida Press, 2006.

Smith, Justin H. *Arnold's March from Cambridge to Quebec: A Critical Study Together with Arnold's Journal.* New York: Putnam, 1903.

Smith, Paul H. "The American Loyalists: Notes on Their Organization and Numerical Strength." *WMQ,* 3rd ser., 25 (1968): 258–77.

———, ed. *Letters of Delegates to Congress, 1774–1789.* Vols. 6–15. Washington, D.C.: Library of Congress, 1980–87.

———. *Loyalists and Redcoats: A Study in British Revolutionary Policy.* New York: Norton, 1964.

Smith, Samuel. "The General's Autobiography: The Papers of General Samuel Smith." *Historical Magazine,* 2nd ser., 7, no. 2 (1870): 81–92.

Smith, Samuel Stelle. *The Battle of Brandywine.* Monmouth Beach, N.J.: Freneau Press, 1976.

Smith, William. *Historical Memoirs of William Smith, 1778–1783.* Vol. 2. Edited by W. H. W. Sabine. New York: New York Times, 1971.

Snyder, Charles M. "With Benedict Arnold at Valcour Island: The Diary of Pascal de Angelis." *Vermont History* 42 (Summer 1974): 195–200.

Sparks, Jared. *The Life and Treason of Benedict Arnold.* Boston: Hilliard, Gray, 1835.

Spring, Matthew H. *With Zeal and with Bayonets Only: The British Army on Campaign in North America, 1775–1783.* Norman: University of Oklahoma Press, 2008.

Starbuck, David R. *The Great Warpath: British Military Sites from Albany to Crown Point.* Hanover, N.H.: University Press of New England, 1999.

Stark, Caleb, ed. *Memoir and General Correspondence of John Stark.* Concord, N.H.: McFarland and Jenks, 1860.

Starke, John, John Schank, and Edward Longcroft. Letter to Captain Pringle, St. Johns, 8 June 1777. "An Open Letter to Captain Pringle." *Bulletin of the Fort Ticonderoga Museum* 1, no. 4 (July 1928): 14–20.

Stauber, Leland. *The American Revolution: A Grand Mistake.* Amherst, N.Y.: Prometheus Books, 2009.

Stedman, Charles. *History of the Origin, Progress, and Termination of the American War.* London: Stedman, 1788.

Steele, Ian K. *Warpaths: Invasions of North America*. New York: Oxford University Press, 1994.

Stegeman, John F., and Janet A. Stegeman. *Caty: A Biography of Catharine Littlefield Greene*. Athens: University of Georgia Press, 1977.

Stephenson, Michael. *Patriot Battles: How the War of Independence Was Fought*. New York: HarperCollins, 2005.

Stevenson, William Flack. *Wounds in War: The Mechanism of Their Production and Their Treatment*. New York: William Wood, 1898.

Stinchcombe, William C. *The American Revolution and the French Alliance*. Syracuse, N.Y.: Syracuse University Press, 1969.

Stokes, I. N. Phelps. *The Iconography of Manhattan Island, 1498–1909: Compiled from Original Sources and Illustrated by Photo-Intaglio Reproductions of Important Maps, Plans, Views, and Documents in Public and Private Collections*. 6 vols. Union, N.J.: Lawbook Exchange, 1998.

Stone, William Leete. *The Campaign of Lieut. Gen. John Burgoyne, and the Expedition of Lieut. Col. Barry St. Leger*. Albany, N.Y.: Joel Munsell, 1877.

——. *Visits to the Saratoga Battle-Grounds*. Albany, N.Y.: Joel Munsell's Sons, 1895.

Stoudt, John Joseph. *Ordeal at Valley Forge: A Day-to-Day Chronicle Compiled from the Sources*. Philadelphia: University of Pennsylvania Press, 1963.

Stout, Neil R. "The Birth of the United States Navy." In *Lake Champlain: Reflections on Our Past*, edited by Jennie G. Versteeg, pp. 216–26. Burlington: University of Vermont Center for Research on Vermont, 1987.

Stowe, G. C., and J. Weller. "Revolutionary West Point: 'The Key to the Continent.'" *Military Affairs* 19, no. 2 (1955): 81–98.

Straus, Oscar. "New Light on the Career of Colonel David S. Franks." *Publications of the American Jewish Historical Society* 10 (1902): 101–8.

Stryker, William. *The Battle of Monmouth*. Princeton, N.J.: Princeton University Press, 1927.

——. *The Battles of Trenton and Princeton*. Trenton, N.J.: Old Barracks Association, 2001.

——. *The Reed Controversy: Further Facts with Reference to the Character of Joseph Reed, Adjutant General on the Staff of General Washington*. Trenton, N.J.: John L. Murphy, 1876.

Stuart, Nancy Rubin. *Defiant Brides: The Untold Story of Two Revolutionary-Era Women and the Radical Men They Married*. Boston: Beacon Press, 2013.

Sullivan, Edward Dean. *Benedict Arnold, Military Racketeer*. New York: Vanguard Press, 1932.

Sullivan, Robert. *My American Revolution: Crossing the Delaware and I-78*. New York: Farrar, Straus and Giroux, 2012.

"Supplies for the Galley *Washington*, 2 October 1776." *Bulletin of the Fort Ticonderoga Museum* 4, no. 1 (Jan. 1936): 21–22.

Syrett, David. *Admiral Lord Howe: A Biography*. Annapolis, Md.: Naval Institute Press, 2006.

——. *The Royal Navy in American Waters, 1775–1783*. Aldershot, U.K.: Scolar Press, 1989.

——. *Shipping and the American War, 1775–83: A Study of British Transport Organization*. London: Athlone Press, 1976.

Taaffe, Stephen R. *The Philadelphia Campaign, 1777–1778*. Lawrence: University Press of Kansas, 2003.

Tallmadge, Benjamin. *Memoir*. 1858. Reprint, New York: New York Times and Arno Press, 1968.

Tapson, Alfred J. "The Sutler and the Soldier." *Military Affairs* 21, no. 4 (Winter 1957): 175–81.

Taylor, Alan. *The Divided Ground: Indians, Settlers, and the Northern Borderland of the American Revolution*. New York: Vintage, 2007.

——. *The Internal Enemy: Slavery and War in Virginia*. New York: Norton, 2013.

Tennant, William. Letter to "my dearest & most lovely partner" [wife, Susannah, in Greenfield, Mass.], Ticonderoga, Oct. 15, 1776. Manuscript letter containing a vivid account of the Battle at Valcour, offered as Item #161, Christie's, Dec. 9, 1994. Copy in Fort Ticonderoga Association research files.

Terrot, Charles. "Naval Action on Lake Champlain, 1776." *American Neptune* 8, no. 3 (1948): 256.

Thacher, James. "The Execution of Major John André as a Spy." *New England Magazine* (May 1834): 353–59.

——. *A Military Journal during the American Revolution*. Boston: Cottons and Barnard, 1827.

Thane, Elswyth. *The Fighting Quaker: Nathanael Greene*. New York: Hawthorn, 1972.

Thayer, Theodore. *The Making of a Scapegoat: Washington and Lee at Monmouth*. Port Washington, N.Y.: Kennikat Press, 1976.

——. *Nathanael Greene, Strategist of the American Revolution*. New York: Twayne, 1960.

Thompson, Ray. *Benedict Arnold in Philadelphia*. Fort Washington, Pa.: Bicentennial Press, 1975.

Tiedemann, Joseph S. "Patriots by Default: Queens County, New York, and the British Army, 1776–1783." *WMQ*, 3rd ser., 43 (1986): 35–63.

Tiedemann, Joseph S., and Eugene R. Fingerhut, eds. *The Other New York: The American Revolution beyond New York City, 1763–1787*. Albany: State University of New York Press, 2005.

Tiedemann, Joseph S., Eugene R. Fingerhut, and Robert W. Venables, eds. *The Other Loyalists: Ordinary People, Royalism, and the Revolution of the Middle Colonies, 1763–1787*. Albany: State University of New York Press, 2010.

Tilley, John A. *The British Navy and the American Revolution*. Columbia: South Carolina University Press, 1987.

Tinckom, Harry M. "The Revolutionary City, 1765–1783." In *Philadelphia: A 300-Year History*, edited by Russell F. Weigley, pp. 109–54. New York: Norton, 1982.

Todd, Charles Burr. *The Real Benedict Arnold*. New York: A. S. Barnes, 1903.

Tomlin, Gregory M. "Valcour Island: Setting the Conditions for Victory at Saratoga." In *Key to the Northern Country: The Hudson River Valley in the American Revolution*, edited by James M. Johnson, Christopher Pryslopski, and Andrew Villani, pp. 269–83. Albany: State University of New York Press, 2013.

Trevelyan, Sir George Otto. *The American Revolution*. 6 vols. New York: Longmans, Green, 1905.

Trumbull, Benjamin. *Journal of the Campaign at New York, 1776–1777*. In *Collections of the Connecticut Historical Society* 7:175–218. Hartford, 1899.

Trumbull, John. *The Autobiography of Colonel John Trumbull.* Edited by Theodore Sizer. New Haven, Conn.: Yale University Press, 1953.

Tuchman, Barbara W. *The First Salute: A View of the American Revolution.* New York: Ballantine Books, 1988.

Tucker, Glenn. *Mad Anthony Wayne and the New Nation.* Harrisburg, Pa.: Stackpole Books, 1973.

Tuttle, Mrs. George Fuller, ed. *Three Centuries in Champlain Valley: A Collection of Historical Facts and Incidents.* Plattsburgh, N.Y.: Saranac Chapter, Daughters of the American Revolution, 1909.

Tyler, John. *Smugglers and Patriots: Boston Merchants and the Advent of the American Revolution.* Boston: Northeastern University Press, 1986.

Upham, George Baxter. "Burgoyne's Great Mistake." *New England Quarterly* 3, no. 4 (Oct. 1930): 657–80.

Upton, L. F. S. *The Loyal Whig: William Smith of New York and Quebec.* Toronto: University of Toronto Press, 1969.

Urban, Mark. *Fusiliers: The Saga of a British Redcoat Regiment in the American Revolution.* New York: Walker, 2007.

Valentine, Alan. *Lord Stirling.* New York: Oxford University Press, 1969.

Van Buskirk, Judith. *Generous Enemies: Patriots and Loyalists in Revolutionary New York.* Philadelphia: University of Pennsylvania Press, 2002.

Van Doren, Carl. *Secret History of the American Revolution.* New York: Viking, 1968.

Varick, Richard. *The Varick Court of Inquiry.* Edited by Albert Bushnell Hart. Boston: Bibliophile Society, 1907.

Volo, James M. *Blue Water Patriots: The American Revolution Afloat.* Laham, Md.: Rowman and Littlefield, 2006.

Wade, Arthur. "A Military Offspring of the American Philosophical Society." *Military Affairs* 38, no. 3 (Oct. 1974): 103–7.

Wade, Herbert T., and Robert A. Lively, eds. *This Glorious Cause.* Princeton, N.J.: Princeton University Press, 1958.

Walker, Lewis Burd. "Life of Margaret Shippen, Wife of Benedict Arnold." *Pennsylvania Magazine of History and Biography* 24 (1900): 257–67, 401–49; 25 (1901): 20–46, 145–90, 289–302, 452–97; 26 (1902): 71–80, 224–44, 322–34, 464–68.

Wallace, David Duncan. *The Life of Henry Laurens.* New York: G. P. Putnam's Sons, 1915.

Wallace, Willard. *Traitorous Hero: The Life and Fortunes of Benedict Arnold.* New York: Harper and Brothers, 1954.

Walsh, John Evangelist. *The Execution of Major André.* New York: Palgrave, 2001.

Ward, Christopher. *The War of the Revolution.* Edited by John Richard Alden. 2 vols. New York: Macmillan, 1952.

Ward, Harry M. *Between the Lines: Banditti of the American Revolution.* Westport, Conn.: Greenwood Press, 2002.

———. *Major General Adam Stephen and the Cause of American Liberty.* Charlottesville: University of Virginia Press, 1989.

Warren, Benjamin. "Diary of Captain Benjamin Warren on Battlefield of Saratoga." Edited by David E. Alexander. *Journal of American History* 3, no. 2 (1909): 201–16.

Washington, George. *The Papers of George Washington: Revolutionary War Series.* Vols.

5–22. Edited by Philander D. Chase et al. Charlottesville: University Press of
Virginia, 1985, 1987, 1988.

———. *Writings of George Washington.* Vols. 6–8. Edited by Jared Sparks. Boston:
Russell, Odiorne, and Metcalf and Hilliard, Gray, 1834–35.

———. *Writings of George Washington.* Vols. 17–20. Edited by John C. Fitzpatrick.
Washington, D.C.: United States Government Printing Office, 1937.

Wasmus, J. F. *An Eyewitness Account of the American Revolution and New England Life:
The Journal of J. F. Wasmus, German Company Surgeon, 1776–1783.* Trans-
lated by Helga Doblin and edited by Mary C. Lynn. New York: Greenwood
Press, 1990.

Watson, Winslow. "The Fortresses of Crown Point and Ticonderoga." In *Munsell's
Historical Series* 3:178–204. Albany, N.Y.: Munsell, 1859.

Watt, Gavin. *Rebellion in the Mohawk Valley: The St. Leger Expedition of 1777.* Toronto: Dundurn, 2002.

Wayne, Anthony. Orderly Book for July 10–Oct. 15, 1776, *Bulletin of the Fort Ticonderoga Museum* 11, nos. 2–4 (1963–64): 93–112; Orderly Book for Nov. 20–
Dec. 1, 1776, *Bulletin of the Fort Ticonderoga Museum* 3, no. 4 (July 1934):
191–98; Orderly Book for Dec. 1–16, 1776, *Bulletin of the Fort Ticonderoga
Museum* 3, no. 5 (Jan. 1935): 218–25; Orderly Book for Dec. 17, 1776–Jan. 8,
1777, *Bulletin of the Fort Ticonderoga Museum* 3, no. 6 (July 1935): 248–60. A
printed transcription of Orderly Book for Oct. 17, 1776–Jan. 8, 1777, appeared in *Munsell's Historical Series* 3:2–140 (Albany, N.Y.: Munsell, 1859).

Webb, Samuel Blachley. *Correspondence and Journals of Samuel Blachley Webb.* Vols.
1–3. Edited by Worthington C. Ford. New York: Burnett, 1894.

Weigley, Russell, ed. *Philadelphia: A 300-Year History.* New York: Norton, 1982.

Weiner, Frederick B. "Military Occupation of Philadelphia in 1777–1778." *Proceedings of the American Philosophical Society* 111 (1967): 310–13.

Weintraub, Stanley. *Iron Tears: America's Battle for Freedom, Britain's Quagmire:
1775–1783.* New York: Free Press, 2005.

Wells, Bayze. *Journal of Bayze Wells of Farmington.* In *Collections of the Connecticut
Historical Society* 7:238–96. Hartford, 1899.

Wermuth, Thomas, ed. *America's First River: The History and Culture of the Hudson
River Valley.* Albany, N.Y.: State University of New York Press, 2009.

Wetenbaker, Thomas Jefferson. *Father Knickerbocker Rebels.* New York: Scribner's,
1948.

Wickman, Donald H. "A Most Unsettled Time on Lake Champlain: The October
1776 Journal of Jahiel Stewart." *Vermont History* 64, no. 2 (1996): 89–98.

Wickwire, Franklin, and Mary Wickwire. *Cornwallis: The American Adventure.* Boston: Houghton Mifflin, 1970.

Wiencek, Henry. *An Imperfect God: George Washington, Slaves and the Creation of
America.* New York: Farrar, Straus and Giroux, 2003.

Wigglesworth, Edward. "Colonel Wigglesworth's Diary Containing His Account of
the Naval Battles on Lake Champlain, Oct. 11 and 13, 1776." In *Autographs:
Letters—Documents—Manuscripts Catalogue No. 1464.* Philadelphia: Stan V.
Henkels Jr., 1932.

Wilbur, C. Keith. *Revolutionary Medicine, 1700–1800.* Chester, Conn.: Globe Pequot
Press, 1980.

Wilkinson, James. *Memoirs of My Own Times*. Vol. 1. Philadelphia: Abraham Small, 1816.

Willcox, William. *Portrait of a General: Sir Henry Clinton in the War of Independence*. New York: Knopf, 1964.

———. "Too Many Cooks: British Planning before Saratoga." *Journal of British Studies* 2, no. 1 (Nov. 1962): 56–90.

Williams, Glenn F. *Year of the Hangman: George Washington's Campaign against the Iroquois*. Yardley, Pa.: Westholme, 2005.

Williamson, Joseph. "Biographical Sketch of Joseph P. Martin, of Prospect, Maine, a Revolutionary Solider." *NEHGR* 30 (1876): 330–31.

Wilson, Barry K. *Benedict Arnold: A Traitor in Our Midst*. Montreal: McGill-Queens University Press, 2001.

Wood, Gordon S. *The Creation of the American Republic, 1776–1787*. Chapel Hill: University of North Carolina Press, 1969.

———. *The Radicalism of the American Revolution*. New York: Vintage Books, 1991.

Wright, Robert K. *The Continental Army*. Washington, D.C.: Center of Military History, 1989.

ILLUSTRATION CREDITS

Page 1 (top): New York from the Hudson: The Mariners' Museum, Newport News, VA

Page 1 (bottom left): George Washington by Charles Willson Peale, 1776: Brooklyn Museum, Dick S. Ramsay Fund, 34.1178

Page 1 (bottom right): Henry Knox by Charles Willson Peale, from life, c. 1784: Independence National Historical Park

Page 2 (top left): Joseph Reed by Charles Willson Peale: Independence National Historical Park

Page 2 (top right): Major General Nathanael Greene by John Trumbull: Yale University Art Gallery

Page 2 (bottom left): General John Sullivan by Richard Morrell Staigg: Independence National Historical Park

Page 2 (bottom right): General Israel Putnam by Dominique Fabronius: Library of Congress

Page 3 (top left): William Alexander, Lord Stirling, by Bass Otis: Independence National Historical Park

Page 3 (top right): General William Howe, Knight: Collection of the Massachusetts Historical Society

Page 3 (bottom left): Admiral Richard Lord Howe: © Superstock

Page 3 (bottom right): George Sackville Germain, 1st Viscount Sackville, by Nathaniel Hone: © National Portrait Gallery, London

Page 4 (top): New York Harbor by Archibald Robertson: Spencer Collection, The New York Public Library, Astor, Lenox and Tilden Foundations

Page 4 (bottom left): General Sir Henry Clinton by John Smart: National Army Museum

Page 4 (bottom right): Charles Cornwallis, 1st Marquess Cornwallis, by Thomas Gainsborough: © National Portrait Gallery, London

Page 5 (top): Britain infantry uniform sketch, 1778, by Philip James de Loutherbourg: Anne S. K. Brown Military Collection, Brown University Library

Page 5 (bottom left): Hessian Miter Cap: Armed Forces History Division, National Museum of American History, Smithsonian Institution

Page 5 (bottom right): British grenadier, holding rifle, c. 1778, by Philip James de Loutherbourg: Anne S. K. Brown Military Collection, Brown University Library

Pages 6–7: Kepp's Bay, August 17th, 1778, by Archibald Robertson: Manuscripts and Archives Division, The New York Public Library, Astor, Lenox and Tilden Foundations

Page 7 (top): *Turtle*, by John Batchelor: www.printsolutions.co.uk

Page 8 (top): *A View of New England Armed Vessels, on Valcure Bay on Lake Champlain,* by Charles Randle: Library and Archives Canada

Pages 8–9: *God Bless Our Armes* by Charles Randle: Fort Ticonderoga Museum

Page 9 (top): *His Majesty's Vessels on Lake Champlain* by Charles Randle: Library and Archives Canada

Page 10 (top left): Benedict Arnold by Pierre Eugène du Simitière: Library of Congress

Page 10 (top right): Benedict Arnold by A. Cassidy: Frick Art Reference Library

Pages 10–11: *The Battle of Valcour Island, 1776,* by Henry Gilder: Royal Collection Trust © Her Majesty Queen Elizabeth II 2015

Page 11 (top): General Sir Guy Carleton by Mabel Messer: Library and Archives Canada

Page 12 (top): *Study for the Capture of the Hessians at Trenton* by John Trumbull: Charles Allen Munn Collection, Fordham University Library

Page 12 (middle): General Charles Lee: Emmet Collection, Miriam and Ira D. Wallach Division of Art, Prints and Photographs, The New York Public Library, Astor, Lenox and Tilden Foundations

Page 12 (bottom): Assunpink Bridge, Trenton, published in the *Columbia Magazine,* May 1789: Trentoniana Collection, Trenton Free Public Library

Page 13 (top): Artistic rendering of Fort Stanwix: University of Texas Libraries

Page 13 (bottom left): Major General Philip Schuyler: Library of Congress

Page 13 (bottom right): Colonel Peter Gansevoort: Benson J. Lossing, *The Pictorial Field-Book of the Revolution* (New York: Harper & Brothers, 1852)

Page 14 (top left): General Horatio Gates by Charles Willson Peale: Independence National Historical Park

Page 14 (top right): James Wilkinson in 1797 by Charles Willson Peale: Independence National Historical Park

Page 14 (bottom left): Lieutenant Colonel Richard Varick by Ralph Earl, 1787, oil on canvas, bequest of Sarah Walsh DeWitt, 1924.4.16: Albany Institute of History and Art

Page 14 (bottom right): Daniel Morgan by Charles Willson Peale, from life, c. 1794: Independence National Historical Park

Page 15 (top left): Benjamin Lincoln by Charles Willson Peale, from life, c. 1781–1783: Independence National Historical Park

Page 15 (top right): General John Burgoyne by Sir Joshua Reynolds: Library of Congress

Page 15 (bottom): A 1768 view of Philadelphia, taken by George Heap. Engraving by Thomas Jefferys: Library of Congress

Page 16: *Fleury's Map of Fort Mifflin:* Division of Rare and Manuscript Collections, Cornell University Library

INSERT TWO, FOLLOWING PAGE 268

Page 1: Battle of Germantown, ca. 1790, artist unknown: Cliveden, a Historic Site of the National Trust for Historic Preservation

Page 2 (top): South side of Washington's Headquarters at Valley Forge in winter: National Park Service

Page 2 (bottom left): John Laurens: Independence National Historical Park

Page 2 (bottom right): Henry Laurens, engraved by V. Green Mezzotinto: Library of Congress

Page 3 (top left): Marie Joseph Paul Yves Roch Gilbert du Motier, Marquis de Lafayette, by Charles Wilson Peale: Independence National Historical Park

Page 3 (top right): Portrait of Alexander Hamilton attributed to William J. Weaver: Indianapolis Museum of Art, Gift of Mr. and Mrs. Eli Lilly, 47.47, imamuseum.org

Page 3 (bottom left): Thomas Conway: The Historical Society of Pennsylvania Portrait Collection

Page 3 (bottom right): Portrait of Mr. and Mrs. Thomas Mifflin by John Singleton Copley: Philadelphia Museum of Art, 125th Anniversary Acquisition. Bequest of Mrs. Esther F. Wistar to The Historical Society of Pennsylvania in 1900, and acquired by the

Philadelphia Museum of Art by mutual agreement with the Society through the generosity of Mr. and Mrs. Fitz Eugene Dixon Jr., and significant contributions from Stephanie S. Eglin and other donors to the Philadelphia Museum of Art, as well as the George W. Elkins Fund and the W. P. Wilstach Fund, and through the generosity of Maxine and Howard H. Lewis to the Historical Society of Pennsylvania, 1999

Page 4 (top): *The Battle of the Kegs:* Picture Collection, The Branch Libraries, The New York Public Library, Astor, Lenox and Tilden Foundations

Page 4 (bottom): *Battle of Monmouth* by Alonzo Chappel: Picture Collection, The New York Public Library, Astor, Lenox and Tilden Foundations

Page 5 (top): Margaret Shippen Arnold by Major John André: Yale University Art Gallery

Page 5 (bottom): Mischianza Lady by Major John André: Cliveden, a Historic Site of the National Trust for Historic Preservation

Page 6 (top): Benedict Arnold's Oath of Allegiance: National Archives and Records Administration

Pages 6–7: The French fleet, under the command of Comte d'Estaing, anchored outside New York, 1778, by Pierre Ozanne: Library of Congress

Page 7 (top left): Major David Salisbury Franks: The Jacob Rader Marcus Center of the American Jewish Archives, Cincinnati, Ohio, americanjewisharchives.org

Page 7 (top right): John Cadwalader: From the University Archives and Records Center, University of Pennsylvania

Pages 8–9: Panoramic view of West Point, New York, showing American encampments on the Hudson River: Library of Congress

Page 9 (top): The *Languedoc* by Pierre Ozanne: Library of Congress

Page 10: Benedict Arnold's July 15, 1780, coded letter offering to sell West Point to the British: Clements Library, University of Michigan

Page 11: The decoded July 15 letter: Clements Library, University of Michigan

Page 12 (top): Beverly Robinson House: Print Collection, Miriam and Ira D. Wallach Division of Art, Prints and Photographs, The New York Public Library, Astor, Lenox and Tilden Foundations

Page 12 (center): The dining room of the Robinson House: Benson J. Lossing, *Pictorial Field-Book of the Revolution* (New York: Harper & Brothers, 1851)

Page 12 (bottom): Colonel Beverly Robinson: Library of Congress

Page 13 (top): Joshua Hett Smith House: Print Collection, Miriam and Ira D. Wallach Division of Art, Prints and Photographs, The New York Public Library, Astor, Lenox and Tilden Foundations

Page 13 (bottom left): William Smith Jr. by John Wollaston: © New-York Historical Society

Page 13 (bottom right): Benjamin Tallmadge by John Trumbull: army.mil

Page 14 (top): A representation of Major John André: Emmet Collection, Miriam and Ira D. Wallach Division of Art, Prints and Photographs, The New York Public Library, Astor, Lenox and Tilden Foundations

Pages 14–15: Figures exhibited and paraded through the streets of Philadelphia, on Saturday, the 30th of September, 1780: Library of Congress

Page 15 (top): John André—Facsimile of a drawing made by himself with a pen the day before his execution: Print Collection, Miriam and Ira D. Wallach Division of Art, Prints and Photographs, The New York Public Library, Astor, Lenox and Tilden Foundations

Page 16: Saratoga Battlefield Memorial: Americasroof/Creative Commons

Endpapers: Map of the Province of New York with part of Pennsylvania and New England, from *George Washington Atlas* (detail): Yale University Library Map Collection

INDEX

challenges for British forces, 64–67, 69
fall of Fort Lee, 31
Gates's southward march and Charles
   Lee's capture, 60, 67–68
Washington in Morristown (1777), 86,
   101, 103–4
Washington's plans to capitalize on
   Trenton success, 77–79
Washington's 1776 retreat to the
   Delaware, 60, 61–64, 65 *map*
—CAMPAIGN OF 1778
British-French standoff at Sandy
   Hook, 216–19, 217 *map*
Old Tappan massacre, 281–82
—CAMPAIGN OF 1779, Clinton's push up
   the Hudson, 247–49, 248 *map*,
   250–51, 262
Newport
British fleet in, 65, 70, 87, 218–19, 252
Clinton's planned assault on French
   fleet (1780), 271–72, 275
New York (city), 4 *map*, 11 *map*, 65 *map*
British-French standoff at Sandy
   Hook, 216–19, 217 *map*
British occupation of, 64–66, 242
British withdrawal to (1778), 204,
   208–9
Clinton's potential abandonment of
   (1778), 201, 209
Hickey's trial and hanging, 3, 5
Kips Bay attack and Inclenberg,
   25–30, 26 *map*, 176
Peggy Arnold exiled to, 323
Washington's decision to evacuate,
   24–25
Washington's plans to attack, 251–52,
   253, 271–72, 273–74
in winter of 1779–1780, 256
See also Hudson River; Long Island,
   Battle of; *specific locations*
New York (colony/state), 33 *map*
loyalist arrests in, 134–35
Tryon as governor of, 92
See also Neutral Ground; *specific
   locations*
—CAMPAIGN OF 1776
Kips Bay attack and Inclenberg,
   25–30, 26 *map*, 176

torpedo attempt on HMS *Eagle*,
   21–23, 194
Washington's retreat to Harlem and
   Battle of Harlem Heights, 24–25,
   26 *map*, 29–31, 204–5
William Howe's arrival (1776), 5–6
See also Long Island, Battle of
—CAMPAIGN OF 1777
Arnold's disputes with Gates, 153–56,
   161–63, 165
Battle of Bemis Heights, 161–67,
   164 *map*
Battle of Freeman's Farm and
   aftermath, 145–51, 147 *map*, 153–57
British positions and strategies, 158
Burgoyne's plans and hopes, 116–20,
   123–24, 131–33
Burgoyne's surrender, 172–73, 178, 179
Clinton's capture of Fort Clinton, 269
Siege of Fort Stanwix, 129–31, 130
   map, 132–36, 141
Stark's victory at Bennington, 133,
   136, 141
See also Saratoga, Battle of
—CAMPAIGN OF 1779
Clinton's consolidation of forces, 252
Clinton's push toward West Point and
   Battle for the Hudson, 247–49, 248
   map, 250–51, 262
Washington's planned assault on New
   York, 251–52, 253
"Notes of the Intrigues and Severe
   Altercations or Quarrels in the
   Congress" (Thomson), xiii–xiv

Odell, Jonathan, 243
Old Tappan massacre, 281–82
Olney, Stephen, 82, 84
Oneida Indians, 131, 134, 135, 156
Oriskany, British and Indian attack at,
   130 *map*, 131, 132, 135
Oswald, Eleazer, 97–98

Paine, Thomas, 62–63, 174, 176, 183
Panther (Indian warrior), 125
Paoli Tavern attack, 157–58, 281, 296
Parker, James, 152
Parsons, Samuel, 30

AVAILABLE FROM PENGUIN BOOKS

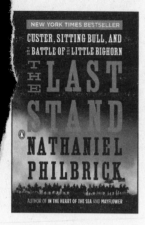

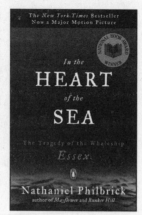

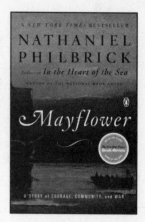

Away Off Shore;
  Nantucket Island and Its People,
  1602–1890

Bunker Hill;
  A City, A Siege, A Revolution

In the Heart of the Sea;
  The Tragedy of the Whaleship Essex

The Last Stand;
  Custer, Sitting Bull, and the
  Battle of the Little Bighorn

Mayflower;
  A Story of Courage, Community,
  and War

Sea of Glory;
  America's Voyage of Discovery,
  The U.S. Exploring Expedition,
  1838–1842

Why Read Moby-Dick?

PENGUIN BOOKS